Advanced BUSINESS

Second Edition

Dan Moynihan & Brian Titley

OXFORD

OXFORD
UNIVERSITY PRESS

Great Clarendon Street, Oxford OX2 6DP

Oxford University Press is a department of the University of Oxford. It furthers the University's objective of excellence in research, scholarship, and education by publishing worldwide in

Oxford New York

Athens Auckland Bangkok Bogotá Buenos Aires Cape Town Chennai Dar es Salaam Delhi Florence Hong Kong Istanbul Karachi Kolkata Kuala Lumpur Madrid Melbourne Mexico City Mumbai Nairobi Paris São Paulo Shanghai Singapore Taipei Tokyo Toronto Warsaw
with associated companies in Berlin Ibadan

Oxford is a registered trade mark of Oxford University Press in the UK and in certain other countries

First published 1995
Second edition 2001

British Library Cataloguing in Publication Data

Data available

ISBN 0 19 832831 1

Typeset by MCS Ltd, Salisbury Wiltshire

Printed in Italy by G. Canale & C.S.p.A., Borgaro T.se, Turin

The publishers would like to thank the following for permission to reproduce photographs:

Ace Photo Agency: 140 *right*, 172 *bottom*, 195 *top*, 260 *middle*, 270, 374 *top left*, 375, 398 *top right*, 414; Barnaby's Picture Library: 75 *bottom middle*, 103, 114, 154 *middle*, 221, 280 *top left & right*, 398 *top left*, 415 *bottom*; Biffa Waste Services: 94; John Birdsall Photography: 495 *top left*; John Bright & Bros Ltd: 398 *middle*; British Health & Safety Executive: 134 *top right*; British Petroleum: 109 *top*; British School of Motoring: 110 *bottom*; British Telecom: 59 *bottom*, 156 *top left*, 156 *bottom left*, 165 *top*, 374 *bottom left*; Philip Davies: 406 *middle*; Ford Motor Company Ltd: 145, 201; Format Partners Photo Library: 332 *top*; Peter Gimbere: 27 *top*; Greater London Record Office: 300 *top left*: Chris Honeywell: 172 *middle*, 177, 181, 184 *left*, 211; I.B.M. 176 *bottom*, 178; I.C.I: 384; K9: 140 *top*; Tony Mays: 300 *top right*; Archie Miles: 406 *bottom middle*; National Coal Board: 430; National Motor Museum: 201 *left*; Nissan: 449; Network: 153; Alan Owens: 405 *bottom right*; Oxford University Press/Chris Honeywell 105, 300 *bottom right*; /Norman McBeath 140 *middle left*, /Terry Austin Smith 467, /J R Tabberner 10S; Alan C Parker/Greenways: 66; Pontin's: 411; Press Association: 33, 71, 77, 195 *bottom*, 297, 616 *top*, 680 *bottom right*, 681 *left*; Sanyo: 20 *middle right*, 32 *middle*, 154 *bottom*, 156 *bottom middle*; Martin Sookias: 18, 54, 58 *top*, 59 *top & middle*, 93, 109 *middle*, 110 *top*, 115, 135, 156 *bottom right*, 163, 165 *top & bottom*, 175, 176 *top*, 179, 184 *right*, 193 *top & bottom left*, 197 *top*, 202, 203, 204, 206, 217, 223, 245, 248 *middle*, 259, 264, 265, 266, 286, 324, 367 *right*, 382 *bottom left*, 416, 483, 495 *middle left & bottom right*, 496, 507, 508, 593, 616 *middle & bottom*, 643, 670, 680 *top*; Sporting Pictures: 246; Tony Stone Images: 127, 154 *top*, 180 *top*, 197 *middle*, 283, 311, 334 *bottom right*; Telegraph Colour Library: 22 *middle and bottom*, 61, 75 *top middle & bottom*, 159 *right*, 160 *top*, 180 *bottom*, 269, 280 *bottom*, 315, 334 *left*, 367 *left*, 374 *bottom right*, 381, 406 *top*, 495 *bottom left*; Tesco plc: 300 *bottom left*; Thames Valley Police: 104; Toshiba: 494; Tropix: 625; Unipart Group of Companies: 139, 193; Van den Bergh Foods Ltd: 198, 647; Voluntary Service Overseas: 673; Volvo Car UK Ltd: 380; Zefa: 334 *top right*, 398 *bottom*

All other photographs courtesy of Oxford University Press

Special thanks to ABTA; British Wool Marketing Board; British Gas plc; British Standards Institute; DHL Worldwide Express; Investors In People; 3i (Investors in Industry); Lacroix Watches; Penguin Books; Rolls Royce plc; TNT.

Contents

Preface

This book aims to provide everything that you need in order to pass the core units in the Vocational A level in Business. The book has been carefully prepared to match closely the Vocational A level course specifications introduced in September 2000.

The book can be used as a course text to support either a course with a high proportion of teacher/lecturer contact time or one with more self-supported study. Students will discover a wealth of activities to help them develop their knowledge and understanding of business and the skills they need to complete the assessment evidence required by the Vocational A level qualification.

As well as helping students to pass their Vocational A level in Business with a good grade, the book has been designed to provide a thorough insight into the dynamic and exciting world of modern business by using a wide range of case studies and real-world examples. Each chapter is packed with up-to-date news articles and statistics to assist students in carrying out research and producing coursework.

Dan Moynihan

Brian Titley

What is Business? A brief introduction

You can choose to start your investigation of business at any point in this book. You do not need to start at Unit 1 and work your way through until the end of Unit 6. For example, you may want to find out about human resource management in business first by studying Unit 4, or begin at Unit 5 with how businesses raise and manage their finance. However, before you do start your course in business it is worthwhile reading this brief introduction to learn a few of the key words and ideas to help you understand the modern business world.

Needs and wants

Everyone needs a minimum of food, drink, and clothing or shelter to protect them from climatic extremes. This contrasts to the diversity of limitless human wants in a modern industrial society. People want cars, video recorders, designer clothes, pop concerts, foreign holidays, for the pleasure they give, not because they are necessary to maintain life and ensure survival.

Today, most people earn money to buy the things they need and want by working in a particular occupation, such as nursing, accountancy, bricklaying, or company management. Very few people attempt to satisfy their own needs and wants by their own direct work. That is, in a modern society, most people rely on others to satisfy their **needs** and **wants**.

Simply defined, **business** refers to the cooperation and organization between people, their materials, buildings, and machines, for the purpose

What is a business organization?

A business organization can be defined as a group of people who cooperate with each other for the purpose of productive activity. A number of features are common to all business organizations:

- **A name**: for example, Sony, Tescos, Unilever
- **A mission statement**: to define the overall purpose of the organization - for example 'to serve our customers'
- **Objectives**: business goals such as optimizing profits, sales revenues, market share
- **People**: business owners, managers, and a workforce with a variety of skills and knowledge
- **An organizational structure**: the chain of command which shows who is in charge, who makes decisions, and who carries them out
- **Rules and regulations**: some set by managers, others dictated by government - for example, concerning health and safety
- **A culture**: a set of common values held by people within the organization - for example, 'to work together to achieve a high standard of product or service quality'
- **Records**: for example, of outputs, revenues, staffing levels, absenteeism, by which to judge performance, and for accounting purposes
- **Rewards and incentives**: to motivate employees and ensure they complete set tasks
- **Specialist functions**: e.g. product design, human resource management, marketing, accounting, distribution, etc.

▼ International specialization

▲ Swiss watches

of productive activity to satisfy human needs and wants. Everywhere you look today, you will see business activity: people shopping in the high street, factories, transport, the provision of parks and refuse collection by local councils, government taxation and expenditures on hospitals and defence, even pollution. The study of business is therefore the study of productive activity, how it is organized, how it creates wealth, and how that wealth is distributed.

What is specialization?

Specialization is a major feature of modern business. It refers to the production of a limited range of goods and services by an individual, firm, region, or even a whole country. For example, despite the output of a wide range of products, Japan is probably best known for its electronic products. Swiss watches, Italian olive oil, Cuban cigars, French wine, and Scotch whisky are all examples of international specialization.

Firms also specialize in particular goods or services. For example, Ford specializes in making cars, McDonald's specializes in fast foods, Esso specializes in drilling and refining oil. Specialization also takes place within a business organization. Most large organizations have different departments that specialize in activities such as personnel, finance, marketing, and design.

▼ Scotch whisky

▲ Japanese videos

Why is trade necessary?

Specialization was the first step towards a wealthier society. People who were able to produce more clothes, pots, food than they themselves needed or wanted were able to exchange their surplus for other surplus items made by other people or communities. Thus, specialization implies a need to trade.

The earliest form of trade involved swapping goods directly and was known as **barter**. However, this was an inefficient form of exchange because it required a **double coincidence of wants**. That is, in order for trade to take place, a person with, say, a pound of apples who wanted to exchange them for some corn, would need to find a person who had surplus corn which they were willing to trade for apples. If the person with corn wanted pears or something else instead, no trade could take place.

Placing a value on a good or service was also difficult. For example, how many apples could be exchanged for a cow, how many cows for a cart, and therefore, how many apples to a cart? Apples and other perishable goods would also rot before too long and so could not be saved to trade at a later date. Because of these problems many people still had to rely on being self-sufficient.

The role of money

Nowadays, trade is easy. You can walk into any shop and make an exchange. Today, **money** is a universally accepted **medium of exchange** for goods and services. Money overcomes the disadvantages of barter:

- It provides a common measure of the value of all goods and services, i.e. all goods and services can be priced in terms of currency units
- It allows people to save and buy goods and services at a later date
- It allows people and business organizations to buy on credit and defer payment for goods and services received

Without money, trade would be difficult and specialization stifled. Money encourages specialization by making trade easier. People are able to specialize in particular tasks and be paid with money for their services. People will accept the money because they know that suppliers of food, clothing, shelter, and all other goods and services will accept their money in exchange.

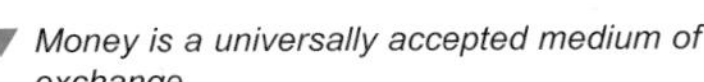

▼ *Money is a universally accepted medium of exchange*

International trade has allowed people all over the world to enjoy a wider range of products and share in technological advances made in different countries.

In the UK today, money includes bank notes and coins, and bank and building society accounts (both current and deposit accounts). Cheques and credit cards are not money but simply a way of transferring money between people and organizations.

How does business create wealth?

Business creates wealth by using natural, man-made, and human resources to make goods and services which people need and want. When goods and services are produced, **resources** are used up - woods, metals, clean air, nutrients in the soil, people's labour, and machines. Businesses will pay the owners of resources for their use. For example, people will supply their labour for wages; landowners will supply land for rent; suppliers of materials and equipment will also be paid to supply them. Business activity, therefore, generates incomes which people can use to buy goods and services. If a business is able to sell its goods and services for more than the cost of the resources it used to produce them, it will make a **profit** - the difference between sales revenues and costs.

Why does business involve choice

The resources used for productive activity are scarce compared with limitless human needs and wants. That is, there are just not enough resources to satisfy everyone's needs and wants. Scarcity of productive inputs implies the need for choice. Businesses must decide how to make the best use of limited resources. Decisions must therefore be taken on three fundamental questions:

- **What to produce?** For example, should resources be used to satisfy wants for food and housing, or should more resources be devoted to the production of computers and tanks?

▼ *Natural resources*

▼ *Labour*

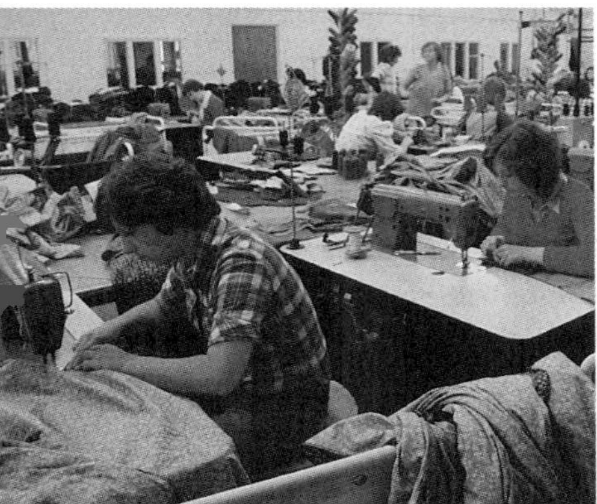

▼ *Capital*

- **How to produce?** Where should production take place? What machines and tools are required? How many workers? What skills do they need?
- **For whom to produce?** Should the old and the infirm get more goods and services? Should more go to those people willing and able to pay the most? Or should everyone get an equal share regardless of their needs? The answer to these questions will depend on people's opinions or value judgements.

What are resources?

The scarce resources available to a business are called **factors of production.** Factors of production can be grouped under three headings:

- **Natural resources** usually called raw materials, include: water from rivers and seas; minerals such as coal and oil; chemicals and gases from the air and deep within the Earth's crust; plants and animals.
- **Labour** describes **human resources.** People provide the physical and mental effort necessary to make goods and services.
- **Capital** describes all those **man-made resources** used to produce other goods and services. To make the task of production easier, man has invented many tools: pens to write with, computers to calculate, screwdrivers, spanners, shovels, drills. On a much larger scale, turbines drive engines, tractors plough soil, roads and railways enable goods to be transported across land, ships and airplanes provide a means of carriage overseas.

Buildings such as factories, offices and shops are further examples of capital goods which help productive activity.

What is an economy?

Choosing how scarce resources should be used is called the problem of **resource allocation.** An **economy** is any system which attempts to solve the problem of resource allocation and decide what, how, and for whom to produce. Within any economic system three main groups of decision-makers can be identified. These are:

- Government
- Private individuals
- Business organizations (including those which seek to make a profit and those, such as charities, which are 'not for profit')

In a market economy such as the UK, most decisions on what, how, and for whom to produce are made by business organizations owned and controlled by private individuals in the **private sector** of the economy. However, some goods and services will also be provided by the government. In **planned economies** such as China and North Korea, the government takes most of the decisions on how to allocate scarce resources. Government authorities and enterprises, owned and controlled by central and local government, form the **public sector** of an economy.

An economy can be of any size and involve any number of people. For example, there is a **local economy** in every village, town, or city. A **national economy** refers to an entire country, such as the United Kingdom. In turn, the United Kingdom is part of the European economy. Indeed, every country in the world can be considered an economy as long as it is involved in productive activity, however small. All the countries in the world together combine to form the **world economy**.

Who are consumers and producers?

A **consumer** is a person who uses goods and services to satisfy their wants and needs. **Consumption**, therefore, involves the using up of goods and services to satisfy wants. When we watch television we are consuming electricity, the television set, and the services of a television company. When we attend college, we are consuming the services of teachers and lecturers. We consume the books we read, the food we eat, the cars we drive, the beds we sleep on, the banks we use.

Business involves the organization of scarce resources into productive enterprises known as **firms**. The people and enterprises who make goods and services are known as **producers**.

Goods and services are produced to satisfy consumer's wants and needs. **Production**, therefore, is any activity which is designed to satisfy wants. A successful business is, therefore, one that has correctly identified its consumers. A firm that uses resources to produce a commodity which nobody wants will soon go out of business.

Where does production take place?

In business it is necessary to distinguish between the different places in which production is organized.

- A **plant** or **factory** will be located at one particular site. Some plants may occupy a large area of land and house many workers and machines, such as a car plant or steel factory. Other plants may be very small, perhaps a small shed where a carpenter carries out his trade.
- A **firm** refers to a business organization, which can own and control any number of plants. For example, as well as offices, Ford UK controls some 13 different plants in the UK where car parts are produced.
- An **industry** consists of a group of firms all producing similar products or services. For example, the car industry consists of all those firms producing cars. Some industries can be dominated by one firm because its scale of production is large compared with competing firms.

Some useful background reading:

Moynihan, D, and Titley, B. '**Economics - A Complete Course**' 3rd edition (Oxford University Press, 2000) Chapters 1, 2 and 19

Business at Work

unit 1

About this unit

Have you ever thought about starting your own business? Or joining an existing business? If you have you will need to know what makes a business work successfully and how to apply that knowledge to your chosen business. For instance, imagine a business owner who doesn't know what customers want, who the business's customers are, and what price to charge. Imagine a salesperson who doesn't know what his or her business is trying to achieve and what makes it different from rival businesses, or a production manager who is unable to explain to staff what quality means.

This unit is about looking at real business. You will consider information provided by businesses and gather your own information from at least one business. A good way of doing this might be to imagine yourself as someone thinking of joining that business as an owner or employee or setting up a rival business to compete with it.

In this unit you will find out about different types of business, their objectives, structures and cultures, and how these affect the way businesses work. You will also examine how all these different aspects of business interact within the business, the different functional areas within businesses and how these operate together to allow businesses to produce goods or services that contribute to the wealth of an economy. You will also find out about the variety of processes used to create goods and services and how and why businesses try to assure the quality of the products they provide.

chapter 1 Production and the Objectives of Business

This chapter examines why and how business organizations undertake productive activities.

What you need to learn

Businesses exist to provide **goods and services**. They change **inputs** (or **resources**, such as labour and materials) into **outputs** to produce the goods and services that meet the wants and needs of their **customers**.

Production is any activity that seeks to satisfy the needs and wants of consumers. You will need to track a production process in order to understand the physical transformations and activities that lead to a finished good or delivery of a service.

From observing the production process you will understand how firms **add value** to their resources. You will need to be able to recognize how firms add value by combining resources to produce goods and services that meet customer requirements.

Quality is an important factor throughout the production process. You need to distinguish between **quality control** and **quality assurance (QA)**. Quality control involves inspecting or testing at various points in the manufacture of a product or delivery of a service. It is usually applied during or after production. However, many businesses use organization-wide approaches to assure quality. This makes quality the responsibility of everyone at all stages in the production of goods and services.

There are numerous quality control and assurance systems including:

- **Total quality management (TQM)**
- **Quality chains and circles**
- **Monitoring and inspection**
- **ISO 9001**
- **Benchmarking**

A total quality approach will combine many of these systems and will involve **staff training and development** in all aspects of quality delivery. You will need to understand and describe the workings and advantages of a total quality approach to productive activity in business.

All business organizations have **objectives** that govern the way they operate. Most businesses aim to **make a profit** from their productive activities, but some will have **non-profit objectives** in **providing a charitable, public or community service**. You need to identify and explain different objectives.

To achieve these objectives businesses may aim to:

- **survive as a business**
- **increase sales or market share**
- **develop a skilled workforce**
- **produce high quality goods or services**

All businesses have particular attitudes, values, and beliefs that make up their **culture**. You need to identify and describe the economic, social, environmental and ethical influences that contribute to a business's culture and describe different business cultures. You should be able to explain how the culture of a business may affect its objectives and help or hinder business success.

Section 1.1

Productive activity

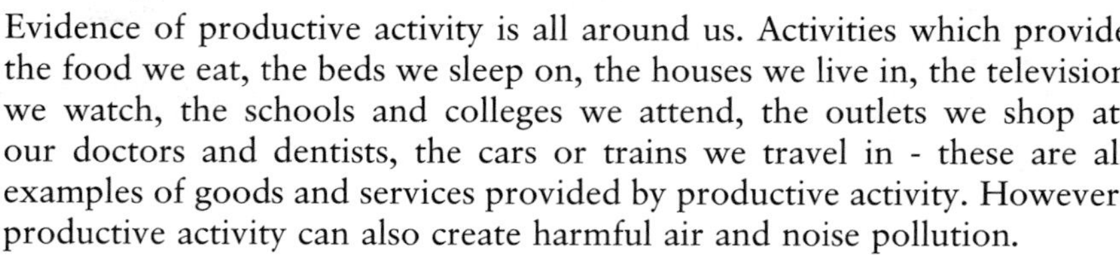

What is production?

▲ *Productive activity*

Evidence of productive activity is all around us. Activities which provide the food we eat, the beds we sleep on, the houses we live in, the television we watch, the schools and colleges we attend, the outlets we shop at, our doctors and dentists, the cars or trains we travel in - these are all examples of goods and services provided by productive activity. However, productive activity can also create harmful air and noise pollution.

Businesses create wealth through their productive activities. They produce the goods and services that consumers demand. **Production**, therefore, can be defined as any activity which is designed to satisfy the wants and needs of consumers. Any activity that fails to satisfy a consumer need or want cannot, therefore, be regarded as a productive activity.

Consumers and producers

In any society most people are both consumers and producers. **Consumers** are people, or other businesses, who demand goods and services to satisfy their needs and wants. For example, when we eat meat and vegetables we satisfy our need for food. When we wear clothes and live in houses we satisfy our needs for warmth and shelter. We use cinemas, compact discs and computer games because we want to be entertained. When a business uses up electricity to power equipment it is satisfying a want to produce other goods and services.

Most people go out to work to earn the money they require to buy the goods and services they and their families need and want. **Producers** are the business owners and business employees who work to supply goods and services, or **products**, to satisfy the needs and wants of consumers.

Combining inputs to produce outputs

Goods and services are the **outputs** of productive activities organized in firms. A **firm** is simply a business organization. All businesses are organizations between people, working together with materials, machines and other equipment to produce a good and/or service. For example, in the production of bread a bakery will first need premises in which to operate. It will then require flour, sugar and salt, fridges, ovens, mixers, ladles, spoons and knives, electricity, and bakers, as well as office staff and equipment - and probably a means of transport.

Workers, materials, power supplies, machines and other equipment are the **inputs** to productive activity. Inputs are likely to have been provided by other businesses, known as **suppliers**. Thus, the bakery also consumes goods and services produced by other firms as well as producing goods for other consumers.

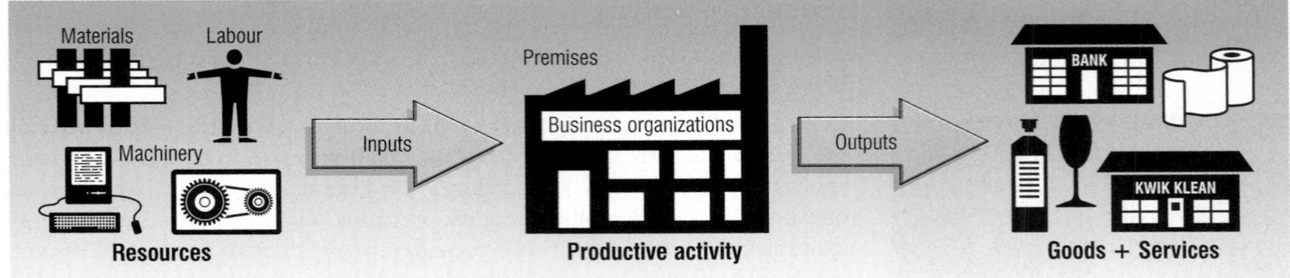

▲ *Productive activity involves combining INPUTS to produce OUTPUTS*

The inputs to productive activity are commonly called **resources**. For convenience economists classify resources into three main categories or **factors of production**. These are:

- **Land** consists of all natural resources, such as water, soil, animals, mineral and ore deposits, and plants
- **Labour** consists of the skills, working time and efforts of people, or human resources
- **Capital** consists of productive 'man-made' resources, such as tools and equipment, machinery, factory and office buildings, vehicles, roads and railways

Factors of production are combined and organized in different amounts and in different ways in different firms to produce different goods and services depending on the production processes required.

Business, therefore, refers to cooperation and organization between the owners of different factors or production for the purpose of productive activity to satisfy consumer needs and wants. There are a great many different types of business producing many millions of different goods and services for consumers in the UK and all over the world.

▼ *Consumer goods*

Types of output

It is useful to distinguish between the many millions of different goods and services produced by business organizations all over the world. A simple distinction is between those goods and services that satisfy the needs and wants of individual consumers and those that satisfy business consumers. We can also distinguish between finished and semi-finished, or intermediate, goods.

A **consumer good** or **service** is any good that satisfies consumers' wants or needs. **Consumer durables** are goods that can be enjoyed or consumed over a long period of time, such as cars, DVD videos and players, washing machines, jewellery, furniture, clothing. In contrast, **non-durable goods** (sometimes called **consumables**) are used up relatively quickly, such as food and drink, petrol, washing powders and newspapers.

Individual consumers will also want **consumer services** such as banking and insurance services, window cleaners, doctors, hairdressers, teachers, telephone providers, and refuse collectors, among many others.

▼ *Finished and semi-finished industrial products*

Some firms choose to satisfy the wants of business consumers for **capital or industrial goods**, such as machinery and equipment, factory and office buildings, and **commercial services**, such as advertising, banking, business insurance, transport and communications.

Natural or 'raw' materials, such as woods, crops and oils, and **semi-finished** goods such as plastics and chemicals, aluminum, glass and component parts, are used to make **finished goods** for individual and business consumers to enjoy. The process of turning natural products into semi-finished and finished products is called **manufacturing** (see 5.7).

Production involves a chain of activities

If the aim of production is to make products to satisfy consumers' needs and wants, the process is not finished until goods and services in the right quantity and of the right quality reach the people and other businesses who want them.

Production involves a **chain of productive activities** linking a number of business organizations - from those that produce natural resources such as coal, wheat and oil, to those that use these materials to make finished goods and services, and finally to those who operate warehouses and shops to sell products to the consumers who want them. Every good or service will have a chain of production linking suppliers with customers (for example, see Figure 1.1).

▼ *Figure 1.1: A chain of production for bread*

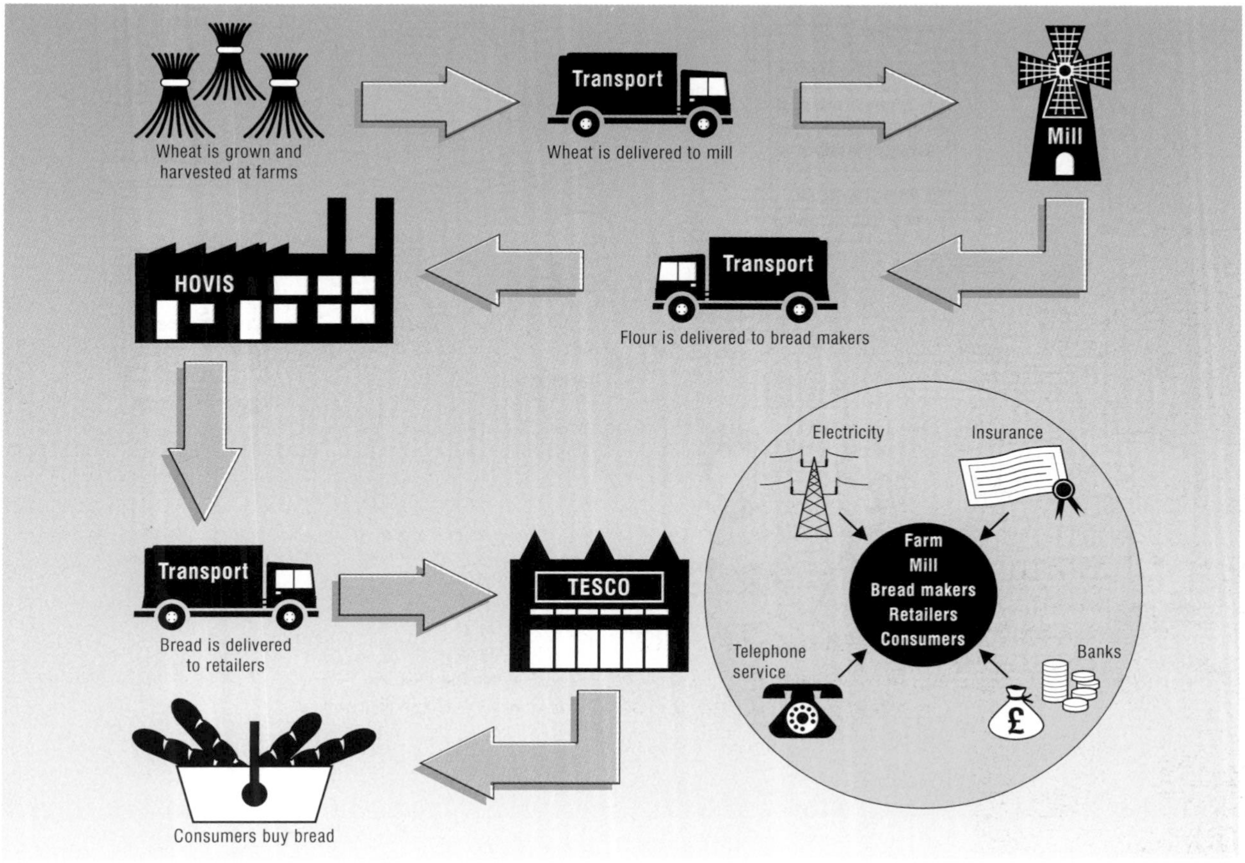

Portfolio Activity 1.1 

1 Below is a jumble of pictures and descriptions explaining how audio compact discs (CDs) are produced

Work in pairs to match each picture to a description. Write down the descriptions to form a chain showing how CDs are produced, from their initial stage to their sale to consumers. Some descriptions can be used more than once.

Descriptions

1 Recording engineers record a group in studio
2 Coal and oil are used to generate electricity for use by firms and households
3 Crude oil is refined
4 Shops sell CDs
5 Transport companies deliver goods and materials
6 Consumers buy CDs
7 Coal and oil are dug and drilled from the ground
8 Chemical firms use oil to produce plastics
9 Insurance firm provides insurance to protect firms from risk, damage or theft
10 Discs are pressed
11 Pipeline carries oil to oil refinery
12 Consumers play CDs
13 CDs are packed into CD cases
14 Banks provide finance for firms

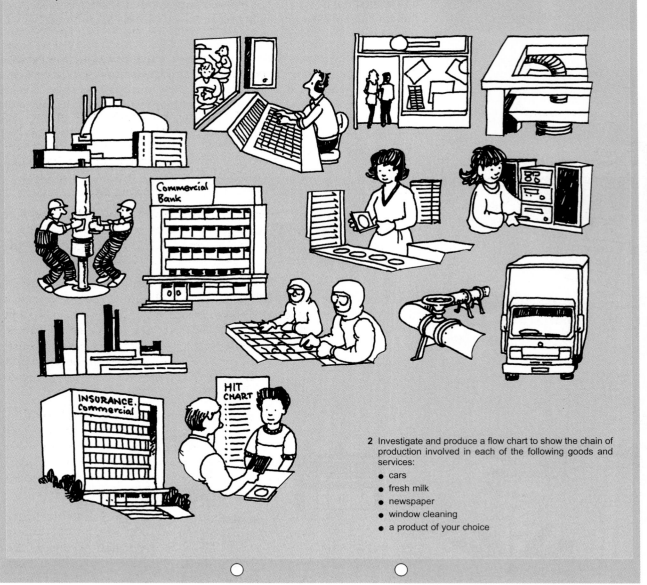

2 Investigate and produce a flow chart to show the chain of production involved in each of the following goods and services:

- cars
- fresh milk
- newspaper
- window cleaning
- a product of your choice

Let us consider the chain of production involved in producing DVD videos for sale to consumers. In the earliest stages, natural resources such as coal and oil need to be extracted from the ground to power electricity stations. Oil, in turn, is the raw material used to produce plastic for the discs and storage cases, which are pressed and shaped by machines. Video editing machines, computers, and recorders are used by engineers to edit and remaster the original video source for the digital transfer to DVDs. The shop is the final destination of the DVD before it is bought. During this process, a great many banks have probably lent money to firms to assist them to complete their part of the chain. Insurance companies have been involved in case of damage or theft and transport companies have delivered raw materials and finished goods to those business organizations that require them.

How productive activity creates wealth

Production involves organizing resources - natural, human and manufactured - to produce goods and services. Unless resources are freely available (for example, air), the owners of these productive resources - land owners, other business owners and employees - will require payment. They will then be able to use their incomes to enjoy the benefit of goods and services bought from other business organizations.

▼ *Adding value in production From these… (inputs)*

▼ *to these (outputs)*

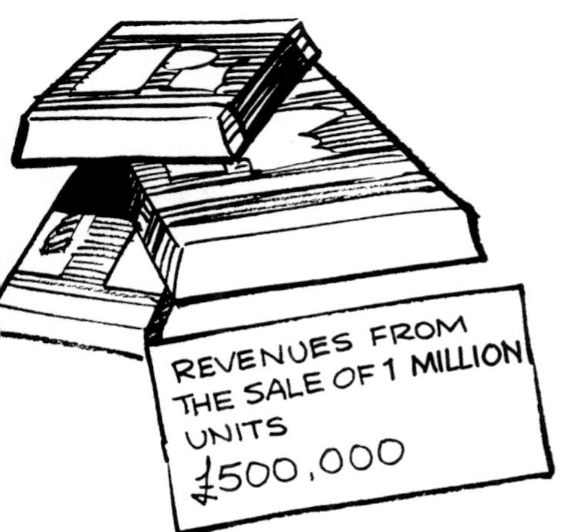

By turning resource inputs into outputs which consumers want and are willing and able to buy, productive activity adds value to resources. For example, a firm that produces 1 million chocolate bars which are sold for 50 pence each but which cost only £200,000 in total to make, has added £300,000 to the value of the resources it used - labour, cocoa powder, milk, paper, plant and machinery, vehicles and power, etc.

In fact, any business organization that uses resources to produce goods or services consumers want is '**adding value**' to those resources. Consider a dressmaker who has bought material from a mill that spins and dyes raw cotton purchased from a farmer (see Figure 1.2 below):

- The farmer sells each bale of raw cotton to the mill for £20. This covers his costs of production and yields him a small profit. The mill can use a bale of cotton to make four yards of material. To allow for a small profit over the cost of the raw cotton and the cost of labour, machines, transport, power, rent, and other overheads, the mill sells the material to the dressmaker for £35. The £15 difference between the price paid for the bale of cotton and the price of the material is the value added, or wealth created, by the mill.
- The dressmaker is able to use the material to make a dress to sell to a shop for £50. This money covers the cost of the material, the dressmaker's labour, the machines she hires, and the power she uses. Any money left over from the sale of the dress after these payments have been deducted is her profit. However, in making the dress for sale at £50 she has added another £15 in value to the resources that have produced the dress.
- The final link in this chain of activity is the shop, which, after deducting the cost of employing shop assistants, power, and rent, plus a mark-up for profit, sells the dress for £70. The shop owner has therefore added a further £20 to the value of the resources that have produced the dress, from the raw cotton in the farmer's fields to the final sale of the finished garment to the consumer.

Firms that provide services are also adding value to the resources they use. For example, a bank provides saving schemes and loans. It will use people's savings to make loans and invest in the shares of limited companies (see 2.2). A bank will earn revenues from interest payments on loans and dividend payments on shares. Out of this money it will pay interest to savers, wages to its staff, electricity bills, invoices for office supplies, rent and rates. Any money left after these payments have been made is the bank's profit - a measure of the value it has added to the resources it has used.

▼ *Figure 1.2: Adding value through a chain of production*

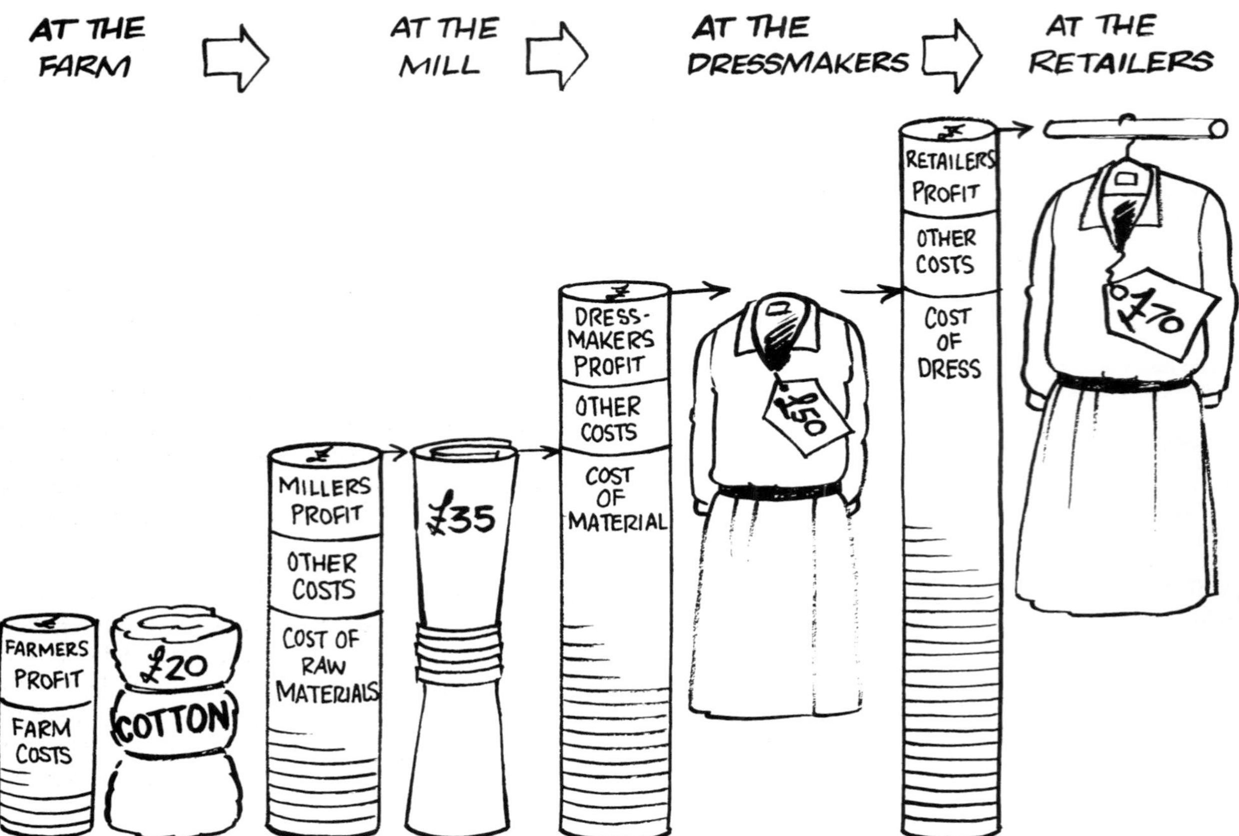

Firms can attempt to maximize the value added to the resources they use, measured as the difference between the cost of those resources and the revenues they generate, by:

- **ensuring the best relationship between the costs of inputs and value of final products.** Most firms will attempt to produce as much as they can from the least amount of labour, materials, and machinery they can. A firm that is able to reduce the amount of inputs it uses but still produce the same amount of ouptut without employing more inputs, has increased **productivity**.
- **reducing the costs of resource inputs.** This can involve employing workers who are willing to work for lower wages or are more productive than existing workers, buying or hiring more efficient machinery, securing supplies of materials from cheaper suppliers, keeping stocks to a minimum to save storage space, reducing waste and accidents at work.

- **quality assurance.** Poorly produced goods and services do not sell but still cost money to make. Making sure that quality is maintained throughout the production process will result in more revenues from given inputs. The management of 'total quality' in firms is becoming increasingly important.

- **marketing.** The marketing of goods and services is an important part of the whole production process (see 8.1). A firm that is unable to supply the right products in the right amounts at the right price, and in the right place, will be unable to sell their products. Marketing helps a firm increase the value added to resources through the production of goods and services, by informing consumers of the existence of the product and persuading them that the price of the product is worth paying.

The ways in which firms add value and improve added value in production are considered in detail in this chapter.

Factors that cause changes in production

The decision by a firm to produce a given level of output of a particular good or service, or range of products, will be influenced by the following factors:

- **Market price.** If the price at which a product is sold does not yield an acceptable profit, then firms will be discouraged from producing that product. Firms that are already engaged in the supply of the product may move their resources into the production of other goods or services, or will attempt to reduce costs to increase profit margins (see 19.3).

- **Availability and quality of resources.** Once a firm has decided what to produce, it must employ the necessary resources to achieve its production targets. Some resources - for example, labour with appropriate skills, or natural materials - may be in short supply, and this will force up the supply price, thereby reducing potential profit margins. Labour must also have skills that are flexible and can be adapted to changes in products, production processes and methods of working. The cost and availability of resources will, therefore, affect the production decisions of firms.

  Increasingly, firms are contracting out non-core activities, such as cleaning and maintenance, and specialist services, to external organizations, rather than employing labour to undertake these tasks on a permanent basis (see 14.6). External organizations will often compete to win contracts with firms, and firms who employ them can therefore insist on quality at competitive prices.

Portfolio Activity 1.2 

A Black Day For Coal

Amid the deluge of figures on the pit closure controversy, two matter above all others. The world price of coal is £30 a tonne. The stuff British Coal now produces is priced at £43 a tonne.

Given this price gap, almost any economic argument for keeping open loss-making coal mines collapses.

The Economist 24.10.1992

Green Sector Urges Tighter Enforcement

Britain's green technology industry called for 'zero tolerance of environmental crime' in order to support sales of air pollution control equipment. It said patchy and relaxed enforcement of air pollution regulations by local authorities was costing the sector billions of pounds in lost business.

Local authorities regulate 12,500 polluting industrial sites under powers granted by the 1990 Environmental Protection Act.

Separately, the government will today be urged by Friends of the Earth, the environmental pressure group, to raise the landfill tax, Britain's first eco-levy.

It published a report suggesting 40 per cent of waste producers had done little to re-use, recycle or minimize their waste in line with the tax's aim of reducing reliance on landfill sites. Raising the tax would encourage more companies to follow the example of the third of businesses that had stepped up waste minimization efforts in response to the tax.

Financial Times, 11.11.1997

New Plant Puts GM In The Fast Lane

IN EISENACH, where once 10,000 East Germans laboured to build 100,000 rattle-trap Wartburg cars a year, Adam Opel is just three months away from its target of producing 125,000 vehicles with less than 20% of the old workforce.

Patrolling the walkway above the newly robotized welding line in the bodyshop, where human beings do just 2% of the work, he tots up the advantages of Opel's showpiece works. According to the measuring standards set by the Massachusetts Institute of Technology, it takes just 18.3 hours to build a car in Eisenach, compared to around 25 at GM's British subsidiary, Vauxhall. 'But the quality is not as good... We make the best Astra in Europe,' he boasts, claiming that cars come off the Eisenach lines with only half a dozen defects each, compared to 14 in Britain.

Financial Times 9.8.1993

'Just in Time' Production Disrupted By Earthquake

Toyota, Japan's largest car maker, yesterday extended assistance to its suppliers hit by the earthquake in Kobe and halted production at all plants for today.

The difficulty in securing supplies from Sumitomo, which makes brake components for Toyota, and Fujitsu Ten, which supplies car audio equipment, was a big factor affecting production at Toyota after the earthquake. The car maker admitted that its Just In Time manufacturing method, which calls for keeping stocks of components at very low levels, meant production was more vulnerable to supply shortages triggered by such disasters.

However, Toyota procures supplies from a number of companies, and the disadvantages of having a low inventory level in an emergency is only one aspect of the Just In Time system which does not affect its overall merits, Toyota said.

Financial Times 20.1.1995

Study the articles above. What factors have affected production in each case? What problems have been, or may have been, caused by these changes?

- **Technology.** Technological advance has resulted in new materials, products, and processes, and has changed the character, working practices, and production methods of many industries. For example, the manufacture of cars is now almost entirely automated. Automation, robotics, computer-aided design and manufacturing, management information systems, and the Internet are all examples of new technology in production. A firm must not only be aware of change, but must also consider the extent to which it can use new technology to keep ahead of the competition.

- **Consumer demand.** To be successful, firms must produce what consumers want and are willing and able to buy. Today, consumers are far more aware of how things are produced. Production processes must reflect growing consumer concern for the environment and the treatment of animals. Firms that fail to cut their pollution, continue to test chemicals on animals, use genetically modified foods, import woods from rainforests (or provide finance to those that do) risk losing customers to those firms who do behave more ethically.

- **Legislation.** A number of laws exist which restrict or prohibit the supply of certain products and set strict guidelines on how production should proceed in the workplace. For example, it is illegal to produce hard drugs, or supply cigarettes and alcohol to minors.

  Growing concern for the environment is being reflected in a number of UK and European Union legislative and tax measures concerning protection, preservation, and pollution (see 6.4). These measures are intended to shape and control production decisions that are potentially damaging to the environment. For example, coal-fired power stations have been forced to fit expensive de-sulphurization equipment to reduce the release of harmful pollutants into the atmosphere. Coal-fired stations are also now being phased out, in favour of cleaner, lean-burn gas-powered electricity-generating plants. Similarly, alternative methods of producing veal meat from young calves had to found when the notorious 'veal crate' method was outlawed in the UK.

  Firms are also required to invest in health and safety measures, such as training, protective clothing, and rest periods for machine operators (see 15.2). Thus, controls on pollution and health and safety at work may raise the production costs of firms, and in some cases limit resource use and production time.

What is productivity?

Production is the total amount of a good or service produced. **Productivity** refers to the amount of output that can be produced from a given input of resources. That is, productivity can be measured as a **ratio of outputs to resource inputs.** Put very simply, a firm that uses 10 units of resources to produce 40 units of output is twice as productive as a firm that uses 10 units of resources to produce 20 units of the same output.

The aim of any business is to combine its resources in the most efficient way. That is, it will attempt to maximize the productivity of its resources in order to produce as much as it can with as little resource input as possible, and at the lowest cost possible. For example, a construction firm that employs 10 carpenters and yet supplies only 1 hammer, drill, and chisel between them has clearly not combined labour and equipment in the most efficient way. By increasing the input of equipment - i.e. providing more hammers, drills, etc. - the firm is likely to achieve a higher level of productivity.

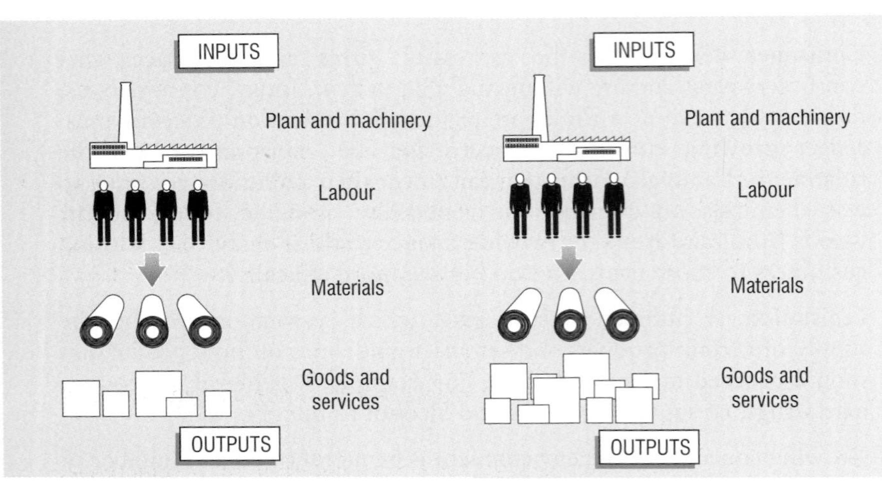

▲ *Productive*

▲ *More productive*

In general, productivity in a firm will increase if more output can be produced with the same input of resources, or if less resources can be used to produce the same amount of output. Thus, raising productivity adds greater value to resources employed.

Combining factors of production

In combining resources for productive activity, a firm can decide to use **labour-intensive techniques** involving a larger proportion of labour than capital (i.e. plant and machinery), or **capital-intensive techniques,** using more machinery relative to labour.

▼ *Capital-intensive*

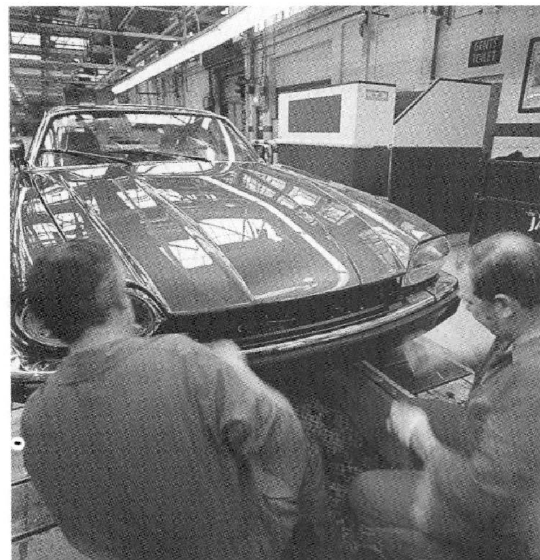

The decision how to combine resources will depend on a number of factors:

- **The nature of the product.** Products in great demand in national and international markets will tend to be mass-produced using a large input of automated machinery.
- **The relative price of labour and capital.** If wages are rising, a firm may decide to employ more capital instead.
- **The size of the firm**. As a firm grows in size, it tends to employ more capital relative to labour.

▼ *Labour-intensive*

FRED'S SHOWING
OFF AGAIN

Measuring the productivity of labour

Although businesses will aim to improve the productivity of all resources, it is usually the productivity of labour that receives the most attention. Workforce productivity is usually measured by assessing changes in the volume or value of output produced in a company.

Labour productivity in a firm can be calculated by dividing output over a given period of time - for example, each day, week, or month - by the number of workers employed. This will give a measure of the average productivity per worker per period:

$$\text{Average product of labour per period} = \frac{\text{Total output per period}}{\text{No. of employees per period}}$$

The **average product** of labour is a useful measure of the efficiency of the workforce. For example, if a company employs 10 workers to produce 200 terracotta plant pots each day, the average product per employee per day is 20 pots. If daily output is able to rise to 220 pots per day without employing additional workers, then productivity will have increased to 22 pots per worker per day.

How easy is it to measure productivity?

A number of problems arise when using measures of the average product of labour. For example:

- Should all employees be included in the calculation of productivity, including cleaners, management, and admin staff? Or should productivity measures concentrate solely on shop-floor workers?
- How can the measure accommodate 'multi-product' plants, where the efforts of employees might contribute to the production of more than one product?
- How can productivity be measured in organizations that produce services, for example, banks or hairdressers?

In a hair salon we might employ a measure of the number of haircuts per hour, but in many ways the salon will be like a multi-product plant, with some people washing hair, others cutting, applying perms, or cleaning. In this case, a better measure of productivity might be achieved by calculating the **value added** per worker per period. This simply means dividing total sales revenues net of costs by the number of employees, to find the average net revenue per worker.

$$\text{Value added per worker per period} = \frac{\text{Total net revenue per period}}{\text{Number of employees per period}}$$

Similarly, measuring productivity in organizations where there is no physical output or sales revenue - for example, the NHS, the Civil Service, or a state school - also poses problems. Here, other measures, such as time spent waiting for operations, or meeting deadlines, or numbers of students obtaining qualifications, have to be used.

Why do firms seek to raise productivity?

The performance of a business organization, in terms of the achievement of certain objectives such as

- business survival
- meeting domestic and international competition
- improving profit
- expanding market share

will depend critically on the level of added value achieved within a firm.

If the same amount of resources can produce more output at the same total cost, then the cost of each unit of output will have fallen. Increasing productivity can therefore lower production costs and increase value added. As costs fall, profit margins rise. A business may also pass on lower costs to consumers in the form of lower prices in an attempt to build and ensure repeat sales at the expense of its rivals.

A firm that fails to increase productivity at the same rate as, or faster than, its competitors will face higher costs and lower profits. Prices cannot be reduced without either sacrificing profits or sustaining a loss. If a firm is unable to offer quality products at competitive prices, then demand for its products will fall. In the long run the firm will face closure, and workers will be made redundant. Adding value is essential to the survival of a firm.

Business organizations in the UK and other developed countries are facing increasing competition from firms in developing economies, such as China, Malaysia, and Taiwan in South East Asia. Wages in these countries are still very low compared with those received by workers in developed countries.

It is therefore vital that firms in the UK increase productivity, reduce unit production costs, and improve product quality in order to compete with overseas organizations and thereby ensure their survival (see 7.4).

Strategies to improve production and productivity

In an increasingly competitive business environment, firms are constantly fighting to raise the productivity of, and add greater value to, their resources. Strategies that aim to improve production and productivity can be grouped into eight main categories. These are:

- secure a reliable source of supplies, and reduce business costs and the need for storage by keeping stocks to a minimum
- introduce total quality control over the whole production process (see 1.2)
- research, develop and introduce new products and/or production processes and working practices designed to reduce waste, improve quality and increase the output from existing input levels of natural materials, capital equipment and labour
- replace old plant and machinery with new, more efficient capital
- increase the amount of new, more productive, capital employed relative to labour

- increase labour productivity through a combination of training for new and improved skills, financial rewards, changes in working methods and management techniques (see 15.2)
- improve safety and reduce accident costs (see 1.4)
- employ more environmentally friendly materials and processes to limit the amount of pollution (see 1.5).

R&D, new production methods, financial incentives to motivate workers, training, investment in new technology, health, safety and environmental measures - all imply higher costs and lower profits in the short run. However, if a firm is able to raise productivity and more than offset these higher costs, the long-term reward will be higher profits, and the ability to compete more vigorously on price and market share with rival firms.

Key words:

Production - economic activity that satisfies a consumer want

Labour-intensive production - the input of more labour relative to capital

Capital-intensive production - employing more machinery relative to labour

Productivity - the ratio of outputs to inputs in a production process, such as the amount of labour input per period of time

Labour productivity - the amount of output produced per unit of labour input

Average product (of labour) - total output divided by the total workforce

Firms - business organizations

Consumers - people and firms who demand goods and services

Factors of production - productive resources

Business - the organization of resources for productive and value added activity

Manufacturing - turning natural resources into finished and semi-finished goods

Consumer durable - a long-lived product that is consumed, or used up, over time

Non-durable goods - goods which are used up quickly in consumption

Capital goods - goods consumed by business customers for productive activity

Semi-finished goods - manufactured goods used in the production of finished products

Finished goods - products ready for final consumption

Value added - wealth created by turning resources into goods and services consumers want

Section **1.2**

Just In Time production and total quality management

Securing supplies

If production is to run efficiently, resources must be available when they are needed. Production will be slowed or held up if a firm suffers shortages of labour, machine breakdowns, and power failures, or if supplies of natural materials and semi-finished components run out. Keeping a sufficient stock of materials or component parts is, therefore, vital to the production process in any firm. Imagine what would happen if Kwik Fit ran out of car-exhausts and tyres to meet consumer demand one weekend!

However, keeping excessive stocks of materials and work-in-progress is costly in terms of storage space, and because it ties up working capital (see 17.1). Because of this, UK firms are increasingly using techniques such as **Just In Time (JIT)** and **Total Quality Management (TQM)**, developed by Japanese industry and used by Japanese firms with operations in the UK.

These and other productivity initiatives are helping more firms to become **lean enterprises.** This means they combine the minimum of resources they can to produce large volumes of the highest quality, with the minimum of waste and stocks, for the lowest possible cost.

Just In Time production

One reason for the high levels of productivity in Japanese industry is the cost reductions achieved by employing **Just In Time inventory control.** This means that suppliers deliver components or materials to production lines 'just in time' for them to be processed. JIT is also known as 'stockless production'.

JIT production is based on the principle that products should be produced when customers need them and in quantities customers want, in order to keep stocks of materials, components, and finished products as low as possible.

For JIT to work, a number of requirements must be met:

- The quality of materials and parts must be high. Poor materials and defective parts can hold up assembly-line production.
- The supplier must be dependable and deliver on time. JIT requires **lead times** between ordering supplies and delivery to be as short as possible. This will be helped if the company and the supplier have a good business relationship.
- It also helps if suppliers are located near the company - but quality and reliability matter more.

Quality assurance

Product quality is an important determinant in the buying decisions of consumers. An organization that fails to assure consumers of quality will lose sales and will eventually be forced to cut back production.

In the past, 'quality control' in many organizations meant inspecting employees' work and products after production had taken place. However, producing poor-quality products and then hunting down the causes in production processes uses up valuable time and resources. Errors are costly.

Total Quality Management (TQM)

To prevent errors happening, Japanese companies have for many years employed methods collectively known as **Total Quality Management (TQM).** These practices have now been adopted by many UK organizations.

The main aim of TQM is to focus companies on the wants of their customers, and on the relationship between suppliers and customers. It involves building-in quality checks at each and every stage in a production process. In this way, problems can be spotted and solved before products complete the production process. Employees are given the responsibility to control the quality of their output, and make changes if and when they detect a problem.

Features of TQM

Empowerment

This means allowing every employee in an organization to use and realize their full potential and abilities. TQM encourages people at all levels in a company to work in teams to analyse production processes and remove waste and inefficiencies. Teamworking improves communication and cooperation in business.

Continuous monitoring and improvement

Kaizen in Japanese means 'continuous improvement'. A business will use TQM to improve productivity, reduce costs, and satisfy consumer wants more effectively than its competitors. However, if a business is to find scope for improvement, production processes need to be continually monitored. **Statistical process control (SPC)** involves collecting data on business performance. Variations in performance, output, delivery times, product quality, materials, employee efforts, absenteeism, can all be analysed to find out what may have caused changes to occur.

Quality circles

These are simply groups of employees, usually between 6 and 12 in number, who work for the same supervisor or line manager. Workers in each circle are responsible for the organization and development of their own jobs. Circle members are trained in problem-solving techniques, in statistical process control, and working in teams.

Each quality circle meets regularly to identify and discuss their work-related problems. They will pass on their findings and any solutions to problems to senior management.

Quality chains

In any business there will be a whole series of suppliers and customers. For example, a secretary supplies a service to a manager. Canteen staff supply a service to a hungry workforce. These **supply chains** will also include customers and suppliers outside the firm. For example, a company may contract the services of another firm to supply and maintain computer equipment. Suppliers must carry out their services to the satisfaction of their customers. Failure to do so may hold up production or result in poor-quality output. TQM places great emphasis on the effective operation of such quality chains and good relationships between suppliers and the firm.

Benchmarking

This involves observing the products and processes of rival companies and then improving on them to satisfy consumers' ever-changing wants.

A firm that is able to demonstrate quality in production and products may be able to display trademarks awarded by independent bodies. For example:

- **The British Standards Institution (BSI)** sets quality and safety standards for a wide range of products. Products meeting the BSI standards are awarded the BSI kitemark to indicate that they have reached the necessary standards. Products awarded the kitemark will have a competitive advantage over those which fail to display the symbol to the consumer.
- The **International Standards Organisation ISO 9001** is a set of international standards on quality management and quality assurance for all manner of products. They can be used by manufacturing and service industries alike. ISO 9001 standards are guidelines firms can use to develop and document the management systems and processes they need to maintain efficient quality control and assurance systems. They include guidelines on product testing and checking, administrative procedures for processing purchase orders and sales documents, and total quality management systems. Business organizations inspected and awarded the ISO 9001 are those who have demonstrated the highest standards. They will have a competitive advantage over organizations that fail to meet ISO 9001 criteria.

- The **Wool Marketing Board** trademark can be used by manufacturers who have produced garments of quality from pure new wool.
- Organizations can register with professional and trade associations if they follow their codes of practice. Examples include the **Federation of Master Builders, Association of British Travel Agents (ABTA),** and the **Advertising Association.**

Portfolio Activity 1.3 

Back to basics on the factory floor

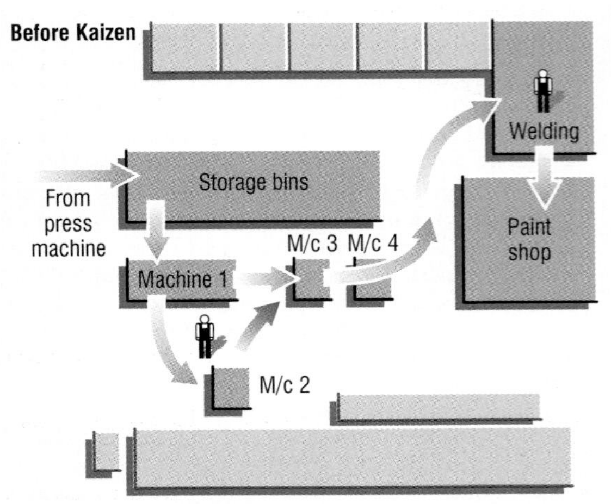

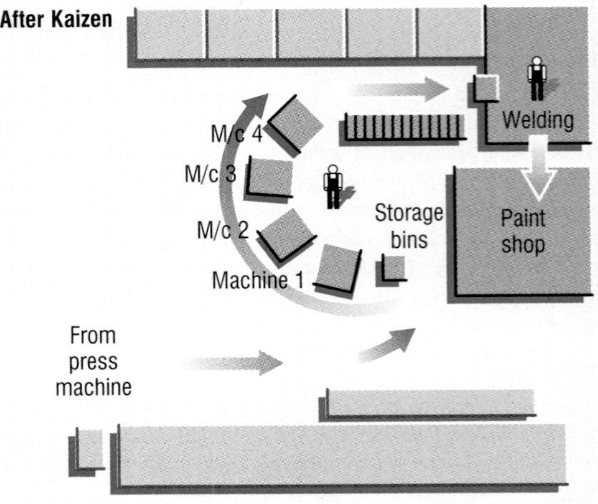

It takes a brave man to allow consultants to tear up his factory and re-arrange it overnight.

At the Paddy Hopkirk car accessory factory in Bedfordshire just before Christmas, consultants inspired by the Japanese concept of continuous improvement – or Kaizen – did just that.

One morning the factory was an untidy sprawl of production lines surrounded by piles of crates holding semi-finished components. Two days later, when the 180-strong workforce came to work, the machines had been brought together in tightly grouped "cells". The piles of components had disappeared, and the newly-cleared floor space was neatly marked with colour-coded lines mapping out the flow of materials.

Overnight, there were dramatic differences. In the first full day, productivity on some lines increased by up to 30 per cent, the space needed for some processes had been halved, and work in progress had been cut considerably. The improved lay-out had allowed some jobs to be combined, freeing up operators for deployment elsewhere in the factory.

One of many Japanese management practices which have been adopted in the west, Kaizen is most frequently applied in larger companies. But it is equally valid in smaller factories. Paddy Hopkirk has sales of £6m a year, but with the help of continuous improvement thinks this can reach £9m.

A central tenet of Kaizen is the elimination of waste. It not only exists in obvious piles of excess inventory. It is also wasteful when an operator makes more movements than is necessary to complete a task because his or her machine is badly positioned.

To reduce one of the biggest sources of waste, Kaizen favours one-piece production, involving as many processes as possible being carried out on a single part consecutively rather than one process being done in a big batch. Parts are only delivered to the next stage of the production or assembly process when they are needed.

Another central theme is the drive to reduce the time wasted in processes that do not add value, like carrying parts or moving from one machine to another.

Financial Times 4.1.1994

Kaizen thinking fires productivity

Ambi-Rad is a European leader in gas-fired 'radiant tube' heating systems. But until recently Mr Brookes, founder and co-owner of Ambi-Rad, was 'too busy' to think about how to increase quality and productivity. 'We were a top-down company with all the new ideas coming from directors' he explained. 'We were worried about the pounds, rather than the pennies'. All that has changed now.

Two years ago Mr Brookes decided that it was time to take action. He set about implementing 'kaizen' thinking under which workers low down in the company hierarchy are given more control over decisions.

Most of the 150 workers at Ambi-Rad's main plant near Wolverhampton, have been divided into eight groups which are each responsible for a specific aspect of making the company's heaters.

Team leaders facilitate new ideas and act as a link between the shop floor and senior managers. One recent idea came from Jean Cokin, an assembly worker for 13 years. She suggested punching holes in a piece of metal in a different place so as to shorten the overall production process. The proposal was implemented, leading to a small but worthwhile change. 'I feel much more involved.' said Ms Cokin. 'As a problem occurs, rather than carry on regardless, we are now encouraged to think a way round it'.

Some of the ideas are very simple, but according to Mr Brookes, suggestions from people like Ms Cokin have taken £300,000 a year off the company's costs. The kaizen scheme has enabled Ambi-Rad to maintain profits at a time of severe difficulties in the engineering business which has been hit by the strong pound and weak demand in important markets.

Financial Times 23.11.1999

1. What is *Kaizen*?
2. Explain how *Kaizen* has been used successfully in the Paddy Hopkirk Car Accessory factory and at Ambi-Rad.
3. **(a)** Gather information on a small local firm, and prepare a short report for management/owners on how they might make use of *Kaizen* to improve productivity. For example, in what ways could their office or factory layout be changed to reduce waste and unnecessary movement? Include 'before and after' layout plans to show the effect of your recommendations.

   (b) What other features of Total Quality Management would you recommend your firm to use? Explain the potential advantages and any disadvantages of your recommendations.

   (c) Make a short presentation of your recommendations to the management/owners of your firm (or members of your group). Discuss your recommendations with them and evaluate your proposals in the light of their comments. For example, what costs and benefits do they think your recommendations, and TQM in general, may have?

Key words:

Job production - producing one product at a time, usually using labour-intensive techniques

Batch production - producing products in batches, for example, of different colours and sizes

Flow production - automated and continuous mass production

Just In Time inventory control (JIT) - keeping stocks and work-in-progress to a minimum by ordering new supplies only when they are needed for production

Lead time - the elapsed time between placing an order for supplies and taking delivery of them

Total Quality Management (TQM) - the continuous improvement of products and processes by focusing on quality at each stage of production

Empowerment - allowing employees to use and realize their full potential and abilities in the workplace

Statistical process control - collecting and analysing data on business performance

Quality circles - small groups of workers each given the responsibility for the organization and development of their own jobs

Quality chains - groups of interdependent suppliers, each one placing an emphasis on reliability and quality

Best practice benchmarking - observing the products and processes of rival companies in order to learn new and better ways of producing

ISO 9001 - a set of international standards on quality management and assurance

Section **1.3**

The impact of technology

chnological advance in medicine

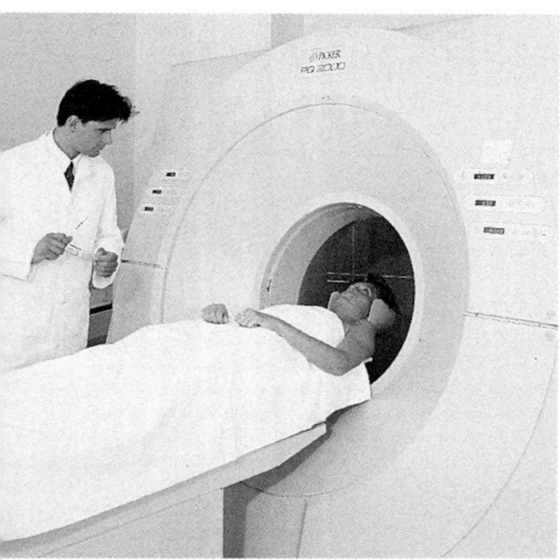

Technological advance

One of the most important factors affecting production this century has been the impact of new technology. For example, advancing technology has brought about the following changes:

- **New products and services**, such as digital versatile discs, mobile phones, flatscreen televisions, automated banking and the Internet
- **New materials**, such as polythene, nylon, and silicon chips for computer motherboards
- **New and more efficient methods of production**, such as computer-aided manufacture (CAM), robotic assembly and welding, genetic engineering to produce hardy vegetable crops, recycling and waste management, laser precision measurements and cutting, 'keyhole' surgery in hospitals
- **New skills**, such as computer technicians, communications engineers, management consultants, genetic engineers

▼ *Technological advance in communications and robotics*

- **Changes in business activities,** such as videoconferencing, direct mailing, wordprocessing, computer-aided design (CAD) and management information systems (MIS). A **management information system** is a restricted network established within an organization to provide managers with information and analysis that will help them in their decision making. In a competitive world the faster this information and analysis is received the better and improvements in computer and communications technology has facilitated this (see 3.3).

Each year, industry spends many billions of pounds on the research and development of new products and production processes. In 1998 some £10.2 billion was spent on R&D in UK businesses alone.

Technological advance has greatly increased the speed, accuracy, reliability, and cost of new capital equipment to business, resulting in a fall in demand for labour in some occupations and industries. For example, the work of once-skilled typesetters and compositors in the printing industry can now be performed by writers and journalists using desktop publishing software. Intelligent robots controlled by computer are increasingly taking over human tasks in manufacturing processes such as car-assembly and food packaging. This is known as **computer-aided manufacture (CAM)** (see 4.2).

What is CAD?

Computer-aided design (CAD) refers to interactive computer software capable of generating, storing, and using geometric graphics. CAD is used by design engineers in many industries for tasks ranging from the development of product packaging to the design of office blocks. The benefits of using CAD are:

- A reduction in lead times between product design and production
- The ability to examine and evaluate a wide range of designs without the need for building 3D prototypes
- The ability to modify designs quickly and easily

The costs of new technology

Despite its undoubted advantages, the increasing use of new technologies in business has not been without cost. Some of the disadvantages include:

- **High 'front-end' costs:** the research and development of new technologies, and their installation and maintenance, are often very expensive. Short-term production costs may also rise if workers need to be retrained, or if labour is laid off and redundancy payments have to be made.
- **Damage to labour relations:** workers may view the introduction of new machinery and production methods with suspicion. Bitter labour disputes between Trade Unions and employers have occurred in the past because of the fear of job losses. New technology has tended to replace manual jobs, but has also created a demand for new, more technical, skills, requiring workforces to undergo retraining.

The substitution of capital for labour in a firm will depend on the type of product and the production process used. In some cases, substitution will not be possible. For example, as yet machines cannot undertake the work of a hairdresser, window-cleaner, economist, or nurse, although clearly many in these occupations will use capital equipment, from hairdriers to computers, to help them in their tasks. In some cases, however, technological advance has increased the demand for labour. For example, the 1980s and 1990s saw a significant increase in the demand for computer technicians and programmers, following growth in the market for personal computers.

Portfolio Activity 1.4 

Investigate the introduction of new equipment in a business organization with which you are familiar. Try to find out:

- The reasons for its introduction
- The cost of the equipment
- The method of finance
- Whether employees were, or will be, given training
- Whether the equipment has replaced labour
- The impact (or expected impact) of the equipment on productivity and quality

Key words:

Technology - the 'science of the industrial arts', that is, the creative processes which help solve problems and improve efficiency

Computer-aided manufacture (CAM) - automated manufacture controlled by computers

Computer-aided design (CAD) - use of interactive computer software to assist design

Substitution of capital for labour - replacing human with mechanical effort

Section **1.4**

Health and safety at work

▼ *Health and safety at work*

In a typical week in Britain, nine workers are killed, a child, an adult, and an elderly person are killed, and 400 people suffer major injuries - all as a result of work-related accidents.

The statistics on work-related accidents in Britain are grim. It is not surprising, therefore, that firms are required by law to provide a healthy and safe environment for their workers and customers (see 15.2). Implementing health and safety measures adds to business costs in the short run. However, a firm that does not consider the interests of its employees is unlikely to achieve its business goals. A healthier workforce, and one that has fewer accidents, is more productive, and will reduce costs in the long run.

Health and safety measures in the workplace include the following:

- Promoting hygienic conditions
- Protecting workers from hazardous substances
- Training staff in health and safety matters
- Providing ear protectors against noise
- Maintaining safety equipment and clothing
- Allowing breaks for lunch and tea so that workers do not become tired
- Providing First Aid kits and training for medical officers
- Controlling workplace temperature
- Reducing workplace air and noise pollution

Clearly, the need for many of these measures will vary depending on the workplace. For example, office workers will primarily need to be aware of fire drills and precautions relating to the prolonged use of computer screens, the movement of office furniture, etc. By contrast, many industrial workers regularly come into contact with potentially dangerous machinery and substances, and will need much greater levels of protection.

Portfolio Activity 1.5 

1. From the articles, explain why it is so important for firms to develop and promote health and safety measures in the workplace.
2. Investigate the health and safety measures employed in your school/college. What improvements would you recommend, if any? To help develop your ideas, it might be useful to collect statistics on past accidents and their causes, to see where improvement might be made. Check with your main school/college office if this information is available.

   Produce a brief report of your findings and ideas to present to senior teachers, following the five-step plan recommended in the article below.
3. Contrast the health and safety measures in your school/college with those employed in another business organization with which you are familiar. Do they differ? If so, why?

Five steps to safety

ADVICE ON how to assess and control risks to health and safety in the workplace is contained in a new free HSE leaflet.

The five steps described in the leaflet are:

- look for the hazards (anything that could cause harm);
- decide who might be harmed and how;
- evaluate the risks arising from the hazards, and decide whether existing precautions are adequate or more needs to be done;
- record the findings; and
- review the assessment from time to time and revise it as necessary.

Work-related illnesses 'costs up to £18bn'

Work-related injuries and illnesses have increased sharply, according to a study of the financial impact of health and safety at work.

The study by the Health and Safety Executive, indicates a 122 per cent increase in the incidence of work-related illness between 1990 and 1995-6, mainly due to the rise in time off work as a result of stress and musculoskeletal disorders.

Work-related injury and illness in the UK annually costs 2.1-2.6 per cent of the gross domestic product, equivalent to between £14.4bn and £18bn. It is estimated to cost employers between £3.5bn and £7.3bn a year in lost output and including insurance - 4.8 per cent of all gross company trading profits.

The study found that workers suffering from work injuries and work-related illness lost £558m in reduced income and extra expenditure. When losses caused by pain, grief and suffering were included in the calculation, this added an estimated £5.5bn to costs.

Financial Times, 25.10.1999

Section **1.5**

Reducing pollution from production

▼ *Noise pollution*

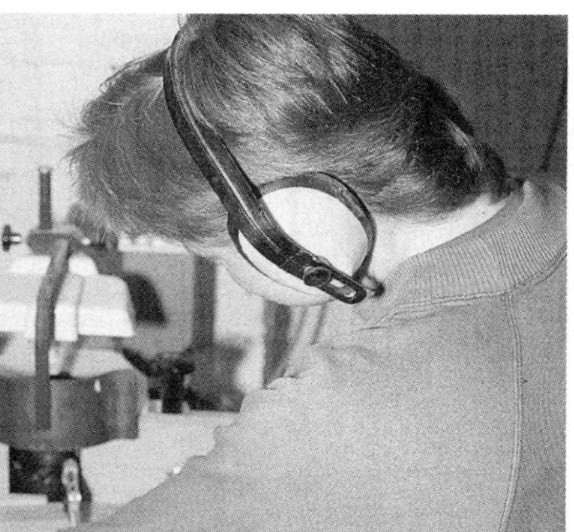

In the working environment

Some production processes result in potentially harmful pollutants being released into the air and some can be very noisy. If employees health and stress levels are not to suffer, employers must make sure that appropriate measures are taken to reduce air and noise pollution. This can be done by issuing employees with protective clothing and equipment. However, wearing masks and ear mufflers may impede worker efforts and so production processes must be investigated for possible solutions. For example, extractor fans, new less noisy equipment and sound proofing could be deployed.

▼ *Chemical pollution*

In the natural environment

However, it is not just workers who may suffer from pollution. Harmful pollutants can be released into the air and water supplies as the result of production in many factories.

Farms may use chemical sprays to protect crops that harm fish and animals. Office work can also result in piles of waste paper. Oil spills can occur at drilling platforms and from tankers. Radiation may leak from nuclear power plants.

Portfolio Activity 1.6 

Life ever after

To discover how green a product is, companies increasingly look at its environmental effects before, during and after production

One study describes how, after Denmark required refillable containers for drinks, Tetra Pak analysed the environmental effects of its non-refillable paper cartons. It showed they could be packed closer together than glass bottles, thus reducing the number of polluting lorry-loads needed to transport them.

The cartons need less energy to refrigerate and cause less water pollution than glass, which must be cleaned. When bottles are discarded, they take up more space in landfills than lightweight cartons. Confronted with such evidence, the Danish government lifted its ban on non-refillable containers, and in 1993 even lifted its tax on milk cartons.

Adapted from The Economist 9.10.1993

Food for thought

In 1988 McDonald's, America's biggest fast food chain, found itself the target of a vociferous campaign by environmental groups against the enormous amounts of rubbish it produced.

The polystyrene 'clamshells' in which McDonald's hamburgers were sold became a vivid symbol of the throw-away society. The company had chosen polystyrene, a light-weight plastic foam with good insulating properties, because it seemed ideal for packaging fast food. But its use meant that a product which took seconds to consume was carried out of the shop in a package that would take centuries to rot. Customers began posting them back to McDonald's in protest. Schoolchildren demonstrated outside its restaurants.

The company saw such protests as a threat to it future survival. Young people, its most devoted customers, were also those who embraced greenery with the greatest zeal.

At first McDonald's expanded recycling at its restaurants. However, the Environmental Defence Fund (EDF) - one of Americas more innovative environmental research and lobbying groups - urged them to reconsider. In a matter of days McDonald's announced it would replace the clamshell, where possible, with a quilted paper wrap made from a layer of tissue between a sheet of paper and polyethylene.

McDonald's continues to work with the EDF. The company now has a number of goals; reduce, reuse and recycle, for example, by reducing the amount of chlorine bleached paper it uses, and using more recycled materials.

Adapted from The Economist 29.8.1992

1. Why did the Danish government ban non-refillable cartons? Why was this ban eventually lifted? What likely effect did these changes have on producers of containers?
2. Why did McDonald's initially choose to supply their products in polystyrene containers? What factors caused them to rethink this choice? What were the likely effects of these changes on production and supply chains?
3. Visit a manufacturing plant. Discuss with workers and managers measures that have been used by the firm to reduce pollution (air and noise) in their working environment and in the natural environment. Why has the firm wanted to reduce pollution? What costs have been involved? If the firm has not employed measures to reduce pollution, make appropriate recommendations. Write up your findings in a word processed report.
4. Assemble examples from newspapers, magazines and TV, that illustrate how firms are changing their production processes to be more environmentally friendly, or in some cases even less friendly, in your opinion. Analyse how these changes are likely to affect business costs and revenues, labour requirements and relationships with suppliers.

Increasing concern for the environment has resulted not only in legislation to control pollution but also firms taking the initiative to make sure they produce goods and services which meet the changing desires of consumers. For example, the *Clean Air Act* and *Environmental Protection Act* set limits on the type and amount of pollutants firms can discharge into the atmosphere, rivers and seas. The Environment Agency for England and Wales and the Scottish Environment Protection Agency are responsible for the control of industrial pollution and waste, and for the regulation of the water environment (see 6.4).

Changing consumer demands for more environmentally products and less damaging methods of production have also resulted in an increasing number of firms adopting many other environmental measures that has changed the way they produce their goods and services. For example;

- wood merchants and furniture makers making sure their supplies are from renewable forests and not tropical rainforests
- fitting catalytic converters on motor vehicles to reduce exhaust emissions
- using new chemicals in fridges and aerosol cans that no longer destroy the ozone layer
- halting the testing of products and ingredients on animals
- using more recycled materials and biodegradable packaging

Unless firms produce the goods and services consumers want, including the way they are produced and the materials they use, firms will not satisfy consumer wants for increasingly environmentally friendly products and will, therefore, fail to achieve their business objectives. It is these we turn to next.

Section **1.6**

Why do business organizations undertake productive activity?

The objectives of business organizations

The people who organize resources in business organizations for the purpose of productive activity are often called **entrepreneurs**. They have the business know-how or the ability to organize production. This is known as **enterprise**.

Entrepreneurs will take the risks and decisions required to make a business organization successful. As a reward for risk taking most entrepreneurs will want to make a **profit** from their productive activities. They do this by producing the goods and services consumers want and are willing and able to pay a price for that is greater than the cost of producing the good or service.

However, some business organizations are set up and run to fulfil **non-profit** motives, for example, providing a **charitable** or **voluntary service** to help people, animals or the environment. In addition, there are government organizations which provide **public services**. Their services may be provided for just a small fee or even free to people who need them.

Providing charitable, voluntary or public services or making a profit are **business objectives.** In order to best achieve these objectives, firms may attempt to fulfil certain other aims first. For example, to achieve the long-term goal of making as much profit as possible, a firm may initially aim to increase sales by spending heavily on advertising, or increase productivity and product quality by investing in staff training. These activities will initially raise costs and reduce profits, but in the long run a successful advertising campaign, improved productivity and better product quality can increase sales, lower business costs and boost profits.

Portfolio Activity 1.7

What do you think are the objectives of the business organizations in the articles and pictures below?

P&O takes on the British Car dealer

A FERRY company today launches the biggest challenge yet to high prices being charged to buy a car in Britain. P&O Stenna Line will import vehicles from the Continent, where they are generally cheaper, and re-sell them at up to 18 per cent less than the standard UK price.

Metro, 1.2.2000

IBM backs Linux to challenge Microsoft

International Business Machines will try to establish the Linux operating system as a major competitor to Microsoft.

The move forms part of the world's largest computer company's attempt to reinvigorate flagging hardware sales and develop e-business software. Microsoft is currently introducing its Windows 2000 family of operating systems.

Financial Times, 11.2.2000

BA to axe 6,500 jobs in drive to boost jobs

British Airways is to shed more than 6,500 jobs over the next three years as it seeks more cost cuts to help finance an ambitious £600m investment programme and restore profitablity.

Financial Times, 1.2.2000

Business Accounts
Year ending 21.12.2000

	£'000
Wages	115
Factory and office rent	40
Materials	350
Electricity	32
Telephone	2
Equipment hire	23
Transport	14
Advertising	36
Overheads	28
Total costs	640
Sales revenue	1,070
Profit	**430**

▲ *Profit is a surplus of revenue over cost*

Making a profit

Most firms hope to persuade consumers to buy their goods and services at a price greater than the cost of making them. Selling goods and services generates **revenue** for a business organization. **Profit** is what is left from revenues after all costs have been paid. A firm that is unable to cover its costs with enough sales revenues will make a loss and could be forced to close down if losses continue.

It is important for a business to make a profit so that it can:

- pay for wages, materials, rents and other bills, and have enough revenue left over to satisfy the business owners who have invested their money in the business
- borrow money from banks and other lenders who will want to be sure the business is successful and can afford to repay them
- use the money to buy new equipment and machinery when it becomes worn out or obsolete

▼ *Table 1.1: The UK's Top Five Profit-makers, 1997-98*

Organization	Main activities	Capital employed £ billion	Turnover £ billion	Pre-tax Profit £ billion	Number of employees
HSBC Holdings	Banking	26.9	18.1	4.5	109,298
Shell Transport and Trading	Oil, gas and nuclear fuels	21.0	32.8	4.3	101,000
British Petroleum	Oil, gas and nuclear fuels	20.6	44.7	3.7	53,700
British Telecommunications	Communications	17.5	14.5	3.0	135,200
Glaxo Wellcome	Chemicals	4.0	8.3	2.9	53,808

The Times 1000, 1998

To help a business make a healthy profit from its productive activities it may be necessary for it to fulfil certain other aims.

Surviving as a business or expanding

In some markets there is so much competition between rival firms to supply that good or service to consumers that the aim of all firms might be simply to survive. That is why some people say 'business is war'!

Staying in business requires making enough money to cover business costs (see 22.2). Survival is often the most important aim of a new business. If the firm can survive, its next aim may be to expand and try to earn a profit. However, for some businesses it is getting more and more difficult just to survive. For example, many small corner shops in cities find that they cannot match the low prices and variety of products in supermarkets. As a result many thousands of small shops have gone out of business in recent years.

Other businesses may seek to grow in size by producing and selling more of their goods and services. This will be easier to do if the consumer demand for their type of good or service is growing (see 5.3). If consumer demand isn't growing, or even falling, a business may only be able to expand if it can attract customers away from rival firms.

To increase consumer demand for its products and grow market share a business will need to make its products more attractive than rival products, by selling at a lower price, by improving the product, and/or by increased advertising. If the business is successful and consumer demand for their product does rise, the firm will have to produce more. All this will cost money, but in the long run it will help the business expand. Alternatively, business organizations will often join together to become bigger (see 6.4).

Increasing sales and market share

If a firm is to make a profit it will need to persuade customers to buy its products. The total number of people willing and able to buy a given product is said to form the market for that product (see 5.1). For example, the **market** for cars and is made up of all the people who want to buy cars. Similarly, the market for oranges is made up of all the people who buy oranges. In fact, every product will have a market if consumers want it.

▼ *Creaming it: Shares in the wrapped impulse ice cream market, UK 1998*

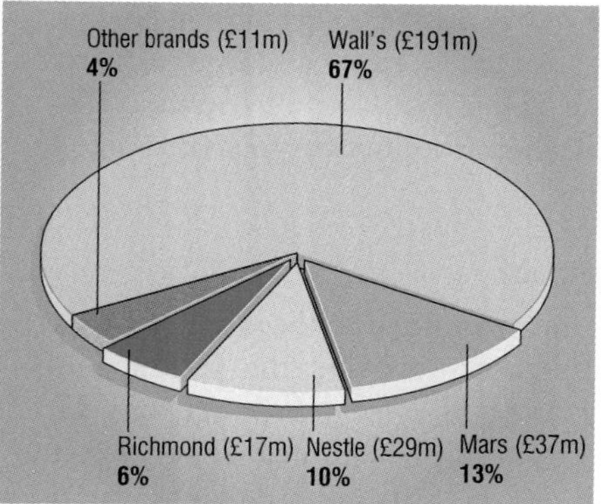

Source: Mintel

Most firms will compete for consumers with rival firms producing the same or similar goods or services. For example, Coca Cola competes with other cola drinks such as Pepsi, Virgin and supermarket own brands. Firms will compete to increase their share of the total market.

The size of the market for any particular good or service can be measured by the value of total sales by consumers of that product. Firms, therefore, compete for a share of the total spending by consumers. Increasing **market share** is, therefore, an important objective for many firms. For example, Wall's dominates the market for ice cream in the UK, with 67% of sales of wrapped ice cream brands in 1998. The next largest ice cream producer, Mars, generated 13% of total UK sales worth £285m in 1998.

A new firm entering a market for the first time may initially price their product very low and spend a lot of money on advertising to attract consumers to buy it. Established rival firms may respond by also cutting the prices of their competing products and increasing advertising. These business strategies can be very expensive for firms. Heavy spending on advertising raises costs and price cutting lowers sales revenues, so profits will fall. However, if a business is successful, it will increase sales and may in future be able to raise its prices so that eventually it will increase profits.

A firm that is able to outsell all it rivals may eventually dominate the market supply of the product. It may become so big and powerful that it can cut prices below the production costs of rival firms and drive them out of business. If a particular product is available from only one supplier, that firm is called a **monopoly** (see 5.2). For example, Railtrack is the monopoly supplier of railway lines in the UK. Rail operators, such as Virgin Trains and Thames Trains, have to pay Railtrack to run trains on their tracks. Railtrack may be tempted to use its monopoly power to make rail operators pay very high charges for the use of their railway lines, but is prevented from doing so by the Government which employs a Rail Regulator to agree with Railtrack what are reasonable charges. Railtrack can be fined if it is found to be using its powerful market position to overcharge. The same goes for any powerful firms who try to overcharge their customers because of their dominant position over the supply of a particular good or service (see 12.5).

Orange cuts call charges and renews war of words

Orange foreshadowed a new price war in the mobile phone industry yesterday when it halved the cost of calls in its pre-pay package and renewed claims that consumers are being ripped off by rivals.

Chief Executive Hans Snook announced that peak-rate calls on Orange pre-pay are being cut from 50p to 25p a minute while its airtime vouchers will no longer expire after a set time. Offpeak is being reduced to 5p a minute.

The Guardian, 28.10.1999

▲ *Price competition is fierce in many industries*

Providing a highly competitive product or service

A business is unlikely to be able to increase its sales and market share if it does not have a highly competitive product. Businesses that produce goods and services which are not very good quality, or are priced too high, or have a poor or out-of-date image, or do not incorporate the latest technologies, or take too long to respond to customer enquiries or complaints, will fail to compete with business rivals that do offer a highly professional and competitive product. For example, would you pay £5 to a window cleaner who always leaves dirt and smears on your windows if another window cleaner offers to make your windows spotless for only £3 or your money back?

Many markets for goods and services are very competitive. For example, people who shop in supermarkets want the widest possible choice of products at the lowest possible prices. This is why price-cutting wars between the big supermarkets chains keep breaking out (see 10.2). Similarly, consumers of computers and other hi-tech equipment always want the latest products and designs and they expect technology to improve every few months. Only those firms that can anticipate what customers will want next and then alter their production to make it for them, will survive.

Improving the quality of a product or service

To make more profit a business might aim to improve the quality of its goods or services. A business can do this by improving the product or service. For example, the packaging or taste of a food product may be improved to make it more appealing to consumers. Technical changes can increase the speed of game play and quality of visual images on a computer games console to meet the demands of young players. Similarly, a doctor's surgery may replace a turn-up-and-wait service with an appointment service to reduce waiting times. A train company may run trains with more carriages during peak hours to reduce overcrowding. However, all these changes may initially increase business costs and so reduce profits.

Consumer tastes, fashion and wants are always changing. Business organizations can improve their existing goods and services to meet these changing demands (see 5.3). Businesses that fail to do so will lose sales and profits.

Developing a highly skilled workforce

It is often said that the most important resource in a business is its people. They are the managers and employees who take the decisions and carry out the day-to-day tasks that run the business. Without highly skilled managers and employees a firm will find it difficult to produce low-cost, high-quality goods or services to outsell rival products. It will lose market share to those firms that do have skilled workforces and ultimately may not survive as a profitable business.

▼ *The most important resource in business*

All business organizations rely on their staff to perform successfully and achieve set objectives. For example, how would a hospital achieve health care objectives without skilled doctors and nurses? Would a bank make a profit if its managers could not take sound financial decisions? Could a charity raise awareness among people and attract donations of money for its cause without people skilled in marketing and charity work? Would a hairdressing salon attract customers if staff could not cut hair? Would electrical shops sell electrical goods if sales staff had no product knowledge or could not operate cash tills?

Managers must be skilled leaders who make the right decisions at the right times to ensure the success of the business. Employees must have the right skills to research and develop new products and processes, to buy materials, components and equipment of the right quality and in the right quantities for production. They must be skilled operators of machinery, produce accurate business accounts, design appropriate marketing campaigns, and provide valued customers services. A business must recruit people with the skills it needs or develop those skills in existing employees through training programmes (see 15.2). It must also seek to retain skilled and valued employees by maintaining good staff relations and offering financial and other rewards.

Not-for-profit objectives

Providing a charitable service

A number of business organizations belong to what is called the **voluntary sector**. Charitable organizations rely on legacies and donations of money to provide help and care for people and animals in need - those without the ability to pay for food or healthcare, and protection from cruelty and exploitation. Charities can also raise money by holding special events, such as fetes and sponsored walks, or even by selling goods, such as T-shirts and Christmas cards. They may also obtain funds from business sponsors and grants from the national lottery and government.

Organizations such as Greenpeace, the RSPCA, The National Trust, Oxfam, and the British Heart Foundation do not aim to make a profit from their productive activities. All the money received by these and other charities are used to cover the cost of their operations, from day to day management and administration, advertising to attract donations, and ultimately (and most importantly) to provide the goods and services to those who need them.

▼ *Charities spend many billions of pounds all over the world each year on good causes*

Charities expenditure in real terms[1] on social protection of the top 500 charities[2]: by function, 1992-93 and 1996-97

United Kingdom	£ Million at 1996-97 prices[1]	
	1992-93	1996-97
Physical disability	297	333
Children	202	255
Cancer	239	228
Mental health	95	148
Blind people	116	133
Other medical and hospitals	193	125
Elderly people	123	111
Terminal care	70	88
Youth	55	66
Chest and heart	44	63
Deaf people	29	46
AIDS	11	10
Total	1,474	1,606

1 Adjusted to 1996-97 prices using the retail prices index.
2 Charities Aid Foundation top 500 fundraising charities.
Excludes administrative expenditure
Source: Charities Aid Foundation
Social Trends 1999

▼ *The objective of the RSPCA is to care for and protect animals from cruelty*

Charitable organizations

There are over 170,000 charities in Britain, all of which have trust status. This means a person, or group of persons, are appointed as trustees of each charity to look after the funds and other assets, such as premises and equipment, of the organization.

Charities are normally exempt from the payment of tax. The Registrar of Charities therefore exercises careful control on the types of activity that can be registered as charities. This is to prevent corrupt business organizations or individuals from setting up bogus charities in order to avoid paying tax on their incomes.

A charitable trust can be set up for the following reasons:

- to help the poor in the UK and overseas - for example, Save the Children and Oxfam
- to provide counselling and advice to those in need - for example, the Samaritans
- to advance education, for example - a voluntarily aided school or public school
- for religious purposes - for example, to restore or maintain an old church
- to protect and conserve the environment and animals - for example, Greenpeace and the RSPCA

Despite the non-profit-making objectives of a charity, it must be managed and run just like any business organization that *does* aim to make a profit. A charity will want to generate as much revenue as possible from donations and other sources to pay for the services it provides to those in need, and to keep costs as low as possible. It will need good managers and skilled workers, and will have to keep detailed financial records.

Charities can go bankrupt if their income is less than their costs, and they can be closed down if it is found trustees have misused money for non-charitable purposes.

Providing a public service

Unlike firms that exist to make a profit, a number of organizations provide goods and services which it is felt everyone should benefit from regardless of their ability to pay for them. Many schools and hospitals, the police and fire services, the Army and Navy, coastguards and street lighting, are all examples of **public services** which are provided to consumers free or for only a small charge at their point of use. Instead, money raised by central and local government from taxes and other revenues is used to pay for the production of public services (see 2.3).

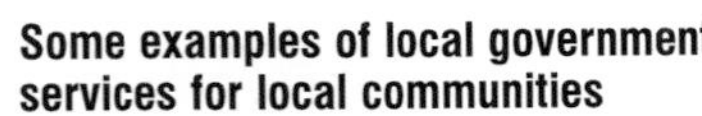

Some examples of local government services for local communities	Some examples of central government services
Street lighting	National Health Service
Refuse collection	Air traffic control
Public parks	Armed services
Libraries	Law and order
Cutting grass verges	Consumer protection
Road sweeping	Immigration services
Local road maintenance	Collection of economic and social statistics
Local community centres	Social security
Fire services	Major road building and maintenance
Family planning clinics	The River Thames flood barrier

▲ *Street lighting, the National Health Service and the Thames Flood Barrier provide public services*

Providing a voluntary service

Some organizations rely on the unpaid skills and help of volunteers to undertake productive activities. They might provide help for homeless people, a counselling service, a refuge for injured animals, a hospital radio station, or run a local sports or amateur dramatics club. Like charities they will often rely on donations of money, revenues from the sale of gifts and other items, sponsors and grants of money from other business organizations and government.

Other not-for-profit organizations

Some organizations may not be registered as charities, may have huge annual turnovers, and may employ many hundreds or thousands of employees, yet still not be in business to make a profit. For example, the Co-operative Society and building societies are examples of **mutual societies** (see 2.2). Any surplus of revenue they make over their costs is ploughed back into the business to the benefit of their members, for example, lower prices for customers of Co-operative Society outlets and higher interest rates for savers in building societies. Similarly, trade unions are run for the benefit of their members who pay a subscription to join them (see 13.4).

In addition, there are **companies limited by guarantee**. They may be owned and run by a small number of shareholders yet have objectives other than making a profit. For example, the League Against Cruel Sports is a limited company (see 2.2). It relies on the same source of revenue as a charity but does not have charitable status. Any revenue it attracts is used to raise awareness of cruel 'blood' sports, lobby the government to ban them, and care for animals that are victim to these practices.

Key words:

Entrepreneur - a person who invests money in starting a business

Enterprise - business know-how and skills

Business objectives - the goals of a business organization

Revenue - money raised from business activities

Profit - a surplus of revenue over cost

Loss - an excess of costs over revenues

Market - all the consumers and producers of a particular product

Market share - how much of the total sales value or volume of a particular product is generated by a business

Monopoly - a firm that dominants the market supply of a particular product or, in the extreme, is the only supplier of a particular product

Voluntary sector - charities and other organizations that do not aim to make a profit and will rely on the help of volunteers to provide their services

Public services - are provided free or below cost by local and central government for everyone to enjoy regardless of their ability to pay for them

Mutual society - a non-profit-making organization run for the benefit of its members

Company limited by guarantee - a private company owned by shareholders that agrees not to profit from its activities

Section 1.7 Business cultures

Many business organizations will express their main business objectives in a **mission statement**. Overleaf are some examples from well-known organizations.

Tesco plc

"Our core purpose is to create value for customers to earn their lifetime loyalty"

Royal Brompton & Harefield NHS Trust

To be the leading national and international centre for the diagnosis, treatment and care of patients with heart and lung disease, creating and disseminating knowledge through research and education.

HSBC Holdings plc

The HSBC Group is committed to five Core Business Principles:

- ***outstanding customer service;***
- ***effective and efficient operations;***
- ***strong capital and liquidity;***
- ***conservative lending policy;***
- ***strict expense discipline;***

through loyal and committed employees who make lasting customer relationships and international teamwork easier to achieve.

British Airports Authority plc

To make BAA the most successful airport company in the world. This means:

- **Always focusing on our customers' needs and safety**
- **Achieving continuous improvements in the profitability costs and quality of all our processes and services**
- **Enabling us all to give of our best**
- **Growing with the support and trust of our neighbours**

Mission statements may also reveal information about the culture of the business organization. Businesses are as individual as societies of people and nations. They have different cultures.

What is an organizational culture?

The **culture** of a business organization is the total characteristics shared by members of the organization. These include their customs, ideals, beliefs, attitudes, habits and skills. The organizational culture will influence the objectives of the business, what it does to achieve them, and how well it is able to achieve them. This might involve:

- how management is structured in the organization (see 2.4)
- the ways people at all levels in the organization interact and communicate with each other (see 3.1)
- the way employees are treated
- the way people dress for work
- how hard people work, their motivation and level of commitment
- administrative procedures (see 4.1)
- rules and regulations
- use of technology
- attitudes towards change (see 2.6)
- the image of the organization in the eyes of local communities, consumers, suppliers and governments (see 12.5)

For example, it is common to hear people say a business has a 'a long-hours culture' or 'a culture that gets the job done', referring either to the hard work ethic and commitment of employees or perhaps the style of managers who expect too much of their staff (see 2.5).

Other organizations may have a 'caring culture' in which employees at all levels of the organizations are valued and treated well, or perhaps they adopt a caring approach to their customers and the environment. We might also compare organizations which have a 'go-ahead' culture and those in which managers and employees resist change and shy away from challenges because they like to do things as they have always done them.

Because a business culture is shared by the organization members, new employees may have to adapt to the culture or leave if they do not 'fit' the culture because it is very different from their own. The cultural reputation of a business can, therefore, either attract new recruits or deter people from applying for jobs in the organization. New members can be introduced to the organization culture formally through induction and other training programmes or informally through the people they work and socialize with in the business. Members who do not easily 'fit' the culture may prove to be disruptive, especially if they begin to influence other employees. This could lead to a lack of co-ordination, affect the image of the organization, and eventually its long-term success.

Influences on organizational culture

An organization's culture is affected by a number of factors. These include:

- The **business environment**. For example, a fiercely competitive environment may encourage employees to pull together and work hard in order to beat rival businesses and ensure the long-term success of their firm and their jobs. This may be encouraged by bonus payments linked to sales or productivity improvements (see 15.2).
- The **economic environment**, which may be harsh. An economic recession may result in falling consumer demand, sales and profits for many business organizations (see 7.1). Tough business decisions may have to be taken including cutting employment levels. At these times the ability of the workforce and senior managers to work together for business survival will be severely tested. In contrast, if the economy and business is booming the business may be able to increase profits and even expand. However, business owners that fail to share the success of their business with their employees, or fail to communicate their expansion plans with them may find they lose their 'hearts and minds'.
- The **working environment** and conditions inside the organization can encourage people to follow the desired culture or cause resentment (see 2.6). For example, is the physical layout friendly and inviting or harsh and cold? Are there on-site leisure facilities, rest areas and canteens? Are work areas and toilets kept clean?
- **Powerful groups or individuals** within the organization, such as a senior manager or a trade union official, may try to impose their ideas on the culture of their organization, or will work hard to gain widespread respect and acceptance for their ideas. A change in senior management or employees can, therefore, cause cultural change within an organization.

- **Social and religious factors** can shape the organizational culture. Divisions can occur and be disruptive. It is important that differences in race, religion, gender, age, and other individual characteristics are respected at all levels in an organization.
- **Business ethics.** Today it is clearly important for business organizations to recognize that consumers do not like to be 'ripped off' by firms who charge high prices and offer poor quality just to make a quick profit. Consumers also want businesses to show more care for people in need, the environment, animals and other creatures. Even if a business doesn't have a particularly caring culture, it may need to present a caring image in order to keep customers happy and profits high. However, it is far easier to introduce changes to business activities that reflect these concerns when an organization does have a caring culture. If it does, all members of the organization, from senior managers down to shop floor workers, can make decisions and organize their day-to-day work in ways that meet with more caring objectives. In turn, the image of the organization will improve both for consumers and people seeking work with the organization.

Portfolio Activity 1.8 

- What are the objectives of the organizations in the articles and statements below?
- Do you think these objectives conflict with, or will help to achieve, the profit motives of these organizations?
- What do these objectives suggest about the culture of each of organization, and/or ...
- the desire of each organization to change its culture or image?

Coke unveils plans to be a 'valued world citizen'

Coca-Cola is looking to forge a series of partnerships with governments to make itself a 'valued citizen' in international markets - and avoid a repeat of the political blunders which tarnished its image last year.

Douglas Daft, the new chairman, said Coke was considering initiatives such as offering its extensive distribution network in India to take polio vaccine into rural areas on the governments behalf.

Carl Ware, head of the company's newly created global public and governmental affairs team, is also examining a similar project in Africa, where Mr Daft said he was 'very aware of the need to address the Aids issue'.

The chairman said the main lesson he had drawn from last year's events was that Coke had not understood the complex changes that had occurred in the European political arena. 'You've got to be sensitive to the needs of these politicians.'

Last week Mr Daft unveiled a major restructuring with 6,000 job losses - the largest in Coca-Cola's history.

Financial Times, 1.2.2000

"Tesco is dedicated to eliminating the need for testing products and ingredients on animals, and is a major financial contributor to the Fund for the Replacement of Animals in Medical Experimentation (FRAME)".

"Our policy on animal testing is as follows:

- Tesco products are not tested on animals by Tesco, by our product manufacturers or by anyone on our behalf
- Ingredients used in Tesco brand products have not been, and will not, be tested on animals by Tesco, or by anyone on our behalf
- Our manufacturers use only ingredients which are known to be safe, ensuring the safety of our customers without further testing on animals
- New products are safety-assessed by experts using data which is already available
- If additional checks are required, these are performed on human volunteers under carefully controlled conditions, or through alternative methods"

Tesco website (www.tesco.co.uk), 16.3.2000

The Boeing Company: *Values*

In all our relationships we will demonstrate our steadfast commitment to:

- **Leadership:** We will be a world-class leader in every aspect of our business and in developing our team leadership skills at every level; in our management performance; in the way we design, build and support our products; and in our financial results.
- **Integrity:** We will always take the high road by practising the highest ethical standards, and by honouring our commitments. We will take personal responsibility for our actions, and treat everyone fairly and with trust and respect.
- **Quality:** We will strive for continuous quality improvement in all that we do, so that we will rank among the world's premier industrial fims in customer, employee and community satisfaction.
- **Customer Satisfaction:** Satisfied customers are essential to our success. We will achieve total customer satisfaction by understanding what the customer wants and delivering it flawlessly.
- **People Working Together:** We recognize our strength and our competitive advantage is - and always will be - people. We will continually learn, and share ideas and knowledge. We will encourage co-operative efforts at every level and across all activities in our company.
- **A Diverse and Involved Team:** We value the skills, strengths, and perspectives of our diverse team. We will foster a participatory workplace that enables people to get involved in making decisions about their work that advance our common business objectives.
- **Good Corporate Citizenship:** We will provide a safe workplace and protect the environment. We will promote the health and well-being of Boeing people and their families. We will work with our communities by volunteering and financially supporting education and other worthy causes.
- **Enhancing Shareholder Value:** Our business must produce a profit, and we must generate superior returns on the assets entrusted to us by our shareholders. We will ensure our success by satisfying our customers and increasing shareholder value.

Boeing website (www.boeing.com), 16.3.2000

Key words:

Organizational culture - the total characteristics (beliefs, attitudes, assumptions, etc.) of an organization's members that influence the way the business operates and its objectives

Mission statement - a brief declaration from a business organization about its main aims and objectives

Useful references

British Standards Institution ***(www.bsi.org.uk)***
Customer Services, 389 Chiswick High Road, London W4 4Al

Charities Aid Foundation ***(www.caf.org.uk)***
Also look in ***www.demon.co.uk/charities***

Department for Trade and Industry ***(www.dti.gov.uk)***
Enquiry Unit, 1 Victoria Street, London SW1H 0ET

Health and Safety Executive ***(www.hse.gov.uk)***
HSE Information Centre, Broad Lane, Sheffield S3 7HQ

Internet key words search: **Charities, TQM, ISO9001**

Test your knowledge

Questions 1–3 share the following answer options:

- **A** Changing the ratio of capital to labour inputs
- **B** Total Quality Management
- **C** Worker empowerment
- **D** Quality circles

Which of the above describe the following strategies to improve productivity in a firm?

1. Organizing labour into small teams

2. Encouraging greater participation in business decision making and problem solving

3. Investment in new plant and machinery

4. The main reason a firm will wish to increase productivity is:
   - **A** To reduce labour input
   - **B** To reduce costs
   - **C** To increase prices
   - **D** To improve quality

5. Quality assurance in business may involve all of the following **except**:
   - **A** Staff training
   - **B** Product testing
   - **C** Compliance with health and safety regulations
   - **D** Closing down the customer service helpline

6. Which of the following organizations is not in business to make a profit?
   - **A** Microsoft
   - **B** Rolls Royce
   - **C** British Heart Foundation
   - **D** McDonald's

7. Just In Time production involves:
   - **A** Supplying a product when the customer pays for it
   - **B** Reducing the lead time between the delivery and processing of materials
   - **C** Increasing stocks of stored components and materials
   - **D** Cutting quality to speed up production

8. Which of the following is a consumer durable good?
   - **A** Washing powder
   - **B** A newspaper
   - **C** Frozen chips
   - **D** A TV set

9. What is the most likely objective of a government-owned organization?
   - **A** To provide a service to the public
   - **B** To expand as quickly as possible
   - **C** To make as much profit as possible
   - **D** To compete with private firms

10. The market share of a business is measured by:
    - **A** The volume of products it makes
    - **B** Total sales of its product
    - **C** Its total production costs
    - **D** Its total advertising expenditure

11. **a** What is production?
    b What is productivity?
    c What objectives do firms hope to achieve by increasing productivity?
    d Explain two ways in which a construction firm might attempt to increase productivity.
    e What strategies could an office employ to improve productivity?

12. **a** What is the difference between capital intensive and labour intensive production?
    b Explain how Total Quality Management differs from quality control.
    c 'The drive for profit and consumers desires for improved product quality will often conflict'. Do you think this statement is true or false? Explain the reasons for your answer.

13. **a** What are factors of production? Give examples.
    b Explain how productive activity adds value to resources.
    c All production involves a chain of activity. Explain, using an example of a good or service of your choice.
    d Why do business organizations undertake productive activities?

14. **a** What is organizational culture?
    b Suggest three factors that may influence the culture of a business organization.
    c Explain, using examples, how the objectives of a business may be influenced by its culture.

chapter 2 Organizing Business

This chapter investigates the types of business organization that exist, their purposes and how management and authority is structured and organized within them.

What you need to learn

Business can be classified in different ways. You need to know whether a business is in the **voluntary, private or public sector**, and understand the differences between different types of business organization.

- The different types of **private sector business organization** are **sole traders**, **partnerships**, **private limited companies**, **public limited companies**, **cooperatives**, **charities** and **franchises**. These business types differ in the way they are financed, controlled, use their profits, and the legal liabilities of their owners.
- **Public sector organizations** are owned and controlled by central and local government. They include **government departments**, **public corporations**, **executive agencies** and **QUANGOs**.

Businesses can change their type of ownership. You will need to understand reasons for change in business ownership and their impact on the liability of owners to repay business debts, access to sources of finance, control and use of profits. Some business owners have **unlimited liability**. If their business fails they are personally responsible for all business debts. Others may have **limited liability**. If their business fails, they can only lose the money they invested in it.

Businesses are structured in different ways according to the way they operate, and according to their culture. The structure of a business can affect the way it works and performs. You need to understand the differences between different organizational structures.

- An organization **hierarchy** shows the **chain of command** in a business from the most senior managers down to managers or supervisors of the lowest rank. A **hierarchical organization** may be **tall** or **flat** depending on the number of layers of management and the span of control of each manager over their staff.
- In a **centralised organization**, authority, responsibility and decision making are concentrated at the top of the hierarchy. In a **decentralized organization**, authority and responsibility are delegated to lower levels of management.
- In a **matrix organization** staff with appropriate skills will tend to be organized into different project teams.

You will need to understand how the market in which a business operates in can influence the organizational structure of the business. This will involve considering the process of **de-layering** and the move towards flatter structures in businesses that operate in fast-changing, dynamic markets.

You will need to understand

- the difference between **autocratic, democratic and consultative management styles** and how they may influence or be influenced by organizational structure
- how the business culture may affect organizational structure and vice versa

Section **2.1**

Types of business organization

There are four main types of business organization in the UK:

- **Private firms** are owned and controlled by private individuals and can range from small one-person businesses to large multinational corporations.
- **Cooperatives** are owned either by consumers who buy from them or by the employees who work in them.
- **Public-sector enterprises** are owned and controlled by government.
- **Voluntary organizations** are private sector organizations run for the benefit of others, often by unpaid volunteers. They do not seek to make a profit. For example, charities are part of the voluntary sector. They rely on donations of money and gifts to provide help and care for less fortunate people, animals and the environment. Some charitable trusts also exist to run schools, churches and social clubs (see 1.7).

▼ *Figure 2.1: Types of business organization*

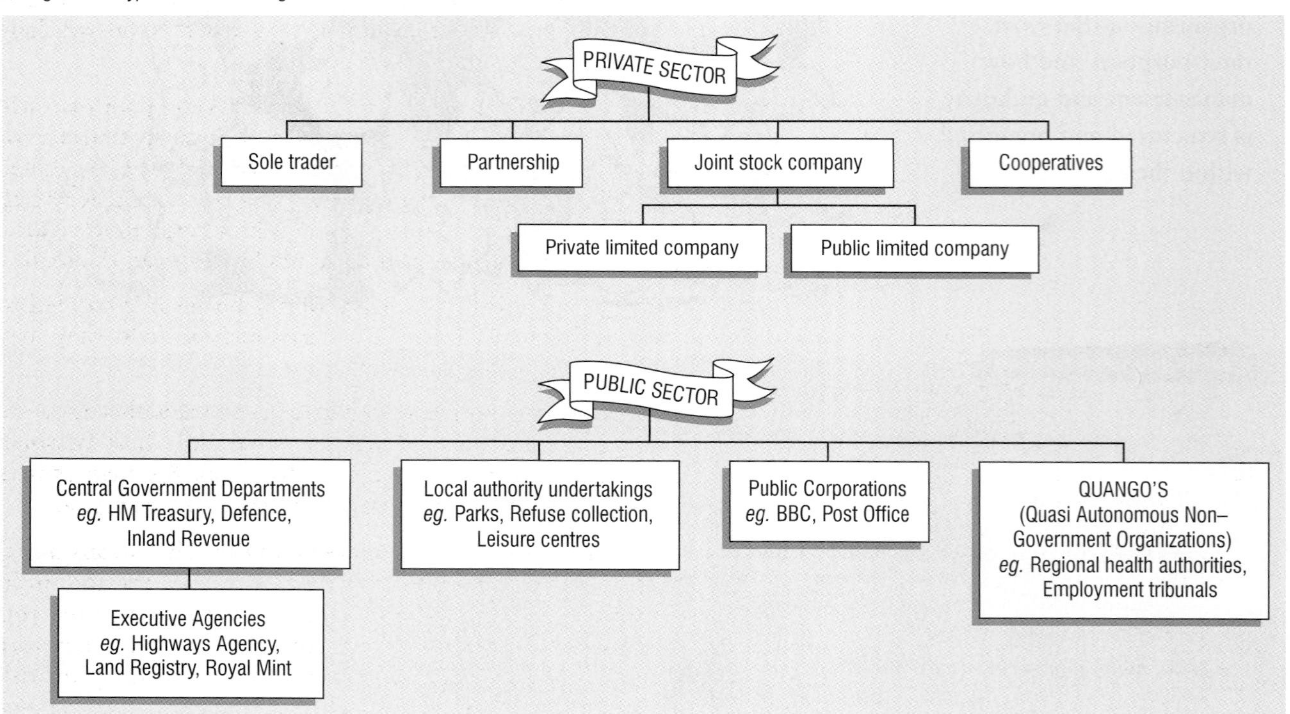

Each type of business organization can be distinguished from other types by considering:

- the business objectives
- who owns the business
- whether the business owners have to repay any business debts
- who controls the organization from day to day
- how the business is financed
- who gets any profits

All of these things can change over time as a business changes its form and type of ownership. For example, as a business grows it may change its main objective from gaining market share to making as much profit as possible (see 1.7). However, in order to grow it may need to raise more finance. To do this the original owners may need to invite new owners to invest in their business. In return the new owners will want a share of any profits. As the number of owners grows it will become more difficult for them all to manage and control the business from day to day. Instead they will employ mangers to run the business on their behalf, but this means the original owners may lose control over their business.

A private individual who wishes to start his or her own business will, therefore, need to consider three main questions.

- **Will I have enough money?** To start a business, an entrepreneur will need **capital.** This is the money used to buy premises, machinery, equipment, and materials (see 18.2). Some businesses will need more capital than others. If a person cannot raise enough money on their own, they may need to find other people, or partners, who will help finance the business and share in its ownership.
- **Can I manage the business alone?** Running a business on your own will often require working long hours and being a 'jack of all trades'. For example, a self-employed carpenter must not only be a skilled carpenter, but will also need to manage the business, do the accounts, advertise, employ staff if necessary, pay the bills, and much more. Setting up in business with other people can help to spread the load.
- **Will I risk everything I own?** The owner of any business is entitled to a share of any profits made. However, if the business fails, they may also be responsible for paying any debts.

 *Unlimited liability*

THEY EVEN TOOK MY CLOTHES!
CLOSED
DEBT COLLECTORS

Some business owners have **unlimited liability**. This means that they are liable to pay all business debts and may have to sell their personal possessions - house, car, furniture, jewellery - to do so. Business owners can be taken to Court and declared bankrupt if debts are not repaid.

However, some business owners enjoy **limited liability**. This means that if their business fails, they only stand to lose the money they invested in it. They will not have to sell personal possessions to raise money to clear business debts. This reduces their risk. An entrepreneur must therefore decide when financing a business whether they are willing to risk everything they own if the business fails. This will influence their choice of business organization.

Key words:

Capital - money used to finance the purchase of business assets, such as plant and machinery

Unlimited liability - when business owners are liable for all business debts

Limited liability - when business owners can only lose the amount of money they invested in a business and are not liable to repay all business debts

Section 2.2

Private sector business organizations

We can distinguish between the different types of private sector business organizations by asking the following questions:

- Who owns the business?
- Who controls the business?
- What is the main source of finance?

▼ *Sole traders*

The sole trader

Ownership and control

The oldest and most popular type of business is the sole trader - a business that is owned and controlled by one person. Many small businesses such as local shopkeepers, market stall traders, plumbers, and hairdressers, operate as sole traders. There are more sole traders in the UK than any other type of business. In fact, many of the very large and successful businesses today started life as sole traders many years ago.

Finance

A sole trader is someone who is self-employed. To start their business, they will usually dip into their own savings or borrow from family and friends. Sole traders will also tend to rely on an overdraft facility at the bank in order to make payments, obtain credit from their suppliers, hire purchase for the purchase of equipment, and credit card companies (see 16.4). However, because sole traders are relatively small and risky business enterprises they will often find it difficult to raise the capital they need to expand. To do this a sole trader may need to consider changing the type of ownership of his or her business.

Sole traders may grow to employ several people or have a number of branches, but so long as there is only one owner the business will remain a sole trader.

▼ *Advantages and disadvantages of being a sole trader*

Advantages	Disadvantages
Easy to set up - there are no legal formalities or fees	The owner may have limited funds and may find it difficult to borrow money from banks
The owner is his/her own boss and can make all the decisions	The owner may have to work long hours and cannot afford to be off sick
The owner keeps all the profits	The owner has unlimited liability
Can be set up with relatively little capital	The owner must be a 'jack of all trades'
Personal contact with customers can encourage consumer loyalty	Small businesses are often unable to benefit from bulk purchase discounts

Partnerships

Ownership and control

Under the Partnership Act 1890, a partnership is defined as an agreement between 2 to 20 people providing capital and working together in a business with the objective of making a profit. Partnerships are common in professions such as doctors, insurance brokers, and vets, although they can also be found in other occupations such as builders, garages, and in small factories. Firms of accountants, solicitors, and members of the Stock Exchange are allowed to have more than 20 partners.

Although it is not required in law, most partnerships operate according to terms drawn up in a **Deed of Partnership**. This is a document that sets out matters such as how much capital each partner has invested in the business and therefore how much they own, how profits (and losses) are shared among the partners, and procedures for accepting new partners. If no agreement is drawn up, the rights and obligations of partners are determined by the 1890 Partnership Act.

Finance

A sole trader may find it difficult to manage a business alone or raise enough finance to expand. A partnership can help overcome this problem. To become a partner in a firm, it is necessary for the prospective partner to buy his or her way into the partnership, thus providing existing partners with additional capital.

Banks may be more willing to lend money to a partnership because the security offered by a group of partners is likely to be more than that of sole trader.

▼ *Advantages and disadvantages of a partnership*

Advantages	Disadvantages
Easy to set up. There are few legal formalities	Partners may disagree
More capital can be injected into the business	Partners have unlimited liability
Partners can have a variety of useful skills, bring new ideas and help decision-making	Partnerships may still lack capital
Partners can cover for each other during periods of sickness and holidays	Profits have to be shared
	A partnership will automatically end, or is dissolved, if one partner resigns, dies, or is made bankrupt

Under the 1907 Partnership Act, **ordinary partnerships** can be turned into **limited partnerships** where at least one partner, known as a **sleeping partner**, has limited liability. Sleeping partners provide capital for the business and take a share of the profits but take no active part in the day-to-day running of it.

Joint stock companies

Joint stock companies are also known as **limited companies.** They differ significantly from sole traders and partnerships in the way in which they are financed, owned, and controlled.

Portfolio Activity 2.1 

Look around your local area and identify businesses that are:

- Sole traders
- Partnerships
- Limited companies

For each business, try to explain why you think the organization, and what it produces, is suited to that particular business type.

Useful sources of information might include:

- Local business phone directories
- Local newspaper articles
- The local council
- The Chamber of Commerce
- Training and Enterprise Councils

Finance

Limited companies raise most of their capital through the sale of shares. Money raised from the sales of shares is known as **permanent capital.** That is, shareholders' money never has to be repaid. If a shareholder wishes to get back the money they invested, they must sell their shares to someone else.

Ownership

Limited companies are owned by their shareholders. Each shareholder has limited liability. The liability to pay company debts should the business fail is limited to the amount each shareholder invested in the company. This gives people the confidence to buy shares in the knowledge that their personal possessions are not at risk.

Control

The day-to-day running of a limited company is undertaken by a board of directors. These are elected by shareholders to run and control the company on their behalf (see 2.5). In a small company, shareholders may be directors. However, in very large companies there may be many thousands of shareholders. In these companies there is a 'separation of ownership from control'.

In addition, limited companies will have:

- **A separate legal identity** - that is, the business exists in law separately from its owners (the shareholders). Unlike sole traders and partnerships, the owners of a limited company cannot be sued for damages, recovery of debt, etc.
- **Strict legal requirements.** The 1985 Companies Act requires all companies to publish financial accounts each year and make these available to all shareholders at an annual general meeting (AGM). In addition, all limited companies must be registered with the Registrar of Companies at Companies House, to whom copies of the financial accounts should be sent. Companies are also required to make their accounts available to any member of the public.

There are two main types of limited company: the **private limited company (Ltd)** and the **public limited company (plc)**. Most of the smaller joint stock companies are private limited companies - there are around half a million in existence in the UK. Plcs tend to be much larger in size but fewer in number.

Private limited companies

The founder members of a private limited company are able to sell shares to raise capital but can only do so to family, friends, and associates. This may limit the amount of money they are able to raise.

Selling shares also means that founder members can lose control of their company unless they retain over 50% of the shares they issue. Because there is one vote per share, the shareholder with over 50% of shares is said to have a **controlling interest.** They are able to outvote all other shareholders on matters such as company policy and the election of directors.

A shareholder who wants his or her money back must sell their shares to another person with the prior agreement of all the other business owners.

Forming a limited company

The promoters of a company are required by law to provide a number of legal documents to the Registrar of Companies:

The **Memorandum of Association** governs the company's relationship with the outside world. It contains important information about the company including:

- The company name (followed by either Ltd or plc)
- The main business address
- The objects of the business, i.e. what it will produce
- A statement of limited liability of the members
- The amount of capital to be raised by issuing shares, for example: £500,000 from the issue of 250,000 ordinary shares with a face value of £2 each
- The agreement of the founder members to form a limited company

The **Articles of Association** control the internal running of the company. These give details such as:

- Procedures for calling a general meeting of shareholders
- The number, rights, and obligations of directors
- Shareholder voting rights

When satisfied that all legal requirements have been met, the Registrar will issue a **Certificate of Incorporation** which permits the new company to start trading.

Single member companies

In 1992, new regulations were introduced under the Twelfth Company Law Directive of the European Union, to allow the formation of private limited companies with just one shareholder.

▼ *Advantages and disadvantages of a private limited company*

Advantages	Disadvantages
The sale of shares can raise capital	Founder members may lose control
Owners have limited liability	Shares cannot be advertised or sold on the stock exchange
The company has a separate legal identity from its owners	Setting up can be expansive because of the legal requirements
Owners can appoint directors on their record of achievement and business knowledge	Financial information must be published
Capital raised from the sale of shares never has to be repaid	An annual general meeting of shareholders must be held each year

▼ *Some well-known public limited companies*

Public limited companies (plcs)

Plcs are among the largest and most successful organizations in the UK. Examples include British Gas plc, Unilever plc and Tesco plc.

Unlike a private limited company, a plc is able to advertise the sale of shares and sell them to members of the general public through the Stock Exchange (see 19.4).

In addition to the advantages and disadvantages of a private limited company, the plc also has a number of others. These are:

▼ *Advantages and disadvantages of a public limited company*

Advantages	Disadvantages
Shares can be advertised	'Going public' can be expensive
Shares can be sold through the Stock Exchange	Some plcs can grow so large that they may become difficult to manage effectively
Large plcs may find it easier to borrow from banks	Risk of takeover by rival companies who have bought shares in the company

Cooperatives

A **cooperative** is an organization formed by people joining together for mutual interest to organize production, make decisions, and share profits. All members have an equal say in running the business and share equally in the profits. There are many different types of cooperative but two main types can be distinguished:

Producer (or worker) cooperatives

These are groups of people who have organized themselves collectively to produce goods or services, as in a farming cooperative. They are able to pool their resources to buy expensive equipment and share equally in decision-making and any business profits.

The number of worker cooperatives grew rapidly during the 1970s when unemployment was rising. The government set up the **Cooperative Development Agency (CDA)** to provide advice and financial assistance to help employees buy shares in the ownership of firms which were faced with closure.

▼ Retail cooperative

Retail cooperatives

The first retail cooperative society was formed in 1844 when a group of workers who were dissatisfied with low pay and high food prices joined together to buy food from wholesalers and take advantage of bulk discounts. The principles of modern retail cooperatives are much the same:

- The cooperative is owned by its members
- Any person can become a member by buying a share for as little as £1
- Members elect a board of directors to run the cooperative
- Each member is allowed one vote regardless of the number of shares they hold
- Profits are shared between members and customers

Today many of the smaller retail cooperative shops have been forced out of business by large supermarkets. In order to compete, a number of cooperatives have formed into larger superstores selling a wide variety of goods and services, normally located on large out-of-town sites. The cooperative movement has also successfully expanded into other activities such as banking, insurance, travel agents, funeral direction, and bakeries. The largest single retailing cooperative is the Cooperative Wholesale Society based in Manchester.

Cooperative societies are governed by the terms and conditions of the Industrial and Provident Societies Acts 1965–1975. Around 11,000 societies are registered in Great Britain. They are responsible to the Registrar of Friendly Societies, to whom they must submit annual accounts.

▼ Wimpy and BSM: two well-known franchises

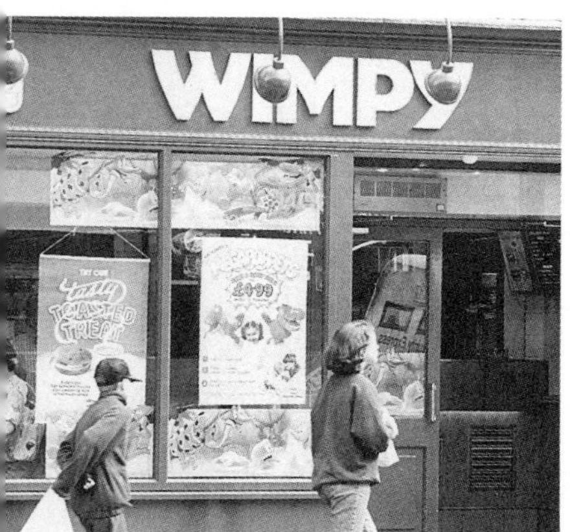

Franchises

This form of business ownership was first introduced in the USA but is now fast growing in popularity in the UK. A franchise is an agreement between two parties:

- The **franchiser** - an existing, usually well-known company with an established market for its product
- The **franchisee** - a person, or group of people, who buy the right to use the trading name of the franchiser and either manufacture, service, or sell its product in a particular location.

Well-known examples of franchise operations include McDonald's, Unigate Dairies, Prontoprint, and Thortons. It is also increasingly common for smaller organizations to franchise parts of their operations. For example, milkmen sometimes franchise their round from the local dairy. Department stores will also franchise space within their stores to other retailers.

To buy a franchise, a business can pay anything from around £15,000 upwards, plus a percentage of their turnover. In return, the established company will often provide training, equipment, materials, marketing, and help finding premises. The advantage to the franchiser is an increase in the market for their product without the need to expand the firm.

In 1998 there were over 750 companies throughout the UK expanding their business nationally through a Franchise Development Programme.

▼ *Advantages and disadvantages of buying a franchise*

Advantages	Disadvantages
Product name and market likely to be well established	Cost of buying franchise could be high
Franchiser will often market and promote the product	A proportion of business profits are paid to the franchiser
Banks may be more willing to lend money to a well-known franchise	Franchise agreement can be withdrawn
Risk of business failure is low	Role of business owners reduced to 'branch manager' Most aspects of business will be dictated by franchiser

Portfolio Activity 2.2

1. What business motives has Uniglobe for selling franchises in its travel agency business?
2. What motives had Richard Soule for buying a franchise in Uniglobe?
3. Your local milkman has asked for your advice. The dairy is offering him the chance to franchise his round. He needs advice on the following concerns:
   - What is a franchise?
   - How does a franchise operate?
   - What are the advantages and disadvantages of buying a franchise?
   - How will he raise finance?
   - What are the sales prospects for doorstep deliveries of milk and dairy products?

   You have agreed to produce a short report for him. You can find out more about this business sector from the British Franchise Association and from Business Franchise magazine.

Turn over to travel . . .

THE collapse of High Street agents Exchange Travel three and a half years ago temporarily halted what should have been one of franchising's more profitable operations – business and retail travel agency franchises.

But now the travel agency franchise is back in the frame, with at least four operators offering franchise opportunities, using modern aids like the international airline booking database to gain access to the 11 per cent of consumer spending that travel represents.

The biggest operator is Canadian-based Uniglobe, which has more than 1,000 offices in the UK, North America, Holland, Belgium and Japan.

This year it is targeting Yorkshire, the East and West Midlands, and the North West, and eight London locations within the M25, for further expansion. Total investment is £120,000 depending on location, including £70,000 working capital and a £15,000 initial franchise fee.

The period of contract is ten years renewable, and turnover is projected at £1 million in year one, rising to £2.5 million in year two, yielding a £640,000 net profit.

Richard Soule, 48, bought into Uniglobe Grosvenor Travel for £150,000 two years ago, using savings from his eight tax-free banking years in the Gulf.

'We service oil companies, Government agencies and local businesses from our Grosvenor Gardens, London, office and are now trading at a turnover of £4.5 million for this year,' he says.

Daily Mail 21.1.1994

Key words:

Sole trader - a business enterprise owned and controlled by one person

Partnership - a business owned and controlled by more than two people

Sleeping partner - a person who invests money in a partnership but takes no active role in running the business

Joint stock (limited) companies - companies which are owned by their shareholders

Private limited companies - companies which cannot advertise share sales and can sell shares only to family, friends, and business associates

Public limited companies (plcs) - organizations able to trade their shares with the general public on the Stock Exchange

Cooperative - an enterprise run and owned jointly by its members, who have equal voting rights

Section 2.3 Public sector organizations

The **public sector** in the UK is made up of organizations which are funded by, and accountable to, central and local government authorities. These organizations affect our daily lives by the way in which they raise money and through the services they provide and rules they make.

Local Government

Local government organizations include the administrative offices of:

- District councils
- County councils (regional councils in Scotland)
- London borough councils

Expenditure and finance

Local authorities provide public services to local businesses and communities such as education, leisure facilities, refuse collection, housing, road maintenance, environmental health and parking enforcement. Some of these services may be provided by private sector organizations paid by local authorities.

Councils raise money in a number of ways:

- mostly from grants from Central Government
- council tax paid by local property owners
- charges for services, such as the use of swimming pools or leisure centres
- rents from council houses
- proceeds from the sale of council houses and council land
- loans

Central Government

Voters elect members of parliament to form the Central Government to be responsible for taking decisions on national issues and controlling the economy (see 6.2). The political party with the most MPs forms the Government.

The main decision-making body in the Central Government is the Cabinet which normally consists of around 21 ministers headed by the Prime Minister. Each minister is appointed by the Prime Minister to be responsible for the activities of a government department. There are around 20 **government departments** including the Department of Trade and Industry (DTI), Her Majesty's Treasury, and the Ministry of Defence. Each department has its own budget to spend on the provision of a range of services and has to submit these spending plans to the Treasury each year for approval.

Civil servants are employed by the Central Government in departments to develop and control economic, social, environmental and foreign policies (see 6.2–6.4). The Scottish Executive and Welsh Assembly are the administrative offices of the Scottish and Welsh parliaments.

Expenditure and finance

Central government raises money mainly from taxes. There are two main types of tax in the UK:

- Direct taxes on incomes and business profits
- Indirect taxes on goods and services, such as Value Added Tax (VAT) and customs and excise duties

Central government also raises money from interest charges on government loans, dividends on shares owned by the government in private companies, and charges for some public services, such as post office deliveries.

Central government uses the money it raises to pay for the provision of public services such as the NHS, social security, major road building schemes and law and order.

In 2000–01 UK Central and Local Government spent around £372 billion paid for from tax and other revenues (see Figure 2.2).

A number of organizations are also under Central Government control.

Executive agencies

A number of public services are provided by executive agencies, such as the Royal Mint, Meteorological Office, Forestry Commission, Land Registry, and National Office of Statistics. These organizations have independent control over how they spend the money paid to them each year by Central Government. Some agencies have been privatized and are now run by private sector organizations.

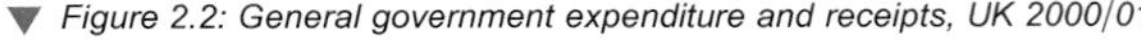

Figure 2.2: General government expenditure and receipts, UK 2000/01

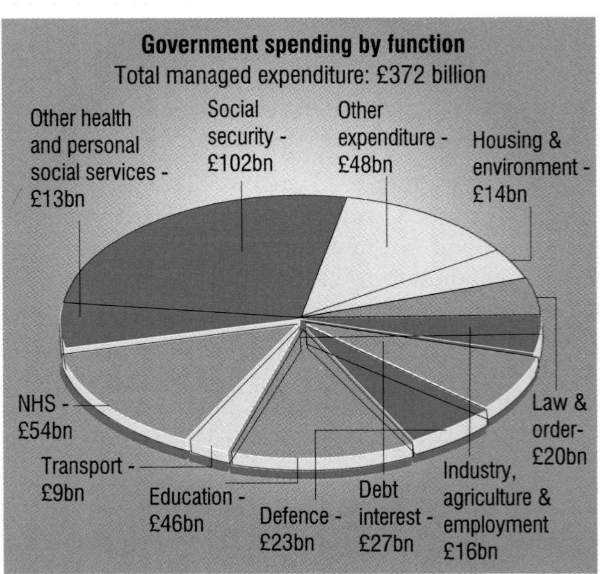

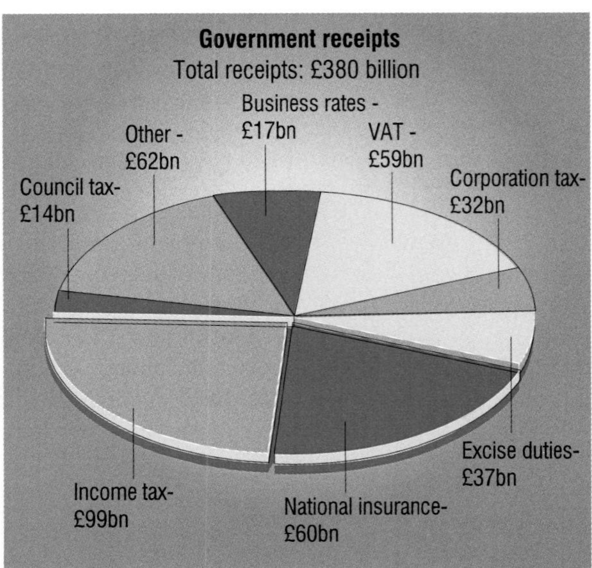

QUANGOs

QUANGO stands for **quasi-autonomous non-government organization.** Quangos are unelected government bodies run by boards of directors to manage a particular government initiative, for example, regional health authorities, research councils, and employment tribunals. Being 'quasi autonomous' means they can be run from day to day rather like a private sector business without the direct control of government officials.

Public corporations

Most **public corporations** are responsible for the day-to-day running of industries owned and controlled by Central Government which sell goods or services directly to consumers. These are called **nationalized industries.** For example, the Post Office is run by a public corporation. However, few industries remain nationalized in the UK today because most, like British Rail and British Telecom, have been sold to private sector organizations (see 6.5).

Public corporations also run the Bank of England, which is not involved in trading activities, and the British Broadcasting Authority (BBC) which is owned by neither the government nor the private sector.

Public corporations have some features in common:

- each is controlled by a Government minister. For example, the BBC is accountable to the Home Office minister.
- each has a Board of Directors who are responsible for the day-to-day running of the corporation. These are appointed by the Government minister responsible for the industry.
- each has a separate legal identity from the Government. This means that legal action can only be taken against a corporation and not the Government.
- each is financed by revenues from the sale of its services to consumers and by Central Government grant (the BBC gets it money from the TV licence fee set by the Government each year and from sale of its programmes).
- each must publish an annual report and financial accounts.
- they do not have to make an overall profit, although public corporations are expected to earn at least an 8% profit on the value of new investments. For example, if the Post Office invested £100,000 in a new equipment it would be required to earn at least £108,000 in revenue from it.
- public corporations may be allowed by Central Government to retain all or some of the profits made to plough back into improving their services. However, the Government may decide instead to use these profits to finance other public services and help reduce taxes.

Portfolio Activity 2.3 

1. Complete the following table of features of different types of business organization:

2. For each of these types of business organization, identify one or two examples, either from your own experience or from other sources, such as a business phone directory or newspaper articles. For each organization, try to find out:
   - Its objectives
   - The types of goods and services it produces
   - How it is financed
   - How it is managed

Type of organization	Who owns the business?	Who manages the business?	Who is responsible for business debts?	Does it publish annual accounts?	Main sources of capital
Sole trader	One person	The owner	The owner has unlimited liability	No	Personal and family savings, bank overdraft
Partnership	2–20 partners				
Private limited company					
Public limited company					Sale of shares to the general public
Cooperative					
Franchise					
Public corporation		Board of directors appointed by government			

Key words:

Central Government - an elected body that operates at national level to control the economy and the overall provision of public services

Local Government - elected bodies such as district councils, county councils and London borough councils, responsible for running local public services

Public corporations - organizations responsible for the day-to-day running of nationalized industries accountable to central government

Quangos - unelected, independent bodies running publicly owned enterprises

Section **2.4**

Organizational structures

Relationships within an organization

Any business organization, whatever its size, whether in the public or private sector, will need to establish an **internal structure**. The internal structure of a business will show:

- Who is in charge
- Who makes the decisions
- Who carries out decisions
- How decisions and information are communicated

That is, the **organizational structure** will establish the relationships between managers and their subordinates necessary to achieve business objectives (see 1.7).

Organization charts

The **formal structure** within an organization can be represented by means of an **organization chart.** Traditionally, an organization chart is constructed with those individuals near or at the top having more authority and responsibility than those at the bottom.

Figure 2.3 shows the organization chart for a manufacturer of American sports fashion clothing. The relative positions of individuals within the boxes show formal relationships, and lines between boxes show formal lines of communication between the individuals.

Departmentalization

The most common method of establishing formal relationships between individuals is by establishing **departments.** A department is defined as a unique group of human resources established by management to perform a particular task within the organization.

- President
  - Vice president sales and marketing
    - UK sales manager
      - Sales Team
    - European sales manager
      - Germany, France, Spain, Italy, Scandinavia
  - Vice president production
    - Stock control manager
    - Dispatch manager
      - IN
      - OUT
        - Relabellers, packers
    - Print and production manager
      - Team leader
        - Belt printers
        - Shift printers
      - Sample manager
        - Samplers
    - Creative art manager
      - Team leader
        - Computer artists
        - Visualizers
        - Table artists
  - Vice president accounts
    - Team leader
      - Accounts clerks
  - Vice president administration and human resources
    - Team leader
      - Admin assistants

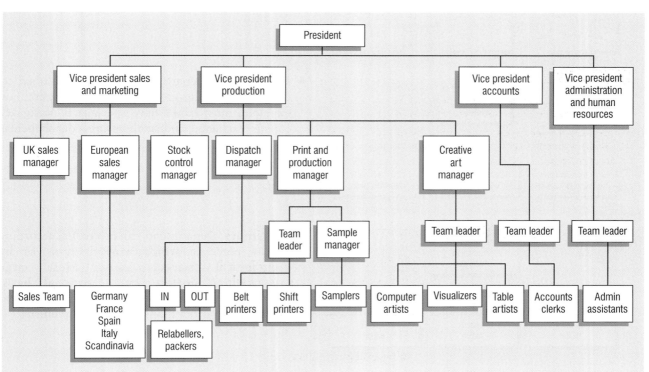

▲ *Figure 2.3: Organization chart for manufacturer of US sports fashion clothing*

▼ *Departmentalization*

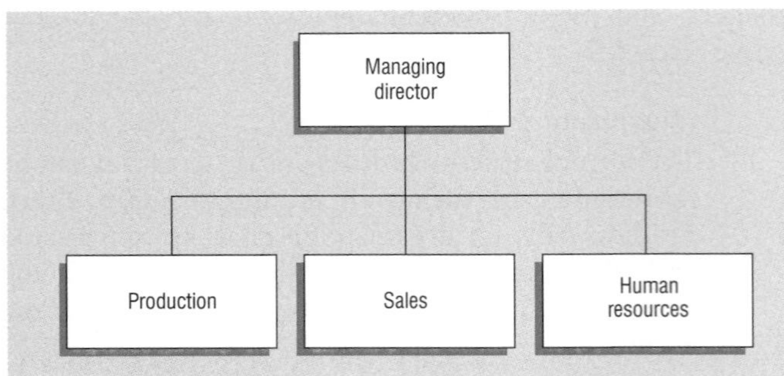

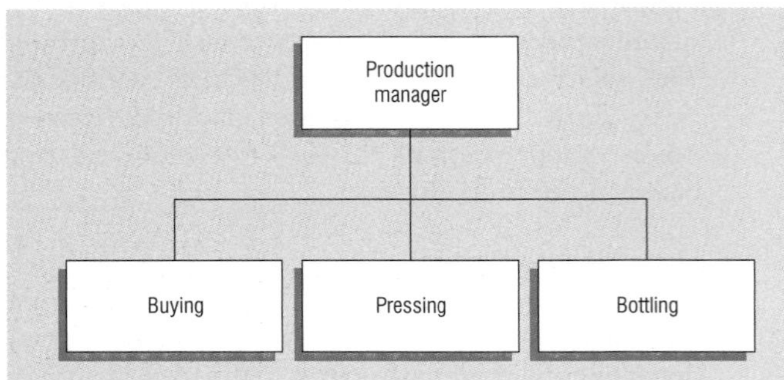

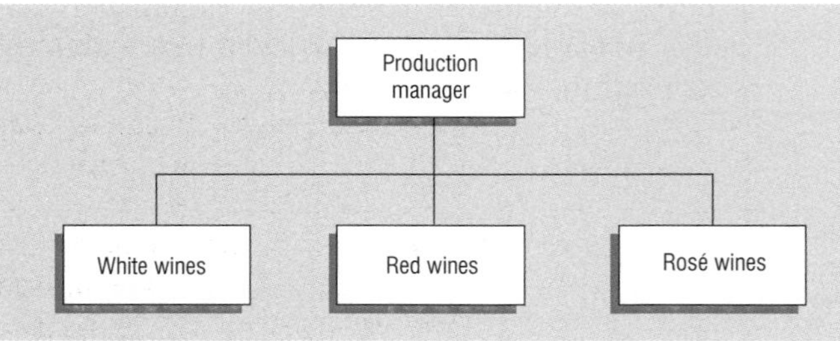

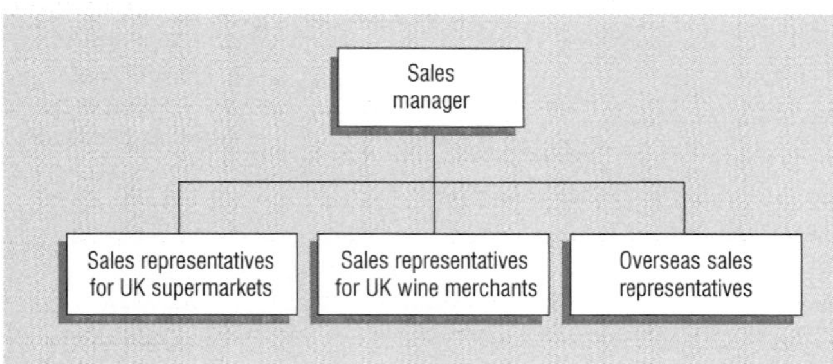

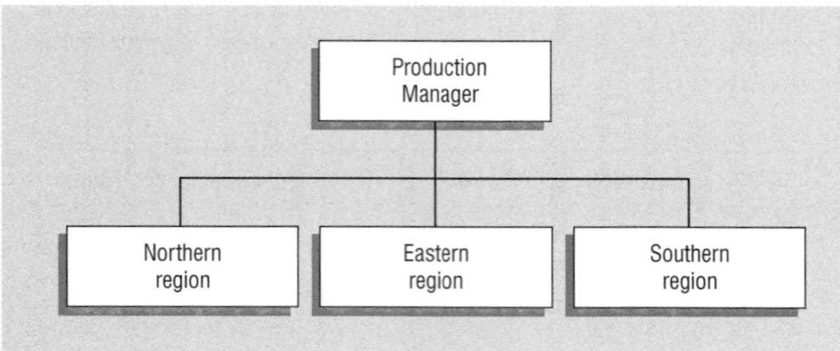

Department groupings can be established in a number of ways. Consider the ways in which a wine producer might be split into departments;

- **By function.** By far the most common method among medium-to-large organizations. Departments are established to perform specific tasks, for example, marketing, finance, production, sales, human resources (see 4.2).
- **By process.** Divisions are based on operations, with each department specializing in a particular task.
- **By product/service.** An organization that produces many different products or brands may find it difficult to coordinate across them. Organizing according to product allows managers to group together the resources needed to produce each product.
- **By customer.** Departments can be established to deal with different groups of main customers. For example, most banks have specialized mortgage, foreign exchange, and small business departments.
- **By territory.** Departments can be created according to the place in which work is done or by geographical market areas. Most large organizations operate on a regional basis. Multinational organizations will have offices, factories, and often shops in different countries.

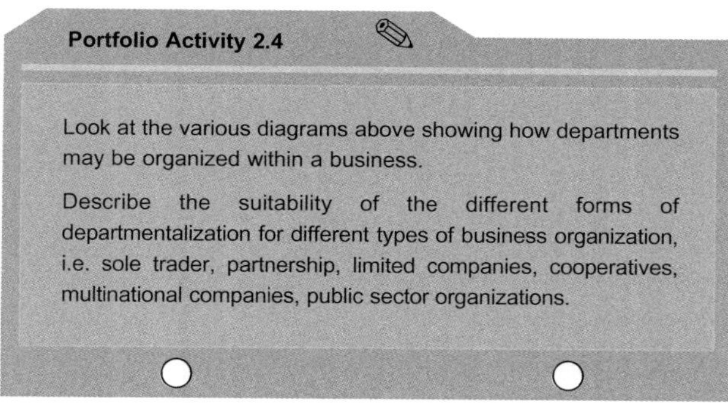

Portfolio Activity 2.4

Look at the various diagrams above showing how departments may be organized within a business.

Describe the suitability of the different forms of departmentalization for different types of business organization, i.e. sole trader, partnership, limited companies, cooperatives, multinational companies, public sector organizations.

Organizational levels and the span of management

When deciding on a firm's organizational structure, management will take into account two important factors:

- The chain of command
- The span of management (or span of control)

The hierarchical organization

The **hierarchy** in a business refers to the layers of management from the most senior managers down to those managers or supervisors of the lowest rank, i.e. 'top-down management'. In a small business there are unlikely to be many layers. For example, in a one-person enterprise - a sole trader - the business owner makes and implements all the decisions as both manager and worker.

Figure 2.4: The hierarchical organization structure

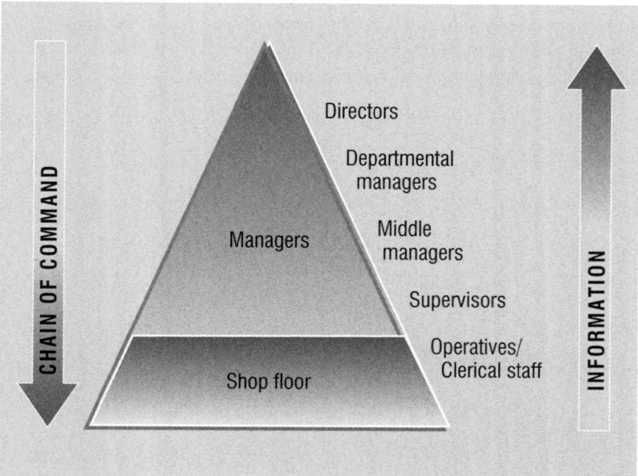

The structure of the **hierarchical organization** is presented as a pyramid (see Figure 2.4). It is narrow at the top indicating few senior managers, while the base, representing a large number of 'shop-floor' operatives or low-grade workers, is broad.

The top layers of management - directors or chief executives - are usually concerned with strategic, long-term plans and policies and with checking that subordinates carry these out. A distinct **chain of command** runs in a line from the top layers of management down through each department in the organization to the 'shop floor'. Orders are passed down this chain of command, while information on which further decisions are taken - sales, revenues, output, staff turnover, etc. - are passed up the organization.

The main advantages and disadvantages of the hierarchical structure include:

Advantages	Disadvantages
Clear management structure	Many layers of communication can slow down speed at which decisions can be implemented
Clear division of responsibility and allocation of authority	Top layers of management may stifle the initiative and motivation of middle managers and subordinates
Organization can be controlled from the top	Senior managers may have limited experience and understanding of functions within the whole organization
	Cooperation and coordination across departments may be difficult

Line and staff functions

There are three main line functions a business organization will have to perform if it is to achieve its objectives. These are:

- Production
- Sales
- Marketing

Individual departments concerned with performing these functions are called **line departments**. Each line department is supervised by a **line manager** who has **line authority** - the ability to give orders concerning productive activities - over his or her subordinates. For example, the production manager has line authority over the production supervisor, who in turn has line authority over machine operatives.

Staff functions are those which support the main line functions of an organization (see 4.2). These are:

- Research and development
- Purchasing (materials and equipment)
- Distribution
- Finance and accounting
- Human resources
- Customer services
- Quality control
- Maintenance (sites, buildings and equipment)
- Communications (see 3.1)
- Information processing

Employees in these areas work across the organization to provide help and advice to all other departments, but have no authority to make decisions in any other department but their own. For example, human resources managers have responsibility for staff matters and welfare in the whole organization, but have no power to hire or fire staff in the production department without the authority of the production manager. **Staff authority** is the right to advise and assist those who possess line authority and other staff personnel.

▼ *Possible line-staff relationships in an organization*

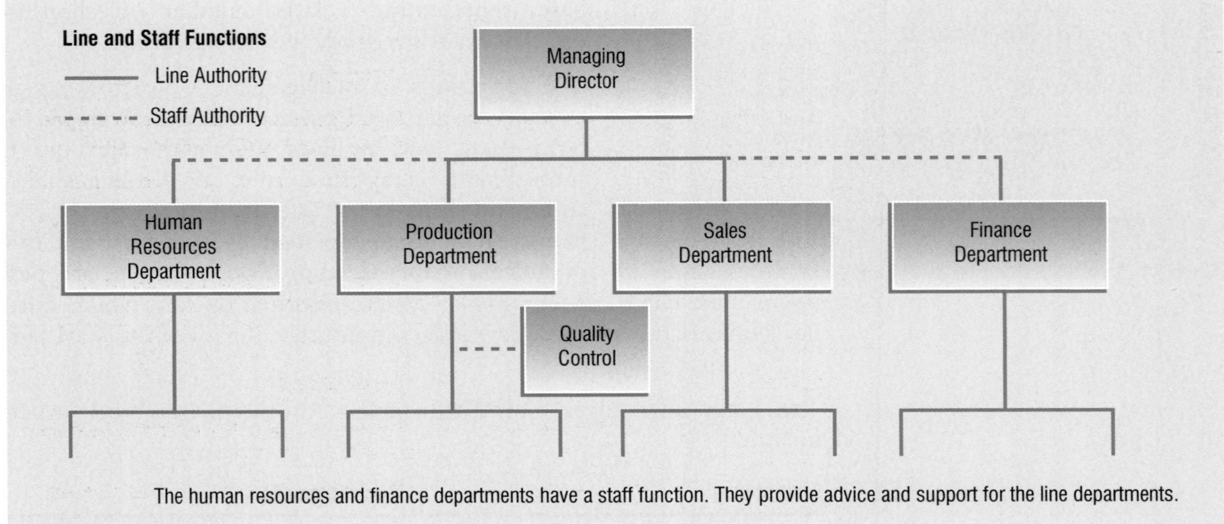

▼ *Figure 2.5: The span of control within organization structures*

Flat and tall organization structures

Within any hierarchy there will be a **span of control.** This refers to the number of individuals a manager supervises. The more individuals in a manager's charge, the wider his or her span of control. Thus, if 5 employees are directly under the control of the production manager, his or her span of control is 5.

In general, the greater the height of the organization chart, the smaller the span of control. It follows that the lower the height of the chart, the greater the span of control tends to be.

Organization charts with little height are usually referred to as **flat organizations**, while those with height are referred to as **tall** (Figure 2.5).

Flat organizations are those which have relatively few or even just one level of management. Many UK enterprises have adopted flatter structures in order to reduce levels of management and bureaucracy, and to give their workforce greater decision-making responsibilities.

Reducing the layers of management in an organization is called **de-layering.** Reducing management layers can speed up communications and decision-making which is important for businesses in fast changing, dynamic markets (see 2.6).

WIDE SPAN OF CONTROL

Advantages	Disadvantages
Fewer levels of management and decision-making	Direct supervision of subordinates can become difficult and management can lose control
Lower supervision costs	Subordinates may have more than one boss
Greater decision-making authority for subordinates can increase job satisfaction	Motivation and output may be impaired if orders become confused
	The structure may become unworkable as business expands

NARROW SPAN OF CONTROL

Advantages	Disadvantages
Allows for tight control and close supervision	Subordinates may feel left out of decision-making process and lack motivation
Communication with subordinates is easier	Management and administration costs are high
	Coordinating decisions of numerous managers can be difficult
	Too much supervision may stifle initiative and motivation

Authority, responsibility, and delegation

Employees in a hierarchy will have varying degrees of responsibility and authority. The higher up the hierarchy, the more responsibility and authority an employee will have. Managers need to have **authority** over their subordinates in order for decisions and policies to be implemented. They have to tell their staff what to do and what is expected of them. Although a task may be delegated, or passed down the chain of command, from a manager to a subordinate, the manager will still have the **responsibility** for making sure his or her instructions are carried out.

Delegation is the process of assigning job activities and corresponding authority to specific individuals within the organization. It is essential because it is impossible for one manager to have direct control over all activities. However, for delegation to be effective, a number of conditions must be satisfied:

- The manager must be sure that the subordinate has a clear understanding of what the assigned task entails and its purpose
- The subordinate must be given the right and power of authority within the organization to accomplish the assigned task
- If necessary, training and guidance should be provided to enable employees to complete delegated tasks effectively
- Whenever possible, tasks should be delegated on the basis of employee interest
- The manager should establish mutually agreed performance criteria for delegated tasks

"I hate to fire people, so I'm ordering you two to fire each other."

Wall Street Journal 11.9.1987

Centralized and decentralized organizations

If a business is **centralized**, authority, responsibility, and decision-making is concentrated at the top of the hierarchy with a few senior managers. 'Subordinates' have little, if any, authority or power to make decisions. The main advantage of centralization is the ability of senior managers to make quick decisions, especially when the business environment is changing rapidly.

A **decentralized organization** is one in which authority and responsibility have been delegated to lower levels of management. Complete decentralization would mean that subordinates would make all the decisions.

▼ *The advantages and disadvantages of centralized and decentralized organizations*

CENTRALIZED STRUCTURE	DECENTRALIZED STRUCTURE
Advantages	**Advantages**
Senior management maintain control of the business and can make decisions quickly from the point of view of the whole organization	Reduces stress and burden on senior managers. Senior managers can concentrate on strategic decisions
Systems and procedures such as human resources, purchasing, advertising, can be standardized and may gain economies of scale (see 22.4)	Subordinates enjoy more decision-making and improved motivation
Reduces risk of duplication of activities and efforts	Subordinates can make decisions based on local conditions affecting their area of work
Senior managers may be more experienced decision-makers	Delegation allows greater flexibility and a quicker response to changing market conditions
	Middle managers can be groomed for senior positions
Disadvantages	**Disadvantages**
Subordinates may lack motivation	More bureaucracy and consultation is involved
Few opportunities for decisions to be made based on local conditions	Slows down decision-making
Senior managers may have little experience or understanding of activities and constraints in individual departments	Decisions taken by different departments may conflict
	Senior managers lose control

In general, the larger the organization, the more decentralized it is likely to be because it would be impossible for senior management to maintain direct control over all business activities. For example, large retail organizations like Tesco's and B&Q which have a number of branches at different locations operate a decentralized structure. Each store will have a manager able to take decisions on staff requirements, store layout, stock control, etc., but who is ultimately responsible to a regional manager and company directors.

Certain functions within a business will always remain controlled from the centre. For example, decisions about budget allocation between departments, advertising, and growth, are likely to be centralized because they affect the whole organization.

The matrix organization

A **matrix organization** is an organization that has been modified primarily for the purpose of completing a special project. The project - for example, the development of a new product - may either be short-term or long-term, with employees with different skills to complete the project borrowed from various departments within the organization to form project teams.

Figure 2.6 shows one way of changing an organizational structure into a matrix organization. A manager would be appointed for each of the two projects and allocated staff with appropriate skills to complete each one. After the projects were completed, the organization could change back to its original structure.

▼ *Figure 2.6: An example of a matrix organization structure*

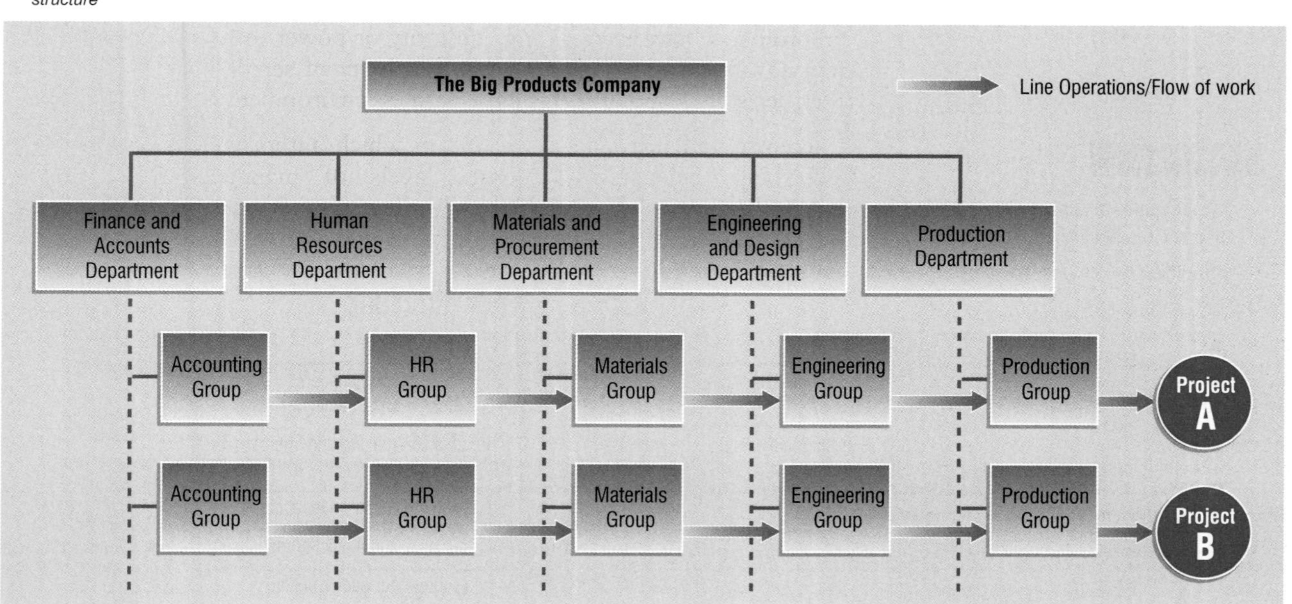

▼ *Advantages and disadvantages of a matrix structure*

Advantages	Disadvantages
Communication within the project team is easier	Employees may have more than one boss
Specialist staff can contribute ideas and help to solve problems	Staff loyalties may be divided between their old department and the project team
Team spirit helps to motivate staff	New lines of authority and communication may be difficult to understand

Portfolio Activity 2.5 

1. How has Barclays Bank plc been reorganized?
2. Why do you think Barclays has been reorganized in this way?
3. Find out how your local Barclays branch is organized. Draw an organization chart for the branch headed by the bank manager/ess.

Taylor reforms Barclays

Mr Martin Taylor, Barclays' new chief executive, yesterday stamped his presence on the UK's largest bank by breaking up its divisional structure and replacing it with a set of management groups reporting directly to him.

His reforms, including the creation of a group offering services to large companies, reduce the influence of Mr Alastair Robinson, head of the former banking division, who was a leading internal contender to be chief executive.

He said Mr Robinson was "a very valuable colleague" but pointed out that he would retire in three years' time. Mr Robinson's remit will include private banking and retail banking in Africa and the Caribbean.

The reforms, which Mr Taylor described as a first step, created groups covering big companies and European retail banking. The new group for UK retail banking will report to Mr Taylor for the first time.

Mr Graham Pimlott, chief executive of merchant banking at the BZW investment banking arm, is to head the group serving large companies.

The bank's former service businesses division – one of three with banking and BZW – will be divided. Mr Joseph De Feo, its chief executive, will retain charge of technology while custody switches to Mr Pimlott's control.

Financial Times 21.4.1994

Portfolio Activity 2.6 

1. Draw an organization chart for your school/ college.
2. What functions does it perform?
3. Describe the type of structure and span of control.
4. From your own experience, what are the advantages/disadvantages of this type of structure?

Key words:

Organizational structure – the various relationships between managers and their subordinates in a business

Organization chart – a graphic illustration of an organization's structure

Department – a group of workers established by management to specialize in a particular task

Line authority – the ability to give orders concerning productive activities, namely the line functions of production, sales, and marketing

Staff functions – those which support the main line functions of an organization, for example, personnel and finance

Staff authority – the right to advise and assist those who possess line authority

Hierarchy – layers of management in an organization

Chain of command – the passage of orders down an organization from top management to the shop floor

Unity of command – the principle whereby any individual within an organization should have only one line manager

Span of control – the number of subordinates a manager supervises

Flat organizations – organizations with relatively few layers of management, each with a relatively wide span of control

Tall organizations – organizations with many layers of management

Delegation – the process of assigning job activities and the authority to carry them out to individuals

Centralized organization – organizations in which authority, responsibility,and decision–making are concentrated at the top of the management hierarchy

Decentralized organization – organizations in which authority and decision–making responsibility are delegated to lower levels of management

Matrix organization – when an organization's structure is modified for the purpose of completing a special project

De-layering – reducing layers of management in an organization to improve communications and decision-making

Section 2.5

Job roles in an organization structure

Directors

The highest level of management in a limited company is the **board of directors.** Directors are elected each year, usually on the basis of their experience and past business performance, and are appointed to run the company on behalf of its shareholders. Some directors may be shareholders in the company themselves.

Directors have a number of responsibilities, some of which are set down in law. These are:

- Organizing the company and its resources into productive activity
- Setting business objectives
- Formulating policies and plans to achieve set objectives
- Monitoring business performance
- Controlling company activities
- Safeguarding funds invested by shareholders and ensuring a reasonable rate of return on their investment
- Determining the distribution of profits
- Preparing and publishing annual reports
- Protecting the company against fraud and inefficiency

Executive directors have full-time responsibilities and are actively engaged in the running of the company. **Non-executive directors** act only in a part-time capacity. These are people employed for their business knowledge and expertise to attend board meetings and provide an independent and fresh view of decision-making. They may also provide useful links with other organizations because of directorships they hold in other companies.

A firm may also invite an employee representative to sit on the board as a non-executive member. Breaking down divisions between management and employees and encouraging worker participation in the decision-making process is increasing in popularity in the UK (see 15.1).

Figure 2.7: Who's who in the boardroom

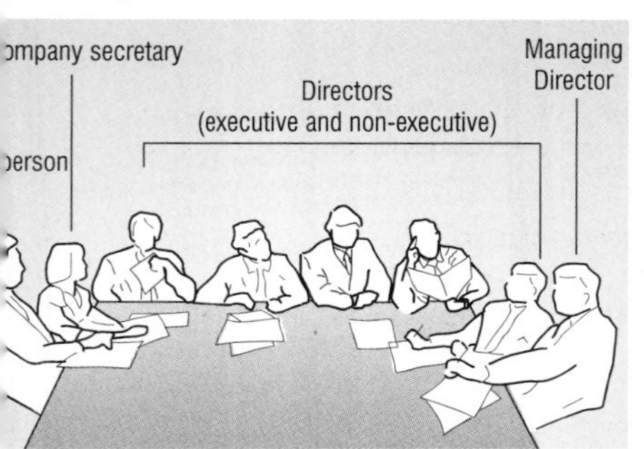

Managing directors

The **managing director**, or **chief executive,** is a director elected, not by shareholders, but by the board of directors to head the organization. The managing director is responsible to the board, and will usually be appointed on the basis of a proven track record in business management.

Specific duties and responsibilities of the managing director include:

- Appointing senior managers
- Implementing company policies designed to achieve business goals
- Supervising and coordinating day-to-day activities within the company
- Developing an organizational culture
- Meeting important Trade Union and government officials, key suppliers, and customers, and taking part in negotiations with them on major issues

Portfolio Activity 2.7 

1. Collect at least five company reports from large public limited companies. These should available to the public on request from the company headquarters or from company websites.
2. From the reports, identify and compare the various functions of the directors.

Other board roles

The **company secretary** is not a director, but an executive officer appointed by the board to carry out administrative duties on their behalf. The company secretary has two main obligations:

- The administration of board and shareholders' meetings, including arranging venues and dates, preparing agendas, recording minutes, etc.
- Ensuring that the company meets all its legal requirements, including compliance with the Memorandum and Articles of Association, reporting changes in company directors, preparing and publishing annual company accounts, etc.

The **chairperson** is elected by the board to chair board meetings. S/he may be either an executive or non-executive member of the board.

▼ *Types of managerial positions available*

Finance Manager

Broad Commercial Role

Up to £50,000 + Car + Benefits **West Midlands**

Outstanding opportunity for commercially focused young finance professional. Wide ranging responsibilities within continuous improvement culture. Director designate position.

THE COMPANY
- Highly successful subsidiary of £500 million plc. Turnover £7 million. Fast growing, 40% compound growth year on year.
- Regarded for product innovation and outstanding customer service.
- Quality focused. Goal to achieve world class manufacturing status.

THE POSITION
- Lead team of 15 in accounts, quality, systems, personnel, warehouse and purchasing functions. Report to Managing Director.
- Ensure the timely and accurate production of financial results. Liaise with divisional and Group Head Offices.
- Develop information systems to support business operations and decisions.
- Significant input into tactical and strategic development of business. Key member of senior management team.

QUALIFICATIONS
- Highly talented qualified Accountant, probably aged between 28 and 35.
- Previous financial management experience within a quality driven company. Ability to combine hands-on/task orientated work with a strategic outlook.
- Bright, resourceful and flexible. Must possess excellent communication and people management skills.

Please send full cv by June 24th, stating salary and ref. GSM2248, to Barkers Response & Assessment, Berwick House, 35 Livery Street, Birmingham B3 2PB

What is management?

Managers influence all aspects of modern organizations. Production managers run manufacturing operations that produce goods to satisfy our wants and needs. Sales managers organize sales teams to market goods and services. Human resource managers provide the organization with skilled and productive employees.

The term **management** is used in two different ways. It can refer simply to those individuals within an organization who are managers. Or it may describe the skills and knowledge used by managers to achieve organizational goals.

Research Manager

London-based business magazine publisher seeks Research Manager.
Responsibilities will include editing two yearbooks/directories; organising market research projects; market data origination, compilation and formatting; and contributing statistical material to company's title.
Successful applicant will have research and directory-compiling experience, and be able to produce reports on Mac/Quark XPress or similar electronic systems.
Good salary and prospects.
Send CV with samples of work to:
Box GAR58, The Guardian, 164 Deansgate, Manchester, M60 2RR.

Korean Store Manager and Sales Manager - London

Top Korean tour group luxury goods store requires a store manager and a sales manager. The store manager will have full profit centre, human resource, procurement and merchandising responsibilities; the sales manager will be responsible for outside sales. Candidates should have at least four years experience in merchandising or sales, speak fluent Korean and English, have a higher education qualification and be prepared to work at weekends.

Please apply with full resume and a covering letter in English & Korean to Box GAR88, The Guardian, 164 Deansgate, Manchester, M60

DDD

BUSINESS DEVELOPMENT MANAGER BASED HERTS

Dendron Limited is an independent company achieving enviable growth with a portfolio of well established and successful brands including Ibuleve, Blisteze, Oz and Stain Devils.

The Business Development Manager will play a central role in leading Dendron's future growth by:-

★ Planning and pursuing sales and profit objectives for a group of Brands.

★ Defining category development potential through new product opportunities and existing Brand Activities.

★ Working with the Dendron Sales Team and major customer accounts to address ongoing and future consumer and category sales requirements.

★ Using Strategic and Budget planning procedures to gain management approval for plans.

We require an experienced Brand Manager who is looking for increased responsibility and personal development.

The rewards include a competitive salary, company car, contributory pension scheme, life assurance and the chance to develop a career with a progressive company.

Write with full details or for an application form contact **The Personnel Department, DDD Limited, 94 Rickmansworth Road, Watford, Herts WD1 7JJ. Telephone: (0923) 229251.**

No Agencies Please

BROCKHILL PARK SCHOOL

Business Manager (New Post)
Salary circa £30,000

Brockhill Park School is an 11-18 mixed school of 1100 students set in extensive grounds including a fully operational farm unit. The Governing Body wish to appoint a suitable person to join the school's Senior Management Team with effect from 1st January 1995 under the leadership of the Headteacher Tony Lyng. The school is going through a challenging and exciting phase of development.

The successful applicant must demonstrate that s/he

* is committed to education in the state sector.
* has the business acumen to effectively manage and develop all aspects of school finances, premises and grounds maintenance.
* the ability to communicate effectively and confidently.
* the personnel management skills to manage a wide range of full-time, part-time and temporary support staff.

For further details please apply to:
Mrs A Amos,
Clerk to the Governors, at the school.
Brockhill Park School, Sandling Road,
Hythe, Kent CT21 4HL

Some definitions of management

Management...

'...entails activities undertaken by one or more persons in order to coordinate the activities of others in the pursuit of ends that cannot be achieved by any one person'

(Donelly, J, Gibson, J, and Ivancevich, J)

'...is the process of designing and maintaining an environment in which individuals, working together in groups, accomplish efficiently selected aims'

(Koontz, H, and Weinrich, H)

'...is the process of working with and through others to effectively achieve organizational objectives by efficiently using limited resources in a changing environment'

(Kreitner, R)

'...is the coordination of all resources through the processes of planning, organizing, directing and controlling in order to attain stated objectives'

(Sisk, H)

Managers have the responsibility for combining and using productive resources - human, physical, financial - to ensure that organizations achieve their goals. All organizations, business, government, charity, even sports teams, need good management to achieve their objectives. Whether or not an organization achieves its aims depends greatly on the quality of its management.

Portfolio Activity 2.8 

Use the job adverts for managers on the previous page and your personal knowledge and observations of managers either in your school/college, place of work experience, etc, to identify and list the general functions managers must perform and the qualities you think they need to carry them out.

As part of this exercise, you might ask to spend half a day observing a manager at work. After you have made your observations, discuss them with the manager in question. Find out whether or not the tasks and behaviour you observed were typical.

▼ *Figure 2.8: Fayol's activities in business operations*

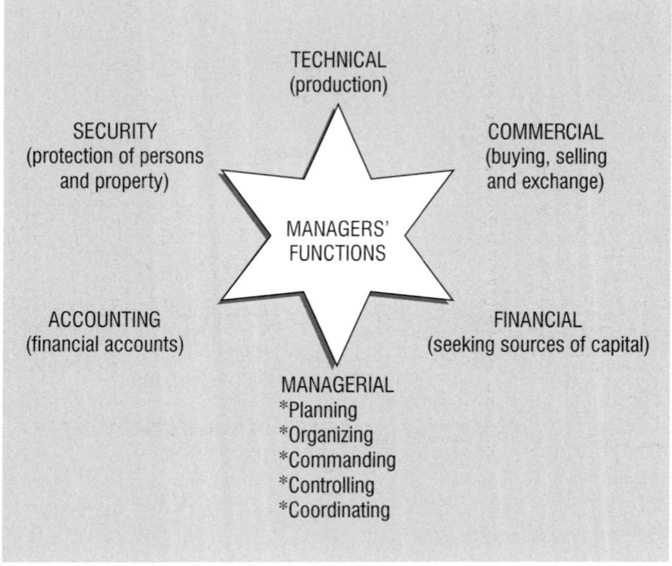

The management process

Management science is devoted to understanding and explaining the role and behaviour of management. Henri Fayol, a French industrialist writing in 1916, has become known as the 'father' of modern management theory, and was one of the first to recognize the need to teach good management skills.

Fayol argued that the activities of any business organization could be divided into six groups as shown in Figure 2.8. His analysis concentrates on managerial activities.

Fayol describes five basic managerial functions. These are:

- **Planning:** setting objectives and choosing strategies, policies, and tasks to achieve them. This will include identifying, and meeting, the training needs of their staff.
- **Organizing:** establishing an intentional structure of job roles for people to play within an organization. The concept of a 'role' implies that people have a definite purpose or objective to fulfil.

- **Commanding:** giving instructions to subordinates to carry out assigned tasks. Managers have the authority to make decisions and the responsibility to see that they are carried out. This function requires managers to be good leaders - motivating, directing, and mobilizing subordinates toward goal attainment.
- **Controlling:** measuring and correcting the activities of subordinates. Managers must make sure that the performance of individuals and departments within the organization meets pre-established standards. If not, they must put in motion actions to correct poor performance and help ensure that plans are accomplished.
- **Coordinating:** harmonizing individual efforts towards the accomplishment of organizational goals. Not all individuals will identify with, or hold, the same objectives as the organization they work for. It therefore becomes a central task of the manager to reconcile differences in the approach, timing, and efforts of individuals to contribute to the goals of the organization. Some have called this function 'the essence of managership'. Each of the managerial functions is an exercise contributing to coordination.

Levels of management

Within most organizations there will be more than one level of management. All managers will carry out managerial functions, but the time spent on each function may differ between the different levels. Top-level or senior managers will spend much of their time on strategic decision-making and planning. Supervisors and lower-level managers, on the other hand, will spend a great deal of time commanding.

The diagram below shows how much time different managers can be expected to spend on each function within a typical organization, and the various objectives they hope to achieve.

Figure 2.9: Time spent carrying out managerial functions

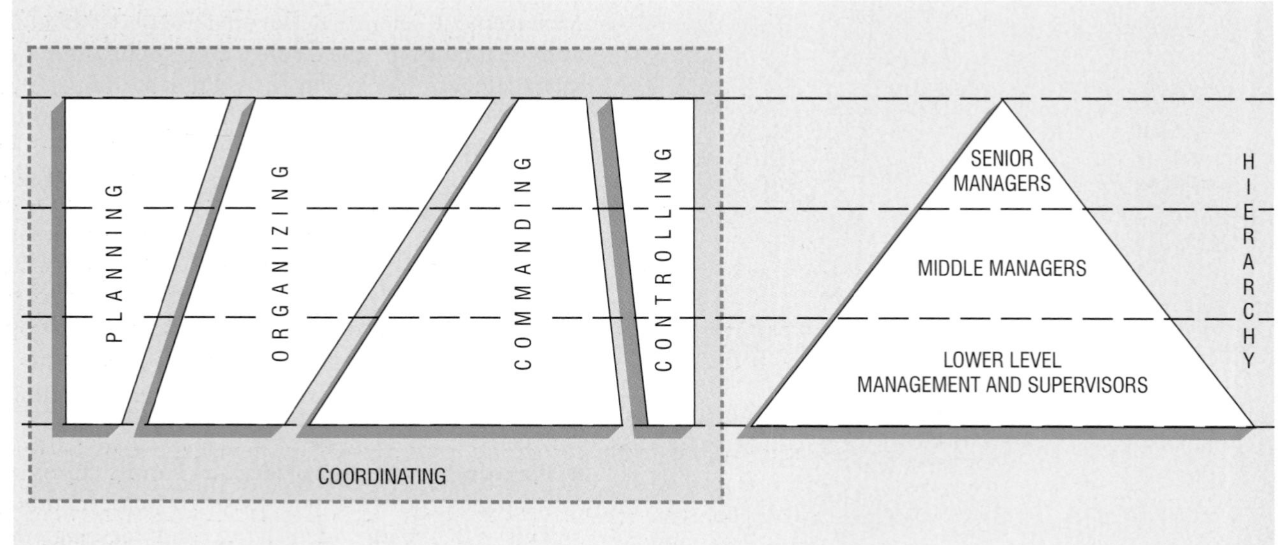

Management styles

How managers carry out their functions and how well they do so will depend on their particular style of management and how their staff react.

We can identify four basic management styles.

▲ *Autocratic management*

Autocratic managers

These managers take decisions alone and expect other members of the organization to carry them out without question. This is a good style to adopt in emergencies when decisions have to be made and actions carried out fast.

However, if mangers are always autocratic, it can create problems. Staff become too dependent on the manager and will not want to or be able to make decisions on their own if their manager is not present. Staff can also become dissatisfied if they are not consulted or think decisions are wrong. If employees are dissatisfied, work will suffer and the business will find it difficult to achieve its objectives.

Persuasive managers

Persuasive managers also take decisions alone but will then spend time persuading organization members that their decisions are right.

By communicating the reasons for their decisions the manager may be able to create more commitment and enthusiasm for the decisions, and the changes they make, among organization members. However, some organization members may still resent that they were not consulted before the decisions were made. Many may still feel the decisions are wrong but will instead simply tell the manager what they want to hear.

▲ *Democratic management*

Democratic managers

Democratic managers allow other organization members to discuss ideas and participate in decision-making. The democratic manager will not attempt to impose their own views. This will help create a high level of commitment to the decisions from organization members and will give them an incentive to carry them out efficiently and effectively.

However, democratic decision-making can be a slow process and may not be appropriate in a fast-changing, dynamic market where quick and sensible decisions are needed to stay ahead of rival firms. Also, decisions can often be compromises which may not be in the best interests of the organization.

Consultative managers

These managers will consult with their staff and other organization members before they come to a decision. The manager will ask for ideas and will take account of the advice of organization members in reaching a decision. However, the final decision is still made by the manager.

The big advantage of this management style is that staff and other members will be motivated to implement the decision and achieve business objectives because they have contributed to the decision-making process. The manager can make more informed decisions in the best interests of the business organization. However, because different people may have different ideas, the decision reached by the manager may still not be accepted by all organization members.

From the above it is clear that managers may adopt different styles at different times depending on the situation, their objective, and the particular staff involved. That is, they may move along a continuum of different styles which involve more or less freedom for subordinates to contribute to the decision-making process (see Figure 2.10). However, the usual style adopted by managers will depend critically on their personality and personal objectives. For example, a manager may adopt an autocratic style because they seek self-advancement and promotion.

Style and structure

Organizations with autocratic and persuasive managers may become more hierarchical over time because they will tend to rule on high and seek to control all aspects of running the business. Managers and staff at lower levels will simply be required to carry out their instructions. In contrast, more democratic and consultative managers may seek to reduce layers of management in order to give other managers and staff more responsibility, and involve them more in decision-making. This change may incentivise organization members to greater effort in order to achieve business objectives.

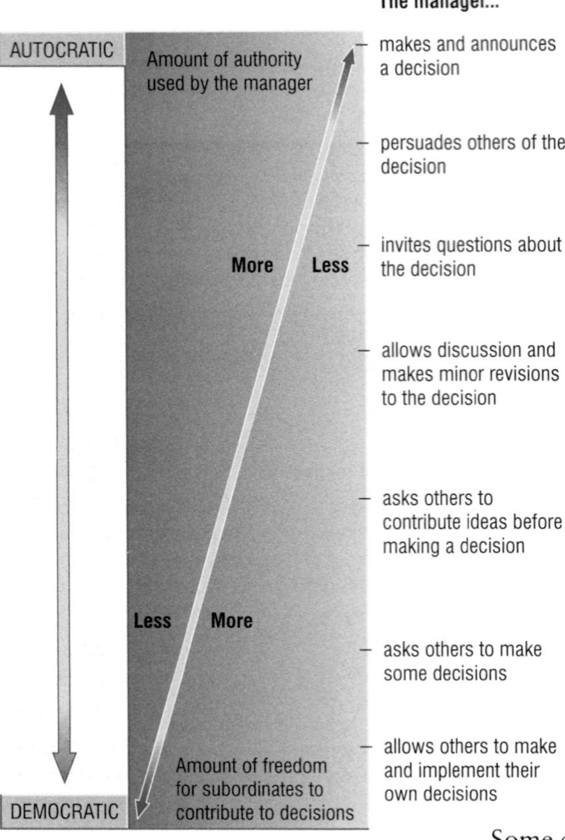
The manager...
AUTOCRATIC
Amount of authority used by the manager
makes and announces a decision
persuades others of the decision
invites questions about the decision
More
Less
allows discussion and makes minor revisions to the decision
asks others to contribute ideas before making a decision
Less
More
asks others to make some decisions
allows others to make and implement their own decisions
Amount of freedom for subordinates to contribute to decisions
DEMOCRATIC

▼ *Figure 2.10: A continuum of management styles*

Management style can also be influenced by the structure of the organization. Changing the structure of an organization can therefore have an impact on management styles. For example, a change from a tall to a flat organization may result in one of the following changes:

- Increased responsibility on individual managers may make them more autocratic, because of the number, importance and speed of decisions they need to make, especially in fast changing and highly competitive business environments

Alternatively,

- Managers may become more consultative and democratic because they can now meet with their staff more often, and involving them in decision-making can reduce the risk of a manager making the wrong decision by only looking at a problem from their own point of view

Consultants and advisers

Organizations known as consultancies are able to provide specialist advice to business organizations, who will often contract their services for special one-off projects. For example, firms of consultants may be brought in to advise on new communication systems, office and factory layouts, marketing campaigns, or new constructions, recruitment procedures, and production processes.

▼ *Consultants: specialist advice at a price*

ACW
Allan C Weller
F.M.S. M.I. Mgt. EURO I.E.

Productivity Improvement Consultant

UK's Leading Authority on M.P.I.P. (Management Performance Improvement Programme)

COMBINING -

- Organisational Analysis
- Operator Involvement
- Problem Solving
- Personnel Development & Training
- Productivity Improvement
- Operational Control

Listed under the D.T.I. Support for Manufacturing Scheme

3 Woodlands Drive, Malpas
Newport, Gwent NP9 6QD
Tel: (0633) 854042

INTERNATIONAL ENQUIRIES WELCOME

Some consultancies, however, may be offered call-off contracts which means that they are paid to provide regular advice as and when necessary - for example, collecting and providing up-to-date economic data from around the world, or giving advice on UK business taxation.

Supervisors

The **supervisor** is usually regarded as the first managerial grade in an organization hierarchy. Supervisors will often be workers promoted off the shop-floor because of their hard work, initiative, and leadership qualities.

The job of the supervisor will vary between organizations but, in general, s/he will be a manager who has had extensive contact with 'shop floor' workers and knows how things should be done 'on the ground'. Supervisors are the first in line to deal with day-to-day operations and problems as they occur - for example, a breakdown in a piece of machinery, staff absenteeism, a hold-up in supplies, etc.

Portfolio Activity 2.9 

These two job adverts are for supervisors in different organizations. Use them to make a list of the general functions a supervisor could be expected to perform, and the personal qualities you think they might need for the job. Draw on any personal experience you have of supervisors in organizations that you know.

SCAFFOLDING SUPERVISOR/ESTIMATOR

MG Scaffolding is a well established scaffolding contractor, and we wish to continue our expansion in the Cambridge area by appointing an experienced Scaffolding/Estimator to join our management team.

To be considered for this position you must be able to demonstrate the following attributes:-

- ★ Minimum of 5 years experience in the Scaffolding Industry.
- ★ Proven skills in the planning, motivation and control of labour, and materials planning.
- ★ The ability to achieve demanding operational and financial targets.
- ★ Flexible and enthusiastic approach to work.

We offer an attractive remuneration package, including competitive salary, performance related bonus scheme, and Company car.

Please apply in writing enclosing a C. V. to:

The Operations Director
MG Scaffold Limited, Industrial Estate
Stanton Harcourt, Oxford OX8 1SL

Croner Publications Ltd, the country's leading publisher in business information is seeking a

SUPERVISOR

to join our Electronic Product Help Desk to promote quality customer care in the developing field of electronic publishing.

As Supervisor, you will be responsible for providing front-line support to subscribers over the telephone, supporting a team of executives and producing a variety of management information and statistics.

A sound educational background to GCSE level (or equivalent) is necessary, together with a working knowledge of PCs, ideally Wordperfect and Lotus spreadsheet packages.

Previous supervisory experience, preferably with a telephone/customer service environment, is essential, together with a mature and flexible approach to work.

As a progressive company, Croner Publications Ltd offers a competitive salary and an attractive benefits package including life assurance, a pension scheme (subject to qualifying conditions), 28 days' holiday and medical cover. Hours of work are normally 35 per week as appropriate, within an 8am - 6pm framework.

Applicants should write, with a CV and details of current salary, to Moira Jevons at:-

Croner Publications Ltd
Croner House, London Road,
Kingston-Upon-Thames, Surrey KT2 6SR

NON-SMOKERS PREFERRED

The operative (or shop-floor worker)

The **operative** is a skilled, semi-skilled, or unskilled worker, whether a machine operator in a manufacturing plant, a bank clerk, a sales assistant in a shop, a trainee accountant, or a truck driver. Operatives, or 'shop-floor' workers, undertake essential tasks directly related to the production of goods and services. In an office environment these workers are known as assistants.

Operatives are at the bottom of the organizational hierarchy. They are responsible to a manager, usually a supervisor. Some may have a high degree of autonomy and responsibility in their jobs - for example, for quality control, ordering stocks, and problem-solving. Others - for example, an administrative assistant - may carry out a narrow range of repetitive tasks, such as filing and photocopying.

Key words:

Board of directors - body elected by shareholders to run a company

Executive directors - directors with full-time responsibilities who are are actively engaged in running a company

Non-executive directors - individuals employed for their expertise or business contacts, who act only in a part-time advisory capacity

Managing director - appointed by the board of directors to implement company policies and supervise and coordinate day-to-day activities

Company secretary - executive officer appointed by a board of directors to carry out administrative duties

Chairperson - elected by a board of directors to chair their meetings

Management - can refer either to people who are managers, or to the various managerial skills and knowledge they must possess in order to achieve organizational goals

Consultant - person, or organization, providing specialist advice, usually under a fixed-term contract

Supervisor - first-line manager with responsibility for day-to-day production issues

Operative - shop-floor worker or office assistant

Section 2.6

Factors that influence the choice of organizational structure

What is structural change?

Many organization structures are **dynamic** - that is, they change or evolve through time. Change will often occur simply as a result of a growth in the size of an organization. But whatever the reason, structural change will be aimed at improving the effectiveness and efficiency of the organization.

There are a number of factors which can influence the choice of organizational structure and prompt change. We can separate these into internal and external pressures:

Internal factors

- **Size:** The larger the organization, the less able top managers will be to control every aspect of the business. Large firms, therefore, tend to have more decentralized and flatter structures than smaller ones. Company directors and/or senior mangers will tend to confine themselves to setting overall objectives and steering the firm, while managers lower down the hierarchy will be responsible for day-to-day activities and the achievement of targets in production, sales, finance, and administration.

- **Location:** Some firms have factories, offices, or shops in more than one location. For example, multinational enterprises operate in several countries. Authority will be delegated to managers in these different locations, since they will be better informed about local conditions, such as labour supply, suppliers, consumer tastes, even languages, currency, and laws.

- **Nature of product:** Management structures tend to be more decentralized in firms supplying goods or services to satisfy specific customer requirements. For example, consider the fitting of double-glazed windows. Responsibility for the measurement and fitting of these windows must rest with those employees who undertake the work. In organizations that mass-produce products for national or even international markets, top-level managers will be able to monitor and control production and marketing efforts more closely.

- **Management style:** The structure of an organization will be a reflection of the particular personalities and management style of top managers. If they enjoy having the power and authority to command all aspects of business activity, then the structure will be tall and centralized, whereas those managers who are more democratic and seek to include employees in decision-making will prefer a flatter, decentralized structure.

- **Changes in working arrangements:** Growing competition has meant that firms are increasingly changing their working methods in an attempt to boost productivity (see 7.1). Work groups are being created in which authority over the organization of tasks and the working environment is delegated to team leaders and supervisors. The idea is that working and problem-solving in groups will provide employees with the incentive and commitment to work harder. Similarly, new production techniques, such as 'Just In Time' production, whereby stocks are ordered and delivered just in time to be processed, require personnel lower down the organizational hierarchy to be able to make quick decisions on the timing and need for further supplies (see 1.2). Such changes in working arrangements have tended to 'flatten' organizational structures and decentralize authority and decision-making.

External factors

- **Increasing competition:** This is perhaps the most important influence on private sector organizational structures. Markets are becoming increasingly competitive at home and abroad. A firm that is slow to react to changing market conditions - for example, new technologies and changing consumer demands - will fail. Passing information up and down a tall chain of command can take precious time and a market opportunity may be missed while top managers decide what to do. Thus, in order to keep pace with changing consumer demands and rivals' marketing strategies, decisions on production, sales, and marketing activities are increasingly being taken by employees 'at ground level'.

- **Entering new markets:** A firm that intends to market a new product may devolve authority and control over the product to an individual department or project group (as in a matrix organization). A firm that enters new markets, especially overseas where there are cultural, language, and legal barriers to overcome, will often need to employ sales and marketing staff with specialized, local knowledge and the authority to take decisions.

- **Technological change:** Businesses have become increasingly aware that communications can be improved by restructuring from hierarchical to flatter structures. This allows information to be transmitted more quickly and easily, and means that managers are given more authority to make decisions. Information Technology is also enabling many office workers to tele-work from home and control their own work tasks and working environment (see 15.2).

- **Change in ownership:** A company that is taken over or merges with another company may often undergo structural change. A takeover occurs when one company buys control of another through the acquisition of shares in the ownership of that company. A firm that is taken over will often lose its original identity and become part of the purchasing or acquiring company.

  A **merger** occurs when two or more firms agree to join together to form a new enterprise with a new legal identity. This is usually done by shareholders of the merging companies exchanging their existing shares for shares in the new organization. The name of the newly created enterprise will normally reflect the names of the merging companies (see 6.4).

  Many public sector enterprises have undergone changes in ownership since 1981. Privatization involves the sale of public sector assets by the UK government to the private sector (see 6.5). British Telecom was the first major state-owned, or nationalized, industry in which shares were

BA to separate online division

British Airways has agreed a radical change to its structure to increase internet sales and help stem its slide in profits.

The airline will separate its internet sales into a new unit in a drive to move half its business - £4.5bn of annual sales - online by 2003. Internet ticketing, airmile accounts and an online check-in will be handled by the new unit, working outside BA's existing headquarters and company structure.

It will be free to market online services more aggressively and sell more travel products from third parties, including non-BA flights. Employees are expected to be offered a stake in the unit, probably through share options.

Financial Times 31.12.1999

▲ *Technological change and competition can drive structural change in business* sold to the private sector in 1984. Since then, many other publicly owned industries have been sold back to the private sector, including British Gas, the electricity supply industry, and regional water supplies. All these industries are now run as public limited companies with boards of directors and business managers, instead of government ministers and public corporations controlling their strategic and day-to-day operations.

Restructuring British Railways

▲ *Rail services in Great Britain are now provided by many different private sector organizations*

In 1948 British Rail was formed by the nationalization of rail services in Great Britain.

The 1993 Railways Act provided for the break-up and privatization of British Rail in the form of the franchising of passenger rail services and the outright sale of all other parts of the business.

From April 1994 the rail industry in Great Britain was substantially reorganized into 80 separate organizations ready for its privatization. Of these, Railtrack became owner of the national rail network, stations, power lines and other infrastructure. It became a public limited company in May 1996 when it was sold to private shareholders.

Passenger rail services were reorganized into 25 Train Operating Companies to be franchised out to private sector companies. Some of these, such as Central Trains, are regionally based; some, like Great Western, serve the old InterCity routes; and others provide London commuter services, such as Thameslink and South West Trains.

On 31 March 1997 British Rail ceased to operate any passenger rail services after the final franchise, to run services on the West Coast Main Line, was awarded to Virgin Trains.

Making a structural change

A major consideration when changing an organization is the way in which people would be affected by the change. A good assessment of what to change and how to make the change will probably be wasted if organization members do not support the change. Managers and employees may resist change because they fear significant changes in their work load and responsibilities, or even job losses. It is therefore important that business owners and senior managers consult with their managers and staff to explain why structural change is necessary, how it can be implemented, and how it will affect them. That is, senior managers may need to adopt more consultative and democratic management styles in order to push through changes, such as restructuring, the introduction of new technology and working arrangements, and new staffing levels (see 2.5).

Unfreezing the organization culture

Resistance to change may be a problem arising from the organization culture. The **culture** of a business organization is the total characteristics shared by organization members. These include their customs, ideals, beliefs, attitudes, habits and skills. The culture influences the way the business operates (see 1.8). For example, if employees have always done things in certain ways then changing their ways, of working to modern,

Some quotes about cultures

'IBM is not everyone's cup of tea, but it is a winner'

'There is a vibrant, intensely commercial personality at Sainsbury, which the potential recruit may react to warmly or positively hate'

'Procter and Gamble people have strong characters, but individual presence is tempered by the influence of the corporation'

From Reynolds, B: The 100 Best Companies to Work for in the UK (Fontana/Collins, 1989)

'Liverpool FCs achievements are the product of its structure... There is a co-operative ethic in which each player's instinct is to maximise the number of goals the club scores rather than the number of goals he scores'.

Some companies - like IBM and Marks and Spencer - have a powerful and identifiable corporate culture... They will often emphasise their dependence on their people. The organization is dependent on them taken as a whole, because the product of the organization is the product of the collectivity... Employees are, in the main, fiercely loyal, and those who find the organization uncongenial leave'.

Adapted from Kay, J : Foundations of Corporate Success (Oxford 1995)

Hitachi union leaders share the managers' concern with the growth and prosperity of Hitachi as a corporation in competition with other corporations.'

From Dore, R : British Factory - Japanese Factory (University of California Press, 1973)

more efficient ways may be resisted. It is, therefore, necessary to understand culture before deciding how members contribute to the achievement of business objectives and the success of the organization. Different organizations may have very different cultures. Combining two or more organizations by merger to form a larger business may, therefore, prove very difficult if the cultures of the individual organizations clash.

A culture will often be determined and formed over time by the dominant group in the organization. Individuals may have allegiances to organized groups which are influential in the way they behave, their beliefs and attitudes. These allegiances may be may be informal and unrelated to their work, such as membership of social, religious or political groups, or directly related to their working situation, such as membership of trade unions (see 13.4). Where the established culture in an organization is to fear and resist change it is necessary for senior managers to 'unfreeze' the culture in order to implement change. In contrast, some cultures may be dynamic and open to new ideas and practices. For example, employees may want to work hard together to stay head of rival firms because they find their work challenging and exciting, and because they know their jobs depend on the continued success of their organization. Alternatively, some cultures may be internally competitive - that is, employees compete with each other for recognition from their managers, pay rewards and promotions. In this culture, employees may be more concerned with their own personal advancement and seek to undermine and withhold information from their colleagues, rather than work together to achieve the goals of their organization. Team building exercises and social events may help to unfreeze such a culture.

Some ways to unfreeze established organization cultures

- Replace top executives and change management teams
- Improve formal and informal communications, for example, by introducing e-mail
- Encourage more consultative and open management styles
- Bring in new recruits and use more staff and management training
- Involve trade unions and employees in decision-making
- Motivate employees through pay and other rewards
- Arrange company parties and other social events to encourage more social cohesion
- Relax some rules and norms - for example, by allowing office workers to wear casual clothes on Fridays
- Spread good news about the organization

Culture Clash at CMB Packaging

CMB Packaging was formed in 1989 as a merger of the old Metal Box company in the UK and Carnaud in France. On the surface there were good reasons to be optimistic about the merger, which formed a combined company worth about £800m. The packaging industry was made up of many small and medium-sized companies facing increased concentration between their major business customers. Mergers had already occurred in packaging and appeared to be relatively successful. The two companies' activities seemed fairly complementary. Carnaud was strong in France, Germany, Italy and Spain, while Metal Box was the leader of the UK market with some Italian activities.

In the event, the real world interfered with the vision and highlighted differences in management styles and cultures. Although this is a common problem even with mergers in the same country, many of the problems could be traced back to cross-country differences. At the top level the president, Jean-Marie Descarpentries, was described as 'flamboyant, a showman, a typical Frenchman full of French management school ideas, like the 'inverted pyramid' with customers at the top and management at the bottom'. By contrast, the old Metal Box group operated with a typical British, top-down, centralised management approach. This clash of cultures at the top led to indecision about the company's strategy and organisation. This in turn led to declining performance.

The conclusion drawn by many people was that perhaps this friendly type of merger is the most dangerous form of cross-European co-operation - particularly if there are significant differences in management style. Unfortunately, management styles are different throughout Europe and present a challenge to European corporate integration. They vary from the autocratic Italian style, to the German consensus approach. If cultures clash, perhaps the best way forward is either through outright take-over - where one culture triumphs over another - or, if this is impractical, through a loose and simple form of co-operation.

Adapted from The Times, 12.9.1991

Culture and the evolution of an organization

Embryonic stage

- In a new business venture everyone pulls together to help make the business a success
- The owners may also be the 'workers' in the business. The culture of the organization is determined by their ideas and personalities
- New employees will be chosen by the business owners according to how well they fit in with their style of working and ideas. In this way the organization develops a culture based on the 'power' the owners have

Growth phase

- Structural change is needed for new developments and as employee numbers grow
- The organization culture may become less cohesive and there could be power struggles
- A role culture may develop based on formal procedures and rules which employees follow to carry out specific functions
- Alternatively, the organization can develop a task culture by organizing project teams to complete tasks

Maturity

- Habits and routines develop as part of the organization culture. New ways of doing things may be resisted
- Senior managers may need to 'unfreeze' the culture in order to make changes. But change may be necessary for the organization to keep ahead of new competition

Decline

- Senior managers may face difficult decisions concerning the future of the organization
- Organization members may fear job losses and so will attempt to resist or slow down necessary changes

?

The evolving organization

Most organization change is incremental, i.e. bit by bit. Organizations tend to evolve over time, moving from one structure and culture to others. However, every now and again changes can be sweeping - for example, a complete reorganization of structure, management teams, working practices, and staffing levels following growth or decline in the business, or change of ownership.

The culture in young enterprise in their 'embryonic stage' is usually shaped by the founders. Once the business survives, their beliefs and visions become embedded in the structure of the organization. This may be called a **'power culture'** because it is the beliefs and decisions of the owners that shape the organization.

However, as the business grows the culture may also begin to change as frictions arise between members who want the business to develop one way and those who desire other options. That is, there may be power struggles. The growth phase also means the introduction of significant numbers of new people into an organization, increasing layers of management, new rules and procedures. A **'role culture'** may develop in which people perform particular functions, such as finance, human resources, design or production, and have formalized job descriptions (see 14.2). In a role culture procedures and ways of working tend to become standardized.

Alternatively, the organization may adopt a **'task culture'** which is project oriented and concentrates on the completion of project tasks rather than carrying out individual functions and procedures. A task culture can be promoted by introducing a matrix structure and teamworking (see 2.4).

As a business matures, habits and routines may form. The culture can become rigid and resistant to change. If the business goes into decline, the organization may face difficult decisions about production and employment levels, and withdrawal from its traditional products and markets. Organization members may find the adjustment difficult. In some cases, the adjustment process may be so slow and difficult that the business owners may choose to sell out to another organization, which may then be able to impose more radical change.

In contrast to the cultures discussed above, some organizations may adopt **'people-centred cultures'**. In these cultures, employees tend to make their own decisions and organize their work as they want. People-centred cultures characterize many voluntary organizations (see 2.1). People-centred cultures may also be found in worker cooperatives (see 2.2). In people-centred organizations decision-making will tend to be democratic but slow.

Portfolio Activity 2.10 

1. How is Coca-Cola restructuring?
2. What motives has Coca-Cola have for changing its organizational structure?
3. Explain what you think the Chief Executive of Coca-Cola meant by "...moving the organization closer to the market, closer to the only place decisions matter".
4. Part of the structural change involves delayering. Explain what this means and how it may affect internal communications and management styles at Coca-Cola.
5. Suggest why the culture of the organization could affect the change process at Coca-Cola.

Coca-Cola cuts 21% of workforce

Douglas Daft, the incoming Coca-Cola chief executive, ushered in sweeping changes yesterday, cutting 6,000 jobs - or 21 per cent of the total workforce - and shifting more responsibility to local units. The group said the cuts, the biggest ever for Coke, will cost about $800m.

He also acknowledged that earnings and volumes may no longer grow at the pace the soft drinks maker has set for many years.

More than a third of the job losses will be at the corporate headquarters, in Atlanta. Coca-Cola, which employs 29,000 people world-wide, will also cut 2,700 jobs overseas, and 800 jobs elsewhere in the US.

Coke's new structure will give regional presidents and their operating units sole responsibility for achieving earnings and sales targets set by headquarters, Mr Daft said.

Financial Times 27.2.2000

Useful references

Moynihan, D. and Titley, B. '**Economics - A Complete Course**' 3rd edn (Oxford, 2000) Chapters 5 and 6

Moynihan, D. and Titley, B. '**Intermediate Business**' 2nd edn (Oxford, 2000) Chapter 6

The Institute of Management ***(www.inst-mgt.org.uk)***
2 Savoy Court, Strand, London WC2R 0EZ

Management Today published monthly by Haymarket Publications ***(www.managementtoday.haynet.com)***

Test your knowledge

1 A US-owned supermarket discount store has recently opened in the UK. In the first year of operation its main business objective is likely to be:

A Gain market share

B Reduce operational costs

C Maximize growth potential

D Restructure the organization

2 Four ex-employees of a large paper mill have started their own business together to manufacture greetings cards. The type of business organization they have formed is a:

A Franchise

B Sole trader

C Partnership

D Public limited company

3 Which of the following is not a private sector business organization?

A Public limited company

B Worker cooperative

C Public corporation

D Partnership

4 If a business owner has unlimited liability it means:

A The business cannot be declared bankrupt

B The owner must meet all debts

C The business has sold shares

D The organization is non-profit-making

5 A public limited company is an organization which:

A Is owned by the government

B Is owned by its workers

C Is listed on the Stock Exchange

D Holds shares in other companies

6 Which of the following is a staff function which supports the main line functions within an organization?

A Marketing

B Finance

C Sales

D Production

Questions 7–9 share the following answers:

The aims of business organizations are many and will include:

A Providing a public service

B Profit maximization

C Expanding sales and market share

D Providing a charitable service

Which of the above could explain the following business activities?

7 Two people selling cold cans of drink for £1 each on a beach during a hot summer

8 An electronics company producing audio recorders that can produce recordable CDs and mini discs

9 Collecting unsold sandwiches from retailers to distribute to homeless people

10 Departments in the organization structure shown below have been organized by:

A Process

B Territory

C Product

D Function

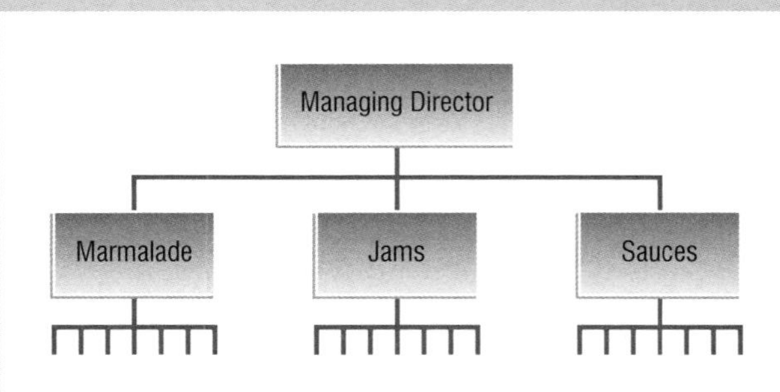

11 Which of the following features do you associate with organizational structures which have a wide span of management, or control?

A Management and supervision costs are lower

B Management can lose control

C Subordinates may have more than one boss

D It allows for tight control and close supervision

12 Which of the following best describes the organizational structure in the chart below?

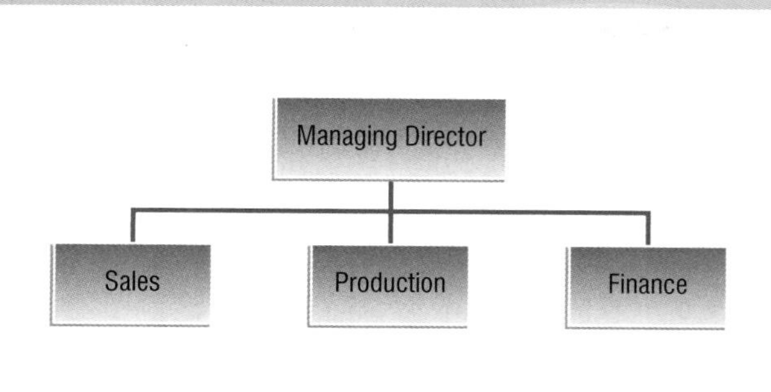

A A centralized, hierarchical structure

B A tall, decentralized structure

C A flat, centralized structure

D A matrix structure

13 **a** Compare the likely objectives of the following organizations:

- ICI (Imperial Chemical Industries plc)
- Royal Society for the Prevention of Cruelty to Animals (a charity)
- A library run by the local council

b ICI is a public limited company (plc). Describe the form of ownership and main method of finance in a plc.

c ICI is also a multinational. Explain what is meant by this.

d Suggest an appropriate organizational structure for ICI.

14 Explain differences between the following types of business organization in terms of ownership, control, and main method of finance:

- Sole trader
- Partnership
- Private limited company
- Public limited company
- Public corporation

15 **a** What is a sole trader?

b Give two advantages and two disadvantages of being a sole trader.

c Jane Bland owns five electrical stores in the Midlands. Explain why her organization will need a structure.

d Suggest an appropriate form of structure for her organization. Give reasons for your answer.

16 **a** What are the span of management and chain of command in an organization?

b What are the span of management and chain of command likely to be like in a tall, centralized organization?

c Suggest one advantage and one disadvantage of a decentralized organization.

d Suggest two factors which might cause a supermarket chain to develop a flat, decentralized structure.

chapter 3 Communications

This chapter examines why businesses need communications systems, the kinds of systems that can be used, and the possible effects of changes to communications.

BUT I DON'T WANT YOU - LET ME TALK DIRECTLY TO THE COMPUTER

What you need to learn

Communication is a two-way process which allows information to be passed between people and organizations.

Businesses need to communicate with a range of individuals and organizations including their customers, their competitors and their suppliers, as well as their own employees.

Good communication within a business is essential if that business is to operate effectively. It is important that you understand the relationship between effective communication and the achievement of business objectives.

You need to be able to identify c**ommunication channels** that exist within businesses and the effect these have on the quality of communication.

Communication channels are the routes along which information is passed. You should be able to compare different channels including:

- **internal and external communications**
- **formal and informal**
- **upward and downward**
- **open and restricted**

Information and communication technology (ICT) has had a dramatic effect on the way communication takes place in business. You need to be able to identify and understand how ICT has changed communications, and analyse the strengths and weaknesses of current developments in ICT for business.

Section 3.1 Why do businesses need communications systems?

Portfolio Activity 3.1 

Identify two possible means of communication for each of the cases given below:

1. A large high street electrical goods chain has 200 stores. Each store needs to regularly update head office about its daily sales, both to provide central information and also to enable head office to order more stock.
2. A multinational company wishes to consult its national managers on plans for new products. It would like the managers to be able to see and hear each other.
3. A solicitor wants immediate written confirmation that a buyer in Spain has written a cheque to purchase her client's villa.
4. The human resources manager in a large UK insurance company wants to send information detailing a new company training scheme to all of its employees.

What is communication?

Communication is a process which enables information to be passed from one person or organization to another. To be effective, communication will require:

- A **transmitter**: a source or sender of information
- A **transmission**: a message or content
- A **channel**: a route through which information is passed, e.g. different employees and organizations
- A **medium**: a method through which information is passed, e.g. a telephone
- A **receptor**: a person or audience to whom the information is sent
- **Feedback**: to indicate whether not the receptor has understood the message

Thus, for communication to be effective, information passed between two parties must be understood and acceptable to those sending it and to those receiving it. If both the person transmitting information and the person receiving it are within the same organization, communication is said to be **internal.** If information is passed between one organization and another, it involves **external communication.**

Success in business depends on being able to respond to changes in the market and to the actions of competitors more quickly than other firms. One very important means of gaining a competitive advantage over rival firms is through fast and efficient communications. Fast and accurate communication means that a firm can find out quickly what is going on in the market and can communicate its response - whether in terms of price changes or the introduction of new or revised products - to its own staff and to customers as quickly as possible. Thus, a business that fails to communicate effectively is unlikely to be successful and meet its objectives (see 1.7).

Who do businesses communicate with?

There are a number reasons why businesses need good communications:

- **to communicate with customers**

The main purpose of any business is to sell or provide goods and/or services to customers. A business that fails to communicate the right information clearly and at the right time to customers is in danger of losing them to business rivals.

Sometimes a business may write to potential customers advertising its new goods or services. However, it is often the customer who first contacts a business - for example, to find out about products and prices. Some may write to complain about a product while others may write to say how pleased they are with the product. In all cases a business should reply quickly to customers with the information they want, for example - a letter that apologizes to a dissatisfied customer and offers a refund or replacement.

▲ *All businesses need to communicate with customers, other organizations and employees on a daily basis*

- **to communicate with other businesses**

A business will need to make regular contact other business organizations if they are customers or suppliers.

A business will have dealings with many different suppliers. Banks, insurance companies, employment agencies, solicitors, accountants, and advertising agencies are all suppliers of business services. Others will provide materials, component parts, fuel, machinery and other equipment. As a customer of these organizations, a business may write to make enquiries, complain or thank them about their services.

Despite being in competition for customers and market share, rival businesses will also share information - for example, to help them compete more effectively against a new business rival, to develop joint training programmes for their employees, to react to government tax and other proposals that may help or harm their businesses, to set up joint ventures, or to work together to solve difficult technical problems.

In addition, a business will also need to communicate with government organizations such as the Inland Revenue, Customs and Excise, Health and Safety Executive, Environment Agency and many more.

- **to communicate with work colleagues**

Everyone who works in a business organization works as part of a team to achieve business objectives (see 1.7). Communication between work colleagues is, therefore, very important.

Communication within a business organization can 'cascade' down the chain of command from managers to their staff, for example, to communicate business objectives, working arrangements, negotiate wages, inform them of other changes and much more. Communications can also rise up through the business hierarchy (see 2.4). Employees can inform more senior managers of production and sales failures and successes, give feedback on training and the performance of their managers, or to react to proposals for changes they feel are not in their interests. It is important for communications to be a two-way process otherwise employees may

▼ *Channels of communication*

EIPT NO. | DATE OF PURCHASE
MODEL NO. | SERIAL NO. | GUARANTEE CARD NO. № 271890
OMER NAME etc. (BLOCK CAPITALS) | AUTHORIZED DEALER'S STAMP
PHONE NO. | DATE OF PURCHASE
WOULD BE GRATEFUL IF YOU WOULD COMPLETE THE FOLLOWING BEFORE
URNING THIS CARD FOR REGISTRATION
Female Age ( )
RQCB0057
S0289H0

feel ignored by their managers. This can reduce their motivation at work and their commitment to the achievement of the business's objectives. A flatter organization structure may help to improve two-way communications.

Channels of communication

We can define a **communication channel** as either a **formal** or **informal** route between people or organizations along which information passes. For example, informal channels of communication can be 'opened' between people at lunchtime and on social occasions. The people involved may discuss business procedures and policy, but sometimes information communicated through this 'grapevine' method may become distorted. On the other hand, formal communication involves information that is entirely necessary to ensure the effective operation and execution of a business activity.

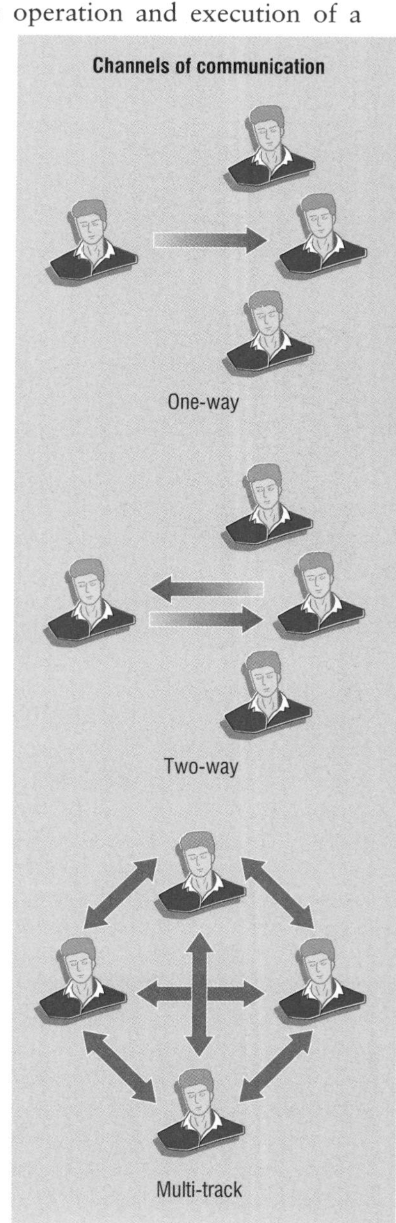

Most channels of communication involve a two-way process, passing information between two or more parties. However, communication can also be a one-way or multi-track process.

One-way channels

These exist to provide people and organizations with information which requires no direct feedback. Here there is only one transmitter and one receptor. Examples might include the announcement of train departure times at a station, or managers passing simple instructions or other information via a 'vertical channel' to workers on the shop floor.

Two-way channels

Here, the communicators must be both transmitters and receptors of information - for example, a group of managers asking employees for their opinions on the introduction of new technology or proposed changes in working methods, and listening to feedback.

Multi-track channels

These exist when information is passed on by one receptor to a number of receptors who are also able to feedback. For example, manufacturers may provide wholesalers with product information which is then passed onto retailers, who in turn give this information to consumers. Wholesalers, retailers, and consumers may then pass their opinions on the product back to the manufacturer.

Open and restricted channels

If a channel of communication is **open**, it means that anyone can share in the information being transmitted. For example, a noticeboard at work is used to transmit information to anyone who reads it.

However, some information will be confidential, and access to it will be **restricted.** For example, if managers are planning to introduce new machinery which is likely to lead to redundancies, they will need information on which to base this decision, but will not wish their workforce to know until their plans are finalized. An organization will also wish to keep new product developments secret, so that rival firms are unable to copy their ideas.

The objectives of communication

Internal communications in a business between owners and managers, managers and other staff, and between office and shop floor workers, will have the following objectives:

- to provide information on a whole range of matters from organizational goals, costs and performance to simple routine matters such as canteen opening times
- to give instructions on a host of tasks that will help the organization function effectively and achieve objectives, such as how to organize production, how to design an advertising campaign, how to fill out order forms, etc.
- to improve team work. Better communication between managers and workers can improve worker morale if they feel their opinions are being considered. Working in teams relies on effective communication between members to get work done.
- to communicate how well individual workers have performed in their jobs either informally or formally via annual job appraisal reviews and to recommend appropriate training and career moves (see 15.2).

The objectives of external communications with other people and organizations will include:

- providing information, such as information on end of year profits to the Inland Revenue or accident statistics to the Health and Safety Executive and so on
- giving instructions, such as orders to suppliers, worker selection criteria to employment agencies, credit arrangements to banks and many more
- confirming arrangements, for example, the date, time and venue for a meeting, or travel times and arrangements with transport operators
- receiving feedback, both internally, for example from workers regarding new working methods, or externally, such as consumers opinions of new products.

Portfolio Activity 3.2 

Investigate the Management Information System in an organization of your choice.

- First establish whether an MIS exists. (If organization members say that they do not have an MIS, then ask how managers obtain information with which to make decisions. All managers need information, and the process by which they receive it will be their MIS, although in some organizations the system may be poorly structured.)
- Find out the information needs of the various managers. (If possible, identify the requirements of the three tiers of management: company directors, middle managers at department level, and supervisors.)
- Identify relevant sources of information within to the organization and from external sources such as government statistics.

Verbal and non-verbal communication

In general, communication can take two forms:

- **Verbal communication** involves people talking either face-to-face or over a telephone or satellite link. It requires oral and listening skills.
- **Non-verbal communication** refers to all other forms of communication which do not require speech. Information is written and transmitted either by hand or on a computer, and will usually be paper-based.

Information Communication Technology (ICT)

The way in which business organizations communicate has changed significantly in recent times. **Information Communication Technology** has revolutionized our ability to store, retrieve, and send information to different users. For example, computers and satellites have improved the quality and speed at which information can be communicated over long distances. Both sound and vision can be transmitted around the world in just a few seconds. The large number of people who have such equipment as telephones, TVs, videos and computers means that business can communicate with a large audience. This is especially important to firms advertising their products to national and international markets.

However, ICT can be expensive to buy and staff may need a lot of training if they are to use the new equipment effectively. People and firms unable to afford new equipment might be excluded from some communications. The security of information is also threatened by telephone bugging and computer hacking (unlawful access to other peoples and organizations computer files).

Portfolio Activity 3.3 

Most organizations today, even some of the smallest, will have a vast array of equipment to aid the process of communication. Below is a list of equipment you are likely to find in a busy office:

- Computer terminal
- Modem
- Fax
- Answer machine
- Mobile phone
- Videophone
- Telephone
- Switchboard
- Pager
- Photocopier
- Tannoy
- Digital TV receiver
- Radio
- Intercom

1. Choose an organization with which you are familiar, and find out how many of these devices they have, how they communicate, and the main types of information they are able to transmit or receive. State whether each piece of equipment is used for one-way, two-way, or multi-track communication.
2. Are there any items of communications equipment that your organization does NOT use or have access to? If so, find out why.
3. Which item, if any, would you recommend your firm to buy or hire to improve communications? Give reasons for your choice.
4. Suggest possible staff training that might be needed to ensure that the new equipment is used effectively and safely.

Key words:

Communication - the process of passing information between people and organizations

Communication channel - a link between people and organizations along which information is passed

Open channels - when information is not confidential and can be shared by anyone

Restricted channels - when information is confidential and is directed to those who need, or have paid, to know

Verbal communication - communicating through speech

Non-verbal communication - paper-based and electronic communication

Section **3.2**

Verbal communication

The easiest way to communicate is simply to talk to people. Today people can talk to each other all over the world using a telephone. However, verbal communication is often complemented by facial expressions - for example, frowning at another person's suggestion - and by body language such as a shrug of the shoulders to suggest indifference. Non-verbal forms of communication such as pictures, graphs, and letters may also form the topic of verbal discussion. Therefore, to be truly effective, verbal communication requires both sound and vision.

Face-to-face communication

The most common method of verbal communication is a face-to-face meeting where people can see who they are talking to. Face to face communications include interviews, such as those held to appoint job applicants (see 14.4), and business meetings.

Where people tend not to meet face to face this can lead to a 'memo mountain' as managers put off talking through difficult issues with people and instead communicate with staff on paper. This lack of direct contact can quickly lead to misunderstanding and also allows the informal 'grapevine' or 'rumour mongers' to take over the channels of communication. In an effective organization there is no substitute for regular face-to-face contact with staff.

Business meetings

Meetings are the most common means of attempting to resolve difficulties and find solutions to problems. Staff at all levels in an organization will be involved at some time in a meeting. However, meetings among managers tend to be the most frequent. Typically, managers will use meetings to:

- Set business objectives
- Monitor progress and business performance
- Discuss new ideas
- Plan for the future
- Discuss and make decisions

Well-run meetings usually require the following key ingredients:

- A strong **chairperson** who is able to keep people to the point and encourage everybody to have their say, yet at the same time prevent certain individuals from dominating
- An **agenda** issued in advance of the meeting, with a clear list of topics for discussion
- A group of people who are capable of keeping to the point and who are willing to listen to each other, make compromises, and reach a solution.
- Someone who is able to take notes of points and matters arising from the meeting for future reference. These notes can be used to produce the **minutes** of the meeting (see 3.3).

Cascading will often follow senior management meetings at which decisions have been made. This involves setting up a series of meetings between lower-level managers, supervisors, and operatives to pass on and discuss the senior managers' business decisions and ideas, and how they will be put into effect.

▼ *Figure 3.1: An example of an agenda for a business meeting*

Notice of Meeting: **Regional Sales Divisions**

Date: 26 March 2001

Time: 2.30 pm

Venue: Head Office, London

Agenda

1. Apologies for absence
2. Minutes of last meeting
3. Action points - budget allocation for ICT
   – new promotion campaign update
4. 'Paris' project: tender proposals for research
5. AOB
6. Date of next meeting

▼ *Figure 3.2: Cascading*

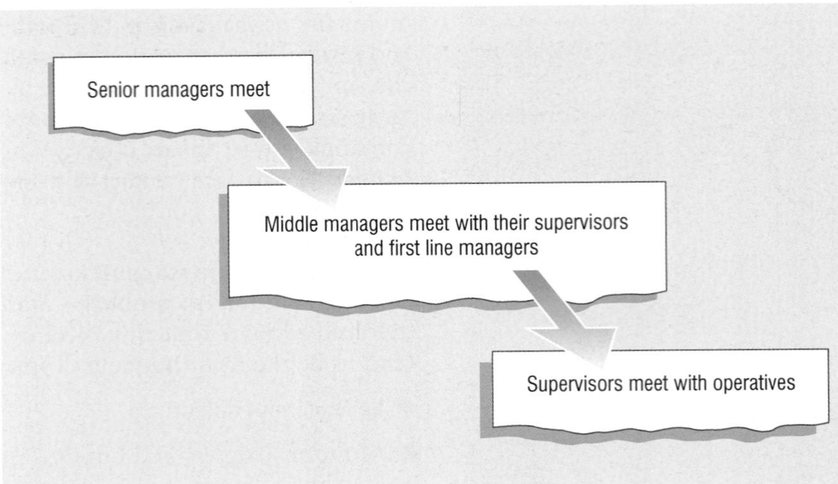
Senior managers meet
Middle managers meet with their supervisors and first line managers
Supervisors meet with operatives

Other types of business meeting

Team meetings - between department managers and their staff teams

Mass meetings - for example, with all the employees, or all the shareholders in a large organization

Presentations - in which one person or group of people present information or demonstrate a product or process to an audience, often using audio and visual methods such as films and slides. Handouts of useful information or speaking notes will also tend to be given to audience members.

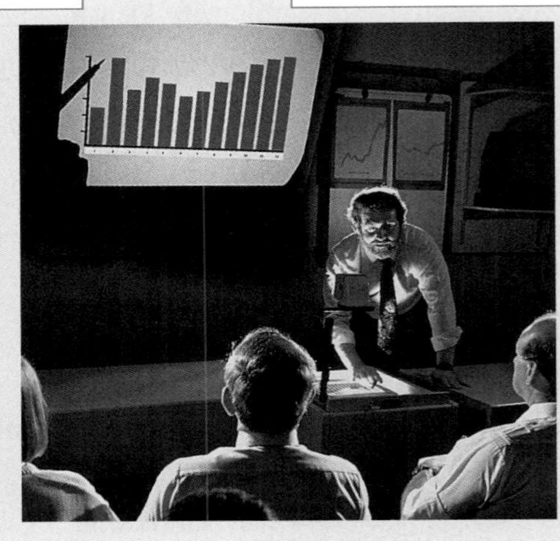

Videophones

These allow users to see and hear each other by means of a built-in camera and small monitor in their telephone sets. Videophones are more expensive to buy than ordinary phones, but they use the same network, and call charges are the same. Business users are likely to find videophones useful because they allow users to make eye contact and to gauge body language, which is an important part of communications.

Videoconferencing

This is a service operated by British Telecom which allows groups of people in different places to be linked using sound and vision. Videoconferencing may be a quicker and cheaper way of achieving a face-to-face meeting than having people travel over long distances. Today, the Internet also allows people to hold video conferences using desk-top cameras linked to their personal computers.

▼ *Videoconferencing can be used for face-to-face communication between people separated by long distances*

Take a look at the problem - Videoconferencing helps decisions

Keith Platt, who runs a £3 million turnover insurance business, has been using British Telecom desktop videoconferencing for just over a year to link six sites around the country. "We did it because we were looking for a competitive advantage in a market where direct sales of insurance are cleaning up the business."

Travelling to meetings in London effectively meant writing off a whole day. Now, by linking up on the videophone, he can save hours at a time - and the cost of travelling. He uses the facilities for board meetings, management meetings, presentations, and training.

"You can resolve a lot more things by talking face-to-face. You can see the body language, negotiate, and come to quick decisions," says Platt, who has spent around £40,000 on video communications equipment.

The cost of video communications is coming down all the time. Whereas five years ago it was strictly for the multinationals, who have hundreds of thousands to invest in large systems with expensive, dedicated transmission lines, the entry cost of videophones is now just a few thousand pounds.

Daily Telegraph 8.11.1994

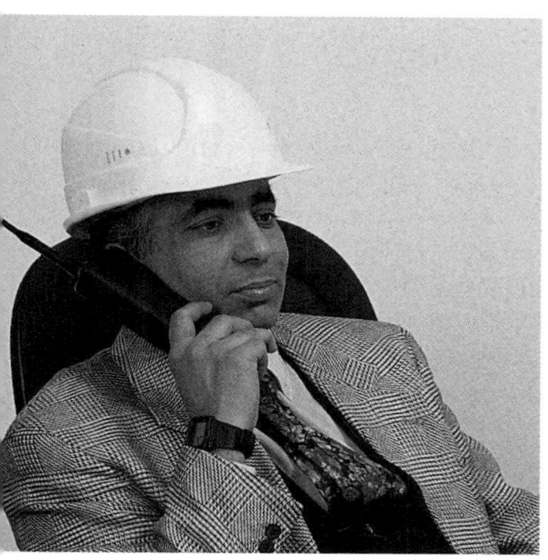

Telephone communications

The telephone is an important piece of communications equipment in business. It allows an organization to talk to its employees, customers and suppliers at any time anywhere in the world. Telephone equipment, network access, and the cost of making calls are all relatively cheap in the UK. This is due to a great number of providers competing to supply the market.

Many businesses now issue **mobile phones** to staff who need to travel away from their offices. This allows them to keep in touch and up-to-date on the latest developments in their business. They can also keep in touch with their customers.

Voice messaging is available to the customers of telephone service providers such as Vodafone and British Telecom. The service allows telephone users to record a message and have it delivered to an electronic 'mailbox'. The user dials the mailbox and uses a personal identification number to listen to the messages. Voice messaging systems are used by business people who travel or who are away from their offices. The advantage of voicemail is that it is useful for communicating out of office hours and between countries where there are time differences.

With new technology, telephones in the near future will also have video screens and people will be able to see who they are talking to. This will mean that business employees will find good communication skills, including their facial expressions, are even more important.

Key words:

Face-to-face communication - talking in person to other people

Agenda - notification to those attending a business meeting of the topics to be discussed and the order in which each will be tackled

Cascading - passing information vertically down the chain of command in an organization through a series of meetings between staff at different grades

Videoconferencing - a BT service which allows groups of people to see and hear each other over long distances

Voice messaging - 'electronic mailbox' facility in which a caller can record a spoken message for a telephone user to listen to later using an personal access code.

Section **3.3**

Non-verbal communication

A large amount of communication is undertaken using non-verbal methods. These can include **memos, minutes, reports, letters, bulletins,** and a variety of **financial documents.** These are used because it is simply not possible to tell everybody everything they need to know using verbal communication methods. Even if there were time to do this, staff are unlikely to remember everything and will need information written on paper to refer to later.

Paper-based communications have an important role in organizations. However, too much paperwork can result in heavy information flows and very poor communication if staff 'switch off' and do not bother to read it.

Internal communications

People in different parts of an organization will often communicate with each other using a variety of non-verbal paper-based methods. Transmitting information in a written paper-based format has the advantage of providing a record of the message, the person(s) sending and receiving the message, and the date of the communication. The key forms of internal communication are as follows:

- **Memorandums**, or memos, are usually sent through the internal mail and are short communications, focusing on a small number of points.
- **Minutes** provide a summary of decisions made and action resulting from business meetings. They are kept for future reference and may be used at a later date to assess the work and action taken by those at the meeting. For example, minutes produced following the meeting to discuss the agenda in Figure 3.1 might be as shown in Figure 3.4.

▼ *Figure 3.3: An example of a memo*

MEMO

To: All senior managers

Date: 15.8.00

From: JP Smith MD

Subject: Meeting on 25.8.00

Meeting cancelled. Rescheduled to 4.9.00 at 2 pm.

Venue unchanged.

Agenda will be sent prior to meeting.

Please phone Kate Morris (x6783) to confirm attendance.

Apologies for inconvenience. JPS

▼ *Figure 3.4: An example of minutes*

KRB
FOODS PLC

Minutes of Regional Sales Divisions Meeting, 26 March 2001

In attendance:

Mr Wood	Sales Director
Mrs James	Scotland & NW
Mr Douglas	NE
Ms Shah	Wales & Midlands
Mr Fawcett	E
Mr Dickens	SW
Mrs Staunton	SE
Mr Hollby	NW Europe

Minutes and Matters Arising:

1. Mr Hallam sent his apologies. Ms Shah to deputize.
2. **i.** Mr Douglas stated that sales figures from North West division had been misquoted in minutes of previous meeting. Correct figure for Q4 2000 was £1.2m.

   ii. Mr Wood explained that purchasing had now received all requests for new ICT equipment. Total bid was £2.7m. Largest element was for networking 160 users in the regional offices at £1.4 million. HQ budget allocation for 2001/2 has now been agreed at £2.4 million. It is envisaged that the current downward trend in prices should mean that all bids can be funded. **No further action required**.
3. Mr Fawcett introduced paper on test-marketing of new 'Champions' chocolate bar in Eastern division territories. Consumer response favourable and sales healthy - 45,000 in first four weeks. A full report was tabled and comments invited before presentation to board of directors on 26.3.01. **Action: All**.
4. Mr Hollby explained that 5 tenders had been received from market research organizations invited to bid for the 'Paris' project to examine consumer preferences for confectionery in France. Tenders ranged in price from £150K to £240K. Before the contract for work is let (end of April 2001) the opinions of divisional heads are invited. Copies of the tender documents were tabled. **Action: All - comments, including nil response, by 14.4.01.**
5. Mrs Staunton was currently working up a proposal for in-store customer purchase incentives. Her report will be ready for consideration by 3.4.01 whereupon division heads will be asked for their ideas on how to implement incentives on a regional basis. **Action: Mrs Staunton to report by 3.4.01.**
6. Next meeting fixed for 27 June 2001 at 2 pm. Venue to arranged.

Portfolio Activity 3.4 

1. Write a memo to your tutor to inform him or her of progress on your assessment work for Unit 1 and your expected completion date.
2. Meet with your class group to plan and discuss your assessments and research. Prepare an agenda to follow and produce minutes after the meeting.

- **Reports** tend to be written for specific reasons, for example, to review the effectiveness of a recent sales promotion, or monitor health and safety at work. Reports summarize large quantities of information and draw readers' attention to key issues which need decisions.

- Some firms produce their own regular newsletters or **bulletins**. These usually highlight important new developments in the firm and provide a chance for management to praise their staff. Other organizations may use a daily or weekly bulletin highlighting key points for staff. This might be pinned to a noticeboard, for example, outside the canteen area where everyone will be able to see it.
- Businesses must keep accurate and up-to-date records of the goods and services they buy and sell, who they buy them from or sell them to, and how much money they receive in revenue and pay out for costs. To do this businesses use a variety of **financial documents** (see 16.2). Financial documents must be clear and easy to fill in otherwise people who complete them may make mistakes. They include purchase orders, invoices, receipts, bank account statements, and customer accounts. Some of these documents will be produced for internal purposes and some will be sent to or received from suppliers and customers.

Portfolio Activity 3.5 

1. Research into the kinds of non-verbal communication methods used in your college/school or any other organization that you know of. Identify the kinds of methods used and survey the opinions of staff on their effectiveness.
2. Produce a brief report on the effectiveness of non-verbal communications in the organization and recommend improvements.

External communications

Advertisements

Business organizations will use **advertisements** to raise awareness of their goods and services. Most advertisements are informal communications and aimed at a large number of people at the same time. They can be informative, such as railway timetables, but most are designed to be persuasive, and aim to encourage consumers to buy the products using attractive promotional images.

Advertisements are considered in detail in Section 10.3.

Business letters

By far the most important formal communication with a customer or another organization is a business letter.

Business letters can be used for many different purposes. Below are just a few examples:

- Arranging and confirming meetings
- Asking job applicants to attend interviews
- Offering jobs to successful applicants
- Providing details of prices and costs estimates for work
- Making complaints to suppliers about poor delivery times or faulty materials
- Asking banks to check the creditworthiness of a customer
- Advertising details of new goods or services to customers
- Making enquiries or seeking information and help from other organizations
- Recording the main points of business conversations
- Writing to members of parliament on matters of concern
- Notifying employees of dismissal or redundancy
- Responding to customer enquiries and complaints
- Direct mailing promotions to customers (see 10.3)

The style and layout of business letters will vary greatly between organizations. However, if a letter is to be effective and create the right impression it must be well presented, to the point, tactful, accurate, and addressed correctly. Figure 3.5 provides an example.

Not all business letters are written from scratch. Many organizations have a range of standard responses - for example, to customer enquiries and complaints. Standard and routine letters can be stored on computers. Modern technology means they can be 'personalized' with individual names and addresses prior to printing. This is very important to a business that wants to send out the same letters to many different people and organizations but wants to give the impression that each letter is a personal communication. This makes it less likely that the person receiving the letter will simply throw it away without reading it.

External post or courier services must be used to send business letters and other paper-based communications to customers and other organizations. A wide variety of delivery services is available, many provided by the Post Office in the UK. These include recorded delivery and insured post, prepaid reply services, parcel post and international post by ship or airmail. There are also many courier services, such as TNT and DHL, who are willing to guarantee times to deliver small or large items all over the world.

▼ *Figure 3.5 : An example of a business letter*

KRB FOODS PLC

Manor House, 17-25 Best Street
London SW34 1EZ
Tel: 020 79189 3440 Fax: 020 79189 3441
www.krb.foods.plc.com

Our ref : KRB1/FS/5.234
Your ref : KRB1/FS/NF2

12 July 2000

Mrs J Bottell
123 Letterman Road
Kingston Upon Thames
Surrey KT1 2FU

Dear Mrs J Bottell

Financial Statement and Accounts 1999–2000

Thank you for your letter and enquiry of 3 July 2000.

We are pleased to enclose a copy of our Annual Financial Statement and Accounts as requested. The latest accounts are for the financial year ending 4 April 2000. An interim financial statement for the first half to 2000/1 will be issued in October.

Please do not hesitate to contact me should you wish to discuss the content of the enclosures in more detail.

Yours sincerely

Nicola Foley

Nicola Foley
Director of Finance
Encs.

Provide a reference number for the receiver to quote in future correspondence. Often a reference will consist of the initials of the person who has dictated it, the typist, the department it is being sent from, and/or the number of the letter.

Always write the name and address of the person or organization you are sending it to on the left-hand side.

Open your letter 'Dear Sir' or 'Dear Madam' (the salutation). If possible, use the person's name.

Write a short subject heading to show what the letter is about.

End your letter 'Yours faithfully' if 'Dear Sir' or 'Dear Madam' have been used, or 'Yours sincerely' if you have used the name of the addressee (the complimentary close).

Sign your letters by hand.

Print your name and job title.

Used if other documents are enclosed with the letter.

Letter heading showing name and address of organization.

Provide a file reference to store the letter in your own organization.

Always date your letter.

Leave line space.

Leave two letter spaces after a full stop and one space after a comma.

▼ *Postal delivery services*

Electronic communications

E-mail (electronic mail)

Imagine the Tokyo office of your organization has asked you to prepare a report on UK sales figures for the last three months. You prepare the report containing text, tables and graphs using desktop publishing software. The Tokyo office wants a hard copy (i.e. paper copy) of the report and a copy of the computer file. You store the computer file on a floppy disk, print out the report and send both by special delivery to Tokyo. However, there is a much easier and quicker way of doing this without the need to send paper or disks over long distances.

E-mail is an increasingly popular means of sending information and business documents without the need to send paper. Computers linked to the telephone network can send and receive computer files containing business documents to and from other computers all over the world. E-mail can be sent via computers either within the same organization, using an Intranet, or between different organizations via the Internet.

To send e-mail all you have to do is call up a file onto your computer or input a letter or message that you want to send. You will then have to type in the e-mail 'mailbox' address of the computer terminal of the person or organization you are sending it to. An e-mail address code is very similar to a phone number except that it will consist of letters and symbols as well as numbers. For example, 'bigbreakfast@planet24.co.uk' is the well-known e-mail address of Channel 4's Big Breakfast TV studios.

Once the e-mail address has been entered the computer will transmit the document over the phone line to the other computer, often in just a matter of seconds even for large amounts of information. The cost of sending the document is charged for in the same way as an ordinary phone call and often costs only a few pence, although the cost will be higher for international transmissions.

A computer at the e-mail address will receive the transmission. The person or organization to whom the computer belongs can then save their file on to their own hard disk or floppy disks and print out the document.

▼ *Low cost or free Internet access and web space for e-mail transmissions is available from a great many providers*

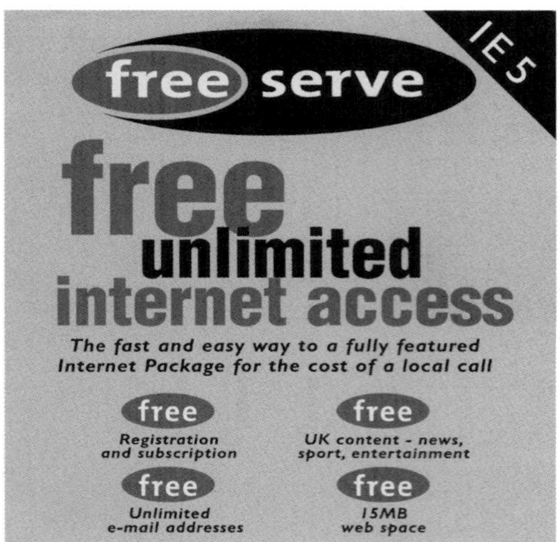

The advantage of e-mail is that a large number of people at different e-mail addresses can be sent the same message at the same time. The message, once sent, will wait in electronic mailboxes in computers for the user to access it.

The Internet

The Internet has revolutionized global communications in just a few years. In the early part of the new millennium it is about to revolutionize the way people and businesses in every country buy and pay for goods and services from all over the world. This is called **e-commerce** (see 11.1). For example, it is now possible to download and read 'on-line' daily newspapers such as *The Sun* or *The Times*, rather than having to go out to buy them.

The Internet is a global computer and communications network linking millions of smaller networks and computers all over the world through land and satellite based telephone connections. It can be used to send e-mails between people and organizations anywhere in the world, or to access the many millions of websites world-wide, set up by individuals and business organizations to provide information or to advertise and sell their goods and services. All this can be done for the cost of local telephone calls.

So what is an Intranet?

An **Intranet** is simply a local computer and communications network within an organizaton - a sort of internal Internet. It can be used for e-mail as well as for information pages, such as jobs and training programmes available to staff in the business, information on the organization structure and senior management team, travel and subsistence arrangements, social events, health and safety matters and copies of standard business documents.

Developing communication networks between computers

A business that wants to use ICT to improve internal information exchange and communications, and develop an Intranet, must link together its computer equipment in some way. This is usually done by creating a **local area network (LAN)**. Networks are either 'wired' together or connected via 'wireless' using radio or infra red transmissions. Access to the LAN can be protected by using a password which users must enter before they can log-on.

At the centre of a LAN will normally be a powerful computer which acts as the file server to all the computers - or workstations - linked in the network. A LAN file server will provide:

- a hard drive on which software is stored
- access to shared software from each workstation
- storage space and back-up for new files created on individual workstations
- temporary storage for files held in print queues for shared printers
- a gateway through which internal communications will pass and can be monitored

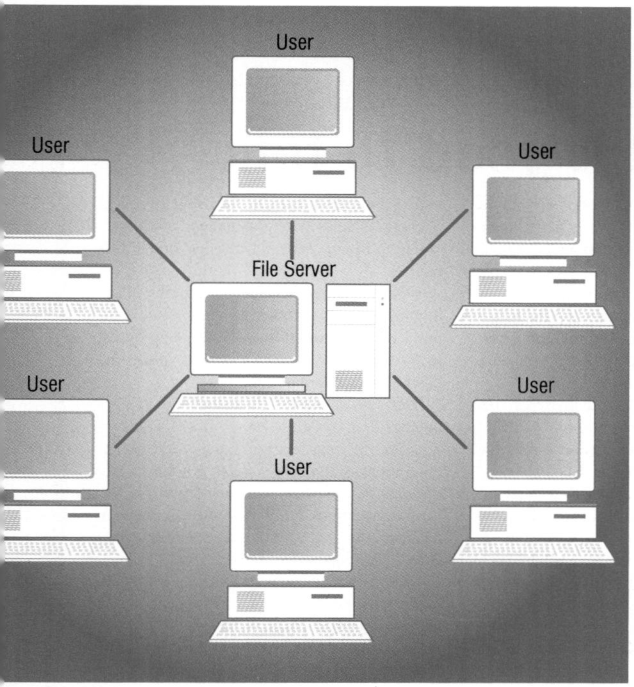

User
User
User
File Server
User
User
User

▲ *A Local Area (computer) Network*

Some LANs do not have a file server. Instead, individual workstations use their own hard disks to store software applications and work files which can be made available to the other workstations in the network. These are called **public files**. Special network software packages can be used to operate this type of network between a number of users.

Computers linked through telephone lines form **wide area networks (WANs)**. Computers are able to talk to each other using the telephone system. WANs can be used to communicate with different parts of the same organization, or even different organizations, at different sites, including those overseas, and with customers.

To create a WAN, both the sender and the receiver of information must possess the following facilities and equipment:

- A computer (either a mainframe or PC)
- A telephone socket
- A telephone line
- A **modem (MOdulator/DEModulator)**
- Communications software to operate the modem

Central to the creation of a WAN is the **modem**. This is a device which can change digital signals to analogue signals and back again. Telephone lines were designed for transmitting audible sounds which are transformed for transmission into electrical 'analogue' waves. Computers, however, send and receive digital signals made up binary code – a series of 0s and 1s. The combinations of 0s and 1s is infinite and can represent an infinite array of different words, numbers, and pictures when converted.

▼ *Figure 3.6: Creating a Wide Area Network (WAN)*

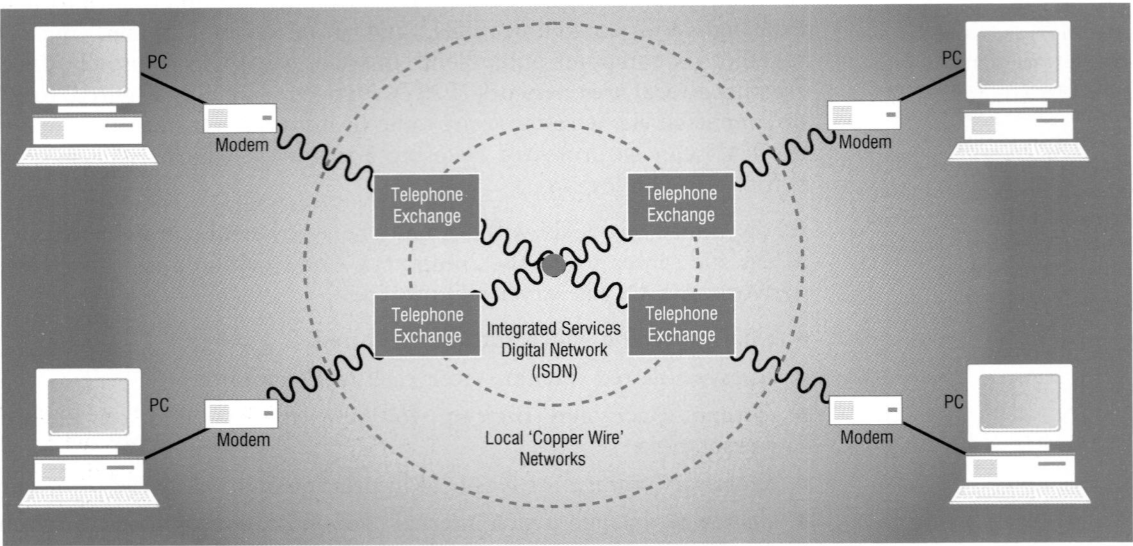

Portfolio Activity 3.6 

What is an Intranet? Use the article below to suggest possible advantages and disadvantages to a business of developing an Intranet.

Companies find it good to talk

IF YOU tell people what is going on you are more likely to retain staff. This conviction is persuading some companies to develop systems of communication that create a sense of community and involvement.

Does in work? Without doubt, according to Cliff Powell, of Mitsubishi Electric. "Our staff surveys used to criticise us for poor communication, so we've worked hard on it," he says. "We set up an intranet where we advertise all our vacancies, detailing the skills that are required and the training that's available. Our record of promotion has been greatly improved and the intranet also brings people together."

AA Insurance introduced a new system of communication three years ago. Treive Nicholas, sales channel development manager, says: "Good communication provides us with a competitive edge. We're in a very competitive business and change is a major issue for us. When people are involved in decisions, they're more likely to be happy. That means they work at their best possible level and customers get a better service. The staff feel more confident; they feel better about coming to work, the difficult periods are easier to overcome - and that helps us to implement changes more easily."

AA Insurance wanted to introduce a system of telephone sales that would halve the time it took to give a quotation and take an order. Senior managers and operators got together for brainstorming sessions.

"We asked our telesales team what they would do to make the process more efficient, what they thought the customers wanted and how the changes should be implemented," says Nicholas. "We recognise that we can't change without the support of staff. If they're suddenly faced with big surprises you go against the grain. We've got hundreds of minds out there and we're trying to engage them, to feed ideas back to the management."

The nuts and bolts of the company's communications strategy include conferences and seminars where workers' views are invited.

Telesales and marketing people get together to formulate forecasts and plans. "The departments are working to the same targets, and relationships have improved," says Nicholas, "Sales now understands what marketing is doing with advertising and direct mail."

BG, the former British Gas, established its intranet a year ago to keep open lines of communication between its 19,000 employees, including those working overseas and some 2,500 of whom are on the road.

Tom O'Connor, BG's head of knowledge-management systems, says: "It has saved us time and money. We put group-wide vacancies on the system every week. It helps people broaden their careers with a sideways move. This is important, because as the organisation has become flatter, the traditional upwards career move is harder to find."

"We provide online training information for people to pick their own packages. There's also an induction programme to help improve people's knowledge of the company. The place where people can find information about the company gets 2m hits a month."

The Sunday Times, 13.9.1998

Telephone lines between UK exchanges are able to carry digital signals, but most lines from exchanges to homes and organizations remain analogue. Modems are therefore needed for computers to communicate with each other until the networks in the UK and overseas become digital. However, most mobile phone networks are already digital - they do not rely on telephone wires to carry their signals. Mobile phones which can send and receive text messages, link to the Internet, and even send and receive colour video images are already available and will become commonplace in the first few years of the new millennium.

▼ Pager

Other telecommunications

Pagers

These are small pocket-sized machines which can alert users to brief but important incoming written messages - for example, asking the owner to contact his or her office urgently. Pagers can ring, buzz and even vibrate when there is an incoming message.

▼ Telex machine

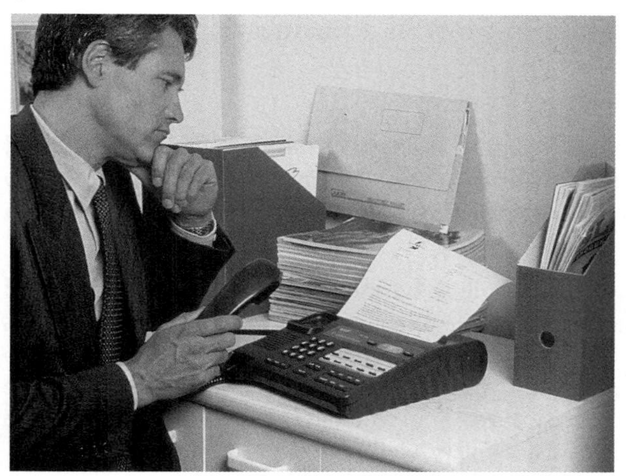

Facsimile transmissions (FAX)

Fax machines are small desktop machines which may be connected to a telephone line. To operate the fax, the user types in the fax number of the recipient of the message. The fax belonging to the sender then rings the receivers fax and establishes contact (this may be heard as a series of screeching tones). Once contact is made, documents placed in the sender's fax machine are read through one page at a time and the details are sent via the phone lines to print out as an exact copy at the receiver's fax machine.

Fax machines are a useful way of sending pictures, drawings, and many other very urgent documents. However, sometimes fax machines might be engaged with other incoming messages or documents although modern machines often have automatic re-dial facilities. The quality of the print out from a fax machine may also be poor on occasion. You will know yourself from talking on the phone to your friends that some phone lines are not always very clear. For the fax machine this means that some transmissions may be unclear. Because of this it is often better to write or type information you intend to send by fax using larger letter and number sizes.

A fax machine is an essential piece of modern business equipment. Prices are affordable even to many of the smallest of businesses. The cost of using a fax is also relatively inexpensive. For most modern machines it will take about one minute to fax ten A4 pages - the cost of a one-minute phone call plus some electricity to power the machine. Larger documents sent by fax and international faxes will clearly be more expensive.

Portfolio Activity 3.7 

Identify a small or medium-sized firm. Assuming that the firm will grow in future, investigate and report on how the business could use modern technology in order to improve communications. Identify potential suppliers of equipment and costs, and also report on the advantages and any disadvantages associated with your suggestions.

Key words:

Memorandum - a set paper-based format for sending information which is urgent or too brief to be sent as a letter

Minutes - a record of who has attended meetings, what was discussed, and what decisions were made.

Reports - documents summarizing large quantities of information and drawing readers' attention to key points

Bulletins - internal newsletters and magazines

Modem - a device, central to the creation of a WAN, which allows computers to communicate with each other over telephone lines

Electronic mail (E-mail) - sending messages between computers over a local or wide area network

Internet - a worldwide computer network linked by modems comprising a vast number of smaller, linked networks

Facsimile (fax) - a means of transmitting documents by telephone line

LAN - a local area network between computers in a business

Intranet - an electronic communications network for internal e-mailing and information circulation in a business

WAN - a wide area network for external communications using computer equipment

Pager - a small portable machine which alerts the user that someone is trying to make contact with them

Voice messaging - a means by which users can send and receive delayed messages using the telephone system

Section 3.4

How good are communications in a business?

Communication breakdowns

Despite spending a lot of time and money on improving the quality and speed of their communications many businesses may still fail to communicate effectively with their customers, staff and suppliers for a variety of reasons:

- **Poor management.** Some people in business may be unprofessional and allow clashes of personality with other staff to affect communications with them. Also, some managers may not recognize their need to motivate employees by allowing them time to consult and become involved in business decision-making. Managers may not always explain the reasons for their decisions very well.
- **Poor design.** Communications may be badly designed or be out of date. For example, a business on more than one site might find it very difficult to maintain good communications and good staff morale if it relies on the postal service for communication. Alternatively, a business might outgrow its existing communications network and find, for example, that its existing computer network regularly breaks down because of work overload.
- **Differences in language or culture or large geographical distances between staff in a firm.** Many large firms have customers and suppliers who are located overseas and may not understand the English language and customs. The same firms may even locate factories, offices and shops in more than one country.
- **Poorly explained or presented messages** can cause confusion and misunderstanding.
- **Prejudices.** Sometimes people interpret a message according to their prejudices. That is they see or hear what they want to and not what is actually being communicated.

- **Internal politics.** Some staff may compete with each other and may hold grievances. In doing so they may attempt to distort communications by spreading rumour and gossip in order to further their own aims rather than those of the business.
- **Physiological barriers.** Some people in business may be partially or totally blind or deaf. Communications can be adapted to the needs of people with special needs. For example, sign language is commonly used to communicate with deaf or hard of hearing workers.

  Braille is used to communicate written text and numbers to blind people. Words and numbers are represented by a series of raised dots on paper or other surfaces, for example on lift buttons. Computers programs are now available to convert text directly into Braille and special keyboards have been made for the blind with Braille keys. Also, new voice-recognition and voice-generation software allow hands-free use of computers.
- **Overuse of jargon.** Not everyone can understand business jargon or technical terms.

SPEAKING TO MD AT HQ OVER THE WAN I SUGGESTED THAT DOWNSIZING FOR JIT IS NOT JUST ABOUT TQM BUT ALSO ABOUT RAISING THE ROCE, TTFN.
? ? ?

The questions all businesses should ask about their communications

Because of the rapid pace of technological change and the pressure to compete with other firms, business organizations are continually reviewing their communications requirements. There are many questions a firm should ask to judge how good it is at communicating, but the most important is:

- **Does the communication meet business objectives?** If a business finds that its sales are falling, its products are always out of date and that it is usually beaten to the market by rival firms, this may indicate that communications with customers - letters, advertisements, telephone calls - are not very good. Internally, a survey of staff morale and motivation can reveal a great deal about the operation and workings of communications within the business.

Other questions include:

- **Was the communication made for the lowest cost possible?** Exchanging information is now faster than ever before, and accuracy has improved requiring less time, effort and power. For example, a large printed business report may take several days and cost several pounds to send by post whereas e-mail can send it in a matter of seconds and cost only a few pence.

  ICT can also be used to perform mundane, repetitive tasks, such as ordering and filing information in a fraction of the time it would take a manual paper-based system. This can free up staff to undertake other productive activities, although it may also mean the business is able to carry out the same amount of work, or more, with less staff and so staff may be made redundant to save on wage costs.
- **Is it value for money?** Compared with its cost, how well does the communication do its job? Are there much cheaper ways of communicating which would work just as well? For example, there is little point in a small firm investing thousands of pounds in building a computer network for e-mail if is not going to be used to send and

▼ *Avoid the dangerious angle... and the Cobra... and the spider*

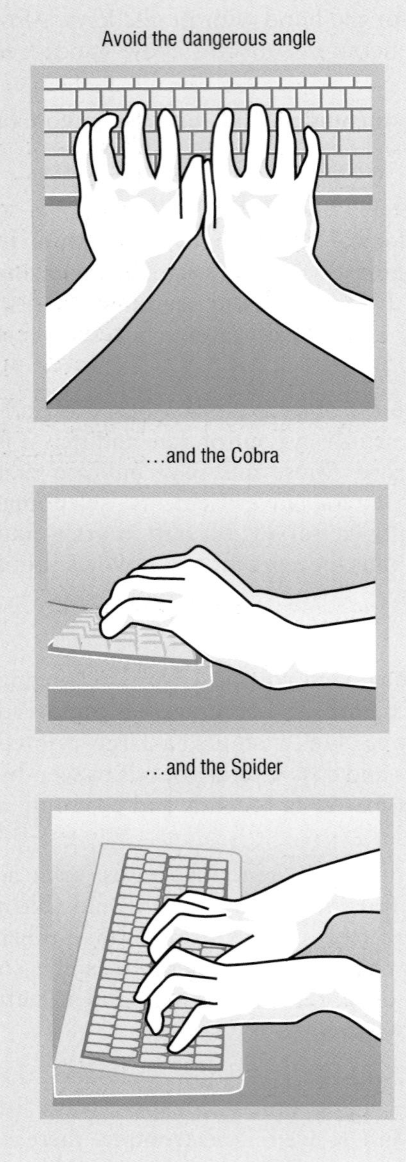
Avoid the dangerous angle
...and the Cobra
...and the Spider

From The Handbook (Preventing Computer Injury) (Ergone International 1994)

receive messages. However, the cost of ICT equipment has fallen significantly over time so even small businesses can afford to buy it and use it. The benefits the equipment can bring to a business more than outweigh the short-term costs of purchase.

- **Does it provide accurate information?** It is essential that information sent and received by a business is error-free. For example, detailed faxes may not always be very easy to read and the receiver may have to interpret words and figures. For example, a supplier may deliver the wrong quantity of materials to firm in response to an illegible faxed order. However, a spreadsheet or document sent by e-mail will reproduce perfectly on screen or output to a suitable printer.
- **How easy is it to use and access information?** New ICT equipment allows businesses access at the touch of a few buttons to a world of information. An organization can find out about a host of useful subjects just by typing in some key words into an Internet search engine which will then provide a list of websites which contain those key words. This may give access to the information a business needs to innovate and develop better products and services for consumers. Useful reports and articles can be downloaded in a just a few minutes. E-mails, with or without file attachments, and faxes can be sent across the world in seconds. However, communication will be of little use if users find operating equipment, like computers and fax machines, too difficult.
- **Are communications secure?** A lot of information stored in computer files and communicated internally by business organizations, such as production costs, new product developments, and staff records, are sensitive and confidential. Although access to electronic information and communications can be protected by password, errors can still occur. For example, e-mails or faxes could be sent to the wrong addresses. Furthermore, computer equipment may be stolen and hackers may be able to break security codes. A business could be open to fraud if unauthorized personnel were able to gain access to confidential information and communications.
- **What is the speed of access?** Paper-based communication is slow, for example, sending a letter or data by internal mail or external post. Technological advance has allowed businesses to send and receive information from anywhere in the world at the touch of a button.
- **What is its impact on information exchange?** Because of improvements in the speed and cost of data exchange from ICT, interaction between individuals and business organizations has increased. For example, from the Internet firms are able to learn of conditions in world markets, such as strikes or wars in countries supplying raw materials, and be able to react immediately to minimize the impact on their business.
- **Do staff need training?** To ensure that full and effective use is made of new communications equipment a business also needs to make sure that users are adequately trained. No matter how user-friendly computers and other equipment are today some basic training will be necessary if employees are to use them to send and receive information.
- **What is its impact on users?** New information communication technology can bring significant benefits. However, increasing demands on users to update their computer skills and to operate a variety of

Old and new styles of keyboard

equipment may cause stress, ill health and lower productivity (see 1.1).

Prolonged use of computers screens and keyboards can result in poor eyesight and repetitive strain injury (RSI) in users' fingers and wrists. To overcome this, many firms make sure their staff are aware of health and safety guidelines on how long they should work at a computer screen without a break, and provide anti-glare screens to fit over monitors. Manufacturers of computer keyboards have responded by introducing alternative designs which help to reduce muscle strain by providing wrist supports and arranging keys in a broad circle around the outstretched hands of the user.

Managers also need to be aware that users may misuse the new equipment. Sometimes local networks can become overloaded by people sending personal e-mails to their friends inside and outside the organization. This can stop important business e-mails getting through. Staff may also use mobile phones issued to them for work purposes to phone their friends and families. This can result in expensive bills for the business. Ease of access to the Internet may result in users spending more time 'surfing' websites for their own enjoyment, and less time being productive. However, managers will need to weigh up carefully the savings they might achieve by outlawing personal e-mails, Internet use and phone calls against the long-term negative impact they could have on employee morale and motivation by doing so.

Key Activity

Your task is to report on a business organization of your choice based on all the things you have discovered about business in Chapters 1, 2 and 3. Obtain the permission of the owners or senior managers to visit the organization, observe people at work, and conduct interviews with staff and customers if necessary.

Your report should contain the following information about your chosen business:

- The business name, main products, location(s) and a brief history
- The production process and quality assurance/control system in the business; the resources it uses; how the business adds value to its resources through productive activity and quality assurance/control; could productivity and quality assurance could be improved in the business?
- The objectives of the business, how the business is attempting to achieve these objectives and what success it has had so far, and/or how it might do better; appropriate tables, graphs and charts showing how numbers of employees, volume of output, numbers of customers, revenues, and/or profits have changed over time, or other supporting information
- The type of business ownership, and the advantages and disadvantages to the business of this type
- An organizational chart showing key personnel, divisions and departments
- A description of the structure, management style and culture of the organization; how these features interrelate and affect each other; and how they can affect or have affected the performance and operation of the business and help it meet its objectives
- How the business communicates internally and externally; what channels it uses, what impact ICT has had on the internal and external communications of the business; how the business's communications could be improved and how ICT could help
- Acknowledgments and sources of information you used

Before you start your report you must draw up a plan of action that prioritizes the tasks you need to complete, how you intend to complete them, when you intend to complete them (i.e. timescale) and the resources you will need to do so, for example, a tape recorder, still or video camera, computer time, access to Internet, etc.

Before you finalize your report, present a draft copy to the business owners or managers. Ask for their comments. Discuss these with them before your produce your final report.

Test your knowledge

1 What is the correct term for records kept of a business meeting?

A Agenda

B Minutes

C Articles

D Memorandum

2 A head office needs to maintain contact with its sales representatives who travel around the UK. What is the best way to do this?

A Fax

B Mobile phone

C E-mail

D Business letter

3 Videoconferencing is a means of:

A Sending text electronically

B Linking staff at different locations using sound and vision

C Communicating using a mobile telephones

D Sending photocopies of documents

4 All of the following are non-verbal methods of communication **except**:

A Memorandum

B Minutes

C Reports

D Meetings

5 If a business installs a new computer into its central services department, what improvements is this likely to lead to?

A Better quality production

B Better motivation amongst workers

C More employment

D Better communications

Questions 6–8 share the following answer options:

Go Ahead is a UK marketing company that devises advertising campaigns for various organizations. The company uses a number of methods to transmit information to its clients. These include:

A Fax

B Telephone

C E-mail

D Paging

Which method is most appropriate to:

6 An informal chat about new campaign ideas with the managing director of a client organization?

7 Sending details of advertising options and costs to the client HQ in New York when a quick decision is needed?

8 Sending weekly sales data for the last five years from the client firm to Go Ahead, so that they can analyse the data and make statistical forecasts?

Questions 9–11 share the following answer options:

A Minutes

B Business letter

C Memo

D Bulletin

Which of the above paper-based communication methods is best used for the following tasks?

9 Informing a senior manager that a meeting has been re-scheduled to another time, date, and venue

10 Recording action points raised at a meeting

11 Informing staff of a change in senior management

12 What type of communication channel would a shop use to pass the following information to all its customers: 'All prices cut by 20%'?

A A one-way channel

B A two-way channel

C A restricted channel

D A multi-track channel

13 **a** What is 'communication' and why is it important to business?

b List three methods of (i) verbal communication, and (ii) non-verbal communication.

c List three pieces of equipment that might be used to produce non-verbal communication.

d Explain the difference between external and internal business communications.

e List three pieces of equipment that can be used for external communications.

14 **a** Suggest two advantages and one disadvantage of installing new Information Communications Technology equipment in a firm.

b What kinds of communications equipment would you recommend for a firm employing a large number of travelling salespeople who need to communicate complex orders back to head office? Explain your answers.

15 **a** What kinds of communications equipment would you recommend for a new electrical chain store needing to despatch customer orders placed in stores from a central depot? Explain your answers.

b Explain briefly some of the main barriers the organization may encounter preventing the effective use of the new equipment.

chapter 4 Business Functions

This chapter examines the different functions a business organization must perform if it is to be productive and achieve its objectives.

What you need to learn

All businesses combine factors or production to produce goods and services. In order for a business to obtain the factors of production it needs, combine them in an efficient way, and provide goods or services that meet with customer requirements, it must carry out a range of **functions**. These include:

- **Research and development**
- **Purchasing**
- **Production**
- **Sales and marketing**

These functions are supported by other functions within a business. These are:

- **Finance**
- **Human resource management**
- **Administration**

Business functions may be organized into **departments** or combined in project teams. You will need to explain how the different functions are connected.

Administrative systems are developed within organizations to organize and perform their business functions. You will need to understand the activities and characteristics of business functions and how each functional area contributes to the running of a business.

You will need to evaluate how well these functions are carried out in a business as this affects the success and efficiency of the business and helps it to meet its objectives.

Section 4.1 The purposes of administrative systems

What is administration?

Portfolio Activity 4.1 

Imagine that you are the owner of a successful small restaurant. You employ five full-time staff, and are kept very busy by regular evening and weekend diners.

Make a list of the typical kinds of routine tasks that would need to be done each week, both by you and your staff.

Can you think of any ways in which the firm could speed up the more repetitive tasks or make the work easier?

Organizing and controlling a business

In a typical business, like the restaurant in Activity 4.1, there are a large number of important jobs which need to be done, and in most cases these will be the same each week or month. A restaurant will need to place regular orders for stocks of food and drink; it will need to check and pay invoices for stock, bank takings, maintain accounts, pay bills and wages, hire and/or train new staff, chase up payments from expense account customers, arrange advertising in the local press, etc. These are the routine tasks which must be carried out repeatedly, but unless they are managed properly, the business will fail. Dealing with these tasks is known as **administration**. Administration is all about the organization and control of business.

The need for good administration

In Chapter 1 we learnt that business organizations combine factors of production - land, labour and capital - for the purpose of productive activity. For most business organizations the main objective of their productive activity is to make a profit for the business owners. Others may not seek to make a profit and will have other objectives, like the provision of charitable or public services.

Productive activity within a business requires a great deal of organization if it is to be done well and achieve set objectives. Any business, therefore, needs to ensure that its administrative system is both efficient and effective:

- **Efficiency** refers to how the organization uses its resources.

The aim will be to combine them in the best possible way to maximize output and minimize costs.

- **Effectiveness** refers to how well an organization achieves its objectives, such as increasing sales and/or profits. Good administration lies at the heart of all successful firms.

In the case of the restaurant, if administration is poor, the business may be slow in paying for supplies. This will mean that suppliers may refuse to trade with them and electricity and telephone services may be cut off because bills remain unpaid. Wages, salaries and overtime of staff may not be calculated correctly and the wrong amounts could be paid at the wrong times, leading to unhappy and poorly motivated employees. The restaurant may not keep proper records of its credit customers and so be unable to chase late payers. In the worst case, it may not be able to organize the ordering and delivery of its stocks of food and drink.

The functions of an administrative system

The way in which a business organizes itself in order to cope with day-to-day tasks is known as its **administrative system.**

An administration system may be defined as a sequence of activities necessary to achieve an objective – for example, to order new stock or to pay for goods received. Administration requires that decisions and procedures follow a set of laid-down guidelines based on good practice. People who carry out these procedures are called administrators.

An example of an administration system

An example of a simple administrative system for processing an order is given below:

1 Order received by the sales department of the firm

2 Warehousing department is informed of the order and checks to ensure that the firm has the right materials to meet it

3 Production department is notified of the requirements of the order

4 Customers informed of delivery date by distribution department

5 Distribution delivers the goods and obtains a Goods Received Note (GRN) from the customer as evidence of receipt

6 Finance department sends out an invoice

7 Credit control department chases up late payment of invoice, if necessary

The main function of an administration system is to provide support for **routine and non-routine functions.** An administrative system provides support services for the entire organization. The main business functions of production, sales and marketing could not operate efficiently without this support.

▼ *Paying wages – a routine function*

Administrative functions can be classed as either **routine** or **non-routine**.

- **Routine functions** are those carried out on a regular basis, such as:

  Organizing financial, physical, and human resources
  Assisting with the smooth production of goods and services
  Assisting with marketing, advertising, and promotions
  Providing accurate and timely information on which to base decisions
  Maintaining sites, buildings, and equipment
  Recording and monitoring business performance
  Meeting external demands for information and legal requirements
  Provide customer service support and dealing with enquiries
  Providing support for quality assurance

  Many of these support functions may be organized into separate departments, for example, finance and accounting, human resources, customer services.

▼ *Dealing with emergencies – a non-routine function*

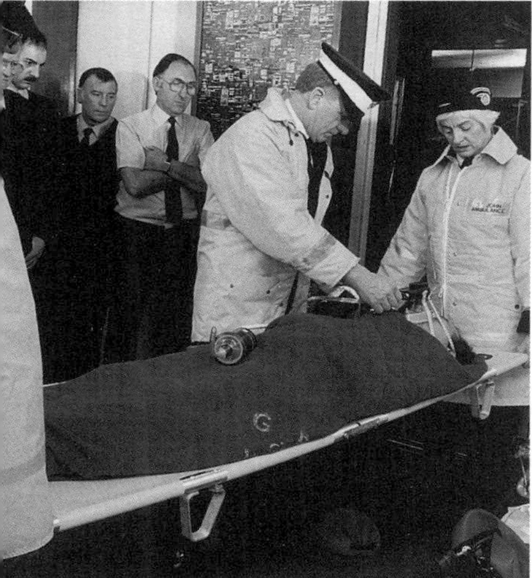

- **Non-routine functions** are those tasks which need to be carried out only at irregular intervals, for example, restructuring the organization, organizing staff cover for absentee workers, dealing with accidents or emergencies, machine breakdowns, legal actions, etc.

The vast majority of business transactions – for example, placing orders for stock, paying wages, loan repayments – occur on a regular basis. Where tasks are routine and predictable, rules and procedures can be established so that the minimum of staff time and thought needs to go into completing the task.

Administrative systems are designed primarily to cope with routine work. However, there will always be some non-routine tasks. For example, a supplier with whom a firm has previously had no contact may require cash payment for their first order. In this case, instead of passing the order through the administrative system, it may need to be passed on to a manager in order that a check can be made on the firm before any money is paid.

A good administrative system will highlight these exceptional or non-routine cases and will have a procedure ready to deal with them.

Portfolio Activity 4.2 

1. Mail and postal delivery seems to be a straightforward process, which many people would suggest does not need an administrative procedure. Having read the article, to what extent would you agree with this view?
2. What problems are created for firms by not having an agreed administrative system for processing 'urgent' mail?
3. Make some suggestions as to what kind of administrative procedure might help.

Mail systems to play a larger role

Mailing is a major part of practically any business activity and includes sending sales letters and promotional material as direct mail as well as issuing invoices and statements vital to business cash flow.

The way in which this is achieved, however, through the use of letter post, parcel post and private courier services is often uncontrolled. For this and other reasons the Royal Mail, rated as one of the most efficient services of its kind in Europe, say that British business has been wasting time and money on this exercise through not having a formal distribution policy.

The key issue, says Colin Bok of the Royal Mail is that while nearly five million packages are sent 'urgently' every day, few businesses agree exactly what is meant by urgent. Only a handful of companies have a clear delivery strategy and know the true cost of distribution, especially that of couriers or fax.

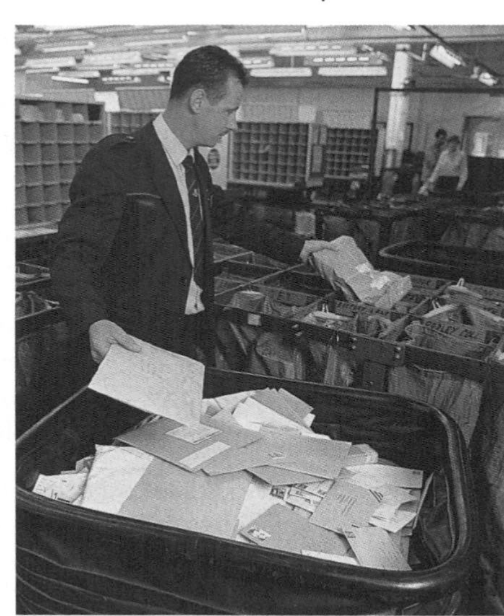

Asked what they thought was meant by 'urgent', 75% of secretaries thought something urgent required immediate attention while only just over half of the managers said 'urgent' meant something had to arrive at a specified time, compared with under 20% of secretaries.

The result is unnecessary cost and confusion as secretaries and other staff double guess what their bosses mean by 'urgent' leading to the 'urgency syndrome' which puts too much emphasis on getting the job done quickly rather than getting it done right.

The policy of most companies in not accounting for post to departments or working groups means that many business managers do not know the true cost of distribution because they have become accustomed to it being a 'cost free area'.

Keith Ward, Professor of Financial Strategy at Cranfield School of Management who contributed to the report, says "by introducing a distribution policy it will help companies control costs and cut out wasted time and money in 'urgently' distributing non-urgent items."

Adapted from Business Equipment Digest, October 1993

Key words:

Administration – the organization of resources to deal with tasks arising from business activities

Administrative system – the way in which a business organizes its human, financial, and physical resources

Section **4.2**

Functions in business

Functional dependency in business

Any business can be viewed as a system of interdependent parts functioning together as a whole to achieve objectives such as improving profit or expanding market share (see 1.7).

Administration involves staff following a set of procedures or rules which set out how things should be done in the firm. Each department or section of a business will operate its own administrative procedures, but all of the systems working within the firm depend on every other system for their own smooth operation. The purpose of an administrative system, therefore, is to bring together all the mutually dependent parts of a business system to make sure they work together in the most efficient way towards the same goals.

Business departments

The most popular way of organizing and administering human, financial, and physical resources in a business system is to divide them into separate departments (see 2.4). Departments allow people to specialize in particular job areas and to improve their skills and performance. However, sometimes organizations will combine the staff who carry out these functions into project teams rather than centralized departments. In project teams, staff will concentrate on the achievement of a specific objective, such as bringing a new product to market.

▼ *Figure 4.1: Departmental functions*

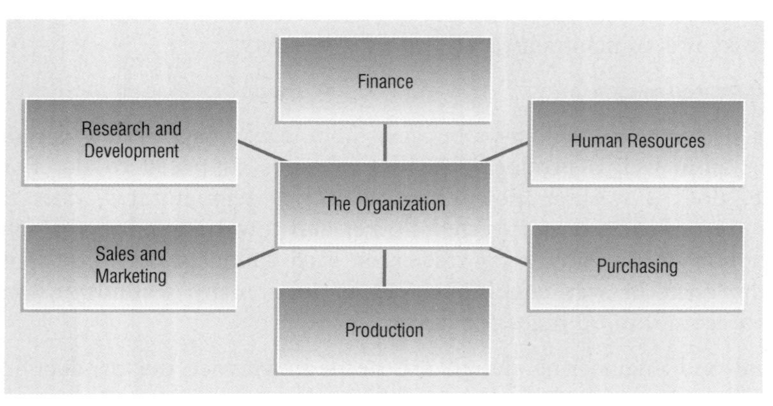

The functions of the various departments one might find in a large organization are detailed below. However, it is important to realize that even in a small organization the same broad functions will need to be performed by staff or owners.

Research and development (R&D)

In a highly competitive business environment, **research and development (R&D)** is increasingly important to the success of a business organization. Each year businesses spend many billions of pounds developing new products and methods of producing them. However successful a product is now, one day it will be replaced by new or better products. For this reason, the future success of most businesses depends upon the work of the R&D department in coming up with new ideas and products which can be developed and sold in the future.

▲ *Meeting consumer wants for improved styling of television sets, and better picture and sound quality has been made possible by research and development by business organizations*

New products are being introduced all the time, especially in the highly competitive consumer electronics market. Every few months, manufacturers of audio and visual consumer electronics equipment bring out new models with different features. Consider the development of television sets over the last few years. They have become slimmer and screen size has increased. They can produce stereo sound, surround sound, and Dolby digital sound from five speakers or more. Widescreen and 'hang-on-the-wall' plasma screen TVs have been introduced. The next generation of TV sets will be able to produce high-definition TV pictures (HDTV) as well as digital broadcast images. Each new development tempts the consumer to replace their old TV set with a new one.

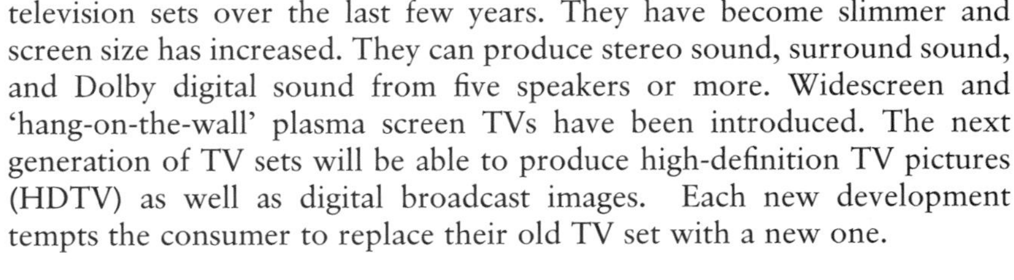

Industrial and engineering design

The aim of many firms is to stay ahead of competition from rival products and firms. This means finding out what consumers want, what they are likely to want in the near future, and developing the ways to produce these products. The marketing department can advise R&D on the results of market research on consumer opinions about products and their wants (see Chapter 9).

Designing new products or improving existing products is called **industrial design.** People who work in R&D on industrial design matters will consider many features of different products including;

- image
- smell
- texture
- user friendliness
- how easy it is to maintain/repair
- incorporated technology
- durability
- taste
- colours
- packaging
- safety
- shape

Product performance will also be very important. **Engineering design** considers how well a product does the job it is supposed to do. For example, does a washing powder work at low temperatures, does it remove grease stains, does it soften clothes and towels? Similarly, it will consider how many miles a car travels on each gallon of petrol, how it holds the road in wet conditions and in how many seconds it can accelerate from 0 to 60 miles per hour.

▼ *Engineers at BAE Systems test a new wing design for a new large aircraft*

Industrial and engineering design are needed, whether the product in question is a highly technical personal computer, a new medicine, an industrial laser, or just a simple cake, children's toy or choc ice.

The R&D Department not only designs new products, or re-designs old ones, but also advises the production department on the best way to produce them in terms of time, cost, materials, assembly and impact on the environment.

The most important consideration in product design is cost - can the product can be produced in the right quantities at a price the consumer is willing to pay? There is no point producing a good or service that consumers cannot afford or are unwilling to pay for because the cost of producing each product is too high. It is the job of R&D staff to work out if the product can be produced at a price greater than cost that the consumer will pay.

What is CAD?

Computer-aided design (CAD) is an interactive computer program which is capable of generating, storing and using geometric graphics. CAD is used by design engineers in many industries to solve design problems - anything from new product packaging to a new office block. The benefits of using CAD are:

- reduction in lead times between product design and production
- a wide range of designs can be examined and evaluated without the need for building 3D prototypes
- modifications and changes are easily made to designs

Many new products that become available to consumers can initially be sold at high prices because they are new, and consumers who buy them can boast to be the first owners of such products (see 10.2). For example, the first home video recorders that became widely available in the early 1970s were priced at £1,000 or more. These early video systems are no longer available. New designs like VHS and Super VHS were introduced and now dominate the home video market. In 2000 a basic VHS machine could be purchased for as little as £75. Instead £1,000 would buy a top of the range DVHS (Digital VHS) machine with a host of features not available on the basic early systems, such as digital picture and sound quality, simultaneous multi-channel recording, up to 49 hours of recording, editing facilities, and so on.

The prices of many consumer electronic products have fallen significantly over time because of technological advances developed by R&D departments in large electronics manufacturers.

Portfolio Activity 4.3 

1. Make a list of all the features of the following goods and services that could be changed to make them appeal more to consumers.
   - chocolate bars
   - a cough mixture
   - computer game consoles
   - public transport
   - passenger air flights
   - motor cars
   - washing powders
   - mobile phones
   - banking services
2. Chart the development of any product or service of your choice through time in a short report using words and pictures. For example, you might like to consider the development of computer game consoles from the very earliest basic machines which contained simple tennis games, through to the Sega megadrive and Nintendo SNES that use cartridges, to the new machines like the Sony Playstation 2 that play high-quality games CDs. However, computer games are likely to be a popular choice for this activity so why not choose something completely different, like toothpaste, oven ready meals, medicines, or a make of motor car?
3. As a class, try to invite an industrial designer in to give a short talk on what they do. If the talk is to go ahead:
   - **a** agree a list of questions you would like to ask about their job beforehand
   - **b** take notes during the talk
   - **c** after the talk, write a short paper on why research and development is so important in modern business and the role of the industrial designer
4. As a class group, discuss how you think the work of a research and development department will depend on other business functions, such as marketing, human resources, and finance.

Purchasing

Staff who make purchases will specialize in buying the goods and services that the firm needs. Items purchased may include the raw materials used in production, the paper and computer supplies used by office staff, new furniture, and other things the organization needs to fulfil its functions. Services bought in from outside firms may include cleaning, painting and decorating, and computer maintenance.

Purchasing staff need to carry out the following jobs:

- advising other departments about the kinds of goods and services available and how well these might meet their needs
- finding and negotiating with suppliers
- buying raw materials, components and machinery for the production department
- ordering other goods and services for the whole organization
- taking delivery of goods
- checking goods and services received against orders
- arranging payment of invoices through the finance or accounts department

▼ *Figure 4.2: The purchasing process*

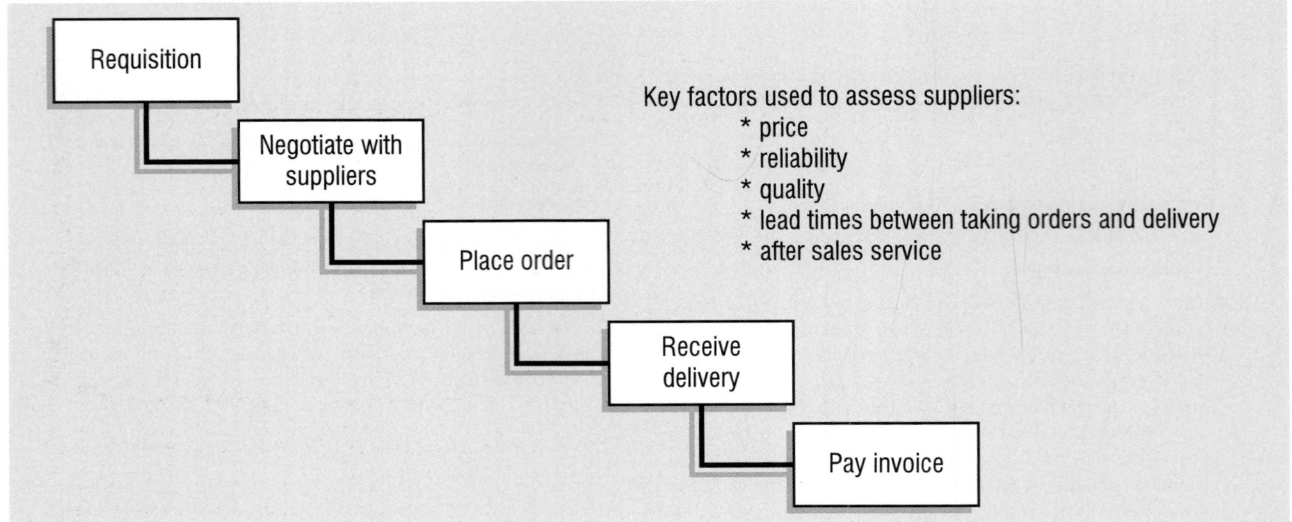

Centralized v. decentralized purchasing

Some business organizations use **centralized purchasing**, whereby the acquisition of materials, components, and other goods and services is carried out by a specialized department. This has the following advantages:

- Staff have, and can build up, specialist knowledge of product qualities and purchasing procedures
- A business is able to take advantage of bulk-buying discounts
- Quality and standards of materials are consistent throughout the whole business
- Storage and distribution can be planned more easily

Decentralized purchasing means that individual parts of a business acquire the goods and services they need themselves. This has the advantage that staff within each area of a business are likely to be more in touch with their needs than a centralized purchasing unit. For example, a retail store manager in a particular locality will be in a better position than his or her headquarters to judge which products are selling well to local customers.

Purchasing, therefore, involves buying materials and other goods and services of the right quality, in the right quantities and at the right price. People who buy supplies will usually become specialists in the particular goods they buy. For example, Nescafé employs people who specialize in securing supplies of high-quality coffee beans to make coffee. Marks and Spencer employs specialists to buy fashion ideas and clothing.

Large firms can often buy in bulk and obtain discounts from suppliers. However, buying materials and other goods in bulk can take up valuable storage space. Because of this many large modern organizations now use a purchasing system known as **Just In Time** production (see 1.2). Under this system materials and components used in production are ordered and then delivered 'just in time' for them to be processed. This allows the purchasing organization to keep stocks to a minimum. For this system to work efficiently suppliers must be reliable in terms of delivery times and product quality. If either is at fault, production will be held up.

Today many functions in purchasing are computerized and conducted over the Internet. For example, it is now possible to send orders, receive invoices, and arrange payment without the need for paper documents (see 16.1).

Portfolio Activity 4.4 

BP Amoco to increase online purchasing to $4bn

BP Amoco will soon be purchasing $4 billion worth of equipment and supplies annually through the Internet, helping it to make huge cost savings, Sir John Browne, chief executive of the oil giant, said yesterday.

Sir John also confirmed that BP Amoco would seek shareholder approval in April to buy back up to 10 per cent of its shares, giving the company scope to return more than £9bn of capital to investors.

He was speaking as BP Amoco reported record fourth quarter profits of $2.3bn - 145 per cent up on the same period last year on the back of higher oil prices and cost cutting.

By the end of 2000 BP Amoco expects to be conducting 95 per cent of its purchasing through 'e-tendering'. So far the group is making savings of 25 per cent on selected supplies by buying online.

Sir John said the savings would not be this great across the board. However, they will be an important component of the $4bn of cost savings that BP Amoco has targeted by the end of 2001.

The company has already achieved $2b.1bn of the cost savings and expects to reap a further $1bn of efficiency gains this year. The savings last year mainly came through a rationalisation programme which cut the workforce by 18,000.

The Independent, 16.2.2000

1. What do you think is the primary business objective of BP Amoco?
2. Why is BP Amoco so concerned with making cost savings?
3. How is the proposed change in BP Amoco's purchasing strategy likely to contribute to its objectives?
4. How have developments in information technology assisted the BP Amoco strategy?

Production

From Chapter 1 we know that productive activity involves combining resources to produce goods and services. Productive activity, therefore, involves all aspects of business organization and is not complete until goods and services reach and satisfy the customers they were intended for.

However, within many business organizations it is usual to find a Production Department, especially in manufacturing firms. The function of the Production Department is to make goods of the right quality, in the right quantity and at the least cost. To do this requires careful planning, monitoring and control.

Production planning

It is essential that a business can supply enough goods to meet consumer demand. This requires careful planning of the whole production process, namely:

- how much should be produced and by when
- the best method of production to use
- what raw materials or components are needed and in what quantities
- how much land or factory space is needed
- what machinery and other equipment is needed
- how many workers are required and what skills they need
- the level of automation in production
- how the product will be packaged and packed for shipment

Production managers must work with staff from the Research and Development Department and Sales and Marketing Departments who will advise on what customers want and how products can be made in order to be as attractive as possible to consumers. In addition, the Sales Department will advise production on the amount of goods or services to produce to meet consumer demand. The Purchasing Department will buy the necessary materials and equipment needed to make the goods, and Human Resources will recruit production workers with the right skills (see 14.1).

Cost is the key consideration in production planning. The cost of materials, equipment and labour will largely determine the cost of each product and, therefore, the price at which it can be sold to make a profit. Resources must, therefore, be combined in the most efficient way in order to reduce the cost of producing each unit of output as low as possible. For example, employing ten people to operate only five sewing machines is clearly not the most efficient way of producing clothes. The cost of each garment will be higher than it would otherwise be if the firm had employed more machines and fewer people.

Monitoring and controlling production

It is important to monitor and control production to make sure there are no problems and that production targets can be met on time. Production control will involve:

- **scheduling** - working out the sequence, and time, in which jobs are to be performed to make or assemble a finished product.
- **monitoring** - this involves checking that work is progressing according to schedule and that production targets will be met. If any problems arise and slow down production, such as machine breakdowns or late delivery of materials, then schedules will need to be rearranged. In addition, it is important to make sure that machines are not over- or under-used, and receive regular maintenance.
- **cost control** - information provided to the Finance Department will allow production costs be monitored.
- **stock control** - production will be interrupted if stocks of materials or component parts run out. The purpose of stock control is to make sure this doesn't happen.
- **quality control** - this involves ensuring that the final product and its features entirely satisfy the consumer. This can be done by inspecting quality at very stage in the production process, including the quality of materials and components, work in progress, packaging and the work of individual employees, even those in other departments in sales, customer services, marketing, etc. This is called total quality management (see 1.2).

A number of these controls have become computerized. For example, orders for more materials can be sent automatically by a computer when stocks fall to pre-determined levels; equipment can be used to check the size, weight and ripeness of different fruits and vegetables; progress can be monitored from data automatically fed into a computer every time products move onto another part of an automated production line.

What is CAM?

Increasingly, computers are being used to automate and control manufacturing processes. Machines such as industrial robots can receive instructions from information entered into a computer. The use of computers in manufacturing is known as **computer-aided manufacture (CAM)**.

In some industries CAM can be directly linked to computer-aided design (CAD) packages. For example, knitting machines can replicate jumper designs planned on a computer. Similarly, industrial robots can learn the shape of cars they are required to paint from computerized images developed using CAD.

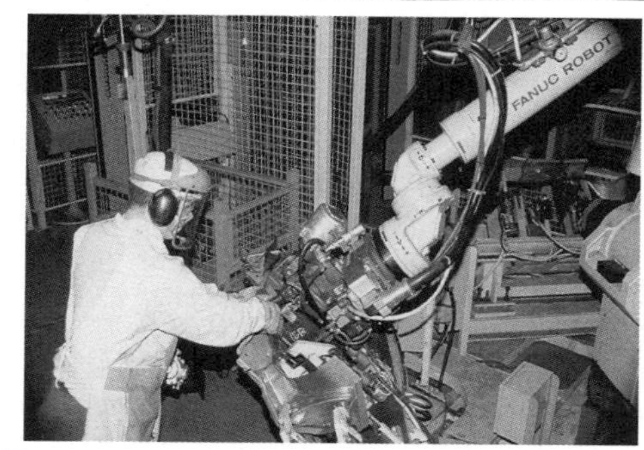

Portfolio Activity 4.5

Arrange a class visit to a manufacturing plant. Take notes during your visit to gather enough information to produce a short report to discuss the following:

- the main functions of the production department
- the number of employees in the production department
- examples of the job titles in the production department
- the type of product made
- how much is produced each day, week or month on average
- the method of production
- how quality is controlled in production
- the types of materials and components used in production
- the types of machinery used
- the level of automation in production
- the layout of the factory floor (include a diagram in your report to show where machinery, stores, etc. are located)
- how production depends on the work of other departments, especially R&D, purchasing, sales and human resources.

Use a word processor to write up your report after your factory visit.

▼ *Advertising is big business!*

Labour outspends BT with £92m advert bill

The Government is now Britain's second-biggest advertiser, spending more than BT, Kellogg's, McDonald's or Coca-Cola.
Industry figures revealed yesterday that the Central Office for Information forked out £92.2 million on advertising in 1999.

Only household giant Procter & Gamble spent more - but it has 160 products to sell, including Ariel, Sunny Delight and Fairy Liquid.
Government adverts included anti drink-driving campaigns as well as nursing and Army recruitment drives.

THE TOP ADVERTISING SPENDERS

Company	1999	1998	%change
Procter & Gamble	£165.4m	£165.7m	-0.1
Central Office of Information	£92.2m	£61.2m	+50.7
Renault UK	£84.9m	£80.5m	+5.5
BT	£84.6m	£104.6m	-19.1
Vauxhall Motors	£84.1m	£83.1m	+1.2
L'Oréal	£67.1m	£58.5m	+14.6
Mars Confectionery	£63.6m	£54.2m	+17.4
Ford Motor Company	£57.4m	£30.3m	+89.1
Kellogg's	£53.0m	£67.1m	-20.9
Van den Bergh Foods	£52.7m	£49.4m	+6.8

Source: Marketing magazine

Metro, 3.3.2000

Marketing

The function of organization members who carry out marketing is to identify what customers will be willing to buy and then to encourage them to buy the product at a price that will earn the organization a profit (see Chapter 9).

There are four main functions of a marketing department in a business:

- **market research** - this involves finding out what different consumers want in terms of products, product features, prices they are willing to pay, where they like to buy products and how they respond to advertising. It can involve holding personal interviews, sending questionnaires through the post, telephone surveys and consumer opinion panels (see 9.3).
- **advertising** - to raise consumer awareness of products. Firms can choose to advertise their goods and services through a variety of media including newspapers, radio, TV, posters and at the cinema (see 10.3). Small firms may prefer to use low-cost adverts in local newspapers. Large firms selling to national or

international markets can afford to produce TV adverts because the payback in terms of increased consumer demand and sales revenues can be huge.

- **promotions** - such as exhibitions and trade fairs, competitions, money-off coupons, sponsoring a football team or tennis star, using special packaging or logos, etc (see 10.3).

- **public relations** - this involves maintaining good relations with other organizations and the general public in order to give a firm a good, and high-profile, image. For example, organizations can sponsor local events and give donations to charities.

The role of the public relations manager

It is the job of the Public Relations Manager and his/her staff to represent their organization to the outside world and make sure it gets well known for good reasons. Their work will include meeting representatives of local communities, pressure groups, for example, Greenpeace and Friends of the Earth, other organizations, local councillors and politicians.

Free publicity is often available from the media. Newspapers, radio and TV are always on the look out for interesting stories about exiting new products and organizations. Public relations managers can provide information to the media using special **press releases** or by giving interviews.

Even the government uses public relations and issues press releases to promote new policies in a favourable way, to show how well their economic policies are working and to limit the damage caused by scandals reported about MPs and cabinet ministers.

Today, many organizations pay outside firms that specialize in marketing to provide marketing services. These specialist agencies can plan and run public relations, advertising and promotional campaigns, and carry out market research.

The Marketing Department will work closely with the R&D and Sales Departments in identifying what customers want, and then in developing attractive products that will encourage consumers to spend their money.

Sales

In many organizations sales and marketing functions will be carried out by one department. However, given the importance of making a sale to business organizations that operate for profit, some firms have a separate Sales Department.

The role of the Sales Department is to create orders for goods and services. The Sales Department may control a sales force whose job it is to visit customers and persuade them to buy.

The Sales Department will be expected to carry out a number of functions fast and effectively. They are:

- responding to requests for information on products, prices, delivery times, methods of payment etc.
- responding to customers orders for goods or services (see 16.3)
- organizing deliveries with the distribution department
- receiving payments by various methods including cash, credit card, hire purchase (see 16.4)

An organization will risk annoying their customers and losing their custom to rival firms if any of the above tasks are mismanaged or take too long. Good sales staff are essential to any organization engaged in selling (see 11.2).

The Sales Department will work closely with marketing in designing advertising and also with production in order to ensure that the right goods are available in the right quantities to meet customer's demands.

Sales departments in most medium-sized and large organizations keep their customer records on a database along with product details and prices etc. Some businesses, like McDonald's, are able to monitor sales of particular products day by day at their UK headquarters by receiving reports from high street stores via electronic mail. This kind of administrative system allows the firm to adjust its promotions, advertising, and prices in response to local conditions.

An important area of sales and marketing is **customer service** (see 11.2). Good customer service can help to improve an organization's image among consumers, resulting in increased sales. Many organizations have customer service departments to look after customers once a sale has been made and to deal with complaints, repairs, providing replacements, etc. A good administrative system will make sure that customer enquiries, repairs, or complaints are dealt with quickly.

Distribution

▲ *Effective distribution involves delivering the right goods and services to the right customers, when and where they want them*

The role of **distribution** is to ensure that goods and services are available to customers when and where they want them. That is, the Distribution Department must ensure that the right goods are delivered in the right quantities at the time agreed with the customer, for the minimum cost. This is called **logistics** - the science of storing and moving goods efficiently (see 11.1).

Distribution may involve the following tasks:

- delivering supplies to other organizations
- choosing delivery methods, eg. by road, rail, air
- vehicle maintenance
- distribution of finished products to wholesalers, retail outlets or direct to consumers
- checking in goods received
- storage
- checking goods out
- monitoring the movement of goods and work in progress within the organization
- monitoring the movement of goods within a retail outlet (i.e. from the stockroom)
- stock control to ensure goods are available when they are required

Some firms run their own transport fleets to distribute goods, while others hire outside contractors to deliver for them. Distribution is an essential department, because no matter what the other departments do, if distribution does not get the right goods to the customer in time, there will be no sale.

Information technology forms the backbone of modern distribution systems. The use of bar code readers means that stock records can be updated regularly and quickly, and new stock automatically re-ordered when a central computer notes that remaining stocks are down to a pre-set level. Many large transport firms use 'routemaster' computer programs which produce a route map for a driver, taking into account the time of day and likely road conditions in order to give the quickest route to a delivery address.

Finance

The key business activities of controlling finance and keeping accounts are usually carried out in the Finance (and Accounts) Department(s).

Securing and managing business finance

It is the job of the accounting manager to make sure the organization has enough capital, either from its own funds and/or form borrowing, to finance its operations (see 23.1). This will include obtaining finance for new projects, such as buying new premises, investing in new machinery or a computer system. The finance manger will calculate if the new project is worth undertaking by comparing the predicted return from the investment (i.e. higher revenues or lower costs) with the cost of the project.

In addition, wages and salaries will often be paid from the Finance Department.

Managing business accounts

Accounts staff will be responsible for recording and analysing all the different financial transactions in the firm (see 16.1). They will keep track of all of the cash entering and leaving the business as well as the amount of credit given to customers and amounts owed by the firm to suppliers. Information about these day-to-day financial activities is recorded in a financial accounting system, which is usually held on computer.

- **Financial accountants** will use accounting records to prepare business accounts. These will include the end of year accounts which summarize how much the business is worth and how much profit it made (see 18.3). These accounts will be made available to the tax authorities and business owners.
- **Cost accountants** will monitor business costs, including those directly related to production, such as materials and machine hire, and costs which arise due to activities such as sales, marketing, human resource management, and even in the Accounting Department.
- **Management accountants** will be expected to provide the managers of the firm with up-to-date financial information to show well the firm is doing at any moment in time and to predict how well the firm is likely to do in the future.

Small organizations may buy in the services of a self-employed accountant or an accountancy firm. Large firms can often afford to employ their own accountants on a full-time basis.

The Finance (and Accounts) Department will work with every other department in an organization. It will need information from Sales on the amount of money coming into the business, from Purchasing on how much it is spending and salaries and from Production on how much is being spent on production etc. The Accounting Department will also set budgets for each department for their future spending and will monitor how actual business performance compares with these financial plans (see 19.1).

Human resources

The most valuable resource in any business organization is its people, or **human resources**. There is a direct relationship between the quality of the workforce and the success of a business.

The size of the Human Resources Department (or Personnel Department) will vary according to the number of people employed in a firm and often with the importance a firm attaches to keeping its staff happy. The larger the firm, the larger the department tends to be and the more specialists it can afford to employ.

All departments in an organization will rely on the Human Resource Department to carry out the following functions:

- the recruitment and selection of staff with the skills and experience the organization needs
- providing employment advice and information
- providing terms and conditions of employment to new employees
- managing changes in working arrangements, for example, due to the introduction of new technology, changing the organizational structure, etc.
- developing and promoting induction courses and training for employees
- handling staff promotions and transfers
- developing and handling staff appraisal procedures
- developing and handling grievance procedures and complaints by staff
- handling employee discipline and dismissal
- dealing with redundancies and redundancy pay
- administering pay and conditions of service, such as holiday entitlements and maternity pay
- taking part in negotiations with trade unions and employee representatives on their pay and conditions
- looking after staff welfare, which can include a staff nurse, and sports and other leisure facilities, particularly in larger organizations
- ensuring health and safety at work guidelines are followed
- keeping staff records for every employee

The main purpose of an administrative system in human resources is, therefore, to develop routines to carry out these functions and maintain accurate records on each employee, including:

- name, address, date of birth, telephone number
- sex, number of dependents, marital status, next of kin
- nationality and place of birth
- National Insurance number
- education history and qualifications
- past and present employment details
- present job, title, responsibilities
- salary or wage rate
- outcome of appraisal interviews
- any disciplinary actions
- training and development undertaken

The functions of a Human Resources Department are considered in detail in Unit 4.

Support services

It is easy to overlook the importance of many other functions and tasks needed in business which simply provide help and support to the main functional areas in an organization.

Consider the list of tasks below. Without many of these a business is unlikely to operate efficiently and effectively and may not achieve its key objectives. Imagine the problems that would arise if an office had no photocopying facilities or up-to-date files, or if waste was never cleared from a factory floor, light bulbs were never replaced, or if a bank had no security.

- Staffing a reception
- Operating the switchboard
- Providing typing/word processing services
- Photocopying
- Data processing
- Filing
- Running the mailroom
- Internal deliveries and collections of post
- Arranging security and cleaning services
- Planning and managing relocations
- Providing staff telephone and office number directories
- Maintaining the premises (i.e. furniture, air conditioning systems, decorations, etc).
- Maintaining computer systems
- Arranging catering and providing canteen facilities

All these various support functions may be combined into one Administration Department.

▼ *Security – a support service that benefits the whole organization*

Support services will often be provided under contract by other organizations employed by the Administration Department. The administrative system must be capable of managing contracts and carefully monitoring the quality of services provided by these other firms, or sub-contractors. A good system will also carefully monitor the views of the internal customers - other employees and managers in the organization - on the quality of the support services provided to them by the sub-contractors.

Catering functions

- Identify catering needs in a firm
- Purchase supplies
- Store food
- Maintain standards of hygiene
- Waste management
- Prepare menus
- Record transactions
- Handle cash

Maintenance functions

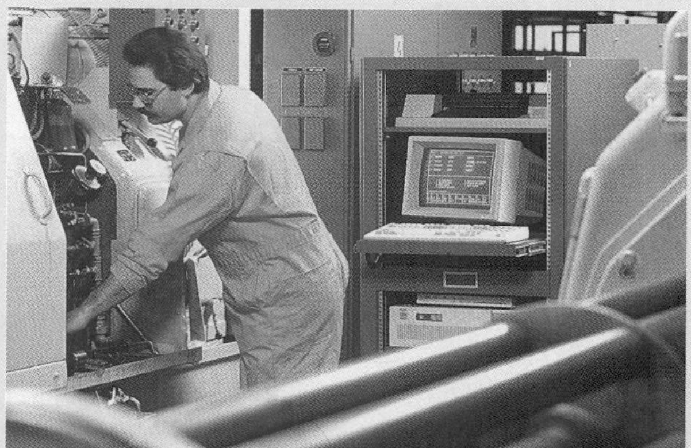

- Create an inventory of all equipment and machinery
- Make regular inspections of all equipment and premises
- Record any faults and repairs undertaken
- Instruct maintenance staff to undertake repairs
- Arrange regular servicing of plant and machinery
- Keep records of maintenance costs

Portfolio Activity 4.6 

1. Investigate the provision of catering and cleaning services in a business organization you are familiar with. In particular:
   - How are they arranged?
   - Who takes responsibility for arranging these services?
   - Why are these services provided?
   - What are the main functions of these services?
   - What other departments/functions in the organization are required to help provide an efficient catering and cleaning service? (*Hint*: Who keeps details of transactions? Who helps recruit staff?)
   - How are service levels monitored?
   - How is Information Technology used, or how could it be used in future?
   - How might the administration of these support services be improved?
2. Write up your findings in a short report.
3. Prepare a short presentation on overhead slides of your findings to give to your study group.

Section 4.3

Evaluating administrative systems

Meeting the requirements of the business

Businesses vary so much in terms of size, structure, location, expertise of staff, and levels of technology used, that no one system of administration will be best for all. Instead, each firm is likely to be better served by creating a tailor-made system to suit its individual circumstances. Bigger firms usually have a greater quantity of decisions to make about purchases, sales, production, finance, distribution, etc., and so will need a more structured and formal system of doing things.

Large firms are able to employ specialist staff to carry out administrative tasks, often aided by the use of computers and other telecommunications equipment such as faxes and modems to link computers through the telephone network. In contrast, in a small sole trader enterprise, most tasks can be undertaken reasonably successfully by just one person doing jobs as and when s/he feels they need to be done.

Sole Trader – Off License

Ordering	Orders placed by telephone daily and given to sales representatives
Stock	Sole trader keeps an informal eye on stock each day and may undertake a formal stock count once a year or month
Distribution	Sole trader employs a delivery boy who makes deliveries in evenings and on Saturdays
Personnel	Sole trader interviews and employs staff her/himself
Accounts	Keeps simple accounts of receipts and payments and hires an accountant to produce annual accounts
Mail	Opens mail her/himself
Written communications	Hand writes orders and letters to suppliers. No internal written communications; the sole trader speaks with staff directly

Public Limited Company – Head office of a large national off-license chain

Ordering	Central on-line computer receives individual orders from shops and generates bulk orders to wines and spirits suppliers. System managed by a specialist staff of purchasing executives
Stock	Computerized warehouse using bar code readers keeps a minute-by-minute record of all stock held and alerts central computer when stocks of some products are running low.
Distribution	Company operates its own fleet of delivery vehicles based at regional distribution depots.
Personnel	A specialized personnel department places recruitment adverts in the national press and operates a national recruitment and training programme from head office
Accounts	Computerized accounts section employing credit control and budgeting executives
Mail	Mail room employing 10 staff equipped with 5 fax machines receiving 2,000 letters per day
Written communications	Word-processed internal communications and electronic mail

▲ *How administrative procedures can differ between a sole trader and a large plc*

In choosing an administrative system, a firm will also consider the following:

Do staff have the necessary skills to operate the system?

For example, are staff aware of the rules and procedures which govern the sending and receiving of invoices, arranging maintenance contracts, hiring staff, etc.? Do they know how to use computerized systems? Staff training in administration and the use of Information Technology can help to improve the operation of an administration system.

What are advantages and disadvantages to individuals?

Does the system reduce or increase the workload of individuals? For example, has the creation of standardized documentation helped to improve the efficiency with which documents are processed, allowing staff to use the time saved to concentrate on other tasks?

Computer software packages are now available which can undertake a number of administrative tasks in a fraction of the time it would have taken manually. But does the firm now expect staff to undertake more tasks as a result? Have the procedures for accounting, organizing human resources, or providing support services become so complex that employees are finding it difficult to remember and cope with them all?

Has the administration system implemented health and safety procedures to reduce the number of accidents in the workplace, such as organizing health and safety training, providing protective clothing, or simply producing staff notices?

Portfolio Activity 4.7 

Select three of the tasks identified in the tables on the previous page and investigate the administrative systems used to deal with them in an organization with which you are familiar.

Compare these with the systems identified by another student in your study group. Report on some of the differences in administrative systems which you have identified and suggest reasons for these differences. To what extent does the design of each system depend on the size and nature of each firm?

What are advantages and disadvantages to the firm?

For example, does the system offer value for money? Do the benefits of using the system in terms of increased productivity and reduced overheads exceed the costs of the system in terms of labour, equipment, materials, training, and running costs? Are some tasks more cost effective if undertaken manually rather than with the help of expensive new computer equipment? Is the system secure? What happens if a computer which contains important documents and records is stolen or breaks down?

Ways of improving administrative systems

A firm may seek to improve the operation of their administrative system in a number of ways.

Monitoring the effectiveness of an administration system

User surveys

One useful way to evaluate the effectiveness and efficiency of administrative systems is to survey the opinions of users. The main users are the staff operating the systems and the customers who purchase the goods or services sold.

There are a range of other business clients who are in contact with firms' administrative systems, including suppliers, government agencies (including the Inland Revenue and Customs and Excise Department), and shareholders. These clients could also provide an insight into administrative efficiency.

The attainment of agreed standards

Administration can be evaluated in each department as well as in the organization as a whole. Administration in a particular department may be judged by identifying the role and purpose of that department and then seeing to what extent its work meets the standards required. For example, a production and distribution department responsible for stock control could have as its aim never to be without any kind of stock for more than one working day and to deliver finished products to customers within three working days.

Staff training and re-training

A workforce that does not understand the correct procedures to follow, or cannot use equipment properly, will not operate a cost effective administration system. Organizations are using training to create multi-skilled workforces (see 15.2). This refers to training to equip people with a wide variety of skills which they can use to good effect in their organization. For example, skills in using computers, word processing, writing and presentation, negotiating, letting contracts, information processing and managing resources, as well as improving any special skills they may have as economists, production engineers, or accountants.

Portfolio Activity 4.8 

For any organization that you know (you could choose your own school or college, for example), identify the various departments and their main purposes.

For each department, decide upon a way of measuring the effectiveness of its administrative systems.

Using your chosen method, evaluate the departmental administrative systems and suggest how the overall efficiency of the business may be gauged. Report on your results.

Choose one department and research in detail the views of the users and customers of the system. Recommend improvements to the system.

Introducing quality standards

In a competitive marketplace, successful firms are those which continuously attempt to improve the quality of their goods and services and production methods.

In order to assist firms to improve the quality of their operations, the **International Standards Organisation** (ISO) has introduced quality standards for firms to work towards. The ISO9001 provides a 'kitemark of quality' similar to the British Standards for Safety, which when demonstrated by firms allow them to display the safety kitemark on their products (see 1.2).

For a firm to demonstrate its achievement of ISO9001, it must introduce a series of management systems and procedures covering areas such as training, design control, production, purchasing, customer services, and quality control. These must be clearly documented and well maintained. External inspectors regularly check that the firm is continuing to follow these documented procedures.

Re-engineering

Business **re-engineering** or **process redesign** provides a way of building new administrative systems into a firm and taking advantage of new technology in order to improve on previous practice. Behind the concept of re-engineering are two key ideas:

- That it is better to re-design all administrative systems in one go rather than to make continual small modifications to an existing system
- That most companies today operate with many thousands of administrative specialists who are judged and rewarded on how well they perform their own specialized tasks, with no concept or interest in how these contribute to the success of the firm as a whole.

By re-engineering and looking at administrative systems from scratch, it is possible to take full advantage of rapid advances in computer technology and falling computer prices in order to build new and better systems.

Introducing new technology

The speed, efficiency and effectiveness of functional areas in business can be greatly improved with the use of modern information communications technology (ICT).

ICT can improve the speed, level and accuracy of internal communications between different functional areas or departments in an organization, and external communications with customers and suppliers (see 3.1).

Valuable information on the business can also be recorded, stored, accessed and processed easily from computer databases, including employee records, financial information, stock inventories, customer and supplier records. It can, therefore, also reduce the need for paper use and file storage space in business.

Key Activity

Investigate business functions in a business organization of your choice. Ideally, this should be the same organization as in your key activity in Chapter 3.

Prepare a short report on the following:

- the main functional areas in the business
- the routine and non-routine tasks involved in performing each function
- who carries out these functions (for example, it might be the owner(s) in a small business, but the staff organized into departments in a large organization)
- functional dependency in the organization, and why it is so important for business success
- how well the business carries out its functions

Key words:

Re-engineering – designing new, more effective and efficient administrative systems to replace old systems

Test your knowledge

1. Which of the following is a non-routine task in a manufacturing plant?

   A Monitoring production costs

   B Recording weekly sales volumes

   C Recording credit sales

   D Dealing with an equipment power failure

Questions 2–4 share the following answer options:

   A Finance

   B Human resources

   C Sales

   D Purchasing

Which of the above administrative functions would be used for the following?

2. Recording and dealing with customer enquiries
3. Handling cash and making payments
4. Preparing a job advertisement
5. Which of the following is not a main function of the Production Department?

   A Production scheduling

   B Cost control

   C Staff recruitment

   D Quality control

6. Which of the following is not a main function of marketing?

   A Market research

   B The preparation of business accounts

   C Promotional campaigns

   D Public relations

7. Which of the following criteria should not be used to evaluate the efficiency of an administrative system in a business renting and maintaining photocopy machines?

   A Reduced call-out times for engineers

   B Reduced market share

   C Quicker despatch of reminders to customers who are late payers

   D Faster despatch of spare parts to engineers from central stores

8. Distribution will involve all of the following tasks **except**:

   A Dealing with customer complaints about delivery times

   B Stock control

   C Checking goods in and out

   D Arranging customer deliveries

10. Which of the following departments in an organization is least likely to be affected by a decision to increase advertising expenditure?

   A Marketing

   B Sales

   C Production

   D Research and Development

11. The following are departments in a large organization:

   - Human resources
   - Finance
   - Production
   - Sales

   a List three tasks the staff employed in each department will be responsible for.

   b Explain why the success of the organization will depend crucially on these and other departments working closely together.

The Competitive Business Environment

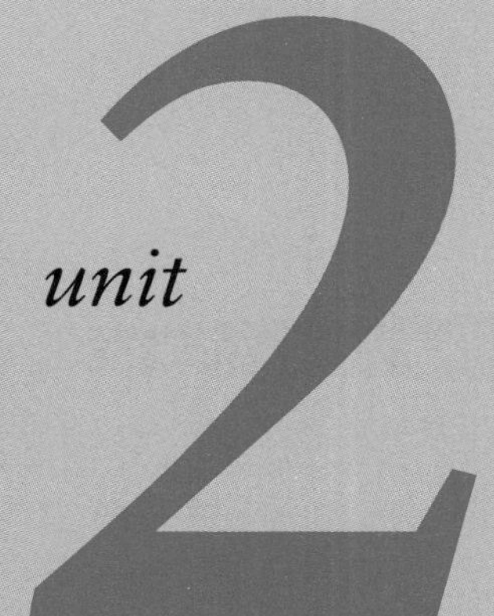

About this unit

To be successful in business you need to know about the environment in which your business operates (see also Chapter 12). Many external factors will affect your business decisions and performance. You will need to anticipate how changes in external factors will affect your business: the actions of competitors in the UK and overseas; how governments will react to decisions that impact on prices, employment and output; the changing wants of consumers and judging what to sell, when and at what price; the decisions of suppliers and judging when to buy and at what price; the reactions of your business shareholders and workers to your decisions. These are also the key elements in what it means to be competitive. A business is unlikely to meet its objectives or survive without an awareness of these key elements.

This unit examines why being competitive is important to business. You will learn what is meant by 'a market' and you will find out how and why businesses and governments try to influence market outcomes.

chapter 5 Competition and How Markets Work

This chapter investigates how markets operate, and how the decisions of consumers and rival firms can affect business.

What you need to learn

A **market** for any particular good or service consists of all those consumers willing and able to buy it and all those producers willing and able to supply it. Markets can be local, national, or international.

You need to identify the **different types of markets** in which businesses operate. These will include:

- **capital goods**
- **commodity**
- **consumer**
- **labour**
- **industrial**
- **internal**

You will need to identify, analyse and evaluate the factors that affect **how markets operate**, how they affect business, and how businesses try to influence market conditions and outcomes.

Market conditions are determined by the interaction of **demand** and **supply** factors. Changes in market demand and/or supply will affect the **prices** at which goods are traded.

Consumer demand is affected by changes in income and tastes, the price and availability of competing and complementary products, and other factors such as advertising and the weather.

Market supply is affected by costs, technology, changes in the prices of other goods and services, business objectives, and government decisions to tax or subsidize supply.

The influence any one business has over supply and the price charged for its goods or services varies significantly between different markets depending on **market structure**.

Market structure affects the amount and intensity of market **competition**. The **globalization** of many markets has tended to increase the number of rival firms supplying the same or similar products and intensify competition between them.

The affect of changes in market conditions over time is reflected in the changing pattern of industry. You need to be able to classify businesses into **primary, secondary and tertiary industrial sectors** and know how to interpret **trends** within and across these sectors that are the results of market changes.

Section 5.1

Markets

What is a market?

The goods and services produced by business organizations are sold in markets. A **market** is defined as consisting of all those consumers willing and able to buy goods and services and all those producers willing and able to supply them. For example, the market for televisions will consist of the producers of televisions and the people who buy them. Similarly, there will be a market for cars, hairdressing, video recorders, window cleaning, and all other goods and services. These are called **consumer markets for goods and services.**

Business organizations will also operate in many other markets, for example:

- **Capital goods markets** - where items such as machinery and vehicles are bought and sold by business organizations
- **Industrial markets** - in these markets the consumer tends to be a large business or government organization investing in a major new and highly specialized engineering project, such as the building of an oil rig, railway, road or dam
- **Commodity markets** - where raw materials such as oil, copper and wheat are bought and sold
- **The labour market** - where people are hired by firms for their services
- **The money market** - where people and financial institutions borrow and lend money
- **The foreign exchange market** - where people and firms buy and sell foreign currencies if they need to trade overseas
- **The property market** - where people and firms buy and sell houses, offices and factories

A market for a good or service can be of any size and can cover any area. It can involve any number of consumers and producers anywhere in the world willing to exchange a good or service. The market for a local newspaper in Kingston upon Thames is likely to be confined to the immediate area surrounding this town, but the market for newspapers such as *The Mirror* or *The Times* is national. Products like oil, sugar, video recorders, and insurance are sold all over the world. These goods and services have international or world markets.

The interaction of consumer demand and producer supply in a market will determine the price at which a product is sold and the quantity sold. Changes in **market conditions** - that is, changes in the level and strength of consumer demand and/or producer supply - can, therefore, influence how individual businesses use their resources.

Portfolio Activity 5.1 

Read the articles below. What factors have caused the prices of the goods and services mentioned to change, and why?

The Pope and the Price of Fish

For over 1,000 years the Roman Catholic Church required believers to abstain from consuming meat on Fridays and instead eat fish. However, a liberalization of the regulation of the church abolished this requirement in December 1966.

Frederick W. Bell studied the impact of this liberalization on the price of fish in New England, USA (with a population approximately 45% Catholic). The study compared fish prices over a ten-year period before the Catholic church abolished the rule with a nine-month period just after. But first he had to correct for the influence of a number of other changing factors on the price of fish: fish imports, prices of close substitutes (poultry and meat); cold storage holdings, and changes in personal incomes, etc. Having corrected for these influences on price, the effect of the liberalization on fish prices can be seen in the following table:

Prices of fish (monthly data 1957-67)

Species	% change in average price due to liberalization
Sea scallops	-17%
Cod	-10%
Haddock	-21%
Whiting	-20%

Bell, FW: 'The Pope and the Price of Fish' in American Economic Review, Vol. 58

The results showed that, for any given quantity of fish, the prices received for fish were lower after the effect of liberalization on demand.

Adapted from Hirshleifer, J: Price Theory and Applications (Prentice Hall International)

Rice price rise

European consumers will soon be paying more for rice because of poor harvests.

Financial Times 20.1.1994

The hotter it gets, the more your Coca-Cola may cost

Coca-Cola is testing a vending machine that automatically raises the price of the world's favourite soft drink when the temperature increases.

Financial Times, 28.10.1999

Orange cuts call charges and renews wars of words

Orange foreshadowed a new price war in the mobile phone industry yesterday when it halved the cost of calls in its pre-pay package and renewed claims that consumers are being ripped off by its rivals.

Chief executive Hans Snook announced that peak-rate calls on Orange pre-pay are being cut from 50p to 25p a minute while its airtime vouchers will no longer expire after a set time. Offpeak is being reduced to 5p a minute.

The Guardian, 28.10.1999

VIDEO GAMES PRICE PROBE

Stores accused of running cartel

MAJOR stores were yesterday accused of operating a cartel to fix the price of video games.

Richard Branson's Virgin Megastore chain, HMV and Britain's biggest electronics retailer Dixons are among the giants facing claims of collusion over the cost of PlayStation titles. Yesterday all these stores increased the price of the most popular games such as Driver and Tomb Raider 3. Some rose 50 per cent from £29.99 to £44.99.

Daily Express, 17.7.1999

Opec considers output rise to avoid pricing row

The Organisation of Petroleum Exporting Countries last night considered a plan to reverse production cuts made last March to try to avoid a confrontation with oil-consuming countries, particularly the US.

The scheme would on paper reinstate as much as 1.7m barrels a day in cuts that over the past year have helped boost the price of crude oil from less than $10 a barrel last February to recent post-Gulf war highs of about $34 a barrel.

But the outcome of the oil ministers' debate depended on persuading Iran, one of the most vulnerable Opec economies, that any sizeable increase would not trigger a price collapse.

Financial Times, 28.3.1999

Christmas cost slides for third year running

The cost of Christmas has taken a pounding from the so-called Wal-Mart effect. The price war among supermarkets, fuelled by the American discounter's acquisition of Asda, has reduced the cost of the average family Christmas to a six-year-low, according to a survey carried out again this year by *The Times*.

The Times, 23.12.1999

Internal markets

Large business organizations will also operate **internal markets** in which different parts of an organization trade with each other. For example, a Production Department will 'demand' labour supplied from the Human Resources Department, materials and components to be bought in by the Purchasing Department, and a supply of finance from the Finance Department to buy new machinery. In turn, the Sales Department will demand finished goods to be supplied by the Production Department at a cost and level of quality that will enable it to sell them to consumers at a profit.

Each part of a business must be aware of the needs of its internal consumers and respond accordingly by supplying the products or services they need at the right time, in the right quantity, at the right quality, and at the lowest possible cost. If one part of the business is unable to do this, it may be shut down and the work placed with a more competitive external supplier. For example, if a business discovered it was paying too much in wages and other overheads for an internal photocopying service then it could invite outside firms to bid for a contract to supply the service at a lower cost. This is called **out-sourcing.** In this way the business is able to reduce costs and improve its competitiveness.

Multinationals are firms with operations in more than one country. They may be able to use their internal markets to their advantage to avoid paying high taxes on profits in some countries. For example, imagine a business that has a factory producing goods in country X and a sales and marketing office in country Y. Taxes on profits are higher in country Y than they are in country X. However, by selling the products at a very high internal price to the sales and marketing office the business is able to report low or zero profits in country Y to avoid paying the tax.

The above example illustrates **transfer pricing.** This refers to the ability of a multinational company to use its internal market to switch profits between countries in which they operate in order to minimize its tax burden.

Key words:

Market - any setting in which trade occurs between consumers willing and able to buy a product and producers who are willing and able to supply it

Market conditions - the level and strength of consumer demand and producer supply in a market

Out-sourcing - reducing internal market operations by buying-in services, such as cleaning, maintenance, and including some manufacturing operations, at a lower cost and/or higher quality than the business could provide itself

Multinational - a global business organization that has operations in more than one country

Transfer pricing - using the internal market in a multinational company to 'price' internal goods and services out of high tax countries into low tax countries to minimize tax liabilities on profits

Section 5.2 Market structure

Why do firms compete?

One of the major determinants of product prices in different markets is the amount of competition between rival suppliers. Markets can be analysed by the amount of competition between firms. In general, the more competition there is between firms to supply a good or service, the lower the price charged to consumers will be. In competitive markets firms will compete by reducing their costs so that they are able to lower prices without cutting into profit margins (the difference between the cost of making each unit and the price it is sold at).

Firms will compete to supply a market to achieve a number of objectives. These are:

- **To increase their customer base.** Firms will compete with each other on price, product quality and through promotional strategies to increase the number of customers buying their products.

- **To increase sales.** Not only will firms seek to increase the number of customers buying their products but they will also hope that existing customers will buy more. Cutting prices can increase sales revenues from products for which demand is price elastic (see 5.6). Advertising and other promotions, such as free gifts, can help to expand sales without the need for price cuts.

- **To expand market share.** The market share of a firm can be calculated as its proportion of total sales (see 1.7). For example, in 2000 Nokia accounted for the production and sale of 32% of mobile phone handsets out of a total of 450 million manufactured worldwide.

Many organizations will aim to increase their share of total sales in a market. The larger an organization's market share, and the more widely established its product, the better able it will be to withstand new competition from new products and firms.

- **To achieve product superiority.** This has two meanings. On one hand it refers to making a product that is clearly better than rival products for reasons of prestige and/or profit. A superior product will help a firm to achieve its objectives of generating sales and expanding market share. But product superiority also means that the product dominates a market by outselling all others - which is not necessarily because it is the best product on the market.

A firm that is able to dominate the supply of a product to market is able to have some influence over the determination of the market price. It is also well placed to fight off competition from smaller rivals.

- **To enhance image.** Firms will also compete on image. Customer perception of an organization will be reflected in sales. A poor image will reduce sales; a good image will help to expand sales and market share.

In response to the growing awareness of environmental issues among consumers, many organizations are trying to present themselves as caring

▼ *Price competition*

▼ *Non-price competition*

and environmentally friendly. For example, the Body Shop prides itself on not testing products on animals, while the Co-operative Bank will only invest money in 'green' companies that have a good environmental record.

Types of competition

We can distinguish between competition between organizations on price, and competition on aspects other than price.

Price competition

Cutting price can expand consumer demand. Hence, competition between firms on price is often vigorous.

Ultimately the ability of a firm to undercut rivals to increase sales will be constrained by market conditions and production costs. Cutting prices to expand sales will reduce the margin between revenues and costs. If a firm is to be in a strong position to compete on prices, it must try to reduce its costs by increasing the productivity of its resources (see 1.1).

There are a number of short-term pricing strategies an organization might use in an attempt to expand sales and market share:

- **Penetration pricing** involves setting product price low to encourage sales. This is especially important for a new or existing firm trying to establish a new product.
- **Expansion pricing** is similar to penetration pricing. Product prices are set low to encourage consumers to buy. As demand increases, the firm can raise output to meet demand and take advantage of economies of scale which will lower the average cost of producing each unit (see 22.4). Lower average costs can either be passed on to consumers as lower prices, or, if prices are held steady, the lower costs will increase the firm's profit margins.
- **Destruction pricing** is a more drastic version of penetration pricing, usually practised by larger firms when threatened by new competition from smaller organizations. The objective is to destroy the sales of competitors by setting price very low - even below costs - and sustaining a loss for a short period of time. Smaller firms, unable to take a loss, will be pushed out of the market.
- **Price war.** In markets where the supply side is very competitive, price wars may develop among rival firms employing the various pricing strategies discussed above.

  Where there is little competition in a market, for example for a new and unique product, a firm may be able to exploit consumers' willingness to pay by pricing at 'what the market can bear'. Competitive pricing strategies are discussed in detail in Section 10.2.

- **Market skimming.** Also known as **price creaming**, this involves charging a high price for a new product to yield a high initial profit from consumers who are willing to pay extra because the product is new and unique. As competitors enter the market, prices are reduced to expand the market.

Market skimming is a practice often observed in markets for new consumer technology such as audio and video products, mobile phones, and personal computers. For example, some of the first recordable CD-ROM drives for computers released on to the UK market by organizations such as Phillips and Yamaha in the early 1990s were priced at around £20,000. In 2000 prices of CD-R drives started from as little as £40.

Non-price competition

When consumers buy a product they are looking not just for low price but also for value for money in terms of the quality of the good or service, its size or shape, colour, smell, or taste. Consumers also look for after-sales care in case anything should go wrong and they might want to exchange their product. Firms can compete on all these facets of a product and service to offer consumers what they want.

Promotion is also very important if consumers are to be tempted to buy one product rather than another. Free gifts, money-off coupons, attractive in-store displays, publicity in magazines - these are all methods that can be used to persuade consumers to buy (see 10.3). Advertising, through media such as television or newspapers, is one of the main ways firms compete for sales. Advertising can be used to present features of a product in an attractive way and to persuade people that a product is better than its rivals. By creating an image for a product in the mind of the consumer, advertising can manipulate consumer wants. Organizations are willing to spend many millions of pounds on advertising because, if used effectively, it can create a want among consumers for a new or existing product. By creating a want and increasing the demand for their product a firm will generate sales and may be able to charge a higher price.

Competition: good or bad for the consumer?

Both price and non-price competition are good for consumers because they can reduce prices and increase the quality and availability of different products. However, advertising and excessive packaging is sometimes considered wasteful. Prices will reflect the cost of these activities and will, therefore, tend to be higher than they might otherwise be.

Portfolio Activity 5.2 

Choose an organization you are familiar with, that sells a good or service. Gather information and write a short report on how they compete with their rival organizations. Try to find out:

- Why do they compete?
- What is their market share?
- Who are their main competitors?
- How do their prices compare?
- What forms of non-price competition do they use?
- How effective have their price- and non-price-competitive strategies been?

What is market structure?

Different markets are organized or structured in different ways. It is tempting to believe that, where there are a large number of firms producing the same product and an equally large number of consumers wanting to buy it, no one producer or consumer has the power to influence market price. This suggests that markets are highly competitive and that, if a firm did try to raise price, it would lose custom to rival producers and soon go out of business.

In reality, very few markets are structured in this way. Perhaps world agricultural markets are the closest examples of what are theoretically known as **perfectly competitive markets**. Because there are so many producers of wheat, barley, and other crops of similar quality worldwide, no one producer is able to price its crop above the prevailing market price.

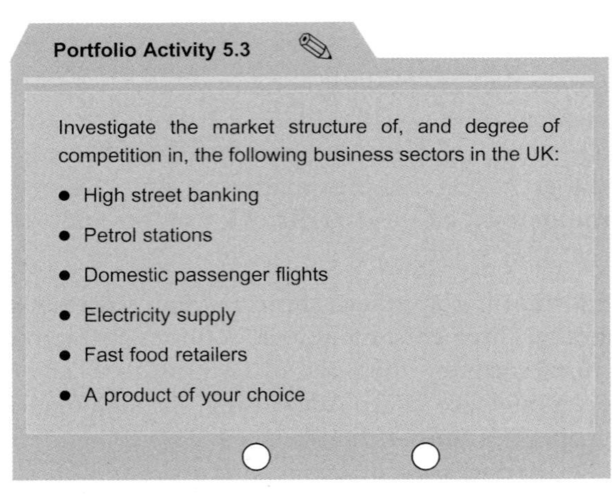

Portfolio Activity 5.3

Investigate the market structure of, and degree of competition in, the following business sectors in the UK:

- High street banking
- Petrol stations
- Domestic passenger flights
- Electricity supply
- Fast food retailers
- A product of your choice

In perfectly competitive markets there are so many consumers and producers of the same product that no one alone can influence the market price - they are all **price takers**. As such, it is hard to understand why firms in perfectly competitive markets, if they existed, would ever compete. For example, what would be the advantage of one farm spending money on advertising wheat? Unless it were able to persuade consumers that its wheat was much better than the wheat of all other producers, it would be unlikely to sell any more at the expense of its rival suppliers. Similarly, it would be unable to cut the price of its wheat below the market price without losing money unless it were able to produce wheat much more cheaply than its rivals. The theory of perfectly competitive markets assumes that all firms have the same production costs. If one firm were able to lower its costs below rival firms, those firms would soon learn how this was done and use the same methods.

Much more interesting and real than the theoretical extreme of perfectly competitive markets in the study of markets is 'small numbers' competition, that is, competition between a small number of firms who dominate the supply of a particular good or service. Most markets are structured in this way. For example, Boeing in the USA and Airbus of Europe compete vigorously as the only suppliers of large civil aircraft in the world. Their size and dominance of this market is able to deter new rival producers from entering the market to compete.

In general, markets are grouped into three broad categories. The table below compares their key characteristics with those of a perfectly competitive market.

Type of market structure	Number of producers	Can producers influence market price?	Do firms compete on aspects of product other than price?	Can existing producers prevent new firms entering market?
'Perfect competition'	Many	No. All firms are price takers	No - products of individual producers are exactly the same	No
Monopolistic competition	Many	Yes - by differentiating their products	Yes - producers try to differentiate their product using brand image	Depends on strength of brand image
Oligopoly	Few	Yes	Yes - fierce competition on product image	Yes
Pure monopoly	One	Yes. A monopoly can be a price maker	No - no competition, so not necessary	Very much - almost impossible for new firms to enter market

▼ *Some oligopolistic markets*

High street banking

Petrol supplies

Paints

Types of market structure

Monopolistic competition

Individual producers will often attempt to modify their own products to distinguish their supply from their rivals. This is called **product differentiation** and is a feature of **monopolistic competition.** It can be achieved by branding - making differences in the design and packaging of products - as well as the creation of different trade names and product images through advertising (see 10.1). In this way an organization can create and maintain consumer demand for their product. Building consumer loyalty to a product reduces the effectiveness of price cuts and advertising as ways to lure customers away from rival firms.

Oligopolistic competition

Today, most markets can be described as 'oligopolistic'. An **oligopoly** exists if a small number of large firms dominate the supply of a particular good or service to a market.

Price leadership is a feature of many oligopolistic markets. In order to avoid price wars, the firms that dominate the market will tend to price their products in line with each other. In extreme cases they may even collude to 'fix' prices. Sometimes, however, agreements to fix prices or play 'follow my leader' break down, and price wars can develop among rival firms.

Cartels are formal agreements between firms to regulate prices and/or output, thereby effectively creating a monopoly. The best known cartel is OPEC (Organization of Petroleum Exporting Countries) which can restrict the world supply of crude oil in order to hold up its market price. **Collusion** to fix prices at artificially high levels is illegal in the UK under the terms of the 1998 Competition Act (see 12.5).

Oligopolistic markets tend to be characterized by aggressive non-price competition for consumers and market share. For example, the growth of shops on petrol station forecourts and the giving of tokens towards free gifts are attempts at non-price competition by a handful of large petrol companies. Similarly, despite the existence of numerous branded products, the washing-powder market is supplied chiefly by two very large producers (a **duopoly**) - Unilever and Procter and Gamble. Their competition concentrates on the creation of strong brand images and customer product loyalty through heavy advertising.

Monopoly

A firm is a **pure monopoly** if it is the sole supplier of a good or service wanted by consumers. For example, until 1998 British Gas plc supplied 100% of households connected to the national gas supply grid in the UK. Today, many different gas supply companies compete to supply gas to firms and households all over the UK.

▼ Blockbuster Video has significant monopoly power in the market for video rentals

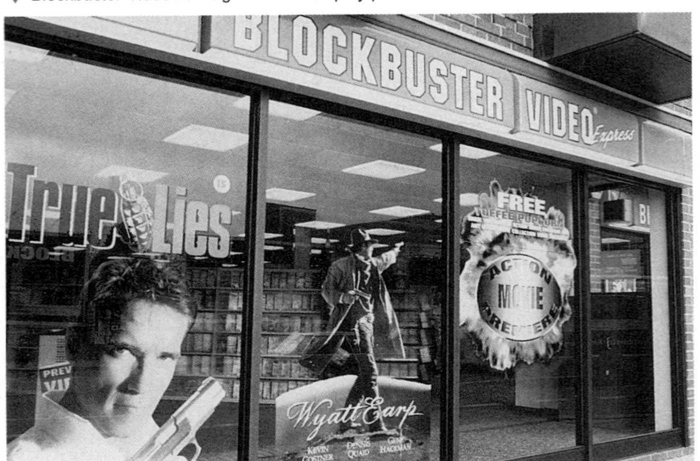

A monopoly faces little or no competition and is therefore able to keep profit levels high by setting a high price for its product. Monopolies are often described as **price makers** because they can restrict the supply to a market to force up the market price. However, in order to do this, the mono-poly must prevent new firms from entering the market. Any increase in supply from new firms will force prices and profits down.

Barriers to entry used by monopolies (and oligopolies) to prevent the entry of new firms into their markets can occur naturally, or can be deliberately created by the dominant firms to force new and smaller competitors out of business.

Natural barriers to entry

New firms may be unable to compete with a monopoly because of the advantages a large firm has simply because of its size.

- **Economies of scale.** By increasing in size, a firm may be able to reduce the average cost of producing each unit of output below the costs of smaller organizations (see 22.4). If one firm is able to produce the entire market supply at a lower average cost per unit than a number of smaller firms put together, then it is known as a **natural monopoly**. The gas, electricity and water supply networks are natural monopolies. This is because it does not make economic sense to have more than one set of gas or water pipes or electricity cables supplying each house, office or factory.
- **Capital size.** The supply of a product may involve the input of such a vast amount of capital equipment that new competing firms find it difficult to raise necessary finance to buy or hire their own. For example, the Airbus Integrated Company will invest around $11 billion to develop the new A380 'super jumbo' aircraft over the period 2000–2005. The new plane will carry up to 650 passengers on two decks, and will be in direct competition with the Boeing 747 'jumbo'.
- **Historical reasons.** A business may have a monopoly because it was first to enter the market for a product and has built up an established customer base. For example, Lloyds of London dominates the world insurance market primarily because of its established expertise dating back to the 18th century.
- **Legal considerations.** The development of new production methods and products can be expensive but can be encouraged by granting innovative producers **patents** or copyright, so as to to prevent other firms copying their ideas and thereby reducing their potential profits. Also, some monopolies are government-owned, for example, the Post Office.

Artificial barriers to entry

While some monopolies occur naturally, others may achieve and retain their powerful market position by creating their own artificial barriers to competition.

Size isn't everything!

It would be wrong to think that all large firms exploit their consumers. Many, because of their size, are able to spend a large amount of money on product improvements and more efficient production processes. Cost savings may be passed on to consumers as lower prices. Monopolies and oligopolies may also face competition from products in other markets and from foreign competition. Increasing global competition has meant many companies have had to grow large to compete with overseas giants (see 7.1).

- **Supply restrictions** can be used to prevent new firms obtaining the supplies of materials necessary for production. If suppliers rely heavily on the orders of a monopoly firm, a threat by the firm to obtain supplies from elsewhere is likely to be very effective in deterring them from supplying rival organizations.
- **Predatory pricing** occurs when the dominant firm in a market cuts its prices - at the risk of losing revenue in the short run - in order to force new and smaller competitors out of business. New firms are unlikely to be able to withstand trading at a loss for as long as the larger, established monopoly. Once new competitors have been forced to close, the monopoly can once again raise prices.
- **Exclusive dealing** involves a monopoly preventing retailers from stocking the products of competing firms. This method of restricting competition is particularly effective if the product supplied by the dominant firm is very popular and the retailer would lose too much trade if they did not sell it. Coca-Cola was accused in 1999 of using this barrier by offering retailers incentives to stock only Coca-Cola products (see Portfolio Activity 12.5).
- **Full line forcing** occurs when large firms refuse to supply retailers unless they stock and sell their full range of products.

Because monopolies and oligopolies have the ability to restrict competition, the UK government has passed a number of laws which can regulate their activities and in extreme cases prevent their formation (see 12.5).

Portfolio Activity 5.4

1. What is an artificial barrier to entry? Explain why it might be against the public interest.
2. What evidence is there from these two articles that artificial barriers are used to restrict entry into the transatlantic air and ice cream markets?

British Midland pledges cheaper Heathrow-US business fares

Business class air fares from London's Heathrow airport to the US are up to 207 per cent higher than from other leading airports in Europe such as Frankfurt, Paris and Amsterdam, according to figures released yesterday by British Midland, the UK's second largest airline.

British Midland has launched an intensive campaign to break into the lucrative transatlantic market from Heathrow, which is currently restricted to only two airlines each from the US and UK.

The carrier cut business and economy fares by up to 35 per cent against the existing competition when it recently opened new routes to Madrid, Milan and Rome from Heathrow.

According to the figures on North Atlantic fares released by the airline yesterday the cheapest return business class fare on the Heathrow-Los Angeles route is £5,138 ($7,744) compared to £1,673 ($2,522) on Milan-Los Angeles.

On the same basis the fare to Chicago from Brussels is £1,864 and from Amsterdam £1,945, while the fare from Heathrow is £4,200.

The figures add fuel to British Midland's longstanding claims that business travellers are being penalised by the terms of the current US/UK bilateral aviation treaty, known as Bermuda II, which is one of the most restrictive in world aviation.

Only two airlines from each country, British Airways and Virgin Atlantic from the UK and American Airlines and United Airlines from the US are currently permitted to fly services between US gateways and Heathrow, the world's busiest international airport.

Financial Times, 5.6.2000

Transatlantic flight costs (£)

To New York	
London Heathrow	3,342
Paris	2,410
Copenhagen	2,024
Amsterdam	1,799
Frankfurt	1,790
Brussels	1,383
Milan	1,210

To Los Angeles	
London Heathrow	5,138
Paris	3,205
Frankfurt	2,695
Amsterdam	2,310
Milan	1,673

Source: British Midland
Round trip fares on non-stop services valid for sale and travel on June 12 2000, Information collated on May 29 2000

Byers up against Walls on ice cream

Court threat as competition ruling singles out market leader

Bird's Eye Wall's, the Unilever frozen food subsidiary, yesterday threatened to seek a judicial review after the trade and industry secretary, Stephen Byers, backed competition commission findings that the manufacturer has been unfairly stifling competition.

Mr Byers accepted the commission's advice that all leading ice cream makers should be prevented from sealing exclusive deals with shops. Wall's will also be barred from keeping other brands out of its freezers, although Mars and Nestlé will be allowed to continue this in an effort to strengthen their competitive position.

'These agreements tie the retailer to a manufacturer and restrict competition and consumer choice' he said.

Mars, which has waged a 10-year battle against Wall's UK dominance, was cock-a-hoop. Walls sells more than two-thirds of all 'impulse' products - ice cream and lollies - sold in small retailers and other outlets.

Mars Confectionery managing director Bill Ronald, said: 'For the first time consumers will be able to buy the ice creams they want, when and where they want and to benefit from competition in the market.'

But Wall's chairman, Iain Ferguson, said the rulings were discriminatory and unworkable, and represented excessive intervention. 'How much regulation can a £300m market take?' he asked. He went on to say the company was consulting lawyers in the belief that some of the rulings may be beyond the secretary of state's powers.

The Guardian, 10.10.2000

Key words:

Market structure - characteristics of a market which determine the behaviour of firms supplying it

Price taker - a firm that has no power to influence market supply or demand and must, therefore, accept the prevailing market price at which to sell its products

Price maker - a firm that is able to influence the market price of a product

Monopolistic competition - a market structure in which a large number of firms compete to supply broadly similar products

Product differentiation - the creation of differences in consumer perceptions of very similar products through brand imaging

Branding - the creation of a brand image for a product through distinctive packaging and advertising

Oligopoly - a market structure with a small number of dominant firms

Market share - the proportion of total sales revenue in a particular market accounted for by a firm or group of firms

Price competition - competition to sell products by undercutting rivals on price

Non-price competition - competition between firms on aspects of product other than price, for example, quality, packaging, free gifts, advertising

Cartel - a formal arrangement between firms to agree prices and/or outputs

Collusion - collaboration between firms to 'fix' prices

Duopoly - when two firms dominate market supply

Pure monopoly - a firm that controls the entire supply of a particular good or service to a market

Barriers to entry - constraints used by existing producers in a market to hinder competition from new firms

Natural monopoly - a firm that controls the entire market supply of a product because production at this scale is the most efficient

Section 5.3 Market demand

What is demand?

Demand refers to the want or willingness of consumers to buy the goods and services produced by business organizations. In order to be an **effective demand**, their wants must be backed up by an ability to pay for goods and services. A business enterprise must attempt to estimate the potential effective demand for their product in order to plan production. To do this, firms can use market research (see 9.1).

Firms can measure the quantity demanded of a good or service at a number of possible prices that may be charged for the product, and over a certain period of time - for example, the number of apples bought per day, videos per week, cars per month or even yearly. This information can be plotted on a graph to derive a **market demand curve.**

In general, all firms observe the following relationship between the price they charge for a good or service and consumer demand:

- As product price falls, the quantity demanded of that product expands
- As product price rises, the quantity demanded of that product contracts (see Figure 5.1).

Portfolio Activity 5.5 

Plotting a demand curve

1. The table below lists possible prices for a 1lb bar of milk chocolate. Collect information from at least 20 people at your school or college on the number of chocolate bars they might buy each month at each possible price. Add up the number they would buy at each price and use this data to plot a line graph in the space provided below. Enter price (P) on the vertical (y) axis and quantity demanded (Qd) per month on the horizontal (x) axis. Label the plotted curve D_1D_1.

(Alternatively enter the data into a computer spreadsheet package to plot an xy graph. Remember to specify the column of prices as your y axis variable.)

2. What does the demand curve look like? Describe the relationship between the price of chocolate bars and quantity demanded.

1LB BAR OF CHOCOLATE

Possible price	Quantity demanded
20p	–
40p	–
60p	–
80p	–
£1.00	–
£1.20	–
£1.40	–
£1.60	–
£1.80	–
£2.00	–

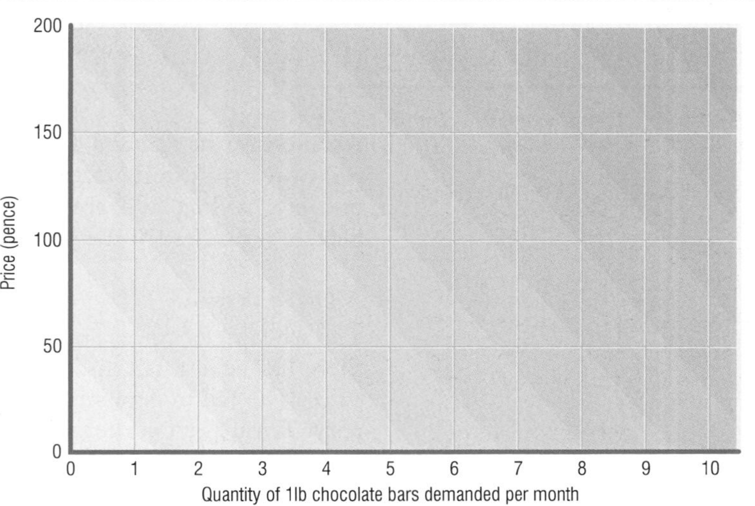

▼ *Figure 5.1: A typical market demand curve*

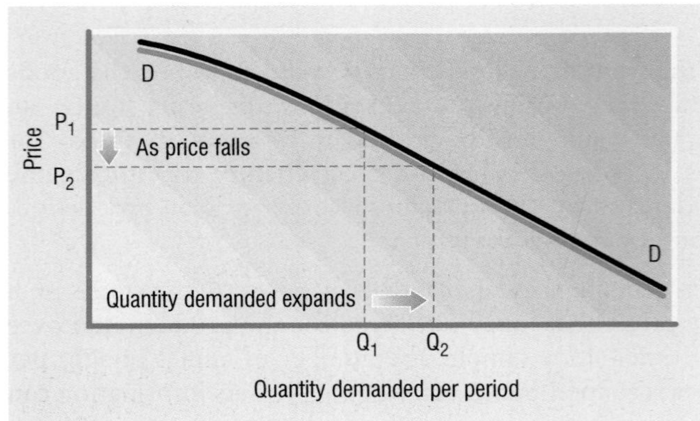

What makes a demand curve shift?

A change in product price causes quantity demanded to expand or contract along a given demand curve. However, over time, consumer demand for a product will be influenced by a number of factors other than price. These will cause the demand curve to shift.

Business organizations sometimes have little control over the conditions that cause consumer demand for their product to increase or decrease. For example, try to think what effect a general rise in household income might have on the demand for goods and services.

An increase in demand

Consider Figure 5.2 below. A firm has estimated the quantity demanded (Qd_1) each week of its blank video cassettes for a schedule of different prices (P). After one year, the firm estimates market demand again (Qd_2) and discovers that consumers now demand more video cassettes at each price than before.

The plotted demand curve D_1D_1 represents the original demand schedule (Qd_1), while D_2D_2 represents the increased level of demand (Qd_2).

▼ *Figure 5.2: An increase in demand*

MARKET FOR 3 HOUR VIDEO CASSETTES

Possible price (£)	Original quantity demanded (000's per week) (Qd_1)	New quantity demanded (000's per week) (Qd_2)
12	50	70
10	60	80
8	80	100
6	110	130
4	150	170
2	200	220

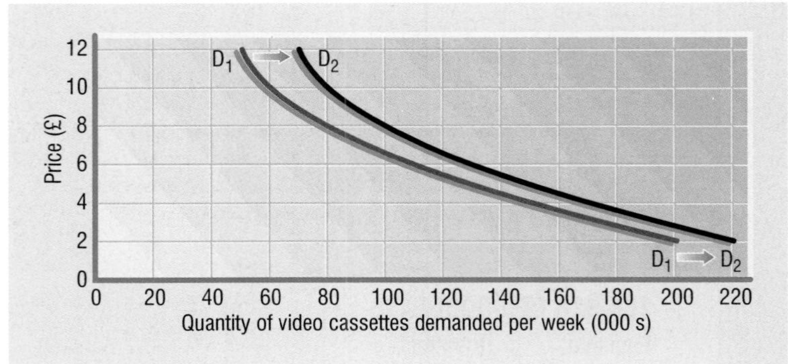

An increase in demand for a good or service can be represented by a rightward shift in its market demand curve. This shows that consumers are now willing and able to buy more of that product than they did before, regardless of the price.

A fall in demand

The schedule of prices and quantity demanded in Figure 5.3 below shows there has been a fall in demand for packets of peanuts at every possible price. The fall in demand is represented by a shift in the market demand curve inwards from the right, from D_1D_1 to D_3D_3.

▼ *Figure 5.3: A fall in demand*

MARKET FOR 1IB BAG OF PEANUTS

Possible price (£)	Original quantity demanded (000's per month) (Qd_1)	New quantity demanded (000's per month) (Qd_3)
1.00	400	100
0.80	500	200
0.60	700	400
0.40	1000	700
0.20	1400	1100

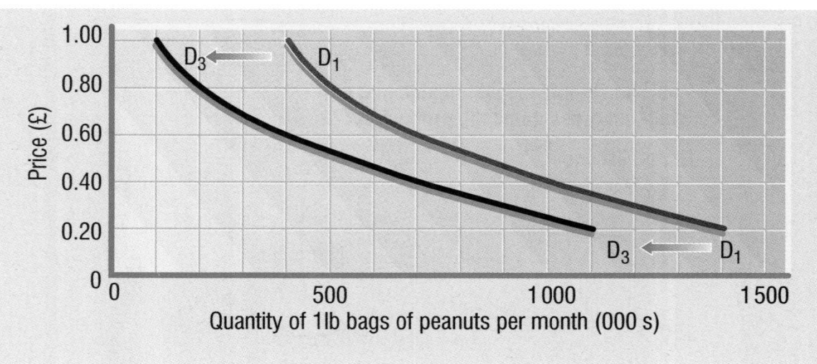

A fall in demand for a good or service can be represented by an inward shift of the market demand curve. It shows consumers as only willing and able to buy less than they did before, regardless of price.

Portfolio Activity 5.6 

Look at these news articles and, for each one:

1. Identify the things that have changed that might affect the demand for the particular good or service in question, or consumer demand for all products.
2. State whether quantity demanded will tend to rise, fall or remain unchanged as a result of the change you have identified.
3. Draw diagrams to show the likely market demand curves before and after each change.

Ministers play down new BSE fears

MINISTERS moved to head off fears of a new BSE scare yesterday after a warning the disease may transfer from one species to another more easily than was previously thought - and without showing any symptoms.

Metro, 30.9.2000

Stocking up for the party season

FORGET socks and bubblebath, according to leading supermarket chains the items most likely to feature on last-minute Christmas shopping lists are condoms, cat litter and champagne.

Sales of condoms are already up by at least 10 per cent on everyday sales and retail insiders suggest that regular figures will have more than doubled by tomorrow.

An Asda spokesman said that it was expecting sales to be 20 per cent above usual for festive season, and Safeway reported that its sales were up 10 per cent. A spokeswoman said: 'People are looking forward to the millennium and stocking up in advance.'

The Times, 23.11.1999

POPULATION CHANGE[1]
United Kingdom

	Population at start of period (000s)
Census enumerated	
1901-1911	38,237
1911-1921	42,082
1921-1931	44,027
1931-1951	46,038
Mid-year estimates	
1951-1961	50,287
1961-1971	52,807
1971-1981	55,928
1981-1991	56,352
Mid-year projections[2]	
1991-2001	59,237
2001-2011	59,954
2011-2021	61,773

1 See Appendix, Part 1: Population estimates and projections.
2 1998-based projections.
Social Trends, 2000

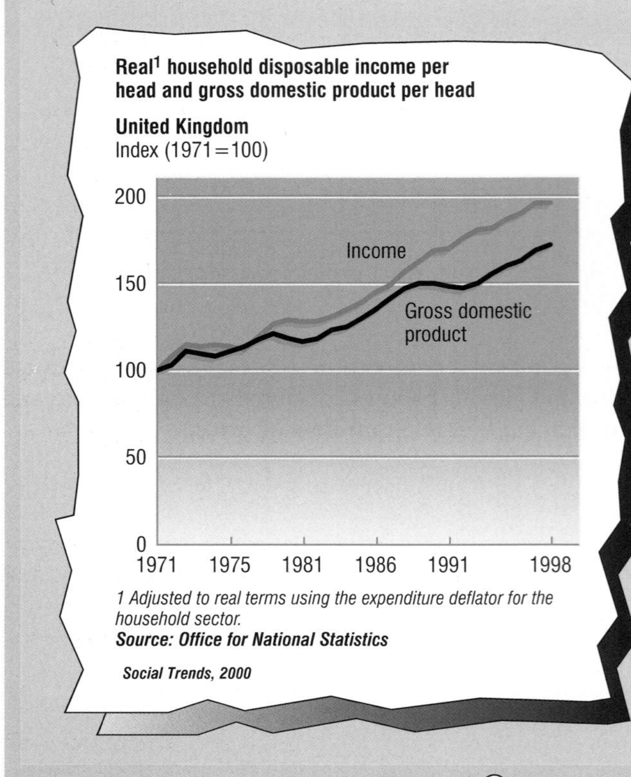

Plunging pound hits US holidays

BRITONS heading for the US on holiday will feel the pinch after the value of the pound fell to a six-year low against the dollar yesterday.

Sterling dipped below the $1.46 mark for the first time since 1994 after trading as high as $1.66 only last November.

The fall also spelt bad news for UK importers who buy most of their raw materials, including oil and gas, in dollars.

However, the pound's decline has given British exporters a boost, allowing them to sell their goods more cheaply on the other side of the Atlantic.

Metro, 30.9.2000

In general, if the demand for a product tends to rise as incomes rise, the product is said to be a **normal good**. If demand falls as incomes rise, the product is said to be an **inferior good**. For example, as incomes rise, people may prefer to travel by taxi rather than bus.

Disposable income refers to the amount of income people have left to spend or save after paying tax on their income. Clearly, any change in the level of personal tax allowances, income tax or National Insurance contributions is likely to result in a change in the quantity of goods and services demanded.

▼ *Figure 5.4: Possible relationships between demand and income*

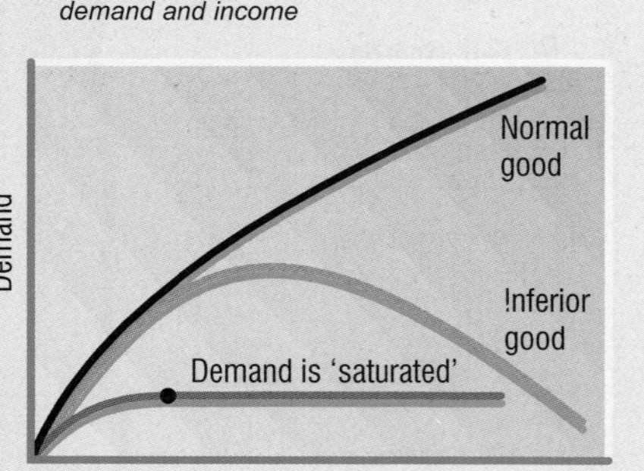

The following factors are likely to cause a shift in the market demand curve for a good or service:

1. Changes in income

Because effective demand is the willingness to buy a product backed by an ability to pay, it is clear that, as incomes rise, consumers will be able to buy more. However, the precise nature of the relationship between income and demand will depend on the type of product considered and the level of consumers' income. For example, a rise in income is unlikely to make most consumers want to buy more salt or newspapers each day or week, but it might allow them to travel less by bus and take the taxi more often, or even to buy a bigger car (see Figure 5.4).

2. The prices and availability of other goods and services

Some of the goods and services we buy need other things, or accessories, to go with them. For example, cars need petrol, compact discs need a disc player, bread is consumed with butter or margarine. These **complementary goods** are said to be in **joint demand**.

▼ *Complements*

Camcorder and cassette

▼ *Substitutes*

Buses and taxis

▼ *Fashion: here today and gone tomorrow…*

1960s

Grunge

If the price of new cars falls, consumer demand for them may expand and in turn generate increased demand for petrol. A rise in the price of compact disc players may lead to a fall in the demand for compact discs.

On the other hand, some goods and services are **substitutes**. A product is a substitute when its purchase can replace the want for another good or service. For example, margarine is considered a close substitute for butter. A rise in the price of one may therefore result in a rise in demand for the alternative. Different holiday destinations are also close substitutes - a rise in the cost of visiting the USA may increase the demand for European holidays.

A business organization will find it useful to gather information on changes in the prices and quality of competing and complementary products from rival producers, because any changes in competitors' products can affect demand and, therefore, sales revenue and profit for their own products.

3. Changes in tastes, habits and fashion

The demand for goods and services can change dramatically because of the changing tastes of consumers and fashion. Carefully planned advertising campaigns based on market research information on consumers can also help to create wants and shift demand curves for the advertised products out to the right.

4. Population change

An increase in population will tend to increase the demand for all goods and services. Population growth in the UK is now negligible. Birth and death rates have fallen and this has resulted in a rise in the average age of the population. The growing number of middle-aged and elderly people has resulted in a changing pattern of demand.

5. Other factors

There are a great many other factors that can affect demand. A hot summer can boost sales of cold drinks and ices. A cold winter will increase the demand for fuel for heating. Higher interest rates can increase the demand for savings schemes but reduce the amount of money people want to borrow, including mortgages for house purchases. Health scares have affected the demand for beef and other meats.

Changes in laws may also affect demand for some products. For example, it is illegal to ride a motorbike without a crash helmet.

Key words:

Demand - the willingness of consumers to buy goods and services at given prices

Effective demand - demand backed by an ability to pay

Market demand curve - a graphical representation of the relationship between demand for a product and price in a market

Normal good - a good for which demand increases as people's incomes rise

Inferior goods - a good for which demand falls as incomes increase

Disposable income - income available to spend on goods and services after income taxes have been deducted

Complementary goods - goods or services which are in joint demand

Substitutes - goods or services which are similar and which compete for consumer demand

Section 5.4

Market supply

The motives for production

Profit or public service?

In a mixed economy such as the UK, goods and services are produced and supplied to consumers by both private sector organizations, owned and controlled by private individuals, and public sector organizations owned and controlled by government bodies and agencies (see 2.2 and 2.3). Some public sector enterprises produce goods and services for sale to consumers, such as a rail journey or a postage stamp. However, many are provided for free at the point of use, such as the National Health Service (NHS), and are instead paid for from tax revenues and government borrowing.

The motive for organizing resources to provide the NHS and a number of other public services, is to provide a service to consumers regardless of their ability to pay. The government also provides a number of goods and services which are of benefit to the nation but which the private sector is unwilling to provide, for example, street lighting, sea defences, and environmental protection. Some publicly provided goods and services are also felt to be too dangerous to be controlled by private organizations, such as nuclear power stations, the armed forces, and law and order.

However, for most private-sector organizations the motive for production is **profit.** Business owners who have invested their money in a business enterprise will wish to earn at least as much from their investment as they could have earned if they had placed their money in a risk-free interest-earning bank account. Profit is the reward for taking a risk and investing money in a business. Business organizations will hope to use their limited resources in the most efficient way to minimize costs and maximize profits.

We can measure the **profit margin** on each unit of output as the difference between the price received from the sale of that unit and the amount it cost to produce. In general, a firm will have an incentive to keep raising output to supply a market as long as the product price exceeds cost. However, the ability of a firm to expand output will depend on the availability of productive resources - raw materials, labour, plant and machinery - and its ability to finance the expansion (see 20.4).

What is supply?

Supply refers to the willingness and ability of producers to make goods and services to satisfy consumers wants and needs.

The **market supply** of a given product represents the sum of the individual supplies of all the producers competing to supply that product to consumers. We can plot information on the amount of a product firms wish to supply to a market on a **market supply curve**. In general, the higher the price, the more of a product a firm will wish to supply because they will expect to earn more profit.

Portfolio Activity 5.7 

1. The following table presents information on the quantity of bean bags that all bean bag producers are willing and able to supply at different prices.

   Plot this information as a line graph in an xy graph space with price on the vertical (y) axis and quantity supplied on the horizontal (x) axis. Join up the points and label the resulting curve the **market supply curve** (S_1S_1).

   Alternatively enter the data into a computer spreadsheet to plot the curve.

Possible price per bean bag (£)	Quantity supplied per month
35	18,000
30	16,000
25	13,000
20	10,000
15	6,000
10	1,500

What does the market supply curve look like? Describe the relationship between product price and quantity supplied.

2. Use the market supply curve S_1S_1 to determine how many bean bags would be supplied at a price of
   - £12
   - £28

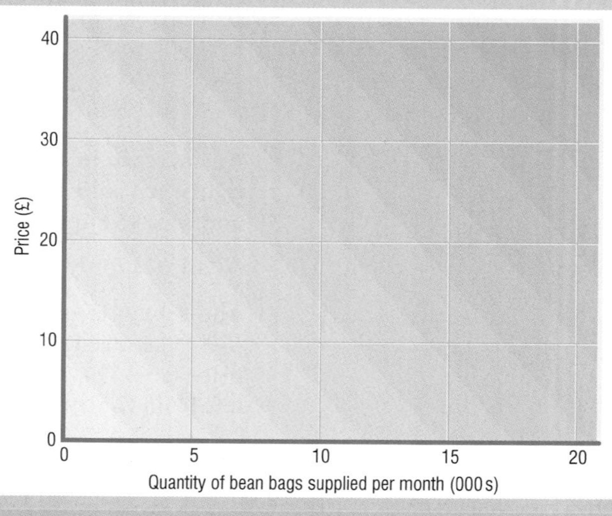

▼ *Figure 5.5: A typical market supply curve*

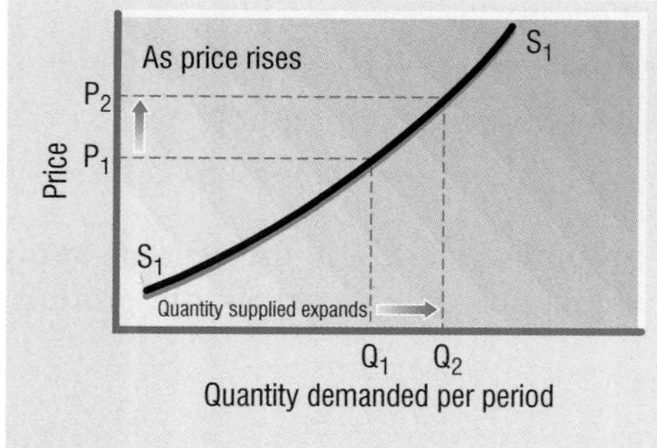

In general, we can observe the following relationships between the quantity supplied of a product and product price (see Figure 5.5):

- As product price rises, the quantity supplied of that product expands
- As product price falls, the quantity supplied of that product contracts

Falling prices will generally be expected to reduce firms' sales revenues and consequently reduce their profit margins over and above production costs.

What causes a supply curve to shift?

A change in the price of a product will normally cause the quantity supplied to expand or contract along a given supply curve. However, changes in factors other than the price of the product can cause the whole supply curve to move.

An increase in supply

The schedule of prices (P) and quantity supplied (Qs) in Figure 5.6 shows that there has been an increase in the supply of disposable razors at all possible prices. The plotted market supply curve S_1S_1 represents the original supply schedule (Qs_1), while S_2S_2 represents the increased level of supply (Qs_2).

▼ *Figure 5.6: An increase in supply*

Price of Razor (pence)	Original monthly supply (Qs_1)	New monthly supply (Qs_2)
50	12 000	15 000
40	11 000	14 000
30	9 000	12 000
20	6 000	9 000
10	2 000	5 000

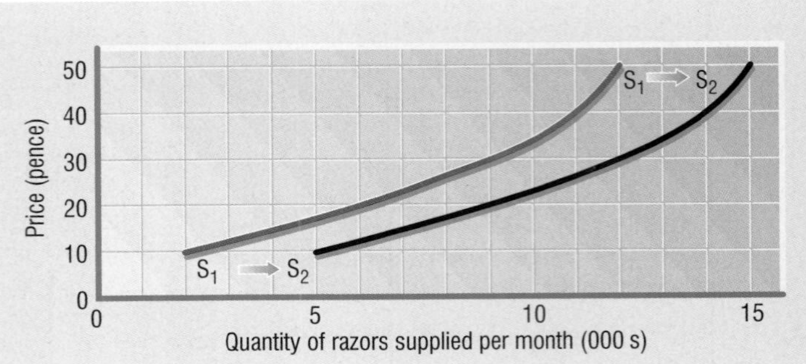

An increase in the supply of a good or service can be represented by a rightward shift in the market supply curve. It shows producers as willing and able to supply more of the product, regardless of price.

A fall in supply

The schedule of prices and quantity supplied in Figure 5.7 shows that there has been a fall in the market supply of potatoes at every possible price from Qs_1 to Qs_3. The market supply curve has shifted inwards to the left from S_1S_1 to S_3S_3.

▼ *Figure 5.7: A fall in supply*

Price of 1lb Potatoes (pence)	Original daily supply (Qs_1)	New daily supply (Qs_3)
100	60 000	40 000
80	50 000	30 000
60	40 000	20 000
40	30 000	10 000
20	20 000	0

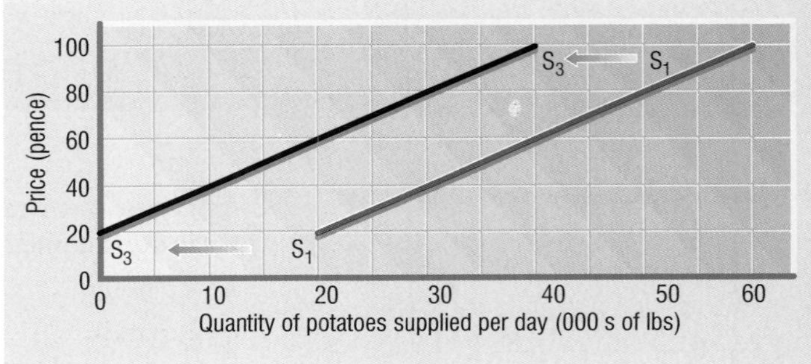

A fall in supply can be represented by an inward shift in the market supply curve. It shows producers as less willing and able to supply the product, whatever the price.

Portfolio Activity 5.8 

1. Look at these news articles and, for each one:
   - Identify the changing factor(s) and the potential impact on the supply of the goods or services in question, or generally.
   - State whether quantity supplied will tend to rise, fall, or remain unchanged as a result of the changing factor.
   - Draw diagrams to show the likely market supply curves before and after each change.

Wine growers to toast climate change

THE south of England could overtake France as a wine-growing region due to the effects of global warming, according to research.

Southern coastal Scotland could also be producing wine within 50 years, if temperatures rise by 2°C as predicted.

Scientists at Oxford University have shown classic red varieties of grape, until now grown in the warmer parts of France and Italy, could become the mainstay of wine production in southern England.

Metro, 23.2.2000

2. Choose a product and investigate the following aspects of supply:
   - Who are the suppliers of your product?
   - What are the characteristics of the product suppliers (i.e. firm size, location, market share, turnover, profit, ownership, etc.)?
   - How do the suppliers compete with each other?
   - Evaluate the supply of the product to consumers in terms of price, range, quality, availability, image.

   Write a short report based on your findings.

   What use could you make of this information if you were considering starting a business to supply the same product?

EU gives farmers a boost by easing pig export ban

BELEAGUERED pig farmers were offered some relief yesterday when the export ban prompted by the out-break of swine fever was scaled down.

The European Commission announced that the general ban on live pigs being exported from England would be lifted.

Daily Mail, 23.9.2000

KEEPING an eye on the shrinking cost of various technologies is also important, say toy manufacturers. Computer chips, for instance, were once formidably expensive, but have now become so cheap that they can be widely used in children's products.

Hasbro has capitalized on low-cost, high-memory chips to produce Talking Barney, a stuffed green dinosaur which says 500 different phrases at random. "Before, six or seven sayings were considered a lot," says Sharon Hartley, vice president of marketing for Playskool, the Hasbro division that makes Talking Barney. "But additional memory has become so cheap now that we've been able to use it in a number of toys."

With the cost of technology diminishing rapidly, toy manufacturers say their products will soon use technologies once thought too expensive even for the adult consumer market.

Financial Times, 21.12.1993

Factors in market supply

The following factors are likely to cause shifts in the market supply curves of goods and services:

1. Changes in the price of other goods

Price changes act as the signals to private-sector firms to move their resources to and from the production of different goods and services (see 5.5). If the prices of pre-recorded video cassettes are falling because demand for them is weak, the potential profit margin between sales revenues and costs will be squeezed and some producers may be attracted to the DVD industry in search of higher profits. This will result in an increased supply of DVD discs. The supply curve for DVDs will shift out to the right as in Figure 5.6.

2. Business optimism and expectations

Fears of an economic downturn may cause some firms to move resources into the production of goods and services they feel will be less affected by falling consumer incomes and demand (see 5.3). For example, high-cost luxury items such as cars and DVD players often fare badly during economic recessions (see 7.1). Conversely, expectations of an economic recovery may result in a re-allocation of scarce resources into new markets, thereby shifting their supply curves out towards the right.

3. Technological advance

Technical progress can mean improvements in the performance of machines, employees, production methods, management control, product quality, etc. This allows more to be produced, often at a lower cost, regardless of the price at which the product is sold. For example, advances in deep-water mining technology and rig design have helped a number of countries to drill for oil in deep oceans once thought too costly to exploit.

4. Global factors

The supply of goods and services can be affected by a variety of factors that cannot be controlled by producers, for example, sudden climatic change, trade sanctions, wars, natural disasters, and political factors. Following the Gulf War in 1990, international restrictions have pre-vented Iraq from selling the oil it produced on the world market. This had the effect of moving the market supply curve of oil in to the left as in Figure 5.7.

5. Business objectives

A firm might seek to increase market share by forcing competitors out of business. This may lead to a fall in market supply.

6. The costs of production

By far the largest determinant of supply is the cost of production, i.e. payments made for raw materials, power supplies, labour, buildings, and machinery.

A fall in the costs of production due, for example, to new technology, will mean that more of a product can be offered at the same price. The profit margin between unit price and unit cost will have increased. The market supply curve will therefore move out to the right. A rise in the cost of production, for example, due to workers winning generous wage rises, or a shortage of raw materials, will have the opposite effect. Market supply will tend to fall at each price.

A firm may actively seek to expand consumer demand for its product in the short run by cutting prices. This will reduce the profit margin between the sales revenues and costs on each item sold. A firm that expands sales will clearly need to raise output in the short run to meet demand. This may initially incur higher costs – paying labour to work overtime, buying in more materials, or more equipment. However, this assumes a firm will be able to finance expansion. Some may be constrained in the amount of money they can raise from retained profits, bank loans or the sale of shares (see 23.3).

By expanding sales and output an organization will hope that in future (the long run) it will be able to reduce the average cost of producing each unit of output, for example, each car, each pair of shoes, or each compact disc. Lower average costs increase potential profit margins between revenues and costs.

Large-scale, or mass, production can reduce the cost per unit of output because there are economies of scale (see 22.4). This is because certain costs incurred by a firm are spread over a larger output. Cost such as rents, rates, lighting and heating, telephone usage and more, are called fixed costs because they have to be paid whatever the size of output produced. For example, consider a firm making cakes. On top of the cost of ingredients and wages, it incurs fixed costs of £1,000 each month regardless of how many cakes it produces. If it makes 1,000 cakes per month the average fixed cost per cake is £1 (i.e. £1,000/1,000). However, doubling output to 2,000 cakes per month reduces the fixed costs per cake to 50 pence and so on.

Large-scale production can also bring cost savings in the form of discounts for buying materials in bulk; lower interest rates on loans from banks, who are happier to lend to well-established large businesses; or even technical economies because the large firm can afford to use new, faster machines and production processes.

Key words:

Profit - an excess of revenues over costs

Profit margin - the difference between the price received from the sale of a unit of output and the cost of producing it

Supply - the willingness of producers to provide goods and services for sale at given prices

Market supply curve - a graphical representation of the relationship between supply and price in a market

Section 5.5

The determination of market prices

Product prices are affected by changes in their market demand and supply. Rising prices are likely to be the result of either a rise in market demand or a fall in the market supply of a product. Falling prices, on the other hand, are the likely result of either a fall in consumer demand for the product, or an increase in supply. The interaction of consumer demand and producer supply will ultimately determine the price at which a good or service is traded.

The **market price** of a product can be found at the point at which the market demand and supply curves intersect. At this price, the amount consumers are willing and able to buy is exactly equal to the amount producers are willing to supply. (In Portfolio Activity 5.9, the market price is determined at 40 pence per chocolate bar. At this price producers will supply 200,000 chocolate bars each week - just enough to satisfy consumer demand).

Portfolio Activity 5.9 

Consider the following market demand and supply schedules for 500-gram milk chocolate bars.

1. Use the table to plot a graph of the market demand and supply curves for chocolate bars.
2. From the table, identify the price at which quantity demanded is equal to quantity supplied. This is known as the **market price**. Label the market price P on your graph.
3. At the market price, producers are willing and able to supply as many chocolate bars as consumers are willing and able to buy. That is, there is an equal quantity traded between producers and consumers. Identify the equilibrium quantity traded in your table and label it Q on your graph.
4. When quantity demanded exceeds quantity supplied there is an **excess demand** in the market. Similarly if quantity supplied outstrips quantity demanded, there is an **excess supply**.

   Using your graph, state whether there is an excess demand or supply at the following prices:

▼ *Figure 5.8: The determination of a market price for chocolate bars*

Possible price of chocolate bar (pence)	Quantity demanded per week (Qd)	Quantity supplied per week (Qs)
70	100,000	420,000
60	120,000	330,000
50	150,000	260,000
40	200,000	200,000

   A 70 pence
   B 50 pence
   C 35 pence
   D 40 pence

5. How do you think firms will alter the price of their chocolate bars if:
   A there is excess demand
   B there is no excess demand or supply?

▼ *Figure 5.9 The determination of market price and quantity traded*

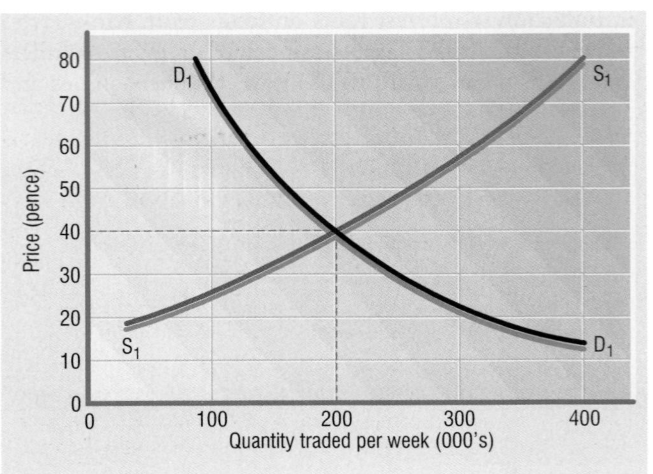

If firms set their prices above the market price - for example, at 80 pence - there will be an **excess supply**. Firms will be producing more chocolate bars than consumers are willing to buy. If consumers are to be persuaded to buy up the excess supply, price will have to fall.

If firms set their prices below the market price, for example at 20 pence, there will be an **excess demand.** There will be pressure on price to rise to 'clear the market'. As the price rises, firms are willing to expand output, while at the same time a rising price causes demand to contract.

The same reasoning applies to any good or service. Only at the market price will consumers' decisions to buy a product match producers' decisions to supply it. There will be no need for price to change unless there is a change in market conditions, i.e. a shift in the market demand or supply curves.

Changes in market price

Four basic movements in the market price for a given product are conceivable if we consider all the possible changes in demand and supply. These are shown in the following diagrams.

▼ *An increase in demand results in more being traded at a higher market price as the quantity supplied expands*

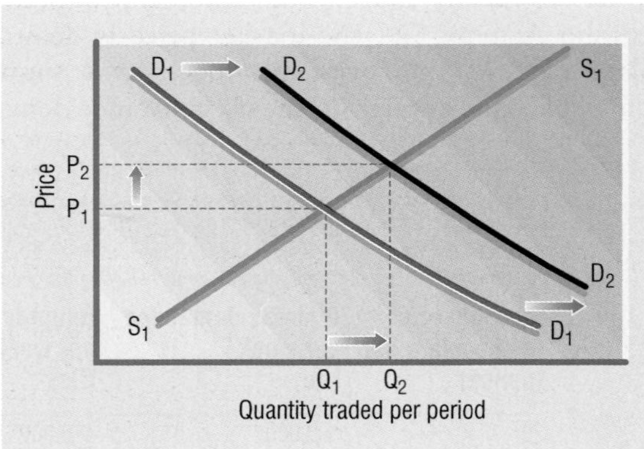

▼ *A fall in demand results in less being traded at a lower market price as the quantity supplied contracts*

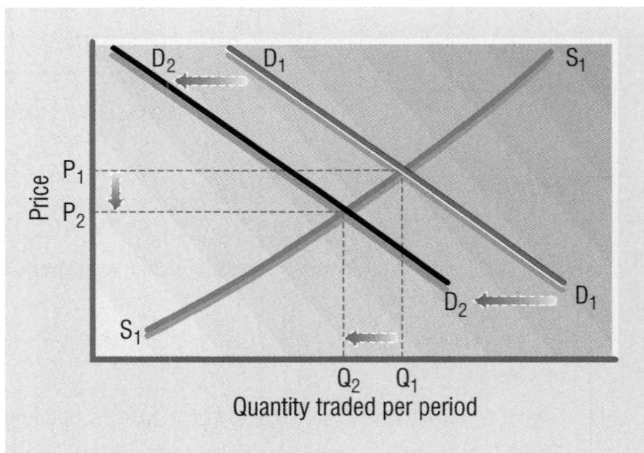

▼ *An increase in supply results in more being traded at a lower market price as quantity demanded expands*

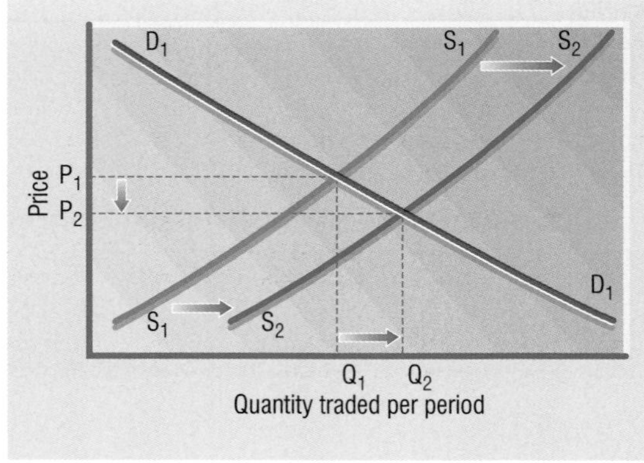

▼ *A fall in supply results in less being traded at a higher market price as quantity demanded contracts*

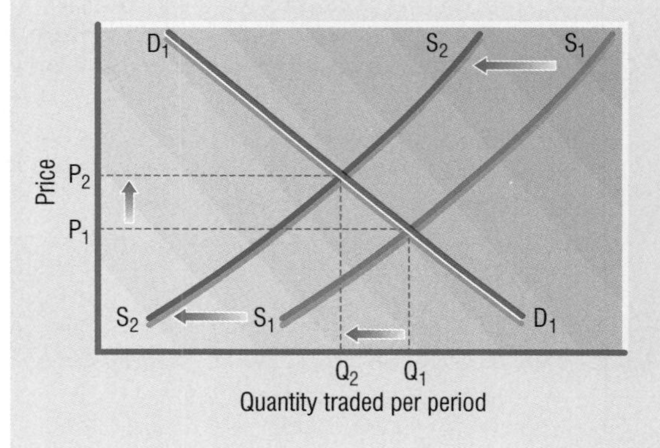

The price mechanism and the allocation of resources

Changes in demand and supply cause changes in the prices and quantity traded of different products. In most economies, changing prices are a signal to producers to increase or decrease the production of different products. For example, a rise in consumer demand for pork will push up the market price and increase the potential for producers to earn higher profits from the sale of the meat. As a result, a number of food producers may be tempted to use more land, labour and capital to breed and keep more pigs. This leaves fewer resources to be used to make products whose prices are lower or falling. The same is true of most products. In this way, consumers get what they want. This is known as the **price mechanism.**

Demand and supply analysis in business

It is important for businesses to be able to analyse the effects of a change in market conditions on price and quantity traded, because of the effect it can have on their revenues, profits, and the allocation of scarce resources. However, the world is always changing, and many shifts in both market demand and supply can occur at any given time. It is difficult to predict the effect on price and quantity traded unless the precise size of the changes in demand and supply are known.

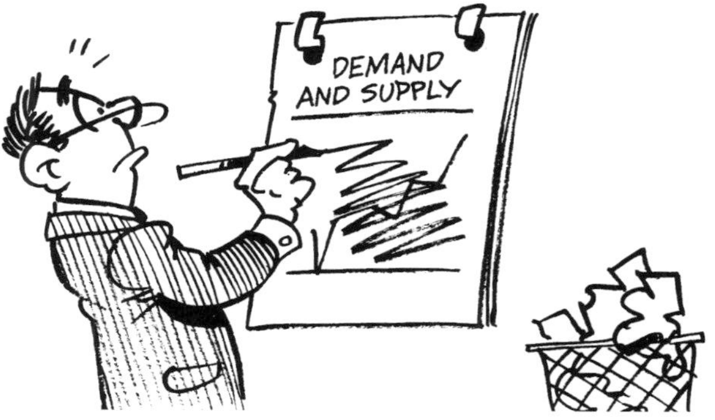

Although drawing demand and supply curves is useful, firms are unlikely to have perfect knowledge of their market demand and supply curves. As a result, they will tend to choose prices for their products which fulfil certain business objectives, for example, pricing to achieve a desired mark-up over cost for profit, or pricing low to increase market share or to force competitors out of business (see 10.2). However, they need to be aware of the forces of demand and supply. As we have discovered, if firms set prices low, there is likely to be excess consumer demand which will cause prices to rise. If prices are set too high, sales will suffer and firms may be left with unsold goods. The only way to sell off surplus stocks will be to lower prices to suit what consumers are willing to pay.

The best any business will be able to do is to examine changes in market conditions as they occur and consider the likely direction of movement in market price and quantity traded. For example, information on the business expansion plans of rival firms could suggest an increasing market supply in the future and downward pressure on prices and profits, thus forcing firms with high costs out of the market. On the demand side, rising interest rates may signal a possible fall in consumer demand for luxury items such as hi-fi, videos and cars, many of which are bought on hire purchase or with the help of loans from banks.

The gathering and analysis of information on market conditions which could affect demand or supply is an important function of business. A business that does not examine or respond to changing market conditions is unlikely to be successful. Large organizations are often able to employ specialist analysts to 'watch the market'. Smaller firms have to rely on the ability and experience of their owners, managers or staff to analyse and interpret changing market conditions.

However, firms are unlikely to alter their prices or output every time there is a change in market conditions. There are high administrative costs involved in changing prices, printing new price lists, relabelling products and communicating the changes to staff. Consumers also tend to dislike rapid price changes. It is hard for them to plan their expenditure if prices are continually going up or down.

Similarly, firms are unlikely to cut production levels, lay off workers and shut down plant every time demand falls. A fall in demand might only be temporary. Only if the slump in demand becomes protracted will firms tend to contract supply. In contrast, a firm is unlikely to invest in new plant and workers to raise output unless it is reasonably sure that high levels of product demand will continue.

Key words:

Market price - the price established in a market for a good or service at the point at which market demand is exactly equal to market supply

Excess demand - when market demand exceeds market supply, usually because price is too low

Excess supply - when market demand is outstripped by market supply, because price is too high

Price mechanism - the influence of changes in market demand and supply, and hence market price, on business decisions to allocate scarce resources to the production of different goods and services

Section 5.6

Elasticity of demand

What is price elasticity of demand?

Producers need to know by how much demand for their products will change, given a change in market price. For example, consider a local bus company that has recently raised its flat rate fare from 70 pence to 90 pence. It discovers that fare revenues collected during peak travel times have increased, but off-peak bus patronage and revenues have fallen. The company concludes that it was unwise to raise off-peak fares. The company made this mistake because it had no knowledge of the price (or fare) elasticity of demand.

Price elasticity of demand measures the responsiveness of quantity demanded to a change in the price of a good or service. Consider two cases:

▼ Figure 5.10

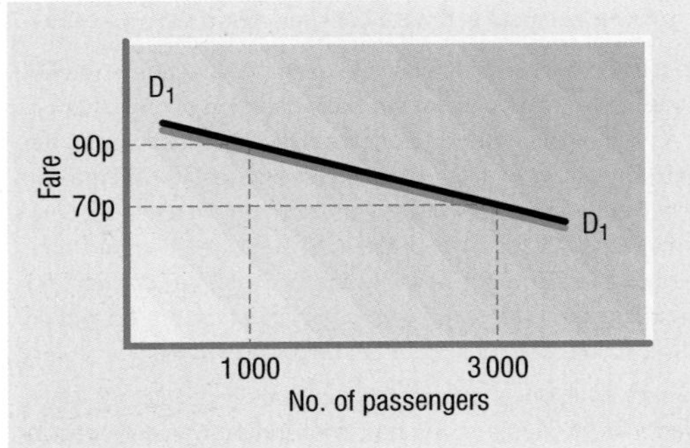

Figure 5.10 represents the market demand curve for off-peak bus trips. It is relatively flat, showing that a small rise in price causes a much larger fall in demand. Here, demand can be said to be relatively **price elastic**. Quantity demanded stretches or changes a lot given relatively small changes in price.

▼ Figure 5.11

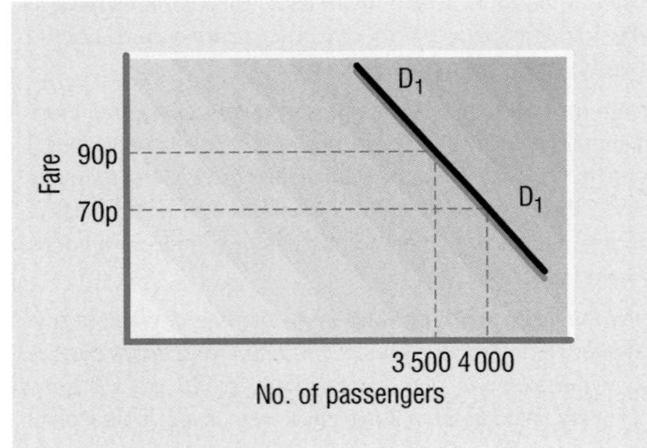

Figure 5.11 could represent the market demand curve of bus passengers who travel during the morning and evening peak, for example, to and from work. It is relatively steep. Even a quite large increase in fares would have only a marginal effect on demand. In this case, demand is said to be **price inelastic**. Quantity demanded contracts or expands very little given small changes in price.

Price elasticity of demand and sales revenues

We can calculate the effect on bus company revenues from the increase in fares from Figures 5.10 and 5.11 as shown in the table below.

Because demand is price inelastic during the peak, raising the flat rate fare has increased revenue. There is only a relatively small reduction in the number of passengers, from 4,000 per weekday to 3,500. However, a significant fall in demand during off-peak hours has caused revenue to fall from £2,100 to just £900. If the bus company wants to encourage increased bus use and raise revenues during the off-peak, it will do best to reduce the off-peak fare, because demand here is price elastic. For example, at an off-peak fare of 50 pence, bus patronage rises to 5,000 passengers and revenues would increase to £2,500 per weekday.

Fare = 70 pence			**Fare = 90 pence**		
No. of passengers per weekday		**Revenue £**	**No. of passengers per weekday**		**Revenue £**
Peak	4,000	£2,800	Peak	3,500	£3,150
Off-peak	3,000	£2,100	Off-peak	1,000	£900
Total	7,000	£4,900	Total	4,500	£4,050

Knowledge of how responsive demand is to price changes will allow a firm to forecast the effect on their revenues of a change in the price of their product. For example, a firm attempting to maximize revenue may actually reduce its product prices if demand for them is highly price elastic. Firms may be able to estimate the price elasticity of demand for their products by looking at past data on price changes and sales revenues, or by using market research to find out how much consumers of a product would buy at different prices.

Measuring price elasticity of demand

The price elasticity of demand for a good or service can be measured in two ways:

- By comparing the percentage change in quantity demanded to the percentage change in price that caused it
- By observing what happens to sales revenues following a change in price

▼ *Figure 5.12: Three cases of price elasticity of demand*

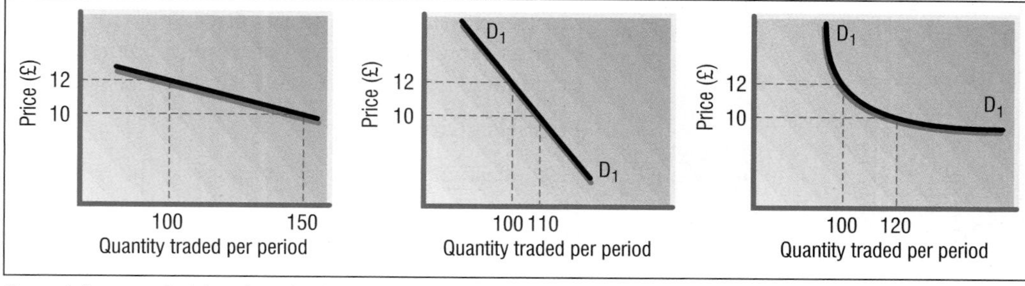

Demand for a product is ***price elastic*** *when:*

- *The market demand curve is relatively flat*
- *The % change in demand is more than the % change in price*
- *A rise in price reduces revenue*
- *A reduction in price increases revenue*

Demand for a product is ***price inelastic*** *when:*

- *The market demand curve is relatively steep*
- *The % change in demand is less than the % change in price*
- *A rise in price raises revenue*
- *A reduction in price reduces revenues*

Demand for a product is of ***unitary elasticity*** *when:*

- *The % change in demand is exactly equal to the % change in price*
- *Revenue remains the same whether the price has been increased or reduced*

Factors which affect price elasticity of demand

1. If the product is a necessity

Basic foodstuffs are necessary for human survival. The demand for products such as bread and flour tends to be relatively price inelastic.

2. How many substitutes a product has

When consumers are able to choose between a large number of substitutes for a particular product, demand for any one of them is likely to be price elastic.

Demand will tend to be price inelastic where there are few substitutes. For example, medicines, petrol, and some foodstuffs, such as milk, have few close alternatives.

Much advertising is aimed at promoting a brand image that suggests the advertised product has few close substitutes, for example, 'Coke, the real thing' (see 8.2).

3. How long a consumer takes to search for alternative products

If the price of a good or service rises, consumers will attempt to search for cheaper substitutes. The longer they have, the more likely they are to find one. Demand for any product is therefore likely to become more elastic in the long run.

▼ *Figure 5.13: Price-elasticity of supply and time Supply is fixed regardless of price at any moment in time*

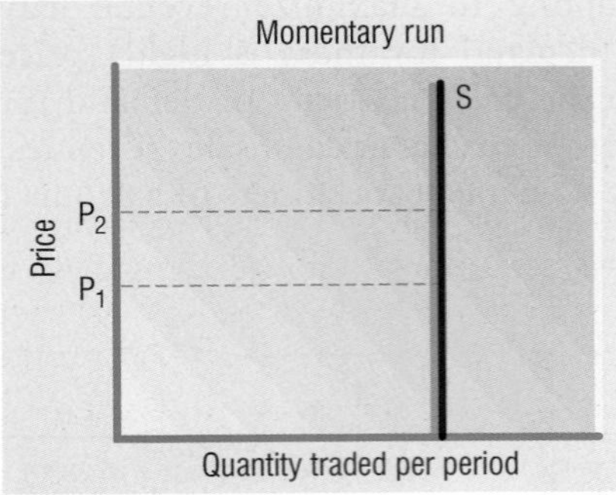

▼ *Supply is price-inelastic in the short run*

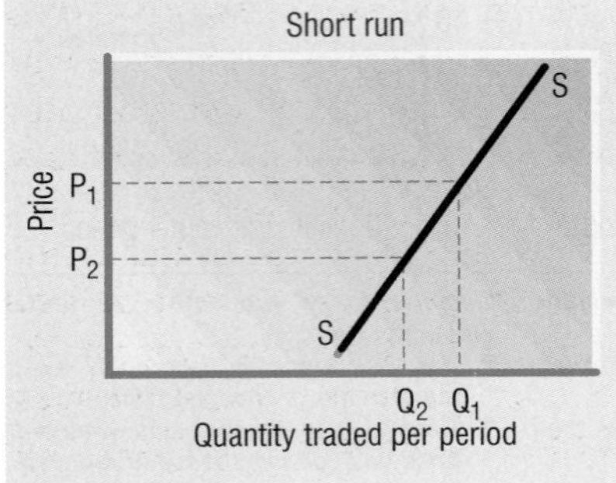

▼ *Supply is price elastic in the long run*

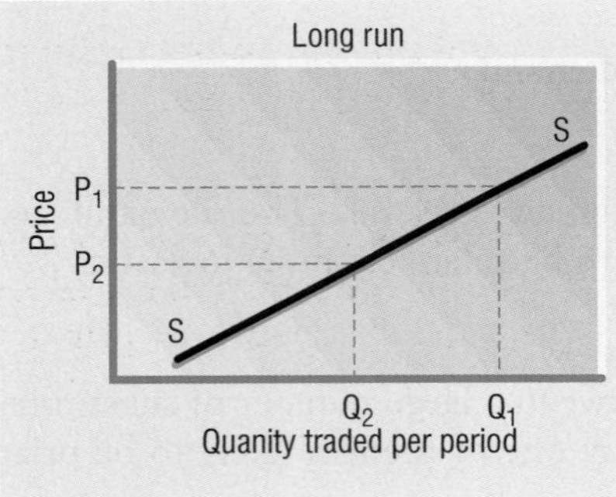

4. The proportion of income spent on a product

Goods and services, like matches, salt, car washes, and newspapers, tend to be price inelastic because they are relatively inexpensive and account for only a small proportion of the average consumer's budget. Any change in their price is therefore likely to have only a minor impact on demand. Demand for these products tends to be price-inelastic.

On the other hand, demand for high-cost, luxury items such as video recorders and cars, tends to be price-elastic. Their purchase will swallow a large proportion of most people's income.

If the percentage change in demand exceeds the percentage change in consumer income that caused it, demand for that product is said to be **income-elastic.** Most luxury goods, like videos and cars tend to be income-elastic. However, if the percentage change in demand is less than the percentage change in income, demand is said to be **income-inelastic.**

Price-elasticity of supply

Price-elasticity of supply measures the responsiveness of supply to a change in price. Supply is said to be **elastic** if a change in price causes a larger proportionate change in quantity supplied of a given product.

What determines price-elasticity of supply?

Time: At any given moment in time, the market supply of a product will be fixed. No more can be supplied whatever the product price. Consider the supply of potted conifer plants for sale at garden centres. If there is a sudden increase in demand, producers will only be able to supply more conifers to the market from their stocks. If they are to increase market supply significantly, producers will need to buy more pots, plant more seeds, and wait for the conifers to grow. Similarly, car manufacturers could not meet a significant increase in demand until they have had time to hire more labour, buy in more materials, and even expand into new premises. In general, supply is more price-elastic in the long run (see Figure 5.13).

Availability of resources: The ability of firms to expand production will depend on some existing resources being unemployed. Failing that, an increase in the supply of natural, artificial, or human resources will be required: for example, an increasing population of working age, the discovery of more oil and mineral deposits, new production methods that can produce more using fewer resources (see 1.4).

Key words:

Price elasticity of demand - the responsiveness of consumer demand to a change in the price of a product

Price elasticity - when demand changes proportionately more than a change in price

Price inelasticity - when demand changes proportionately less than a change in price

Unitary elasticity - when the change in demand is in equal proportion to a change in price

Section 5.7

Trends in industrial sectors

Changes in consumer demand, technologies and methods of production have over time greatly affected the industrial make-up of the UK and many other developed countries. Today, service industries such as banking, retailing and communications, produce over 70% of the total value of UK output and employ over 75% of the UK workforce. This compares with a period around 300 years ago when most people worked in agriculture, and just 100 years ago when most employed people in the UK were engaged in mining and manufacturing activities. For example, in 1947 some 720,000 miners produced 150 million tonnes of coal each year. By 1999, there were fewer than 9,000 people employed in UK coal mining, producing an annual output of 40 million tonnes. This trend decline continues.

What is an industry?

Business activities are often classified by grouping together firms producing the same goods or services into industries. An **industry** consists of all those firms producing the same good or service. For example, the construction industry consists of all those firms engaged in building homes, offices, shops, factories, roads, hospitals, or even small garages or patios. The oil and gas industry consists of firms like Exxon, BP Amoco, and British Gas that extract and sell fossil fuels. The retailing industry consists of firms that operate shops, mail order catalogues, home shopping channels on TV, and outlets through which consumers can buy products. One of the most important developments in retailing in recent years has been the introduction and growth of e-commerce, or shopping via the Internet.

Industrial sectors

Because there are so many different types of industry it is often useful to divide them up into three broad industrial sectors, or groupings.

The primary sector

The primary sector consists of firms which produce natural resources by growing plants, like wheat and barley, digging for minerals like coal or copper, or breeding animals. Primary firms are grouped into **primary industries**.

Primary industries
Farming
Fishing
Mining
Quarrying
Oil and gas extraction
Forestry
Water supply

Primary means these industries are the first stage in most production chains, as many of the raw materials grown or dug out of the ground are used to produce something else. Primary industries are sometimes called **extractive industries**, because they extract natural resources from the Earth.

The secondary sector

Secondary firms use natural resources provided by primary industries to make other goods. For example, a dairy will take milk provided by a farm and turn it into cheese and yoghurt. Iron ore is turned into iron and steel. Oil is refined into petrol and other fuels, and is also used in paints and plastics. Oil, coal, and gas are used to produce electricity.

Using raw materials to make other goods is known as **manufacturing**. Firms involved in manufacturing, and those engaged in construction, are known as **secondary industries**.

Some secondary industries
Aerospace
Clothing
Vehicles
Steel
Electricity
Computers
Processed foods
Furniture
Construction
Metal goods
Food products

The tertiary sector (or service sector)

A great many firms do not produce physical products but provide services instead. Firms in the service sector are grouped together as **tertiary industries.**

It is usual to divide tertiary activities into two groups:

- Firms that produce **personal services**, such as doctors, hairdressers, window cleaners, tailors, teachers, and gardeners.
- Firms that produce **commercial services** for other business organizations, such as selling goods in their shops, transporting them, business banking, finance and insurance, advertising services, and communications.

Some tertiary industries
Education
Banking
Insurance
Wholesaling
Retailing (Shops etc)
Public Administration
Leisure
Health
Distribution
Advertising
Transport
Communications

Because retailing - selling goods and services to final consumers - is such an important commercial service on which other firms rely, people often make the mistake of thinking that tertiary industries provide the final link in the chain of production for most goods and services. In fact, retailing is only one of many tertiary industries. Without a great many other commercial services like banking and insurance, transport or advertising, many primary, secondary, and other tertiary firms would find it very difficult to produce anything at all.

Developments in industrial sectors

Significant changes have taken place in the industrial make-up of the UK over time. We can examine these changes in terms of the number of people employed and the amount of output from each of the major industrial sectors.

The decline of the primary sector

Many years ago, most people in the UK relied on farming and other primary industries, such as coal and tin mining, for jobs and incomes. Today, the picture is very different.

During the Industrial Revolution in the UK, which is thought to have started in 1760, millions of workers left farming and mining to get jobs in the new factories producing textiles and clothing, rolling stock for the new railways, ships, and industrial machinery.

The new manufacturing industries consumed large amounts of raw materials such as coal for power, iron and steel, wood, and rubber. An increasing amount of these raw materials were imported from cheap sources overseas.

Because an increasing number of people no longer worked the land to provide their own supply of food, there was an increase in the demand for food from workers employed in factories. Despite the falling number of farm workers, new farming technology and cheap food imports from

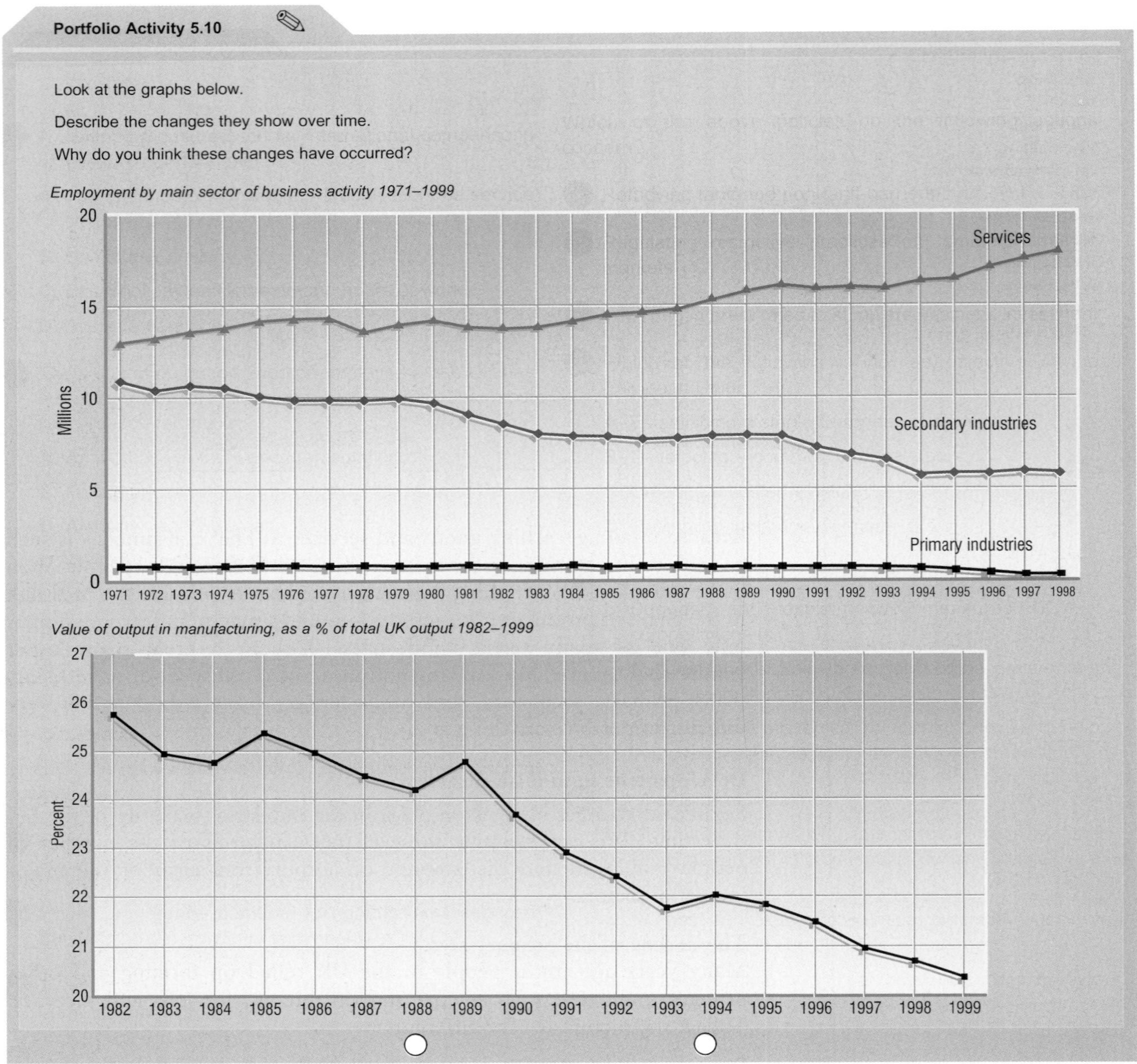

overseas ensured that an ever-increasing supply of food could be provided for the growing number of manufacturing workers in towns and cities.

Portfolio Activity 5.10
Look at the graphs below.
Describe the changes they show over time.
Why do you think these changes have occurred?
Employment by main sector of business activity 1971–1999
Millions
Services
Secondary industries
Primary industries
Value of output in manufacturing, as a % of total UK output 1982–1999
Percent

By 1999 primary industries employed around 500,000 workers - just 2% of all workers in the UK. This compares with 3.8% of workers employed in primary industries in 1971.

The value of goods and services from the primary sector has grown over time, but has fallen as a proportion of the total value of output from all industries in the UK . This is because the output of secondary and tertiary industries has increased faster than output from primary industries. In 1971 primary sector output accounted for just 4% of the value of total UK output. This share had fallen slightly by 1999.

▼ *Declining*

▼ *Growing*

The decline of manufacturing

Despite the strong growth in UK manufacturing employment and output during the eighteenth and nineteenth centuries, this industrial sector is now in decline. Many jobs have been lost from manufacturing industries and their contribution to the total UK output of goods and services has fallen.

Between 1971 and 1999, almost 4 million jobs were lost from manufacturing industries in the UK. Over the same period the proportion of the total value of UK output provided by these industries fell, from 41% in 1971 to around 20% in 1999. This has been termed **deindustrialization.**

Additionally, the UK share in the output of manufactured goods from all over the world has fallen, and the UK now spends more on foreign manufactured goods (imports) than it earns from selling its own manufactured goods to foreign countries (exports). Before 1983 the UK had always sold more manufactured goods overseas than it imported each year.

A number of reasons have been suggested for the decline of manufacturing industry in the UK and many other developed countries:

- The biggest decline in manufacturing has been in old industries such as textiles, iron and steel production, shipbuilding and railway locomotives. These have been replaced by new manufacturing industries making new products with new technologies.
- Increasing competition from business organizations overseas, many in newly industrialized countries, such as Japan and, more recently, China, Malaysia and Taiwan, where wages and, therefore, product prices tend to be cheaper.
- A number of UK firms have closed down and moved their operations to newly industrialized countries because wages there are lower.
- As people have become wealthier they have been spending more on personal services such as banking, property and car insurance, financial and legal advice, leisure activities and improved communications. As a result the service sector has grown rapidly.
- More recently, manufacturers have blamed the high value of the UK pound against other currencies. This means overseas countries have to spend more pounds on UK exports of manufactured goods. UK exports have become more expensive to buy and so demand for them has fallen.

▼ *The decline of employment in 'old' manufacturing industries*

Employee jobs, United Kingdom, 1948–98

						thousands
	1948	1958	1968	1978	1988	1998
Coal mining	794	782	482	295	118	16
Ports and docks	156	156	136	66	36	25
Railways	572	495	293	250	155	89
Steel production	268	306	329	271	99	48
Shipbuilding	245	215	156	147	58	20
Agriculture	784	577	385	372	316	312
Motor vehicle manufacture	280	316	475	474	108	101
Textile manufacture	993	931	737	488	228	180
Column totals	4,092	3,778	2,993	2,363	1,118	791

Labour Market Trends, July 2000

▼ *Hi-tech manufacturing*

However, some manufacturing activities in the UK have been growing: hi-tech electronics equipment, chemicals, petroleum products, and aerospace. Output, jobs and exports have been increasing for many business organizations in these industries. These are relatively new manufacturing industries, all using the latest technologies, lots of hi-tech equipment and requiring highly skilled manufacturing workers. They have taken over from old labour-intensive engineering industries as the pace of technological innovation and change has increased, sweeping away products and manufacturing processes of the past and introducing new products and new ways of making them.

The growth of services

With the rapid growth in the incomes and wealth of many workers in the UK over the last 70 years, many people have been taking more leisure time and have used more of their money to spend on consumer services. Many millions of people now work in shops, offices, transport, communications, financial services, and other tertiary sector jobs.

Between 1971 and 1981, services like banking and insurance created a total of 1.8 million jobs. By 1981, around 61% of all employees in the UK were employed in the service sector.

Between 1981 and 1999, services had created almost 4 million jobs. By 1999, some 18 million people were employed by the service sector around 75% of all UK employees. The service sector now produces around 70% of the total value of UK output, up from 55% in 1971.

Some of the most significant trends in services in recent years have occurred in the sectors below.

- Growth in consumer spending has led to a rapid expansion in retailing. In 1988 UK consumers spent £300 billion on goods and services and just over 3 million people were employed in retailing. By 1999 total consumer spending had risen to £540 billion and the number employed in retailing was over 4 million. One of the biggest developments in retailing in recent years has been the growth of e-commerce, or shopping over the Internet.
- Around £45 billion was spent on having meals out and accommodation in 1998 compared with £14.5 billion in 1985. Employment in hotels

Portfolio Activity 5.11 

1. Below is a jumbled group of reasons for the rapid increase in the importance of the tertiary sector in the UK and other developed countries. Match up each reason for growth with its possible effect on the service sector in the economy.

Reasons for growth

- Rise in consumers' incomes, allowing them to spend more on luxury goods, e.g. TVs, videos, cars
- Increase in peoples' savings as incomes have risen
- Increase in number of tourists, as people can afford to travel more
- Increase in number of people wanting to own their own home
- Reduction in the number of hours many people work each week (the average working week of full-time employees in the UK in 1999 was 38.2 hours)

Impacts on service sector

- More solicitors, building societies, estate agents, and insurance services
- Increase in demand for leisure activities and leisure centres
- Increase in number of large shops and shopping centres
- More holiday shops, restaurants, and hotels
- Increase in banking and financial services

2. What evidence is there of growth in the service sector in your local town? Conduct a local business survey using business telephone directories, and from your own observations. Your local authority, Chamber of Commerce, and Business Link office may also provide useful information.

and restuarants also increased, from just over 1 million employees in 1985 to 1.32 million in 1998.

- Spending on recreational and cultural services increased from £9 billion in 1985 to over £20 billion in 1998. Employment in businesses providing these services grew from 490,000 employees to 535,000 over the same period.
- Although the National Health Service provides free and subsidized health care, spending on private health care and insurance has increased significantly in recent years. In 1998 spending on private health care and insurance was £3.3 billion, up by 350% on 1985. Around 1.5 million people are employed in health services in the UK. This includes many nurses and doctors as well as people employed in the administration of health services and providers of health insurance.
- UK household expenditure on financial services was £30 billion in 1998 compared with £14 billion in 1985. The financial services sector of the UK includes banks, credit card companies, building societies and insurance companies. Together, these sectors employed just under 1.1 million people in 1998, up from 750,000 employees in 1985.

Rising incomes mean more people want to save more, and also want to borrow more to buy houses, cars, luxury holidays and other goods. In 1998 loans made by UK banks summed to over £2,000 billion, compared with £589 billion in 1985 and just £167 billion twenty years earlier. Increased wealth has also increased demand for insurance, and increasing foreign travel has boosted the demand for foreign exchange services. Credit and debit card use has also risen significantly. Over 3.7 billion individual purchases were made with a credit or debit card in 1997 compared with just over 400 million in 1985.

Today, many banks are offering 'home banking' services for customers over the Internet. As home banking increases, banks will be able to shut some high street branches and save on costs of staff and premises.

Key words:

Industrial sector - a group of industries undertaking broadly similar business activities, such as manufacturing or the provision of service industries

Primary sector - industries which produce natural resources

Secondary sector - industries which use natural resources to produce other goods, including the construction of buildings, roads and other infrastructures

Manufacturing - using natural and man-made materials to produce semi-finished and finished goods

Tertiary sector - industries which provide services, such a retailing and communications

Deindustrialization - the decline of manufacturing activity in terms of its share of total employment and output

Useful references

Moynihan, D. and Titley, B. '**Intermediate Business**' 2nd edn (Oxford, 2000) Chapter 5

On-line help on how markets work is available from The Biz/ed net at *bized.ac.uk*. Type in key words **competition** and **markets**.

Test your knowledge

1. There is an increase in the demand for oranges. This could be explained by:

   A An increase in imports of oranges

   B A fall in the price of apples

   C A successful advertising campaign for oranges

   D Poor weather reducing the supply of oranges

2. Which of the following would cause a movement along the market demand curve for gloves?

   A A rise in consumer income

   B A fall in the price of gloves

   C Severe weather conditions

   D A change in consumer tastes in knitwear

3. In order for a consumer's demand for a new car to be effective, that consumer must have:

   A A want for the car

   B A need for a car

   C An available supply of cars

   D An ability to pay for the car

4. The market demand for bread is very price inelastic. This could be explained by the fact that bread:

   A Is a basic necessity

   B Has many competing products

   C Accounts for a large proportion of household expenditure

   D Is poorly advertised

5. The graph shows two demand curves for compact disc players in a local hi-fi shop:

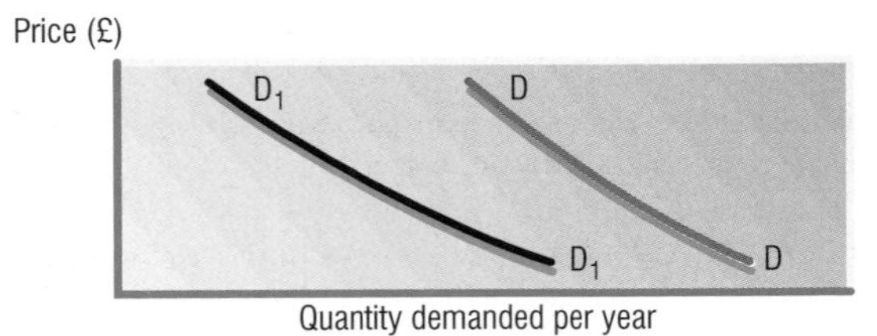

   Which factor will have caused the movement from DD to D_1D_1?

   A A fall in the price of vinyl LPs

   B An increase in the rate of income tax

   C A fall in the price of compact discs

   D A fall in the supply of laser components for disc players

6. BT has cut charges for phone calls made during off-peak periods. Revenues have increased as a result. It concludes that off-peak demand for phone calls is:

   A Price inelastic

   B Price elastic

   C Unrelated to price

   D Of unitary elasticity

7. The graph below shows a change in the market supply of microwave ovens.

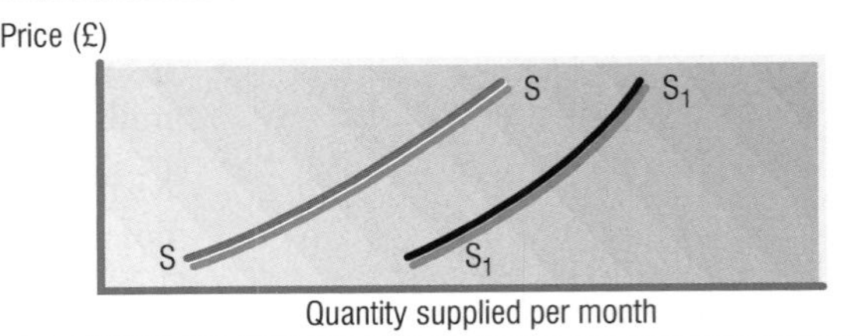

   The shift in the supply curve from SS to S_1S_1 may have been caused by:

   A A rise in the price of gas ovens

   B A fall in production costs

   C An increase in demand for microwave ovens

   D A rise in the market price of microwaves

8. The ability of a producer to supply a good at a given price will be affected by:

   A A change in consumer income

   B A change in the amount of imported goods

   C A change in production technology

   D A change in the price of the good

9. A firm that supplies 100% of a market is known as:

   A An oligopoly

   B A sole trader

   C A pure monopoly

   D A duopoly

10 Which of the following is NOT a feature of an oligopolistic market:

A A small number of firms supply the market

B Heavy advertising of products

C Strong product brand images

D Price wars

11 The most likely explanation for the decision by a business owner to turn his sweetshop into a video film rental shop instead is:

A Consumer demand for video film rental is falling

B Consumer demand for confectionery is rising

C Consumer demand for video film rental is rising

D Consumer demand for all goods and services is falling

12 Increasing competition in a market is likely to:

A Raise market price and the quantity sold

B Lower market price and the quantity sold

C Raise market price and lower the quantity sold

D Lower market price and raise the quantity sold

13 Firms will compete to achieve all the following objectives except:

A Increased market share

B Higher sales revenues

C Product superiority

D Lower market prices

14 **a** Suggest two reasons why firms compete to supply a market with a good or service.

b What is the difference between price competition and non-price competition? Explain your answer using examples.

c What is 'monopoly'?

d Other than price, suggest two ways in which a monopoly can restrict new competition to supply a product.

15 You work for a new company that is about to launch a new mobile phone network. In preparation you will need to provide answers to the following questions:

a What factors are likely to affect the demand for mobile phones?

b What is the likely relationship between consumer demand for mobile phone services and the price per minute of each call?

c What impact will your organization have on the supply of mobile phone services?

d What will determine the market price for mobile phone services and how many calls are made?

e What will happen to market price if there is a fall in demand for mobile phone services?

16 'Potato prices rocket after crop failure'

a Consider the headline above and explain, using appropriate diagrams, why the price of potatoes increased.

b What is 'effective demand'? Why is it important to firms selling to make a profit?

c What will be the likely impact on the market price for potatoes if there is a corresponding rise in demand for them?

17 Explain, the likely impact on the market price of butter and the quantity sold of each of the following events:

A Income tax is raised by 2%

B The price of milk used to make butter rises

C The price of margarine increases

D A successful advertising campaign declaring 'butter is best'

E The cost of equipment used to make butter falls

chapter 6 Government Policy and Business

This chapter examines why and how the government intervenes in markets and government policies affect how businesses operate.

What you need to learn

Business activity and competition can have both positive and negative effects, on consumers, employees, other businesses, the environment, and the general health of the economy. You need to understand **why and how governments intervene in markets** to influence business activities.

You need to know about **Competition Policy** and the functions of the UK and European Union **Competition Commissions**, and the ways in which UK and EU governments act to protect consumers and the environment.

Government plays a key role in managing the economy and market conditions. You need to understand the effects on business of government policies to control the economy and how business can be affected by:

- **public expenditures**
- **taxation**
- **subsidies and grants**
- **interest rates**
- **exchange rates**
- **laws and regulations**
- **privatization**

Section 6.1

Government intervention in markets

Market failure

What is wrong with the market?

In Chapter 5 we learnt how the allocation of resources to different markets is determined by the individual decisions of producers and consumers. Producers will increase their output of goods and services in response to effective consumer demand. A rise in demand forces up market price, providing firms with a profit incentive to extend supply. In this way, freely working markets:

▼ Market failure?

- Respond quickly to consumer wants
- Produce a wide variety of goods and services to meet diverse consumer wants
- Encourage the use of new and more efficient methods of production in order to maximize profits for business owners.

However, the market system may not always produce an outcome that is beneficial to all. For example:

- Resources will be employed only if it is profitable to do so.
- Large and powerful monopolies may develop.
- The market may fail to provide certain goods and services such as street lighting, law and order, and defence if private firms find it difficult to charge a price for these to individual consumers based on the amount they have consumed.
- The free market may encourage the consumption of harmful goods. For example, producers may be willing to supply dangerous drugs to consumers who are willing and able to pay for them if there are no legal constraints to prevent them doing so.
- Private firms and consumers may ignore the damaging social and environmental effects of their production and consumption decisions.
- The system allocates more goods and services to those consumers with the most money. The needs of the poor can often be ignored.

In many countries, therefore, governments intervene in markets in an attempt to correct some of the ways in which it fails to produce a satisfactory outcome, either in terms of the market price of the product or the quantity traded.

Why do governments intervene in markets?

The governments of the UK and the European Union (EU) have a great deal of power to intervene in product markets (see also 7.3). The reasons why successive governments have used this power are:

1. To regulate prices set by private firms with a significant command over the market supply of a product who may use this power to restrict supply and force up market price.
2. To increase or regulate the amount of competition for supply in markets dominated by a one or a handful of large firms.
3. To counteract anti-competitive activities, such as price fixing rings.

Portfolio Activity 6.1 

The articles below describe intervention by the UK government in a number of product markets.

UK yards win share of £1.25bn MoD order

The Ministry of Defence yesterday ordered ships from yards in Scotland, Northern Ireland and north-east England.

Geoff Hoon, defence secretary, said the UK portion of the £1.25bn order would secure 2,000 shipbuilding jobs and create 1,000 new ones.

UK industry and trade unions, however, were disappointed that four of the ferries, to be operated under a £950m private finance initiative contract by Andrew Weir Shipping, will be German built.

Navy ships are built in Britain, but as the ferries are commercial, the MoD insisted it was bound by European Union procurement rules.

Financial Times, 7.10.2000

Consumer boom raises pressure on interest rates

People are spending more of their income than at any time since the boom years of the late 1980s, according to figures published yesterday. The news re-ignited fears that interest rates may need to rise further to choke inflation.

The savings ratio is at its lowest level since the autumn of 1988, when Britain's last big spending bonanza triggered a disastrous surge in inflation that tipped the economy into recession.

Financial Times, 30.6.2000

Cheers – cough up

The price of a pack of 20 cigarettes rose 11p last night as The Chancellor of the Exchequer continued government policy of trying to cut the number of smokers by increasing tobacco duty above the rate of inflation.

Daily Telegraph, 1.12.1993

Oftel calls on BT to cut charges for customers

BT could be forced to introduce annual price cuts for all its customers, industry watchdog Oftel said yesterday.

The company is required to reduce yearly charges by 4.5 per cent for the 80 per cent of BT residential users who make the fewest calls. But after a 12-month review of BT's prices, Oftel found the company could extend the cuts to ensure greater competition in the sector. It suggested a range of options from an extension of the existing arrangement to an overhaul of the pricing system. It said: 'Oftel considers that for many customers there is little choice of provider and for lower residential users little competition for calls. This suggests that some form of regulation to restrain BT's retail prices will be required.' BT welcomed Oftel's proposals but said it believed the sector was more competitive than the watchdog had made out.

Metro, 7.3.2000

COWBOY builders face a Government crackdown to protect householders from shoddy work and conmen.

Under a new scheme, properly-trained and qualified traders will carry an official Government-approved identity badge.

The move follows thousands of complaints to ministers and consumer groups about builders, plumbers and other craftsmen who botch jobs or charge too much.

Sunday Mirror, 5.11.2000

'Tax rise by 2003' fear for Labour

MINISTERS last night admitted the chances of post-election tax cuts were slim.

They may even have to order tax HIKES to fund a £68billion spree on schools, hospitals and transport.

Deputy Chancellor Andrew Smith confirmed a Labour Government will be forced to borrow in 2003 to pay for its spending commitments.

The Sun, 31.10.2000

1. What impact will each of the measures described above have?
2. Explain each of the measures used by the government.
3. For each market, suggest why the government has intevened.
4. Consider the price elasticity of demand for cigarettes. Suggest whether or not the actions taken by government will have the desired effect on consumption. What will be the effect on tax revenues? Explain your answers.
5. Gather information from newspapers and other sources on various measures taken by government to influence prices in different markets. In each case record why the action was taken and the mechanism used to influence price, and explain whether or not you consider the action will be successful.

4. To protect consumers from misleading marketing and unscrupulous trading practices.
5. To encourage the consumption of a product by keeping prices low, or discourage consumption by keeping prices high. For example, the price of petrol is kept high to conserve a valuable natural resource, but also to discourage car use to reduce harmful exhaust emissions.

   In contrast, much health care is provided free of charge at the point of use to encourage people to seek help and advice. For example, if vaccinations against harmful communicable diseases were charged for, fewer people would want them and the disease could spread.
6. To raise the incomes of some producers in order to encourage them to continue to supply their product. For example, farmers' incomes have often been protected because if they go out of business a valuable domestic source of food supply is lost.
7. To stabilize prices in markets susceptible to dramatic changes in the conditions of supply and therefore price. For example, unforeseen weather conditions can cause large variations in agricultural harvests. Resulting price changes can discourage both consumption and production.
8. To protect environmental and social interests, such as public health and moral concerns, such as the exploitation of child labour.
9. To protect employment and employee rights.
10. To provide goods and services that benefit people and the economy but which private sector firms would be unwilling to supply because their production would be unprofitable – either because people cannot afford to pay a price for them above costs or because it would be difficult to charge individual consumers according to how much they benefit from them. Examples include: street lighting, roads, defence, police and a legal system, sea defences, the Thames flood barrier, etc.

How do governments intervene in markets?

The UK Government can use a number of measures to intervene in markets to influence price and the quantity traded, either directly or indirectly by influencing consumer demand or producer supply.

- **Macro-economic policy.** This refers to measures that attempt to influence the performance of the entire economy in terms of the rate of general price inflation, unemployment, growth in total output, and the balance of overseas trade. The overall level of taxation, public expenditure, and interest rates are policy variables which can be used to effect changes in all markets (see 6.2).
- **Micro-economic policy.** This refers to policies that are directed at individual product markets. For example, specific taxes like those on cigarettes, and subsidies to areas of high unemployment (see 6.3).
- **Legislation and regulation.** Governments can pass laws which regulate business activities. There are a variety of laws to restrict anti-competitive behaviour and regulate the environmental impact of business operations (see 6.4).

The government has also set up a number of 'watchdogs' which set standards of service and regulate price increases in certain industries. For example, the Office of Water Services (OFWAT) regulates the privatized water supply companies (see 12.5).

- **Public ownership and privatization.** In the past, one way to regulate industries that had significant market power or to protect jobs in firms that were in danger of closing was to take them into public ownership. That is, the government would take over the ownership and control of these organizations. However, since 1979 government administrations in the UK have returned many public sector activities to the private sector under a programme of privatization (see 6.5).

The following sections consider these measures in more detail.

Section **6.2**

Macro-economic policy

Government policies to control the economy

What is macro-economics?

Macro-economics is the study of how an economy works as a whole, including the overall level of income and prices, total employment and unemployment, the base rate of interest, total savings and investment, the rate of growth in total output, the balance of overseas trade, and the currency exchange rate.

Government macro-economic objectives

Like most governments in the developed world, the UK government has four main macro-economic objectives. These are:

- To achieve low and stable inflation in the general level of prices (see 7.2)
- To increase employment
- To encourage economic growth, i.e. growth in total output
- To secure a favourable balance of payments (i.e. between inflows from inward investment and payments for UK exports, and outflows from UK investment overseas and payments of imports - see 7.1)

It is assumed that if the government can meet these objectives it will create an economic climate which is favourable to business. For example, it is argued that high inflation destroys business confidence and jobs. Business will find it difficult to plan ahead if the costs of their materials and equipment are rising quickly.

When prices rise quickly, consumers cannot afford to buy so many goods and services and so demand falls. People may also save more to protect the value of their savings which are worth less as inflation rises. In addition, if the UK rate of price inflation is higher than other countries, UK goods become less competitively priced and overseas demand for UK exports will fall.

▼ Aggregate demand

▲ Consumer spending

▲ Investment

▲ Public expenditure

▲ Exports

As firms experience a fall in demand, they cut back production and shed resources, including labour. Unemployment will therefore tend to rise.

Controlling aggregate demand

Central to the success of macro-economic policy is the control of the level of **aggregate demand** in the economy.

Aggregate demand refers to the demand of all consumers of UK goods and services in the very widest sense. That is, consumption of goods and services by the public, investment in new plant and machinery by firms, expenditure on goods and services by the Government, and spending on UK exports by other countries.

Rising aggregate demand is normally characteristic of **economic recovery** and **boom** (see 7.1). Most business organizations experience rising sales and order books. To fulfil orders and meet demand, firms may create employment opportunities and invest in expanding their capacity to produce. However, if firms are unable to keep pace with rising demand, stocks will fall and firms will tend to increase their prices. During an economic boom, when total demand outstrips the supply of all goods and services, prices will tend to rise rapidly. Rising prices will eventually choke off demand and, if incomes fail to keep pace with prices, demand will start to fall.

Falling aggregate demand is characteristic of **economic recession** or **slump**. Trading conditions become difficult as demand for goods and services falls and firms experience rising stocks and falling orders. Prices are likely to fall as supply exceeds demand – or at least rise less fast. If recession continues, firms will cut back production. Investment in new research and development and machinery will also suffer as long-term plans are cut back. Unemployment tends to rise and growth in the productive capacity of the economy will falter.

The Government is able to influence the level of aggregate demand for goods and services and, therefore, business trading conditions and employment opportunities, by using a number of **policy instruments**. These are:

- The general level of taxation
- The general level of public sector expenditure
- The base rate of interest

These policy instruments are used because:

- the amount consumers have to spend on goods and services depends on their level of personal **disposable income**, i.e. income after the deduction of tax
- as the interest rate rises, firms tend to reduce their investment in new capital goods, such as machinery
- total public expenditure accounts for around 39% of total demand in the UK

- as interest rates fall, the value of the pound in terms of foreign currencies tends to fall, reducing the price of UK goods and services sold abroad.

Fiscal policy

Using taxation and public expenditure to influence the level of aggregate demand in the economy is known as **fiscal policy**.

Fiscal policy involves changing the level of public spending and/or taxation to influence the level of aggregate demand. In 2000–01 the total managed expenditure of UK government was £372 billion compared with tax and other receipts of £380 million – around 39% of the total national income of the UK economy (see Figure 2.2). Changes in public spending and taxation can, therefore, have a big impact on the economy.

- During times of economic recession when trading conditions tend to be poor and unemployment relatively high, the government can give the economy a **fiscal boost** by cutting taxes and/or increasing public expenditure. Increasing capital expenditure, for example, on the construction of new roads and hospitals, will create employment opportunities for firms and people in the construction industry. As the number of people employed increases, the level of expenditure on goods and services will tend to rise.
- During times of high inflation when high demand may be forcing up prices, the Government can increase taxes and/or reduce public spending. The same actions will not only affect the demand for UK goods but will also reduce the demand for goods and services imported from abroad if the balance of overseas trade is unfavourable (see 7.2).

There are two main types of tax the UK Government can charge:

- **Direct taxes** (collected by the Inland Revenue) are levied directly on the incomes of people and firms, and include income tax, corporation tax, capital gains tax and inheritance tax (see Table 6.1). Raising income tax will reduce people's disposable incomes and reduce the level of aggregate demand in the economy. Conversely, cutting corporation tax on business profits will raise the amount firms are able to re-invest in new plant and machinery or pay in dividends to shareholders. In 2000 the UK had one of the lowest rates of corporation tax among the major industrialized countries, and the lowest starting rate of corporation tax (10%) for small and medium sized enterprises (SMEs) in the European Union.

▼ *Table 6.1: Public sector receipts*

	£ BILLION	
	Outturn	**Projections**
	1990–00	**2000–01**
Inland Revenue		
Income tax (gross of tax credits)	95.9	103.8
Corporation tax (gross of tax credits)	34.2	32.2
Tax credits	–3.0	–4.9
Petroleum revenue tax	0.9	2.0
Capital gains tax	2.1	3.0
Inheritance tax	2.0	2.3
Stamp duties	6.9	8.3
Total Inland Revenue taxes (net of tax credits)	**139.0**	**146.7**
Customs and Excise		
Value added tax	56.4	59.2
Fuel duties	22.5	23.2
Tobacco duties	5.7	7.4
Spirits duties	1.8	1.8
Wine duties	1.7	1.7
Beer and cider duties	3.0	3.0
Betting and gaming duties	1.5	1.5
Air passenger duty	0.9	1.0
Insurance premium tax	1.4	1.7
Landfill tax	0.4	0.5
Customs duties and levies	2.0	2.1
Total Customs and Excise	**97.3**	**103.0**
Vehicle excise duties	4.8	4.9
Oil royalties	0.4	0.6
Business rates	15.3	17.0
Social security contributions	56.4	59.8
Council tax	13.0	13.9
Other taxes and royalties	8.3	8.8
Total taxes and royalty receipts	**334.6**	**354.7**
Accrual adjustments on taxes	4.3	2.9
less VAT and own resources contribution to EU budget	–5.7	–6.6
less PC corporation tax payments	–0.4	–0.4
Tax credits	3.0	4.9
Interest and dividends	3.4	5.2
Other receipts	17.9	19.6
Current receipts	**357.1**	**380.3**
Memo:		
North Sea revenues	2.6	5.3

Treasury 'Pre-Budget Report', November 2000

- **Indirect taxes** (collected by the Customs and Excise Department) are levied on goods and services, and therefore only have an indirect effect on incomes via spending. The main indirect tax in the UK is Value-Added Tax (VAT). Indirect taxes also include customs duties on the price of some imported goods and excise duties on such items as cigarettes, alcohol, and petrol. Licences for motor vehicles and televisions are also forms of indirect tax.

Raising indirect taxes will at first add to price inflation in the economy because they are added either as a percentage, or as a lump sum, to the price of goods and services. However, as prices rise, people will find they are

What is the Budget?

Each year (usually in March) the Chancellor of the Exchequer presents the government plans for public spending and revenues for the next 12 months to Parliament. This is known as the **budget**.

The government uses the budget to announce new taxes, abolish old taxes, or revise tax rates. Increases or cuts in spending on different activities, for example, defence, transport, the health service, are also announced in the budget.

If a central government plans to spend more than it expects to raise in tax revenues, there will be a **budget deficit**. In contrast, a central government that budgets for a surplus expects to raise more in tax receipts than it plans to spend.

Total public sector revenue also includes taxes raised by local authorities, interest on loans made by Government, and dividends on shares held by public sector organizations. These amounts are relatively small compared with receipts from income and other taxes. Total public sector spending also includes spending by local authorities and public corporations.

If total public sector spending exceeds total receipts in any one year, the public sector must borrow the difference by selling interest bearing bonds to the private sector. The amount the public sector needs to borrow is called **public sector net borrowing**.

In 2000–01 the UK budget was in surplus by around £17 billion so the Central Government was able to repay some of the **public sector net debt** - the total stock of borrowing by the public sector (around £315 billion in 2000–01). A repayment of debt is indicated by net borrowing being negative (see Figure 6.1).

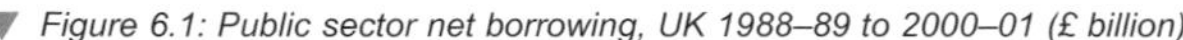

Figure 6.1: Public sector net borrowing, UK 1988–89 to 2000–01 (£ billion)

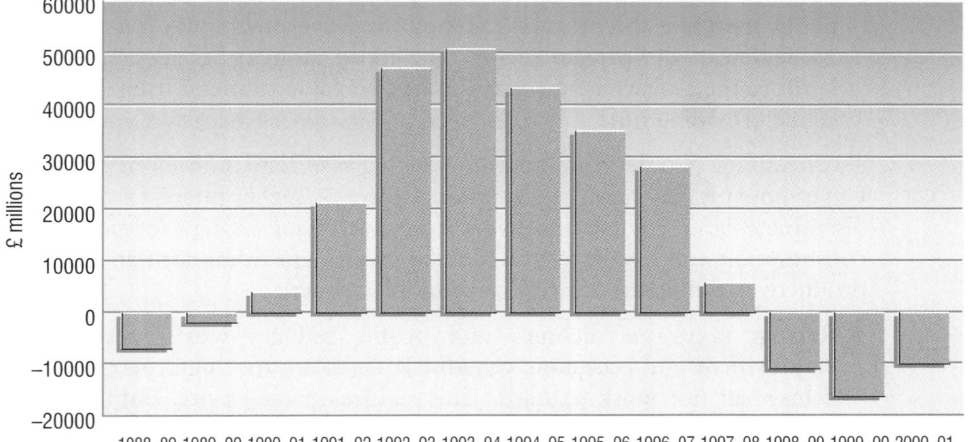

HM Treasury

unable to buy as much with their incomes and so demand for many goods and services will fall. Cutting indirect taxes will have the opposite effect.

Indirect taxes can also be used selectively to influence the demand and supply of individual goods and services as part of micro-economic policy in the UK (see 6.3).

Employees' National Insurance Contributions (NICs) are not strictly a tax although they are levied as a percentage of earned income in much the same way as income tax. Thus, by raising or lowering NICs the government can affect the level of disposable income and, therefore, consumer demand for goods and services.

Problems with fiscal policy

Using fiscal policy to contract aggregate demand during inflationary booms and to expand demand during economic recessions has been called **stop-go policy.**

It is a policy that many economists have criticized. They have argued 'stop-go' fiscal policy has not worked in the past. Instead inflation and unemployment got much worse in many countries. For example, in the UK during the 1970s and 1980s when the rate of price inflation climbed as high as 25% over a 12-month period and more than 3 million people became unemployed. This is because:

- **Fiscal policy is cumbersome to use:** It is difficult for a government to know precisely when and by how much to expand public spending or cut taxes in a recession, or cut spending and raise taxes during a boom.

Boosting aggregate demand by increasing public spending and/or cutting taxes may cause an economy to 'overheat'. That is, demand may rise too much and too quickly. If the amount of goods and services to buy does not rise as quickly as demand, there will be demand-pull inflation. On the other hand, the Government may cut spending and raise taxes by too much following a period of high inflation causing unemployment to rise.

- **Public spending crowds out private spending:** To finance an increase in public spending and/or cut in taxation the Government may borrow the money from the private sector. The more money the private sector lends to the Government the less it has available to spend itself. This is called **crowding out.**

To encourage people, firms and the banking system to lend money to the Government it may raise interest rates. However, higher interest rates may discourage other people and firms from borrowing money to spend on consumption and investment. Reducing investment in modern and more productive equipment can reduce economic growth.

- **Raising taxes on incomes and profits reduces work incentives, employment and economic growth:** If taxes are too high, people and firms may not work as hard. This reduces productivity, output and profits. As productivity falls firms' costs increase and they are less able to compete on product price and quality against more efficient firms overseas. As a result demand for their goods and services will fall and unemployment will rise.

- **Expansionary fiscal policy increases expectations of inflation:** As a result, people will push for higher wages to protect them from higher prices in the future. Rising wages increases production costs and reduces the demand for labour. This in turn causes a cost-push inflation and rising unemployment.

▼ *Figure 6.2: General Government expenditure as a percentage of Gross Domestic Product*

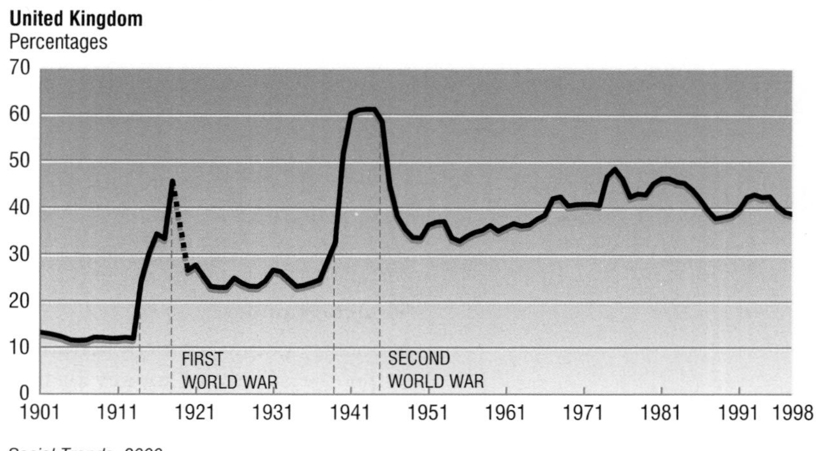

Social Trends, 2000

Fiscal rules

In recent years, successive UK governments have accepted the above arguments and no longer use fiscal policy to try to boost aggregate demand in recessions and cut demand in booms. Instead, they have adopted a number of fiscal rules which govern public spending and borrowing. These are:

- current and capital expenditures are managed and controlled separately. This is so that the costs and benefits of long-term capital investments, for example in new roads, hospitals and school buildings, can be easily identified
- the Government should only borrow money to pay for public investments and not to fund current spending on public sector wages and consumables, such as stationery
- public sector debt as a proportion of GDP should be kept at a low and stable level, so that debt interest payments do not become a burden.

These fiscal rules help to keep public spending and borrowing under control so that interest rates and taxes can be lowered. Lowering taxes on profits and incomes can give firms and people more incentive to work harder and raise output. Lowering interest rates can reduce the cost of borrowing for firms and people. Many firms will often borrow the money they need to invest in new technologically advanced equipment to help improve their competitiveness (see 7.2).

Portfolio Activity 6.2 

Working in groups:

1. Gather information on the most recent budget from newspapers such as the *Financial Times* and *The Independent*, business magazines, bank reports, and budget statements available from the Treasury.
2. Examine the information carefully and identify the key budget changes and how they might affect business activity either directly or indirectly through their impact on the macro-economy.
3. Working on your own, pick a number of key changes to analyse the effects in some detail and produce a word-processed report summary.
4. The report should also record the reaction of business owners and managers you are in contact with. Arrange to phone or visit them when they have some spare time and ask them how they feel the budget changes will affect their business. How do their reactions compare with your own thoughts?
5. Discuss your findings within the group. To what extent do you feel the Government should intervene in business and economic activity?

Monetary policy

Monetary policy refers to actions taken by a government to try to control either the supply of money in the economy or the price of money. The price of money is the interest rate in the economy – what it costs to borrow money or the reward for saving or lending money. The base rate is the main interest rate in the economy and is the key instrument of monetary policy (see Figure 6.3).

'Tightening' monetary policy involves raising the base rate of interest to make borrowing money more expensive, and saving money more attractive. As a result, the demand for goods and services will tend to fall. Firms will also tend to borrow less to invest in new plant and machinery.

It follows that reducing interest rates can boost demand in the economy during economic recessions.

Monetary policy and overseas trade

Interest rates in the UK can also affect the price of goods we buy and sell overseas by influencing the value of the UK currency sterling on the foreign exchange market (see 5.1).

An increase in interest rates relative to those offered in other countries will increase the demand for interest-bearing deposits in the UK. People overseas will wish to increase the amount of money they keep in UK banks and other financial institutions. However, to do this they must buy UK pounds sterling with their own currencies. As with any other good, as the demand for pounds increases, so does their price in terms of other currencies.

As the value of the pound rises, exports of UK goods and services sold overseas become more expensive and demand for them is likely to fall. However, the price of imports the UK buys from overseas will also fall, thereby reducing **imported inflation**. The level of UK imports of raw materials for use in UK industry is significant. Falling import prices can reduce production costs which can be passed on to UK consumers in lower prices.

▼ *Figure 6.3: The Bank of England base rate of interest, 1969–1999*

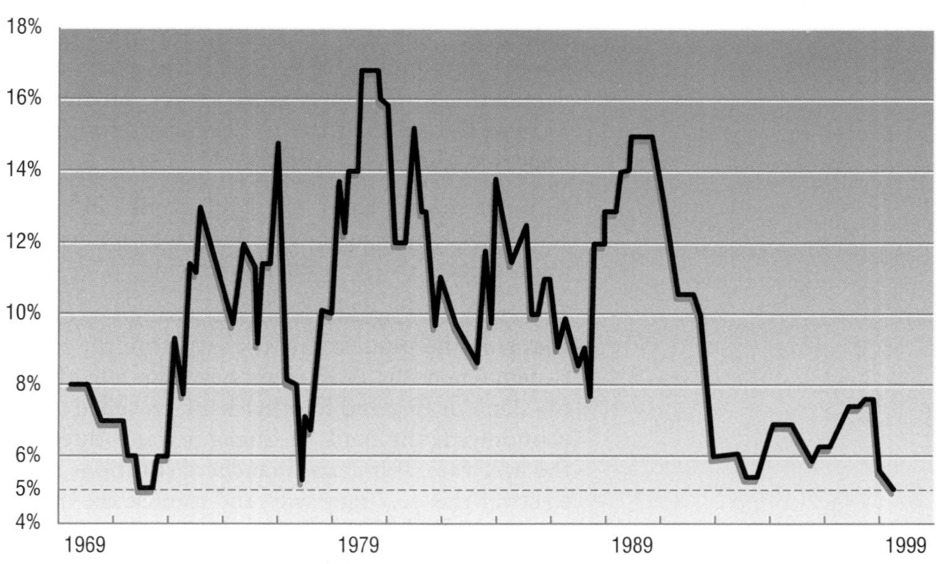

Economic Trends

When there is downward pressure on the pound, imports will tend to become more expensive. In a bid to reduce the inflationary impact of a fall in the value of the pound, interest rates will often be raised.

It follows that reducing interest rates can help reduce the value of the UK pound and the prices of UK exports overseas. This may create an increase in the demand for our exports and result in export-led growth in the UK economy.

The role of a central bank

A central bank in an economy is the bank of a government, and it will help support its fiscal and monetary policies. It is responsible for looking after tax and other revenues received by the Government, managing payments for public spending, and holding gold and foreign currency reserves. A central bank will also oversee the operation of the banking system and will make loans to high street and other banks in the economy.

The Bank of England is the central bank in the UK. In 1997 it was given independence by the new UK Government to set the level of interest rates required to meet the Government's inflation target of no more than a 2.5% increase in the general level of prices each year. That is, the Bank of England has to decide when, and by how much, to raise or lower interest rates in the economy in order to keep price inflation low and stable. It does this with the help of a **Monetary Policy Committee** (MPC). The Governor of the Bank of England is head of the MPC.

Controlling interest rates

The MPC is a panel of economists who meet each month to help the Bank of England make its decision on interest rates using up-to-date information and forecasts of movements in the general price level, wages, real output, exchange rates, and other economic variables.

If the information and forecasts suggest price inflation could rise, the MPC will tend to raise interest rates. Raising interest rates will tend to reduce the demand for borrowing from consumers and firms. If they borrow less money, they will have less money to spend and aggregate demand will fall or rise more slowly. Higher interest rates will also tend to raise the value of the UK exchange rate and hold down the prices of imported goods and services.

If, on the other hand, the MPC thinks inflation is likely to fall and the economy is in danger of sinking into an economic recession, it may cut interest rates to encourage borrowing.

The Bank of England is able to change interest rates in the economy by changing the interest rate it charges on the loans it makes to the banking system when it is short of money. The rate of interest charged on loans by the Bank of England to other banks is called the **base rate** of interest in the economy. If the Bank of England wants interest rates to rise, it will raise the base rate. If it costs financial institutions more to borrow money, then to cover this cost they will tend to raise the interest rates they charge their customers for loans. In this way an increase in the base rate causes a general rise in interest rates throughout the economy.

If the Bank of England wants to reduce interest rates, it will lower the base rate on loans to the banking system. As the cost of borrowing from the Bank of England falls, financial institutions can lower their interest rates.

Portfolio Activity 6.3 

Interest rate held as growth picks up

Interest rates were put on hold yesterday amid signs that seven cuts in the cost of borrowing since October 1998 have fuelled a boom in the housing market in the south and a resumption of economic growth.

With sterling showing signs of weakness against the dollar on the foreign exchanges, threatening to increase import prices, the Bank of England's monetary policy committee voted to leave its base lending rate at 5%.

The City believes that having succeeded in stimulating activity the MPC will eventually switch its attention to heading off a rise in inflation, which it is charged by the government with keeping at 2.5%.

But most economists say it is premature to conclude that the next move in borrowing costs will be up. Despite rapidly rising house prices in London and the south-east, prices overall remain relatively subdued. The latest Halifax house price index shows prices rising nationally at an annual rate of 6.6%, compared with a peak of more than 30% in the late 1980s.

Moreover, sterling's persistent strength against the euro - which cuts import prices and restrains export sales to Britain's largest market - and weakening wage growth suggest that borrowing costs may have further to fall.

The Guardian, 9.7.1999

1. What is the role of the Monetary Policy Committee in the UK?
2. Describe what has happened to interest rates in the UK since the MPC was formed, and why the MPC made these decisions.
3. How is the Bank of England able to change interest rates in the UK economy?
4. Explain how the high value of sterling against the euro 'cuts import prices and restrains export sales' from the UK.
5. What impact is an increase in interest rates likely to have on businesses? (Hint: think about the likely impact it will have on consumer demand, business investment, demand for exports and the prices of imported materials.)

Key words:

Macro-economic policy – government actions designed to influence the whole economy

Aggregate demand – the total amount of demand for goods and services in an economy by consumers, firms and governments at home and overseas

Economic recession – a period of falling aggregate demand, rising unemployment, and falling output

Economic recovery – a period of rising aggregate demand, output and prices, and falling unemployment

Disposable income – income left to spend or save after taxes on income and National Insurance Contributions have been deducted

Policy instruments – levers which can be used by government to influence macro-economic variables such as price inflation and unemployment

Fiscal policy – using taxation and public expenditure to influence the level of aggregate demand

Fiscal boost – lowering taxes and/or raising public spending to raise aggregate demand and generate business and employment opportunities

Direct taxes – taxes levied on incomes, such as corporation tax on company profits

Indirect taxes – taxes raised from expenditure, such as VAT

The Budget – the government's annual plans for levels of taxation and public expenditure

Budget deficit – when the government plans to spend more than it expects to raise from taxes in a given year

Public Sector Net Borrowing – the amount the government must borrow in a year to cover a shortfall of government revenues below public expenditure

Public Sector Debt – the total amount of outstanding government borrowing

Monetary policy – the use of interest rates to influence the level of aggregate demand in the economy and the foreign exchange rate

Foreign exchange rate – the value of one currency in terms of another, for example £1 = US$1.5

Imported inflation - price inflation caused by rising imports prices due to a falling exchange rate

Bank of England - the central bank of the UK

Base rate - the Bank of England's interest rate

Monetary Policy Committee (MPC) - a panel of experts who meet each month to advise the Bank of England on whether or not UK economic conditions require a change in the base rate of interest

Section 6.3 Micro-economic policy

What is micro-economics?

The study of **micro-economics** focuses on how individual markets work and not how the whole economy works. Thus, it considers how prices are determined by the forces of demand and supply in particular markets.

Micro-economic policy instruments

Unlike macro-economic policy instruments, which are intended to affect the overall level of income, prices, and employment in the economy, micro-economic policy instruments are targeted at particular markets in an attempt to influence the market price and quantity traded.

A number of policy instruments are available:

- Setting price ceilings and floors
- The selective use of indirect taxes
- The selective use of tariffs and quotas on imports
- The selective use of public expenditure

Price floors and ceilings

Governments can impose a fixed price in a given market (see Figures 6.4 and 6.5). For example, during the Second World War the prices of many goods in short supply were kept artificially low in the UK. If the prices of

▼ *Figure 6.4: A maximum price*

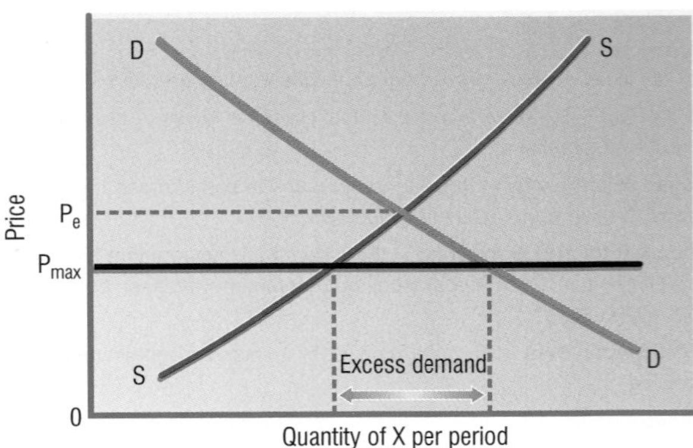

Price ceilings
If a maximum price (P_{max}) is fixed below the free market price (P_e) it will result in an excess of demand. 'Black markets' supplying goods at higher prices to those who can afford to pay may develop.

▼ *Figure 6.5: A minimum price*

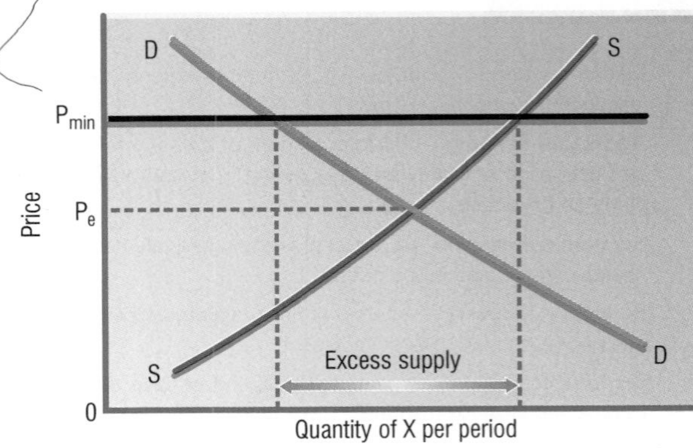

Price floors
A minimum price floor (P_{min}) imposed above the free market price (P_e) will cause an excess of supply over demand.

▼ *Figure 6.6: The effect of VAT on supply*

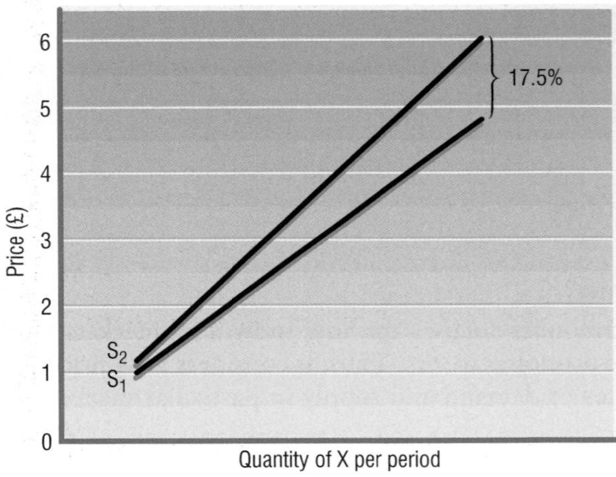

▼ *Figure 6.7: The effect of a 50p excise duty on supply*

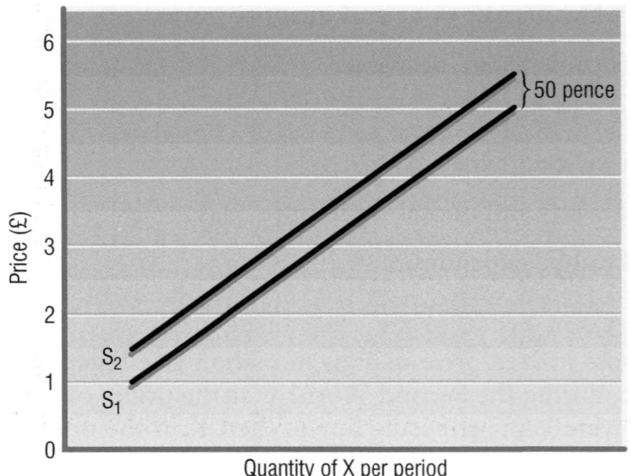

goods, such as eggs and meat, had been allowed to find their free market price, the shortage of supply would have pushed their price beyond the reach of most people. At various other times, UK governments have imposed ceilings on rents in the rented accommodation market. These controls were not always sccessful. Price floors have often been used in agricultural markets to protect farm incomes (see also CAP, 7.3). Cheap imported food and advances in technology mean that most consumers in developed countries can buy their food at a lower cost from foreign producers than from domestic farmers. This has, in part, led to falling wages and employment in agriculture in developed countries during the last fifty years.

However, the use of price floors in agricultural markets has often encouraged over-production and surplus produce must be withdrawn from the market if prices are to be kept high.

More recently, the UK Government has introduced minimum wage legislation, placing a floor below which the wages of workers cannot fall (see 15.2). Business representatives argued that minimum wages being set too high would increase costs and could reduce the demand for labour.

Indirect taxes

Indirect taxes, namely VAT and Customs and Excise duties, can be used to influence the price and quantity traded of selected goods and services. **Value-Added Tax** (VAT) is an **ad valorem tax**. This means the tax is levied as a percentage of the price of a commodity. VAT, currently set at 17.5% in the UK, is levied on most goods and services.

Apart from raising revenue, indirect taxes are often used to discourage over-consumption of tobacco, alcohol, and petroleum products.

A tax additional to the price of a product can be regarded as a cost and will therefore shift the supply curve upwards by the amount of the tax.

Sharing the burden of tax between consumers and producers

Imposing a tax on a product does not necessarily mean that the price of that product will be raised by the full amount of the tax.

This is because producers might reduce their own prices so that the after-tax price does not discourage consumers from buying their products. Clearly, in this way the tax is a cost to producers because it will reduce their sales revenues and profits.

Portfolio Activity 6.4 

1. These three articles illustrate how VAT can be used selectively to achieve different government objectives in different markets. Explain what these objectives might be in each case and why the EU and UK governments might want to achieve them.
2. In each case, suggest what will be the likely impact of the VAT measures on consumers, businesses and employees.
3. The article 'New VAT squeeze on juices' suggests that the price of one litre of juice 'will rise by the full 17.5% VAT from £1.95 to £2.30'. Explain why some producers may be unwilling to pass on the full amount of the tax to consumers.
4. Investigate indirect taxes on goods and services. What products are exempt from VAT, and why? To what products are customs and excise duties applied, and why? What changes were made to these taxes in the last budget and why? What are the effects of these taxes on consumers and business?

New VAT squeeze on juices

A TAX on healthy fresh fruit drinks is to be imposed next month.

The new VAT squeeze caused uproar last night as the Government rushed it through the Commons in 90 minutes.

A litre of orange juice will go up from £1.95 to £2.30 in supermarkets.

Industry sources grimly predicted a fall in sales, threatening 2,000 jobs – most in South Wales and Northamptonshire.

Labour slated the $17\frac{1}{2}$ per cent tax as "wicked".

But the Treasury claims it is fair to treat fresh fruit juices the same as other drinks.

Tory MP Sir Teddy Taylor called the move "a disgrace".

He said: "This means that VAT has been introduced on to a fresh food without Parliament having had the opportunity to debate it."

Daily Mirror, 4.11.1993

Brussels in push for VAT on internet sales

The European Commission is expected to adopt a proposal this week making life far more difficult for US companies hoping to make sales over the internet in Europe.

The measure would eliminate a tax loophole which has made it possible for merchants based outside the EU to avoid levying Value Added Tax on their products.

'Obviously the US will have a problem with this as American companies will be taxed despite having no physical presence [in the EU].', said Robert van Brederode, president of KPMG-European VAT & Customs Services.

Currently US companies can sell items such as software, music, information and other electronic services to buyers in Europe without having to account for VAT on any sale.

The Commission wants to bring the sale of these virtual goods into line with that of tangible items such as CDs and books for which suppliers are required to register for VAT in the EU.

While the Commission hopes the move will level the playing field between US and European businesses, though, it may still leave companies based outside the EU with some advantages.

Under the rules, non-EU suppliers could register in one single EU state and charge VAT according the rules of that state.

This would allow a company to register in a state with low cost jurisdiction, thus retaining a competitive advantage.

For instance, at 15 per cent, Luxembourg, has one of the lowest VAT rates, while Denmark's represents one of the highest rates at 25 per cent.

Financial Times, 5.6.2000

From April 2000, the rate of VAT on installations of certain energy saving materials in all homes was reduced from 17.5 per cent to 5 per cent. The energy saving materials that qualify for the reduced rate when installed in homes by contractor are:

- insulation for walls, ceilings, roofs, lofts, water tanks, pipes and other plumbing features;
- draught stripping for windows and doors;
- central heating system controls, including thermostatic radiator valves;
- hot water system controls; and
- solar panels.

From HM Treasury 'Pre-Budget Report', November 2000

Tariffs and quotas

Tariffs are taxes placed on the price of selected goods and services imported from overseas in order to discourage their consumption and hence reduce a balance of payments deficit (i.e. when outflows of money from the UK, in payment for imports and investments overseas, exceed inflows of money from abroad). A **quota** is a physical limit on the amount of goods that can be imported from overseas.

The European Union is committed to removing these barriers to free trade between member countries but imposes a common tariff on all goods imported to EU member countries from non-EU countries (see 7.3).

Subsidies

Subsidies are grants of money or tax allowances provided by the government to selected organizations to protect production and jobs and, in some cases, to keep prices low.

Loss-making activities: Subsidies are often paid to loss-making activities. For example, a number of franchised passenger rail service operators are paid an annual subsidy to keep trains running on loss-making lines. If these subsidies were not paid, either fares would have to rise or the lines would be closed.

Protection of infant industries: New firms and industries often find it difficult to start up and compete with well-established, larger foreign competitors. It is sometimes thought that these industries should be protected from competition from cheap foreign imports. Governments may subsidize infant firms to lower their costs of production in the hope that they will eventually grow strong enough to be able to compete. However, many industrial subsidies are now outlawed by World Trade Organization rules on foreign trade (see 7.3). Subsidies used to lower costs of domestic firms give them an unfair advantage over rival overseas firms who may be more efficient.

Regional policy: The Government provides aid to business organizations in those parts of the UK designated as **Assisted Areas** in an attempt to regenerate employment, incomes, and demand in areas of industrial decline. Grants for new capital and plant are available to firms that are able to demonstrate that their productive activities help to create new jobs, or safeguard existing ones (see 23.3). The availability of regional grants may influence the location decisions of new firms.

The EU is also able to offer **structural funds** to contribute towards the cost of actions to deal with structural economic disparities within the EU (see 23.3).

Environmental protection: Subsidies might also be used to encourage more environmentally friendly activities, for example, by subsidizing the construction of recycling facilities and plants. Similarly, selective taxation can discourage activities that harm the environment. Taxes on petrol were raised by at least 5% above inflation each year during the 1990s to reduce the demand for petrol and thereby reduce harmful pollutants from car use. Since March 2001 motorists have paid an annual vehicle excise duty linked to the level of carbon dioxide emissions from new vehicles and the type of fuel used. The more a car or van pollutes, the more the duty payable. Similarly, the landfill tax is designed to encourage firms to recycle more of their waste rather than simply dumping it at landfill sites.

Key words:

Price ceiling – a maximum price imposed in a market above which market price will not be allowed to rise

Price floor – a minimum price imposed in a market below which market price will not be allowed to fall

VAT – Value Added Tax levied on most goods and services

Ad valorem tax – a tax levied as a percentage of the market price of a good or service, such as VAT

Subsidies – grants of money paid to certain firms to cover their production costs in part.

Regional policy – UK and EU measures to promote business and employment opportunities in areas of industrial decline and high unemployment

Section **6.4**

Legislation and regulation

A number of laws exist in the UK to protect consumers from unfair and anti-competitive trading and to safeguard the environment from abuse by business.

Competition policy

Underpinning government **competition policy** is a view that anti-competitive and restrictive behaviour by firms in dominant market positions is against consumers' interests. Much legislation and government action to increase the degree of competition in markets has, therefore, aimed to outlaw restrictive practices and mergers that are thought to be against the public interest (see 12.5).

Merger activity refers to all forms of amalgamation between firms. Amalgamation occurs when two or more firms join together to form a larger enterprise. There are two main ways business amalgamation can take place: takeover or merger.

Takeovers

A takeover occurs when one company buys control of another through the **acquisition** of shares in the ownership of that company.

Takeovers can be **hostile** or **friendly**. A hostile takeover occurs when managers and shareholders in a company resist another firm's bid for ownership. This will normally require the predator company to raise additional funds to purchase ownership. A friendly takeover occurs when one firm invites or allows another to take control. This may be because the firm cannot raise the necessary finance to expand or is struggling to survive in a competitive market.

Mergers

A merger occurs when two or more firms agree to join together to form a new enterprise with a new legal identity. This is usually done by shareholders of the merging companies exchanging their existing shares for new shares in the new organization. The name of the newly created enterprise will normally reflect the names of the merging companies, for example, PriceWaterhouseCoopers formed from the merger of the well-known global management consultants Price Waterhouse and Coopers and Lybrand.

Reasons for merger activity

The main reason for amalgamation between two or more organizations is to expand market share and increase market power. Other reasons for mergers may include:

- **To enter a new market.** For example, in early 2000 UK brewer Scottish and Newcastle bought the Kronenbourg Brewing Group in a deal worth £1.8 billion. The take-over elevates S&N to the top brewer by turnover in the UK and France, and number 2 in Belgium and Italy.
- **To defend market position.** A predator may launch a hostile takeover bid for a competing firm, or two firms may agree to merge to warn off competition or counter the threat of a hostile takeover by a rival.
- **To secure the supply chain by merging with a supplier.**
- **To enjoy economies of large-scale production** (see 22.4).
- **For the purpose of asset stripping.** An **asset stripper** will aim to buy up another company at a market value which is less than the value of its total assets (see 18.2). It will then close down any loss-making operations and sell off the more lucrative parts of the acquired firm at a profit.

Merger activity has increased in recent years, but only around 5% of all mergers are referred to the competition authorities. Many firms have combined to form larger, sometimes global, enterprises in order to compete more effectively in increasingly global markets.

Competition laws

The Monopolies and Trade Practices Act 1948 established a Monopolies Commission to investigate dominant firms to see if they acted in the public interest, and recommend further action if they were found to be abusing their market power. The **Monopolies and Mergers Act 1965** extended the powers of the Commission to investigate mergers and takeovers and created the Monopolies and Mergers Commission (MMC).

The **Fair Trading Act 1973** established the **Office of Fair Trading (OFT)** with responsibility for the administration of all policy relating to competition and consumer protection. The OFT is further responsible for monitoring merger activity and referring cases to the MMC for investigation.

The **Competition Act 1998** set up the **Competition Commission** to take over the functions of the Monopolies and Mergers Commission, and to undertake Fair Trading Act inquiries into mergers and monopolies. The Commission has legal powers to ban business behaviour which damages the interests of consumers or which abuses monopoly power. Individuals and firms who are found guilty of anti-competitive behaviour can appeal to the Competition Commission and seek damages in the law courts if they believe that their reputation has been unfairly damaged or they have been unfairly fined.

Portfolio Activity 6.5

1. What is a merger?
2. From the articles, list the companies involved in mergers. Which markets do they operate in? What business reasons can be given for their desires to merge?
3. List the US, UK and European Union government competition authorities involved in the investigations of the mergers reported in the articles. Why are these authorities concerned about them?
4. Research and produce a factsheet for business on competition policy in the UK and European Union using computer software. This should include a description of the role of competition policy, practices that are outlawed, why mergers may be referred for investigation, and the responsibilities of the OFT, Competition Commission and the EU. Recent examples of OFT and Competition Commission investigations from newspaper articles and the internet can be included to illustrate points made in your factsheet.

Byers refers NTL and Vivendi to OFT

Trade and Industry Secretary Stephen Byers stopped the furious pace of consolidation in the media industry in its tracks yesterday by referring two big transactions to the Competition Commission. Mr Byers rejected one set of advice from the Office of Fair Trading and ordered the commission to investigate NTL's proposal to buy the residential business of Cable and Wireless Communications.

But he accepted the watchdog's advice to require scrutiny of the stake taken by French media and utilities company Vivendi in British Sky Broadcasting. The move comes as a warning to fast-growing media companies that European regulators and governments will not stand by while groups seek powerful positions in the European market.

The referrals sparked outrage in the City and among cable industry executives. One TV executive said the move would benefit Rupert Murdoch, who controls BSkyB, because it would hinder Vivendi in its attempts to force him to merge the satellite broadcaster with Canal Plus, the French group in which Vivendi holds a 49% stake.

The referrals also delay the cable industry as it gears up to launch digital TV services in competition to BSkyB and ONdigital.

Mr Byers said he was referring NTL's takeover of the CWC business because he was concerned about the reduction in the number of cable operators from three to two.

He said: "Effective competition in these markets is of central importance to the consumer." His concerns centre on the delivery of pay-TV services. The Competition Commission will report by 25 February.

By contrast, his decision to refer the Vivendi stake is in line with advice given to Mr Byers by John Bridgeman, Director General of Fair Trading.

The Office of Fair Trading had been examining Vivendi's purchase of a 24% stake in BSkyB and its appointment of a senior executive to the satellite broadcaster's board.

The trade and industry department said Mr Byers "considers the acquisition raises competition concerns in respect of the market for film and sports rights and for conditional access technology in the UK". The DTI added that the referral did not prejudge whether a merger of the two companies would be against the public interest.

The Guardian, 13.11.1999

AOL/Time Warner tie-up faces anti-competition scrutiny

Competition commissions on both sides of the Atlantic are sceptical about the implications of the recent AOL and Time Warner merger.

When the £125bn merger between US media giants AOL and Time Warner was announced in January, it was obvious that it faced a long walk through the regulatory minefield.

The two companies have been under intense scrutiny on both sides of the Atlantic, from the Federal Communication Commission in Washington and the European Commission in Brussels, and it's easy to see why.

AOL is the dominant internet service provider in the US and co-owns AOL Europe with German media giant Bertelsmann. Time Warner controls cable access to about 20% of all US homes and has plenty of media content thanks to its CNN, Warner Brothers and Warner Music subsidiaries.

The EC told the companies last month that the merger "would create a dominant position in the markets for online music delivery, music software, internet dial-up access, broadband internet access and integrated broadband content" that would "significantly impede" competition.

The picture is further complicated by the proposed £14bn merger between UK music group EMI and Time Warner subsidiary Warner Music. Some analysts call this the "first cousin" of the AOL deal, as it will provide even more content for Warner cables and AOL portals, but it has made the tough-talking competition commission even more sceptical.

The companies involved have indicated they would make concessions to allow the merger to proceed. These are said to include a Time Warner pledge that it will make its music content available on other internet systems. EMI and Warner will also make their music compatible with three other software music players not owned by themselves or AOL, for at least five years. Finally, AOL has guaranteed that for three years it will not force content providers who link up with AOL in the US to make a commitment to AOL Europe.

The concessions are wide-ranging, and EMI and Warner Music have also offered to spin off labels and publishing rights, but they don't address the sheer scale, and main point, of the merger. AOL Time Warner would be a vertically integrated media giant, with powerful interests in content, the internet and cable. The possible dominance of the internet music download market is a key concern for the EC.

The Guardian, 11.9.2000

Consumer protection

Consumer protection is about helping consumers get a fair deal when they buy goods and services. Many years ago there was very little consumer protection. The basis of the law relating to the sale and advertising of products was known as *caveat emptor* – 'let the buyer beware'. Consumers had to make purchases at their own risk.

However, a vast array of goods and services are available to consumers today, many imported from overseas. Consumers cannot be expected to have the detailed technical knowledge to evaluate all the different products available. More than ever before, they must rely on business organizations for information and advice on what to buy.

A number of organizations exist to advise consumers and protect their interests from large powerful producers who may be tempted to misinform or be economical with the truth. For example, the Consumers Association publishes the *Which?* magazine series which carry expert product evaluations. TV programmes such as *Watchdog* perform a similar role and publicize consumer complaints.

A large number of laws exist relating to safety, price, advertising messages, choice, and quality of goods and services (see 12.5). For example, the Food Safety Act 1990 states that all food must be prepared and sold in hygienic conditions, and all pre-packed foods must display a list of contents.

The emphasis in law has changed from *caveat emptor* to *caveat vendor* – 'let the seller beware!'

Regulation (and deregulation)

A vast array of rules and regulations apply to business activities in the UK, from the conditions in licenses for public houses and taxis, to shop opening hours and health, safety and environmental standards. An increasing number of regulations from the EU are also affecting UK business, from issues such as the treatment of cider as wine for taxation purposes to the appropriate name for soya milk.

The **1994 Deregulation and Contracting Out Act** streamlined and removed around 450 statutory regulations on business. Some of the regulations were clearly out of date and needed to be replaced, whereas others were thought to be too restrictive and reduced the competitiveness of UK firms. Areas covered in the act included restrictions on shop opening hours, children in pubs, building society lending, and rules applying to mergers. The legislation also allowed the contracting out of public sector services to private firms.

The removal of unnecessary regulations and 'red tape' continues to ease burdens placed on business, especially smaller ones. For example, in April 2001 a number of measures were introduced to ease the administrative burden on small and medium-sized enterprises of making VAT returns.

However, many other regulations on business activities have been introduced or tightened. Many of these regulations aim at improving

How bendy is yours?

In 1988 the European Commission created four cucumber classifications, setting standards for each class – including the amount of curve per 10 cm. Top class cucumbers had to be practically straight. Other cucumbers – the ones with kinks in – were quite legitimate but unclassified.

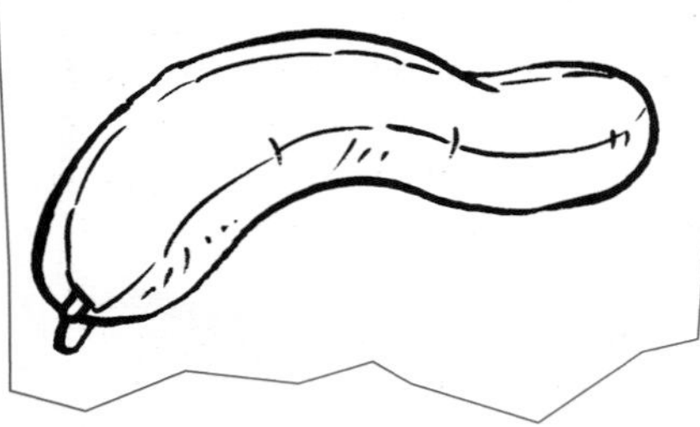

▼ *De-regulation*

Legal oddities in line for abolition

One of the strongest arguments for the government's drive against red tape is the sheer oddity of some of the regulations being abolished.

For example, methylated spirits cannot be sold between 10pm on Saturday and 8am on Monday. Meths drinking, the Department of Trade and Industry says, is a thing of the past, so legislation enacted 105 years ago can be repealed.

Scottish hairdressers are not allowed to open on Sunday, English haircuts on the Sabbath are apparently legal.

Shops need a specific licence for selling kettle de-scaler. It is classed as a poison.

Financial Times, 20.1.1994

A taste of the 450 measures to be swept away:

- A change in the basis of Health and Safety legislation. At present, outdated legislation cannot be removed unless it is replaced
- Changes in the definition of a newspaper proprietor under competition law. The present requirement to investigate newspaper mergers catches some deals not involving newspapers at all
- Companies which have ceased trading will be allowed to apply to be struck off the register, thus being relieved of their Companies Act obligations
- Shops and supermarkets in Scotland will be allowed to sell alcohol on Sunday between 12.30pm and 10pm. This is now prohibited, though pubs are allowed to sell alcohol all day
- The act requiring employment agencies to be licensed is to be repealed.
- Goods vehicles and public service vehicles must now have their licences renewed every five years. This is to be replaced by a system of continuous licensing
- Local authorities will no longer be responsible for the supervision of slaughterhouses
- Duplication in rules for the design and construction of buildings will be eliminated
- Paperwork on the transfer of waste will be simplified
- Several new areas of public service will be subjected to market testing. These include the administration of civil service pension schemes, the enforcement of milk hygiene and the invalid vehicle scheme

product safety standards and protecting the environment - for example, night flying and aircraft noise restrictions at airports, and a statutory approvals process for the use of pesticides in farming.

Environmental protection

The **Environmental Protection Act 1990** and a growing body of European legislation on the environment regulate the behaviour of firms in the UK, and these are enforced by the Environment Agency and the Scottish Environmental Protection Agency. Taken together, these laws control many thousands of different industrial processes which might, if unregulated, cause noise or chemical pollution in the air, on land, and in water supplies. Local Authorities also monitor some 30,000 industrial processes for unacceptable levels of pollution in their local communities. Firms found guilty of breaking anti-pollution laws can be fined heavily.

Many firms are now voluntarily developing their own codes of practice regarding the environment due to pressure in the market from consumers. An increasing number of firms are producing environmental performance reports along with their end-of-year profit and loss statements and balance sheets (see 18.2). The Confederation of British Industry (CBI) has also issued guidelines stressing that 'firms should establish policies to secure openness in safety, health and environmental information and should make adequate arrangements for their application in practice'.

Key words:

Competition policy – government actions that aim to increase the degree of competition in markets

Merger activity – amalgamations between two or more firms, usually with the intention to increase market share

Takeover – when one firm buys a controlling interest in another firm

Merger – when two or more firms agree to combine their operations

Asset stripping – buying up another firm at a low price with the intention of selling off its assets at a higher price

Office of Fair Trading (OFT) – government body responsible for the administration of all policy relating to competition and consumer protection in the UK

Competition Commission - the UK competition authority. It has the task of implementing UK competition policy and has the power to ban behaviour which damages the interests of consumers or which abuses monopoly power

Deregulation – the removal of statutory restrictions on competition

Section **6.5**

Public ownership and privatization

Public ownership

Following the end of the Second World War a number of industries were nationalized in the UK, including coal, steel, and the railways. Nationalization refers to the transfer of a whole industry from private to public ownership by the passing of an act of parliament forcing the private owners of firms to sell their shares to the government. Nationalized industries are defined as those public corporations which trade directly with consumers.

Nationalized industries 1982

British Coal
National Girobank
Electricity (England and Wales)
British Airways
N of Scotland Hydro Electric
British Airports Authority
S of Scotland Electricity
British Rail
British Gas
British Waterways
British Steel
National Bus Company
British Telecom
Scottish Transport Group
Post Office
British Shipbuilders
London Transport
Civil Aviation Authority

Why were industries nationalized?

UK governments have in the past taken into public ownership entire industries, such as railways, coal, and shipbuilding, for the following reasons:

- **To promote economies of scale:** As firms grow in size they may be able to lower the average cost of producing each unit of output. Economies of scale refer to cost savings associated with large-scale production (see 22.4). Some industries need to be very large, even to the extent that they become a monopoly supplier, in order to take full advantage of the cost savings large-scale production can bring.
- **To control natural monopolies and avoid wasteful duplication:** Imagine five different private firms competing to supply gas to your home. Five sets of pipes would be required where only one is necessary. In this case competition between firms would be wasteful.

  A firm is a **natural monopoly** if the most efficient size of that firm is one that supplies the whole market. Examples of natural monopolies include the supply of gas and water through pipelines, and electricity through the National Grid. In a natural monopoly resources can be combined in the most productive and cost-effective way. State ownership enabled these industries to develop to their most efficient size. However, in private hands such large firms may abuse their market power to push up prices to consumers (see 5.2).
- **For safety:** Some industries, such as nuclear energy, were thought to be too dangerous to be controlled by private entrepreneurs.

- **To protect employment:** Some firms were nationalized because they faced closure as private sector loss-making organizations. For example, in 1975 the UK Government rescued British Leyland to protect the jobs of car workers.

- **To maintain public services:** Private sector firms will not continue to provide goods and services if they make a loss. Under public ownership, loss-making services, such as rail lines and postal services in remote areas, or supplies of gas or electricity to households that consume very little, can be subsidized using tax revenues.

British Gas plc
Offer for Sale
by
N M Rothschild & Sons Limited
on behalf of
The Secretary of State for Energy

Under the Offer for Sale in the United Kingdom and separate offerings in the United States, Canada, Japan and Europe

4,025,500,000 Ordinary Shares of 25p each are being offered

at 135p per share

of which 50p is payable now,

45p is payable on 9th June, 1987 and

40p is payable on 19th April, 1988

Privatization

Since 1979 most nationalized enterprises and many other public sector activities in the UK have been returned to the private sector. **Privatization** involves private firms taking over public sector activities. It can take many forms:

- **The sale of public sector assets:** Here, shares in government-owned nationalized industries are sold to the general public and private sector firms. The first most significant sale was in 1984 when shares in British Telecom were sold (see Figure 6.8).

  Privatization also includes the sale of major assets owned by the Government. For example, in 1982 the Government sold 51% of shares in Britoil, a part of the British National Oil Corporation (BNOC).

  The Government also sold shares it once held in private sector companies, such as British Petroleum, ICI, Cable and Wireless.

- **Joint ventures with the private sector:** In other cases, privatization can take the form of joint ventures between public sector concerns and private firms, for example the UK Government in 2001 intended to operate London Underground train services jointly with private sector firms in a 'Public Private Partnership'.

- **Contracting out:** Many local authorities now invite private sector firms to compete for jobs such as refuse collection, parking enforcement, school catering, and road-sweeping. This is known as **tendering.** Contracts are awarded on the basis of a private firm providing a low-

THE PRIVATIZATION PROGRAMME
SALES TO DATE

1979–80	British Petroleum ICL Suez Finance Company and other miscellaneous
1980–81	Ferranti Fairey North Sea Oil-Licenses British Aerospace Miscellaneous and small NEB
1981–82	British Sugar Cable and Wireless Amersham International National Freight Miscellaneous plus Crown Agent and Forestry Commission land and property sales
1982--83	Britoil Associated British Ports Sales of oil licenses, oil stockpiles miscellaneous
1983-84	British Rail Hotels Cable and Wireless
1984–85	Enterprise Oil British Gas onshore oil Sealink ferries Jaguar cars British Telecom
1985–86	British Airports Royal Ordnance factories
1986–87	British Gas
1987–88	British Airways British Airports Authority Rolls Royce Leyland Bus and Truck
1988–89	British Steel Trustee Savings Bank British Leyland
1989–90	Regional Water Authorities
1990–91	Electricity Area Boards
1991–92	Electricity Generation
1992–93	British Coal
1994–96	British Rail
Future Sales	National Air Traffic Service British Nuclear Fuels Executive Agencies

▲ *Figure 6.8: The privatization programme*

▼ Local services are now operated by private firms

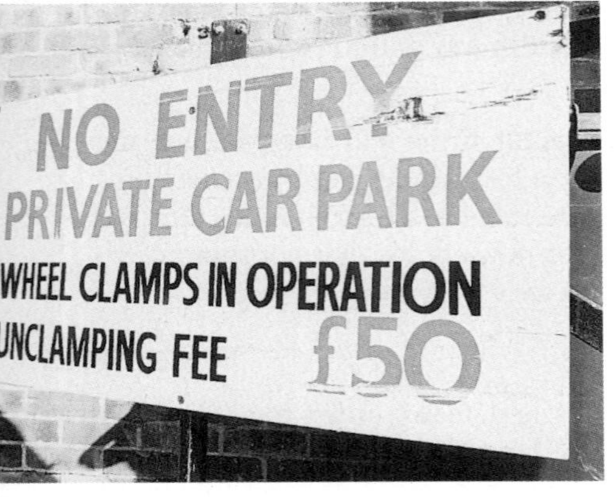

▼ A deregulated bus service

price, quality service. Also, private firms can now build and operate prisons on behalf of the Government. Former police duties, such as prisoner escort services, are also under contract to some private firms.

- **Franchising:** In 1994 the Government split British Rail up to form Railtrack, a new body responsible for track and signalling infrastructure, and a number of separate train operating organizations responsible for providing passenger services over given areas of network (see 2.2). Private sector organizations are invited to bid from time to time (usually around every 7 years) to run these train-operating companies under franchise to the Government. For example, in 1996–97 Virgin Trains was successful in winning the franchises for West Coast Main Line and Cross Country services.

Franchises to run the passenger rail services are awarded subject to certain conditions concerning minimum service standards (frequency and punctuality of trains), quality standards, and other requirements such as allowing through ticketing and the provision of passenger information. Franchised operations are accountable to the industry regulator, the Strategic Rail Authority which has the power to award and take away franchises, and control fares on certain routes. The Health and Safety Executive regulates rail safety.

- **Deregulation:** Deregulation does not involve a transfer of ownership between the public and private sector. It refers to the removal of state controls limiting competition in markets (see 5.2). An example is the provision of bus services, which are free to be provided by private operators in most major UK cities.

The arguments for privatization

- **To stop government abuse of monopoly power:** Because consumer demand for commodities such as gas and electricity tends to be price inelastic, it has been argued that governments have in the past simply raised prices to fund increases in public expenditure.
- **To increase efficiency:** It has been argued that public sector activities were inefficient and provided poor services because they faced no competition and did not have to return a profit. Privatization allows these enterprises to operate for profit. Competition and profit provide the incentive to greater efficiency to reduce costs, lower prices and improve quality.
- **To raise government revenue:** For example, the sale of British Gas shares raised over £6 billion.
- **To give ownership to the people:** People have been encouraged to buy shares in the ownership of privatized industries. As shareholders, they have the right to vote on how these companies should be run and can earn dividends on their shares when these companies make profits.

The arguments against privatization

- **Competition breaks up economies of scale:** If the most efficient size of a firm is one that supplies the whole market for a particular product, then breaking that firm up into a number of smaller competing firms will be inefficient and raise costs and prices.

- **The public interest is no longer protected:** Services that make a loss will be closed by private sector firms aiming for profit. The privatization of the rail network has raised fears that rail services to remote areas and off-peak services which do not earn a profit will be closed.
- **It does not return ownership to the people:** Instead, most shares in the ownership of privatized industries are held by large financial institutions such as banks and insurance companies' funds. Many have also been snapped up by non-UK companies.
- **Private monopolies exploit consumers:** Those opposed to the sale of nationalized industries argue that privatization has created private sector monopolies able to restrict output to force up prices.

In order to prevent this, the UK Government has set up a number of industry regulators which are able to control prices and set service standards in privatized industries. For example, Ofgem (the Office of Gas and Electricity Markets) regulates the gas and electricity supply industries (see 12.5).

Key words:

Nationalization – transferring the ownership of private sector firms in an industry to the public sector

Nationalized industries – public sector enterprises which trade directly with consumers

Privatization – the transfer of public sector assets and activities to private individuals and firms

Useful references

HM Treasury **'Pre-Budget Report'**, published every November by The Stationery Office ***(www.the-stationery-office.com)***

Any good quality national newspaper the day after the Budget in March each year

Competition Commission *(www.Competition-Commission.org.uk)*
New Court, Carey Street, London WC2A 2JT

Environment Agency for England and Wales ***(www.environment-agency.gov.uk)*** for advice on environmental protection policy, laws and enforcements

Her Majesty's Customs and Excise *(www.hmce.gov.uk)*
New Kings Beam House, 22 Upper Ground, London SE1 9PJ for advice on customs and excise duties

Her Majesty's Treasury *(www.hm-treasury.gov.uk)*
1 Parliament Street, London SW1P 3AG for information on UK fiscal and monetary policy, Budgets and pre-Budgets

Inland Revenue *(www.inland revenue.gov.uk)*
Somerset House, London WC2R 1LB for advice on UK tax policy

Office of Fair Trading ***(www.oft.gov.uk)***
Fleetbank House, 2–6 Salisbury Square, London EC4V 8JX for information on consumer protection and competition laws

Internet key words search: **monetary policy, interest rates, VAT, Budget**

Test your knowledge

Questions 1–3 share the following answer options:

- **A** Raise income tax
- **B** Raise selected excise duties
- **C** Raise public expenditure
- **D** Cut interest rates

Which of the above policies would you advise the Government to use in an attempt to:

1. Increase employment opportunities?
2. Reduce the consumption of cigarettes?
3. Increase consumer borrowing?
4. Corporation tax rates on company profits have been reduced in recent years. Fiscal policy is being used in this case to:
   - **A** Encourage firms to lower their product prices
   - **B** Enable firms to pass on higher dividends to shareholders
   - **C** Encourage firms to invest in new plant and machinery
   - **D** Encourage firms to pay higher wages

Question 5–7 share the following answer options:

- **A** To boost employment
- **B** To control pollution
- **C** To increase competition
- **D** To protect domestic food supplies

Which of the above objectives do the following organizations or policies seek to achieve?

5. Regional Policy
6. Competition Commission
7. The Environment Agency
8. Which of the following is unlikely to be a reason for the privatization of public sector activities?
   - **A** To increase business management and efficiency
   - **B** To give consumers more choice
   - **C** To break up economies of scale
   - **D** To raise government revenue
9. Which of the following is **not** an argument in favour of imposing restrictions on imports?
   - **A** To reduce domestic unemployment
   - **B** To protect domestic firms from foreign competition
   - **C** To increase consumer choice
   - **D** To protect an infant industry

Questions 10–12 share the following answer options:

- **A** Competition policy
- **B** Regional policy
- **C** Fiscal policy
- **D** Monetary policy

Which of the above policies:

10. Uses interest rates to influence the general level of economic activity?
11. Regulates monopolies and merger activity?
12. Provides financial assistance to new and existing firms in areas of high unemployment?
13. **a** Suggest and explain four reasons why the UK Government intervenes in product markets.
    b What is fiscal policy? How can the policy be used to help create employment and business opportunities?
    c What is monetary policy? How can it be used to boost investment in new plant and machinery by business?
    d Using examples, explain how indirect taxes can be used to influence the price and quantity traded of particular goods and services.
14. **a** Suggest and explain two reasons why entire industries in the UK were taken into public ownership in the past.
    b What is privatization? List two industries that have been privatized in the UK.
    c What are the arguments for and against the privatization of rail services in the UK?
    d Explain the role of the Competition Commission in UK competition policy.

chapter 7 International Competitiveness

This chapter examines the competitiveness of UK industry, and how the European Union and the World Trade Organization affect businesses trading internationally.

What you need to learn

Increasingly competition between business organizations is global.

You need to understand the meaning of **international competitiveness** and how multinationals and other businesses operating in international markets try to be competitive.

You also need to explain how the following factors can affect the competitiveness of an international business:

- the trend towards increased freedom of trade and the role of the **World Trade Organization**
- the effect of barriers to trade - trading pacts, tariffs, quotas
- the **European Union**, European Monetary union and the single market

Section 7.1

The performance of UK industry

International competitiveness

The globalization of markets

Competition between business organizations for sales, market share and ultimately business survival, has become intense and global. Businesses seeking expansion have outgrown their home markets and successfully penetrated market overseas. This has been driven by a number of key factors:

- real incomes around the world have grown giving consumers more buying power
- consumers can buy on-line from different businesses located anywhere in the world using the Internet
- barriers to trade and competition between different countries are being dismantled
- businesses have grown and merged to form huge multinational organizations able to compete globally against other multinationals and forcing smaller local businesses out of their home markets

The world's top 20 brands, 1999

Brand name	Country	Industry
Coca-Cola	US	Beverages
Microsoft	US	IT
IBM	US	IT
General Electric	US	Diversified
Ford	US	Automobiles
Disney	US	Entertainment
Intel	US	IT
McDonald's	US	Food
AT&T	US	Telecoms
Marlboro	US	Tobacco
Nokia	Finland	Telecoms
Mercedes	Germany	Automobiles
Nescafe	Switzerland	Beverages
Hewlett-Packard	US	IT
Gillete	US	Personal care
Kodak	US	Imaging
Ericsson	Sweden	Telecoms
Sony	Japan	Electronics
Amex	US	Financial services
Toyota	Japan	Automobiles

Source: Interbrand

Financial Times, 2.2.2000

Many of the biggest multinational companies in the world are mainly Japanese or Amerian. Their company, brand and product names are known and instantly recognized the world over, e.g. Coca-Cola and Sony. The world's top 10 brands in 1999 were all of US origin.

However, among the world's top 50 global industrial giants in 1998 were key UK companies British Petroleum, British Telecommunications and Shell Trading and Transport (as part of the Royal Dutch/Shell Group, one of the largest companies in the world). BP has since merged with the US oil company Amoco, and it now has business operations in around 100 countries.

Table 7.1 illustrates the huge scale of some of the UK-based multinationals.

Other well-known UK multinational companies include HSBC Holdings (banking), Bass (brewing), Marks and Spencer (retailing), British Airports Authority (transport and retailing services), BAE Systems (aerospace and defence), Rio Tinto (mining), and Imperial Chemical Industries (chemicals).

▼ *Table 7.1: The top 3 UK multinationals, by turnover 1998*

UK Multinationals 1998	Principal activities	Capital employed £ billion	World sales £ billion	Total employees
British Petroleum	Oil & gas exploration, marketing, oil refining, and chemicals	20.5	44.7	53,700
Shell Trading and Transport	Oil & gas exploration, marketing, oil refining, chemicals, coal mining	21.0	32.8	101,000
British Telecommunications	Communications	17.5	14.5	20,250

The Times 1000, 1999

However, most UK multinationals are small compared with some of the US giants such as Microsoft (IT) and General Electric (aerospace, electronics, investments, etc.) and huge Japanese corporations such as Toyota (automobiles) and Sony (electronics).

Portfolio Activity 7.1

Here is a list of names of multinational organizations. Try to find out their country of origin, the number of countries they operate in, their main products, and any recent indicators of their business performance. Tabulate the information in an appropriate format.

Coca-Cola	BP Amoco	Ford
Ciba Geigy	Seimens	GEC
Du Pont	Peugeot	Nestlé
Fiat	AT&T	Wal-Mart
Sony	Mobil	Nissan
McDonald's	Phillip Morris	Procter & Gamble

Of the world's one hundred largest economic entities in 1998 in terms of annual income, 52 were multinational companies and 49 were countries. Multinationals are responsible for around two thirds of total world trade and entire world industries can be dominated by a handful of these large global organizations. For example, 60% of the world trade in bananas is controlled by just three multinational firms. General Electric was the biggest company in the world in 2000 with a market value over £600 billion.

What is competitiveness?

To meet the challenges presented by the globalization of markets UK industry must be able to compete in home and overseas markets. The performance of the economy and the standard of living in the UK will ultimately depend on the ability of UK businesses to compete.

For a business, **competitiveness** means meeting consumers' needs more efficiently and more effectively than its rivals. For an economy as a whole, the Organization for Economic Cooperation and Development (OECD) defines competitiveness as *'the degree to which it can, under free and fair market conditions, produce goods and services which meet the test of international markets, while simultaneously maintaining and expanding the real incomes of its people over the long term'*.

The ability of UK businesses to compete in international markets and to promote growth in total output and incomes, therefore, requires sustained improvements in productivity and product quality, and reductions in production costs at a rate which exceeds those of countries overseas (see 1.1).

How competitive is the UK?

There are a number of indicators of the changing competitiveness of UK industry as whole over time. Four of the most important and revealing indicators are changes in:

- Real Gross Domestic Product (GDP)
- UK share of world trade
- Output per employee
- Unit labour costs

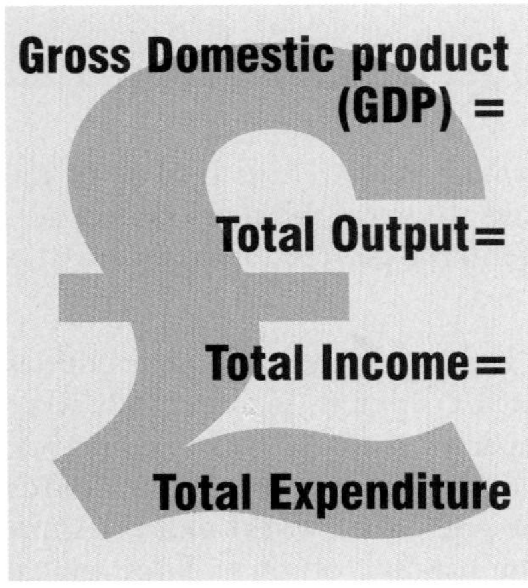

Gross Domestic product (GDP) =
Total Output=
Total Income=
Total Expenditure

Gross Domestic Product

If all the firms in an economy manage to produce more goods and services in one year compared with the previous year, the result will be **economic growth.**

Gross Domestic Product (GDP) is a measure of the total value of all goods and services produced in a country per period. Because the production and sale of goods and services generates incomes for the owners of resources – i.e. labour and suppliers of materials and machinery - GDP is, therefore, a measure of the total or national income of a country. Also, because by definition the national income will be spent on goods and services, GDP is a measure of the total expenditure on UK goods.

Revenues from the sale of goods and services will tend to rise each year, simply because prices rise. Economists say this represents a rise in nominal GDP. However, in order for there to be economic growth, the total output of goods and services must also rise. That is, there must be an increase in real output, or real GDP. An increase in real GDP refers to an increase in the quantity and/or quality of goods and services available for an economy to enjoy, and therefore, an increase in real national income.

Figure 7.1 shows the rise in both nominal and real GDP between 1975 and 2000. Over this period, GDP, measured at current market prices, increased from £105 billion to £935 billion - an increase of 790%! However, after deducting the effect of price inflation on the value of goods and services, real GDP, measured in constant prices, expanded by only 76% over this period - an average increase of 2.3% each year. We might expect this long-term trend rate of growth to continue in the UK. However, in the short term, real GDP can fall during an economic recession, or rise even faster than the trend during a boom. For example, during the economic recession in the early 1990s, UK real GDP fell by 1.5%.

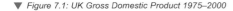

Figure 7.1: UK Gross Domestic Product 1975–2000

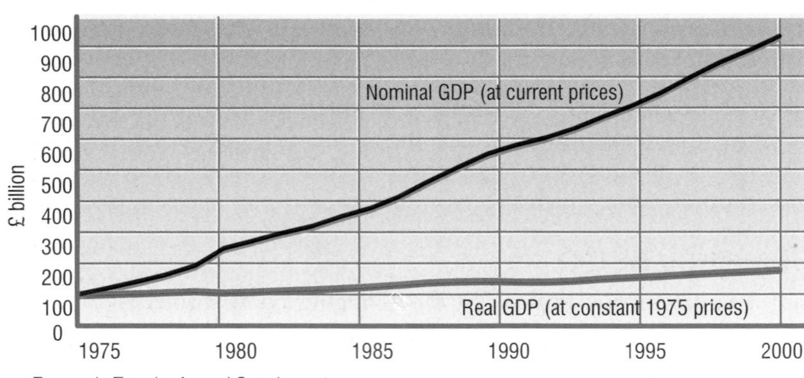

Economic Trends, Annual Supplement

Despite the increase in real GDP enjoyed by the UK, some other countries have done much better in the past (see Figure 7.3). Growth rates in real GDP of 4–5% per year were achieved in many of the developed economies of Western Europe, North America, and Japan.

The business cycle

The continuous fluctuations in real GDP around a long-term trend rate of growth are called the **business cycle** or **trade cycle**. Four stages can be identified in one complete cycle:

1. During an **economic recession** or **slump**, as in the UK in the early 1990s, real GDP tends to fall below trend (see Figure 7.2). There is negative growth. Recessions are characterized by falling output and rising unemployment as a response to falling consumer demand and business investment. Price inflation tends to fall as firms cut prices in a bid to boost sales and maintain shares in shrinking markets. Business profits tend to fall, and an increasing number of firms will close as the slump deepens. However, falling consumer demand for imported goods may improve the balance of international trade.
2. A **trough** occurs when the economy has reached the bottom of the business cycle. Consumer demand and business investment will be low, but will have stopped falling. Unemployment will be high.
3. During an **economic recovery**, incomes and demand start to rise. Stocks of goods will fall, and businesses will respond by increasing output and their recruitment of staff. Unemployment will begin to fall. Growing business optimism may boost investment spending. However, growing demand will tend to suck in more imported goods, and the balance of trade may deteriorate.
4. During a **boom**, real GDP will be rising above trend, as in the mid-to-late 1980s in the UK (see Figure 7.2). Consumer demand, output, sales, and profits will all be buoyant. Unemployment will be low. However, if the supply of goods and services is unable to expand fast enough to meet demand, there will be price inflation.

Economists suggest that the UK completes a full cycle in economic activity every 8 to 12 years.

▼ *Figure 7.2: The UK business cycle*

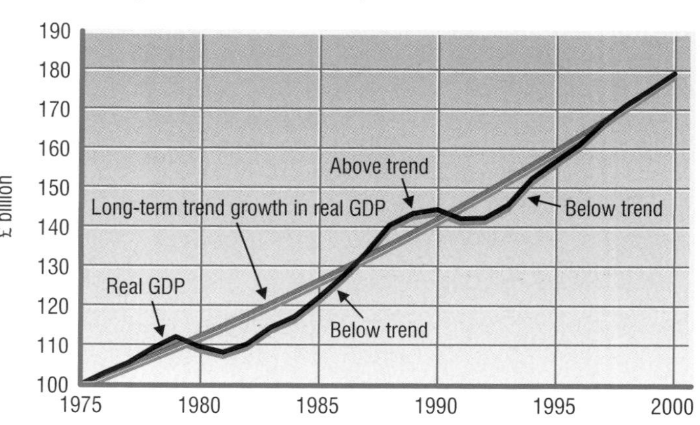

▼ *Figure 7.3: Growth in real GDP, selected countries 1983–2001*

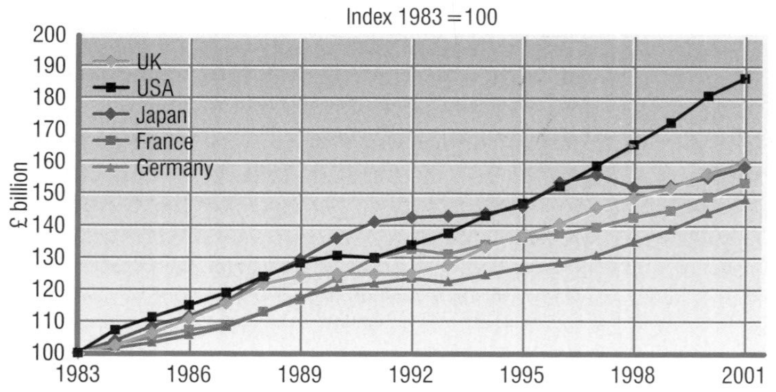

OECD Economic Outlook, June 2000

However, more recently, growth in many developed western countries has slowed down. In some cases, real GDP growth has even turned negative during the world economic recession in the early 1990s as firms cut back their production, and more recently in 1998/99 in Japan. Some of the most significant growth rates since 1990 have been observed in the **emerging markets** of Latin America and South East Asia. For example, real GDP in China has expanded by over 7% real each year since the mid-1990s.

Despite substantial growth in the GDP of **newly industrialized economies** such as China, Malaysia, and Brazil, these countries remain relatively poor. In some cases the average income per head of their populations in 2000 was no more than £350. They present developed countries like the UK with both an opportunity and a threat: they are **emerging markets** for exports of UK-produced goods and services, but also present firms with growing competition in their home and international markets, because they are able to produce goods and services with low-cost labour and are aggressively pursuing business expansion and productivity growth. However, in terms of GDP per head of population the UK lags behind many of her major competitors (see Figure 7.5). This poor performance is primarily due to lower labour productivity in UK industry, whether measured by output per person employed or by labour costs per unit of output.

▼ *Figure 7.4: Growth of real GDP, developing economies 2001**

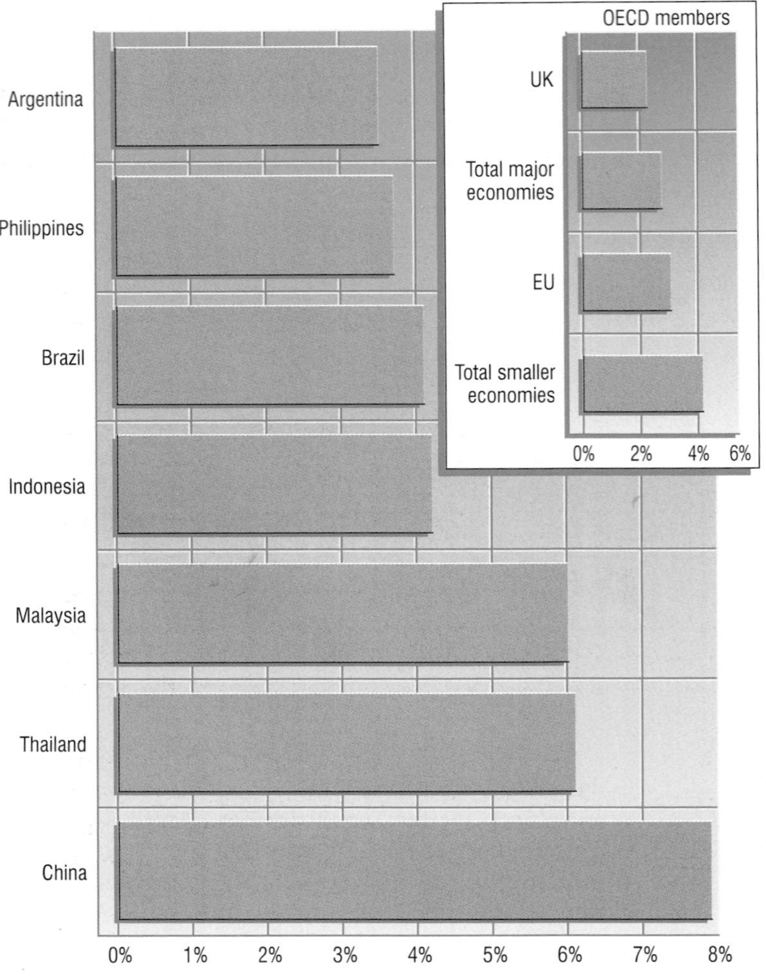

** OECD forecasts*
OECD Economic Outlook, June 2000

▼ *Figure 7.5: Gross Domestic Product per head of population, international comparison 1997 (UK = 100)*

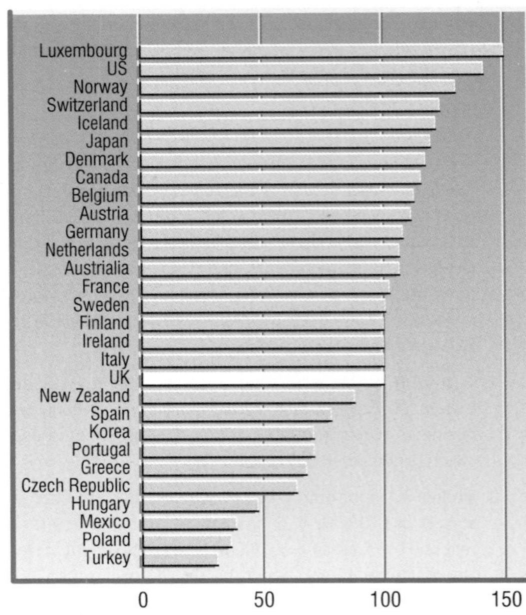

Portfolio Activity 7.2 

1. Compile an economics and business diary, by collecting newspaper and economics/business magazine articles about the current economic climate in the UK over the next 12–24 months. Include data on changes in GDP, retail sales, investment, industrial output, price inflation, unemployment, overseas trade, and government economic policy, etc.

   From your findings, what stage would you say the UK has reached in the business cycle? Does the information you have collected give conflicting views of recovery or recession in the UK?

   Write a brief commentary at the end of every month to explain emerging trends in the UK economy, and how these compare with other countries, as highlighted by the articles you have collected.

2. Obtain up-to-date data on GDP, price inflation, unemployment, overseas trade, etc., from publications such as *Economic Trends*, the *Monthly Digest of Statistics,* and *Labour Market Trends.* Plot graphs of the historical series for these economic variables to include in your diary to illustrate the emerging trends you have discussed.

OECD Member Countries (2000)

Major economies	Smaller economies	
USA	Australia	Mexico
Japan	Austria	Netherlands
Germany	Czech Republic	New Zealand
France	Denmark	Norway
Italy	Finland	Poland
United Kingdom	Greece	Portugal
Canada	Hungary	Spain
	Iceland	Sweden
	Ireland	Switzerland
	Korea	Turkey

International trade

In common with other countries, the UK trades with foreign countries in order to:

- Obtain those goods and services it cannot produce, such as many raw materials and other components required to make goods and services in UK industry

- Benefit from a wider variety of goods and services
- Take advantage, where possible, of lower production costs and prices of some goods and services produced overseas
- Expand the markets for UK goods and services, so that UK firms can grow in size and benefit from economies of scale (see 22.4)

Overseas trade not only involves the buying and selling of goods and services, but also trade in currencies necessary to make payments to foreign countries.

Goods and services bought by the UK from overseas are known as **imports.** An import, therefore, represents a flow of money out of the UK. To pay for imports, UK firms must exchange UK pounds for foreign currencies. The sale of UK pounds will tend to reduce their market price or exchange rate. (See Chapter 5 for a discussion on how the forces of demand and supply affect the market price of goods and services.)

Goods and services produced by UK firms and sold overseas are **exports.** The sale of exports generates a flow of money into the UK. Foreign countries must buy UK pounds with their currencies in order to pay UK exporting firms. The demand for the UK currency, sterling, tends to push up the UK exchange rate.

The balance of payments

The difference between flows of money into and out of the UK is known as the **balance of payments.** If payments overseas exceed payments received from abroad, the balance of payments will be in deficit. The net outflow of money from the UK will tend to reduce the sterling exchange rate on the world currency markets.

There are five main categories of trade and international payments for trade:

- **Trade in goods.** This involves trade in physical commodities, such as oil, machinery, foods, chemicals, cars, video recorders, etc. If payments for imports exceed payments made for exports, the balance of trade in goods will be in deficit (see Table 7.2).

Table 7.2: The UK balance of payments on current account (£ million)

	1975	1980	1985	1990	1995	1999
(A) Exports of goods	19,451	47,493	78,291	102,313	153,725	165,667
(B) Imports of goods	-22,696	-46,164	-81,707	-121,020	-165,449	-192,434
(C) Balance of trade in goods (A+B)	**-3,245**	**1,329**	**-3,416**	**-18,707**	**-11,724**	**-26,767**
(D) Exports of services	7,352	15,002	23,635	31,188	48,687	63,982
(E) Imports of services	-5,959	-11,285	-17,016	-27,178	-39,772	-52,444
(F) Services balance (D+E)	**1,393**	**3,717**	**6,619**	**4,010**	**8,915**	**11,538**
(G) Income balance	604	-1,428	12	-588	5,976	8,332
(H) Current transfers balance	**-317**	**-452**	**-988**	**-4,258**	**-6,912**	**-4,084**
Current balance (C+F+G+H)	**-1,565**	**3,166**	**2,227**	**-19,543**	**-3,745**	**-10,981**

CSO UK Balance of Payments ('The Pink Book')

- **Trade in services.** This involves international trade in services such as tourism, insurance, and banking. For example, if a UK resident visits a foreign country on holiday, the money s/he spends there represents a flow of money out of the UK and so is classed as an **import**. Conversely, if a foreign shipping firm insures its fleet at Lloyds of London, the premiums paid into the UK are an **export.**

- **Income balance.** Flows of income to and from the UK consists of employment incomes from cross-border and seasonal workers and, more significantly, investment incomes from foreign investments, assets and liabilities. Inflows of investment incomes include dividends paid on shares held by UK residents in foreign companies located in the UK and overseas, interest payments on UK loans made overseas, and profits paid to UK owners of overseas businesses. Outflows of investment incomes include profits paid to overseas owners of businesses in the UK, interest payments on foreign loans to the UK, and dividends on shares in UK companies held by residents of other countries.
- **Current transfers.** These are composed of central government transfers (e.g. taxes and payments to and from the European Union – see 7.3) and other transfers (e.g. gifts in cash or goods received by private individuals from abroad or receipts from the EU where the UK government acts as the beneficiary of the transfers).
- **The balance of payments current account** is a measure of international trading performance. If the total of flows of money out of the UK (for imports of goods and services, employment and investment incomes and current transfers) exceed flow of money into the UK (for UK exports, employment, investments and transfers), then the current account will be in deficit.

The UK share of world trade

The UK is usually a net importer of goods, but the current account balance has tended to hold up, because it has traditionally performed well on services. This is chiefly due to London being a recognized international centre for banking, insurance, and finance. Figure 7.6, however, shows that since 1986, a worsening deficit in trade in goods has overshadowed the surplus from trade in services, such that the current balance became

Figure 7.6: The UK balance of payments current account, 1975–1999

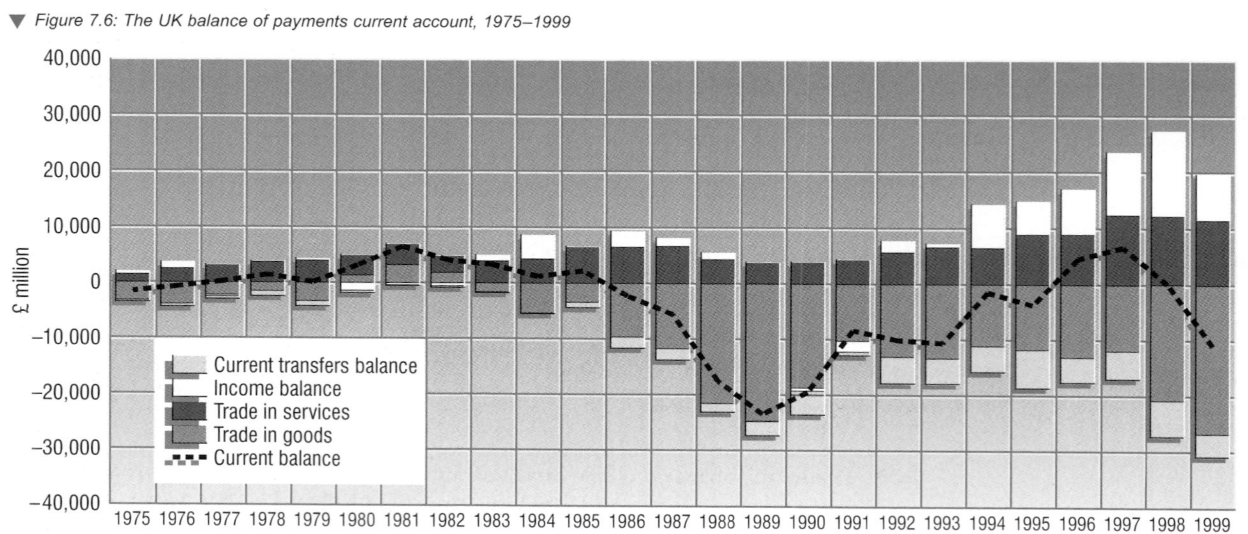

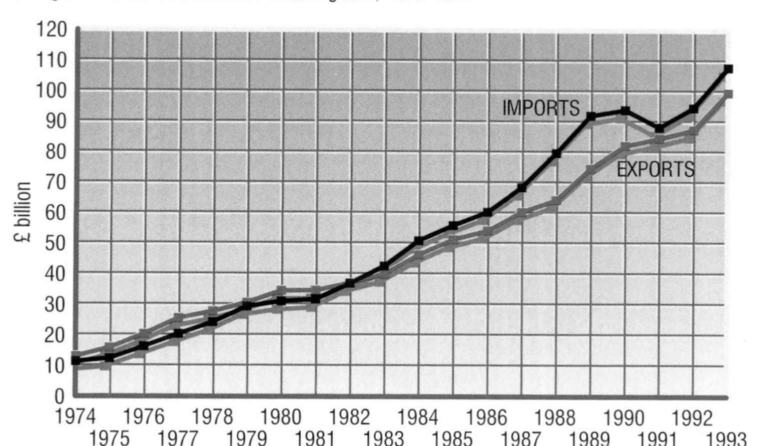

Figure 7.7: UK trade in manufactured goods, 1975–1999

negative. Competition from other financial centres such as New York and Tokyo has also tended to reduce the balance on invisible trade.

The UK has always been a major exporter of manufactured goods, notably machinery. Until 1983, the value of UK exports of manufactures had always exceeded imports. For example, in 1975, UK revenues from the export of manufactures were 25% higher than the value of UK imports. However, in 1983, the balance of trade in manufactures turned negative for the first time in recorded history, and has remained in deficit ever since (see Figure 7.7).

Finished and semi-finished manufactures still account for around 80% of total UK exports of goods, but their share of total world export sales has declined significantly over time. In 1950, the UK accounted for 25% of world export sales of manufactures. By 1970, this share had fallen to 11% and in 1999 was around 5%.

Figure 7.8 shows that in 1985, the UK share of total world export trade in goods was 5.3%. Since then it has fallen to around 4.8% of a market worth in excess of £5,470 billion in 1999. At the same time, countries such as Japan, the USA, and a number in South East Asia, were able to increase their share of total export sales.

However, the amount of imports entering the UK has increased over time. The UK accounts for around 6% of the world trade in imports. The emerging markets of South East Asia have taken an increasing proportion of world imports as their economies expand and industrialize.

Figure 7.8: Shares in world trade

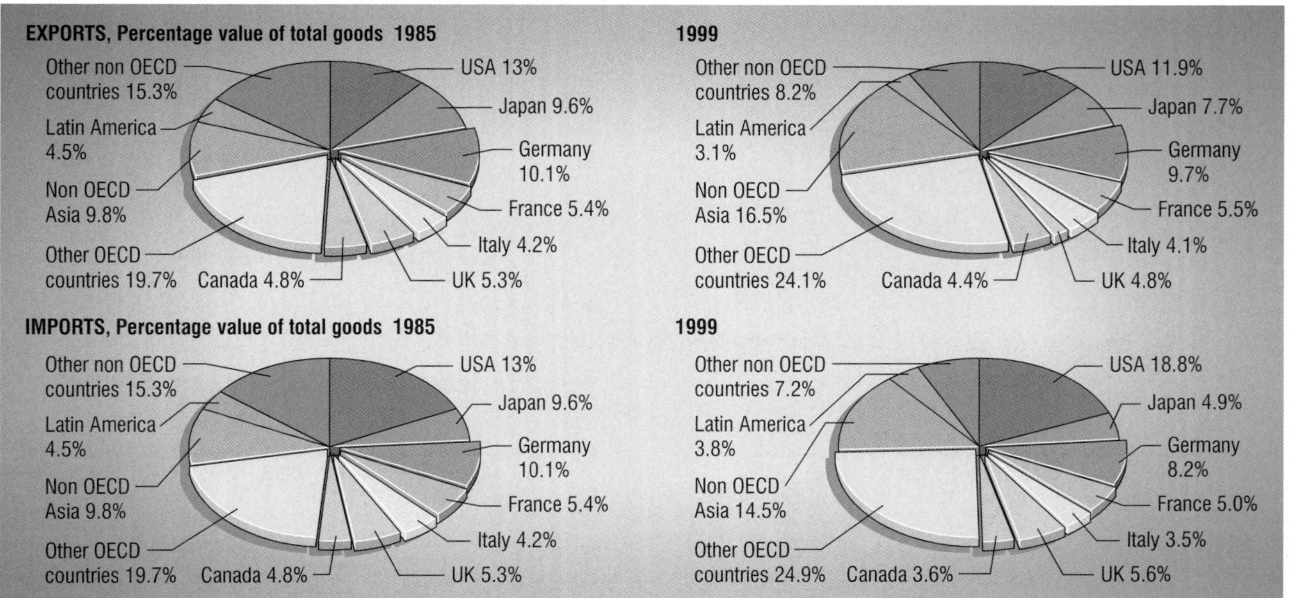

OECD Economic Outlook, December 1994, June 2000

▼ *Figure 7.9: UK exports by region*

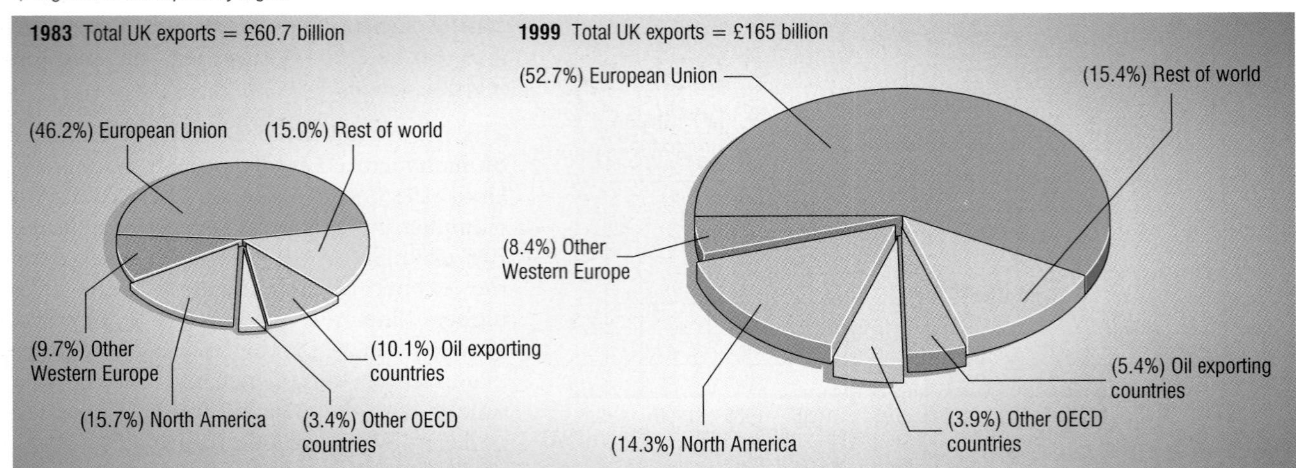

Annual Abstract of Statistics, 1994, 2000

Competitiveness and currencies

Competitiveness in world trade is often measured by reference to the relative prices of imports and exports, and the **Sterling Effective Exchange Rate Index**.

The *Index of Relative Export Prices* published in ONS *Economic Trends* is a measure of the average value of UK exports of manufactures, divided by a weighted average of the value of exports of manufactured goods from all other countries expressed in the same currency value. A fall in the relative price index suggests increasing price competitiveness for UK exports.

The **Sterling Exchange Rate Index** measures the average value of the pound against the currencies of all her trading partners. A fall in the index indicates that the average value of the pound has depreciated. This will reduce UK export prices, but raise the price of imports to the UK. An appreciation in the value of the pound against other currencies will raise export prices, but lower import prices.

▼ *UK Relative Export Prices Index*

▼ *UK Sterling Exchange Rate Index*

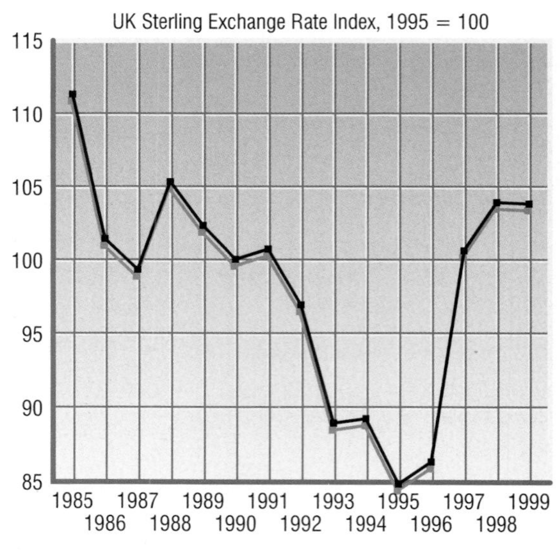

Since joining the European Union (EU) in 1972, the UK has enjoyed a growth in her share of intra-EU export trade. In 1958, the UK sold just 22% of her total visible exports to all the other countries who made up the EU in 1994 (see 7.3). By 1983, this share had risen to 46%. In 1999, the EU imported around £95.5 billion of visible exports from the UK, some 53% of total UK visible export sales worth £165 billion (see Figure 7.9).

The UK has also enjoyed a growth in her exports to the emerging markets in Asia, while the share going to North America, the largest market for UK goods, has remained relatively stable at around 14–15% since 1990.

Output per employee and unit labour costs

The value of output per employee is an average measure of the productivity of labour. It is calculated in official statistics as follows:

$$\text{Value of output per person employed} = \frac{\text{Real Gross Domestic Product}}{\text{Total number of employees}}$$

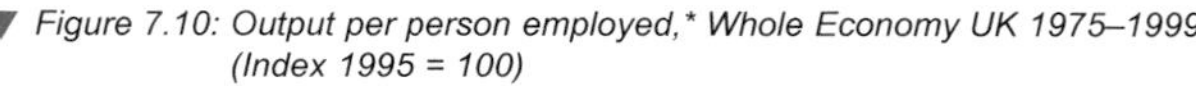

▼ *Figure 7.10: Output per person employed,* Whole Economy UK 1975–1999 (Index 1995 = 100)*

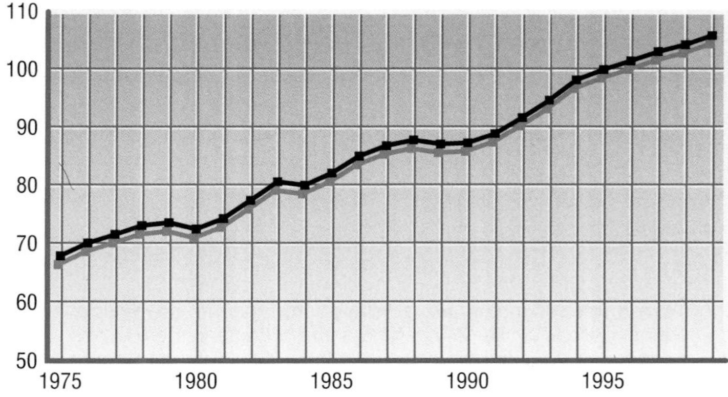

European Economy, 1999 Review

Figure 7.10 shows that significant improvements have been made in the productivity of the employed UK labour force in recent years. The value of output per person employed increased by 55% between 1988 and 1990. However, this is unlikely to have been solely due to the increased efforts of the workforce. Increases in productivity will also occur due to:

- Technological advance in equipment and production processes
- The closure of inefficient plants and organizations
- Changes in working practices

Unit labour costs

Increases in productivity reveal nothing about the cost of production. If, for example, real wage costs (wage increases over and above inflation) have risen faster than productivity, firms will be less competitive.

Unit labour costs for the whole economy can be calculated by dividing the total wage bill for all employees by the total volume of output in the economy. In cash terms, labour costs per unit of UK output increased by 445% over the period 1975–1999. However, Figure 7.11 shows that, after deducting the impact of price inflation on wages, real labour costs per unit were around 10% lower in 1999 than they were in 1975.

However, this still compares unfavourably with many other countries where real unit labour costs have fallen faster, by around 15% over the same period in other European Union member states and in Japan.

▼ *Figure 7.11: Real labour costs per unit of output, Whole Economy UK 1975–1999 (Index 1991 = 100)*

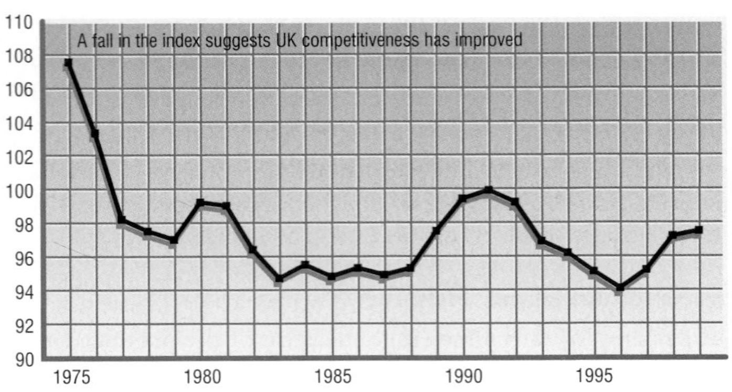

European Economy, 1999 Review

Figure 7.11 also reveals notable changes in the competitiveness of UK industry over time. Between 1988 and 1990, unit labour costs increased significantly as workers managed to secure wage increases without corresponding productivity gains. In fact, output per employee fell at the same time (Figure 7.10).

International comparisons

If productivity levels are poor and wage costs are high, firms will find it difficult to compete with rival companies who are more efficient. Firms with higher productivity and lower costs will be able to sell their products at lower prices and increase their market share.

If foreign firms are more competitive than UK companies, consumers in the UK will tend to buy cheaper imported products. Also, UK companies will find it difficult to sell their products overseas. Falling demand for UK products at home and overseas can cause rising unemployment.

It is, therefore, important to examine levels and changes in productivity and unit labour costs over time in the UK, compared with her main overseas competitors.

UK competitiveness

The UK Government publication 'Competitiveness - our partnership with business UK' (DTI, September 1997) highlighted the productivity gap between UK industry and industries overseas (see Figures 7.12 and 7.13).

'On manufacturing productivity, it is clear that, while there have been improvements, we still lag well behind, whilst the overall size of the sector has declined.'

'Across the economy as a whole, the gap in productivity performance is similar to that for manufacturing and there is less evidence of the gap being closed in the 1980s. This points to a gap in service sector productivity as well. Overall the picture shows the UK behind all other major competitors except Japan on GDP per hour worked.'

▼ *Figure 7.12: Manufacturing productivity, output per hour worked UK = 100*

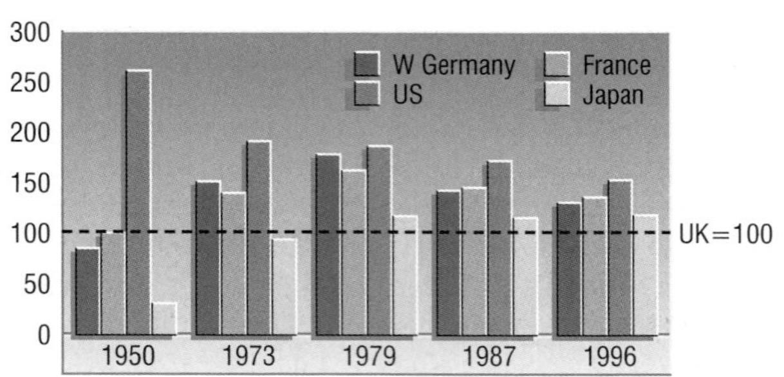

Source: van Ark: 1979 and 1996 figures extrapolated using IMF data

▼ *Figure 7.13: All industries productivity, output per hour worked UK = 100*

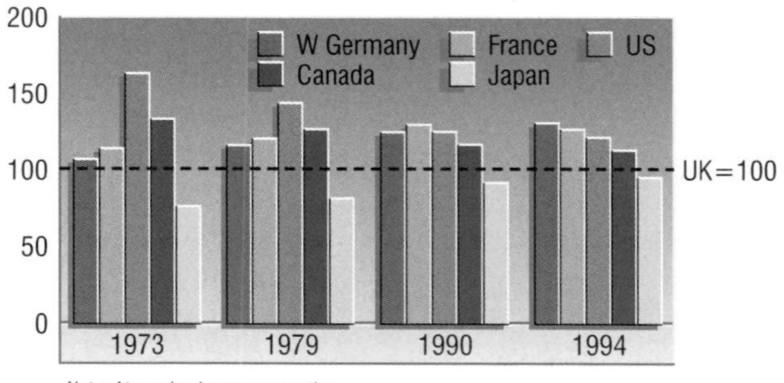

Note: At purchasing power parties.

Source: DTI calculations from ONS, OECD and Eurostat data

Portfolio Activity 7.3 

Look at the statistics on changes in output per worker and unit wage costs for the USA, Japan, and selected EU member countries below. Produce a short report to present to your group covering the following topics:

1. Explain how output per worker and unit labour costs are calculated. Why are they useful measures in business?
2. Suggest which countries have become more competitive and which have become less competitive over time by comparing the changes in output per worker and unit labour costs.
3. What might explain these differences between countries?
4. Plot four graphs each one showing changes in unit labour costs and productivity for the UK, the European Union, the USA, and Japan. When unit labour costs are rising faster than output per worker, profit margins in industry are likely to be falling. If productivity increases faster than unit labour costs, the reverse is probably true. Describe what is happening in each graph.

PERCENTAGE ANNUAL CHANGES IN

	Real output per person employed						Real unit labour costs					
Country	**1995**	**1996**	**1997**	**1998**	**1999**	**2000**	**1995**	**1996**	**1997**	**1998**	**1999**	**2000**
Belgium	1.8	0.7	2.7	1.5	0.9	0.7	-1.20	-0.61	-1.33	-0.93	0.42	-0.63
Denmark	3.0	1.5	1.0	0.5	1.3	2.1	-0.31	-0.74	0.95	0.42	0.63	-0.83
Germany	1.8	1.5	2.3	1.8	1.1	2.3	0.00	-0.40	-1.51	-1.43	-0.10	-1.46
Greece	1.2	2.8	3.8	0.3	2.1	2.4	1.56	-1.33	1.56	0.61	-0.91	-1.41
Spain	0.9	1.1	1.1	0.2	0.4	1.0	-2.66	-0.63	-0.53	0.32	-0.64	-0.75
France	1.2	1.3	1.9	2.1	1.3	1.5	-0.31	-0.10	-1.13	-0.52	0.10	-0.73
Ireland	4.2	3.9	4.9	3.8	3.4	3.6	-5.05	-2.66	-2.73	-4.38	-1.41	-1.31
Italy	2.9	0.8	1.4	0.6	0.3	1.4	-3.69	0.33	0.11	-4.80	0.46	-0.91
Netherlands	0.8	0.5	1.0	1.0	0.9	1.1	-0.81	-0.20	-0.92	-0.31	0.93	-0.21
Portugal	3.6	2.3	2.1	0.9	1.7	2.4	-1.67	0.74	-0.84	-1.17	0.75	0.43
UK	1.2	1.3	1.7	1.1	0.4	2.0	-1.14	-1.05	0.00	1.17	2.10	0.31
European Union average	1.7	1.3	1.8	1.3	0.9	1.8	-1.13	-0.31	-0.83	-1.15	0.53	-0.74
USA	0.2	1.8	2.1	2.1	2.1	1.6	-0.51	-1.12	-0.21	1.04	0.62	0.92
Japan	1.3	4.6	0.3	-2.2	2.1	1.1	0.69	-1.97	0.80	1.69	-2.15	-2.00

European Economy, 1999 Review

Key words:

Economic growth - an increase in the volume and/or quality of output (ie growth in real GDP)

Gross Domestic Product (GDP) - the value of the total output produced by UK-owned resources

National income - the total income of all UK individuals and organizations, also measured as the value of GDP

Business cycle - continuous fluctuations in real GDP around some long-term trend rate of growth. Growth below trend is characteristic of economic recession, while growth above trend takes place during an economic boom

Newly industrialized countries - low-wage economies that are developing their industrial base and represent emerging markets for exports from developed economies such as the UK

Imports - flows of money out of the UK in payment for goods and services from overseas

Exports - flows of money into the UK in payment for UK goods and services sold abroad

UK exchange rate - the value of the UK currency sterling in exchange for currencies of other countries

Trade in goods - overseas trade in physical commodities

Trade in services - international trade in services

Balance of payments - the difference between flows of money into and out of the UK for the purpose of inward and outward investment or payment for exports and imports

Current account - the balance of trade in visibles and invisibles

Unit labour costs - the cost of labour per unit of output

Section **7.2**

Government action to improve UK competitiveness

Government economic objectives

The UK Government's overall economic objective is to promote sustained economic growth in the total output by establishing a stable economic environment for business, based on low and stable price inflation. The Government argues that without this, uncertainty will stifle business and employment opportunities, and businesses will be discouraged from investing for the future and developing the products on which UK prosperity depends.

▼ *Figure 7.14: UK price inflation (percentage annual change in the all times Retail Prices Index), 1960–2000*

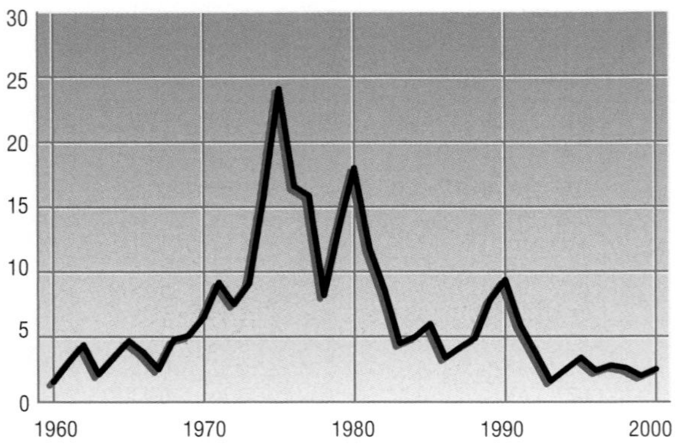

Economic Trends, Annual Supplement 2000

Low and stable price inflation

It is argued that high and volatile price inflation of the kind experienced during the 1970s destroyed jobs, stifled economic growth, and increased the demand for imports from countries with lower price inflation than the UK, thereby causing a balance of payments deficit. At one point, the annual rise in the average level of prices in the economy reached 25%.

Since October 1992 the UK government has set an explicit target range for annual inflation of 2.5%. If inflation is likely to rise above this measures will be taken to try to bring it back down (see 6.2).

Measuring price inflation

Inflation may be defined as a general and sustained rise in the prices of goods and services. It is measured by calculating the percentage increase in the price level over successive time periods - per month, or per year.

The **Retail Price Index (RPI)** is the main 'headline' measure of price inflation in the UK. It expresses the percentage change in the average level of prices of a 'basket' of some 600 different goods and services, in terms of movement in a single number series. The goods and services in the 'basket' are selected as representative of those purchased by the 'average' UK household, based on a sample of 7,000 households. Approximately 150,000 price quotations are recorded each month by government statisticians from a large number of retail outlets across the UK.

In the **base year**, the average price of the RPI basket is assigned the number 100. If, on average, the price of the basket increased by 10% the following year, the RPI will be calculated as 110. If, over the next year, the average price of the basket rises by 12%, the RPI will be recorded as 123.2 (110 x 1.12).

Taking the year 1960 as a base, the RPI increased from 100 to 1348 by 2000. That is, over this period, the prices of goods and services in the basket had, on average, increased by 13.5 times their original 1960 prices.

The **RPI-X** Index excludes mortgage interest payments from the RPI because they are affected by changes in interest rates.

The **Producer Price Index (PPI)** is calculated from the price movements of approximately 11,000 materials and products purchased and manufactured by UK industry. Increases in material prices paid by producers are likely to feed through to retail prices after a time-lag.

Government policy and inflation

Government policy for reducing inflation recognizes the following possible causes of rising price inflation:

- **Demand push inflation** occurs when the total demand for goods and services in the economy exceeds the total output or supply. As a result, prices will be forced up.
- **Cost push inflation** occurs when rising production costs are passed on to consumers in the form of higher prices. Production costs can rise either because workers push for wage increases above increases in productivity,

What is wrong with inflation?

The UK government argues that low inflation - and the confidence that it will be *kept* low - is essential for better economic performance and improved competitiveness. This is because:

- Inflation distorts the price signals in markets on which firms base their decisions about what goods and services to produce. Changes in relative prices become confused by general inflation. Even with general price inflation of only 5% per year, prices double every 14 years.
- High inflation creates uncertainty, which leads to reduced business investment in new plant and machinery - the engine of future economic growth. If firms are unsure about future prices and levels of inflation, they will be less willing to take risks and invest in long-term projects.
- High UK inflation relative to other countries reduces demand for UK exports, but increases the demand for cheaper overseas imports in the UK, thereby destroying jobs at home. Between 1989 and 1999 UK inflation averaged 5.7% per year, somewhat above her major European and non-European competitors.
- High inflation erodes the purchasing power of money. People are able to buy fewer goods and services than they did before, and so demand for goods and services tends to fall.
- As the purchasing power of money falls, lenders of money tend to push up interest rates to compensate. Savers will also demand higher interest rates to protect the value of their savings. As interest rates rise, borrowing becomes more expensive for consumers and firms.

▼ *Price inflation: How does the UK compare?*

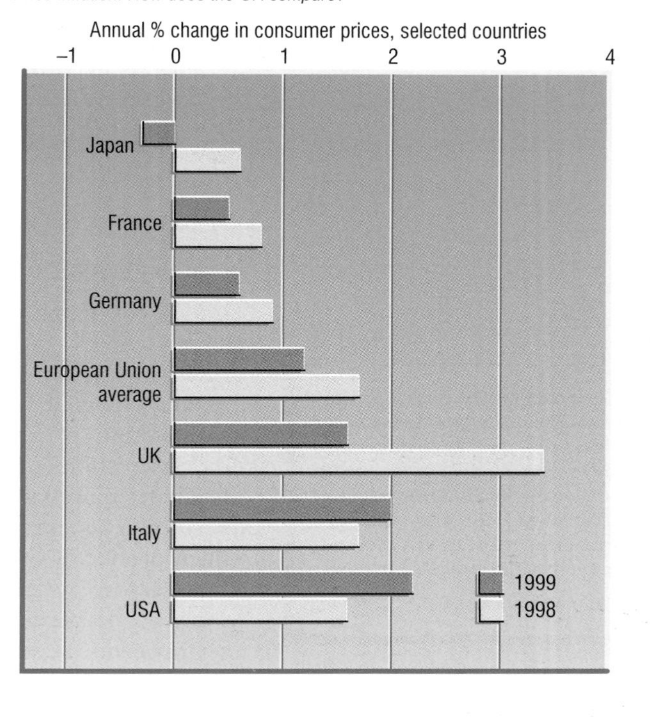

or if the price of materials and components rise. Many economists believe that inflation rates in excess of 20% experienced in the UK in 1974 and 1979 were the result of massive crude oil price increases agreed by the main oil-producing nations.

- **Imported inflation** is said to occur as the result of a fall in value of UK sterling on the foreign exchange market. This will increase the price paid for materials, semi-finished, and finished manufactures, and services purchased from overseas.

Given these possible causes of inflationary pressure in the UK economy, the following government policy measures to control inflation have been developed:

- **Fiscal policy** to control rapid increases in demand for goods and services by raising taxes and/or lowering government spending (see 6.2)
- Using **interest rates** to stabilize the UK exchange rate to encourage exports and to reduce imported inflation (see 6.2)
- **Supply side policies** to improve the ability of UK industry to expand output to meet demand and to reduce business costs and prices. These include:
  - Reducing the burden of taxation on incomes and profits to encourage effort and investment (see 6.2)

- Competition policy to encourage price competition (see 6.4 and 12.5)
- Privatization: allowing private sector firms to supply goods and services formerly provided by central and local government (see 6.5)
- Deregulation to remove out of date restrictions on competition and business (see 6.4)
- Promoting skills through an investment in education and training (see 15.2)
- Support for the 'knowledge-driven economy'
- Removing barriers to international trade (see 7.3)
- Encouraging inward investment (see 7.3)

> "The modern world is swept by change. This new world challenges business to be innovative and creative, to improve performance continuously, to build new alliances and ventures. But it also challenges Government: to create and execute a new approach to industrial policy."
>
> *The Rt Hon Tony Blair MP*

Encouraging the 'knowledge-driven economy'

A knowledge-driven economy is one in which the generation and exploitation of knowledge has come to play the predominant part in industrial competitiveness, and the creation of jobs and wealth. Knowledge facilitates more rapid scientific and technological advances which can allow businesses to innovate in products and production processes. It can help them produce more and different products faster, more cheaply and better than before. High-tech, knowledge-intensive manufacturing industries, such as aerospace, computers and communications equipment, and pharmaceuticals, and knowledge-based services such as telecommunications, computer and information services, finance and banking, are growing in importance in terms of the value of their output and employment.

The UK Government recognizes the importance of continued investment in research and development (R&D), new technologies and the workforce skills needed to promote UK competitiveness across many different industries. It is able to encourage firms to undertake this investment by providing a stable economic environment, and through a number of direct measures:

- funding skills training in new technologies (see 15.2)
- allowing expenditures on research and new technologies to be offset against corporation tax on company profits plus an additional R&D tax credit to help small and medium sized businesses invest in R&D
- establishing the Foresight programme to develop visions of the future and bring together the knowledge and expertise of business, science and government
- Business Link advice centres (and equivalent offices outside England - see 20.5) have Innovation Technology Counsellors available to provide local advice and help with European Research and Development initiatives
- grants for individuals and small/medium sized businesses to review, research, or develop technologies leading to commercial products
- LINK is a mechanism for supporting collaborative research partnerships between UK industry and the research base. It provides financial support to individual programmes of pre-competitive science and technology research

- the Patent Office helps small firms to protect their business ideas, inventions and logos by offering advice about patents, designs, trademarks and copyright
- targeted financial and other supports at hi-tech knowledge-based industries, such as aerospace, which may otherwise find it difficult to raise finance from banks to fund high-risk R&D investments with potentially long and uncertain payback periods

What is investment?

Investment is defined as the act of buying new and often improved plant and machinery by private and public sector business organizations. Investment spending is, therefore, a source of demand and revenue for producers of business premises, machinery and other man-made resources. Investment spending is also known as **gross domestic fixed capital formation**.

Some investment expenditure will be to buy new assets to replace man-made resources - premises, machinery and other equipment - which are old, worn out and no longer productive. Simply replacing old equipment does not add to the ability of firms to increase their output. However, investment in new and additional premises, machinery and other equipment will expand productive capacity.

New investment by business is, therefore, essential if the productive capability of the UK economy is to grow. Investment in new technologies can also mean faster, more efficient production, less wasteful and better quality production. This can lower the cost of producing each unit of a good or service and, therefore, improve the competitiveness of UK industry.

It is often argued that UK firms are reluctant to invest compared with other countries because business owners are often uncertain about the profits they will earn from new investment. For example, in 2000 UK industry and government invested a total of £155 billion in artificial (non-natural) resources, the equivalent of some 18% of the total value of UK output of all goods and services. This compared with around 25% of total output in Japan and 21.2% in Germany (see Table 7.3). This suggests that these other countries are devoting a far larger proportion of their total national outputs to investment in new plant and machinery than the UK. However, these figures do not tell us how much of that spending is to replace old and worn out equipment or to increase productive capacity.

▼ *Table 7.3: Gross domestic fixed capital formation, as a % of GDP in selected countries*

	1970	1980	1990	2000*
United Kingdom	18.9	18.0	19.3	18.4
Germany	25.5	22.6	21.0	21.2
France	24.3	23.0	21.2	19.4
Portugal	23.2	20.2	26.4	27.9
Italy	24.3	24.3	20.2	19.1
European Union	23.8	22.0	20.9	20.5
USA	18.0	20.2	16.8	20.3
Japan	32.2	31.6	32.2	25.0

European Economy, 1999 Review
**** forecast***

Portfolio Activity 7.4

1. What is international competitiveness and why is it important?
2. What are the reasons for the UK's relatively poor performance according to the article?
3. How is the UK Government trying to improve UK competitiveness? Investigate and report on current policies by visiting the Department of Trade and Industry website at ***www.dti.gov.uk*** or by writing to the DTI for information.

Britain slips in global competitiveness league

INADEQUATE training and education have helped to push Britain down the global competitiveness league, according to a report out yesterday.

The UK has tumbled from fourth to eighth in the league, according to the annual study published by the World Economic Forum. Taiwan, Canada, Switzerland and Luxembourg have all leapfrogged Britain in the competitiveness race.

Sophisticated financial markets and access to venture capital are among the UK's competitive advantages cited in the report. However, these strengths were partly out-weighed by shortcomings in both schools and corporate training courses.

Competitive disadvantages include "adequacy of average years of schooling, quality of scientists and engineers and attention to staff training".

The study, produced by business luminaries such as Professors Michael Porter and Jeffrey Sachs, put Singapore at the top of the competitiveness league for the second successive year. Singapore's flexible labour markets, openness to trade and high levels of education have helped the economy to maintain its competitiveness despite the crisis in Asia. Hong Kong slipped from second to third.

The US replaced Hong Kong as a second in the league, earning praise for the strides the economy has made in the field of technology.

However, the study said a bubble economy could be developing in America, and predicted the US boom could fade by this time next year.

The Times, 14.9.2000

Key words:

Inflation - a sustained increase in the general level of prices, usually measured as a rate of increase per period of time

Retail Prices Index (RPI) - a record of the average price level of a representative selection of some 600 household goods and services over time. Changes in the RPI per period provide the headline rate of price inflation in the UK

Producer Prices Index (PPI) - a record of movement in the average price of some 11,000 materials used in manufacturing

Gross fixed capital formation - investment in new and replacement plant and machinery

Section 7.3 Government action and international trade

Trade policy

Markets are becoming increasingly global as real incomes rise in countries all over the world. UK business will be unable to keep pace with international competitors without easy access to overseas markets. Eliminating barriers to free trade and cross-border investment will increase business and consumer choice, and reduce the cost of goods and services.

The UK trade policy operates as part of the **European Union (EU)** policy on trade, and trade agreements administered by the **World Trade Organization (WTO).**

▼ *Figure 7.15: The European Union in 2000*

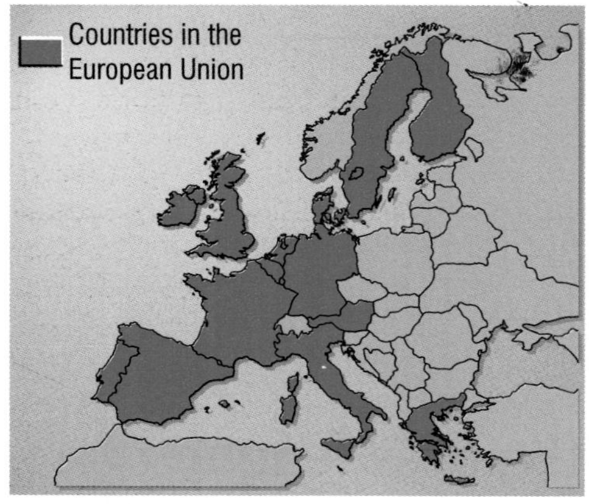

The European Union

The European Community (EC) began in 1958 when six countries - West Germany, Italy, France, Belgium, the Netherlands, and Luxembourg - signed the Treaty of Rome, committing themselves to the formation of a common market.

By 1993, the UK, Spain, Portugal, Greece, Eire, and Denmark had also joined, making a total of 12 member states (the 'EU12') and forming a market of over 350 million people.

On 1 January 1995, the number of EC countries increased to 15, as Austria, Finland, and Sweden became full members. Turkey and Cyprus have also applied for membership, with many more considering joining, such as the former communist countries of Poland and Hungary. On 7 February 1992 the EC became known as the European Union (EU).

Decision-making in the EU

There are five main groups which influence decision-making and ensure that decisions are upheld in the EU:

- The **European Commission** is the executive of the EU and makes proposals on policy and legislation.
- The **Council of Ministers** is made up of foreign secretaries from the governments of each member state, who are responsible for all major community decisions on such issues as industry, transport, agriculture, and finance.
- The **European Parliament** consists of elected members from all over the EU. The EU Parliament has powers to approve or recommend changes to the Council's position, but has no powers of veto.
- The **Economic and Social Committee** acts in an advisory capacity to the Council. It is made up of employees, Trade Unions, and independent representatives of the member states.
- The **European Court of Justice** ensures that EU laws are observed in member states and deals with any disputes.

Other international trading agreements

Many other countries have agreed to trade pacts (or trade blocks) to form customs unions or 'free trade areas' on a regional basis. That is, they work together to 'free' trade between their members but attempt to restrict imports from outside using tariffs and controls on volumes, known as quotas. These aims have been achieved with varying degrees of success.

Examples include:

NAFTA (North American Free Trade Areas): including the USA, Canada and Mexico. The Caribbean Basin Initiative of 1999 seeks to extend NAFTA to Latin American and Caribbean countries

European Free Trade Association (EFTA): including Iceland, Norway, Switzerland and Liechtenstein

Common Market for Eastern and Southern Africa (COMESA)

There are also many sub-regional pacts, such as the **Caribbean Community** and the **Central American Common Market**

EU objectives

The EU has a number of broad objectives which will dramatically alter the way in which people live and conduct business.

To form a customs union

Before the EU was set up European countries used to impose tariffs on imports from each other. This meant, for example, that people in France would have to pay much more for goods imported from say Germany and the UK. In this way the French Government hoped it would encourage French people to buy goods and services from producers in France even if they could be imported at lower prices from overseas. Because of this **protectionism**, many firms were unable to sell their goods and services abroad and this raised unemployment among European workers.

The EU has formed a **customs union** and has removed all taxes on trade between EU members. So now, for example, the UK can export freely to all other EU members. However, many imports coming into the EU from non-EU countries are taxed in order to make them more expensive and so discourage EU consumers from buying them. This tax is called the **common external tariff.**

The common external tariff is designed to protect business and jobs in the EU from cheap imports from outside the EU. Tariff rates applied to the price of imported goods and services have to be the same in each EU country otherwise there would be problems. For example, suppose the UK applied a 20% tariff to the price of imports from non-EU countries while France only applied a 10% tariff. A Japanese firm exporting to the UK could first export their products to France and then ship them to the UK without incurring extra tax.

To encourage freedom of movement

The EU wants to remove all barriers to the free movement of goods and services, business and personal investments, and people across EU borders. People in the EU are free to live and work in any member state and be entitled to the same conditions of employment, health care and social security benefits as anyone else in their chosen member country.

To operate a Common Agricultural Policy

The European Community felt that it was vital for Europe to produce its own food and not rely on foreign supplies. In order to achieve this aim the EC introduced the **Common Agricultural Policy (CAP).**

Under the CAP farmers are guaranteed a high price for their produce by the EU Government. However, this has often caused farmers to overproduce every year. Excess supplies are bought up by the EU Government.

Portfolio Activity 7.5 

1. What evidence is there from the article that the EU operates a customs union?
2. Why is Sony objecting to this EU policy?
3. How is the EU customs union designed to protect businesses and employment in EU member countries?

Sony threatens to sue Brussels

Sony, the Japanese electronics manufacture, may take legal action against the European Commission if it does not change its tariff classification of the PlayStation2 games console.

Sony believes the Commission's recent decision to designate PlayStation2 a video game player, liable to a levy 2.2 per cent duty on every console imported into the region, is unfair.

The group says PS2 - which has a 128-bit microprocessor, a DVD player, and the potential to connect to the internet - is as sophisticated as a computer and should be classified as one. No duties are levied on computers imported into Europe.

"We will file suit if PS2 is going to be classified in a different tax category, the with 100 per cent certainty Sony will have to take some action," said Ken Kutaragi, president of Sony Computer Entertainment.

The tiff began when Sony Computer Entertainment Europe (SCEE) applied to the UK Customs and Excise department (HMCE), which helps the Commission process duty applications, to designate PS2 a computer. The department rejected the application last month on the grounds that PS2 was not significantly different from its predecessor, PlayStation, released in 1995 as a video game player.

Financial Times, 2.11.2000

The CAP has been criticized because it has often resulted in huge stockpiles of surplus produce and high food prices for EU consumers. The excess output cannot be sold in the EU because it would cause food prices to fall and reduce farmers' incomes. The food stockpiles are also very expensive to store and so are sold off cheaply to non-EU countries. Sometimes the surplus food is fed to animals or even destroyed.

Recently subsidies have been redirected to encourage more organic and less intensive farming methods.

To provide help to less prosperous regions in the European Union

The EU regional policy provides money to less developed areas in the EU by providing jobs and improving schools, housing, roads, etc. (see 23.3).

To establish a single European market

The **Single European Market** (or **internal market**) was created on 1 January 1993. EU members agreed to remove all remaining barriers to movement and free trade such as frontier checks at custom posts, cumbersome importing documents designed to raise importing costs, different national product and safety standards, the application of separate - and sometimes unnecessary - health checks, and major differences in indirect taxation such as rates of VAT, excise duties, and duty-free allowances.

To create Economic and Monetary Union (EMU)

On 7 February 1992 the heads of state of governments of the European Community signed the Maastricht Treaty agreement on European Union. The main focus of that agreement is the creation of a framework for **European Economic and Monetary Union (EMU)**, involving the creation of a single currency and common economic policy.

For the agreement to come into effect in full, each member state has to approve it. Not all have done so. Denmark voted against the Treaty and the UK opted not to adopt a single European currency for the time being. This means the UK Government will have to have a Parliamentary vote before it can join. EMU involves the creation of single European currency and common economic policies. The single European currency was given the name the 'euro' at a meeting in Madrid in 1995.

Member countries that met the Maastricht criteria in 1998 were able to qualify for the third stage of the EMU which began on 1 January 1999. At this time eleven member countries introduced the euro and transferred control over interest rates to the European Central Bank. Between January and June 2002 their national currencies will be withdrawn. Remaining EU members who meet the Maastricht criteria will be allowed to join stages 2 and 3 of EMU at a later date if they wish to do so.

To make sure EU members keep to the Maastricht condition on Budget deficits they all agreed a **stability and growth pact** at a meeting in Dublin in 1996. This agreement is designed to prevent national EU Governments spending more than they raise in tax revenue and running up deficits in excess of 3% of their GDP. A country will be penalized if the Government budgets for a deficit of more than 3% unless the country is in a deep recession and increased Government spending is needed to boost aggregate demand (see 6.2).

EMU: a three-stage plan

Progress towards European Economic and Monetary Union involves following a three-stage plan:

1. Increased coordination of fiscal and monetary policy between EU members, and completion of the internal market
2. A gradual transfer of economic decision-making power from national central banks, such as the UK Bank of England and the German Bundesbank, to a new single European Central Bank
3. Fixing the value of exchange rates between EU member currencies, a single European monetary policy, and the eventual replacement of national currencies by a single **European Currency Unit (ECU)**.

The Maastricht Treaty states that member states wishing to join EMU Stage 3 must meet the following conditions:

- **Inflation:** annual average price inflation to be within 1.5% of the rate of price inflation of the three EC member states where it is lowest
- **Interest rates:** average long-term interest rates over 1 year to be within 2% of rates in the same three member states
- **Budget deficit:** member states must not have a deficit between public expenditure and tax revenues that is considered 'excessive'
- **Exchange rates:** the national currency of the member country must have been within the narrow band of the European **Exchange Rate Mechanism (ERM)** for at least two years

The European Exchange Rate Mechanism (ERM)

What is ERM?

The ERM was the first step towards economic and monetary union in the EU and the introduction of a single European currency. The ERM requires member states to agree exchange rates between their currencies and then 'fix' them. Interest rates could be used to stabilize currency rates. National central banks in EU member countries would also buy up or sell a particular EU member currency in order to raise or lower its value, if necessary, to keep it at the agreed exchange rate.

Exchange rates in the ERM are pegged to the value of the strongest currency in terms of its value against the currencies of non-EU member countries. For many years, the strongest currency in the system was the German mark, being an indication of the strength of the German economy. When the UK joined the ERM in October 1990 the value of sterling was fixed at £1 = 2.95 Dm. As the value of Dm appreciates or depreciates against non-EU currencies so too will all the other currencies tied to it in the ERM. Thus, if £1 = 2.95 Dm = US$1.5, then an appreciation of the Dm would take their values to say 2.95 Dm = US$1.7 = £1.

Currencies in the ERM are allowed to fluctuate within a narrow band around the strongest currency. When the UK joined the ERM in October 1990 there were two bands set at 2.25% and 6%. The first band allowed currency values to rise above or fall below its fixed rate by up to 2.25%. The wider band allowed the values of weaker currencies to vary by up to plus or minus 6%. Sterling initially joined the wider band which included the currencies of Spain and Italy.

Why did the UK leave the ERM?

During September 1992 increasing pressure on the UK pound due to a large balance of payments deficit and uncertainty about the UK economy, caused the value of the pound to fall to its lower limit of 2.78 Dm, i.e. 6% below its value on entry to the ERM. Speculation that the pound would be devalued caused many financial institutions around the world to sell their holdings of sterling, causing the value of the pound to fall further.

▼ *How the ERM works*

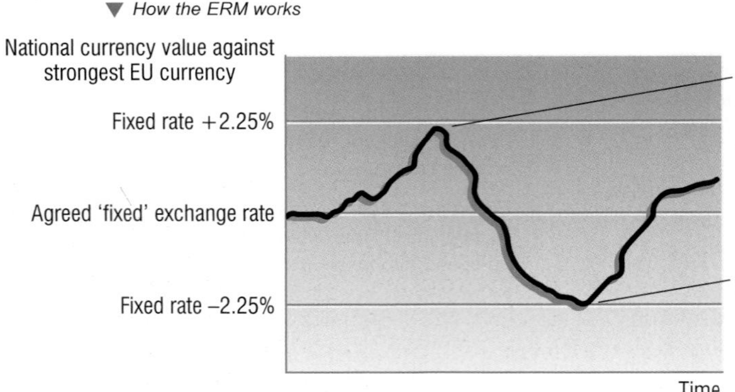

A government must take actions to reduce the value of its national currency if it has risen to the top of the band. These are increasing the supply of the currency on the foreign exchange market and/or lowering interest rates.

A government must take actions to increase the value of its national currency if it has fallen to the bottom of the band. These are buying up their currency on the foreign exchange market and/or raising interest rates.

Intervention by the Bank of England and other central banks in Europe failed to support the pound. Billions of pounds in foreign currency reserves were used to buy up pounds in an effort to raise the value of the pound. Interest rates were also raised from 10% to 15% briefly in an attempt to attract foreign investors to place their money in UK bank accounts, by first converting their currencies into pounds. However, the value of the pound continued to fall below its ERM floor and so the UK withdrew from the ERM on 16 September 1992.

Because of this experience many think the ERM is unstable and the UK has yet to rejoin. In 2000 confidence in the good health of the UK economy meant that the pound was strong and its value was high against other currencies. Some economists have argued the pound would need to fall in value before it could rejoin the ERM. However, a fall in the value of the pound would increase the price of imports and boost imported inflation.

What is the euro?

The final step towards economic and monetary union in Europe is the introduction of a single currency and transfer of decision-making on European interest rates and monetary policy to a **European Central Bank (ECB)**. This will have a big impact on the way businesses in the UK and other countries conduct trade with euro zone member countries.

The **euro** is the name given to the money, or currency, that will replace the national currencies of the EU member countries. So, for example, by mid-2002 the French franc, German deutschmark, Spanish pesata and other EU currencies will not exist. Instead people in these countries, or travelling to them, will use euros to buy and sell goods and services. Even UK pounds and pence may be replaced with the euro one day.

Eleven EU countries started using the euro on 1 January 1999. Countries using the euro form the **euro zone**. Only the UK, Sweden, Denmark and Greece have not joined the euro zone, although Greece hopes to meet the Maastricht criteria soon to be able to join.

The euro will be used alongside existing currencies until they are withdrawn from use in 2002. This is so people have time to get used to paying for goods and services in euros. One euro is worth about 6.5 francs in France, 1.95 marks in Germany, and 1936 lire in Italy. These rates are fixed until national currencies are eventually phased out in July 2002.

The role of the European Central Bank

The creation of a European Central Bank (ECB) accompanied the introduction of the euro. Its main objective is to keep price inflation low and stable across the euro zone. To do this it takes decisions on the single monetary policy and interest rate for the euro zone. If it thinks price inflation will rise, it is likely to raise interest rates, and it will cut them if it believes price inflation will fall. The ECB also holds and manages the foreign exchange reserves of all the member EU states.

▼ *The euro will replace national currencies in 2002*

The Euro rates

GERMANY	1.95583	marks
FRANCE	6.55957	francs
ITALY	1936.21	lire
HOLLAND	2.20371	guilders
SPAIN	166.386	pesetas
PORTUGAL	200.482	escudos
FINLAND	5.94573	markka
IRELAND	0.787564	punts
AUSTRIA	13.7603	schillings
BELGIUM	40.3399	francs
LUX'BOURG	40.3399	francs

Portfolio Activity 7.6 

Imagine the day comes when UK has joined in the single European currency and has replaced pounds and pence with euros and what this might mean. Read the quotes below and use them to make a list of the advantages and disadvantages of joining the euro. Do you think it is a good or bad idea for the UK to scrap its national currency in favour of the euro? What are the likely impacts of a decision to join the euro zone on UK businesses? Discuss in your class group.

Female holidaymaker: "Everytime I went on holiday to say Spain or Portugal I would have to change my pounds into pesetas or escudos. Foreign currency exchanges usually charged a commission to do this of around two or three percent. Then if I had any foreign notes left over after my holiday I would have to change them back into pounds and pay commission again. Now I don't have to do this. Using euros makes it so much easier and cheaper."

Businessman: "We might have to close down next year if demand for goods overseas doesn't pick up. Exports are way down and I have already laid off 30% of my workforce. I blame the high fixed value of the euro. If we had kept the pound its value could have fallen against other currencies like the US dollar. This would reduce the price of our exports overseas and help boost demand for them."

Shopkeeper: "Don't talk to me about the bloomin' euro. When we first joined I had to price everything in pounds and euros. All my price lists and catalogues had to be reprinted. Then when the pound was finally replaced I had to reprint them all again!"

Male holidaymaker: "Shopping overseas was never easy for me when there was lots of different national currencies. For example, I was in Italy a few years ago. A bottle of wine in a restaurant cost me 8,000 lire. That's expensive I thought. Then I realized it was only around £3 because there were over 2,600 lire to every pound. Now everything is in euros I can easily compare prices in different countries."

Female politician in 'Anti Euro Party': "The European Central Bank has set interest rates too high for the UK. The UK is in recession and needs to have lower interest rates to stimulate demand for goods and services. However, because inflation is high in the rest of Europe the ECB has raised interest rates. This will just create unemployment in the UK."

Business man: "We import many component parts from suppliers in mainland Europe. Paying for them in euros has reduced our costs. Trade has increased because we have been able to cut our prices. And as we sell more we need to import even more from Europe. When we had the pound import prices would fluctuate because of changes in exchange rates. For example, we could order £100,000 of components from Germany one morning when the pound was worth 2 marks, and by the afternoon the cost could have gone up to say £105,000 because the pound had fallen to 1.9 marks."

ECB spokesperson: "The ECB is committed to bringing down inflation across the European Union. Because of this commitment interest rates can be lower than they would have been in some individual countries. This is because some countries have a poor inflation record. If people think there is a risk of higher inflation they will press for higher wages. As a result a country will have to raise interest rates. People will believe the risk of inflation is lower if there is a strong ECB controlling inflation in their countries."

The ECB heads the **European System of Central Banks (ESCB)** which is made up of the national central banks of all the EU countries, including the Bank of England in the UK (see 6.2). The Bank of England is a member of the ESCB with special status because the UK is not in the ERM and has not introduced the euro. This means it is allowed to take decisions on monetary policy and interest rates in the UK but does not take part in decision-making concerning the single monetary policy for euro countries.

It is the job of the ESCB central banks in the euro zone to apply the interest rate and meet the inflation targets agreed with the ECB in their own countries.

Arguments for and against the euro

The UK has yet to adopt the euro and commit itself to replacing the pound with the single European currency. The issue is very controversial. There are a number of arguments for and against joining the euro.

Potential benefits of the euro

- **Reduced transaction costs:** If there is just one European currency, consumers and businesses within the EU will no longer need to exchange pounds for Spanish pesetas, or French francs for Irish punts when travelling to different EU countries or paying for their imports. Changing money into foreign currencies costs money because many banks and foreign exchange agencies charge commission to do so. This will help to reduce business costs of foreign trade.
- **Increased European competition:** Because all prices will be quoted in euros, comparing prices in the different member countries will be easier. There will be no need to convert prices in one currency to another. Because of this people may be more tempted to shop around for the best deal, either during the course of travelling or via the Internet. This will increase price competition between suppliers in the different EU countries.
- **Reduced exchange rate uncertainty:** International trade between EU members may become less risky and cheaper. This may encourage more trade and help create jobs. This is because businesses will no longer have to pay for imported goods and services in foreign currencies which can rise or fall in value against their own currency. For example, if the French franc falls against the German mark, French businesses will have to pay more for imports from Germany. Because they now use the euro, this will no longer happen. However, the euro can still change in value against non-member currencies like the US dollar and Japanese yen.
- **Lower interest rates:** If the European Central Bank can show it is firmly committed to keeping inflation at a low level across the euro zone, it may be able to do so with lower average interest rates. Low interest rates will reduce the costs of borrowing by business organizations to pay for new investments that will help improve their technological capabilities and competitiveness. In contrast, individual countries with a poor inflation record may have to keep interest rates higher and for longer to control inflationary surges in consumer demand.

- **Increased inward direct investment:** A European Union with a single currency forms a very large market for goods and services. Firms from Japan and other non-EU countries may be tempted to set up factories, shops and offices in the EU in order to sell their goods and services into this large market. This is called **direct inward investment** from overseas (see below). In this way firms from non-EU countries are able to avoid the common external tariff on their goods.

Potential costs of the euro

- **National Governments will no longer be able to use economic policy to control inflation and unemployment in their own countries:** This is because EU countries that have entered stages 2 and 3 of the EMU rely on the European Central Bank to set interest rates across them. They are also committed to a budget deficit of less than 3% of their GDPs. A member country with high inflation relative to the others is likely to want higher interest rates than the ECB would set. A country with relatively high unemployment may want much lower interest rates and to increase public spending (see 6.2). Joining in the euro prevents it from doing this.
- **Changeover costs:** Introducing the euro will cost businesses money. These additional costs will be passed onto consumers as higher prices. The costs arise because firms will have to change all their price lists, menus, catalogues, wage payments and accounts into euros. The Government will also have to change its public accounting, taxation and social security systems.

MPs say euro switch to cost business billions

A cross-party group of MPs warned business it could face a multi-billion pound bill from preparing to operate in euros, with small firms hit hardest. Parliament's Trade and Industry Committee accused the government of shying away from the subject for political reasons.

"The potential costs to business of joining the euro are high, to be measured in billions not millions," the committee said in a hard-hitting report. "The government is unwilling even to discuss the costs to business of UK membership of the euro, let alone to estimate them."

Neither of the two National Changeover Plans published so far by the government properly addressed the costs of switching to the single currency, it said.

Prime Minister Tony Blair says he will join the euro after next year's expected election but only if the economics are right and the public support it in a referendum.

Polls show as much as 70 per cent of the population want to keep the pound. But firms will increasingly have to deal in euros whether Britain adopts the euro or not.

The committee took evidence from a wide range of industry groups who said companies could spend two percent or more of their turnover switching over computer systems and making other preparations for the single currency.

The British Retail Consortium told the committee changing tills and computer systems would cost the average retailer 1.2 per cent of turnover. Small businesses may spend as much as 2.6 per cent.

A survey by accountants KPMG found companies expecting to spend five times as much switching their systems to deal in euros than they did to counter the Millennium Bug.

For the banking sector, the British Bankers Association said estimates had put the cost at 1.2 per cent of operating costs for each of the three years it expected changeover to last.

"The government should produce guidance on planning and budgeting for IT projects for euro conversions at the earliest opportunity after a decision is made," the MPs concluded. "We recommend that, should there be a 'yes' vote on a single currency referendum, the government encourage businesses to prepare financial plans for the changeover as soon as possible."

London Reuters, 16.11.2000

The World Trade Organization

What is the WTO?

The **World Trade Organization (WTO)** was established in 1995, replacing the General Agreement on Tariffs and Trade agreed between many trading nations in 1947. The WTO was formed following GATT discussions between 1986 and 1993 and agreements reached in Switzerland on 15 December 1993.

The WTO is the only global international organization dealing with the rules of trade between nations. At its heart are the WTO agreements, negotiated and signed by the bulk of the world's trading nations and ratified in their parliaments. The goal is to help producers of goods and services, exporters, and importers conduct their business. In June 2000 the WTO had 138 countries as members, accounting for over 90% of all world trade by value.

The WTO's overriding objective is to remove barriers to free trade. It does this by:

- Administering trade agreements
- Acting as a forum for trade negotiations
- Settling trade disputes
- Reviewing national trade policies
- Assisting developing countries in trade policy issues, through technical assistance and training programmes
- Cooperating with other international organizations

Portfolio Activity 7.7 

1. What is the role and purpose of the WTO?
2. Describe the trade dispute between the US and the EU. Explain how the US scheme allowing US companies to avoid paying tax on their export incomes could give them an unfair advantage over EU companies and 'violated trade rules'.
3. What are the advantages of free international trade to UK consumers and business?
4. What are the possible disadvantages of free trade to UK businesses and employees?

US and EU seek to calm trade dispute

The US and European Union yesterday sought to take the heat out of their dispute over an American scheme that enables companies to avoid taxes on export income. The moves followed a World Trade Organisation ruling that it violated trade rules.

Charlene Barshefsky, US trade representative, said Washington disagreed with the ruling but respected its WTO obligations and did not want to jeopardise ties with the EU.

The case is the most important in the WTO's history. Failure by the US and EU to settle it could add to the strains on their relationship created by bruising recent conflicts over WTO rulings against the EU's banana import regime and ban on hormone-treated beef.

"We will seek a solution that ensures that US firms and workers are not at a competitive disadvantage," Ms Barshefsky said. "It is neither in the interest of the US nor the EU to allow this case to damage our bilateral relationship."

Lawrence Summers, US Treasury secretary, said the Foreign Sales Corporations scheme was important to US companies, but that Washington would "work closely with the Europeans, the business community and the Congress to achieve a solution".

EU officials said yesterday it was for Washington to make the next move. "Our door would be open to discuss how to go about the implementation of the findings," the European Commission said.

The ruling upholds a WTO panel finding last year that the FSC scheme was an illegal export subsidy and must be repealed or amended by October 1 – five weeks before the US elections. Citing US Treasury figures, the EU says the scheme saved US exporters $3.5bn (£2.2bn) in tax last year, though the US says the value of the subsidy is much smaller.

Financial Times, 25.2.2000

Encouraging inward investment

UK government policy is to encourage both inward and outward investment.

Some WTO trade disputes

Below is just a handful of trade disputes the WTO dealt with between 1996 and 1999.

United States – Standards for Reformulated and Conventional Gasoline imports, complaints by Venezuela and Brazil (WT/DS4). The US announced implementation of WTO recommendations as of 19 August 1997.

Japan – Taxes on Imported Alcoholic Beverages, complaints by the European Communities, Canada (WT/DS10) and the United States (WT/DS11). The period for implementation was set by the Arbitrator at 15 months from the date of adoption of the reports, i.e. it expired on 1 February 1998. Japan presented modalities for implementation which were accepted by the complainants.

United States – Restrictions on Imports of Cotton and Man-Made Fibre Underwear, complaint by Costa Rica (WT/DS24). The US announced that the measure at issue expired as of 27 March 1997.

Brazil – Measures Affecting Desiccated Coconut imports, complaint by the Philippines - no implementation issue in view of the result.

United States – Measure Affecting Imports of Woven Wool Shirts and Blouses, complaint by India. The US announced that the measure was withdrawn as at 22 November 1996, before the Panel had concluded its work. Therefore, no implementation issue arose.

Canada – Certain Measures Concerning Periodicals, complaint by the United States. The implementation period was agreed by the parties to be 15 months from the date of adoption of the reports, i.e. it expired on 30 October 1998. Canada has withdrawn the contested measure.

European Communities – Regime for the Importation, Sale and Distribution of Bananas, complaints by Ecuador, Guatemala, Honduras, Mexico and the United States. The period for implementation was set by arbitration at 15 months and 1 week from the date of the adoption of the reports, i.e. it expired on 1 January 1999. The EC has revised the contested measures.

India – Patent Protection for Pharmaceutical and Agricultural Chemical Products, complaint by the United States. The period of implementation was agreed by the parties to be 15 months from the date of the adoption of the reports, i.e. it expired on 16 April 1999. India undertook to comply with the recommendations of the WTO within the implementation period.

European Communities – Measures Affecting Meat and Meat Products (Hormones), complaint by Canada and the United States. At its meeting on 26 July 1999, the WTO authorized the suspension of concessions to the EC by the United States and Canada in the respective amounts determined by the arbitrators as being equivalent to the level of nullification suffered by them.

Inward investment refers to the setting up of foreign-owned multinational companies in the UK. By far the biggest foreign investors in the UK are US and Japanese companies. The UK attracts more US and Japanese business investment than other EU member countries.

Outward investment refers to UK investment overseas. The setting up of UK companies abroad provides access to foreign consumers, allowing UK-owned business to sell more goods overseas and improve the balance of international payments.

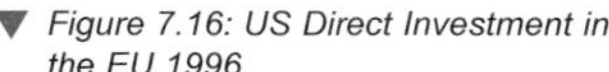

Figure 7.16: US Direct Investment in the EU 1996

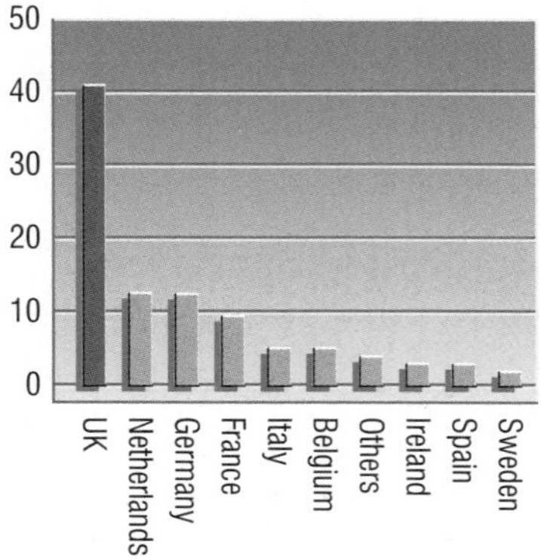

US Department of Commerce 1997
From 'Invest in Britain', DTI, 1998

Figure 7.17: Japanese direct investment in the EU 1951–3/1996

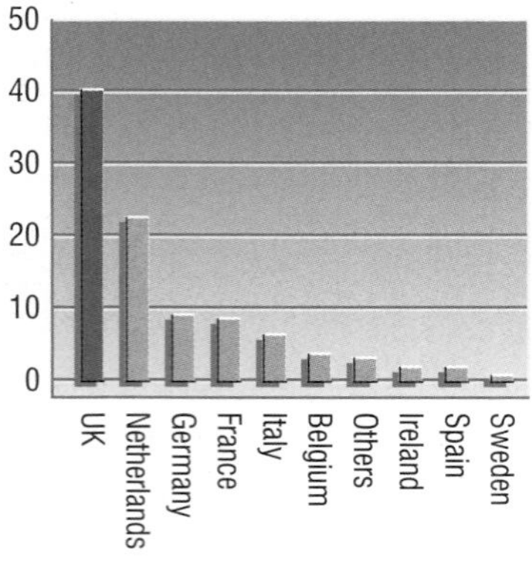

Japanese Ministry of Finance

The government publication 'Competitiveness: Helping Business to Win' (HMSO, 1994) suggested inward investment has the following benefits:

'Inward investment brings world-class production techniques, technical innovation and managerial skills, which can be transferred to local companies. It has revived the international competitiveness of some sectors of UK industry, such as vehicles.'

Key words:

European Union (EU) - organization of European countries, formerly the European Community, which seeks closer economic and political union between members

Customs union - a group of countries with free trade between them and a common external tariff, like that of the EU

Tariff - a tax placed on an imported good

Single European Market - an agreement by EU member countries to remove all barriers to free trade between them

Common external tariff - tariff placed on goods imported to the EU from non-EU countries

Common Agricultural Policy (CAP) - interventions in agricultural markets by the EU government to stabilize farm incomes in member countries

EMU - European and Monetary Union to create a common currency and macro-economic policy in EU member countries

ERM - the European Exchange Rate Mechanism which fixes the exchange rates of the currencies of EU member countries as a prelude to the introduction of a single European currency

The euro - the single European currency

Euro zone - those EU member countries which have adopted the euro

European Central Bank - the Bank of EU Government which will be responsible for decision-making on European interest rates and monetary policy

World Trade Organization (WTO) - established to oversee recent GATT agreements and to further promote free trade

Inward investment - the setting up of foreign-owned enterprise in the UK

Outward investment - UK investment overseas

Section 7.4 Business strategies

What can businesses do to improve their competitiveness?

In the last section we considered how the government can help UK industry to improve its ability to compete in international markets for goods and services. But what can individual firms do for themselves?

Throughout this book we consider the various ways in which businesses can improve their performance in terms of increased sales, market shares and profits (see 1.7). If these objectives are to be achieved, then businesses must employ strategies that increase output for a given input of human, man-made and natural resources. That is, firms must aim to improve their productivity and lower their costs of production (see 1.1).

Strategies firms have been using to improve their ability to compete for customers and market share include:

- investing in new faster and more efficient machinery and production processes. For example, new technologies such as robotics and computers have revolutionized many manufacturing processes (see 1.3).
- expanding the scale of production to spread fixed costs, such as rent, rates, insurance and other overheads, over a larger output and thereby lowering the average cost of per unit of output (see 'economies of scale' 22.4).
- increasing marketing efforts to increase sales, expand market shares and to enter new markets (see 8.2). Marketing will also include using market research to find out about changing consumer wants and the development of new and existing products to satisfy their wants (see 9.1).

- training employees to improve and broaden their skills, and introducing more efficient working methods, for example, team working, quality circles and flexitime (see 15.2).
- re-designing jobs to improve employee motivation (see 15.1) and increasing the flexibility of human resources by introducing more part-time and temporary employment contracts (see 13.2).
- streamlining administrative procedures and changing the structure of the organization to improve the communication of information on which business decisions are made and the speed at which decisions are implemented by employees (see 4.1).
- cost control by monitoring spending by individual departments, negotiating discounts with suppliers, changing the method of business finance from high-cost loans to cheaper sources of funds (see 23.2).

A firm will be able to judge the effectiveness of these strategies on their business performance in terms of:

- increased market shares
- higher sales volumes and revenues
- lower labour costs and improved productivity
- improved products and service quality

For the UK as a whole, the effectiveness of both business and government strategies will be measured in terms of meeting the following objectives:

- economic growth in the national output
- increased export volumes and revenues
- an increased share of the world export market
- low and stable inflation
- an increased standard of living, as measured by the growth in incomes, a wider choice of goods and services, better quality goods and services and less wasteful, more environmentally friendly production

Key Activity

A business magazine has asked you to write an article about an industry of your choice to examine:

- the market conditions that affect businesses in the industry
- the degree of domestic and international competition in the industry, and how this is changing
- how it is affected by current policies of the UK and EU Governments
- how competitive the industry is and what businesses are doing to improve their competitiveness
- future prospects for businesses and employees in the industry

Your article should be produced using computer word processing software and submitted to the magazine (your tutor) initially in a draft form for comment before your finalize the article.

You can enhance the presentation of your article by using a two-column text format and scanning in relevant photographs you have found or taken yourself.

Your article should:

- Describe the industry you have chosen in terms of: the industrial sector it operates in; products and production processes; numbers of businesses and employees; turnover; market shares of the different firms in the industry; exports; recent trends.
- Analyse the demand and supply conditions that affect businesses in the industry: Is the market expanding or contracting, and if so why? What impact have recent changes in market conditions had on the industry (in terms of sales turnover, numbers of firms and employees, exports, etc.)? Is competition increasing and becoming more global? What different forms of competition are there between firms operating in the market? What is the market structure like? How do businesses in the industry try to influence consumer demand and the actions of rival firms, and why?
- Evaluate the impact of different government policies on the industry. This should include government policies to control the overall level of activity in the economy and policies aimed specifically at the market in which the industry operates. How has the government intervened in the market and why? How has the industry responded to changing government policies?
- Assess the impact of increasing international competition on the industry. How competitive is the industry? How is the industry responding to the globalization of markets? What impact has the single European market had on businesses in the industry and how are they preparing for the possible introduction of the single European currency, the euro? What impact is the euro likely to have on the way these businesses operate?
- Use relevant sources of information including UK and EU Government statistical publications; news reports and articles; interviews with managers and employees of firms in the industry; company annual reports and information from company websites.
- Include tables and graphs showing relevant business statistics to support your arguments.

Useful references

The **European Commission** publishes useful statistics in **'European Economy'**. Visit the European Commission website at ***europa.eu.int/comm/index.htm*** or write to the European Commission, 200 rue de la Loi/Wetstraat 200, B-1049 Brussels, Belgium.

'Our Competitive Future – Building the Knowledge Driven Economy' (DTI, December 1998). For this and further information about government initiatives to improve UK competitiveness contact the **Department of Trade and Industry (*www.dti.gov.uk*)**, Enquiry Unit, 1 Victoria Street, London , SW1H 0ET.

The Office of National Statistics produces the following statistical publications:

- *Annual Abstract of Statistics*
- *Economic Trends*
- *Monthly Digest of Statistics*

Visit the ONS website at ***www.ons.gov.uk*** or write to ONS, Public Enquiry Services, 1 Drummond Gate, London SW1V 2QQ.

World Trade Organization (*www.wto.org*)
rue de Lausanne 154, CH-1211 Geneva 21, Switzerland.

Internet key words search: **competitiveness, international trade**

Test your knowledge

1 A common measure used for international comparisons of workforce performance is:

- **A** The total number or workers employed in the service sector
- **B** Unit labour costs
- **C** Basic holiday entitlements and hours of work
- **D** Average earnings

2 The value of output per worker employed in the UK has more than doubled since the early 1960s. The most likely reason for this is:

- **A** An increase in the working population
- **B** Falling prices
- **C** A shorter working week
- **D** Technological advance

Questions 3–5 share the following answer options:

- **A** Imported inflation
- **B** Cost push inflation
- **C** Demand pull inflation
- **D** Deflation

Which of the above types of price inflation will the following changes tend to give rise to?

3 Rising real wages outstripping labour productivity improvements

4 Rising aggregate demand for goods and services outstripping the growth in total supply

5 A fall in the value of UK sterling on the world foreign currency markets

6 Which of the following is an import to the UK?

- **A** UK machinery sold abroad
- **B** Japanese investment in the UK
- **C** A UK resident taking a holiday in Spain
- **D** A Greek shipping firm insuring their fleet in the UK

Questions 7–9 share the following answer options:

- **A** Competition policy
- **B** Monetary policy
- **C** Trade policy
- **D** Fiscal policy

Which of the above policies do the following actions concern?

7 Removing tariff and non-tariff barriers

8 Regulating restrictive practices of dominant firms in markets

9 Lowering interest rates to stimulate business investment

10 Which of the following is not an objective of the European Union?

- **A** Establishing a single European currency
- **B** Developing a common monetary policy
- **C** Creating a customs union
- **D** Restricting inward investment

11
- **a** What is meant by international ‘competitiveness’?
- **b** Suggest and explain two measures of UK competitiveness.
- **c** Suggest and explain three policies the government could use to improve UK competitiveness.
- **d** Suggest three strategies a firm might devise to help improve its ability to fight international competition.

12
- **a** What is ‘price inflation’?
- **b** Give three reasons why an important objective of the UK Government is to maintain low and stable price inflation.
- **c** Suggest and explain three major potential causes of price inflation in the UK.
- **d** List and explain two major policy initiatives the UK Government is using in an attempt to improve competitiveness.

13
- **a** Briefly describe what has happened to the UK share of world exports over time, and suggest two possible reasons for these changes.
- **b** What is the purpose of the Single European Market in the European Union?
- **c** Give two examples of newly industrialized countries, and suggest why they present both a threat and an opportunity to developed EU member countries, such as the UK and Germany.

Marketing

unit 3

About this unit

Marketing is not just about advertising or selling. It involves finding out what kinds of design, packaging, prices, distribution, promotion, and after-sales service different kinds of customers want, and satisfying their wants in a way that will encourage them to buy and to keep on buying a particular product. It is about understanding the customer and ensuring that goods and services match existing and potential customer wants. It is also about looking at and trying different ways to influence the wants and buying behaviour of consumers.

In this unit you will investigate the marketing process, from conducting research about market needs to evaluating the success or otherwise of a marketing strategy. You will examine the principles and functions of marketing in business and the way in which successful marketing contributes to income and profit generation. The portfolio activities will give you insight into the process of devising successful marketing strategies and the opportunity to devise your own.

chapter 8 The Principles and Functions of Marketing

This chapter considers the main functions and underpinning principles of marketing, and what makes marketing successful.

SO, IF YOU WANT TO MAKE A TASTY PROFIT JUST ADD YOUR PRODUCT, PRICE AND PLACE, AND THEN SPRINKLE LIBERALLY WITH PROMOTION
THE MARKETING MIX
PRODUCT
PRICE
PLACE
PROMOTION

What you need to learn:

Marketing is essential to the success of any business. Its primary aim is to enable businesses to meet the needs and wants of their actual and potential customers, whether for profit or not.

You need to understand that if marketing is to be successful it must:

- **understand customer wants and satisfy their expectations**
- **understand and keep ahead of competition**
- **communicate effectively with customers**
- **co-ordinate its business functions to achieve marketing aims**
- **be aware of constraints on marketing activities**

You need to understand how these criteria for successful marketing are related to the central aim of marketing - meeting actual and potential customer wants. You should also understand the importance to many businesses of developing and maintaining a relationship with their actual and potential customers and other business stakeholders, such as government and lobby groups.

Section 8.1

What is marketing?

The need for marketing

Most private-sector business organizations aim to make a profit from the sale of goods and services to satisfy consumer wants. However, there are a number of organizations that do not aim to make a profit - for example, some organizations in the public sector and charities. However, almost all organizations will need to market their goods and services. **Marketing** can promote sales and higher revenues, while for charities it can generate a stream of donations and increase the take-up of the services they provide.

Marketing principles

Markets are dynamic. They are in a constant state of change due to fluctuations in the economy, changes in the behaviour of competitors, the introduction of new technology, and alterations in government policy. Because of these changes, it is necessary for firms to continually alter and develop their product ranges and promotional strategies to match ever-changing consumer wants.

After sales service

Distribution

Some definitions of marketing

'The identification, satisfaction and regeneration of customers wants at a profit.'

Marketing is not just about advertising or selling. Marketing involves finding out what kinds of design, packaging, pricing, distribution, advertising, promotion, and after-sales service different kinds of customers want, and satisfying their wants in a way that will encourage them to buy a product over and over again. Marketing affects every department in an organization and the prosperity of the whole organization depends upon successful marketing.

'Marketing involves identifying and providing what the customer wants both now and in the future.'

Successful firms are those which can identify and produce what the market wants next and keep ahead of the competition.

'Marketing is War!'

Marketing is about competition between rival firms for a limited amount of consumer spending. Winners in the marketing battle will prosper by increasing their market share and earning more profits. Losers will be eliminated and driven out of business. For example, in the UK fast food market, firms like Wimpy lost their dominant market position when they failed to respond to the threat posed by the US firms McDonald's and Burger King, who, by the late 1980s, had successfully taken over the market.

In-store promotions

Advertisements

Prices

Marketing involves the application of the following principles:

- **Anticipating market opportunities.** Businesses need to identify gaps in markets for new products, or new uses for established products, and be aware of markets in which sales are expanding. For example, in the late 1990s the market for mobile communications was expanding rapidly.
- **Satisfying consumer expectations.** Consumers will expect the right product to be in the right place at the right time and with the right price and promotion. For example, if the price of a product is above expectations, consumers will not buy it. Similarly, if a high-quality product is priced too low, consumers may be suspicious.
- **Generating revenues (and profits).** The purpose of marketing is to maximize sales through advertising, promotion, and pricing strategies. Expanding sales will increase revenues and the potential for profit. Charities can also generate donations through careful marketing.
- **Utilizing technological developments.** Technological developments can increase the speed at which a firm reacts to the identification of a market opportunity. New machine and production processes can speed up production and reduce costs. Consumers will also expect the latest technological developments in goods and services, such as computer games, home shopping and banking, mobile phones, etc.
- **Maximizing the benefit to the organization.** Marketing will only be cost-effective if the additional income it generates exceeds the costs involved and ensures the long-term survival of the business.

Portfolio Activity 8.1 

Yo-Yo becomes a money-spinner

Nick Nuttall and Jody Scott on a piece of new technology that a revived interest in an old favourite

A TINY clutch operated by springs and ball bearings has fuelled a boom in sales of yo-yos not seen for a generation. Purchases of the 2,000-year-old-toys have reached a peak over recent months with sales now running at more than 150,000 a week.

Makers and yo-yo enthusiasts claim the renaissance is attributable to a patented clutch mechanism that automatically rewinds the yo-yo up its string. The clutch allows novices to master moves such as "Walking the Dog" quickly and easily. Children used to take weeks to learn complex moves and would become bored and frustrated but the clutch means a person can become an accomplished user within hours.

In the past, said Gerry Masters of the British Association of Toy Retailers (BATR), many yo-yo fans did not perfect the tricks until the fad, which reappeared every few years was almost over, but the new breed of yo-yo caters to the shorter attention spans of today's children.

The clutch is the brainchild of the US company Yomega. Matt Woodruffe of TKC, which promotes Yomega products in Britain, said that the other element in the current success was the way yo-yos are being promoted. Players meet at shops to demonstrate their skills and are graded as bronze, silver, gold or platinum, based on the tricks they can carry out. Mr Woodruffe said that once a player had reached gold level s/he was presented with a £20 plus model. Those achieving platinum would be rewarded with a top-of-the-range £100-plus model, such as Silver Bullet or Metallic Missile.

But it is not just the top-end models that are selling well. A spokesman for Becks toy shop in London, says the £4.99 Thunderstorm is also a hit with schoolchildren. Gerry Masters of the BATR estimates children have an average of two yo-yos each, and some may own as many as ten. "They are buying them a bit like fashion accessories - perhaps to go with their sports shoes" he said.

Adapted from The Times, 8.10.1999

1. To what extent do you think the new Yo-Yo products and promotions show evidence of the application of marketing principles?
2. How does the Yo-Yo example match the definitions of marketing given above?
3. Research the main marketing objectives for any organizations that you are in contact with. Compare your findings with those of other students. Are they similar? If not, why do they differ?
4. Study the range of marketing activities for any organization that you know. Compare your findings with other students. Do organizations differ in the way they market themselves? If there are differences, do they depend upon the size of the firm, line of business, business sector, etc?

Section 8.2

▼ Digital Satellite TV, mobile phones, personal computers - expanding markets in the 1990s

The objectives of marketing

Marketing objectives and functions

The goals of marketing will reflect the overall objectives of business such as profit maximization, growth, or the provision of a charitable service. Marketing objectives will therefore differ from company to company but are likely to include some or all of the following:

- **Analysing market needs.** Market research can be used to gather information about consumers' buying habits and spending patterns (see 9.1). Firms will use this information to identify market opportunities for new products and marketing strategies.

- **Growth - developing new products.** A firm may set the goal of developing the new product or modifying its existing product range to satisfy consumer requirements. Product development can involve the modification of existing product lines, the creation of new products, and technological breakthroughs (see 10.4). For example, the development of laser and fibre optic technology has brought us products such as compact discs and cable television, as well as applications in the healthcare and defence industries.

- **Growth - entering a new market.** A business must choose wisely which markets to enter to sell its products. It may target overseas markets or particular groups of people within a market - for example, luxury cars aimed at high-income groups.

- **Growth - increasing sales or market share** (see 1.7). In a contracting market, i.e. one where where consumer demand is falling, a firm may aim to keep its total sales the same, while sales in the industry as a whole shrink. This can only be achieved at the expense of competitors' sales and with the help of a very aggressive marketing policy. In expanding markets, for example, in digital satellite and cable TV systems, it is possible that all firms in the industry will benefit from rising sales, and so the marketing strategy required need not be so aggressive.

- **Increasing profitability or cashflow.** A marketing campaign may be designed to meet profit, cashflow, or in the case of a charity, fundraising targets. A marketing strategy may involve increasing the price of a product, coupled with heavy advertising designed to re-position the product in the consumer's mind as being of higher quality or possessing characteristics which somehow justify the new, higher price. Placing the product in the right retail outlets will also help to promote sales and profits (see 11.1).

- **Optimizing customer perception of organization and/or product range.** Marketing to increase consumer awareness and improve the image of an organization and product is an important objective in competitive and quickly changing markets. A firm may wish to improve the image of its product range, either by changing and 'improving' the products, or by simply re-marketing them as being improved or different in some way - for example by re-launching the product with a new trademark or logo. Similarly, a firm can enhance its image by sponsoring sports events, making public donations to charities, or simply by improving customer services and after-sale care.

▼ *Improving products and product image*

- **Managing the effects of change and competition.** Market conditions of demand and supply are in a constant state of change due to fluctuations in the economy, changes in the behaviour of competitors, the introduction of new technology, and alterations in government policy (see Chapter 5). Firms therefore need to continually alter and develop their product ranges to match ever-changing consumer wants and keep pace with the product and marketing developments of rival firms.

Portfolio Activity 8.2 

1. Some products have such well-known trademarks or symbols that it is often possible to advertise them without using words or pictures. How many of the symbols opposite can you recognize? Where would you expect to find them? What products do they advertise?
2. Choosing the right name for a product is often as important as what is said about them in an advert. What type of products are these brand names for?

Bic	Wispa	Old Spice	Tipp-ex	Cornetto
Radox	Heineken	Imperial leather	Mars	One2One

3. **(a)** Choose any product - for example, a chocolate bar, a can of fizzy drink, or perfume. Think of 10 names to call your product and design a series of logos (using a computer graphics package if possible) that are both informative and create the image you want for the product.

   (b) Conduct a survey of at least 20 people in your college. First, ask them what product they think each name and logo is for, and record their answers. Then reveal the identity of the product and its intended characteristics - e.g. taste, smell, design, etc. Conduct the survey again, asking which name and logo best describe the product.

   (c) Describe your product, list names and logos, and present the survey results as tables and graphs in a brief report. Which name and logo would you recommend, if any, and what modifications would you advise?

Key words:

Marketing - the anticipation, identification, satisfaction, and regeneration of consumer wants by business

Marketing objectives - marketing goals that a business will seek to achieve

Section 8.3

What makes marketing successful?

▼ *Marketing a family event*

Understanding customer wants and satisfying their expectations

Effective marketing means that firms must consider every aspect of the business from the perspective of their customers. For example, IKEA, the Swedish furniture company provides basic flat-packed furniture. The product range in itself is simple, but the marketing includes cartoon films and playrooms for children, Swedish food, and heavy marketing through home delivery of free catalogues. Through marketing, IKEA is in effect selling not just flat-packed furniture, but a family event. In this way, marketing is said to add value or increase the attractiveness of the product to the final consumer.

Understand and keep ahead of competition

Most businesses have competitors. Successful firms not only have to provide what customers want and will pay for, they also have to satisfy their wants and expectations better than business rivals. This means firms must be prepared to continuously update and change the products, prices, promotions and places of sale they offer to meet customer demands. To do this, firms need to undertake regular market research to keep up to date with the changing wants and expectations of consumers and actions of rival firms (see Chapter 9).

How do firms compete?

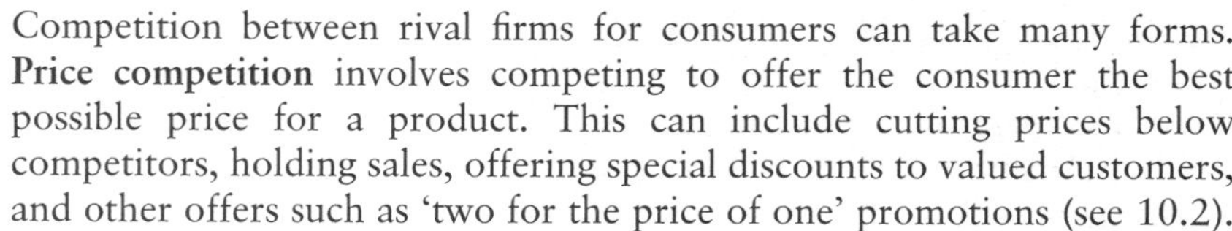
Competition between rival firms for consumers can take many forms. **Price competition** involves competing to offer the consumer the best possible price for a product. This can include cutting prices below competitors, holding sales, offering special discounts to valued customers, and other offers such as 'two for the price of one' promotions (see 10.2).

Firms can also compete on aspects other than price, for example by trying to outdo each other on product quality and performance, introducing new products before rivals firms do, providing better customer services and after-sales care, placing the product in many more retail outlets than rival firms, and also through better advertising and other promotional strategies. These are all forms of **non-price competition** (see 10.3).

Mobile mayhem at supermarkets

LEADING supermarket chains said yesterday they had sold mobile phones worth millions since cutting the cost of pre-paid packages by up to 50 per cent three days ago. A spokesman for Tesco, which started the price war on Monday by cutting the cost of all its pre-paid mobiles to £49.99, said: "We have sold over £2 million worth of mobile phones since we reduced the price". Tesco is selling pre-paid mobiles from all four major networks - Cellnet, One2One, Vodafone and Orange - all the one price. The packages would normally sell for between £69.99 and £79.99 from high street phone retailers or the networks themselves. Meanwhile, Asda, which cut the cost of its mobiles to just £39.99, admitted that in some stores it had experienced problems getting the phones on the shelves quick enough for customers.

Metro, 15.9.1999

▲ *Price and non-price competition between rival firms can be fierce*

Product versus market-orientated firms

Some firms are **product-oriented.** They introduce new products to a market because they have discovered how to make them, and not because a marketing activity has revealed a consumer want for the product.

Product-oriented firms concentrate on products and production processes. For example, Sinclair Electronics developed and launched the C5 - the first low-cost, mass-produced electric car. This was a technical breakthrough, but the product was a failure because Sinclair had not researched the market. There was little consumer enthusiasm for the product.

A **market-oriented** firm will continually review and analyse consumer wants and modify their product and marketing strategies accordingly. Market-orientated firms tend to be more successful than firms that concentrate on products and processes, because they produce what the market wants. For example, the Japanese Sony Corporation continually adapts its products and product ranges to meet consumer requirements. Because the investment needed to develop and launch products such as the Walkman, 'Digicam', and Mini-disc onto international markets is so huge, Sony must be sure that their marketing is very effective.

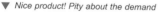

▼ *Nice product! Pity about the demand*

Product or market orientation?

What causes a firm to concentrate on product or on the market?

The type of product

Firms producing industrial goods are more likely to concentrate on product. Products like brain scanners and weapon systems are developed for highly specialized markets.

Business objectives

If a firm aims to maximize profits or sales, it will need to be fully aware of consumer wants and adapt its product and approach to marketing accordingly.

Market structure

A firm that faces fierce competition is more likely to be market-orientated. It must know exactly what consumers want or it will lose them to rival products.

The size and nature of the market

In markets that are small and specialized, firms will tend to be product-orientated - for example, antique dealers, craft industries, scientific and specialist magazines.

Mass marketing involves a business aiming its products at large national and international markets. This contrasts with **niche marketing** where a business aims a product at a particular, often very small, segment of a market. However, successful niche markets, for example, connoisseur hi-fi produced by small specialist firms like QUAD and Naim Audio, can attract larger firms like Pioneer and Sony, who are able to offer 'high-end' products at a lower price.

Communicate effectively with customers

A great deal of information needs to be communicated quickly and clearly to customers about the goods and services offered by business organizations. A business that fails to communicate effectively, or as well as rival firms, with its existing and potential customers will not be successful.

Business organizations will provide information to customers in a variety of ways. These can be oral communications with business employees and sales staff, or in written form (see 3.1). Written information will include product brochures and instruction manuals, price lists and menus, product guarantees, customer account statements and safety notices.

What customers need to know

Customers may contact an organization to find out information on a variety of different matters:

- The name of a member of staff to contact
- Details about goods and services provided by the organization
- Latest prices
- Product features, including technical details
- How to place an order
- Delivery dates
- Discounts available
- Accepted methods of payments
- Credit facilities
- Product guarantees
- After-sales care, including refunds and repairs
- Product leaflets, brochures, and other sales literature available
- Company policy on giving refunds and making exchanges
- How to register a complaint
- Where to go for more information or advice

One of the main ways businesses communicate with actual and potential customers is through **promotions** (see 10.3). Almost every organization will at some time or another engage in promotional activities to let consumers know about the business and the goods or services it provides. Small local businesses, large national and international firms, charities, government organizations, even your school or college - all use promotions to send messages to consumers. These messages may be on posters and leaflets, in letters and catalogues, advertisements in newspapers and magazines, or on the TV or websites, even on footballer's shirts. They can be **informative messages**, such as the opening times, product weight or a bus timetable, or **persuasive messages** that try to persuade consumers that the product being promoted is better than rival products and is worth buying.

'Mind the gap'

This Wonderbra advert is one of a number created by Susanna Hailstone of the TBWA advertising agency. Weekly sales soared by 7,000 after the striking poster campaign was launched.

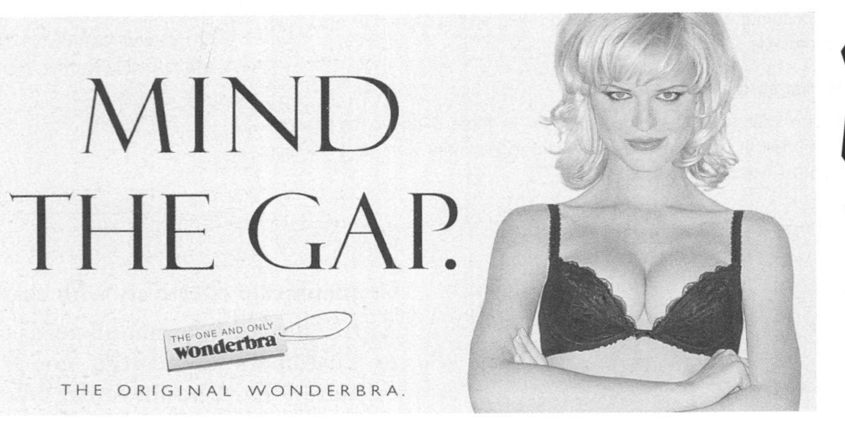

First impressions often last, and so creating a poor first impression is likely to lose customers in business. A customer who contacts a business for the first time to make an enquiry and is kept waiting or misinformed is unlikely to forget the experience and will shop with rivals firms. A customer who is offended by an advert or cannot understand a poorly produced instruction manual will also buy rival products in future.

Co-ordinate its business functions to achieve marketing aims

All departments in a business will contribute to marketing and the achievement of business aims (see 4.2). New products need to be researched and developed. They need to be produced in the right quantities, at the right time, to the right quality and cost. These and marketing activities need to be financed and costs and revenues accounted for. And, if the marketing strategy is successful in generating more sales, customer service staff need to be on hand to deal with more enquiries and orders from customers. Unless these activities are co-ordinated, marketing and the business will not be successful.

For example, imagine a new advertising campaign has created demand for a new product but people are unable to buy it. This may be because the Production Department has failed to produce enough because the Finance Department could not raise enough finance to expand production capacity, or the Purchasing Department has not bought in enough materials. Or it is a failure of the Sales Department to process customer orders efficiently. Whatever the reason, potential customers will soon lose interest and buy a rival product instead and the marketing function will have failed.

Be aware of constraints on marketing activities

A business must take account of a number of constraints when designing and introducing a new marketing strategy (see 12.5). Any business that is not aware of these constraints is unlikely to achieve its business aims and, worse still, could end up appearing in law courts and being fined heavily and/or its owners imprisoned.

Affordability and profitability

Marketing activities, such as research, new product development and advertising, can be expensive. For a marketing strategy to be effective, a firm must weigh up these additional costs against how much it can afford, and the benefits the strategy may yield in terms of improved corporate image, higher sales and increased profits.

Legal constraints

Because most businesses aim for profit, some may be tempted to mislead consumers about the prices, quality and availability of their products. They may also attempt to cut their costs by using substandard materials, disposing of waste in harmful ways, and not ensuring high standards of hygiene and safety in their workplaces or retail outlets. All these practices are illegal. The governments of the UK and the European Union have introduced laws and organizations which seek to protect the interests of consumers and the environment from poor business activity. Businesses must make sure their marketing strategies do not fall foul of these laws.

▼ *A number of organizations set and monitor business standards in the travel industry*

Industry codes of practice

Many industries have drawn up voluntary codes of good practice and organizations to encourage member firms to follow them. Examples, include the **Federation of Master Builders** and the **Association of British Travel Agents (ABTA)**. The advertising industry also has its own regulator, the **Advertising Standards Authority (ASA)**. It advises on good practice, and will investigate complaints from members of the public and rival firms.

Ethical, environmental and social constraints

Ethics are the values, or moral code, of individuals and society, which govern behaviour and business conduct. Sometimes profits can be more important in business than ethics. Some businesses may seek to mislead consumers about their products and their conduct to generate more sales and profits. Some practices are clearly against the law, but there may be many things a business can do within the law that may be considered unethical by many people. For example, the testing of cosmetics and chemicals on animals is legal, but many consumers dislike this and prefer to buy products not tested on animals. It is, however, illegal to describe a product as not tested on animals when it or its ingredients have been. Similarly, it is legal to cause damage to rainforests by cutting down trees to sell for wood, but it is illegal to mislead consumers about where the wood came from.

All the things that help to make marketing successful will be explored in detail in the chapters that follow in this unit.

Portfolio Activity 8.3 

1. What evidence is there from these articles that the organizations concerned have or have not put the main principles of marketing into practice?
2. Do you think these organizations are market- or product-oriented? Use evidence from the articles to support your views.
3. How are the organizations changing their marketing strategies and why?
4. Suggest other marketing strategies the organizations might use to keep existing customers and attract new ones.

Tellycom 2000

ORANGE is set to launch the world's first mobile video phone within weeks.

Users will be able to see each other as they talk, thanks to a four-inch screen.

The £500 superphone - just seven inches long - will also allow owners to store and replay favourite TV clips, access weather and traffic maps and connect to the internet to send e-mails and receive faxes.

An Orange research team has worked in secret to steal a march on competitors - and confound experts who thought the first mass-market video phone was years away. An Orange spokeswoman said: "Orange wasn't prepared to wait and developed its own technology. We anticipate a great deal of interest".

Engineers have strengthened the Orange network's signals so it can carry enough data to transmit moving pictures. None of its rivals - Vodafone, Cellnet or One2One - have the technology to do this yet.

The Mirror, 23.10.1999

The Mail forces Sainsbury's to label 'Frankenstein foods'

SAINSBURY'S is to label hundreds of products containing 'Frankenstein food' derivatives in a major victory for Daily Mail readers.

The country's second biggest supermarket chain revealed the U-turn yesterday amid allegations that it had been 'misleading' shoppers.

Foreign biotech companies such as U.S.-based Monsanto, the food industry and the Government have been accused of forcing genetically-modified (GM) food on to the nation.

Consumers are angry that the products were introduced without any proper consultation or any study on their long-term effect on human health.

Sainsbury's had refused to label products containing the derivatives of crops such as soya and maize which have been genetically modified.

It argued that, because the DNA of the GM crop did not exist in the derivatives - for example, lecithin and oil from soya and modified starch from maize - there was no need to label.

Yesterday, however, Sainsbury's issued a statement saying: 'We have decided to label products which contain GM soya lecithin and GM soya oils, in addition to labelling products containing GM soya. The first labelled products will begin to appear on the shelf in the next couple of months.'

'We will be informing customers about this with a new, updated leaflet.'

Sainsbury's original policy put it out of step with rivals such Tesco, which labels the derivatives. GM ingredients are used in huge range of products - approximately 60 per cent of supermarket foods - from curry ready-meals to chocolate puddings and steak pies.

Now Sainsbury's, which continues to refuse to label the derivatives of GM maize, will have to either reformulate its products or order new packaging for many own-label products.

Daily Mail, 10.2.1999

Key words:

Promotions - marketing communications with customers

Product orientation - a business approach which places emphasis on production processes and product

Market orientation - a business approach which places emphasis on consumer wants

Mass marketing - marketing aimed at selling products in huge quantities in large national and international markets

Niche marketing - marketing aimed at small, often specialized, market segments

Test your knowledge

1 Which of the following is not a primary objective of marketing?

- **A** Reducing production costs
- **B** Market penetration
- **C** Maintaining market share
- **D** Influencing consumer wants

Questions 2–4 share the following answer options:

- **A** New packaging
- **B** A new advertising campaign
- **C** A new consumer helpline and help desk
- **D** A new company logo

Which of the above marketing activities could help achieve the following business objectives?

2 Satisfying customer requirements

3 Increasing market share

4 Improving corporate image

Questions 5–7 share the following answer options:

- **A** Distributing DVD video discs and audio compact discs through supermarkets
- **B** Cutting product price below costs to compete with a new business rival
- **C** Investigating trends in consumer spending from published data sources
- **D** Developing multimedia games software for computers

Which of the above would satisfy the following marketing principles?

5 Utilizing technological developments

6 Anticipating market opportunities

7 Generating revenues

8 Which of the following is an example of a persuasive promotional message?

- **A** A bus timetable
- **B** A price list at a wood suppliers
- **C** An advert for summer holidays in Greece
- **D** A customer safety notice by escalators in a shopping mall

Questions 10–13 share the following answer options:

- **A** Satisfying customer expectations
- **B** Keeping ahead of the competition
- **C** Communicating effectively with customers
- **D** Awareness of constraints on marketing activities

Which of the above criteria for successful marketing are the following initiatives most likely to satisfy?

10 Sending out business letters to customers advising of new shop opening times

11 Introducing wheelchair ramps at railway stations for disabled passengers

12 Developing the lightest, thinnest and most powerful laptop computer

13 Labelling all goods with their ingredients and country of origin

14 **a** What is marketing?

b Explain three key principles which underpin marketing.

c Explain, using simple examples, what a business will need to do to make its marketing successful.

chapter 9 Researching Customer Wants

This chapter examines sources of marketing information and data collection methods appropriate to a firm researching their market and developing new and improved products and promotions to satisfy consumer wants.

What you need to learn

A business has to explore the wants and expectations of consumers, and the activities of rival firms before it can develop a marketing strategy. To do this business organizations will use different methods of **market research** and sources of data.

You need to know how **primary research** is carried out, and how to interpret primary research data for use in developing marketing strategies.

Primary research methods you should be able to use and understand include:

- **interviews, focus groups and consumer panels**
- **questionnaires and surveys**
- **sampling**
- **test marketing**

You need to know the uses and sources of **secondary research** data.

You need to be able to use these methods and interpret your research findings.

You will need to understand the purposes of marketing databases and how they are used to provide information about:

- **customer behaviour, such as customer preferences and buying habits, product substitution, and sales trends for new and existing products**
- **the market, such as market share, market segments, and competitor activities**

Different market research techniques are suitable for different products and businesses. This is related to **the cost of conducting the research, the speed of retrieval and accessibility of data**, and **the validity and accuracy of the data gathered**.

It is vitally important that market research data is fit for the purpose intended and representative of those consumers of interest. If not, there is a high risk that the research data will be biased and the wrong marketing decisions taken.

Section 9.1

What is market research?

▼Face-to-face interviews with potential consumers

The identification of consumer wants

A business will only be successful if consumers want and can buy what it produces both now and in the future. **Market research** can reduce the risk of producing products that do not appeal to consumers by helping a firm to discover information about their consumers.

Market research involves the gathering, collation, and analysis of data relating to the consumption and marketing of goods and services. The purpose of such research is to identify whether there is want for a particular product - a **gap in the market** - or whether a want can created among consumers by persuasive advertising (see 10.3).

Market research information

In order to identify consumer wants for **consumer goods and services** and **capital goods**, firms need to gather information on the following:

- **Consumer behaviour.** For example, how do consumers react to TV advertising or advertising on the radio? Do they like free gifts? How do they react to price changes and new products?
- **Buying patterns and sales trends.** How do buying habits differ between different regions, income groups, age groups, sexes, races? How do buying patterns change over time? Which markets are expanding - i.e. show rising consumer demand and sales? Which markets are contracting - i.e. show falling consumer demand and sales?
- **Consumer preferences.** How do consumers react to different products, styles, colours, tastes, retail outlets, methods of payment, promotional devices, etc?
- **Activities of rival firms.** How do competitors adapt their products and prices to meet consumers' wants? How well do their products sell? What is their market share? What marketing strategies and what new products are they developing?

Once a firm has identified the kind of market research information it needs, decisions can be taken on how to get the information, how much to spend on collecting it, and how often to undertake research.

A firm also has to consider what it will do with the information it collects. For example, if research shows sales of recordable CD players are rising while sales of mini-discs are falling, will the firm increase advertising expenditure on mini-discs or will it shift production towards CD-R machines? Collecting market research information alone will not make an unsuccessful firm successful. Good decisions have to be taken on the basis of the information collected.

Market research and business decision-making

Market research will provide information to a firm on whether the customer will buy the product, and on the design features, colours, packaging, prices, and kinds of retail outlets that consumers prefer.

Figure 9.1: The stages of market research

STAGE 1

Decide on the purpose of market research. What information do you need? What action will be taken as a result of research findings?

STAGE 2

Decide the most appropriate methods of research given information requirements, time and budget constraints.

STAGE 3

To obtain the information required, how many people should you ask and what type of consumers should they be?

STAGE 4

Undertake the research

STAGE 5

Analyse the results, draw conclusions and make marketing decisions based on the findings.

Portfolio Activity 9.1 

1. Using the article below, identify as many reasons as you can to explain why market research is an important business activity.
2. Why might it sometimes be very difficult for a firm to act on the results of its market research?

Let The Customer Be Your Guide

When Julian Rankin and Michael Osborn set up their lighting business in London in 1985 they had definite plans for the future. They had set their sights on establishing their company, Ora Lighting, as a manufacturer of well-designed high-quality light fittings.

But instead of being able to sell their range of lighting products they found that seventy percent of their work was special one-off product development. "We tried to steer away from that and impose our own standard ranges of products on the market, but as a small company we didn't have the marketing muscle."

The partners sought advice under the government's Enterprise Initiative. The advice they got from a consultant was to go with the market rather than try to fight it. Now at a time when many competitors have gone out of business, Ora has a turnover of £500,000 and record order books.

Ora's initial approach is not unusual. "A lot of companies think they know who their customers are but never talk to them to find out what they really want. There is a lot of pride involved for someone who has built up his business, he doesn't want somebody telling him he has got it wrong."

Creating a more professional approach to marketing is hampered by widespread ignorance of what marketing actually is. Marketing is not just about selling, instead marketing goes to the heart of a business, determining its field of activity and choice of products. It starts with market research in order to build up a knowledge of customers and competitors. It moves on to designing products or services to suit the market-place and pricing them at the highest level the market will bear.

Businesses which take market research seriously often face painful choices. They may have to give up a cherished product to move into a more promising area. But the alternative to making what your customers want, could be making, and selling, nothing at all.

Adapted from The Financial Times 5.10.1993

Additionally, research will help to identify the kind of consumer who is likely to purchase the product. For example, market research can reveal information on consumers' likely age range, sex, geographical region, favourite leisure pursuits, and lifestyle. This information will assist in the creation of appropriate marketing strategies to attract customers (see 8.3).

Product development

Take a look around your house. The chances are that you will have a television, a video recorder, a telephone, a compact disc player, a microwave, and a number of other household appliances. Few of these products would have been found in a house 50 years ago. Go back 150 years, and there would have been no cars, aircraft, or plastics, and few of the medicines that we take for granted today. All of the products we are able to enjoy today are the result of innovations and technological breakthroughs.

▼ *Figure 9.2: The scope of market research*

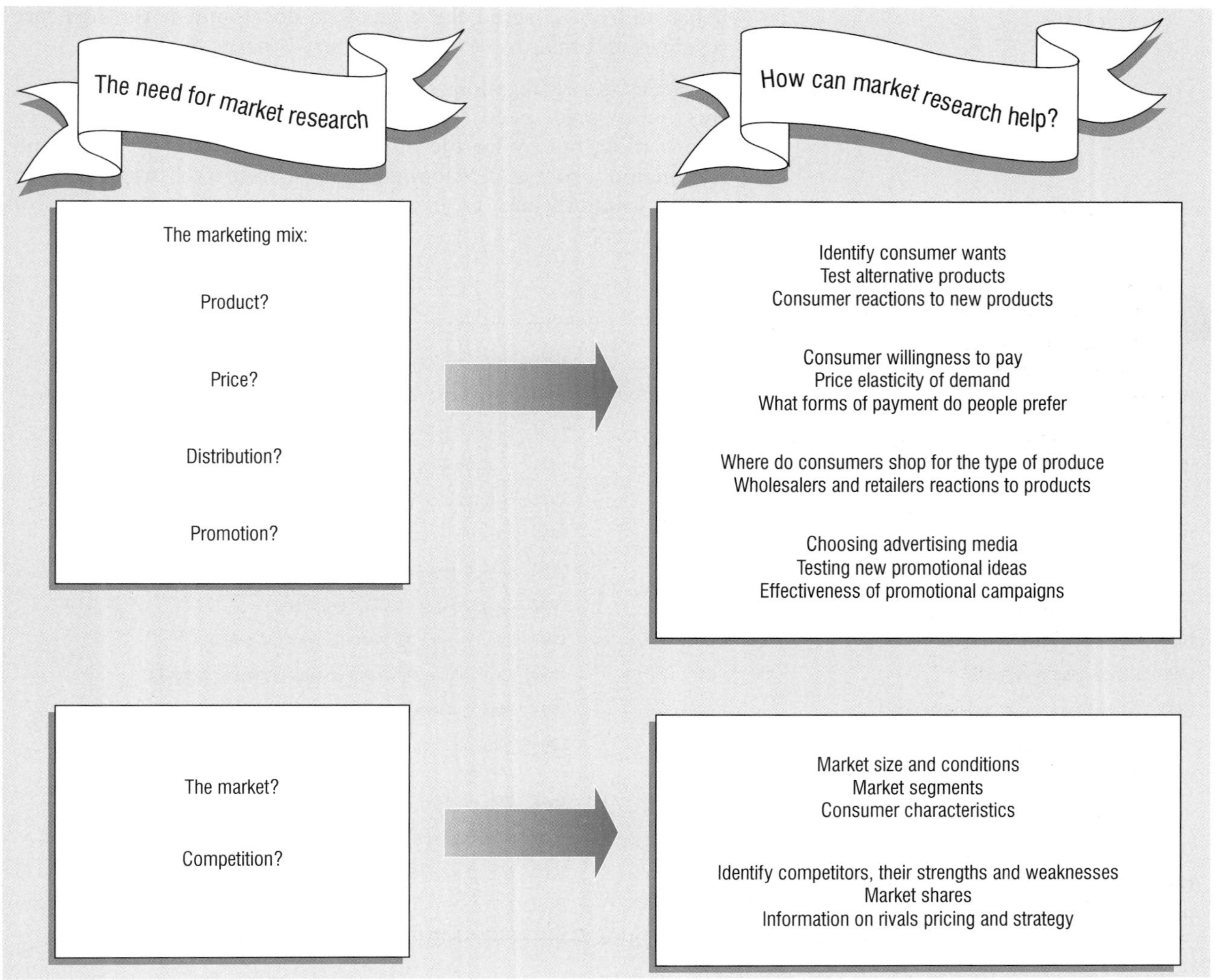

Because fashion, tastes, technology, levels of competition, and the economy are always changing, the market for goods and services is also in a state of continuous change. Change means that firms are increasingly keen to find new products to out-sell their rivals, and new processes to reduce their production costs. This process is called **research and development (R&D).**

- **Research** is the investigation and discovery of new ideas
- **Development** involves putting ideas into practice

R&D is financed and carried out mainly by businesses, government, and higher education institutions. It is defined as '*creative work undertaken on a systematic basis in order to increase the stock of knowledge, including knowledge of man, culture and society, and the use of this stock of knowledge to devise new applications*'. Sometimes the process can take many years to complete, and success is not always guaranteed. For example, the Concorde supersonic aircraft took around 30 years to develop, yet it has still not covered the cost of its development through fare revenues and sales to other nations and is never likely to.

In 1999, UK organizations spent over £10 billion on R&D. Part of this will have been spent on collecting market research information, but by far the most money is spent on product and production process development. Some research may result in simple modifications to existing products and processes - for

Some important product developments since 1900

1900 Kodak manufacture the first mass-produced camera

1903 *Daily Mirror* newspaper is published

1908 Henry Ford promotes the sale of the first Model T car

1919 First flight across the atlantic by Alcock and Brown

1927 Warner Bros release first 'talking picture' in USA

1928 Limited TV transmissions in USA and UK

1930 Electric kettle introduced

1935 IBM market first electric typewriter

1938 Dupont develop non-stick Teflon

1939 ICI develop polythene

1943 Lazlo Biro invents ball-point pen

1955 ITV brodacasts begin in the UK

1947 British Rail formed

1948 National Health Service created

1956 Bikinis introduced

1957 First supermarket opens in UK

1960 Pentel produce felt-tip pen

1963 IBM develop wordprocessing for computers

1966 Fibre optics developed

1967 Laser beams developed in USA

1971 Intel develop first microchip

1975 BIC market first disposable razors

1982 Channel 4 starts broadcasting

1984 First breakfast TV shows launched in UK

1992 Sega launches CD megadrive

1993 Stereogram 3D pictures become popular

1994 QVC home shopping channel is launched in UK

1994 National lottery launched in UK

1994 First quad speed CD-ROM and rewritable CD-ROM drives on sale

1996 Private companies take over UK passenger rail services

1998 DVD players and discs launched in Europe

2000 Video mobile phones introduced

example, package re-design such as the ringpull can or paper liquid carton. Modifications can help to reduce production costs and may prolong the commercial life of an existing product (see 10.4).

Some new products and processes are invented by private individuals and inventors purely by chance. For example, 'cats eyes' in roads were the result of the inventor seeing light reflected in broken glass in a road. Inventors can sell their innovations to firms who are willing to produce them for sale. New inventions and ideas can be protected by **patents** which prevent them being copied by other people and firms.

Occasionally, private inventors and organized R&D can result in **technological breakthroughs** leading to the discovery of entirely new products or processes. For example, microchip technology has allowed the development of desktop computers capable of doing work once carried out by computers that filled entire rooms. The invention of lasers has opened the way to the development of micro-surgery in medicine, advanced military weapons, and digital compact audio and video disc players.

Key words:

Market research - the gathering, collation, and analysis of data relating to the consumption and marketing of goods and services

Consumer goods and services - any commodities that directly satisfy a human need or want

Durable goods - products consumed over a long period of time

Non-durable goods - products which are used up quickly

Capital goods - products which are used as an input to further productive activity and which do not satisfy an immediate consumer want

Product development - the production of new products or the modification of existing ones

Research and development (R&D) - investigating new ideas for products and processes with a view to commercial exploitation

Patents - a licence to protect ideas from being copied

Section 9.2 Sources of marketing information

Information requirements

Information collected by market research can be either **qualitative** or **quantitative**:

- **Quantitative data** refers to numbers - for example, the value and volume of sales per period of time or numbers of shoppers per week - which can be presented in a numerical or graphical format.

- **Qualitative data** refers to information concerning the motives and attitudes of consumers. It focuses, not on how consumers behave, but *why* they behave in certain ways. Qualitative data is a useful supplement to quantitative data. It is sometimes the only source of information when numerical data is scarce.

There are two main sources of market research information: **primary research,** where researchers gather information about the market themselves; and **secondary research,** where researchers use information that has already been collected by other people and organizations.

▼ *Figure 9.3: Sources of information*

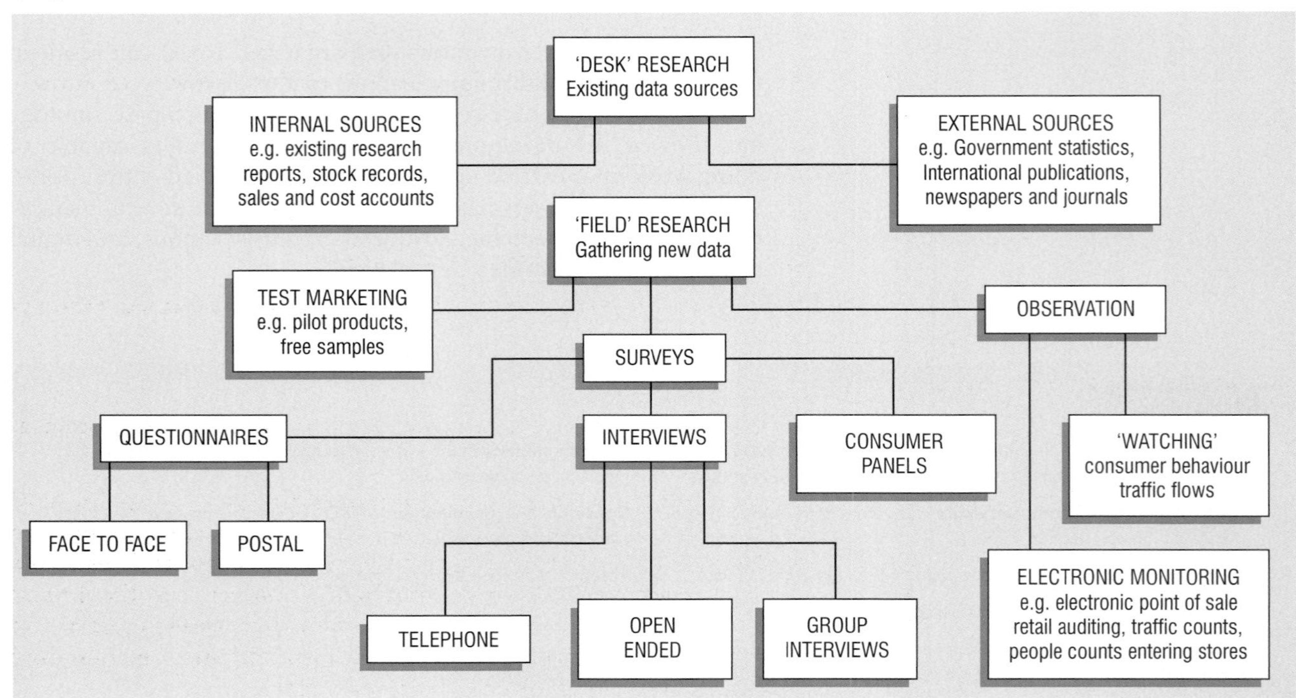

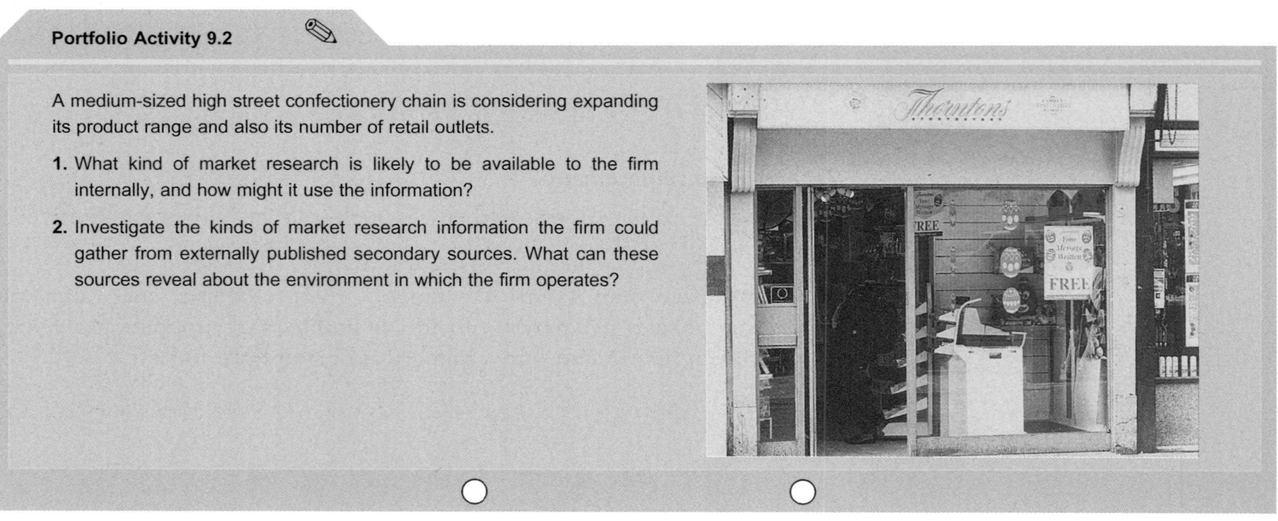

Portfolio Activity 9.2

A medium-sized high street confectionery chain is considering expanding its product range and also its number of retail outlets.

1. What kind of market research is likely to be available to the firm internally, and how might it use the information?
2. Investigate the kinds of market research information the firm could gather from externally published secondary sources. What can these sources reveal about the environment in which the firm operates?

Secondary data

So-called **desk-based research** makes use of **secondary data**, or data which has already been collected for another purpose. Sources of secondary data may be found both within a business and from outside the firm.

Internal sources

Most firms will find that the experience of their staff and internal business records provide valuable information about the past performance of products. Sources of internal information may include:

- Existing market research reports
- Data on the success of various past promotions
- Distribution data on delivery times, and customer details
- Shopkeepers' opinions on products
- Stock records and product quality audits
- Sales records showing seasonal variations in sales
- Accounting records showing cost variations
- Databases of information built up on customers via returned warranty cards or Internet use

External sources

Secondary information is also available from outside the firm, often at little or no cost, from a variety of organizations:

- **UK government statistics.** The government publishes a vast array of information on all aspects of the economy, business, and the population. Publications such as *Social Trends, Regional Trends,* the *Census of Population,* the *Family Expenditure Survey*, and the *Annual Abstract of Statistics* provide useful background marketing information about regional and national population characteristics, income and expenditure patterns and trends, and much more.
- **Specialist business organizations.** A number of organizations specialize in market research and produce regular reports which can be bought by the public. Examples include Neilsons Retail Audit, Mintel, and Dun and Bradstreet.
- **Consumer databases.** sorted into different groups of consumers with similar characteristics, can be purchased from specialist marketing agencies and 'list brokers'. They build consumer profiles classified by age, gender, income, spending habits, and other characteristics, from a mixture of population census data, questionnaires, electoral-roll information, and (in America) credit card data.

Additionally, many sources of highly specialized secondary market research exist on computer databases and are available to firms with computer links at a charge. These include surveys by the Economist Intelligence Unit, the Financial Times Business Information Service, and

Customer profile system offer

A small, privately held UK company has developed a machine capable of analysing the behaviour of millions of consumers, providing managers with hitherto unobtainable competitive marketing information.

It could prove to be a key weapon in the fast-growing electronic business world, where retailers and service providers potentially have huge numbers of customers but interact with them only through the internet.

Companies that have used the machine, a massively parallel computer system developed by Whitecross Data Exploration, are making bold claims for its effectivness.

The Whitecross system is a combination of special analytical software and superfast hardware, which lends itself to the marketing needs of telecommunications companies where vast quantities of calling data have to be analysed.

Financial Times, 23.12.1999

economic reports by the OECD (the Organization of Economic Cooperation and Development).

- **International publications.** Organizations such as the World Bank, United Nations, and European Commission publish a wide variety of papers and journals containing economic and social data on different countries which are useful to market researchers.
- **Competing firms.** Public limited companies (plcs) are required to produce annual reports on their activities. A rival firm will be able to obtain information about company profits and sales from these reports.
- **The media, TV, and newspapers** will often carry features on economic, business, and social patterns and trends.

Key words:

Quantitative data - numerical information

Qualitative data - expressing values in words; for example, the weather is very hot, hot, cold, or very cold.

Primary research - new market research data gathered by a researcher

Secondary research - desk-based research using existing data from a variety of sources

Secondary data - data already gathered for another purpose

Internal data sources - sources of market research data available from within a firm

External data sources - sources of market research data available from other organizations outside the firm.

Section 9.3 Primary research

Primary market research data

Primary data is information which is newly created by field research. Because primary information is newly created, it tends to be more expensive to gather than **secondary data** which is already in existence.

The major advantage of primary data is that, because it is fresh data gathered for a particular purpose, it is likely to match the firm's requirements more closely. It will also be up-to-date and exclusive to the collector.

In the past, most market research was undertaken by specialist research firms like Gallop, Mori, and the Market Research Bureau (MRB). However, new technology means that many firms can carry out their own research. Large superstores can obtain primary marketing information using bar-code readers which immediately register patterns of

▼ *Electronic point-of-sale systems provide valuable consumer data*

sales with a central computer. **Electronic Point-of-Sale (EPOS)** systems are now used in nearly all large supermarkets and many other stores. For example, the head office of the McDonald's fast-food restaurant chain can monitor sales in every store daily and can measure the sales response of different products to particular kinds of promotional activities. This gives McDonald's an edge in being able to react very quickly to the market.

Sampling

All of the possible consumers in a market for a particular product taken together are called the **target population.** A survey based on primary research information from the whole population in a market is called a **census.** Because all possible buyers are surveyed, data gathered from a census is likely to be very accurate - and exceptionally expensive in all but the smallest markets.

Because of the expense involved in gathering data from the whole population, researchers usually survey a small part of the whole market. Selecting some of the market for research is called **sampling.**

Methods of sampling

The main methods of sampling are:

Random sampling

In a random sample, every member of the population has an equal chance of being surveyed. Random sampling reduces the chance of bias, but may generate some surplus information because people other than those in the target market may be selected.

Systematic random sampling requires that every *n*th member of the population is surveyed, e.g every 20th after the first has been selected at random. One drawback is that the sample may not be a random representation of the whole market.

Stratified sampling

This method involves dividing the sample into market segments made up of particular kinds of consumers, based on existing knowledge of their representation in the entire market population. For example, the market for a certain type of computer game may be 75% male, aged between 13 and 17.

Quota sampling

Truly random sampling requires that particular members of the target market are surveyed. This is time-consuming and expensive because it requires very large sample sizes to ensure that the sample is unbiased. A way of avoiding having to ask particular people questions is for market researchers to focus on a quota of people with certain characteristics. For example, a researcher may be instructed to survey 250 males between the ages of 45 and 65 and 100 males over 65. The danger is that those sampled either may not possess these characteristics, or may not be representative of the whole market.

Due to its low cost, quota sampling is the most popular method and is often used by survey organizations like National Opinion Polls, Mori, and Gallup.

Methods of collecting primary data

Face-to-face survey

A popular method of obtaining primary data is face-to-face questioning based on a pre-designed **questionnaire.** This method is cheap and has the advantage of allowing the interviewer to target particular kinds of people.

Open-ended interview

The advantage of an open-ended interview is that it is flexible. Using this method, the interviewer works from a list of subjects of interest, rather than specific questions. The interviewer can therefore ask questions as s/he wishes and can guide each interview as s/he feels best. This method is useful when the subject is of a confidential or embarrassing nature, or when a very complicated and specialized topic is being researched.

Telephone survey

Telephone surveys allow researchers to target particular respondents by geographical area. However, this method clearly rules out people not listed in the directory and those without telephones, which can cause bias.

Postal surveys

It is possible to select a market research sample through postal sampling. The biggest drawback is that people receiving postal questionnaires may view them as 'junk mail' and throw them away. Postal surveys work best when the customer is given an incentive to reply, perhaps entry into a prize draw or a promise of a free gift.

The Rise of Pester Power

If your child is aged three to 12, watch out. The admen have targeted them as the next big thing in consumer power.

Research by Saatchi and Saatchi shows children are an irresistable business opportunity. The advertising agency has uncovered a terrifying statistic that children influence more than £31 billion spending by adults. A Marketing to Children conference in London last year named this phenomenon "pester power", and cheerfully attributed it to the guilt of working mothers.

Among these powerful consumers, our savvy London kids are coming under the most intense scrutiny. McCann Junior, a new division of marketing agency McCann Erickson, now interviews groups of children within the M25 area about their changing tastes every week.

Adapted from the Evening Standard, 15.4.1999

Consumer panels

A firm can test consumer opinion by inviting a group of potential customers to give their views on products and asking them to allow their spending decisions to be monitored over a period of time. Using a panel, researchers might ask people to keep records of their purchases over time in order to measure the impact of advertising or of trends in fashion. This method gives a picture over time, rather than just a snapshot of current buying habits, as with the questionnaire.

Observation

Simply observing consumer behaviour - for example, monitoring TV and radio audiences for particular programmes and regions, or counting traffic on roads and at car parks - can generate a great deal of useful market research information. Some firms will use **focus groups** of consumers to monitor spending patterns and behaviour over periods of time.

▼ *Wispa bars were launched initially, with great success, in the Tyne Tees TV region in late 1981 prior to national release. They were still selling well in 2000*

Experimentation

Sometimes a new product or advertising campaign will be tested on a sample of the target population, perhaps in a particular region of the country. Because of the high cost of launching a product on a national or international market, **test marketing** (or **field trials**) reduces the risk of making expensive mistakes. If consumers in the test dislike certain aspects of the product or campaign, the firm can make modifications prior to launch.

Rules for designing questionnaires

Questionnaires are the most useful method of gaining primary data from consumers. They may be used in face-to-face surveys, telephone surveys, and postal surveys. Administration of questionnaires is much easier today thanks to the use of handheld electronic data processing machines. However, a badly designed questionnaire can yield poor or inaccurate information.

Portfolio Activity 9.3

Below is an example of a badly designed questionnaire. Look at the questions and see if you can identify what is wrong.

1. Do you ever take a bath? YES/NO
2. When did you last take a bath? ______________
3. What is the chemical composition of your present bubble bath?

   ____
4. How much water do you use in your bath?
   - 50 litres
   - 100 litres
   - 150 litres
   - More than 150 litres
5. You do use bubble bath, don't you? ______________
6. Where do you buy it? ______________
7. How much would you pay for bubble bath?
   - Less than £1
   - £1
   - £1.50
   - £2
   - More than £5
8. Do you think the price and scent of bubble bath is important? YES/NO

A number of rules must guide the design of a questionnaire. These are:

1. Questions should not be offensive or embarrassing for people to answer. If they are, people will either not answer, or not tell the truth. For example, how often people take a bath may be seen as a personal question by many respondents.
2. Questions should be easy for people to understand and not require specialist knowledge which most people do not possess. For example, most people would not know the chemical composition of their present bubble bath.
3. Questions should not require people to make calculations in their heads. Most people will not be able to calculate the volume of water in their bath tubs. If they give an answer, it is likely to be wrong.
4. Questions should not be loaded or encourage consumers to reply in a particular way. Leading questions like 'You do use bubble bath, don't you?' will encourage people to say 'Yes', even if this is not true.
5. Questions should be designed to limit the number of possible responses that can be made. For example, the question:

   'What price would you be willing to pay for one litre of bubble bath:

   (a) less than £1?

   (b) £1 to £5?

   (c) more than £5?'

is more likely to give a useful answer than an open-ended question asking how much someone would pay for bubble bath. It is hard for people to give an exact price, but much easier to indicate an ideal range.

6. Questionnaires may be open or closed in design. **Open questions** allow a wide variety of responses and do not pin the respondent down to particular answers. Such questions are likely to lead to fuller, and more varied answers than closed questions.

   Closed questions ask respondents to respond either 'Yes' or 'No', or to pick an answer from a limited range of options, known as **multiple choice questions**. Closed questions lead to a narrower range of responses and make analysis of data much easier. However, they prevent respondents giving opinions or introducing new and unexpected thoughts on the product.

The questions in Figure 9.4 were part of a survey containing 45 questions about customer ownership of different brands and types of electrical appliances, shopping habits, use of health and beauty products, hobbies and activities, motoring, smoking, and personal finances. The customer survey was undertaken by Indesit, a manufacturer of electrical appliances for the home, including cookers, freezers, washing machines and dishwashers. Indesit uses completed surveys to build customer lifestyle profiles to inform future product and promotion design.

Choosing the best method of gathering research information

Once the sampling method has been chosen, the next step is to decide exactly how the information will be gathered from the sample. Firms can use a variety of methods of collecting information, including face-to-face interview, postal questionnaire, consumer panel, or electronic data gathering using the latest retail auditing technology.

There is no one 'best' method of gathering information. Whichever method a firm chooses, it will need to weigh up the advantages and

Portfolio Activity 9.4 

1. What sampling method and research method do you think the Guardian survey used, and why?
2. What types of business organization are likely to be interested in the findings of the survey?

Students Reject Couch Potato Lifestyle

Students are likely to spend roughly half the national average hours watching television and listening to radio, according to a new survey by the *Guardian*.

Graduate Facts, a survey of more than 2,000 students, found that they watch around 12 hours of TV and listen to about 11 hours of radio a week, compared with the national average of 27.16 hours and 20.8 hours respectively.

The survey found that students are more likely to read broadsheet newspapers. Of those surveyed, 23 per cent read the *Guardian* most often, compared with 16 per cent for the *Independent* and nine per cent for the *Times* and *Daily Telegraph*.

The *Guardian* plans to re-interview the students several times as part of a tracking study.

▼ *Figure 9.4: An example of a questionnaire*

INDESIT CUSTOMER SURVEY

Thank you for taking part in this Indesit survey. Every single reply will help us understand what our customers really want from our products — so your opinions count!

The survey includes questions about domestic appliances. There are also some more personal questions about you and your family. *If you'd prefer not to answer any of the questions, just ignore them!* In return for your answers, you'll receive £100 worth of money-off coupons plus Free Entry into our Grand Prize Draw. So do please spare a few moments to tick the boxes in this survey and post it back to us within 14 days in the envelope provided. You don't need a stamp.

EXAMPLE: **Do you drink tea?** 1 ☑ Yes 9 ☐ No

1. ABOUT YOUR PURCHASE

01 Thinking about the magazine, what did you think of its content?

	Very Good	Average	Poor
Articles	1	4	7
Offers	2	5	8
Overall	3	6	9

02 Please indicate which of the following you own, its brand and how old it is. (Please tick one in each column)

	Washing Machine	Tumble Dryer	Dishwasher	Fridge	Fridge Freezer	Freezer	Gas Cooker	Electric Cooker
Ariston	01	01	01	01	01	01	01	01
Belling	02	02	02	02	02	02	02	02
Beko	03	03	03	03	03	03	03	03
Bosch	04	04	04	04	04	04	04	04
Candy	05	05	05	05	05	05	05	05
Cannon	06	06	06	06	06	06	06	06
Creda	07	07	07	07	07	07	07	07
Electrolux	08	08	08	08	08	08	08	08
Flavel Leisure	09	09	09	09	09	09	09	09
Fridgidaire	10	10	10	10	10	10	10	10
Hoover	11	11	11	11	11	11	11	11
Hotpoint	12	12	12	12	12	12	12	12
Indesit	13	13	13	13	13	13	13	13
Lec	14	14	14	14	14	14	14	14
Neff	15	15	15	15	15	15	15	15
New World	16	16	16	16	16	16	16	16
Parkinson Cowan	17	17	17	17	17	17	17	17
Stoves	18	18	18	18	18	18	18	18
Tricity Bendix	19	19	19	19	19	19	19	19
Whirlpool	20	20	20	20	20	20	20	20
White Knight	21	21	21	21	21	21	21	21
Zanussi	22	22	22	22	22	22	22	22
Other	23	23	23	23	23	23	23	23
Age in Years								

03 Have you had to have any of the above appliances serviced or repaired in the last 12 months? (Please tick all that apply)

1 ☐ Washing Machine
2 ☐ Tumble Dryer
3 ☐ Dishwasher
4 ☐ Refrigerator
5 ☐ Fridge Freezer
6 ☐ Freezer
7 ☐ Gas Cooker
8 ☐ Electric Cooker

04 Do you have extended warranty cover on any of the appliances listed below?

	Manufacturer's Warranty	Retailer's Warranty	Insurance Company's Warranty	None
Washing Machine	01	09	17	25
Tumble Dryer	02	10	18	26
Dishwasher	03	11	19	27
Fridge	04	12	20	28
Fridge Freezer	05	13	21	29
Freezer	06	14	22	30
Gas Cooker	07	15	23	31
Electric Cooker	08	16	24	32

05 Which of the following events led you to buying these appliances.

	Washing Machine	Tumble Dryer	Dishwasher	Fridge	Fridge Freezer	Freezer	Gas Cooker	Electric Cooker
Kitchen re-fit	01	08	15	22	29	36	43	50
Moving house	02	09	16	23	30	37	44	51
Marriage	03	10		24	31	38	45	52
Having children	04	11		25	32	39	46	53
Retirement	05	12		26	33	40	47	54
Had a windfall	06	13		27	34	41	48	55
Previous appliance breakdown	07	14	21	28	35	42	49	56

06 If you bought because of moving house, did you buy before or after moving? 1 ☐ Before 2 ☐ After

07 Which three of the factors listed below normally influence your decision to purchase a particular model (Rank top 3 – please tick ONE in each column)

	1st	2nd	3rd
Features	01	13	25
Promotional offer/credit	02	14	26
Friend/relative recommendation	03	15	27
Retailer advertising	04	16	28
Choice of colour	05	17	29
Value for money	06	18	30
Style/Appearance	07	19	31
Manufacturer advertising	08	20	32
Repurchasing similar model	09	21	33
Salesperson's recommendation	10	22	34
Brand reputation	11	23	35
Other	12	24	36

08 From the list below, please indicate your top 3 retailers in order of preference for the purchase of your domestic appliances.

01 Apollo
02 Energy centre
03 Comet
04 Co-op
05 Currys
06 House of Fraser
07 John Lewis
08 Independent Retailer
09 Allders
10 Mail Order
11 Miller Brothers
12 Northern Electric
13 Power House
14 Granada Rental
15 Scottish Power/ Electricity Plus
16 Tempo
17 Other

1 ☐☐ **2** ☐☐ **3** ☐☐

09 When you replace any of the appliances listed below, how likely are you to buy the same brand?

	Washing Machine	Tumble Dryer	Dishwasher	Fridge	Fridge Freezer	Freezer	Gas Cooker	Electric Cooker
Would most probably buy the same brand	01	04	07	10	13	16	19	22
Would seriously consider other brands	02	05	08	11	14	17	20	23
Would prefer a different brand	03	06	09	12	15	18	21	24

10 Would you consider replacing any of your other non-Indesit appliances with an Indesit appliance? 1 ☐ Yes 9 ☐ No

11 How satisfied are you with the performance of your product(s)?

	Washing Machine	Tumble Dryer	Dishwasher	Fridge	Fridge Freezer	Freezer	Gas Cooker	Electric Cooker
Very satisfied	01	05	09	13	17	21	25	29
Satisfied	02	06	10	14	18	22	26	30
Not particularly satisfied	03	07	11	15	19	23	27	31
Very dissatisfied	04	08	12	16	20	24	28	32

12 Have you ever had to contact Indesit for service or enquiry?
1 ☐ Yes 9 ☐ No

13 If yes, what was the purpose of your call?
1 ☐ Appliance breakdown
2 ☐ Needed help to operate appliance
3 ☐ Wanted to buy product warranty
4 ☐ Enquiry about other products
5 ☐ Other

14 How satisfied were you with the service we provided as a result of the call?
1 ☐ Very satisfied
2 ☐ Satisfied
3 ☐ Not particularly satisfied
4 ☐ Very dissatisfied

15 Are you on the internet? 1 ☐ Yes 9 ☐ No

16 Would you be happy to receive product information and offers from Indesit on the internet? 1 ☐ Yes 9 ☐ No

17 Would you consider shopping for domestic appliances on the internet?
1 ☐ Yes 9 ☐ No

disadvantages, using a variety of criteria. These can be identified in the form of questions:

- **Fitness for the purpose** - will the survey collect the data required?
- **Cost** - how much will it cost to collect the data?
- **Speed** - how long will it take to collect data?
- **Accessibility** - how easy will it be to collect data?
- **Accuracy** - how accurate will the data be?

The first step in any research process is to define what information is required, and which consumers need to be surveyed. For example, consider a firm manufacturing baby foods who want to find out if parents and babies like their new recipes, and what price to charge for them. The firm would be ill-advised to gather information by taking a random sample of people leaving a supermarket. A better approach would be to arrange a consumer panel of parents and babies. Panel members might be chosen from details of new births from the register of births, deaths, and marriages.

Each survey method will perform differently on selection criteria, and firms need to determine which features are most important to them before going ahead. For example, if a business is in a highly competitive market like consumer electronics, it will want to bring new products to market very quickly to keep ahead of its competitors. In this case, speed is likely to be more important than cost. Alternatively, a small firm, inexperienced in market research, may choose whichever method is easiest to use.

A large drugs company investing many millions of pounds in the research and development of new products may consider that accuracy is the most important criterion. The greater the amount of information gathered, the more accurate marketing predictions and policies are likely to be.

Limitations of market research

In spite of very large expenditures on market research, around 90% of all new products fail after they have been launched. Market research may sometimes fail because buyers' wants may change more quickly than firms can gather information. When this occurs, researchers say that the data is **biased.**

Bias can arise in primary data in a number of ways:

Sampling bias

If market research is to be of use to a firm, the sample of people chosen for interview must reflect the views and behaviour common to the whole population. If not, the sample will be biased.

Questionnaire bias

Questionnaires must be carefully designed. Leading questions may encourage or force people being interviewed to give particular responses, which may not represent their actual behaviour or views.

Interview bias

People conducting a survey may not always pick people at random. For example, a young male interviewer may be drawn towards asking more young females then he would have done if the selection was purely random.

Response bias

Some people may give misleading or unrepresentative answers to questions simply because they cannot remember how many times they have used a particular good or service, or how they felt about it. Some people may even lie!

Key words:

Target population - all possible consumers of a product

Random sample - a representative group of consumers taken from the total population at random

Sampling - selecting a sample of consumers from the target population

Stratified sample - a sample of consumers selected to have characteristics in the same proportions found in the population as a whole

Quota sample - a sample achieved by selecting respondents until predetermined numbers of individuals with specified characteristics have been interviewed

Systematic sample - a non-random sample formed of every *n*th person

Face-to-face surveys - interviews with potential buyers usually conducted at random in the street

Telephone survey - research conducted by telephone interview

Postal survey - a questionnaire sent and/or returned through the post

Open-ended interview - interview based around a series of topics for discussion rather than set questions

Consumer panel - a group of consumers who allow their buying behaviour to be monitored over time

Electronic monitoring - observation of sales or consumer behaviour using computer technology

Test marketing - testing a product or advertising campaign on a sample of consumers prior to national or international launch

Section 9.4 Investigating the buying habits of consumers

Dividing up the market

Information about the buying habits of different types of consumers is extremely valuable to business organizations. They need to know about the types of consumers who want to buy their products so that they can develop new products and promotions that will appeal to them.

In order to make decisions about the type of products to make, packaging, prices, advertising, and other promotions, business organizations will want to know about the following:

- The type of goods and services consumers buy
- How much they buy
- How often they buy

These **buying habits** will tend to vary between different groups of consumers depending on:

- Their age
- Their gender
- Where they live
- Their lifestyle, tastes, fashions, and preferences

It is precisely because of our different buying habits and characteristics that such a vast array of different goods and services are produced by business organizations to satisfy our wants.

Market segments

In order to plan products and promotions, firms divide up the people who are likely to buy their product into different groups known as **market segments**. Each market segment consists of consumers with similar characteristics, such as age, sex, location, and or lifestyle.

Buying habits will differ between different market segments. For example, the type of clothes and cars bought by young people on high earnings will be very different to those bought by families. However, the buying habits of consumers in the same market segment are likely to be broadly similar. For example, most young parents will buy disposable nappies and baby foods frequently.

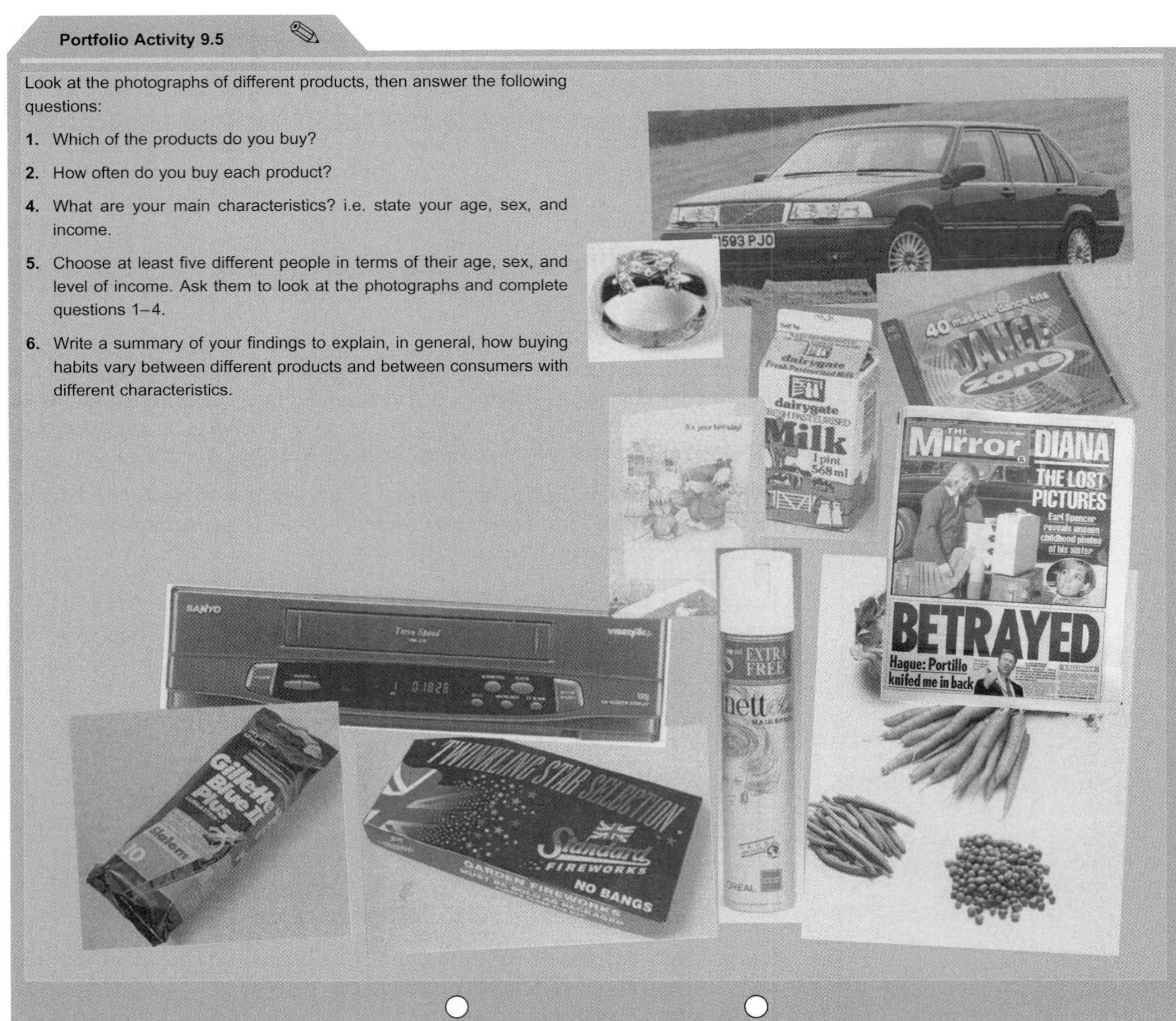

Portfolio Activity 9.5

Look at the photographs of different products, then answer the following questions:

1. Which of the products do you buy?
2. How often do you buy each product?
4. What are your main characteristics? i.e. state your age, sex, and income.
5. Choose at least five different people in terms of their age, sex, and level of income. Ask them to look at the photographs and complete questions 1–4.
6. Write a summary of your findings to explain, in general, how buying habits vary between different products and between consumers with different characteristics.

▼ *Products and promotions can be aimed at particular target audiences*

Target audiences

Firms can use information on the buying habits of different market segments to design products, advertising, and other promotions that will appeal to them. A market segment that has a particular product aimed at it - for example, teenage pop magazines or holidays for the over-50s - is known as a **target audience**.

Buying habits

The type of goods and services we buy depends on our needs and wants. Most people, regardless of their age, sex, income, or location, have the same basic needs for food, clothing, and shelter. However, the type of food, clothes, houses or flats, and other goods and services we buy will differ because we have different tastes and levels of income.

Needs also vary because of our health and age. Disabled and elderly people tend to have different needs to other people and therefore buy different goods and services.

Our wants as consumers are vast and differ between people. However, some general patterns emerge. For example, young people are more interested in pop music and street fashions than middle-aged people or pensioners. People on high incomes are more likely to use the services of financial advisors and banks.

Level of buying

How much we buy depends on how much money we have and how much of it we want to spend.

In general, the more money a person has, the more s/he tends to spend on goods and services. However, even people with the same amount of money will spend different amounts on different goods and services. That is, people have different propensities to spend. One person may prefer to save money rather than spend it all. Similarly, one person will want to buy the most expensive, top-of-the-range DVD player, while another may be content with a DVD player with basic features at a much lower price. Much will depend on their particular preferences.

Frequency of buying

How often a consumer buys a particular product depends largely on the type of product rather than their particular preferences.

Some people may be able to afford a new car each year, but in general cars and other expensive items that last a long time, like jewellery, carpets, and televisions, are bought infrequently. Firms that make these products therefore have to rely on attracting new customers in order to keep sales high.

Some goods and services, such as bread, meat, washing powders, and newspapers are bought regularly by nearly everyone. These products are used up quickly, and repeat purchases have to be made every day, week, or month. Banks are used frequently by people to pay in and withdraw money. Some people may visit a hairdressers on a regular basis, while others prefer to grow their hair long and will only pop in for a trim now and again. Consumer demand for some goods and services is seasonal. For example, Easter eggs at Easter, suntan lotions during the summer, fireworks for 5th November, and cards, trees, and decorations in the run up to Christmas.

▼ *Targeting holidays at different age groups*

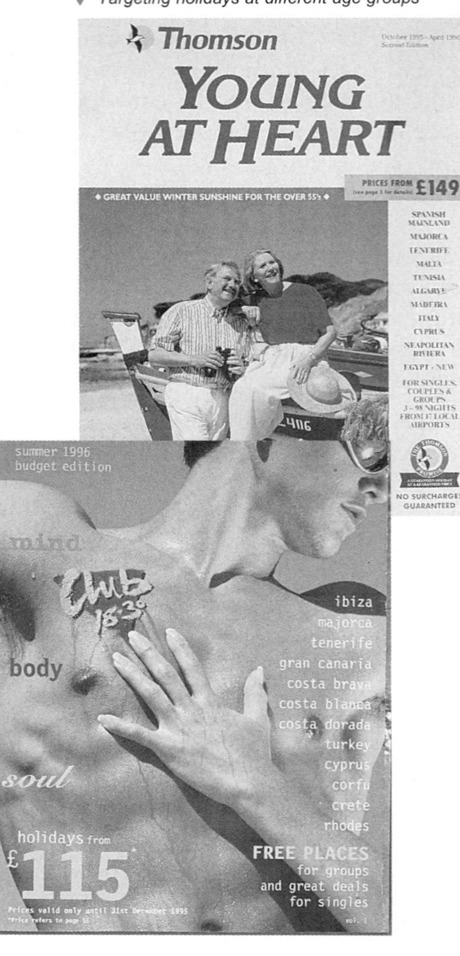

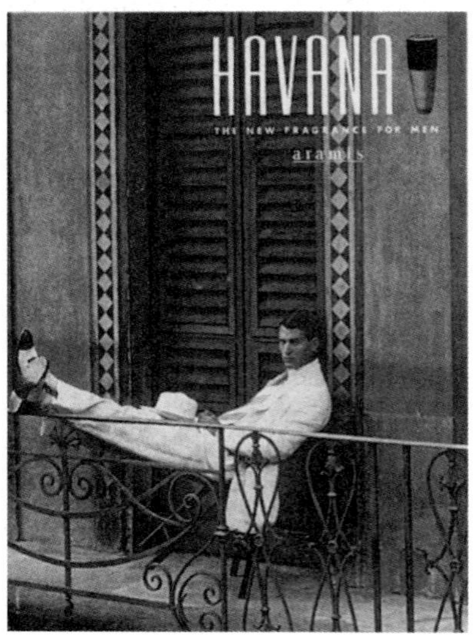

Consumer characteristics

Age

Our needs, wants, and buying habits tend to change as we grow older. Consumers can therefore be divided up into market segments separated by age. For example, the package holiday industry has designed special holidays and selling strategies aimed at the 18–30 age group, parents with young children, and the over-50s.

Businesses which depend heavily on selling products aimed at particular age groups will be very interested in government population forecasts. For example, producers of baby clothes and foods will be especially keen to know if birth rates are likely to rise or fall.

Birth and death rates in the UK are quite low. Fewer babies are being born, and more people are living longer. In 1998 there were 12.8 million people aged under 16 in the UK, compared with 14 million in 1971. On the other hand, there were around 9 million people over 65 years of age in 1998 compared with 7.8 million in 1971. The number of people over 65 in the UK is forecast to increase to over 12 million by 2021. These changes in the age structure of the UK population will affect the pattern of consumer demand.

Gender

Men and women have different buying habits and tend to be attracted by different kinds of promotions and marketing activities. For example, a recent study found that when shopping, men were more likely to pick up and look at products coloured either blue or green, while women are more likely to look at products packaged in lighter shades.

In the UK at present, women live on average nearly seven years longer than men. Therefore, goods and services aimed at the elderly are more likely to be bought by women, and so advertising needs to be designed with this in mind.

Firms and advertising agencies study the different buying habits of men and women, and design products and advertising for them accordingly. However, they have to be careful, because in many cases products used by one sex are bought as gifts by the other. For example, men buy their wives and girlfriends perfume and lingerie, and women buy their boyfriends and husbands aftershave and boxer shorts.

Portfolio Activity 9.6

1. Collect some examples of advertisements clearly aimed at different age and gender groups. For each one, decide who the advert is aimed at and the message(s) it contains.
2. Visit your local shopping centre and investigate shops and products clearly aimed at different age and gender groups.

   For example, you might want to compare the products, decor, and atmosphere in the following outlets:

   - **Holidays on offer in travel agent's**
   - **Clothes shops**
   - **Restaurants**

   In each case state what age/sex group the products and/or outlets are aimed at, and how they are designed to attract their target audience.
3. Write a short report on your findings, discussing how firms target their advertising, products, and retail outlets at consumers in different age and gender groupings.

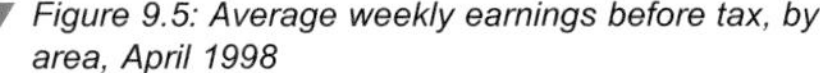

▼ *Figure 9.5: Average weekly earnings before tax, by area, April 1998*

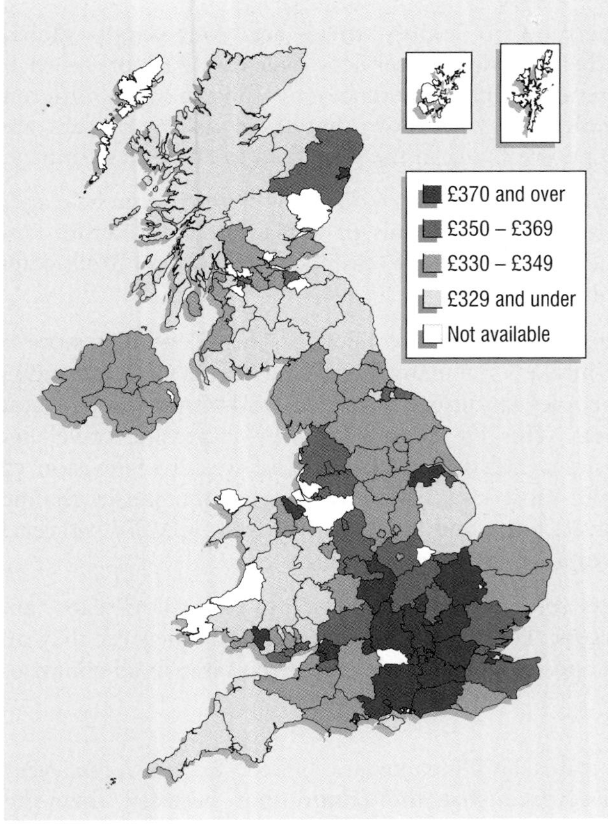

Social Trends, 1999

The characteristics of consumers in different geographic regions

Incomes and buying habits differ between regions of the country. This is shown by the map in Figure 9.5, which gives details of average gross weekly earnings per person in April 1998 in the different regions in the UK. The highest earnings were in the South East, in particular in Greater London, where average weekly earnings were £500. Cornwall was amongst the lowest with average gross weekly earnings below £300. Firms can use this geographical information to divide consumers into groups by region in order to target their products and advertising.

Not only are there regional differences in incomes, but lifestyles also differ according to the region, leading to different spending patterns and different opportunities to sell products. For example, research shows that in Scotland people tend to consume more fried food and cigarettes than the rest of the country. This information will be of special interest to firms attempting to sell health foods. Particular features of different parts of the country also present opportunities for targeting products. For example, can you think of any products that are likely to sell well at seaside resorts in England, ski resorts in Scotland, or at major tourist attractions such as Stonehenge, the Tower of London, or Edinburgh Castle?

Television regions are often used as a way of identifying regional boundaries and of creating regional market segments. Television advertisements can then be designed to appeal to consumers in particular regions.

The UK age/sex structure

Figure 9.6 shows an age–sex pyramid for the UK population in 1997. The number of males and females in the population are shown on the horizontal axis, while the vertical axis shows the ages of each group.

The United Kingdom has an ageing population. In 1961, around 12 per cent of the population were aged 65 and over and 4 per cent were aged 75 and over. This had increased to 16 per cent and 7 per cent respectively in 1997.

▼ *Figure 9.6 : UK population pyramid, 1997*

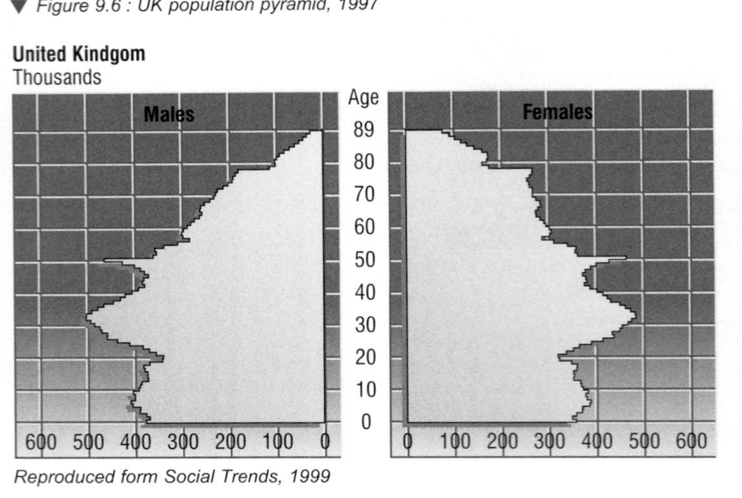

Reproduced form Social Trends, 1999

Consumers in different countries

Markets and competition to supply them are increasingly global. Businesses that sell their goods and services overseas therefore need to know about characteristics and preferences of consumers in different countries. For example, did you know that there are more cars and televisions per 1,000 people living in the USA than in any other country?

Differences in consumer buying habits in different countries can be caused by differences in income and standards of living, lifestyle, culture, and beliefs. As an example, you only have to think of the different foods eaten by people in different countries.

But did you also know that Marks & Spencer opened its first store in China in 1995? The markets for many goods and services are expanding internationally as people in different countries discover more about products sold overseas. This has been helped by increasing travel and tourism between counties and the globalization of western television via satellite. For example, most countries now receive the music channel MTV. As a result, music, films, and fashion advertised on MTV can reach consumers spread over a very wide geographical area.

Examples of products sold globally include Coca-Cola, Levi jeans, and McDonald's hamburgers. These products are identical wherever they are sold, and advertising and selling methods can be the same in all countries.

Consumer lifestyles

Lifestyle, economic status and income are linked, but in recent years researchers have discovered that the relationship between them has become less clear. For example, a semi-skilled builder may drive an expensive sports car while a city lawyer may prefer to drive a Mini.

Lifestyle segmentation involves identifying how groups of people choose to express their personality. Using market research into consumer lifestyles, firms build up profiles which provide information about potential customers.

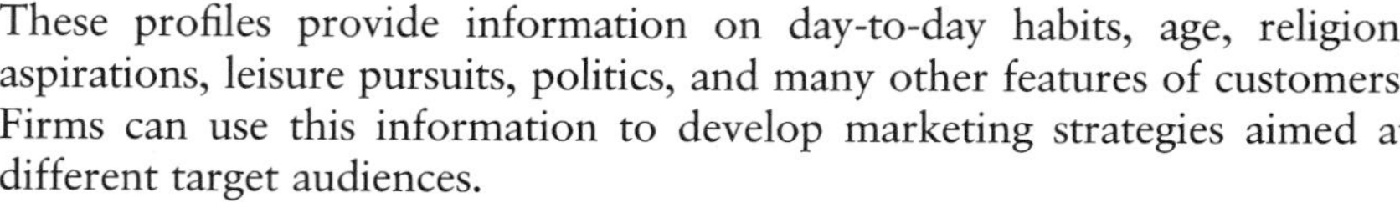

These profiles provide information on day-to-day habits, age, religion, aspirations, leisure pursuits, politics, and many other features of customers. Firms can use this information to develop marketing strategies aimed at different target audiences.

Because many people want their lifestyles to be more glamorous and exciting, products are often marketed in a way that suggests that buying those products will allow them to lead the lifestyle they want.

- **Socio-economic group (SEG)**: Firms will often divide up potential consumers into different socio-economic groups which rank people by their occupations, which in turn are often closely related to levels of education and income. People within each SEG tend to have similar lifestyles and buying habits.

▲ *This advertisment for the RAV4 is aimed at young, affluent males - and projects an appealing image and lifestyle to these consumers.*

▼ *Table 9.1: Socio-economic groups, UK 1999*

Socio-economic group	Occupations	% of population
A Upper/Upper middle class	Higher managerial, administrative, or professional	2.8%
B Middle class	Intermediate managerial, administrative, or professional	18.6%
C1 Lower middle class	Supervisory or clerical and junior managerial, administrative, or professional	27.5%
C2 Skilled working class	Skilled manual workers	22.1%
D Working class	Semi-skilled and unskilled manual workers	17.6%
E Very low income earners	Unemployed, state pensioners, disabled, and casual workers	11.4%

Joint Industry Committee for National Readership Surveys, JICNARS

A new social class classification is to be used in government statistics from 2001.

The National Statistics socio-economic classification (NS SEC) will have 7 main occupational classes;

1 higher managerial and professional
2 lower managerial and professional
3 intermediate occupations
4 small employers and own-account workers
5 lower supervisory, craft and related
6 semi-routine occupations
7 routine occupations

In addition, there will be a class for those who have never worked and the long-term unemployed.

Research has shown that consumer habits do vary by social class. For example, different classes have quite different media preferences. Upper class people show preferences for magazines and newspapers, while lower social classes show a preference for television. Even in their TV viewing habits, classes show different preferences, with upper classes favouring news and drama programmes and lower classes preferring soap operas and quiz shows.

There is also some research evidence to suggest that people with more education are more likely to buy cheaper own-label products rather than expensive brand labels. The suggestion is that more educated people are more willing to risk such products because they are less influenced by the heavy advertising that goes with the popular brand names.

Researchers typically use six main categories of social class or **socio-economic groups (SEGs)** to segment the population as in Table 9.1.

- **Tastes and preferences**: Everyone has different likes and dislikes. That is, our tastes vary, although firms clearly rely on enough people having broadly similar tastes in order to mass-produce many items.

  Our tastes are influenced by a variety of factors, including what is pleasing to the eye as well as pleasing to the tastebuds. Not everyone likes eating hot, spicy Indian or Thai food, whether they are rich or poor. However, rich people may prefer to eat such food in exclusive restaurants, while people on lower incomes may get theirs from a local takeaway.

  Tastes are also likely to be influenced by those around us - family, friends, and acquaintances. For example, you may choose to listen to certain types of music or play particular sports to fit in with your friends. Similarly, people may buy cars, take holidays, and wear clothes that are associated with particular socio-economic groups. For example, high-income groups may prefer to spend their money on BMW or Mercedes cars, Caribbean cruises, winter ski-ing holidays, and designer clothes.

  Preferences are similar to tastes in many ways. For example, we all have our preferences in music, clothes, food, drinks, etc. Many consumers like to eat cereal in the morning, but some will prefer to buy Sugar Puffs rather than other brands, while others may prefer Harvest Crunch to Cornflakes.

  Both our tastes and preferences, and therefore our buying habits, can change with age, fashion, and moral views. For example, increasing numbers of consumers now prefer to buy products which have not been tested on animals or which harm the environment. These consumers have been termed 'conscience spenders' or 'green consumers'.

- **Fashion**: Changes in fashion affect the buying habits of consumers. Most fashionable goods have a relatively short product lifecycle. This means that new products experience rapid sales growth, a peak in sales, and then start to decline in popularity - all in a relatively short space of time. For example, toys, games, and T-shirts introduced to tie in with the release of a big Hollywood film, such as *Toy Story 2* or *Star Wars - The Phantom Menace*, have lifecycles of only a few months while the film is popular.

  Changes in fashion are particularly evident in the clothing industry. For example, after the 1960s and 1970s it was no longer fashionable to wear flared trousers. In the 1990s designer labels, such D&G, Nike, Calvin Klein and French Connection UK became fashionable. Each season, clothes designers release their new collections which eventually influence the colours and styles many people will wear. Producers of clothes tend to target their new products and adverts at younger people because they tend to follow fashion more closely than other groups of consumers.

A large drugs company investing many millions of pounds in the research and development of new products may consider that accuracy is the most important criterion. The greater the amount of information gathered, the more accurate marketing predictions and policies are likely to be.

Key words:

Market segment - consumers with similar characteristics who are willing and able to demand a particular product

Target audience - a market segment that is targeted by firms to promote particular products

Socio-economic groups (SEGs) - occupation and lifestyle groupings

Section 9.5 Investigating consumer trends

Information on sales

The aim of market research is to identify market opportunities. An important aspect of research is to track sales in order to try to forecast those products which are likely to experience rising sales and those which for which sales will decline. Falling sales indicate falling profitability and declining market opportunities. Rising sales indicate an opportunity to expand market share and profits in the long run.

Producers must try to predict what consumers will want next, and provide it before their competitors do, otherwise they risk failure. A firm that does not produce what consumers want, or produces it too late, will not be successful. A **trend** in consumer demand refers to the general direction of change over time. Trends can operate in both directions. If sales are rising, this suggests an upward trend in demand. If sales are falling there is a downward trend.

▼ *Figure 9.7: How to recognize a trend in consumer demand*

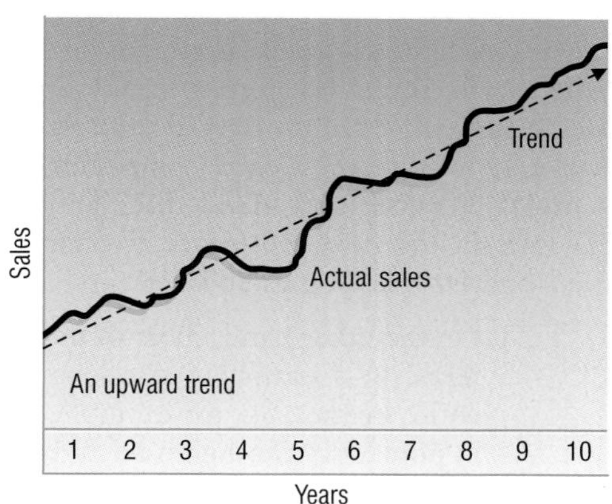

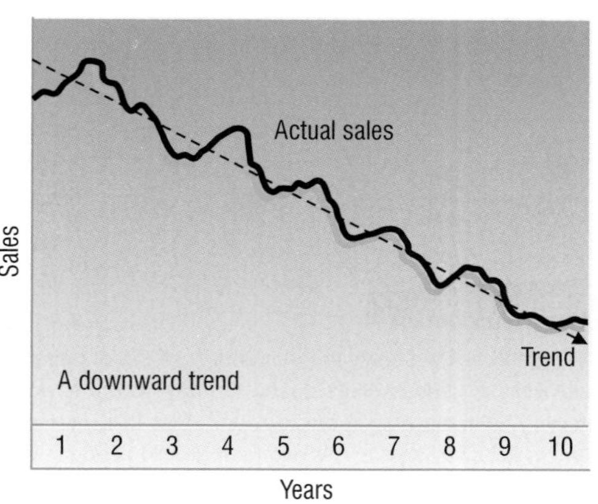

▼ *Figure 9.8 : Trends in UK household expenditure, 1971–1997*

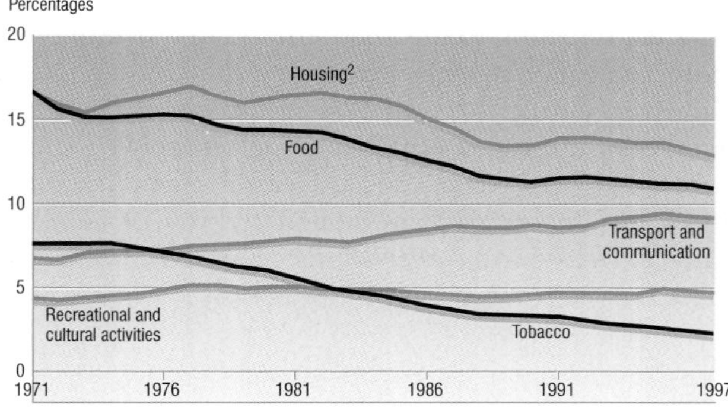

1 At constant 1995 prices
2 Includes rents, rates and water charges, but excludes expenditure on home improvements, insurance, community charge and council tax.

Social Trends, 1999

For example, Figure 9.8 shows how household spending patterns have changed over time. Between 1971 and 1997 expenditure on food as a percentage of total household expenditure fell from 17% to 11%. However, households are now devoting more of their total expenditure to travel and communications, and to housing. Over the same period the number of cars and owner-occupied dwellings in the UK more than doubled. This is related to rising incomes and changing aspirations. Between 1971 and 1998 household income more than doubled in real terms.

Changes in consumer demand which continue in the same general direction for two to three years or more are usually considered to show a long-term trend. A long-term downward trend in consumer demand for particular goods and services can spell trouble for those firms that produce them. Firms may be tempted to switch production to those goods and services which show a continuing upward trend.

Short-term trends

Other changes in demand can be very short-lived, some lasting for as little as a few days, such as the increase in demand for flowers on Mothers' day each year, or tickets for a pop concert. Other short-term changes in demand may be seasonal - for example, the rise in demand for suntan lotion for three to four months each summer, or the increase in demand for toys before Christmas each year. All are examples of short-term trends in consumer demand.

Other short-term trends in demand for particular goods or services may be observed for a year or two before the general direction of demand changes. Many will be to do with changes in tastes and fashion. For example, the craze for Ninja Mutant Turtle toys was relatively short-lived. By the time you read this book, a more recent, but similar craze for Pokémon computer games and toys may be over, and demand for them will be falling.

Some short-term trends in consumer demand

You will be able to think of many different examples of short-term trends in consumer demand for different goods and services.

Here are just a few:

- Sales of tickets to a pop concert
- Sales of Christmas cards
- Sales of special editions of newspapers and magazines
- Sales of foreign holidays during the summer
- Sales or rentals of a new video film release
- The surge in demand for electricity at around 6–7 pm when people get home from work

Short- and long-term trends

Long-term trends in demand usually occur for all the products in the same market. For example, there has been a steady growth in the number of compact discs purchased over time, while the demand for vinyl LPs has fallen so markedly that many record companies no longer make them. Now, sales of DVD music and video discs and players seem likely to overtake CD sales in the next few years. Similarly, the trend decline in demand for all cigarettes is long established.

Square eyes

The graph below shows the percentage of the population who watch television at various times during the day. There is a rising trend in viewing numbers from 6 pm to 8 pm. After this, numbers of viewers start to fall away again. This two-hour growth period in viewing figures is a short-term trend. Not surprisingly TV adverts are more expensive to show at this time of day than at any other time.

▼ *Radio and television audiences throughout the day*

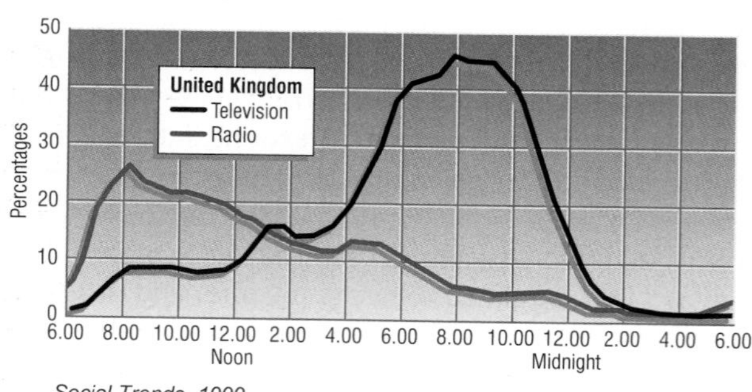

Social Trends, 1999

On the other hand, short-term changes in demand often relate to a particular good or service, rather than the entire market. So, for example, pop groups may decline in popularity through time and sell less CDs, despite the growth in sales of CDs in general. Similarly, despite the long-term decline in demand for cigarettes, sales of a brand called 'Death' cigarettes increased after they were launched, but the increase was short lived.

Short-term trends in consumer demand may move in a different direction to the long-term trend. For example, more and more tourists are visiting the UK each year. However, during the Gulf War in Kuwait in 1990, the number of tourists visiting the UK fell sharply - a short-term downward trend - because of the fear of terrorist attacks on American planes. Similarly, tourist numbers tend to fall during the winter compared with the summer.

Past trends

Some trends in consumer demand have developed over many years. For example, in the UK over the last hundred years, there has been a steady trend towards more home ownership and less private renting of accommodation. At the same time, there have been trends towards increased car ownership and more holidays abroad. Most homes now have a television, refrigerator, and telephone. Thirty years ago, very few homes had these items. The reasons for these observed long-term trends in consumer demand are many. Some of the most important are:

- **Most people in the UK now have more money to spend.** This has enabled them to spend more of their incomes meeting their wants, for example, video recorders, jewellery, holidays. The increased use of credit cards to boost our spending also reflects a change in people's attitude towards debt.
- **People work fewer hours than many years ago.** This has given them more time for leisure activities, and has increased demand for holidays, sport centres, DIY and garden centres, restaurants, and pubs.
- **Social attitudes have changed.** More women now go out to work and have less time to look after their families. This has caused an increase in demand for time-saving appliances such as microwave cookers and dishwashers. Also, less people go to church today. Until recently, shops have been prevented from opening on Sunday because of pressure from churchgoers.
- **Couples are marrying later and having fewer children.** This has meant a growing number of single people, an increase in the number of households, but a fall in their average size. This has helped to increase the demand for household furnishings and appliances. Some large retail outlets have even introduced 'singles shopping nights' where people can meet.
- **People have become more health-conscious.** We now take more exercise, smoke fewer cigarettes, eat less fatty foods, and drink more fruit and herbal drinks.
- **There is growing concern for the environment** - so-called 'green consumerism'. This has affected the way many goods and services are produced and the types of products stocked by many shops. It has increased the demand for products which are not tested on animals and do not release harmful pollutants into the air, and for foodstuffs produced by organic farms.
- **Technology has advanced rapidly.** This has meant that once high-cost products such as televisions, CDs, computers, and video recorders have come down in price and can now be afforded by many more people.

▼ *Rising incomes, changing tastes, cultural factors and technological advance have resulted in significant changes in consumer demand over time*

Sales[1] of CDs, LPs, cassettes and singles

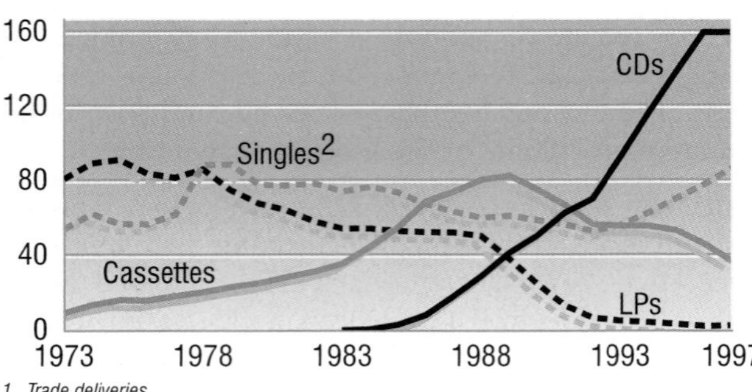

1 Trade deliveries
2 All formats combined (7", 12", cassette and CD)
Source: British Phonographic Industry

Social Trends, 1999

Holidays[1] taken by Great Britain residents, by destination

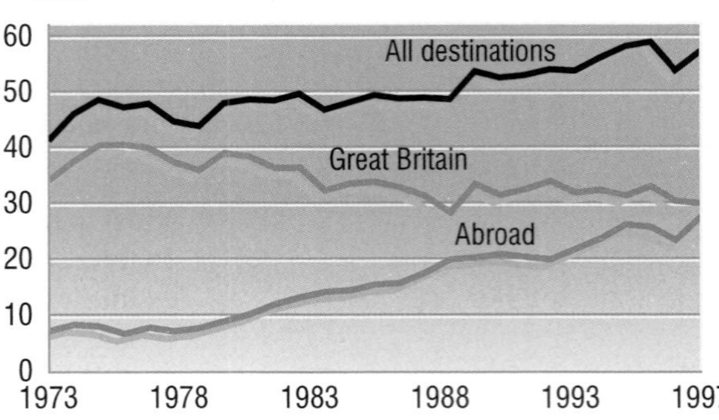

1 Holidays of four nights or more
Source: British National Travel Survey, British Tourist Authority

Social Trends, 1999

Future trends

Firms investigate past trends in demand in order to predict what might happen in the future. For example, sales of tobacco in Western countries have been falling for many years, and it is likely this long-term trend will continue. Tobacco firms have responded by trying to sell more cigarettes in Third World countries.

Sales of computer PC-DVD and CD-RW drives have been growing steadily recently, and again it seems reasonable to guess that this trend will continue. However, guessing at the future using the past can be dangerous, because the future may be completely different. Some experts suggest that the Internet will make text, sound, and video available to all homes on demand in the near future, and that this could make CD and DVD discs redundant.

It is possible to identify a number of current trends in consumer demand which are likely to continue into the future. For example, the growth of the 'green consumer', healthy diets and eating, more computers, and increased cinema attendance are sales trends which have all been growing in recent years. However, technology, fashions, and tastes are changing all the time, and this can lead to new and unexpected changes in demand in the future. Businesses will use market research to try to predict future trends in consumer demand and shopping patterns.

Useful references

- Office for National Statistics, 'Social Trends' (published annually)
- Also visit the Market Research Society web site at ***www.marketresearch.org.uk***
- **Internet** key words search: **Market research**

Portfolio Activity 9.7

You are a market analyst for Supreme Supermarkets plc, an organization that owns and operates 100 food stores across the UK. Use the information below to prepare a report for the manager of the Purchasing Department suggesting how the supermarket should alter their product range over the next five years.

Justify your recommendations using secondary data on forecasts of economic and demographic variables (for example, growth in GDP, lifestyle changes, etc.). Present your ideas formally to the Purchasing Department (your class), using graphs and overhead slides. Expect them to challenge your ideas and prepare appropriate responses.

▼ *Changing patterns in the consumption of food at home, Great Britain*

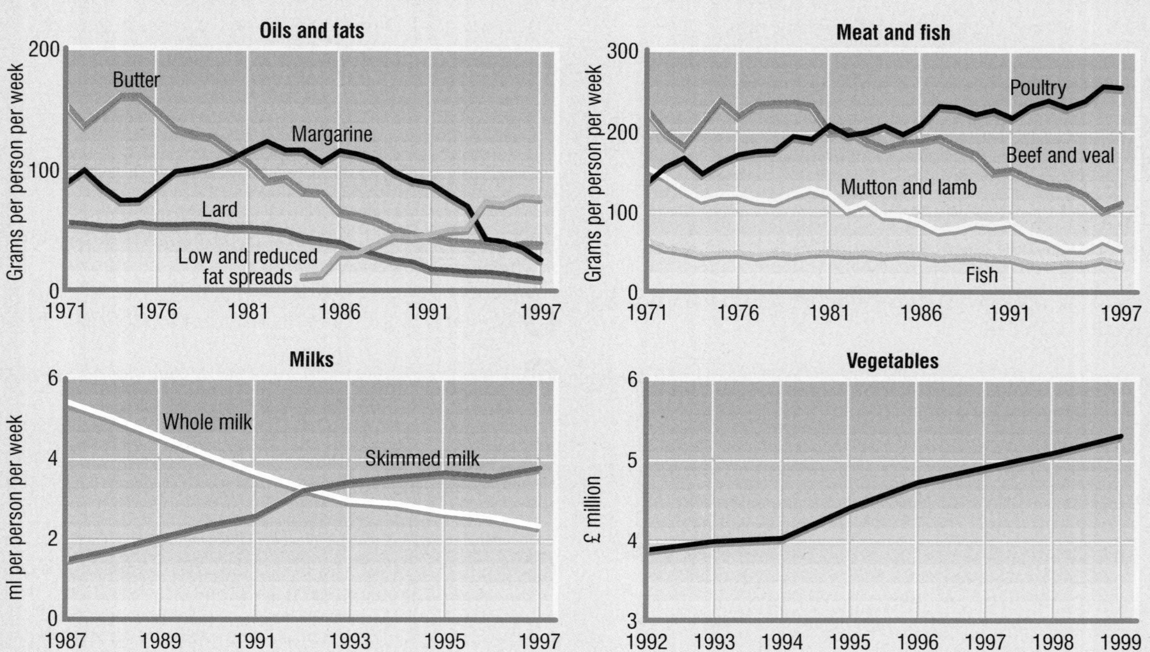

Diet-conscious add years to life expectancy

Better diets, medical care, housing and social habits are helping to make Britain a healthier place to live. A baby boy born today can expect to live until he is 75 and a girl should reach 80. In 1901, life expectancy was little more than 45 years.

The number of cot deaths has more than halved between 1901 and 1999, with the rate down to just 0.7 per thousand live births.

Infant mortality generally has fallen to just under 6 per thousand births, almost half the level in 1981. Changes in diet have been a key factor in improving adult health care.

The consumption of fish and poultry has been rising while that of red meat (such as beef and veal) has been falling. There has also been an increase in low and reduced fat spreads in preference to butter or margarine. In 1997 consumption of butter was only half that in 1984 while consumption of low fat spreads rose more than sixfold over the same period.

The amount of fresh fruit eaten by people has also increased. In 1975 each person in Britain ate an average of 500 grams of fresh fruit each week at home; by 1997 this had risen to over 700 grams. In contrast, consumption of vegetables is now only slightly higher than in 1975 at just under 750 grams in 1997.

However, the type of vegetables consumed changed during the period, with consumption of fresh green vegetables declining and that of other fresh vegetables, such as aubergines, parsnips and mushrooms, increasing. More recently, there has been a significant growth in demand for food products produced organically without the use of chemicals.

Over the last 25 years cigarette smoking among men has fallen from 52 per cent to 29 per cent, and from 41 per cent to 28 per cent among women. However, regular cigarette smoking by children is on the up and giving cause for concern.

Similarly, alcohol consumption is rising. The current Department of Health advice is to limit consumption to less than 21 units a week for men and 14 units for women. However, the proportion of men and women consuming over these amounts has been increasing, particularly among women. The percentage of women drinking more than 14 units a week increased form 9 per cent to 14 per cent between 1984 and 1997.

Adapted from The Times, 27.1.1994 and Social Trends, 1999

Test your knowledge

1 A company decides to undertake primary research because it:

A Is simple to collect

B Is low cost

C Provides qualitative information

D Can be tailored to suit the research

Questions 2–4 share the following answer options:

The following are examples of research methods:

A Telephone interviews

B Postal surveys

C Electronic monitoring

D Face-to-face interviews

Which method would you advise a firm to use in the following situations?

2 When an instant response is required to test a TV advertising campaign

3 When the background to the research needs to be explained in full and requires detailed understanding

4 When respondents wish to remain totally anonymous

Questions 5–7 concern the following information:

A DIY superstore intends to carry out some market research. It has identified the following possible methods:

A Desk-based research

B Interviews

C Observation

D Electronic monitoring

Which method should the store choose if:

5 They want to calculate their share of the total DIY market?

6 They want to find out what people buy, and why?

7 They want to find out patterns of movement around aisles in the store?

8 Which of the following is NOT an example of a secondary source of data?

A A newspaper article

B *Social Trends*

C *Economic Trends*

D A questionnaire

Questions 9–11 share the following answer options:

A Telephone interview

B Postal survey

C Test marketing

D Personal interview

Which of the above methods of primary research have these advantages and disadvantages?

9 No need to train interviewers but a poor response rate

10 Time consuming and expensive, but individual questions can be probing and answers detailed

11 Reduces risk of expensive national product launch being ill-designed but consumer preferences may differ by area

12 **a** Give an example of a consumer durable, and a capital good for industrial use.

b Suggest and explain two ways a firm might gather market research information for each of the examples you have given above.

c Suggest two criteria a firm might use in deciding which method of research to use.

13 **a** Why do firms research their markets?

b What is the difference between primary and secondary market research data?

c What is product development? Explain how it is often based on market research information.

d Suggest two sources of secondary market research data a firm might use to develop a new washing powder.

chapter 10 Marketing Strategies (1): Pricing and promoting the product

This chapter examines product pricing strategies and the methods used to communciate with consumers.

What you need to learn

Businesses need to combine a set of **marketing strategies** in a way that meets consumer needs and wants. You need to understand the range of marketing strategies used, the connections between different strategies, and the need for a coherent mix of strategies.

The **marketing mix** consists of all those activities including research, product development, pricing, promotions, distribution, selling and customer services, that a firm will need to undertake in order to attract and keep customers.

Firms can adopt different **pricing strategies** depending on their costs (such as **cost plus pricing**), the level and strength of consumer demand (for example, **penetration and expansion pricing**, **cream skimming**), and the amount of competition (**predatory and destruction pricing**).

Firms will **communicate** with their customers through **promotions**: **branding**, **advertising**, **direct mail**, **public relations**, **sales promotions**, **sponsorships**, **product presentation**, **direct selling**.

You need to be able to evaluate the marketing strategy for a good or service according to marketing principles.

Section 10.1 Implementing the marketing mix

▼ *Figure 10.1: Elements in the marketing mix*

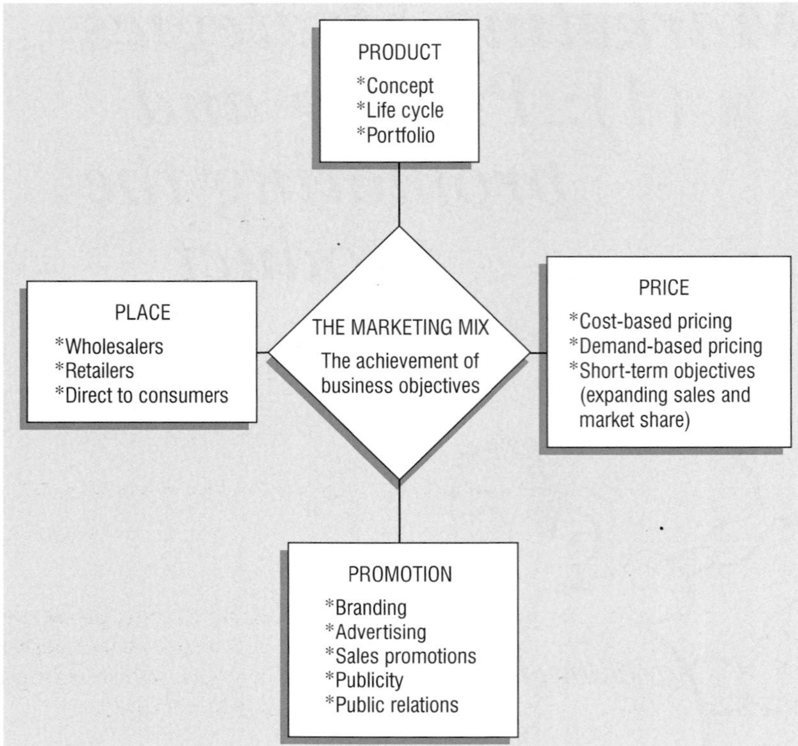

What is the marketing mix?

When consumers buy a product, they are attempting to satisfy a wide range of desires. The **marketing mix** refers to the combination of elements within a firm's marketing strategy which are designed to meet or influence the wants of customers in order to generate sales. It is the role of the marketing department in any organization to co-ordinate the planning, organization, and implementation of the marketing mix across the whole organization.

The marketing mix of any organization will be made up of four main components:

- Product
- Price
- Promotion
- Place

If a firm is to be successful it must get all four elements right.

A good marketing mix will encourage customers to build up loyalty to a particular product or product range. Additionally, many firms producing items such as hi-fi and video equipment ensure repeat purchases for their products through **built-in obsolescence.** This means that products either last for a limited timespan and then wear out, or have to be frequently updated.

▼ *Built-in obsolescence: the Ford Fiesta in 1978 and 2000*

Differentiated and undifferentiated marketing

In considering the marketing strategies of different organizations, we can distinguish between **differentiated** and **undifferentiated** marketing.

Differentiated marketing

Not all consumers will want the same things from a product. For example, when buying a hi-fi system, some people may want very high-quality sound, others will look for features and gadgets, while others may desire maximum volume and the latest technology. In such markets, firms will need to adopt a **differentiated** marketing strategy. This involves marketing a product in different ways to different groups of people or market segments, so as to emphasize different aspects of the same product.

In an extreme form, a firm may use concentrated marketing aimed at only one market segment. This can often be a successful and cost-effective method of marketing for small firms serving niche markets. Examples might include polo equipment aimed at high-income groups, student rail passes aimed at people under 26 years of age, or magazines such as *Kerrang* aimed at young people who like heavy metal music.

Undifferentiated marketing

The strategy of broadcasting a single message about a product to the whole market is known as **undifferentiated marketing**. This tends to be used where the product is **homogenous** - that is, where the product cannot be differentiated by producers to suit the needs of different market segments. For example, potatoes used to be advertised by the Potato Marketing board on behalf of all potato producers, because the product satisfies a basic need for food which is common to all con-

▲ *The government-subsidized Potato Marketing Board was closed down in 1997*

Product

The product is central to the marketing mix. Consumers buy goods and services to satisfy a variety of desires. A firm must be aware of these desires if it is to operate successfully in the market. A firm is not just selling a product, but a whole concept to the consumer (see Figure 10.2).

After-sales service
Design
Colour
Producers image
Concern for environment
5 Years Parts & Labour Free
Shape
Availability of parts
Size
Customer helplines
Guarantee
Low energy use
Taste
Size
Concern for environment
Design
Texture
Colour
Smell

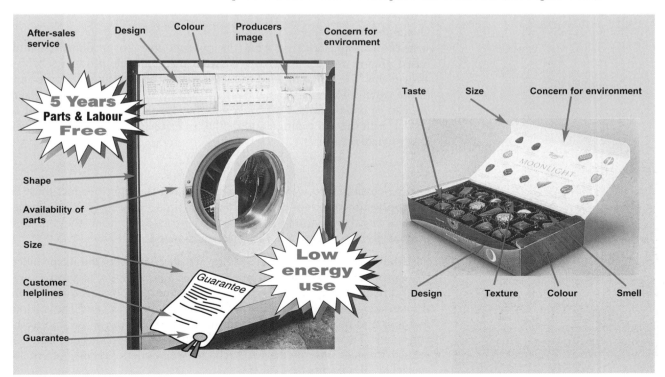

▲ *Figure 10.2: The product concept*

Price

The prices of all goods and services are likely to vary over time as market conditions alter and marketing objectives change from - say - launching a new product to maximizing profit from it.

Three major factors influence the pricing policies of firms:

- Costs of production
- The level and strength of consumer demand.
- Degree of competition in supply

Short-term objectives, such as responding to the threat of new competitors, or the need to extend the life of the product, may also affect pricing strategies (see 10.2).

Cost-based strategies

Cost-based pricing strategies involve setting price with reference to the costs of production.

Firms will normally calculate the average cost of producing each item before adding a mark-up over cost for profit. However, in the short run, a firm may price below costs, thereby sustaining a loss, in order to promote a new product or fend off competition from rival firms. The aim will be to expand sales and market share.

As sales expand, the firm will be able to increase output and reduce the cost per unit. Cost savings associated with an increase in the size of a firm - for example, the ability to buy in bulk and receive discounts - are known as **economies of scale** (see 22.4).

Demand-based pricing

Instead of basing price on what the product costs to produce, **demand-based pricing** asks the question: 'At what price will the product sell?' To answer this, the firm will need to look carefully at consumers' perceptions of the worth of a product - i.e. their willingness to pay - and at the pricing policies of competitors. Only then will they be able to produce a good or service with the right design and quality to fit the market, and at the right cost to yield a profit.

Place

For the consumer to want to make a purchase, the right product must be transported to the right place at the right time - otherwise the customer will not buy. It will also be necessary for a producer to hold stocks of their product to respond quickly to consumer demand.

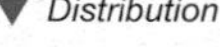

▼ *Distribution*

Distribution refers to the methods by which consumers obtain products from producers. It is a significant element in a firm's costs, and so requires careful management. The firm will need to consider physical distribution, the storage and transportation of goods and services, and the various methods and outlets through which the good or service can be sold to the consumer. These methods will include selling direct to the consumer or selling through **intermediaries** such as wholesalers, retail outlets, or specialist sales agents (see 11.2).

Choosing the distribution channel

A business will need to choose the most efficient channel of distribution for its products: one that will allow them to make their products available to consumers quickly, when they want them, and at minimum cost. Factors to consider will include the following:

- **How big is the market?** Large markets spread over a wide area will usually require intermediaries. International sales may require agents with knowledge of overseas markets and trade regulations.
- **How large is the producer?** Large firms may have the finance and personnel necessary to run their own distribution network of vehicle fleets, warehouses, and even retail outlets.
- **Who are the consumers?** Consumers of low-value, mass-produced goods normally expect to obtain them quickly and easily at retail outlets. Industrial consumers will often require technical details and will deal directly with a manufacturer or agent. They may be willing to wait some time for their order to be fulfilled.
- **What is the product?** Highly specialized or personalized goods and services will require direct contact between producer and consumer. Perishable goods will need to be sold quickly, so speed will be a key factor. Low-value goods sold in bulk are likely to be distributed through intermediaries, thus relieving the producer of the need for, and cost of, storage. New products may meet with some resistance from retailers and may require alternative means of distribution.
- **What is the product image?** Sometimes a firm may wish to restrict the sale of its products to certain shops and stores in order to preserve an exclusive product image.

Promotion

Promotion involves providing information to consumers about products through a variety of media, and attempting to influence buying decisions by stressing certain features. 'Influence' may become 'persuasion' when firms attempt to stress product features which may be more imaginary than real (see 10.3).

Above- and below-the-line promotion

Above-the-line promotion aims at mass markets through independent media such as TV, radio, and press advertising.

Below-the-line promotion refers to the use of media over which the producing firms have more control, allowing them to target their products more closely at particular consumers. Examples include exhibitions, packaging, and in-store sales promotions.

Branding:

- Creates consumer loyalty
- Distinguishes the product from its rivals
- Can help firms justify charging higher prices to their consumers

▲ 'Beanz meanz Heinz'

▲ 'You either love it or hate it'

Branding

Most forms of promotion seek to create an image to go with the product. **Brand imaging** is an important part of a firm's marketing strategy. Underlying all successful branding is the principle that people not only buy products, they also buy images. For example, Volkswagen advertised the typical VW driver as an affluent, care-free, attractive, professional type of person. The advertising slogan spoke of 'VW people'. The campaign was successful as a large market segment identified with or wanted to be like the kind of people portrayed as 'VW people'. Sales of the cars rose accordingly.

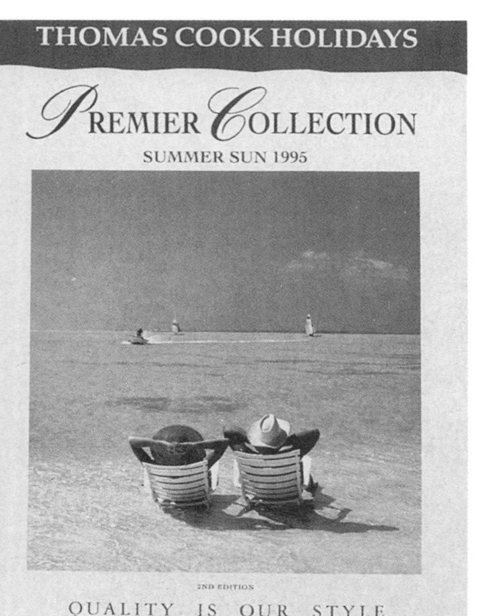

THOMAS COOK HOLIDAYS
PREMIER COLLECTION
SUMMER SUN 1995
2ND EDITION
QUALITY IS OUR STYLE

▲ 'Don't book it, Thomas cook it!'

Old brands top lists of nation's shoppers

The British have often been accused of being stuck in their ways and clinging to tradition. And a new study has found that as far as their grocery is concerned it is true.

Research into shoppers' buying habits showed that although people are willing to try new products, they quickly return to the brands they know best.

The study, by market research company AC Nielsen and Checkout magazine, found that of the country's 1000 top selling brands, 39 per cent have been on the market for 50 years or more. The study found only nine per cent have been launched in the past ten years.

The country's favourites

These best-selling brands, all introduced at least 50 years ago, are a marketing man's dream:

Coca-Cola soft drink
Walker's crisps
Nescafé coffee
Persil washing powder
Andrex toilet roll
Heinz tomato soup
Pepsi soft drink
Brooke Bond PG Tips tea
Kit Kat chocolate
Anchor butter
Tate & Lyle sugar
Kellog's Corn Flakes cereal
Weetabix cereal
Mars chocolate bars
Kleenex tissues
Wrigley's chewing gum
Cadbury's Dairy Milk
Birds Eye frozen peas
Kitekat cat food
Typhoo tea
Colgate toothpaste
Bisto gravy mix
McVities Homewheat biscuits
Oxo stock cubes
Shredded Wheat cereal
Tampax tampons

Metro, 26.8.1999

The world's top 10 brands

Coca-Cola
Microsoft
IBM
General Electric
Ford
Disney
Intel
McDonald's
AT&T
Marlboro
...all are US-owned

Financial Times, 2.2.2000

If branding can make consumers believe that the branded product is better than others, they will be willing to pay a higher price for it. As many rival products are virtually identical, the only way in which a particular one can be made to stand out is often through aggressive branding. This is usually achieved through the use of a brand name, catchphrase, distinctive packaging, and, in the case of soap powders, a scented or coloured powder.

A firm can choose a separate brand name for each of its products or use one name for the whole range. For example, brand names like McDonald's, Sainsbury, and St Michael cover a range of products. Marketing using these brand names means that promoting one product helps the others in the range. However, if one product in the range is not up to standard, this can badly affect the image of the others.

Portfolio Activity 10.1

Consider the following product ranges:

- Washing powders
- Biscuits
- Canned soft drinks
- Toilet rolls and tissues
- Tea and coffee

For each product range investigate:

- The brand names of products (including supermarket own-label brands)
- The images that are created for each brand
- How they are promoted (including advertising, sales promotions, publicity material, etc.)
- The different groups of consumers (or market segments) aimed at by different brands

Fast-moving consumer goods (FMCGs)

Consumer goods such as washing powders, biscuits, canned drinks, and crisps are used up relatively quickly by consumers who may need to make frequent repeat purchases. To meet the high demand for these and other so-called **fast-moving consumer goods**, both retail outlets and manufacturers must frequently re-stock.

Competition among producers to supply FMCGs is fierce. In order to capture market share, producers tend to produce a range of similar products aimed at particular market segments consisting of different groups of consumers with shared characteristics and buying habits (see 9.4). Although there is very little difference between products, distinctive images and brand names can be created for each product in a range by heavy advertising and by the use of different packaging. For example, biscuits such as 'Jammy Dodgers' may be aimed at the youth market segment, while the image created for Bendicks chocolate biscuits is one of luxury and decadence to capture demand from affluent middle-aged and middle-income consumers. Images created for washing powders can emphasize smell, 'whiteness', softness, colour stability, and environmental concern, with each particular image being aimed at a different market segment.

Producers will often spend large amounts of money advertising brands to create customer loyalty and to ensure repeat purchases for their products. This enables them to price their products at a premium, because consumers have been made to believe they are getting something which is worth a higher price. However, in recent years, increasing competition from supermarket own brands and changing consumer attitudes have reduced the demand for well-known brands such as Heinz baked beans and Coca-Cola. Supermarkets have also used the power of advertising and price discounts to create an image of 'value for money' for their own-label brands.

Portfolio Activity 10.2

1. What are brands?
2. Explain how brands are created and why.
3. What business aims do the firms mentioned in the article below have in providing free books and equipment for schools?
4. The National Federation of Parent Teacher Associations is concerned that the promotional messages contained in free exercise books do not openly persuade pupils to buy brands. Instead, companies like C&A are encouraged to promote more educational messages in their advertising. Do you think this makes any difference, given the objectives of marketing? Explain your answer.

Brands enter the classroom

As pupils return to school this week for the autumn term, some will find their exercise books have changed. Instead of the usual dull covers they will feature corporate logos and messages from sponsors such as Weetabix and PepsiCo.

Marketing company Lasting Impressions is giving its Jazzy Books to 700 primary and secondary schools in Britain. If the scheme is a success, it hopes to provide every pupil in Britain with free exercise books.

Marketing to schools is not new. The National Consumer Council estimates companies spent £300m ($489m) marketing to schools last year. Tesco, the supermarket chain, allows parents to collect points towards the purchase of school computers. But this is the first time companies have paid for essential resources.

"Schools spend £10m on exercise books each year," says Neil Eastwood, Lasting Impressions' programme manager. "Under this scheme they get the books free so cash can be used for other essential purchases."

Mr Eastwood says sponsors' messages are vetted to ensure they do not overtly advertise brands. "We have an ethical panel run by the National Confederation of Parent Teacher Associations that makes sure the messages and the artwork are suitable for use in schools. Sponsors are not allowed to say, 'Buy our product'."

The company ran a pilot scheme this year sponsored by retailer C&A and glue brand Pritt to assess the reactions of teachers, parents and pupils.

"We ran messages promoting courtesy and consideration for others, and one page of the book features clothing which carried reflector strips so that children can be seen in the dark," says Mary Sangster, advertising manager for C&A. "We see our involvement as a corporate awareness campaign."

PepsiCo is sponsoring the books. "We get involved in a lot of things that are of value to the community but it doesn't necessarily mean that our name will be splashed across the front page," the company says.

But teachers and parents, unions and local education authorities have expressed concern about increasing commercialism in the classroom. One scheme causing disquiet is being proposed by Essex-based marketing company Imagination for School Media Marketing. It plans to pay 300 secondary schools £5,000 a year to carry poster advertising in school corridors, gyms and dining halls.

Financial Times, 1.9.1997

▼ *Examples of contracting and expanding markets in the 1990s*

Contracting markets	Expanding markets
Typewriters	Multi-media personal computers and software
'Doorstep' milk deliveries	Organic foods
Animal furs	Mineral waters
Tobacco and cigarettes	Herbal drinks
TV repairs	Widescreen TVs
Vinyl LPs	DIY
Coal and solid fuels	Mobile phones
Duplication equipment	Digital Versatile Discs
Beef and veal	Aromatherapy

The marketing mix and the growth of organizations

Business organizations aiming for growth in their size and scale of production can do so in a number of ways:

- through developing new products to sell
- by expanding their share of a market
- by entering new markets at home or abroad

Product development

Consumer wants are always changing because of various factors - fashion, social and cultural change, growing incomes, new legal requirements, and many more (see 9.5). It is important that firms keep pace with changing wants and develop existing or new products that people will continue to buy. The development of products and their performance in markets are considered in sections 9.1 and 10.4.

Contracting and expanding markets

If consumer demand for a particular good or service is falling over time, the market for that product is said to be shrinking or contracting. Firms making that good or service will suffer declining sales and profits.

Competition for remaining customers will be fierce among firms and some may close down.

If, on the other hand, consumer demand for a particular good or service is rising over time, the market for that product is said to be expanding. Those firms already producing the good or service will attract new customers and experience rising sales and profits. They may have to expand production to meet demand and it is likely that other firms will be attracted to the market.

Building market share

Entering a new market will often require a firm initially to charge a relatively low price for its products to attract customers away from established rivals. Heavy advertising and in-store promotions to raise customer awareness about the product will also be necessary. For example, advertising for a new drink called Red Bull was prolific in the summer of 1995 with a number of humorous cartoons being shown on prime time television and posters with the catchy slogan 'It's amazing what a Red Bull can do!'. In this way marketing was being used to gain a foothold in the large canned soft drinks market and to build sales and market share. Red Bull is now a well-established product.

Key words

Marketing mix - the elements of a firm's marketing strategy designed to meet consumer wants and generate sales. The four main elements are product, price, place, and promotion.

Differentiated marketing - marketing a product in different ways to different market segments

Concentrated marketing - marketing aimed at one particular market segment

Undifferentiated marketing - marketing a product in the same way to the whole market

Homogeneous products - products which cannot be differentiated

Built-in obsolescence - commodities which are frequently updated or produced in such a way that they wear out relatively quickly

Cost-based pricing - pricing products according to their cost of production

Demand-based pricing - pricing policies based on market conditions and consumer willingness to pay

Economies of scale - cost savings resulting from an increase in the size of a firm

Distribution - the process of getting products from producers to final consumers

Promotion - attempts to influence the buying decisions of consumers.

Above-the-line promotion - promotion aimed at mass markets through independent advertising media such as TV, radio, cinema, and newspapers

Below-the-line promotion - promotional methods such as packaging, trade fairs, in-store merchandising, targeted more closely at the customers of a particular firm

Branding - creating a distinctive name and image for a product to differentiate it from rival products

Fast moving consumer goods (FMCGs) - frequently bought, branded products which are heavily advertised and aimed at different groups of consumers.

Section 10.2

The pricing decision

What determines prices?

Deciding on the price at which to sell a product is one of the most important decisions an organization can make. If price is set too high, consumers may be unwilling to buy the product. If price is set too low, a firm may not be able to cover its costs of production.

The prices of all goods and services are likely to vary over their product life-cycles as the marketing objectives of different organizations change - for example, from launching a new product, to maximizing profit from the product (see 10.4). At any given time, short-term objectives, such as the need to fight off new competitors or to extend the life of the product, may affect the pricing strategy of a firm. Pricing low to generate sales and fight off competition may cause a firm to lose money in the short term. However, in the long run, if a firm is to stay in business it must be able to cover its costs of production with sales revenues.

Three major factors can, therefore, be identified as influencing the pricing decisions of firms. These are:

- The costs of production (and the desire for profit)
- The level and strength of consumer demand
- The level of competition among producers to supply the market

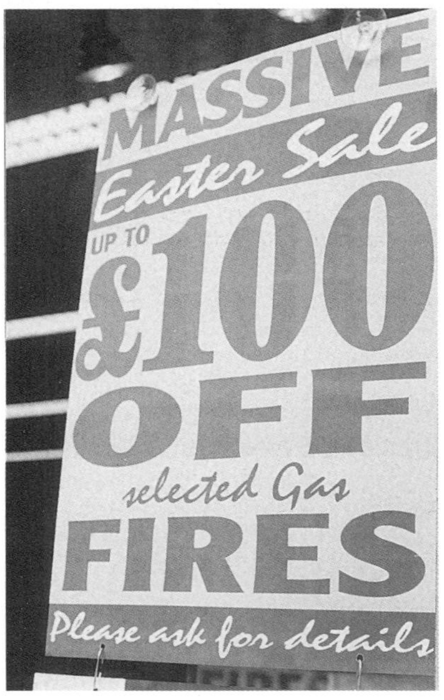

▼ *Promotional pricing to boost sales*

Factors influencing pricing decisions

Prices set by a firm with reference to its costs of production will be greatly influenced by the particular aims and objectives agreed by the organization.

The need to survive

Underlying all business is the need to survive. To do this, a firm must be able to generate enough revenue to cover its costs of production. This is of particular importance to non-profit-making organizations such as charities. All donations or monies they receive are spent on their particular activities. That is, income should exactly equal costs. However, because flows of income and expenditures do not necessarily occur at the same time, charities must be careful not to overspend and operate at a loss.

The desire for profit

Covering costs may ensure business survival, but most business owners also want to earn a profit from their activities. The level of return on their investment will need to be at least as much as the interest they could have earned by placing the money in a bank account instead. In order to earn this profit, they will need to set a price for their product which will generate revenues to exceed production costs.

Expanding sales

When a firm enters a market for the first time with a new product, its long-term objective may be to maximize profit, but in the short term it will have other aims as well. For example, in order to ensure a successful launch for the product, it may decide to pitch price low and cut its profit margins to the bone. If there are a number of other similar products already on the market, it may need to keep price at this low level in order to build market share and maximize potential sales. If sales do not match expectations, it may find itself left with underused capacity, in terms of labour, stocks of materials, machines, and other equipment.

However, in other circumstances, launching an entirely new and unique product may allow a firm to pursue a high-price strategy. Consumers may be willing to pay a premium price for a new product. A high selling price may also be the only way the firm can justify the high cost of product research and development (R&D) and an initial supply. It may be that sales will need to expand before a firm can benefit from cost savings associated with mass production and be able to pass these on to consumers in the form of lower prices.

External factors influencing pricing decisions

Setting price with regard only to the costs of production ignores the constraints imposed by external factors such as:

- The level of consumer demand (see 5.3)
- The amount of competition among producers (see 5.2)
- Government intervention in product markets (see 6.1)

▼ *Figure 10.3: What influences the pricing decision?*

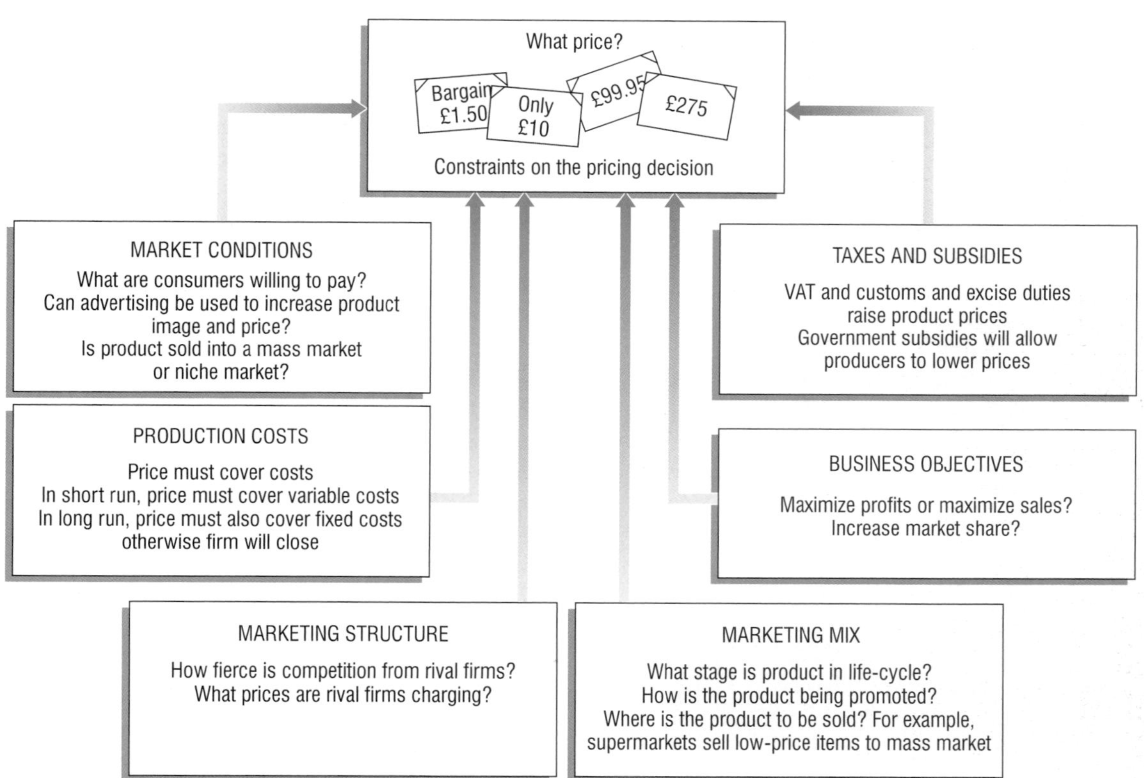

Cost-based pricing methods

If a firm is to survive in the long run, it must be able to cover its costs of production. If revenues do not exceed costs, it will make a loss. It may be able to sustain a loss for a while, but in order to continue operating, it must generate enough revenue to cover wage bills and pay for materials and power, rent and rates, and other overheads.

Cost-plus pricing

This involves calculating the cost of producing each unit of output, and then adding a mark-up for profit. For example, if a firm produced 10,000 units of a product costing £20,000, the **average cost** would be £2 (see 22.4). A 10% profit mark-up would mean that units would be priced for sale at £2.20 each.

Marginal cost pricing

The addition to total cost resulting from the production of an additional unit of output is known as the **marginal cost** (see 22.4). A decision to expand output by one or more units will be based on an assumption that unit price will be at least sufficient to cover marginal costs, such that the total profit earned on all previous units is not reduced.

▼ *Figure 10.4: Cost-based pricing*

Sometimes firms will price just above marginal cost in order to use up spare capacity and ensure that at least a small contribution to fixed costs is made. For example, consider an airline selling flights to New York. Whether the plane flies full or half-empty, it will incur the same fixed costs for fuel, flight crew, and staff. Suppose 80% of seats at the standard fare are sold, yielding a reasonable profit on the flight. In an attempt to fill the plane, the airline can offer remaining seats at bargain prices. The marginal cost of each additional passenger will be small - just the cost of additional administration and on-board refreshments. As long as the fare price more than covers these small additional costs, the airline will be able to add to its profit.

Problems with cost-based pricing

Cost-based pricing strategies make no allowance for the market and what people are already paying for similar products. Once a mark-up for profit has been added on top of allocated costs per unit, the product price may be too expensive compared with rival products, and the firm will find it difficult to make sales. In the short run, therefore, a firm may be forced to cut price and take a loss in order to fight off competition.

▼ *Flight bargains offered by 'bucket shops' - an example of marginal cost pricing to use up spare capacity*

Evening Standard 29.12.1999

Demand-based pricing

Market- or **demand-based** pricing strategies tend to involve pricing products at 'what the market will bear'. That is, producers will price high if consumer demand is high. For example, high prices are often charged for unique products, like rock festivals and designer clothes, because demand will normally outstrip supply.

Instead of reflecting what the product costs to produce, demand-based pricing asks: 'At what price will this product sell?' In adopting this approach, firms will need to carry out careful market research to find out what consumers are willing to pay, and also study the pricing policies of their competitors. Only then will they be able to produce a good or service with the right design and quality to fit the market, and at the right cost to yield a profit.

Short-term pricing objectives

The product price charged by a firm will largely depend upon the target market for the product and the objectives of the firm. For example, in some markets, such as supermarket own-brand products, firms will need to adopt a low-price strategy to attract customers away from well-known brand leaders. In other markets, high price can actually be an attraction because it lends exclusivity or 'snob appeal' to the product. Products in Hamleys Toy Shop in London's Regent Street, for example, are sometimes priced 400% above those for the same toys in high street shops, yet the toys will still sell because of the exclusivity and image of the store.

▼ *Figure 10.5: The relationship between price and consumer information requirements*

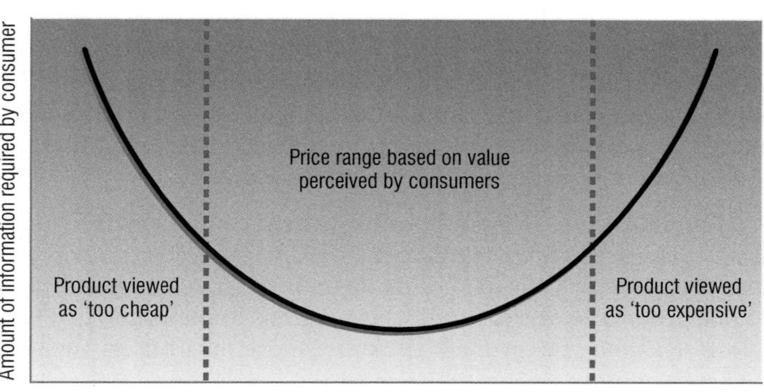

Adapted from 'Directing the Marketing Effort' by R Willsmer (Pan)

If customer's perception of the product does not match the price, extra marketing effort will required to justify the difference (see Figure 10.5). This is true whether the price is lower or higher than the customer would normally expect to pay. Both 'bargain' prices and excessively high prices are likely to arouse suspicion. The greater the difference between the consumer's expected price and the actual selling price, the greater the marketing effort required to convince the customer that the price charged is justifiable.

Market skimming

This strategy, also known as **price creaming,** is often used when there is little competition in a market. It involves charging a high price for a new product to yield a high initial profit from consumers who are willing to pay extra because the product is new and unique. As competitors enter the market, prices are reduced to encourage the market to expand.

Market skimming is a practice often observed in markets for audio and video products. For example, Sony and Phillips were the first manufacturers to release compact disc players in the UK during the mid-1980s. Initially, the players were priced at £500 or more. By 2000, there existed a bewildering variety of CD players, some priced as low as £25.

Penetration pricing

This strategy is used by firms trying to gain a foothold in a new market. It is a high-risk, high-cost strategy that tends to be confined to large firms who supply mass markets.

Penetration pricing involves setting product price low to encourage consumers to try the product and to build sales. This will also encourage retailers and wholesalers to stock the product and in doing so reduce their demand for competitors' goods and services. In addition, the firm may boost sales by lowering price if demand is price-elastic (see 5.6). Cutting price tends to increase total sales revenue if demand is price-elastic.

However, in markets where the supply side is very competitive, a **price war** may develop among rival firms. Any rise in sales from price cuts may be shortlived, as rival firms slash prices in an attempt to retain their market shares. It is often said that only the consumer wins in a price war.

Expansion pricing

This is similar to penetration pricing. Product prices are set low to encourage consumers to buy. As demand increases, the firm is able to raise its level of output and take advantage of economies of scale, which will lower the average cost of producing each unit (see 22.4). Lower average costs can either be passed on to consumers as lower prices, or, if prices are held steady, the lower costs will increase the firm's profit margins.

Price discrimination

This is used when a firm is able to charge different prices to different groups of consumers. For example, rail companies have different fares for peak and off-peak travel. Similarly, British Telecom charges different rates for telephone calls made at peak and off-peak times.

Price discrimination is only possible when consumers are unable to undercut higher prices by reselling the product from low-price markets to higher-priced ones. Thus, it is often possible to charge different prices for the same product or service in different regions of the country or world, if the cost of sending the product elsewhere more than offsets any saving in price between areas.

Competition-based pricing

Where there is fierce and direct competition between suppliers to a market, firms will often adopt **competition-based** pricing strategies.

Price leadership

This will tend to occur where firms are reluctant to start a price war by cutting their prices. They will therefore tend to price their products in line with those charged by their competitors. In some cases, a dominant firm may take on the role of **price leader**, and rival firms will raise or cut prices as dictated by the dominant firm. **Price leadership** tends to occur in markets dominated by a handful of large and powerful suppliers, such as petrol retailing.

Destroyer pricing

A more drastic version of penetration pricing, **destroyer pricing** is used when the objective is to destroy the sales of competitors' products, or to warn off new entrants to the market. Trading losses resulting from destroyer pricing strategies cannot usually be maintained for long. Freddie Laker, owner of Laker Airways in the 1980s, accused large airlines of operating destroyer pricing on transatlantic air routes, causing his business to collapse.

Competition remains fierce on some heavily used routes in the UK and Europe to provide low-cost no-frills air travel between major airline operators, such as British Airways, and new smaller rivals such as easyJet. In 1999 easyJet accused BA of subsidising the losses made by its subsidiary airline, Go, because it was selling tickets below cost in an attempt to attract passengers away from rivals. Low-cost airline operator Ryanair soon ran into difficulties trying to compete with larger rivals, for example, setting air fares as low as £17 for a one-way trip to Edinburgh. Price wars between low-cost airline operators in the UK and in lucrative overseas markets, such as the USA, continue.

Wal-Mart's takover of Asda is expected to drag UK retailers into damaging price wars

Is this the end of life as the British consumer knows it? Wal-Mart, the world's most formidable retailer, has arrived in the UK and is widely expected to transform the shopping experience for Britain's 55m inhabitants.

Almost overnight, UK retailers will find themselves facing price wars on everything from food to cosmetics and clothing to household goods. Customers should enjoy huge discounts of 10 to 15 per cent on their basic shopping needs.

Financial Times, 15.6.1999

Price wars

In the late 1990s many major supermarkets in the UK were also accused of entering into **price wars** on many products. Price wars will often develop in markets where the supply side is very competitive and established businesses are threatened by new entrants.

Price wars are not popular among firms even though they frequently occur. This is because engaging in a price war is a very high-risk strategy. Gains tend to be shortlived as rival firms continually slash prices in an attempt to steal custom from each other. Only the consumer benefits in the long run, as firms' profits margins are drastically reduced by successive price cuts without a sustained increase in demand for their products.

However, where there is little competition in a market, for example for a new and unique product, a firm may be able to exploit consumers' willingness to pay by pricing at 'what the market can bear'.

Problems with demand- and competition-based pricing

Cost-based pricing ignores the influence of the market conditions of consumer demand and supply on price. Conversely, the main problem with price-setting with reference to market conditions is that it may ignore the production costs which a firm must at least cover through sales revenues if it is to survive.

As long as a firm is able to cover its variable costs of production in the short run, it can continue production and carry on with objectives such as launching a new product or expanding market share. However, a firm cannot go on making a loss indefinitely. Eventually it must be able to pay for its fixed costs of production, namely rent, rates, and overheads (see 22.3). In the long run, therefore, pricing decisions must take into account total costs, including fixed costs, as well as market conditions. If a firm is only able to cover its costs by setting its product price higher than rival products, then to make sales and survive, it will need to examine the scope for cost-cutting and increasing productivity (see 1.1).

Portfolio Activity 10.3 

1. What is a 'price war'? What evidence is there from the articles that supermarkets chains are engaged in price wars?
2. What motives has Asda for cutting the prices of a number of products?
3. What will be the likely impact of the price war on other organizations?
4. Collect evidence from competing supermarkets to support the view that they are engaged in price wars:

   (a) Compile a list of items that are likely to appear in a typical household's weekly shopping basket.

   (b) Find out the price of these items from 3–4 different supermarkets in your area every 2 weeks for a 20-week period. How do prices change over time, and how do they compare between your chosen supermarkets?
5. Collect evidence from newspapers on price competition in other markets. Keep a scrapbook, and write a brief evaluation of each article you find. For example, list the main organizations competing on price, their motives, and what their pricing strategies have achieved so far.

Asda discounts starts bitter pill price war

ASDA tomorrow opens a second front in its war with the pharmaceutical industry when it trebles its range of own-label remedies. Most will be half the cost of leading brands, while some will offer discounts of "several hundred per cent".

An advertising and promotional campaign will accompany the launch of around 30 painkillers, cold cures and vitamin pills. It signals Asda's determination to smash the price-fixing agreement for over-the-counter drugs which it claims cheats consumers, providing "ridiculous profits" of more than £280 million a year.

The move has been condemned by high street chemists who fear they may soon go the way of bakers and grocers, who have already been forced out of business by the supermarkets. Profits from prescriptions have been eroded by government cuts and the in-store pharmacies introduced by large out-of-town retailers.

Adapted from The Sunday Telegraph, 21.5.1999

Asda wades into music price war

Asda has cut the price of CDs and videos, and threatened yesterday to use its buying power to force the music industry to take the price of chart albums below £10.

The company, now owned by the world's largest retailer, Wal-Mart, said it would reduce the price of chart CDs to £11.99 and will absorb that from its own profit margins.

But, at a meeting with the six leading record labels in the UK last week, Asda said it wanted the music industry to absorb a further £2 reduction which would take the price of CDs below £10.

The discount - the second price reduction from Asda in a year - follows the launch of a promotional offer from Boots which has knocked a third off the price of some CDs and raised speculation of a price war.

David Inglis, general manager of entertainments for Asda, warned that if record companies did not agree to work with Asda it would be prepared to use its market clout to try to achieve its goal.

The Guardian, 23.11.1999

Key words:

Demand-based pricing - pricing policies based on market conditions and consumer willingness to pay

Market skimming - high-price strategies used to maximize profits from a new product in the short run when there is little competition

Penetration pricing - low-price strategies aimed at boosting total sales and expanding market share

Price discrimination - charging different prices to different market segments for the same product

Cost-plus pricing - setting product price equal to average cost, plus a mark-up for profit

Competition-based pricing - setting prices with reference to prices charged by rival firms

Price leadership - when rival firms in a market set their prices in accordance with those charged by a dominant firm

Destroyer pricing - low-price strategies adopted by a firm or group of firms to force competitors out of the market

Loss-leader - an unprofitable product which continues to be produced and sold because it has a positive effect on the sales of other products produced by the same organization

Marginal cost pricing - setting price equal to or just above the cost of producing an extra unit of output

Section 10.3 Communicating with consumers

Marketing communications methods

Marketing communication involves providing information, through a variety of media, about a product to target audiences of consumers, and attempting to influence their buying decisions by stressing certain features of the product. 'Influence' may become 'persuasion' when firms attempt to stress product features which may be more imaginary than real. The key methods of marketing communication are:

- Advertising
- Public Relations

- Publicity
- Sales promotions
- Direct marketing

▼ *Figure 10.6: UK advertising expenditure by media, 1998*

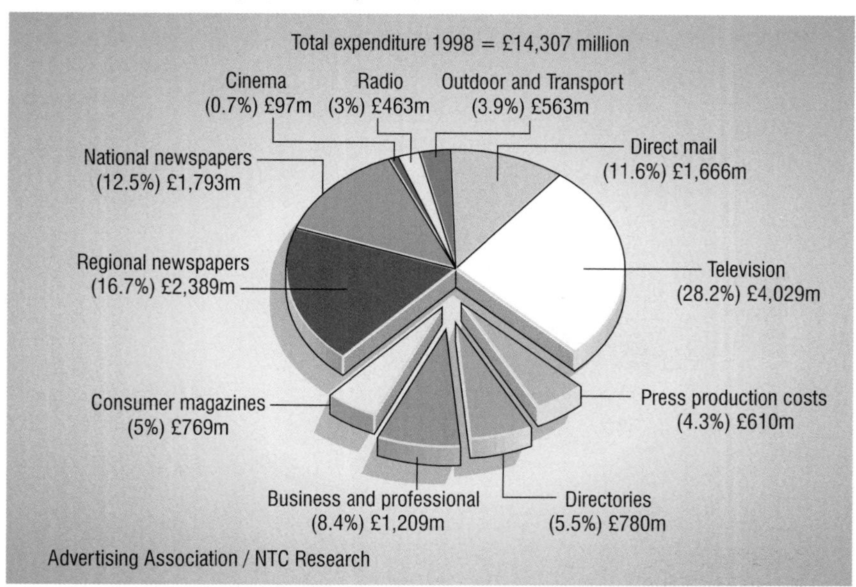

Advertising

Advertising is the main method of promotion used by business. Spending on advertising has grown over time as the real disposable income of households has increased. In 1998, a total of £14.3 billion was spent on advertising in the UK. However, advertising alone will not sell a product; it must be supplemented with other aspects of the marketing mix, including promotion by the sales force, in order to be successful.

Advertising media

Newspapers and magazines

There are over 11,000 different newspapers and magazines available in the UK, ranging from national daily newspapers to free local newspapers and specialist magazines of limited circulation. Advertising is an important source of revenue for these publications.

In 1998, 56% of all adults read a daily newspaper. Thirty-four per cent of all males read either the *Sun* or the *Mirror*.

The Press

- National daily newspapers
- National Sunday newspapers
- Regional daily newspapers
- Local weekly papers
- Local free newspapers
- Consumer magazines
- Specialist interest magazines
- Trade and professional magazines

Informative and persuasive advertising

The purpose of **informative advertising** is to provide the consumer with information about the product. Examples of purely informative advertising include bus and train timetables and classified advertisements in the local press or phone directories.

Informative or persuasive?

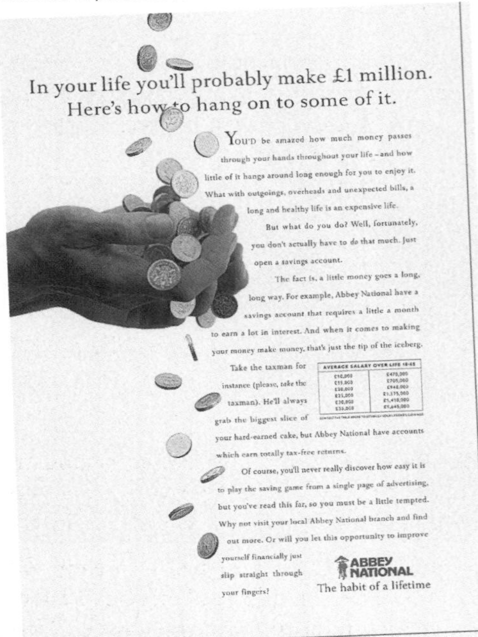

Persuasive advertising is designed to encourage consumers to buy a certain product rather than competitor products. Such advertising will focus on differences with rival products which may be true, or may simply be created by clever advertising. One manufacturer ran a very successful soap-powder advertising campaign for many years claiming that their product washed 'whiter than white' - a meaningless phrase which nevertheless influenced the buying habits of many consumers.

▼ *Figure 10.7: ITV advertising market shares*

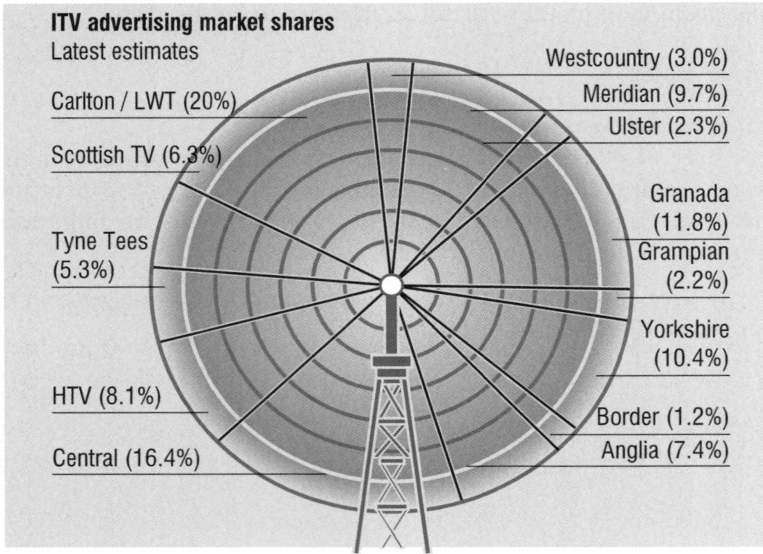

Marketing Pocket Book, 1999

Television

Television is an ideal means of advertising to reach mass markets, offering the benefits of movement and sound to promote products and services. Commercial television covers the whole of the UK, and advertisements can be broadcast to reach the whole population, or targeted at particular ITV regions.

Due to increasing sales of digital satellite and cable systems, there are now an increasing number of commercial TV stations in the UK. Because their market is still relatively small, the cost of advertising on these channels tends to be much lower than on ITV and Channel 4, where a 30-second peak-time advert, shown just once, could cost as much as £25,000 (Carlton TV, 1999).

Cinema

In 1998, 125 million people went to the cinema in the UK. Because of recently growing audiences, advertisers have begun to increase their use of cinema advertising and are now designing adverts specially for cinema release.

Radio

Radio listening has also increased in recent years. There has been a significant growth in the number of local commercial radio stations, whose main source of funding is revenue from adverts. Local radio provides a relatively cheap and effective means of advertising for many medium-sized and even smaller firms.

The Internet

Modern information communications technology can store and transmit visual images, text and sound over the telephone network to anyone who has a computer linked by modem to the 'world-wide web' or **Internet.**

People can use the internet to visit the 'websites' of many different organizations for information on the goods and services they offer. Advertising on the internet can be informative or persuasive. Web pages can also be interactive. This means the user can select different options and the website can react to their choices, for example, by advertising other products or offering price discounts.

Some organizations also provide secure websites so that people can enter their credit card and address details to order goods and services. Buying and selling over the internet is called **e-commerce**, and is becoming increasingly popular (see 12.2).

Other advertising media

Large **posters** placed in highly visible sites can be a relatively cheap and effective means of grabbing peoples' attention. Smaller posters placed on the side of buses and taxis, on railway stations, and in airports can be seen by large numbers of people. Sports venues are also popular sites to place posters on hoardings.

Adverts for products can also be placed on the packages of other products - for example, on matchboxes, carrier bags, and T-shirts - and even on hot-air balloons.

▼ *Advertising spending 1998 by product group*

Product group	£m
Retail and Mail Order	1712
Motors	924
Financial	712
Food	575
Toiletries & Cosmetics	438
Leisure Equipment	403
Holidays, Travel & Transport	367
Publishing	321
Drink	293
Household Stores	258
Pharmaceutical	245
Entertainment	177
Government	135
Charity & Educational	80
Institutional & Industrial	74

Advertising Association, 1999

▼ *Figure 10.8: Choosing advertising media*

Advertising media		Plus points	Minus points
National newspapers		Coverage is national Reader can refer back to advert Product information can be provided	Use of colour limited Smaller adverts tend to get 'lost' among others Readers often ignore adverts
Regional and local newspapers		Adverts can be linked to local conditions Can be used for test-marketing before national launch	Reproduction and layout can be poor Average cost per reader relatively high due to more limited circulation
Magazines		Can use colour Adverts can be linked with feature articles Adverts can be targeted in specialist magazines	Adverts must be submitted a long time before publication Competitors' products often advertised alongside
Radio		Can use sound and music Relatively cheap to produce Growing number of stations Audiences can be targeted	Non-visual Message usually short-lived Listeners may switch off or ignore adverts
Television		Creative use of moving images, colour, and sound Can use visual endorsements by well-known personalities Repeats reinforce message Growing number of channels Adverts can be regional	High production costs Peak time can be expensive Message short-lived Viewers may ignore or switch over during adverts
Cinema		Creative use of images, colour and sound Adverts can be localized Adverts can be targeted at age groups at different films After decline during 1980s audiences increasing again	Limited audiences compared with other media Audience restricted to mainly younger age groups Message may only be seen once due to infrequent visits to cinema
The Internet		Easy and relatively cheap to set up web pages Can present colourful moving images and sounds Adverts can be interactive Internet is worldwide and accessible 24 hours a day	Not everyone has access to a computer or the internet Web pages need to be updated regularly and quickly Increased risk of credit card fraud may put off people ordering goods over the net using their credit cards
Posters		Good cheap visual stimulus Can be placed near to points of sale National campaigns possible	Only limited information possible Susceptible to vandalism and adverse weather

Publicity

There are a variety of ways a firm can publicize its organization and products:

- **Sales literature** - handouts, leaflet drops, promotional booklets
- **Signs** - on buildings or in windows; for example, pub signs
- **Vehicle livery** - vans and lorries painted in colours and logos associated with a business organization
- **Stationery** - letterheads and logos on paper and documents
- **Point-of-sale** - promotional stands, posters, leaflets at checkouts and shop counters
- **Product placement** - display of products on the sets of major TV and film productions, free gifts, and **product endorsements** from well-known TV and sports personalities who are paid to wear or use particular products.

▼ *Leaflets and signs provide useful and relatively inexpensive publicity*

Public Relations (PR)

Public Relations involves actions undertaken by a business in the hope of obtaining favourable, and often free, publicity. This is especially important to a firm trying to develop a corporate image or fending off bad publicity. Types of Public Relations activity can include:

- **Press releases:** published statements issued to the media, often offering stories and facts that can be treated as news items
- **Sponsorship:** funding of sporting, cultural, or social events in return for the display of the sponsor company's name and logo. Sponsors may also have an exclusive right to sell their products at the event.
- **Lobbying:** attempts by business or non-profitmaking organizations to influence or persuade decision-makers or those in positions of power. For example, pressure groups like Greenpeace and Friends of the Earth will often lobby Members of Parliament and businesses in an attempt to force changes in the laws governing the treatment of animals and the natural environment.
- **Community relations:** creation of links between businesses and local community groups, with firms contributing professional expertise to voluntary organizations, providing jobs and training to disadvantaged groups, and sharing advice and resources with smaller local companies. The benefits include an improved image for the business, and therefore a greater willingness on behalf of consumers to accept its products and brands.

▼ *Sponsoring a major sporting event is an effective method of improving public relations*

Portfolio Activity 10.4 

1. Collect sales literature produced by various organizations to promote their products and raise awareness.
2. Study how images and messages are used in the leaflets. Prepare a short report of your findings.
3. From your investigations, design and produce a sales leaflet on a product of your choice, using a desktop publishing package.
4. Find out how business organizations locally and nationally are helping your community. What are their motives?

Sales promotion methods

In-store merchandising

Whilst advertising may bring the customer into a shop, in-store promotions or merchandising are usually required in order to encourage customers to make the purchase at the point of sale. Such promotions may take the form of the use of display material, attractive stands, posters, free samples, and attractive and friendly sales representatives.

In shops, careful thought is also given to design and layout. Sometimes exits are intentionally hard to find, to encourage customers to browse a little longer. Sweets are strategically placed at checkouts to encourage children to pressurize their parents into buying them whilst queuing.

We have ways of making you buy!

Imagine this: a visit to the supermarket in the not-so-distant future. Park your car, grab a trolley, and set off down the first aisle. You plan to buy a jar of your favourite coffee - but even before you reach its shelf, a video ad on the small screen attached to your trolley alerts you to a new coffee which is on offer.

Even before you've scanned your shopping list, your attention is grabbed again. The air is scented with coconut oil. Best buy that suntan cream now, you think, before the Summer holidays.

And so it goes on. The experience of shopping is about to change forever. During the next couple of years, the arrival of sophisticated electronics will change the habits of a generation. Shelves will talk to the customer as s/he walks by, shoppers will add up their own bills with handheld scan guns, and shoplifters may be banished, as electronic tags are embedded in the packaging of every supermarket product.

Interactive couponing machines will be installed so that, using bar-codes, the machine can monitor purchases and issue personalized on-the-spot discount coupons to persuade shoppers to buy a rival product next time. For example, Pepsi could negotiate with the supermarket the right to have discount coupons issued for its six-packs of cola each time a similar sized pack of Coke is scanned at the checkout.

The main attraction of developing electronic wizardry is simply to sell more goods by targeting the consumer more directly.

Adapted from The Sunday Times 26.12.1993

▼ *Competitions, money-off coupons and free gifts are often effective sales promotion methods*

Other sales promotion methods

- **Competitions:** firms will often run competitions, details of which are displayed on product packaging. To ensure repeat sales, the competition entrant will often be required to collect coupons as proof of purchase.
- **Free mail-ins:** firms may provide free gifts to consumers who collect coupons from product packaging.
- **Money-off coupons:** in magazines, on product packaging, or delivered by direct mail, to encourage sales of a particular product
- **Loyalty incentives:** consumers may be encouraged to remain loyal to a particular product if they are provided with an incentive. This may involve accumulating points which can be used to gain money off future purchases or exchanged for a specific product. For example, petrol station chains such as Shell and Esso give coupons to their customers which can be exchanged for 'gifts'.
- **Sales staff incentives:** firms may offer performance-related pay and gifts to encourage staff to make more sales. For example, staff can earn commission based on a percentage of the sales revenues they generate.

Direct marketing

Direct marketing allows manufacturers to deal directly with consumers without the need for retail outlets or wholesalers (see 11.2). Direct marketing is the fastest-growing method of selling products in the UK.

Mailshots

These are increasingly popular with some manufacturers and can be sent to the homes of thousands of potential consumers. The mailshot contains product details and an order form. Mailshots are usually personalized using modern computer technology, with each letter showing the individual customer's name and address. However, much mailshot marketing is viewed by consumers as 'junk mail' and ends up in the bin.

Portfolio Activity 10.5 

1. What is *direct marketing* and how does it differ from other forms of marketing?
2. Why does the article suggest the first direct marketers were local shopkeepers?
3. Explain the terms *mass production*, *mass retailing* and *mass marketing*.
4. Why is direct marketing becoming so important?
5. With reference to Chapter 8 and the factors that help to make marketing successful, explain why firms must 'track what each customer buys, talk to him/her, and tailor products especially for him/her'.
6. The article lists various ways of direct marketing, including mailshots and via the Internet. Investigate, collect and evaluate 10 different examples of direct marketing. How good or bad are they? How do they measure against the criteria for successful marketing?

Direct hit

THINK of the junk mail clogging your letterbox, or those annoying cold calls during supper, and direct marketing seems a modern curse. That is because so much of it is so crude. But behind those unwanted offers and fake-prize draws lies an important change in marketing. This is a move away from mass marketing, which starts with a product and finds customers to buy it, towards an information-led, one-to-one marketing, which may ultimately sell each individual a customized product.

The reason for this change is computer technology. Its falling costs and increasing power are allowing 'mass-customised' manufacturing, the gathering and manipulation of vast amounts of personal data and, for the first time, a ready way for customers to tell producers directly what they want.

The new form of direct marketing is a big step up from today's crude version. But it is also on some ways a step back. The first direct marketers were trusted local shopkeepers. Compared with today's direct marketers, whose best stab at the personal touch, is a pre-printed letter with a misspelt name, the local shopkeeper really knew his customers - remembering when to order a favourite piece of fabric for one, suggesting a new cough syrup to another.

The transformation of direct marketing from its local origins into advertising's downmarket cousin dates from the birth of mass production, which allowed manufacturers to produce standardised goods in huge quantities for sale in chain stores to unseen buyers.

With mass retailing came mass advertising. Without direct contact with the consumer, manufacturers could not know who was buying what; only what was selling. Mass advertising established a link between a product and millions of faceless consumers. Brands - promoting a short, memorable message - were part of this relationship. The result has in many cases been fantastically successful: for example, Coca-Cola has created a drink that is instantly recognised among many millions of loyal customers.

But as advertising costs have risen and the number of media have increased, mass marketing has become harder and more costly. That plus new computer technology, has pushed direct marketing into the limelight. Its full potential is only just being grasped.

The low costs of direct marketing have created a huge and fast-growing industry - made up of direct mail, telemarketing, database marketing, the Internet and free-phone TV, radio and print mail order advertisements.

Yet most direct marketing remains clumsy. Britain's Direct Marketing Association admits its members waste large amounts of money sending mailings to dead people; typical success rates for most mailshot campaigns in developed countries are no better than 2%. Steve Dapper, chief executive of Rapp Collins, a big direct-marketing agency, complains that consumer data are sold too freely, leading to pesky cold calls and junk mail. The trouble is that direct marketing is still driven by the same thinking as mass marketing.

Smart companies are trying to change this by gathering information first hand from customers. Doubleclick, an American Internet advertising company, sends specific advertisements to people who browse the web, depending on where they are, the time of day and what they are looking at. These advertisements can produce response rates of over 25%. Others such as Tesco, a British supermarket, analyse electronic point-of-sale information as people shop, making it possible to change prices at different times of day or to tailor selections to suit local customers.

Now direct marketing is on the threshold of something new. At its heart is a change in the relations between customers and businesses, so that each customer is treated differently. According to Steve Dapper, firms must do three things; track what each customer buys, talk to him/her, and tailor products especially for him/her.

The Economist, 9.1.1999

Mail order advertisements

Many firms specialize in selling direct to the consumer through advertisements placed in newspapers, specialist magazines, and other publications. Customers may order products such as computers, cameras, and much more by simply telephoning the firm and quoting a credit card number.

Telesales

Some businesses employ sales staff to telephone potential customers in order to sell them goods and services. This method gives the advantage of allowing the firm to tailor their selling effort to suit the customer. However, many customers do not like being telephoned at home by sales people, and the success rate for such calls is not high.

Home shopping

The development of communications technology such as digital satellite and cable television and the Internet has enabled producers to get closer to their target audiences. For example, 'Shop!' is a home shopping channel, providing 24-hour advertising and product reports enticing viewers to buy direct from the screen. Home shopping at on-line retailers, or e-tailers, via the **Internet** is becoming increasingly important (see 11.2).

Key words:

Informative advertising - seeks to provide consumers with product information

Persuasive advertising - seeks to influence and persuade consumers to buy a product

Advertising media - different means of advertising to consumers, such as TV, cinema, and radio

Public Relations (PR) - activities such as sponsorship and lobbying, aimed at raising organizational and product profile

Sales promotions - methods used to generate sales and repeat purchases, such as money-off coupons, competitions, and customer loyalty incentives

Direct marketing - methods of promoting products direct to consumers, for example, by mailshots, mail order, and telesales

Section 10.4 Product performance

Evaluating marketing communications

The effectiveness of marketing communications in targeting their audience and delivering the right message can be judged by a number of factors:

- **Sales (volumes, values, and growth).** Businesses will often set annual targets for sales levels in both absolute terms and in terms of growth. For example, a company may set an objective to sell 10% more units than last year and attain a total of £3 million in revenues. Failure to achieve these targets may indicate a failure of marketing communications.

- **Repeat sales.** Firms which sell fast-moving consumer goods rely on repeat purchase of their products by consumers. For example, a firm that sells biscuits will try to use marketing communications to ensure that once the consumer has finished the packet, they will immediately want to purchase another one.
- **Brand loyalty.** Through advertising and promotion, a firm will try to make very similar products, like washing powders, appear different and better than their competitors. Creating a strong brand image with which consumers can identify will encourage repeat sales.
- **Extending product life-cycles.** Changes in consumer wants and spending patterns over time will mean that most products have a limited commercial lifespan. However, through appropriate marketing, demand for a product can be maintained and the lifetime of a product extended.
- **Consumer awareness.** Marketing can be judged as effective if it heightens awareness of the product among consumers. If consumers are able to remember a catchy name, logo, or advertising jingle for a product, then there is greater chance they will buy it.

▼ *Figure 10.9: The product life-cycle*

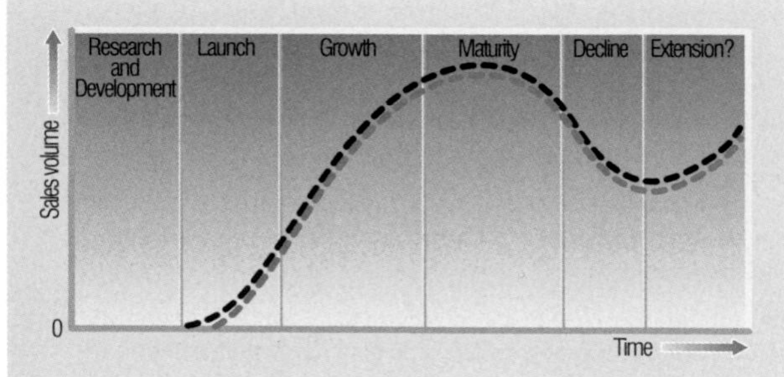

Product life-cycles

Like people, products are born and will eventually die as consumer demand and technology move on. Goods and services change and develop during their lifetimes, and marketing objectives will need to change to match changes in the product. A major marketing tool to help a business plan for the future is **product life-cycle analysis.**

The commercial stages through which a product may pass are known as the product life-cycle. For example, when a new product is launched, it is likely to be relatively unknown, and marketing will need to persuade potential customers, distributors, and retailers to purchase it. The marketing objective will be to get the product established, with sales rising as quickly as possible. On the other hand, a firm with an established product and a large market share may wish to concentrate on making as much profit as possible by creating a strong brand image with higher prices.

There are five main product life-cycle stages:

1. Research and Development
2. Launch
3. Growth
4. Maturity
5. Decline

A sixth stage, known as **Extension** is possible where a firm may wish to re-launch an old product as 'new' or 'improved'.

Stages in the product life-cycle

Stage 1: Research and Development (R&D)

At this early stage, a business will research the market to find out what the consumer wants and whether it is possible to make and sell the product at a profit. R&D involves research into all aspects of the product, including technical aspects of production, packaging, pricing, and possible market segments.

Stage 2: Launch

This is a very expensive stage in the life-cycle because the product is new and the firm may have to charge consumers a low price and invest heavily in informative advertising to ensure that the market becomes familiar with it. A good example is the launch of Digital Versatile Discs (DVDs) on the home cinema market in 1998–99.

Stage 3: Growth

During the growth stage, sales will start to rise and advertising will shift from being primarily informative to persuasive advertising to ensure continued demand for the product. Many products falter at the growth stage, when sales fail to take off in spite of heavy marketing. This tends to indicate insufficient care in Research and Development, and/or a poor advertising strategy.

Stage 4: Maturity

At maturity, the product should be well-known and established, and reaching its maximum level of sales and profitability. However, by this time, new firms may be entering the market, and advertising will be needed to maintain market share. Mature products include Kellogs Cornflakes and Oxo cubes, while mature industries include soap powders and newspapers.

Stage 5: Decline

Eventually sales for all products will start to decline. This can be caused by changes in fashion, or, more likely, by new technology which either replaces the product or allows competitors to offer a new or improved version at a lower price.

Stage 6: Extension

It is possible to extend the life-cycle of a product by convincing customers that the product is somehow different or better than before. Most successful extension strategies start well before the product goes into decline. For example, Oxo cubes were used during the war to give the flavour of meat to other foods when there was very little meat available. After the war, when the supply of meat increased, the life of Oxo was extended by relaunching it as a means of enhancing the flavour of real meat.

▼ *Figure 10.10: Different product life-cycles*

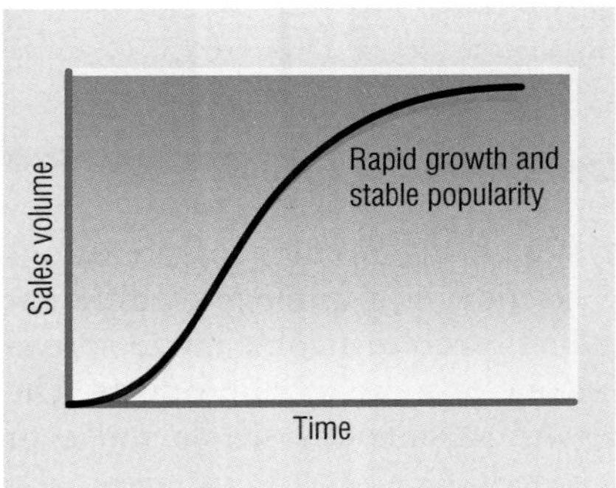

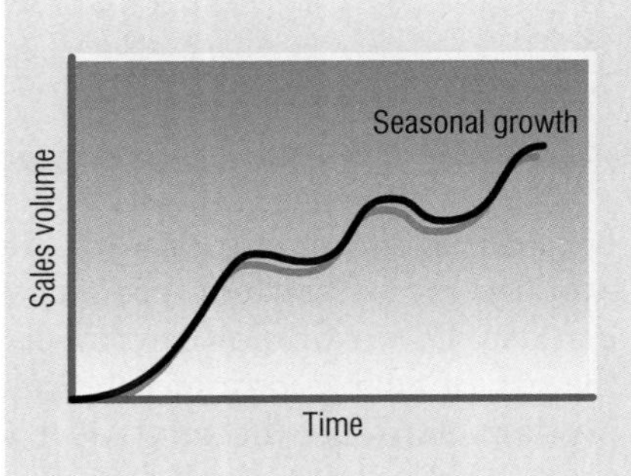

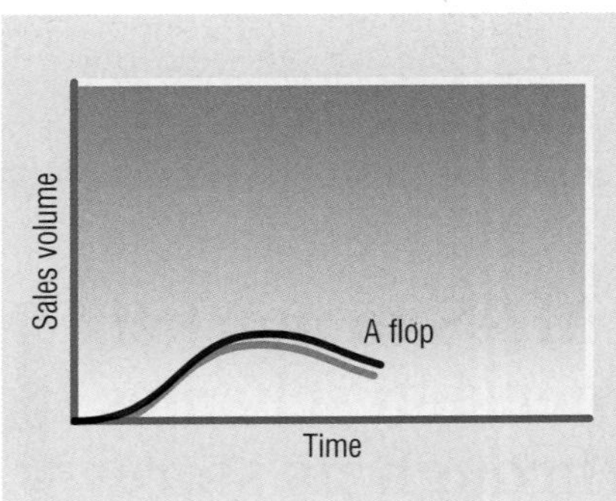

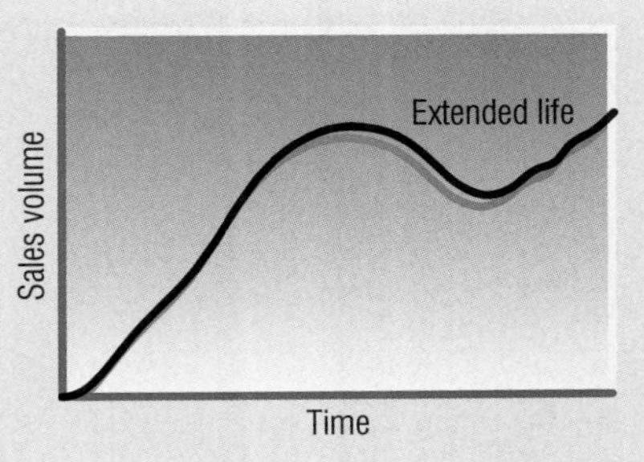

The product portfolio

Although different products have life-cycles of different lengths, it is true to say that on average, most life-cycles are getting shorter and shorter. In consumer electronics, new models of camcorders, TVs, and DVD players are launched every three to six months. Shortening product life-cycles are due to rapid advances in technology and heavy international competition in markets where consumers expect to be able to buy the latest developments.

A matter of life and death

Think of music reproduction. The wind-up gramophone of my grandparents' generation is extinct. In three human generations, five sorts of listening hardware - Edison's cylinders, brittle 78rpm records, vinyl LPs and singles, cassettes, CDs - have arrived and become pre-eminent; yet already two have gone. This list does not even include total failures. Eight-track tape and quadraphonic sound died out because they were ill-adapted to capture consumers' money. The heyday of cylinders was ended by discs, which were better adapted for feeding off the world of the consumer.

New Scientist, 6.2.1993

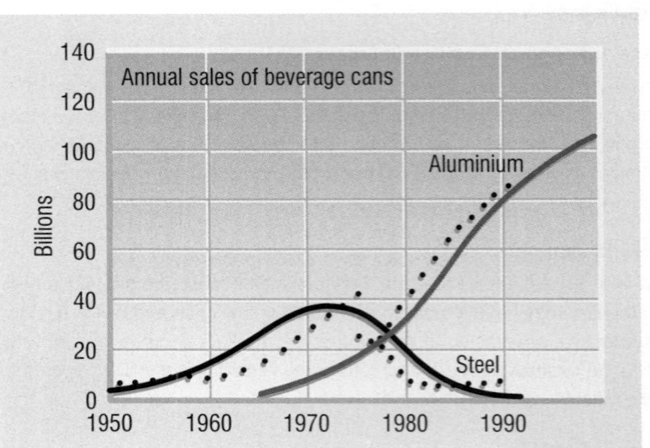

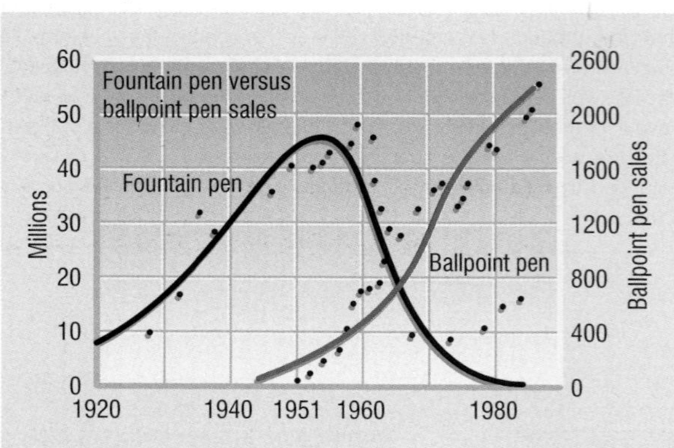

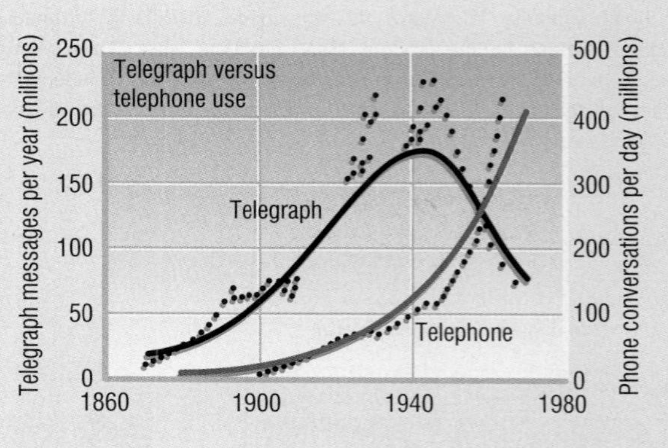

M&S to market pension schemes through its stores

Marks & Spencer, the UK's most profitable retailer, is to offer life and pensions products from next year in addition to its existing financial services.

Financial Times 2.2.1994

Because of shortening product life-cycles, many modern organizations produce more than one product and operate in a number of different markets. **Diversification** into other products enables a company to spread the risk of falling consumer demand for one or more of its products. The **product portfolio** (or **mix**) of a firm will include the whole range of products they offer, including all the brands, line extensions, sizes, and types of packaging available.

▼ *Figure 10.11: Managing the product portfolio*

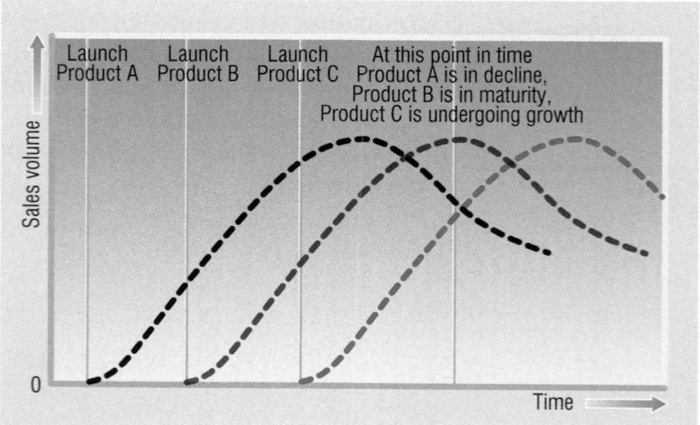

Portfolio Activity 10.6

1. What is a product life-cycle? From the article, what stage do you think the brands Tango and Brylcreem are in their life cycles?
2. What marketing strategies did the producers of Tango and Brylcreem use to extend the profitable lives of their products?
3. Suggest alternative extension pricing and promotional strategies that the producers of the two products could have used instead. Give reasons for your suggestions.

Brylcreem: Sales UP 100%

THE PROBLEM: Sales were plunging.

THE BRIEF: To update the Brylcreem styling range, giving it a sophisticated and stylish image, away from the old red and white tubs.

WHAT THEY DID: "We opted for a very masculine look, using a tyre-tread theme which conjures up powerful images," says David Rivett, chief executive of the company given the task of re-vamping the hair cream's packaging.

"Cars and sex have connotations that could be associated to these products."

THE RESULT: Sales up 100 per cent on last year.

DESIGN CONSULTANTS: Design Bridge Structure.

New-look Brylcreem, left, and the old image, below

The Mirror, February 1999

Tango: Sales UP 50%

THE PROBLEM: Sales were levelling at 150 million litres in 1992. "We needed to take radical action," says Britvic marketing boss David Atter.

THE BRIEF: To get the message across that Tango was different from other fruit drinks.

WHAT THEY DID: Broke several rules, one being that you can't put a fruit drink in a black can.

In fact, the black made the colour of the fruit even more stark. This year Tango got a second make-over, to make it clear it was more than just an orange fruit drink.

RESULT: Sales rose by nearly 50 per cent a year to 220 million litres. It is the No.1 fizzy fruit drink.

DESIGN CONSULTANTS: Wickens Tutt Southgate.

Tango before, left, and after

Key words:

Product life-cycle - an analysis of the different stages which a product will pass through, and associated sales at each point

Extension strategies - methods used to extend the marketable life and sales of a product

Diversification - producing a range of commodities for different markets

Product portfolio - the mix of products marketed by a firm at a given point in time

Useful references

The following magazines are published weekly and are available from larger branches of WH Smith or on order from local newsagents:

- *Campaign*, Haymarket Business Publications Ltd., 30 Lancaster Gate, London W2 3LP
- *Marketing*, Haymarket Business Publications Ltd., 30 Lancaster Gate, London W2 3LP
- *Marketing Week*, Centaur Communications Ltd., St. Giles House, 50 Poland Street, London W1V 4AX

The following books are published annually by NTC Publications Ltd, Farm Road, Henley-on-Thames, Oxfordshire RG9 1GB *(e-mail: info@ntc.co.uk)*:

- Advertising Association Statistics Yearbook
- Marketing Pocket Book

Also visit the Advertising Association web site at *www.adassoc.org.uk*

Internet key words search: **Advertising, Promotions, Marketing**

Test your knowledge

1 Which of the following is unlikely to be a important objective of penetration pricing strategies?

A Increasing market share

B Launching a new product in a competitive market

C Maximizing sales revenue

D Maximizing short-term profits

2 You are a business manager in a large established firm. A new firm has entered the market and threatens to reduce your market share. Which of the following pricing strategies would you advise your organization to adopt in the short term?

A Market skimming

B Destruction pricing

C Price discrimination

D Contribution pricing

3 Which of the following is **not** an example of price discrimination. Charging different prices for the same product:

A In different countries

B At different times of the day

C In different years

D To different groups of consumers

4 The product life-cycle is an essential part of:

A After-sales service

B Planning future marketing activities

C Knowing when the firm will have to shut down

D Planning how long the product will last before it wears out

5 Which of the following can be used as a means of extending a product life-cycle?

A Marketing to existing market segments

B Retaining the existing packaging and advertising

C Altering packaging and advertising

D Maintaining present pricing policies

6 Maturity in a product life-cycle is characterized by:

A Steadily growing sales

B Steadily falling sales

C Fierce advertising with competitors

D High and stable sales

7 Direct marketing methods used by a producer will include:

A Selling direct to retailers

B Placing mail order adverts in magazines

C Using persuasive TV advertising

D Employing agents to sell products direct to consumers

8 Which advertising media will best suit producers aiming their products at niche markets?

A Specialist magazines

B Sky Movies Channel

C *The Mirror* newspaper

D Posters near to point of sale

9 Which if the following methods would you use to promote the launch of a new product to a mass audience?

A Sales leaflets

B Placing an advert in a popular daily newspaper

C A TV advert

D Direct mail

Questions 10–12 share the following answer options:

A Lobbying Members of Parliament

B Adverts in local newspapers

C Competitions requiring collection of five proofs of product purchase

D Sponsoring a school fete

Which of the above methods would you recommend to organisations with the following aims?

10 A firm wishing to improve community relations

11 Animal rights campaigners wanting an end to fox and stag hunting with dogs

12 A firm wanting to create product loyalty

13 Which of the following is **not** an element of the marketing mix?

A Product

B Price

C Personnel

D Promotion

14 **a** Suggest and explain a pricing strategy a firm could adopt to launch a new product.

b How might established firms in the same market adapt their pricing strategies in the face of the new competition?

c Explain using examples what price discrimination is.

d Explain why a holiday company may offer foreign holidays at bargain prices within a few days of their departure dates.

15 A new disco is about to open in your local town centre.

a What is the likely target audience of the disco?

b Recommend three ways the owners could promote their disco to their target audience.

An existing disco nearby has been open for 10 years and is now experiencing a fall in entrance numbers.

c What does this suggest about the stage in the product life-cycle of the existing disco?

d Recommend two promotional methods the existing disco might use to extend their product life-cycle.

16 **a** What is *branding*?

b Suggest two ways a firm might create a strong brand image for a new chocolate bar.

c What pricing policy would you advise the firm to pursue in launching the new chocolate bar. Give reasons for your recommendation.

d Explain the possible benefits of marketing to a charity.

chapter 11 Marketing Strategies (2): Placing and selling the product

This chapter investigates how business organizations distribute and sell goods and services, and the services they need to offer to attract and retain customers.

AND NOW IF YOU WOULD BE SO KIND AS TO FETCH THAT BOX OFF THE TOP SHELF
OUR STAFF WILL BEND OVER BACKWARDS TO HELP YOU

What you need to learn

Businesses need to combine a set of **marketing strategies** in a way that meets consumer needs and wants. You need to understand the range of marketing strategies used, the connections between different strategies and the need for a coherent mix of strategies.

Distribution aims to get the right products to the right places at the right time to meet customer expectations and secure their purchases.

Effective **customer service** is required to support a customer who has bought or is thinking of buying a good or service.

Selling goods and services is vital for the success of a business. It will greatly depend on the quality and motivation of staff in customer service and the physical conditions of the sales environment.

You will need to be able to evaluate the marketing strategy for a good or service according to marketing principles.

Section **11.1**

Placing the product - distribution

What is distribution?

An organization can spend millions of pounds on developing and advertising products, but if the right product is not in the right place at the right time for a consumer to buy, then all this money and effort will have been wasted. The objective of distribution is to make sure this does not happen.

Distribution is a significant element in a firm's costs and so will require careful management. Firms will need to consider physical distribution, storage and transportation of goods and services, and the various methods and outlets through which a good or service can be sold to a consumer.

Unless the distribution method, location, image, and quality of sales advice offered at the place of sale are right, the customer will not buy. Place of sale is a key ingredient in the marketing mix (see 10.1).

Effective logistics

Logistics is often called the science of moving things. Effective **logistics** in business is about managing the process of distribution so that the right goods and services, get to the right consumers, in the right place, in the right quantities and at the right time as quickly and cheaply as possible.

Logistics, therefore, concerns

- controlling the availability of goods and services
- improving speed of delivery
- identifying and using the best channels of distribution to consumers
- **availability of goods and services:** No organization can stock everything that may be wanted by a customer. Many specialize in providing a narrow range of goods and services. For example, an electrical shop will concentrate on the supply of home appliances, such as microwaves, video recorders and washing machines. However, nothing is more frustrating than to find out that a producer or retailer does not have the item that you want. It is even worse if you had telephoned first only to be told that the goods were in stock.

Many large stores now have advanced computerized stock control systems linked to bar code readers at their cash tills. The bar code readers scan every item leaving the shop and automatically update the central stock records, so that at any moment the computer has a complete record of what is available in the store. In the most advanced systems used by large supermarkets, the computer is set to automatically generate an order for new stock when the existing stock reaches a certain level.

For example, if it takes two days for a supermarket to receive a delivery of toilet rolls after placing an order, and the supermarket sells 2,500 toilet rolls every day, the supermarket knows it must place a new order when its stocks are down to 5,000 rolls. By the time the existing stock has run out, a new delivery will have been received. By using new technology in this way, large stores are able to keep control of their stocks and should be able to avoid disappointing customers by being out of stock.

How firms can improve the availability of goods and services

There is no point trying to stock everything customers may want. First, a business would tie too much money up in stocks, some of which may remain unsold, and secondly, their storage would take up too much space.

However, some firms have successfully diversified into other products in an attempt to offer customers more choice. For example, many petrol stations also offer on-site supermarkets. Blockbuster video also rents and sells computer games, music CDs, soft drinks, crisps and sweets. However, before a business makes this decision it will use market research to find out what more their customers want.

If an ordering and delivery service are introduced, it is important that it is simple to use by a customer, and that sales staff are honest about how long products will take to be delivered.

Sometimes consumers require a very wide range of goods and services. In this case it is important for an organization to operate a fast ordering and delivery service. However, it is pointless pretending to a consumer that a product can be obtained in a few days if it cannot.

A significant number of mail order firms selling products such as computer CDs, music and electronic equipment, advertise in specialist magazines, listing a vast range of stock, most of which they do not actually hold. The reason for this is that it would simply be far too expensive for firms to carry all of the stock that a customer might possibly require. These firms trade in the hope that if an item is ordered they can get it quickly.

- **speed of delivery:** The time taken between an order for a good or service being placed and taking delivery is called the delivery **lead time.** There is increasing pressure on suppliers from their individual and business customers to reduce lead times. It is frustrating to wait a long time for something you have ordered to be delivered. A firm that is able to guarantee the shortest lead time between receiving an order and making delivery is likely to gain more customers than slower rivals.

Lead times will often depend on the type of good or service being supplied. For example, highly specialized items such as hand-crafted furniture or industrial robots are likely to be made to order. They cannot simply be supplied from stock kept in a warehouse. For example, there is a waiting time of around two years to receive a new Rolls-Royce car.

Business customers will often rely on delivery lead times being as short as possible. This is because many now operate just-in-time production

How firms can improve speed of delivery

A business should always be honest to customers about when they can expect to receive the goods and services they have ordered. In the event of delivery being delayed, the same organization should contact the customer in good time to arrange an alternative. It is very annoying having to wait for a delivery that never arrives!

The speed of delivery is largely dependent on the time it takes for the supplier to process an order. Taking orders and receiving payment confirmation by phone, fax or via the Internet can speed up the rate at which orders are turned around. Some organizations are even able to promise next-day delivery from their central warehouses or a 24-hour emergency call out service for service providers, such as car mechanics and plumbers, for an additional charge.

Delivery times may also be improved by changing the method used to deliver items, for example, by using special delivery and courier services rather than first or second class post. Delivery by road may also be improved by planning ahead the best route to take. New technology such as Routemaster can help drivers plan the most direct routes to their destinations and alert them of any congestion along the route as they drive. Delivery by air to overseas customers is fast but can be expensive, especially for heavier items.

systems whereby materials needed in production are ordered and delivered just in time for them to be used (see 1.2). In this way these firms can keep their stocks of raw materials and components to a minimum to reduce storage costs.

- **Channels of distribution:** A **channel of distribution** refers to the route a producer uses to reach the final consumer of the product. The four main routes are illustrated in Figure 11.1.

▼ *Figure 11.1: Channels of distribution*

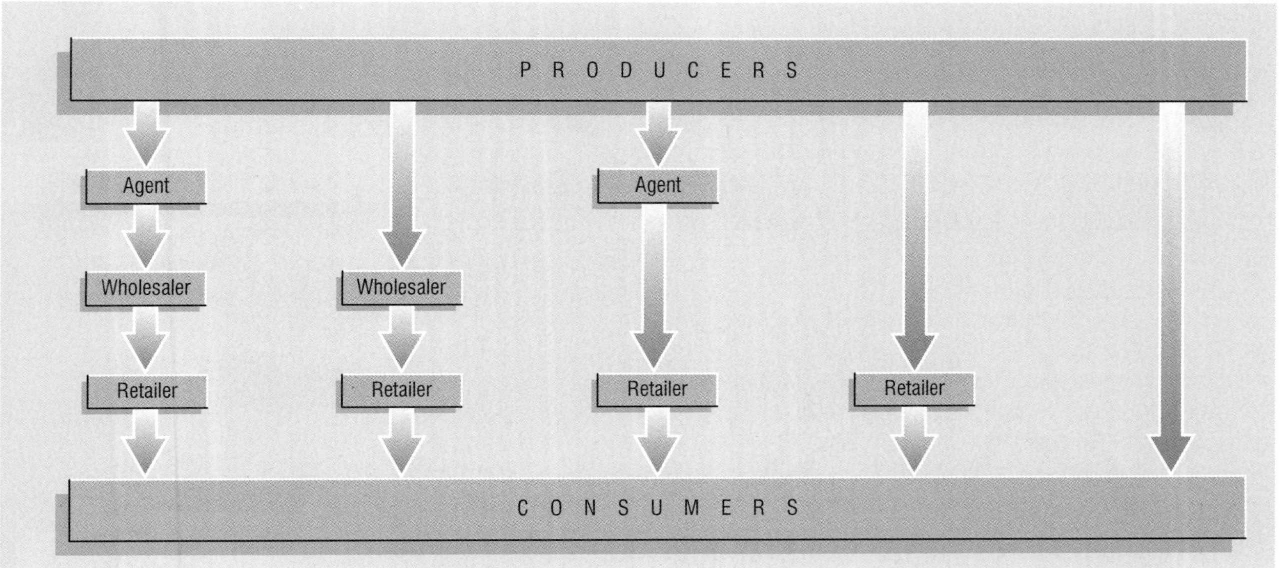

There are two main types of distribution channel:

- **Direct** from the product producer or service provider to the consumer. **Direct sale methods** include **factory sales, telesales, personal selling, TV and radio sales, pyramid selling** and **mail/phone/fax/Internet order**.
- **Indirect** through an external organization, such as a wholesaler, retail outlet, distributor, or agent. These organizations are known as **intermediaries**.

Distribution channels can be either national or international, involving sales to consumers and other organizations overseas. In some cases, a distribution channel can be made *exclusive* by restricting the number of outlets at which a product can be sold. For example, Dixons has an exclusive deal with Sanyo to sell one of their popular camcorder models.

Some producers distribute directly to the consumer from their factories or to their own retail outlets. For example, a bakery will need to get its products into the shops very quickly before they pass their sell-by date. To guarantee that shops stock their goods, some manufacturers will often own their own chains of retail outlets, and deliver direct. For example, many breweries own public houses. This gives them the advantage of a guaranteed outlet for their beers. It also allows the manufacturer to take all of the profit.

Other manufacturers may prefer to concentrate on making the product, and leave storage, selling, and distribution to outside specialist firms.

Indirect distribution via intermediaries

Wholesalers buy in bulk from manufacturers and are prepared to sell in smaller quantities to local retailers. This can be to the advantage of both the manufacturer and the retailer.

▼ *Figure 11.2: The function of the wholesaler*

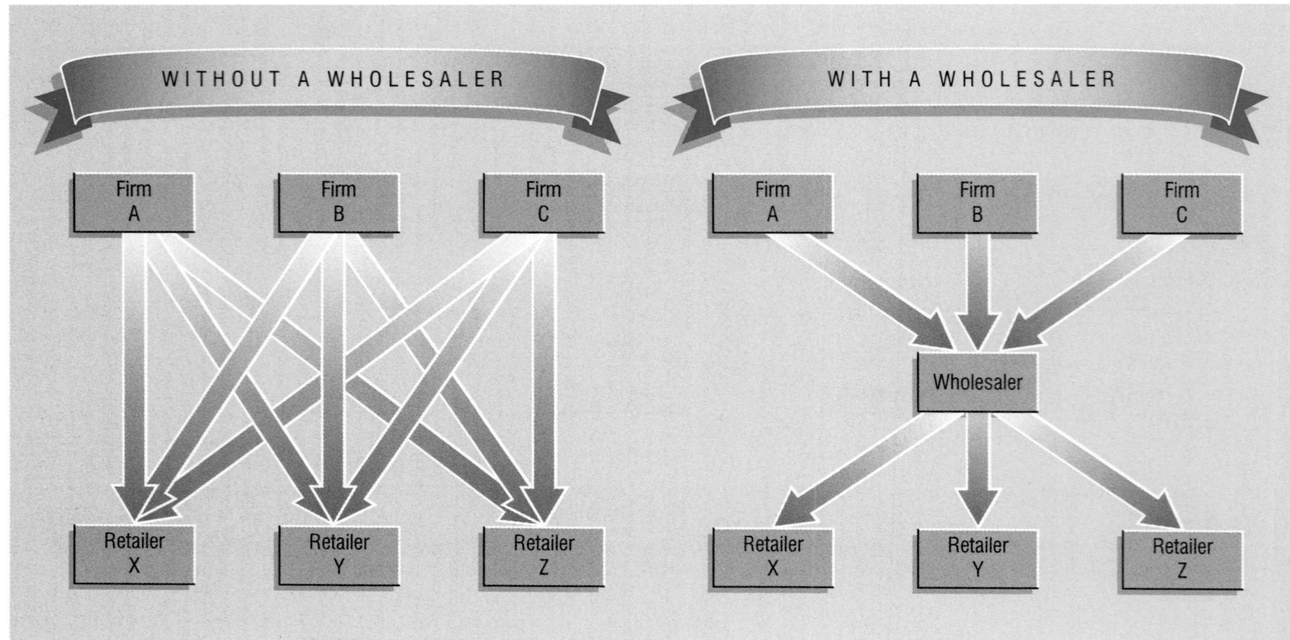

The advantages of using a wholesaler are as follows:

Advantages to the manufacturer:	**Advantages to the retailer:**
The wholesaler will:	**The wholesaler will:**
• Buy in bulk and pay for storage	• Allow the retailer access to a wide range of products from different manufacturers
• Bear cost of transport to customers/retailers	• Provide a delivery service
• Relieve manufacturers of the cost of administering orders to many customers over a wide geographical area	• Provide information on new product lines
• Provide a source of market research information from contact with retailers	• Sometimes help with storage and give credit

The disadvantages of using a wholesaler

Use of a wholesaler adds to the cost of the final product and so raises the price charged to the consumer. This also reduces the share of profit for the manufacturer and retailer. Because of this, wholesaling has gone into decline in recent years as manufacturers have tried to keep the wholesalers' share of the profit for themselves by selling direct to retailers or straight to the final consumer.

Retailers

The **retail sector** consists of shops and stores who often provide the final link in a chain of distribution from the manufacturer to the final consumer. Retail outlets may either buy products direct from the producer or from a wholesaler, before adding their own mark-up on prices to charge the final consumer in order to cover their overheads and for profit.

A growing number of manufacturers now prefer to use their own distribution networks to sell directly to large retail outlets such as Sainsbury's, Marks & Spencer, and WH Smith. Some retail chains are so large that they take on many of the functions of the wholesaler themselves. They also buy and store in bulk, splitting up stock for distribution to their stores all over the country, or even the world. These large chains can reach many millions of consumers in different markets, and so are often able to influence manufacturers, demanding high product quality and guaranteed delivery times.

Recent trends in retailing

Growth in consumer spending has led to an expansion in retailing. In 1988 UK consumers spent £300 billion on goods and services and just over 3 million people were employed in retail trades. Ten years later, total consumer spending had risen to £540 billion and the number employed in retailing was over 4 million. There have also been many changes within the retailing industry and the way people shop over the last few years.

Some major changes have taken place in retailing over the last 20 years. These include:

- Retailing has become dominated by large multiple retail organizations, such as Tesco, B&Q, and Boots. In 1997, 92% of total retail spending by UK consumers was in only 20% of shops. Many small independent shops have been unable to compete on price and product range and have gone out of business. Others have joined together to form small voluntary chain groups such as Spar, Londis and Happy Shopper, so that the shop owners can benefit from bulk buying discounts from wholesalers and produce their own label brands for sale.
- There is increasing competition on prices and product ranges between large retailers as they try to attract shoppers away from each other. Price wars have broken out among many large supermarket groups. They have also offered bonus schemes to customers who remain loyal, such as cheap flights and bigger price discounts, and made many improvements to customer services, such as free buses for the elderly and home deliveries. Shops that do not offer good value for money and good service will quickly lose customers.
- Many large retailers offer their own credit cards for their customers to use and will often give additional rewards, like money-off points, if they use the cards to buy things in their shops. This promotes customer loyalty.
- Huge shopping complexes have been developed in large towns and out-of-town areas. These offer many shopping and leisure facilities 'under one roof' for many thousands of people to use. This has caused decline in many older and smaller shopping centres. Government planning controls now restrict the development of new out-of-town complexes because they encourage people to use their cars more, causing congestion and pollution.
- Many large retailers now sell many different goods and services. For example, Tesco is a food supermarket chain but now has large superstores that also offer computers, clothes, hi-fi and audio equipment, petrol, books, CDs and videos, and even banking and insurance services.
- Supermarkets and other retail chains are selling more and more of their own-label products. Own-label products are often cheaper than manufacturers own brands, like Coca-Cola or Heinz Baked Beans.
- Late night and Sunday shopping have been introduced, giving consumers more flexibility when to shop.
- There has been a growth in the number of convenience stores, especially on petrol and railway station forecourts. These shops pick up 'passing trade' from commuters and motorists.
- Many large retailers also offer 'home shopping' via the Internet.

Portfolio Activity 11.1

Consider the trends in retailing above. What changes in consumer demands do you think might have helped to cause these trends?

Agents and brokers

Agents are used by producers to obtain sales on their behalf. For example, travel agents sell holidays for tour operators and earn a **commission**, or share of the profits, for doing so. When entering a new foreign market, a firm will often seek the help of a business or individual with local knowledge to act as an agent to help with sales, distribution, and advertising in the overseas market.

Brokers are often used by producers to buy and sell commodities in bulk, such as tea, sugar, gold, and other metals on international markets. The bulk is then usually broken up to be sold on to processing industries.

▼ *Mail order adverts*

▼ *Mail order catalogues*

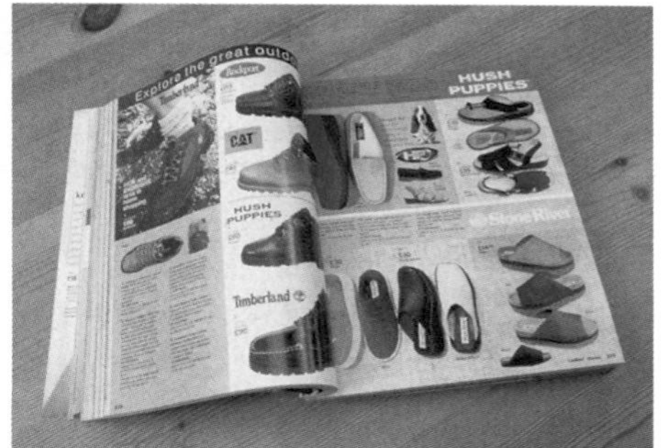

Distribution direct to the final consumer

Direct selling cuts out the intermediary and allows the manufacturer to deal directly with consumers. This is the fastest-growing method of distribution in the UK. Direct selling methods include:

- **Mail-order advertisement:** many firms specialize in selling direct to the consumer through advertisements placed in newspapers, specialist magazines, and other publications, or by sending mailshots direct to potential customers. Products such as computers, cameras and camcorders, even garages, can be ordered simply by telephoning the firm and quoting a credit card number, or by filling in a printed form and sending it off with a cheque.
- **'Factory' sales:** these are organized by the manufacturer direct to final consumers, either by allowing customers into factories every now and again to sell off surplus or old stock at 'knock-down prices'; by opening up a shop on site, or by mail order. For example, many farms have opened farm shops to sell their produce. Similarly, customers can buy cars 'straight off the production line' at the showrooms at Ford Motors in Dagenham, Essex.
- **TV and radio sales:** an increasing number of mail-order adverts are appearing on TV and radio with the benefit of sound and vision. With a growing number of commercial radio stations and cable or satellite TV channels, the cost of advertising via these media has fallen.
- **Mail-order catalogues:** companies such as Great Universal Stores plc which operate mail-order catalogues are simply large wholesalers who deal direct with the general public, splitting bulk into individual items, and allowing the consumer to pay in instalments. The cost of credit and home delivery, which can often take up to 4 weeks, tends to be reflected in higher prices. As a result, the importance of mail-order catalogues in total sales has declined in recent years.
- **Personal selling:** this involves personal contact with the consumer by company sales representatives, either over the phone (telesales), or face-to-face at meetings and 'on the doorstep'. Experienced sales teams can explain how the product works, give demonstrations, and tailor their marketing approach to suit the individual requirements of each consumer. However, personal contact can be expensive, and often consumers react adversely to 'doorstep' sales or being bothered on the phone.
- **Pyramid selling:** this system is used successfully by a number of companies, notably the American company Amway, who produce a wide range of products including soap, jewellery, and perfumes from their factories in the USA. These products are sold directly to consumers in many countries, including the UK.

  The principle of pyramid selling is that individuals agree to make regular purchases of a company's products to sell on to other consumers - often their family and friends - in their spare time. At the same time, each new salesperson aims to recruit others who are willing to buy

IF ALL ELSE FAILS SIMPLY STICK YOUR FOOT IN THE DOOR
KWIK KLEAN KARPET

▼ *Personal selling is not always welcomed by consumers*

products in bulk from them, in order to sell on to other consumers. The incentive to recruit new salespeople is that the person recruiting will earn a percentage of the sales they make. Clearly, the salesperson at the top of the pyramid stands to make the most money by earning a percentage of the sales of each person below him or her.

Salespeople at the bottom of the pyramid often make little money, as people are not always willing to buy products such as cleaning liquids and soaps in bulk for their own use, and on a regular basis - especially from companies they do not know. Selling to friends and family can also be awkward. The result is that the goods bought by sales recruits to sell on to other consumers often remain their own!

▼ *Figure 11.3: How pyramid selling works*

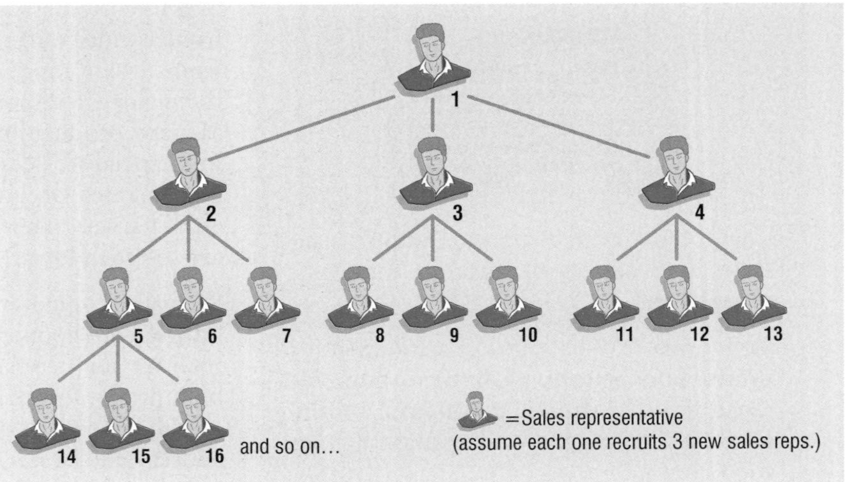

(assume each one recruits 3 new sales reps.)

Portfolio Activity 11.2 

1. What channels of distribution and sales methods would you use for the following products? Explain your reasons:
   a) Life insurance
   b) Crude oil
   c) Ice cream
   d) Computers
   e) Hamburgers
   f) Furniture
   g) DVD films
   h) Farm tools
2. Undertake research to find out how these commodities are distributed and sold by real-life organizations.
3. Investigate the distribution channel(s) used by an organization of your choice. For example, if you choose a retail outlet, follow the channel back to the manufacturers of the various products sold. If the organization manufactures goods, follow the distribution channel forwards to the final consumer.

▼ *Change is fast – example growth in Internet book business*

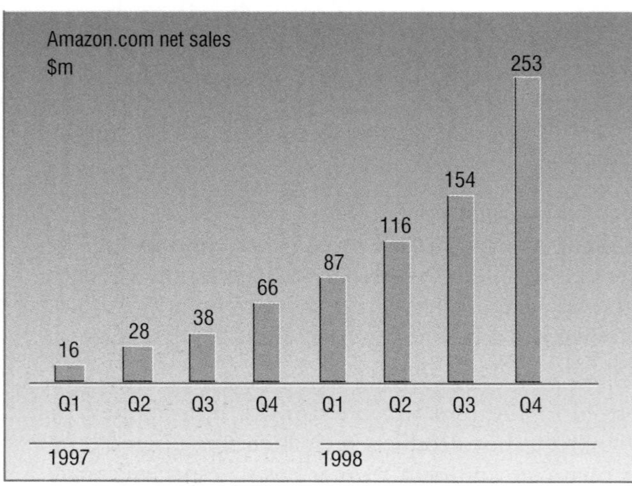

Source: Amazon.com

How e-commerce has helped Rover

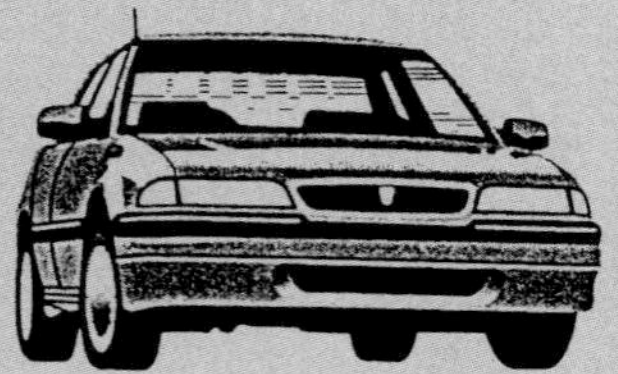

Using Electronic Product Definition and links with suppliers through the Red-X programme.

Delivered 6-month reduction in production introduction time and 75% reduction in build problems, mainly attributed to supplier integration through e-business.

Source: UK CALS Industry Council

E-commerce

One of the biggest developments in distribution in recent years is the sale of goods and services over the Internet. This is called **e-commerce**, and it is expected to revolutionize the way people and firms buy and distribute products.

Spending in the UK using e-commerce was £3 billion in 1999 and is expected to be £9.5 billion in 2001. In contrast, American consumers spent $8 billion on Internet shopping in 1999 with business-to-business e-trade of $43 billion.

E-commerce is important because of the way it is impacting on the structure of business. It is bringing many organizations closer together with their suppliers, reducing costs and delivery lead times, and improving the quality of shared information.

In the business-to-consumer area, businesses can market their products direct to customers over the Internet, respond quickly to their e-mail enquiries, and improve overall customer satisfaction. Consumers can also benefit from a wider range of goods and services, at lower prices, from a wide range of suppliers. For example, Wal-Mart, the major US discount chain, carries more than ten times as many product lines on its website as in its largest store. In financial services, e-banks such as Egg and First-e offer higher rates of interest than the high street banks to attract savers. They are able to do this because their costs are so much lower.

Specialist computer programs called 'search engines' and 'intelligent shoppers', or 'shopbots', are available on the Internet for people to search for suppliers offering the best prices for the goods they want anywhere in the world. To make purchases, customers have to enter their address and credit card details and send them over the Internet to their preferred supplier. These details can be protected by password to stop other people hacking into these web sites and misusing credit card details.

Portfolio Activity 11.3 

Look at the excerpts from newspaper articles below and suggest how e-commerce is affecting UK business, and the likely advantages and disadvantages of growth in e-commerce.

Think small and grow

The Internet is closing the gap between big business and smaller companies. It is giving smaller businesses the opportunity to find better value deals and become better informed.

The Guardian, 30.9.1999

Credit fraudsters stalk the Net

The boom in Internet shopping is fuelling a massive rise in credit card fraud. Consumers who pay for goods over the Net are 20 times more likely to fall victim to fraud than if they pay at a till or over the telephone.

The Guardian, 12.9.1999

Tesco sets its sights on global power

Britain's biggest supermarket group yesterday brushed off the threat of a food price war and outlined bold new plans for international expansion and for selling books on the Internet.

The company - which already has 75,000 on-line grocery shoppers - is due to double the number of stores servicing them. It says business is already profitable and has gone into partnership with a mail order company, Grattan, to sell household goods on the Internet.

The Guardian, 22.9.1999

Goodbye Mr Taxman

The Institute of Directors is right to warn that the government could lose £10bn a year in VAT revenues as a result of the expected swing towards trading on the Internet. But the loss of tax is not a reason for trying to slow down the pace of e-commerce because, as Bill Gates reminded us last week, anyone who does not do business on the net will face ruin in five years time.

It is not just VAT that is at risk because it will also be difficult to tax the incomes of people who are (say) working in the UK on a software product and sending the finished product electronically to the US or Australia. Who even knows who they are?

The Guardian, 2.9.1999

Price of entry to brave new world

The 1999 World Competitiveness Report places the UK 13th in the number of computers per capita and 11th in the extent of Internet connections. A panel of experts judged us as 21st in the extent to which electronic-commerce was developed for business use. In all of these areas we are out-performed by five or six other European countries, plus the USA, Canada, Singapore, Japan, Australia, and New Zealand.

Two of the reasons for this dismal performance are self-imposed. We have inadequate telecommunications provision. Telephone costs here are far higher than in Germany, Japan, Italy, the US and Canada. Another reason is "bandwidth" - the capacity of a communications channel to transfer data. Relatively few UK users have anything other than two copper wires through which to connect to the world, so the potential for multi-media use, rapid file transfer or video conferencing is very limited. In addition, we rank only 14th in the world, and 10th in Europe in the number of telephone lines per 1000 of population.

The Guardian, 25.9.1999

Net sales force retail rethink

A TENFOLD INCREASE in on-line sales will force retailers to overhaul their strategies, according to a report from research analyst Verdict. It predicts that in the next five years the on-line proportion of total retail sales will grow from 0.3% to 3%, totalling £7.4 billion.

Verdict reported that the largest portion of on-line sales will be grocery shopping at £2.3 billion.

The growth in on-line sales has been helped in part by people's increased access to the net. On-line shopper's buying habits have also changed, with books taking over from software as the main on-line purchase - in 1999 31% of internet users bought books compared with 16% for music and films and 11% for software.

e.business, February 2000

▼ *How E-commerce can reduce prices for the consumer*

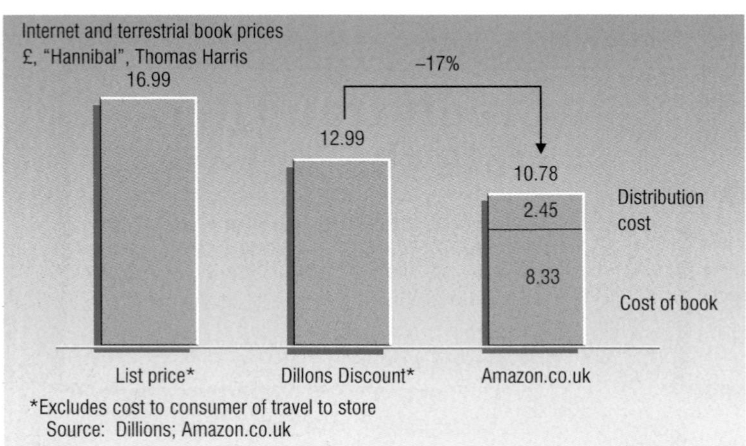

E-commerce will revolutionize the way people and businesses order, buy and supply goods and services in the 21st century. The UK government wants to encourage e-commerce in the UK. Firms that fail to provide internet services may lose out to those who do. This could mean increasing spending on goods and services from overseas and rising unemployment in the UK.

The advantages of e-commerce	Possible problems with e-commerce
• Increased competition to supply goods and services will help to lower prices and improve customer services	• Suppliers will be forced to offer internet shopping services in order to compete. Traditional businesses may close
• More firms can sell and supply direct to consumers and reduce use of whole-salers and retailers. This will save distribution costs and help reduce prices for consumers	• Fierce e-competition may result in some firms having to close down
• An increase in consumer demand for many goods and services provided over the internet. This will benefit many firms and help boost wealth and job creation	• Increasing imports and more money flowing out of the UK if consumers increase purchases from overseas suppliers
• People will not have to travel to shops so often. This will help reduce traffic congestion and pollution in many major shopping centres	• Falling Government tax revenues as UK consumers switch spending from UK suppliers to overseas suppliers, and download some products directly into their homes (e.g. software, music)
	• Increased risk of credit card fraud

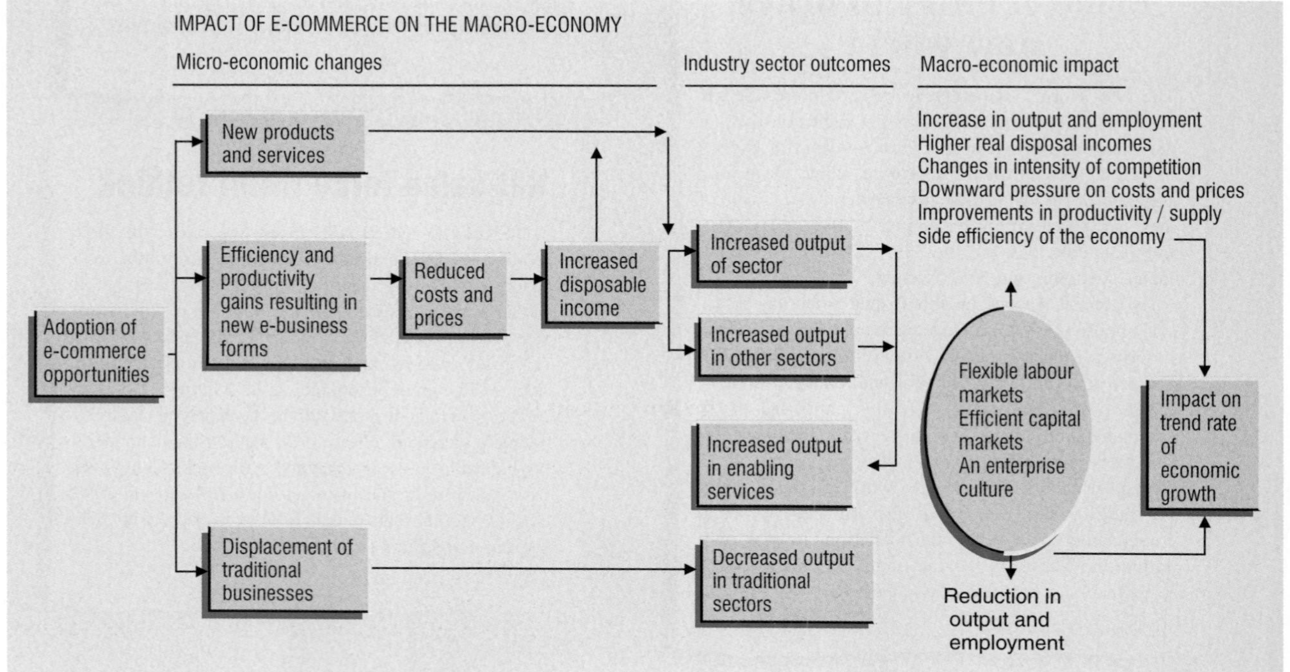

Source: 'Winning the race for e-commerce', Cabinet Office, 1999

Physical distribution

Whatever the channel used to sell a product to the final consumer, most will require movement of goods from one place to another using various modes of transport. Firms will need to consider the relative costs of transport by road, rail, sea, or air, against the speed and possibility of damage, or deterioration of goods. For example, transport by air is very expensive for bulky items, but is a fast method of transporting smaller items over long distances, especially overseas.

Risk of damage to fragile products can be reduced by using packaging materials, while refrigeration units can be used to transport perishable products such as meats and vegetables.

Some large organizations have their own vehicle fleets to transport goods by road within the UK. Distribution facilities are also provided by a large number of private operators such as DHL and TNT, who are willing to guarantee delivery times to their customers all over the world.

Key words:

Distribution - the process of getting products from producers to final consumers

Logistics - planning and controlling the efficient distribution of goods and services

Lead time - the time it takes to deliver a good or service from receiving an order

Distribution channel - any route taken by a firm to get their product to the customer

Intermediaries - firms which act as links in a channel of distribution, such as wholesalers, retailers, agents, and brokers

Commission - an incentive payment made to sales representatives, calculated as a percentage of sales revenues

Direct distribution - methods of distributing products direct to consumers, for example, by mail order, TV and radio adverts, or telesales

Pyramid selling - a method of selling direct to consumers by recruiting sales representatives who are willing to buy products in bulk before personally selling them on to the final consumer

E-commerce - the sale of goods and services over the Internet

Section 11.2 Closing the sale

What is selling?

Selling can be defined as a personal communication to a customer to make a sale. This contrasts with marketing communications, such advertising, which are not personalized (see 10.3).

Selling is the final link in the distribution chain and is vital for the success of a business. Market research, product development, pricing, and promotion strategies will all have been wasted if an organization cannot 'close the sale'.

Sales communications methods

Producers of goods or services who distribute them directly to the final consumer rely heavily on the skills and efforts of their sales teams to generate sales revenues. If distribution is through an intermediary, then each organization must rely on the sales efforts of every organization in the channel to work towards expanding sales.

Poor sales from one organization will feedback through a distribution channel. For example, if a retail outlet is unable to sell its stock of chocolate bars, it will reduce its order for them from the wholesaler. As stocks build up, the wholesaler will reduce its order from the manufacturer of the chocolate bar. Eventually the manufacturer may take the decision to reduce production and either switch resources to another item, or axe the product altogether.

If sales teams in each organization involved in a channel of distribution are to be effective in making and expanding sales, they will need to be fully informed of product details, new lines, discounts offered, and the various selling techniques they can use to make a sale. The objective of various sales communications methods is to do just that: to inform and motivate sales teams to generate sales.

Sales communication methods include:

- **Sales campaigns:** these can be used to promote an individual product or the product range of a particular manufacturer. A campaign may be agreed between the manufacturer, wholesalers, retailers, and agents in a distribution chain. The sales forces within these organizations will promote the product vigorously, offering price discounts for bulk orders, and distributing promotional materials such as posters, leaflets, or even free gifts and samples to give away. The campaign will also usually be supported by heavy advertising on TV and through other media, such as newspapers and magazines.

▼ *Delegates attending sales conferences are keen to learn about new products, promotional strategies, and selling techniques.*

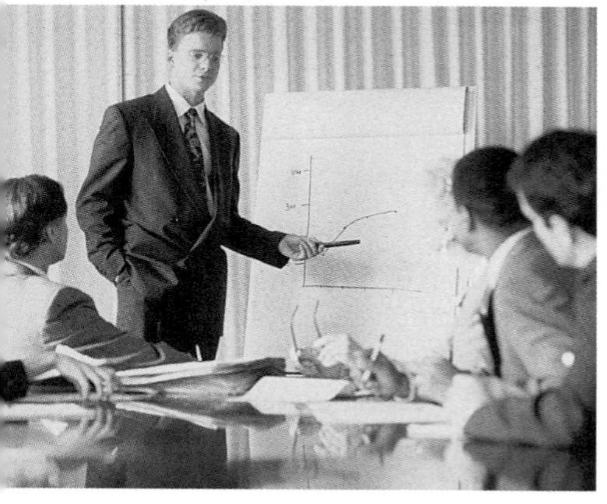

- **Sales conferences:** these can either be internal to an organization or, more likely, will involve sales staff from different organizations sharing a common interest in the promotion of a particular product. New product developments and sales techniques can be discussed in lectures and seminars.

- **Sales meetings:** these are internal meetings of sales teams, often from different regions, used to discuss sales performance and set targets for improvement. Meetings may be confined to regional managers of sales teams who will then 'cascade' with their sales teams (see 4.2). Pyramid selling relies heavily on sales meetings, with outsiders often being invited in an attempt to recruit them into the sales teams.

- **Sales letters and memos:** these can be sent out to sales teams on a regular basis to update staff on sales performance, provide product information, news of price discounts and new product lines, sales campaigns, future conferences, and meetings.

- **Trade fairs and exhibitions:** often combined with sales conferences, these are used primarily to promote products directly to consumers - especially to industrial buyers. They are also a useful forum for sales teams from different organizations to investigate rival products and discuss selling techniques. Technical staff will be on hand to demonstrate products and gauge consumer reaction. Well-known examples include the Stitching and Knitting Show, the Motor Show, the Ideal Home Exhibition, and Confex, a trade fair to advertise the services of firms who specialize in the organization and design of exhibitions, stands and advertising.

Providing customer service

Good customer service is vital to business success today. An organization that cannot deliver good customer service will have wasted marketing effects to attract consumers and will fail to close sales. Consumers are demanding continually higher levels of customer service from business organizations. Those that fail to satisfy the expectations of consumers will lose existing and prospective customers to rival firms who can.

Imagine you go into a shop and are made to wait fifteen minutes while a sales assistant has a chat with a friend on the telephone. Then, when the assistant serves you s/he is off hand and unable to give you a demonstration of the product or to tell you much about it. The till area is also very dirty and they will only accept cash payments. You prefer to pay by credit card.

When you get the product home you find out that the item you have bought doesn't work properly or that parts are missing. You take it back to the shop and the staff do not seem to care and are reluctant to change it or refund your money.

The chances are that you will think twice about buying from this business again. Not only will you not buy again, you will also advise others not to buy. The firm will lose your repeat custom and it will lose some new customers as well because it failed to provide you with the standard of customer service that you expect.

More and more firms today are understanding the need for good customer service because it is good for sales and profits. The horror story given above is unlikely to happen, but even if just one part of it occurs customers may go elsewhere. The simple rule in business is that good products do not sell themselves. Only good products, with good customer service and marketing, will sell.

Features of good customer service

An organization that fails to provide good customer service could end up spending more effort dealing with complaints than selling goods and services. Its customers will be lost to organizations that can keep their customers happy.

Good customer service involves many aspects of the operation of a business organization. For example:

- **Staff** should be:
  - well trained and motivated
  - friendly and provide a prompt service
  - helpful and polite
  - clean and tidy

- dressed smartly
- knowledgeable about products, methods of payments, the layout of the business premises, and consumer protection laws, etc.
- able to provide information and advice

- **Premises** should be:
  - clean, tidy, and well presented
  - equipped for people with special needs, e.g. having ramps for people in wheelchairs and with prams and pushchairs
  - easy to find your way around
  - well signposted
  - fitted with safety features, such as fire exits, wide doors and steps, handrails on stairs, emergency telephones in lifts, etc.
  - able to satisfy customer expectations. For example, if customers are expected to pay a big membership fee and large monthly subscriptions to join and use a fitness and leisure centre they will in turn expect all the latest fitness equipment, luxuriant and comfortable surroundings, clean and safe shower and changing areas, a good bar and restaurant, trained fitness staff, a large swimming pool, sauna, jacuzzi, and ample parking facilities.

- **Products** should be:
  - reasonably priced
  - of good quality
  - reliable and safe
  - provided with clear instructions, if appropriate
  - guaranteed, if appropriate

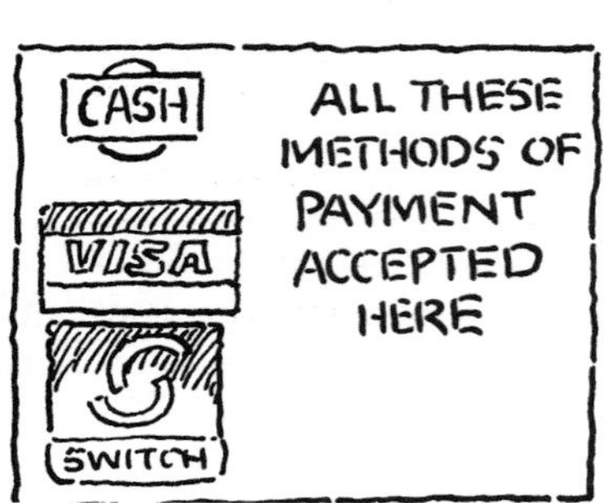

- **Sales administration** should have the following features:
  - customer orders should be fulfilled quickly
  - delivery services should be prompt and reliable
  - product catalogues, price lists and information leaflets should be up to date and perhaps offered free of charge
  - customers should be allowed to pay for goods and services in a number of different ways: cash, credit or debit card, cheques, on hire purchase, etc.
  - loyalty cards and bonus schemes should be introduced for loyal customers who make repeat purchases

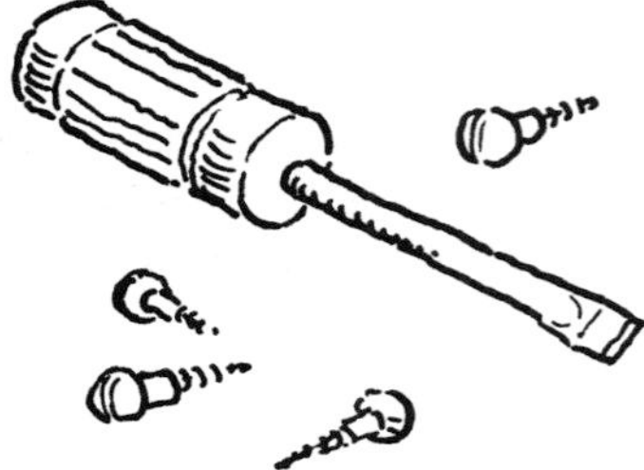

- **After-sales care** should:
  - provide a prompt and reasonable repair service
  - deal with customer complaints quickly and sympathetically
  - exchange goods and give refunds without quibble

- **Care for the environment.** Customers are genuinely concerned about the environment and want firms to make significant improvements in the way they make their products. Ways in which this might be done include:
  - undertaking regular 'green' audits
  - recycling waste
  - conserving energy - e.g. turning off lights when not in use
  - using more recycled materials and biodegradable products
  - stopping the testing of chemicals and finished products, such as cosmetics, on animals
  - only buying wood from renewable forests
  - buying products from only those suppliers who have a good environmental record

Clearly not every organization will offer customers all the same features of customer service. For example, you would expect to find a clean and hygienic toilet in a restaurant but you are unlikely to find a toilet in a record shop. Similarly, you would not expect car mechanics providing a service in a car repair centre to be smartly dressed or very clean. In fact you may be put off taking your car there if they are!

Portfolio Activity 11.4 

1. Using the checklist of good customer service features above, investigate customer service in a business organisation of your choice. For example, this could be:
   - a retail outlet, such as a shop, bank, sandwich bar, or hairdressing salon
   - a service provider, such as a window cleaner, car mechanic, or painter and decorator, bus and rail services
   - an office, such as a job centre, council offices or a government department
   - an e-tailer selling goods over the Internet
   - a factory
   - a local hospital, school or college

   You may need to adapt the checklist to suit the particular activities of the organization you choose. For example, the product features above would not apply in a factory, hospital or school.

   In some cases you may have to ask permission to be on the organization's premises. In other cases, you will simply be just another member of the public looking around.

2. Write up your findings in a short report using a word processor. Your report should contain:
   - an introduction, describing your chosen organization, its name and location
   - your impression of customer service in the organization, i.e. how well you think it lives up to the feature of good customer service listed above
   - what the organization could do to improve its customer service

Meeting customer needs

Good customer service is all about responding to customers needs and satisfying their expectations. Consumers will contact a business organization for a variety of reasons. Whether they make contact in writing, on the telephone or in person, customers will need one or more of the following from a business organization:

- to obtain information
- to make a purchase
- to obtain a refund or exchange
- to complain
- to receive after-sales care

In addition, there are those customers who may have **special needs**. For example, disabled people, people with sight or hearing difficulties, people with small children, and many more who may have other needs as a customer of an organization.

All customers will need, and expect, to receive fair, honest and efficient treatment. Staff training can help employees identify their customers and their needs, and to be more able to respond to those needs.

Customers need information

First impressions often last. In business, creating a poor first impression is likely to lose customers. A customer that contacts a business for the first time is unlikely to forget if they were kept waiting and treated badly. How sales staff greet people and deal with their enquiries is, therefore, of vital importance. In all cases, enquiries should be dealt with politely and quickly.

Even if an employee cannot answer an enquiry s/he must still offer the customer help. This can be done by taking a note of their name, contact address or phone number, and then passing these details on to another member of staff to follow up the enquiry. An employee should never say they cannot help a customer, unless of course the customer has contacted the wrong organization in the first place.

It is also important to keep customers informed about any developments which may affect their enquiry. For example, by advising a customer, on the phone or in writing, when the item they want or have ordered is ready for collection or when delivery can be made.

In many cases, customers who make general enquiries are satisfied simply to receive leaflets and brochures that provide them with basic facts about the organization and their products.

Customers need to make purchases

Most business organizations rely on external customers buying their goods and services in order to stay in operation and earn a profit. The same is true even of non-profit-making organizations such as charities and National Health Service hospitals. If a charity fails to attract donations or if a hospital fails to attract patients sent to them by local doctors, then they face the risk of closing down.

Customers can make purchases by visiting an organization in person or by placing an order over the telephone or in writing. Individual customers make most of their purchases by visiting shops. Business customers are more likely to place orders for the products they want. In some cases they may even be visited by sales representatives from suppliers who will take their orders.

Before making their purchase, many customers will want some advice on product features and performance. It is, therefore, important that staff involved in sales know about the products they are selling. If staff in an organization are unable to provide advice the customer may be put off making the purchase and take their custom elsewhere.

Some items require more **product knowledge** than others. For example, the most a customer may want to know about vegetables sold in a grocer's shop or supermarket is 'are they fresh', or 'how can I cook them'? However, a customer deciding between alternative video recorders may want to know technical details about the quality of the picture and sound, can it be used for video editing, how many channels can it store, and how long can the timer be set for?

Technical experts with very specialized and detailed knowledge will be needed to explain about many industrial products such as weapon systems, medical instruments and drugs, and production machinery.

It is equally important that staff in service industries know about the services they provide to customers. For example, a person selling insurance would need to know about all the different types of insurance available, what they do and do not cover, and the premiums payable. Similarly, a hairdresser could be asked to advise on styles, types of shampoos to use, hair colours and perms.

Sometimes customers will want advice and information on other matters relating to their purchase, such as whether the product can be delivered, whether its guaranteed, the method of payment they can use, and whether credit terms are available. The decision whether to buy or not from an organization could be based in part on these additional factors.

Consumers can now make payment for their purchases in a variety of ways. Businesses must have the facilities to accept different methods of payment, including cash, credit cards, store cards, debit cards, cheques, money-off coupons, credit notes, etc. Sales staff must know the procedure for accepting different methods of payments and processing - for example, what documentation is required, what information from a credit, debit or store card is needed, and how the payment method is to be authorized (see 16.3).

▼ *Lack of product knowledge can put off customers. But don't try to be too technical*

AND THIS SIR IS THE OOGIMAFLIP OVERRIDE BUTTON ON THE THINGYMMBOB TO ALLOW THE WHATCHUMMACALLIT TO OPERATE IN QUARK MODE.

▼ *Figure 11.4: Accepting payments by credit card.*

1. Sales assistant checks card number against published list of stolen or missing cards.

2. Card is 'swiped' through electronic till point or manual device to transfer impression of raised numbers on the card onto an issued document. Different cards may require different documents.

3. If manual method is used, the assistant must fill in purchase details on the document and phone the credit card company to obtain clearance for the amount of the purchase.

4. Sales assistant notes clearance code number issued by the credit card company on the document,

5. Customer signs till receipt or card purchase document.

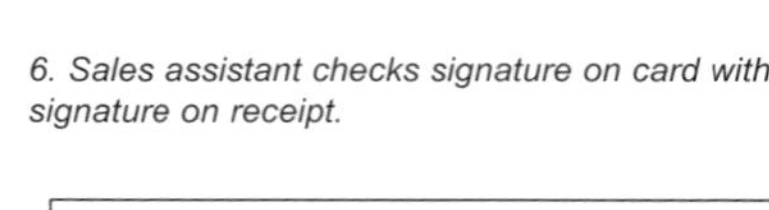

6. Sales assistant checks signature on card with signature on receipt.

Customers need after-sales care

A useful way to promote customer loyalty and repeat purchases is to follow up the purchase with after-sales care. This is especially important when the customer has received a service or personalized product, such as carpet cleaning or double-glazing. A follow-up telephone call or personal visit can establish if the customer is satisfied, or what can be done to overcome any dissatisfaction they may have.

After-sales care also extends to providing spare parts, technical advice, or arranging repairs and maintenance. Customers need to have confidence that they can find help if anything goes wrong. Organizations that fail to provide this kind of help will soon lose out to rival firms that do offer after-sales care.

Customers may need to obtain refunds or exchange products

All businesses should have an agreed policy on what staff should do if a customer wants to exchange goods they have purchased or to obtain a refund. Such a policy is an important part of good customer service because if the public feel that a firm is unfair in its treatment of them after having bought a faulty good or even a good about which they have changed their mind, this can damage future sales and the long-term reputation of the business.

Whatever the refund or exchange policy is, it must be in line with consumer laws such as the **Trade Descriptions Act** and **Sale of Goods Act** which are designed to protect the customer (see 12.5). Customers who return faulty or sub-standard goods have a legal right to a refund - they do not have to accept an alternative product, credit note or gift vouchers (even though sometimes shop staff try to persuade customers to do so).

Many large high street stores, including BHS and Mothercare, will exchange goods if the purchaser returns them but will only give a refund if the customer has a receipt. Comet Warehouses will only exchange goods if they are returned within 14 days of purchase. Most retailers of computer software and computer games will not exchange any goods unless there is a genuine fault. This is because the customer may have made a copy of the computer software or may have used the software in a way which could have infected it with a computer virus.

▼ Many retail organizations set aside a small area staffed by experienced employees to deal with customers who want to return goods.

A number of organizations have policies which offer consumers more than their legal minimum entitlement. For example, firms are not required by law to exchange goods simply because customers have changed their mind about what they want, but some firms may be willing to exchange goods in this situation, as long as they are still in their original packaging. They may even decide to do so if the customer does not have a receipt. These kinds of 'no quibble' exchange and refund policies mean that customers become more confident about buying goods, because they know they can take them back if necessary.

Customers may need to complain

Even in the best-run organizations, customers will sometimes feel that they have been treated badly or unfairly. A complaint may be directed at a particular member of staff, a product that is faulty or sub-standard, or at the procedures used by an organization.

A good business will always listen to customer complaints and take them seriously. Firms can learn a great deal about how to improve their business by listening to customers who have a genuine grievance. Even if a customer is unhappy now, they are likely to be more satisfied in the long run if the firm has a well understood and clear policy of listening to customer complaints and taking corrective action.

Most large organizations have clear guidelines for staff to follow when dealing with, and monitoring, complaints. Consider the procedures used to deal with the following complaints:

Mr Smith telephones his telephone company to complain about being overcharged on his quarterly bill.

Telephone company records details of the customer and complaint in a paper or computer file.

Telephone company writes to Mr Smith the next day to acknowledge his complaint and to assure him that it will be investigated.

Telephone company investigates complaint: it finds that Mr Smith has been overcharged due to a computer error.

Telephone company writes to Mr Smith to apologize for the mistake and for any inconvenience it may have caused. A new bill for the correct amount is issued.

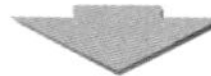

Telephone company contacts Mr Smith to ask him if he is satisfied with his new bill or if any further action is necessary.

Mrs Jones takes back the hairdryer she bought last week because it keeps overheating. She complains to the sales assistant who served her that the product is faulty.

The sales assistant apologizes and directs Mrs Jones to the Customer Help Desk.

A member of staff at the Customer Help Desk examines the hairdryer and apologizes for the inconvenience caused by the sale of the faulty item.

Mrs Jones says she would like a replacement.

The Customer Help Desk provides a new hairdryer. They test the replacement and check that Mrs Jones is satisfied.

The member of staff who dealt with Mrs Jones records details of the complaint and the action taken.

How to cope with unhappy customers: some golden rules

- Show concern for the customer's feelings - be sympathetic and listen
- Note down the important details
- Do not make excuses or try to cover up
- Never lose your temper - it will only infuriate the customer even more
- Always inform the customer clearly about how the complaint will be dealt with, how long it will take, and who should be contacted next
- Always show your customers you care
- If a customer is abusive or threatening, withdraw and seek assistance from senior staff or even the police

▼ *Organizations that do not provide for people with special needs will lose their custom*

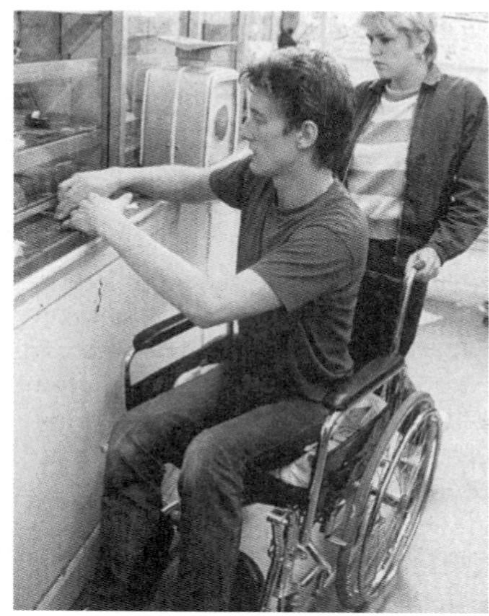

Some customers have special needs

Some customers may have special needs which require particular attention by an organization. These include people who are:

- Blind or partially sighted
- Deaf
- Physically handicapped
- Mentally handicapped
- Elderly
- Foreign visitors
- With young children

There will also be people who need help in an emergency, for example, if they faint, are robbed, or taken ill. In these cases, assistance is required quickly. Staff may need to administer First Aid themselves or contact other staff members who can help. They will also need to be aware of procedures to evacuate customers from buildings during a fire or bomb scare.

Today, many organizations are keen to look after people with special needs. An organization that does not offer services for people with special needs will lose their custom to organizations that do. For example,

disabled people can only shop where there is good access and facilities for wheelchairs. Even a single small step outside a shop can prevent disabled people from entering. It is just as easy in most cases to provide a wheelchair ramp as it is to provide a step. These customers may also need help to open doors, reach shelves, and carrying shopping.

Blind customers need to be able to take their guide dogs into shops with them. Because they will be unable to see the objects they want to buy, they will rely on staff with good product knowledge to provide clear descriptions. Some blind and partially sighted people may need staff to escort them around business premises, rather than simply giving them directions.

The mentally handicapped and foreign visitors may have difficulty expressing their needs and making themselves understood. Staff need to be patient and listen carefully and provide the help they need. Deaf people who can lipread will also need staff to speak slowly and clearly to them.

Elderly people are often confused by new technology and products, and take tonger to make up their mind what to buy. Staff should never get impatient, and should be prepared to spend more time explaining product details, methods of payment, arrangements for delivery, and other features. Elderly people may also have difficulty with steps and doors, and may need help getting around a store and carrying their purchases.

Even families with young children have special needs and are more likely to visit stores where children are clearly welcomed and catered for. For example, IKEA stores have a supervised playroom and a cartoon cinema to entertain young children while their parents shop for furniture. This is good for parents, but it is also good business for IKEA.

Customers with special needs require more time, care, and attention than other customers.

How firms can improve access for customers with special needs

Many people still have problems gaining access to buildings and different modes of transport. An organization may improve the accessibility of their premises and services by providing the following features:

- Ramps for wheelchairs and pushchairs that are neither too steep or too long
- Installing automatic doors to replace old or heavy doors that may be difficult to open
- Providing wide lifts and toilets for people in wheelchairs
- Signposting the layout of facilities in business premises
- Installing voice synthesizers in lifts to give details of floor numbers and warnings to stand clear of the doors
- Providing staff to help customers pack and carry their shopping and open doors for them

Many of these features can be 'designed into' new premises with ease. However, it may be difficult to add them to old buildings.

Portfolio Activity 11.5 

1. What, apart from the meal itself, do customers in fast food retail outlets expect the organization to provide? Support your answer by reference to the article and by observing customers in queues and at tables in a fast food outlet.
2. From the article, and your observations, are fast food retailers meeting the needs of their customers?
3. Suggest two likely business objectives of fast food organizations. In the light of your answer to Question 2, do you think the achievement of these objectives is being helped or hindered by the quality of customer service provided?

Secret test criticises fast-food service

By Diane Summers, Marketing Correspondent

Fast-food restaurants, popularly viewed as providing the ultimate in well-drilled friendliness and service, in reality rate worse than banks or, in some respects, passenger rail services, according to customers who secretly tested them.

A large-scale "mystery shopping" exercise, involving visits to 2,500 retail outlets by researchers posing as consumers, found that fast-food staff scored below the average for all retailers on friendliness, politeness and helpfulness.

Almost 20 per cent of staff forgot part of the order and 15 per cent delivered something that had not been asked for. Twenty-five per cent of staff failed to repeat the order as a check that it had been taken correctly. Shoppers also found that almost 20 per cent of restaurants had a litter problem.

The company which conducted the research, the Grass Roots Group, based in Tring, Hertfordshire, sent researchers to a total of 154 branches of McDonald's and Burger King for the study.

Financial Times, 17.1.1995

Evaluating customer service

There are a number of ways to judge the success of a business organization in meeting the needs of consumers:

- **The improved image of the business.** Good customer relations will improve the image of an organization and will generate repeat trade and customer loyalty.
- **The impression left with customer.** If refunds are dealt with quickly and without fuss; if complaints are followed up immediately; if information is accurate and freely available, and products and customer services reliable, then the customer will form a favourable impression of the organization and is more likely to deal with them again in future.

  Market research and monitoring customer complaints are two ways an organization might observe changes in customer perceptions of products and image.
- **Business performance.** Improved image and customer relations can be measured in terms of increased cashflow from sales. This ultimately will feed into higher profits.

Customer care is top priority

The chairman of London Transport is putting customer care at the head of his agenda.

"People can talk about infrastructure. They can talk about equipment. Certainly these things are important, but I think that the single thing that has the biggest impact on the public is their perceived attitude of the staff."

London Direct No.11, October 1994

The role and responsibilities of sales staff

The quality of sales staff is of vital importance in the marketing mix (see 10.1). Despite heavy investment of time and money in product development, pricing strategies, advertising, and other promotional methods, no organization will succeed in the marketplace if sales staff fail to carry out their duties adequately.

Sales staff in retail outlets or those involved in telesales or door-to-door selling are no longer expected simply to operate tills, telephones, or give product demonstrations. The duties and responsibilities of sales staff are expanding, and training is essential if they are to perform these well. However, training is often overlooked or poorly designed.

Portfolio Activity 11.6 

1. Visit a retail outlet of your choice and observe various sales staff in operation. Make a note of the tasks they are required to perform and how customers benefit from them.
2. Now examine the duties and responsibilities of sales staff who sell products or services directly to consumers over the telephone. Arrange to phone the sales department in an organization of your choice. Ask the sales assistant if they would mind answering a few quick and simple questions about their duties and responsibilities to help you with your project. Have your questions prepared and make a note of their answers.
3. From your notes compiled in Questions 1 and 2, draw up a list, with explanations, of the main duties and responsibilities of sales staff in general.

The main duties and responsibilities of sales staff are to provide:

- **Customer care.** Looking after a customer while they make up their mind is important if they are not to feel rushed into a decision. This could involve helping them try on garments in a shop, giving them a cup of tea and somewhere to sit while they wait at the hairdresser's, or just giving them time to browse without interrupting. Looking after the customer in a helpful, friendly, and caring way increases the chance they will purchase from the organization and remain loyal to it in the future.
- **Point-of-sale service.** This can be as simple as placing shopping in carrier bags for customers, providing product information, or checking that electrical goods work properly before they leave the shop.
- **Product knowledge.** Few consumers have the ability or time to investigate the full range of products available. For example, products such as computers and camcorders are technically very complex, and many are imported from overseas where product standards may differ. Customers will often rely on sales staff, either in a shop or on the telephone direct to the manufacturer, to provide them with technical details of product performance, and to recommend best buys. They will be disappointed if staff are unable to give these details and may go to another organization to make their purchase.

- **Sales information and help.** This can involve providing information on product lines, how to order goods or services, and credit facilities available, or simply pointing out where customers can find the product they are looking for.
- **Taking payments and giving refunds.** Sales staff must know how to receive and process different methods of customer payments, and how to give refunds, quickly and efficiently with minimum fuss.
- **After-sales care.** Sales staff can contact customers to check they are happy with the good or service they have received, provide technical advice and assistance, and arrange replacements, remedial work or repairs, if required.
- **Dealing with customer complaints.** Sales staff must be able to deal with customer complaints in a sympathetic and helpful manner and, if necessary, pass them on to a member of staff who has the responsibility.
- **Knowledge of customer rights.** Sales staff must be aware of, and comply with, the requirements of laws introduced to protect consumers from misleading advertising and sales practices, and unsafe or unhealthy products.
- **Feedback.** Sales staff are often the 'eyes and ears' in the market for goods and services. They can provide valuable market information on changing customer wants, willingness to pay, and perceptions of products and corporate image.
- **Prospecting.** In many organizations, prospecting and investigating sales leads is done by telephone. Sales staff pick telephone numbers and phone potential customers to see if they are interested in purchasing a particular good or service. This is a popular method used by organizations selling advertising space in newspapers or magazines, and by double-glazing and home security firms.

  However, prospecting can also be undertaken by sales staff in shops. Many customers enter shops to browse, not knowing exactly what they want. A sales assistant can offer help and advice, and in so doing, promote various products to customers in the hope of making a sale. A good salesperson will learn to recognize a **buying signal** that suggests a customer is happy with the hard or soft 'sell'.

▼ *Sales staff must know the requirments of consumer protection laws*

BUT YOU SAID IT WOULDN'T STRETCH IN THE WASH

Whatever the tasks sales staff perform they must always carry them out in a friendly and helpful manner. Customers want to feel their custom is valued, and that they are getting good advice and attention. Unfortunately the trend towards bigger organizations and e-commerce has meant friendly, personal service is under pressure. Staff can seem abrupt because they are concentrating on speed of service and, in some cases, there is no contact with staff at all any more because sales are handled electronically.

Many businesses are now retraining their staff in how to be friendly towards their customers and serve them efficiently. For example, staff can receive training in how to respond to e-mails from on-line customers, their telephone manner, and even in simple things like smiling and saying 'Hello' or 'Good morning', making eye contact, saying 'Thank-you' and 'Goodbye'. All these things can help to make a good impression with the customer and encourage repeat custom. However, staff who try to be too friendly can put off customers just as much as those who are too abrupt.

▼ Over freindly

▼ Too abrupt

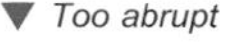

▼ Just right

Sales administration

One of the main responsibilities of sales staff is to ensure that the **administration** and **processing** of sales is quick and cost-effective. Customers will soon become dissatisfied if staff are slow to process their orders or arrange credit, and poor sales administration can lead to higher costs and lower sales.

With the increasing use of computerized administrative procedures, processing nowadays can be considerably easier and quicker, but sales staff need to have the right training. Sales procedures include:

- **Processing orders.** This involves receiving orders for goods or services over the counter, by phone or fax; checking the order against stock; advising the customer of availability, prices, acceptable methods of payment, and delivery dates, and entering this information on computer or paper records.
- **Credit clearance and control.** Increasingly, both organizations and private individuals are making payments on credit extended to them either by the organization from which they are making a purchase, or from a credit card or loan company.

Sales staff will be expected to administer and control the giving of credit. This will involve the following tasks:

- Completing credit agreement documents
- Checking the creditworthiness of a customer with the accounts department in the organization, credit card company, or bank
- Establishing a credit limit for each customer based on feedback from the accounts department, credit card company, or bank
- Sending out reminders for late payment
- Chasing bad debts.

- **Processing customer accounts.** This will involve itemizing purchases on credit made by individual customers, adding up their total bills, sending out accounts, and receiving payments. As many of these tasks are now computerized, sales staff must make sure that the correct details of purchases are entered into the right accounts.
- **Working out delivery schedules based on priorities and routes.** Staff must ensure that deliveries are prompt, and that the right goods reach the right customers in good condition. Routes should be planned to minimize transport costs and travel time betwen different delivery addresses.
- **Maintaining security.** This concerns keeping records of customer names, addresses, payments and accounts confidential, as well as handling money securely.

Key words:

Selling - a personal communication to a customer to make a sale

Sales communications - methods used to inform and motivate sales staff, including sales meetings, conferences, and trade fairs

Customer service - all aspects of business operations that are of interest or concern to customers, including motivation of sales staff, physical conditions of premises, product reliability and after-care, efficiency of sales administration, care for the environment

Sales administration - processing customer orders, purchases, payments and deliveries

Useful references

'Retail Pocket Book', published annually by NTC Publications Ltd, Farm Road, Henley-on-Thames, Oxfordshire RG9 1GB (*e-mail: info@ntc.co.uk*)

'e.business' , published monthly by Crimson Publishing, Vigilant House, 120 Wilton Road, London SW1V 1JZ (*www.ebusiness.uk.com*)

Look at **trade and professional magazines** in larger branches of WH Smith and other newsagents, for example, 'The Grocer', 'Retail Newsagent', 'Caterer and Hotelkeeper'

Internet key words search: **Retailers, Wholesalers, Distribution**

Test your knowledge

1 A direct sales method that can be used by a producer is:

A Selling direct to retailers

B Placing mail order adverts in magazines

C Using persuasive TV advertising

D Employing agents to sell products direct to consumers

2 Duties and responsibilities of sales staff in an organization are likely to include all of the following **except**:

A Providing product information

B After-sales care

C Making repairs

D Giving refunds

3 Which of the following is an indirect sales method?

A Factory sales

B Using wholesalers

C Door-to-door selling

D Pyramid selling

Questions 4–6 share the following answer options:

A Information

B Refund

C Product demonstration

D Spare parts

Which of the above customer needs could be satisfied by the following customer services?

4 A technical telephone 'hotline'

5 An after-sales service department

6 Point-of-sale services

7 Which of the following Acts protects the consumer from false claims made about products?

A Sale of Goods Act

B Weights and Measures Act

C Trademark Act

D Trade Descriptions Act

8 Sales staff may be expected to undertake the following administrative tasks **except**:

A Analysing the results of market research

B Processing orders and organizing deliveries

C Credit clearance and credit control

D Prospecting

9 Which of the following is an indirect method of distribution?

A Pyramid selling

B Mail order

C Agent sales

D Telesales

10 **a** What is distribution, and why is it important?

b What is a wholesaler?

c Give two advantages to a manufacturer and a retail chain of using a wholesaler.

d Suggest two reasons why wholesalers are declining in importance.

11 **a** Suggest three needs customers have in making a purchase other than for the products they intend to buy.

b Suggest and explain three services that sales staff in an organization will be expected to provide in order to meet the customer requirements you have listed in (a).

c How would you evaluate the performance of an organization and its sales staff in meeting the needs of customers?

d Outline two sales communications methods an organization could use to inform and motivate their sales staff.

12 **a** What is an indirect distribution channel?

b Explain the role of a wholesaler, retailer, and agent in an indirect distribution channel.

c Suggest and describe three sales methods a manufacturer could use to distribute products direct to the final consumer.

d What distribution channel and sales method would you advise the following organizations to use for their products. Give reasons for your recommendations.

i A large firm selling industrial lasers to a worldwide market

ii A small carpet cleaning firm serving a localized market

iii A manufacturer of frozen foods

iv A distributer of DVDs, CDs and computer games

chapter 12 Analysing Marketing Opportunities

This chapter considers how and why businesses develop different marketing strategies and the analytical tools they use to help them do so.

What you need to learn

To develop a marketing strategy you will need to use market information to analyse the **competitiveness** of your good or service and to gain an understanding of the environment within which the business is operating. You will need to be familiar with **PESTLE** and **SWOT** analyses for generating information on the business environment.

You need to understand how businesses will develop different marketing strategies depending on environmental factors. You need to distinguish between the following strategies:

- **market penetration**
- **new product development**
- **entering new markets**
- **diversification**

Using analytical models such as the **Ansoff matrix**, you should be able to identify the circumstances in which the above strategies may be appropriate. You need to understand the importance of innovation, creativity and insight when identifying strategies for changing market position for new product development.

You also need to know how to use the **Boston matrix** to make judgements about the portfolio of products marketed by a business.

It is also important to consider the following constraints on marketing activities:

- industry-based constraints, such as the **Advertising Standards Authority**
- ethical, environmental and social constraints, such as **business stakeholders** and **pressure groups**
- legal constraints, such as the **Trades Description Act** and **Competition Act**

Section 12.1 Analysing the business environment

What is the business environment?

Most firms have to compete with others to sell their goods or services. A firm that is **competitive** will stay one step ahead of the competition. It will correctly anticipate consumer wants, and produce the product consumers want, when they want it, at the price they want, in the right quantities, and at the right place of sale. It will do this faster, better and at a lower cost than rival firms. A firm that is competitive will be more productive than competing firms, have lower average costs of production, and will strive for continual improvement.

Firms that compete with each other are engaged in a 'war': to win market share, customers and revenues, and to stop rival firms taking away their market share, customers, and revenues. The battlefield is the business environment in which those businesses operate and as in a real war, the battlefield is always changing. Consumer wants, shareholders objectives, rival marketing strategies, and the laws that govern how businesses operate will all tend to change over time. A business that fails to understand the environment it operates in and is unable to plan for or cope with change, will not be successful. In contrast, a business that has analysed its business environment will be able to devise strategies and tactics to maintain a **competitive advantage** over rival firms.

The business environment is influenced by:

- changes in the weather and the **natural environment**
- the actions of rival firms introducing new products, prices and advertising campaigns in the **competitive environment**
- changes in the attitudes, expectations and purchasing decisions of consumers determine the **social environment** in which businesses operate
- changes in laws and other controls by central and local government determine the **economic, regulatory and legal environment** that affects business
- the skills, actions and expectations of employees, shareholders and financiers in the **internal environment** of a business

The natural environment

The physical or natural environment will always have a big impact on the way businesses operate. Changes in the weather can damage crops and increase the prices paid by food manfacturers and consumers. The weather can also affect consumer buying patterns (see 9.5).

Fierce storms, floods and earthquakes can cause extensive damage, and firms need to ensure that they have adequate insurance cover (see 20.3).

There is increasing awareness among consumers that business activity can affect the natural environment. Oil spills and waste chemical dumping have resulted in local environmental disasters, while globally the burning of fossil fuels has caused atmospheric pollution, acid rain, and climate change.

The competitive environment

The degree of competition between firms supplying the same or similar goods and services will depend on a number of factors. Michael Porter of the Harvard Business School in the USA developed a useful framework that classifies the various forces of competition under five headings for each industry. These are:

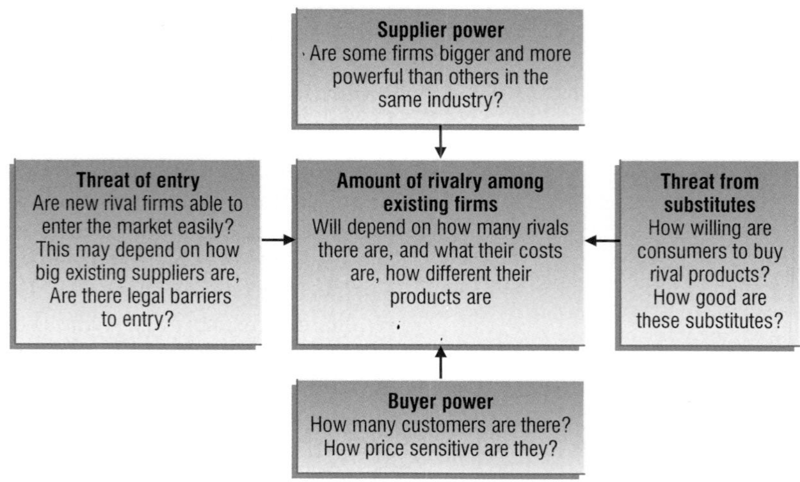

Supplier power
Are some firms bigger and more powerful than others in the same industry?
Threat of entry
Are new rival firms able to enter the market easily? This may depend on how big existing suppliers are, Are there legal barriers to entry?
Amount of rivalry among existing firms
Will depend on how many rivals there are, and what their costs are, how different their products are
Threat from substitutes
How willing are consumers to buy rival products? How good are these substitutes?
Buyer power
How many customers are there? How price sensitive are they?

So, for example, in industries in which there are many different suppliers, consumers are very price-sensitive and the product has close substitutes - for example, margarine is a close substitute for butter, and rail travel is a close substitute for domestic flights - competition will tend to be fierce. Similarly, where there are many rival suppliers of similar size and only one major buyer, rival firms will compete vigorously for sales. For example, the UK Government is the main customer for defence equipment in the UK, and export sales are often limited by security considerations.

▼ *The social environment - the attitude, beliefs and actions of consumers and pressure groups - influences business decisions*

The social environment

The social environment is people. People are consumers and through their spending decisions they will determine the success or failure of many business organizations. Consumer spending patterns will be determined by their income, tastes, values, beliefs, and attitudes (see 9.4).

By making choices on which products to buy, people have a major influence on what firms produce. In recent years consumers have become more health-conscious, and more concerned about the environment and the treatment of animals. For example, many consumers may now prefer to buy from firms known to promote a more caring image towards the environment and animals, such as The Body Shop, Tesco and The Co-operative Bank.

Consumers' views can also be influenced by pressure groups - who are themselves groups of concerned consumers. These can be small groups fighting local issues (such as the closure of a railway line or the building of a new superstore), or major international lobby groups (such as Greenpeace and Friends of the Earth), fighting issues such as pollution, whaling and cruelty to animals.

The economic, regulatory and legal environment

The actions, policies and laws of local and central Government in the UK and the government of the European Union can have a major impact on businesses. The possibility of changes in ruling governments and changes in their policies is a source of great uncertainty for many businesses, and when changes occur they can have a major impact on the business environment.

EU and UK governments have passed a number of laws and regulations which aim to protect consumers, workers and the environment from the possibility of being mislead or mistreated by businesses (see 12.5 and 20.3). Owners of firms found breaking these laws can be fined heavily or even imprisoned. Conforming with laws and regulations can raise business costs.

Government economic policy aims to create economic conditions in which businesses can prosper by keeping price inflation low and stable, stimulating consumer demand, and encouraging employment. However, the actions governments take to achieve these conditions can impact significantly on business. For example, to control inflation in the UK the government may raise taxes and interest rates. Raising taxes on business profits will reduce after tax profits. Raising taxes on people's incomes will reduce the amount of money they have to spend on goods and services. Raising interest rates will raise costs for businesses repaying bank and mortgage loans (see 23.2).

The impact of government policies on business are considered in detail in Unit 2.

The internal environment

The ability of a business to survive changes in its external environment, prosper and achieve its business aims will depend very much on its workers, managers and the people and other firms who provide the business with finance. The skills and attitudes of employees, including the quality of management and the confidence investors have in the business, will affect the performance of the business. For example, if employees think they are being treated unfairly by the business, they may take disruptive actions which can raise costs and lose the business custom. If the people and organizations who finance the business lose confidence in the ability of managers to take decisions that will improve sales and profits, they may replace the managers or withdraw their financial help.

Shareholders are the owners of limited companies (see 2.2). They will want to make sure business managers are making profits so that they will earn a return on the money they have invested in their shares. Shareholders will often vote on who they want to manage the businesses they own and how they should be managed.

Analysing the business environment

Before a business decides on a strategy - what to produce, how to produce it, what price to charge, where to place it for sale, and how to promote it - it must examine its environment and plan ahead for any changes in the environment that may have a negative impact on the organization. Only then can it design a strategy that has a good chance of success.

The purpose of environmental analysis is to inform strategy development to minimize any potential damage to the business from change and maximize the advantages. Analysing the business environment cannot provide all the answers and guarantee success, but not doing so will almost certainly result in business failure.

There are two useful methodologies a business can use to examine its environment.

PESTLE analysis

A **PESTLE analysis** should identify and evaluate:

- environmental factors that should or do influence business strategy
- trends and possible/probable environmental developments, opportunities or threats that could affect the business in the future

PESTLE analysis focuses on external factors, breaking them down into a number of categories. It allows a business to identify exactly what changes the outside world may hold for the organization in the foreseeable future.

▼ *Figure 12.1: A PESTLE table*

Political	Economic	Social	Technological	Legal	Environmental
Changes in : UK and overseas governments Government policies Taxation Public expenditure	Changes in: Economic growth Interest rates Inflation Unemployment National income Exchange rates	Changes in: Population size Age distribution Income distribution Level of home ownership Educational attainments Social mobility Lifestyles Working conditions Attitudes to work and leisure Environmental awareness	Changes in: Spending on research and development by government and industry Speed of technology transfer New materials and processes Developments in information communications technology Improvements to existing equipment	Changes in: Health and safety law Employment regulations Competition laws EU directives Consumer protection laws	Changes in: Pollution controls Waste disposal Parking restrictions and congestion charges

A PESTLE analysis will consider the implications of any one or all of the above changes on:

- the organization structure and objectives
- customers
- the industry/marketplace
- suppliers
- rival firms
- other stakeholders, such as shareholders, local communities

Portfolio Activity 12.1 

Research an organization of your choice. This should include discussions with the business owners and/or senior managers.

1. Find out what changes your chosen organization has gone through in the past two or three years:
   - List the most significant changes that have affected the way the business operates
   - For each change identify whether the organization took any action to anticipate the effects of the change
   - What other business environmental influences have been particularly important to the organization in the past?
   - Are any of these influences more or less significant now, and in the future, for the organization and its competitors?
2. Organize the main influences you have identified that are important to the business, now and in the future, under the main PESTLE headings.
3. What actions could the business take now to the minimize the potential for negative impacts and maximize the advantages of changes that could affect the success of the business in the future?

Figure 12.2: A SWOT matrix

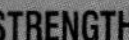

STRENGTH	WEAKNESS
any particular skill, competence or unique selling point a business has which will help it gain and retain a competitive advantage. A business strength could also be its product quality, reputation or customer service	any aspect of the company which may hinder the achievement of specific objectives such as limited experience of certain markets/technologies, extent of financial resources available
OPPORTUNITY	**THREAT**
any feature of the external environment that can be advantageous to a firm, such as significant market growth or customer loyalty	any environmental feature that will present the business with problems or hinder achievement of its objectives, such as increased competition from new firms, or increases in wages and business taxes

MATCHING

SWOT analysis

A **SWOT analysis** considers the strengths and weaknesses of the business and its current strategy, and the opportunities and threats the business environment may present the firm in the future. The aim is to identify the extent to which the current strategy of an organization and its more specific strengths and weaknesses are relevant to, and capable of dealing with, the changes taking place in the external business environment.

A business can use SWOT analysis to design a new strategy or revise an existing one that maximizes its strengths, minimizes or overcomes any weaknesses, makes the most of opportunities, and reduces threats.

Factors thought to determine the strengths, weaknesses, opportunities and threats of a business are usually presented in the from of a matrix, but it is important to note that

- effective SWOT analysis also requires some evaluation of the relative importance of the different factors under consideration
- factors are only relevant if they are important to consumers
- threats and opportunities are conditions presented by the external environment and they should be independent of the firm

Figure 12.3: A SWOT analysis for 'Island Airways'

STRENGTH	WEAKNESS
Recognized national brand name and image Low costs Profitable Efficient operation Mainly modern aircraft fleet	Low passenger numbers and revenues Some loss-making routes Out-of-date equipment Some old and noisy aircraft Low skill levels
OPPORTUNITY	**THREAT**
New international routes Improve passenger numbers and revenues Training to improve skills Outsource some services, such as catering and cleaning Diversify, into airport ownership and	Down-turn in economy Competition from established international airlines New noise laws Loss of key personnel, including pilots New low-fare/no-frills start-up

The matrix in Figure 12.3 is an example of a SWOT analysis for a small national airline company offering domestic flights between the different islands that make up the country.

Having constructed a matrix of strengths, weaknesses, opportunities and threats, a business can make use of the matrix in guiding strategy formulation. The two major strategic options are as follows:

- **Matching:** This involves finding, where possible, a match between the strengths of the organization and the opportunities presented by the market. For example, the airline in the above example may be able to reduce fares to boost passenger numbers and revenues without reducing profit margins significantly in the short term because it is has low costs.

Strengths which do not match any available opportunity are of limited use, likewise opportunities which do not have any matching strengths may be difficult to take advantage of. So, for example, unless the airline above has competencies in running an airport and airport retail outlets it is an opportunity that is probably best left unexploited. It may also find it difficult to compete on international routes if its brand name and image only have national recognition.

- **Conversion:** This requires the development of strategies which will convert weaknesses into strengths in order to take advantage of some particular opportunity, or converting threats into opportunities which can then be matched by existing strengths. The airline in the example above may plan to train its workforce to improve skill levels. It might also undertake market research to find out when and where people want to fly to most. It could then revise its timetable to cut loss-making routes and improve passenger numbers on others.

Portfolio Activity 12.2 

Imagine you are an entrepreneur planning to start up one of the following small businesses:

- car showroom
- DVD video rental shop
- landscape gardening service
- home hairdressing service
- website design consultancy
- travel agency
- electrical wire manufacture

1. Pick three of the businesses listed opposite and in groups identify:
   - the strengths each business will need to be successful and may already have (for example, its small size)
   - the marketing opportunities they may have and should plan to exploit
   - possible threats posed by rival firms and products, legal constraints and other influences – what can and should the businesses do to reduce these threats?
2. For one of your businesses in task 1 above, list the external (PESTLE) environmental factors that could affect the design of the business strategy .

Key words:

Competitive advantage – any one factor or group of factors that benefits a firm over rival firms in competition

PESTLE analysis – an evaluation of the environmental influences - political, economic, social, technological, legal and (natural) environmental – that can and do influence business strategy

SWOT analysis – an evaluation of the strengths and weaknesses of a business organization, and the opportunities and threats the external environment presents to it

Section 12.2

Figure 12.4 : The Ansoff matrix

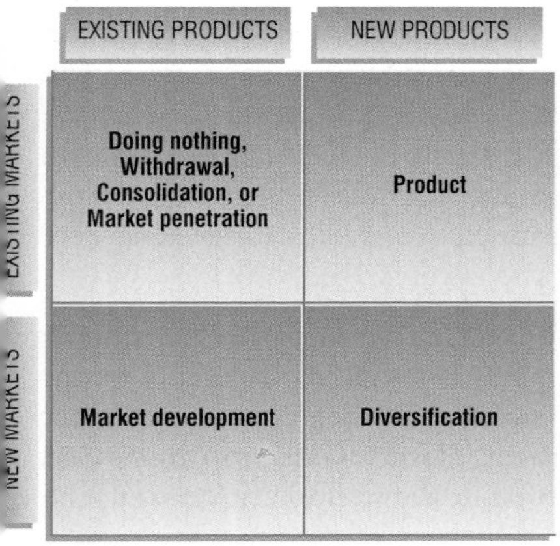

	EXISTING PRODUCTS	NEW PRODUCTS
EXISTING MARKETS	Doing nothing, Withdrawal, Consolidation, or Market penetration	Product
NEW MARKETS	Market development	Diversification

Developing a marketing strategy

The Ansoff matrix

The first step in developing a marketing strategy is analysing the current and future state of the business environment, and identifying the strengths and weaknesses of the business. The next step is to use this information. The strategy should draw on the business strengths to make the most of its opportunities, overcome weaknesses, and reduce threats. The **Ansoff matrix** is a simple planning tool that can help with strategy development. It is based on the need for business organizations to do 'opportunity searching' and identifies four possible strategic directions.

The Ansoff matrix recognizes that in order to grow a business has to consider both its markets and products. The combination of existing and new products and markets provides different marketing opportunities. These are:

Promoting existing products in existing markets

The **do-nothing strategy** involves sticking with an existing strategy. This may be appropriate in the short term when the business environment is static or when the firm is waiting to see how things develop. However, in the long term such tactics are unlikely to be realistic or beneficial.

Withdrawal may take place through the closure or sale of the business. It may be an appropriate strategy if:

- there is a significant and irreversible fall in demand for the product
- the business is making a loss
- the firm has been badly affected by competitive pressure and environmental change

Consolidation takes place when a firm concentrates its activities on those areas where it has established a competitive advantage and focuses its attention on maintaining its market share. When this strategy has been caused by falling profits, the situation is often called **retrenchment**. This may involve the firm in seeking to lower costs, increase quality and increase marketing activity.

Market penetration involves selling more of the existing product to increase market share as opposed to just maintaining it (see 1.7). When the overall market is growing, penetration may be relatively easy to achieve, because the absolute volume of sales of all firms in the market is growing and some firms may not be able to satisfy demand. In static or declining markets, a firm pursuing a market penetration strategy is likely to face intense competition from rival firms.

▼ *Simple business ideas - major business successes*

Developing new products for existing markets

New product development involves a firm in making significant modifications, additions or changes to its existing product range, but using the security of its established customer base. In industries that carry out a lot of research and development, product development may be the main thrust of strategy because product life-cycles are short and because new products may be a natural spin-off from research and development (see 10.4). However, new product development can be risky and expensive, and it requires insight to make a decision about whether to go ahead with it. It is important to research what consumers want before releasing new products to identify if there is a 'gap in the market' (see 9.1).

Many of the products we take for granted today started as the innovations or ideas of private individuals. For example, Percy Shaw became a multi-millionaire after inventing 'cats-eyes' for roads. The idea came to him after seeing his car headlights reflected in broken glass. Swedish brothers Gad and Hans Rausing made over £5 billion from their simple invention, the TetraPak milk carton.

As long as customers want or need the new product, being first to market with the new product can mean success for the business and increased revenues.

Promoting existing products in new markets

Market development can include entering new geographical markets, perhaps overseas, promoting new uses for an existing product, and entering new market segments (for example, making a product appeal to people in other age groups). The aim is to increase sales of the existing product to other groups of consumers. If successful, this has the effect of broadening the customer base and reducing the risk of a fall in demand in any one market threatening the viability of the business.

For example, Rolls-Royce in Derby is one of the leading manufacturers of jet engines for aircraft in the world. It exports engines all over the world and has even developed jet engines to power large fast ships, to help in the drilling for oil and to drive turbines to produce electricity. This is a good example of market development.

Developing new products for new markets

Business organizations can grow by producing different types of goods and services at different stages in their product life-cycles. This is called **diversification.** Businesses diversify because diversification reduces risk. If consumer demand for a particular good or service falls, those organizations that supply the good or service will suffer and may eventually have to close down. If those same businesses also produce many other goods and services, a fall in demand for one may be offset by a rise in demand for their other products.

Firms can diversify by combining with rival firms, by buying up existing businesses or starting new ones. They can also combine with their suppliers and even their major business customers. In this way, a firm is more able to produce more and better products for consumers, faster and cheaper than rival firms. A firm that is able to do so may have a much better chance of achieving business aims of more sales revenue, a bigger market share and more profit (see 1.7).

- **Horizontal diversification** is the development of activities which are complementary to or competitive with the organization's existing activities. In many ways it is also similar to market penetration. For example, British Petroleum and the US company Amoco joined forces in 1999. Both companies are active in oil and gas extraction and the manufacture of petroleum products. It enabled the companies to combine to grow their global market share.

  The Virgin Group of companies is an example of horizontally diversified organization in the tertiary sector whose offerings include financial services, entertainment, retail outlets, holidays, and rail and air travel. The high-profile Virgin brand name and image is a valuable marketing device for all these operations.

  Horizontal diversification can allow firms to spread overseas and provide significant cost savings from large-scale production. These are called **economies of scale** (see 22.4). For example, the employment of more specialized machines and labour, the spreading of administration costs and bulk buying, and loans on more favourable terms from banks because large firms are less risky and more likely to repay their loans

- **Vertical diversification** involves spreading into different stages of the production process. For example, BP Amoco is a vertically diversified organization because it drills for oil, refines oil into petroleum products, and then retails petrol at petrol stations. Similarly, many major beer brewers also own public house chains.

  Organizations that diversify vertically do so to make sure they have a ready source of supply of the natural resources or components they need, and/or to ensure they have retailers willing to sell their products to consumers.

- **Conglomerate diversification** involves a firm producing different goods and/or services, which at face value seem to bear little or no relation to its existing products or markets. For example, Unilever is a firm famous for its detergents but with diversified interests in food, chemicals, paper, plastics, animal feeds, transport and tropical plantations.

Portfolio Activity 12.3 

Read the articles below. What marketing strategies are the firms pursuing according to the Ansoff Matrix? Explain the reasons for your choice in each case.

C&A to close all 109 UK stores

C&A, the pan-European retailer owned by the secretive and wealthy Brenninkmeijer family, is quitting Britain after 78 years on UK high streets.

The company, which was losing about £1m a week in the UK, admitted yesterday it had failed to compete with discount retailers such as Matalan and brands such as Gap.

C&A's departure, far from relieving pressure on other middle-market retailers such as Marks and Spencer and BHS, could allow discounters and brands to expand in the UK.

C&A said it would close all its 109 UK stores, ranging from large shops to department stores, during the next six to nine months. The 4,800 UK staff were told yesterday morning.

Financial Times, 16.6.2000

Acquisitions bolster First Technology

First Technology, which makes crash-test dummies and safety sensors, said recent acquisitions had strengthened its position in technology that makes cars more comfortable for drivers.

As well as daytime lighting and automatic climate controls, the group is to provide sensors for General Motors' in-car navigation and internet access programme.

It will also start production of sensors that automatically activate headlights.

Sales of sensors from Control Devices, a US-based sensor and circuit-breaker maker bought for £89m in 1999, rose 23 per cent in the year to April 30. This helped US sales rise 76 per cent to £54.3m.

Financial Times, 30.6.2000

Teenagers go for sports shop chain

PROMOTIONAL campaigns targeting fashion-conscious teenagers helped sports shop chain John David Sports increase profits by almost a quarter last year. The Lancashire based company which has 133 shops, saw profits before tax leap to £12.21 million for the year ending March 31. Shareholders will get a total dividend of 6p.

Metro, 15.16.2000

Harvey Nicks opens doors to boutiques

Harvey Nichols, the luxury department store and restaurant group, is bringing its own designer chic to the high street with plans for about 10 boutiques selling food, clothing and cosmetics.

Joseph Wan, the chief executive who yesterday reported a 6 per cent rise in annual pre-tax profits, said Harvey Nichols intended to expand substantially the range of own label products currently focused mainly on food, which would be sold in the boutiques.

Financial Times, 21.6.2000

1,800 new jobs at telecom firm

A CANADIAN telecoms company yesterday announced it was creating 1,800 jobs in the UK to meet the demands of booming Internet use.

Nortel Networks is to spend £66 million expanding production of its 'next generation' Internet systems.

The jobs will be created at Nortel plants in Paignton, Devon, and Monkstown, Northern Ireland.

The company said more employees were needed to meet demand for its optical Internet systems, which speed up access and data transmission across the net.

Nortel said it had won 17 out of the last 20 European contracts for 'next generation' equipment, including work for BT, MCI, Worldcom and JazzTel.

The UK jobs and investment are part of a plan to create 5,000 jobs worldwide and invest £250 million to triple production capacity during next year.

Metro 3.11.1999

Key words:

Ansoff matrix – a simple analytical tool that assists strategy development based on a consideration of products and markets

Consolidation – a strategy that concentrates on an existing competitive advantage to maintain market share for an existing product, usually when the market is static or shrinking

Market development – a strategy that seeks to promote an existing product in new markets at home or overseas

Market penetration – a marketing strategy that seeks to grow the market share for an existing product

Horizontal diversification – increasing the range of products which are complementary to or competing with the existing products

Vertical diversification – spreading into different stages of the production process

Conglomerate diversification – spreading into unrelated business activities and products

Section **12.3**

Comparing marketing strategies

Choosing between alternative strategies

A business may have several different strategies it can choose to pursue based on an analysis of environmental factors and its strengths, weaknesses, opportunities, and threats. Senior managers must therefore decide which strategy is the best one to adopt for the business. There are no hard-and-fast rules for choosing between alternative strategies, but a number of techniques have been developed which may be of some help. These include:

- **product life-cycle theory**
- **the Boston 'growth share' matrix**

Product life-cycle theory

Like living organisms, products are born, evolve, reach maturity and eventually die. Some have a revenue earning potential longer than others, but generally product life-cycles are shortening (see 10.4).

The most appropriate marketing strategies based on life-cycle theory are those which correctly anticipate products reaching market maturity and release new products or modify existing ones as sales of others decline. Cash-flows and profits are related to the product life-cycle.

For each product in the portfolio the appropriate marketing strategy will depend on its stage of life. During the early stages the strategy should concentrate on correcting product problems in design, features and positioning so as to establish a competitive advantage and promote product awareness through advertising. During the growth stage when sales are rising the strategic concern should focus on distribution capabilities to make sure enough is produced to meet demand.

During product maturity competition tends to grow and marketing efforts should concentrate on maintaining customer loyalty. Extension strategies can prolong the profitable life of products entering the decline phase by updating the product and by heavily promoting a new product image so that its life-cycle is started again or maturity is extended.

▼ *Figure 12.5: The Boston 'growth share' matrix*

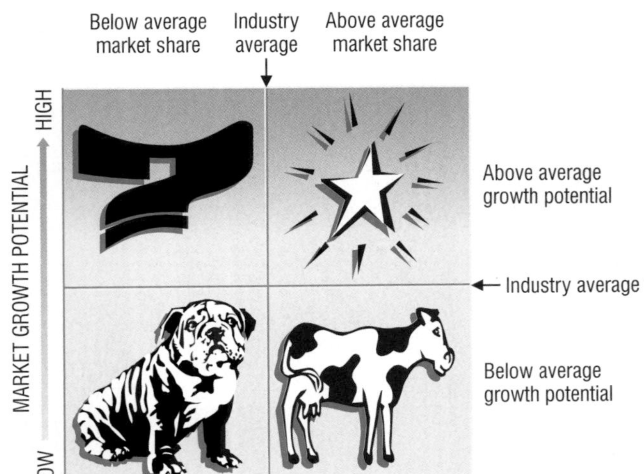

The Boston 'growth share' Matrix

The Boston matrix was developed by the Boston Consulting Group and is a useful analysis tool to understand the product/service portfolio in multi-product firms. The Boston matrix classifies products (or businesses) on the basis of their (1) expected growth rate (on the vertical axis) measured by expected growth in sales revenues, and (2) market share relative to rival products.

The underlying assumption in the growth-share matrix is that a larger market share will enable the business to benefit from economies of scale, lower unit costs and thus higher profit margins.

The Boston matrix suggests there are four types of business or product. These are:

- **Dogs** have low expected growth rates and low relative market shares. A business should stop producing or sell off its 'dogs'. (This is called **divestment.**)
- **Question marks** have a low market share compared with other firms in the same industry but have good growth potential. They are currently at a competitive disadvantage and need investment to correct any weaknesses they have.
- **Stars** have both a high market share and high growth potential. However, they will require significant cash investments to do this through product redevelopment and promotions.
- **Cash cows,** as their name implies, earn a business significant revenues and profits. They have a strong market position in markets that have reached maturity. These products can be 'milked' for profit because they require very little investment to keep them going.

Businesses and their products can be located on the matrix and arrows can be used to indicate where each one is thought to be heading. For example, will a question mark become a star or a dog? Will a star eventually become a cash cow?

This type of presentation is useful because it can help a business answer a number of questions:

- Is there a reasonable balance in the product portfolio?
- Is the business trying to invest in too many new products?
- Are there products that should be dropped?
- Is there a need for immediate new product development?

The most appropriate marketing strategies based on the Boston matrix are those which aim to keep a balanced portfolio of goods or services ensuring that there are enough cash-generating products to match the cash-using ones.

Portfolio Activity 12.4

Look at the Boston matrices for three different multi-product firms. Their products have been positioned in the matrices and arrows used to indicate likely changes to their market positions and growth potential.

For each one, say whether or not you think the business will experience problems and suggest, giving reasons, what strategies they should adopt.

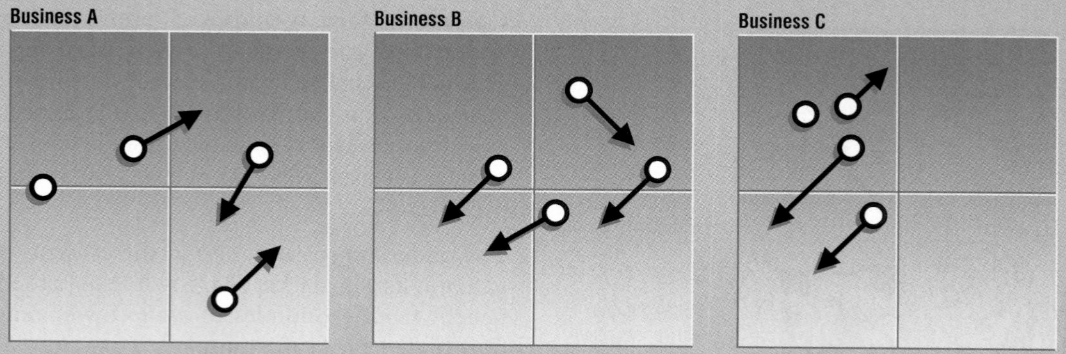

Business A

Business B

Business C

Problems with analytical models

Some of the analytical tools we have considered above have received criticism, largely because they are so simple. Managers who use them may overlook the need to undertake rigorous analysis of their external and internal environment for formulating and implementing strategy. As a result, managers may make the wrong choice based on incomplete or erroneous data. For example, the Boston matrix concentrates only on two dimensions of product markets, size and market share, and therefore may encourage marketing management to pay too little attention to other market features. Products which have a big market share and show significant revenue growth are not necessarily the most profitable.

Secondly, a competing firm who knows you are using a certain model can anticipate your strategic moves and be able to maintain a competitive edge over your business.

In conclusion, therefore, these analytical tools should be used with care. They cannot replace detailed analysis but can help to reduce complex relationships into easy-to-understand problems and solutions.

Key words:

Boston matrix - a simple analytical tool for comparing different strategies and product mixes. It classifies products (or businesses) on the basis of (1) the expected growth rate (on the vertical axis) measured by expected growth in sales revenues, and (2) their market share relative to rival products. It identifies four main types of product:

Stars – are products with high market standing and growth potential

Cash cows – are established products with high market shares but little further growth potential

Question marks – are products currently trading at a disadvantage which, if put right, could have high growth potential

Dogs – are products with growth potential and a low market share

Divestment – moving resources out of the production of particular prouct(s) either by selling off or liquidating a business

Section 12.4 Constraints on marketing strategies

Business stakeholders

All businesses have **stakeholders** - that is, people or other organizations who have an interest in or influence on the actions and performance of business. Stakeholders can, therefore, influence the design of marketing strategies.

Stakeholders in business include:

- **consumers**
- **employees**
- **shareholders**
- **communities**
- **government**

The wants of consumers dictate to businesses what and how to produce, and at what price. Rising consumer demand can benefit business. Falling consumer demand can result in falling sales and profits, and possibly closure of many businesses.

Employees provide their labour and skills to produce the goods and services consumers want and therefore help a business achieve its objectives (see 1.7). However, finding and recruiting the right workers can be expensive (see 14.1). Workers also demand good working conditions and wages. Employee demands for higher wages can increase business costs, and may disrupt production if they take industrial action to secure their demands.

Stakeholders also include people and organizations who provide businesses with the finance they need to start-up and pay for day-to-day business costs, such as rents and business rates, wages and the cost of materials (see 22.2). A business may borrow money from a bank or building society. These financial organizations will want to make sure the businesses they lend to will be successful and run well by their managers so that they will be able to afford to repay their loans. If a business cannot repay a loan, it may have to sell off its stocks of finished goods and materials, machinery and premises to do so. This could mean the business is unable to continue.

Shareholders own limited companies, and they will want to make sure their business managers develop strategies to maximize profits so that they will earn a good return on the money they have invested in their shares. Shareholders will often vote on who they want to manage the businesses they own and how they should be managed.

People who live in local communities and the national community also have an interest in the activities of firms, because they expect businesses to produce their goods and services without damaging the environment and the health and wellbeing of people nearby.

Finally, the Government is an important stakeholder in business because it relies on the activities of businesses to create jobs, incomes and economic prosperity for the country. The Government also has an interest in business because it relies on them to produce the tax revenue with which it pays for the schools, hospitals and other provision of the public sector. The Government also affects business through the policies it uses to control price inflation and employment in the UK economy (see 6.2).

In order to be successful, businesses need to identify who their main stakeholders are and then act in ways which balance the needs of the various stakeholders involved. For example, a local community may want local firms to produce as quietly and with as little pollution as possible, whereas shareholders may wish the firm to spend as little money as possible on pollution control in order to maximize profits. Sometimes business organizations are forced by law to account for the needs of particular stakeholders. For example, the Government has passed a range of anti-pollution laws, in order to prevent businesses from damaging local and global environments, and other laws to protect the rights of consumers.

Iceland to go 100% organic

Supermarket chain Iceland is to switch its entire vegetable range to organic.

The 'bold move' followed a survey by the retailer suggesting three-quarters of customers would prefer organic goods if they were cheaper than current prices.

Iceland is also considering completely organic poultry and fish ranges. The store yesterday pledged its decision would mean no extra cost to the customer.

But it warned shareholders it would need an extra annual investment of around £8 million by December 2001 to back up its pledge.

Metro, 15.6.2000

How consumer choice can affect marketing strategy

Consumers

Changes in consumer demand for goods and services occur for many reasons (see 5.3). The main reasons are changes in the amount of money consumers have available to spend over time, and changes in their attitudes, tastes and wants.

Changes in demand for some goods and services may also occur because of concerns over the way they are produced. For example, demand for organic food products has increased because of health fears over the use of chemicals and drugs in the production of crops and meats. Farmers and food manufacturers may have to change the way they produce food products in order to survive. Similarly, there has been an increase in demand for 'cruelty-free' products such as cosmetics that have not been tested on animals. Firms that continue to test their products on animals may suffer falling sales. The spending decisions of consumers can, therefore, affect the way goods and services are produced and marketed.

More and more business organizations today are adopting a 'customer focus'. This means that they concentrate their activities on attracting and keeping customers, by finding out what consumers want and providing these products, in the amounts they want, when they want them, and at prices they are willing to pay. Customers expect accurate product information, high standards of service and quality and reasonable prices.

Employees

Employees are key stakeholders in business. They depend for their livelihoods on the incomes they earn from work and also upon the prospects available to them for career progression. The majority of successful firms recognize the importance of their staff to the success of a business strategy, and they spend a great deal of time and effort in training and developing their workforce and improving their working conditions so that their employees are happy and motivated (see 15.1).

A business that fails to increase productivity, improve product quality and introduce modern technology is unlikely to stay competitive against rival firms and products. However, some employees will dislike changes in their working arrangements and the introduction of new technology. If workers feel their jobs are threatened by new machinery and changes in working arrangements, they may take actions to disrupt their businesses. This can mean lost output, lost sales, and higher costs for the businesses affected. For example, workers may vote to go on strike so that the business has to close down until the dispute is settled. In this way the interests of employees can conflict with strategy.

Shareholders

Shareholders are the owners of limited companies (see 2.2). Shareholders can be individuals or other organizations, such as pension fund companies and banks. By buying shares in a company they provide that company with finance.

The main concern of shareholders is that their companies pursue successful strategies and make profits. Shareholders will benefit in two ways from profits. First, they will earn dividends each year on their shareholdings. The more shares a person or organization holds and the more profits their company makes, the more dividends they will receive. Secondly, the more successful their company, the more their shares will be worth and the more easily they can sell their shares at a profit.

The owners of large limited companies will not necessarily be the managers of those companies. Instead the owners employ managers, or directors, to run their companies from day to day. This is known as the 'divorce of ownership from control'.

In large companies, owners may only be consulted on very important business issues. However, if the owners do not like the way their directors are running their business or if company sales and profits are falling, they may replace their management teams. Where there are many hundreds or thousands of shareholders in a public limited company, that company will hold annual general meetings at which its shareholders can vote on the management team. Shareholders with voting rights can either attend an AGM or vote by post.

Conflicts between managers and owners of companies can often occur. For example, managers may want to spend more on expanding the businesses they control. Shareholders will want the return on their shares from profits to be as big as possible. Spending more on new premises and machinery will reduce profits, and could land the company in trouble if it expands too much and cannot sell enough to pay its extra costs.

Similarly, the managers of one company may resist being taken over by another because they do not want to lose their jobs. Shareholders in that company may, however, welcome a takeover by another company if it means they can sell their shares at a higher price or will earn more profit.

However, company managers depend on shareholders for their jobs and incomes. In the long run they must make their companies successful and profitable or will risk losing their jobs. Furthermore, an unsuccessful company will not be able to attract more shareholders to raise more finance.

Communities

People can have an influence on business activities even if they are not consumers of the products they provide. Communities are collections of people and will reflect their culture, attitudes and values. Communities can therefore be local, national or international. Developing good public relations is often a key element of many marketing strategies (see 10.3).

For example, do you live near or visit areas close by to factories, offices, shops, farms, mines and quarries, or an airport? If so, you will have an interest in the actions of the businesses that own or use these facilities even if you do not buy their products. You may be concerned because you, your family or your friends use and enjoy these facilities, are employed at them, or work in other businesses that supply them with goods and services and therefore depend on them for employment and incomes. You may also be concerned about the impact these firms have on the environment.

For example, people who live near large airports may be concerned about the increasing number of flights, especially at night, pollution from aviation fuel, and increasing traffic congestion on roads leading to the airports. A decision to expand an airport could also mean knocking down nearby houses and woodland to build new runways and terminals. However, many local people may work at their nearby airport and a decision to expand could create more employment, not just at the airport but in nearby shops and hotels, and on rail and coach services which take people to and from the airport.

Green victory over oil explorers

Whales, dolphins and coral reefs in the North Atlantic will benefit from a victory by environmentalists over the Government and the oil industry yesterday.

A High Court Judge ruled that the Government had failed to apply the European Commission's habitat and species directive in awarding licences for oil exploration in the Atlantic frontier.

Lord Melchett, an executive director of Greenpeace, said that the ruling by Judge Maurice Kay meant that Tony Blair had been forced to put conservation before oil exploration.

Green campaigners said that the victory would limit oil exploration and force the Government to survey marine life between 12 and 200 nautical miles from the coast to identify any vulnerable species and designate sites as special conservation areas.

"The decision is a huge victory for whales, dolphins and coral reefs. The Government should learn from this and review whether it can afford to continue to license new oil exploration given the damage that it will cause to marine life and the global climate" he said.

The Times, 6.11.1999

▲ *The actions of some firms can have widespread impacts of concern to people in many countries*

But even if you do not live near to business activity, the actions of firms can still affect you. For example, when the oil tanker the Exxon Valdez ran aground in Alaska, spilling its cargo of oil into the sea and along the coast, it caused widespread pollution, and many fish, birds and marine animals died as a result. Although few people lived along the coast affected, many people all over the world were upset about the level of pollution caused. Similarly, the burning of fossil fuels such as coal, oil and gas in many production processes can cause widespread air pollution and is thought to have contributed to global warming. That is, the activities of firms can be of interest not just to local communities, but also to national and international communities if they have a large impact on the environment.

People can make their concerns about business activities known to firms by writing to them or refusing to buy their products. For example, in 1991 the Italian fashion giant Benetton was forced to abandon the testing of chemicals on animals after a ten-day boycott of their products by many people all over the world. This was a well-organized international campaign but many campaigns are local and small. For example, local rail users may group together to protest to their local rail company about changes to their services. They may also write to their local councils or members of parliament, organize marches, and place adverts in newspapers.

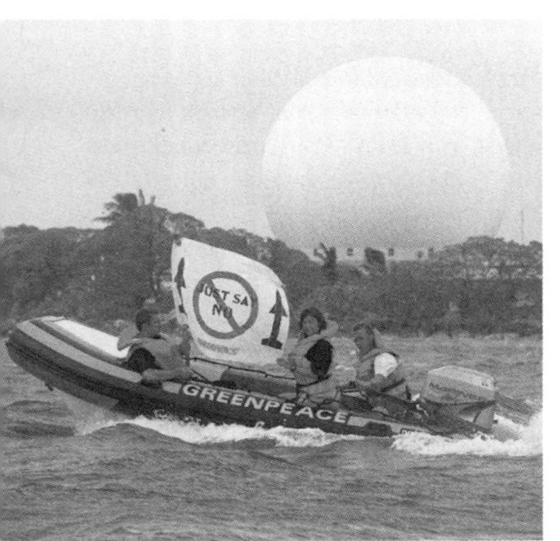

Lobby groups or **pressure groups** are groups of people or organizations with an interest in influencing the actions and decisions of firms and governments. For example, Greenpeace and Friends of the Earth are well-known international lobby groups who aim to protect the environment from pollution, while the World Society for the Protection of Animals campaigns against cruelty to animals.

Lobby groups can be very powerful because they can create a great deal of bad publicity and persuade consumers not to buy goods and services. Bad publicity and the threat of falling sales is often enough to persuade some firms to change their decisions and actions.

Legal constraints

Consumer protection

Because most private sector firms are in business to make profits, some may be tempted to develop marketing that will mislead their customers – for example, by making exaggerated claims about their products to increase sales or by overcharging them. To prevent firms behaving in ways that are against the best interests of their customers, the UK Government has created **consumer protection laws**, and organizations to enforce them, such as local **Trading Standards Offices** and the **Office of Fair Trading** (see below).

UK consumer protection laws make it an offence to:

- supply a good or service which is not in a satisfactory condition or is of poor quality
- give false written or spoken descriptions of goods and services
- mislead consumers about the true price they will pay for a good or service, by excluding any hidden charges, interest charges or value- added tax
- make false statements about price reductions, for example, by suggesting the sale price of a product is 50% off the recommended price when it is not

Key consumer protection laws

Weights and Measures Act 1963

Pre-packaged products must display the weight or volume of the contents. This Act makes it an offence not to disclose this information and to sell short measures. Certain products must be sold in fixed amounts - for example, milk can only be sold in pints or litres.

Trade Descriptions Act 1968

This Act makes it an offence to mislead consumers in advertising. Descriptions of goods and services must be accurate and must not make false claims. The Act makes it illegal to claim that a good is in a 'sale' unless it has been sold at the higher price for 28 consecutive days in the last 6 months. It also makes it an offence to give misleading information on prices. Under this act a number of farmers were prosecuted in 1998 for describing their cattle as coming from BSE-free herds.

Consumer Credit Act 1974

This protects consumers when they buy goods or services on credit, such as hire purchase. For example, credit brokers must obtain a license, provide a copy of any credit agreement to the consumer, always be truthful, and not charge exorbitant interest rates. Advertisements for credit must state the annual percentage rate of interest (APR).

Sale of Goods Act 1979

This has three main parts:

i Goods must be of merchantable quality - that is, not be damaged, broken, or flawed in any way.

ii Goods must be fit for the purpose they were made for, and this must be made known by the seller. For example, if you ask for trousers that can be machine-washed, a shop cannot sell you trousers that can only be dry-cleaned under the pretence they are machine-washable.

iii Goods must fit the description given of them. For example, if a box of matches is said to contain 250 matches, then it should not contain any less.

If any of these conditions are broken, the shopkeeper must either provide a satisfactory replacement, or refund the consumer's money.

Consumer Protection Act 1987

Under this Act it is a criminal offence for producers to supply goods which are unsafe. The Act also lays down rules governing the use of such terms as 'sales price', 'reduced price' and 'bargain offer'. Prices advertised in this way must be genuine reductions.

Food Safety Act 1990

The main purpose of this Act is to ensure that all food and drugs on sale are pure and wholesome. The Act states that all food must be prepared and sold in hygienic conditions. Prepacked foods must display a list of ingredients, and advertising must not mislead consumers about the nature of the food and drugs.

Property Misdescription Act 1991

The main legislation for dealing with false descriptions, the Trade Descriptions Act, has never applied to descriptions of land or property, only to goods. So, for instance, a house described by an estate agent as being in a quiet secluded area when in fact it was on a main road would not have been covered by the Trade Descriptions Act. Because of concerns about the number of inaccurate descriptions applied to property the Director General of Fair Trading recommended the Property Misdescription Act of 1991.

- sell or possess goods for sale which are unsafe
- give customers short weights or measures
- demand payment for goods delivered to customers who did not want them
- prepare and sell food in unhygienic conditions, or with harmful ingredients
- not offer customer refunds, even if they cannot produce a receipt
- restrict competition, for example, if a group of firms agree to all charge the same high price or to work together to force new rivals out of business

Competition policy

Most firms that aim to make a profit will compete with rival producers in an attempt to get more customers and establish a dominant position in the market. As a dominant supplier a firm has more control over the price it can charge to consumers. If a firm, or group of firms acting together, can see off existing competition and establish barriers to entry to new competition it may then abuse this market power by misleading consumers, cutting product quality and raising prices in order to make huge profits. **Competition policy** refers to measures that can be taken by a government to control the behaviour of firms that are thought to be anti-competitive and acting against the public interest. It can involve:

- **Prohibition:** A **monopoly** is a firm that dominates the supply of a particular good or service. It may use this market power to overcharge customers who have no other choice of supplier, and provide poor-quality goods or service. A **pure monopoly** is the only supplier in a market. Monopolies can be banned or forced to break up. For example, in the 1980s large UK beer breweries were forced to sell off many of the pubs they owned. This was because smaller brewers were unable to find pubs that would sell their beer. In this way the large brewers were restricting competition and customer choice.
- **Regulation:** A government can allow a private sector monopoly to continue but pass laws to make sure it acts in the public interest. For example, in the UK the Strategic Rail Authority regulates the behaviour of passenger train operating companies, and the Office of Gas and Electricity Markets (Ofgem) regulates the prices and services of gas and electricity supply companies.
- **Impose fines:** Fines can be imposed on firms who are thought to be abusing their market power and overcharging consumers.

Before any of these actions are taken it is important for a government to investigate each case of anti-competitive behaviour and then decide which action is appropriate. A monopoly need not necessarily be anti-competitive and bad for consumers.

For example, in 1976 Rank Xerox had a virtual monopoly in the supply of photocopiers with 96% of all sales in the UK. For every £1 it invested in its operations it made an extra 40 pence in profit. Rank Xerox was investigated by the UK Government but was found to be acting in the interests of consumers. This is because Rank Xerox was the first firm to develop and mass produce photocopiers. Its high profits were a reward for the risk the company had taken by investing a huge amount of money in a revolutionary product. Similarly, recent mergers between large UK brewers like Bass and Carlsberg-Tetley were allowed to go ahead because the new larger firms will be able to compete more effectively against huge overseas brewers selling their beers into the UK, and move into rapidly growing markets for beer in Asia and South America.

Competition policy in the UK is put into practice by a number of key organizations:

- **The Office of Fair Trading:** This important office was created by the Fair Trading Act of 1973. It is a Government Agency that watches and investigates the conduct of trade and protects the consumer against unfair or restrictive practices. The Office of Fair Trading (OFT) is run by the Director General of Fair Trading (DGFT).

  The OFT collects information on, and makes surveys of, all types of trading practices used by firms. If the information reveals anti-competitive behaviour the DGFT has the power to fine those firms responsible up to 10% of their annual sales revenues.

- **The Competition Commission:** The Competition Commission was set up by the **Competition Act 1998.** It came into force in March 2000 and took over the functions of the previous competition watchdog (the Monopolies and Mergers Commission) and Fair Trading Act inquiries into mergers and monopolies. It has the ability to ban behaviour which damages the interests of consumers or which abuses monopoly power.

  Individuals and firms who are found guilty of anti-competitive behaviour by the DGFT can appeal to the Competition Commission and seek damages in the law courts if they believe that their reputation has been unfairly damaged or that they have been unfairly fined.

- **Industry regulators:** Following the privatizations of British Telecom, British Gas, the Electricity Area Boards, British Rail and the Regional Water Authorities in the UK, the Government created a number of industry regulators. These organizations regulate prices and service quality in these industries because the private sector firms have considerable regional and national market power over the supply of their products. There are few substitutes for their services for consumers. As more competition is introduced into these industries regulation can be reduced.

Industry regulator		Regulate...
OfTel	Office of Telecommunications	Telecommunications industry
OfWat	Office of Water Regulation	Water supply
Ofgem	Office of Gas and Electricity Markets	Gas and electricity generation and supply
ORR	Office of the Rail Regulator	Railtrack plc
SRA	Strategic Rail Authority	Passenger rail services

- **The European Commission:** The European Commission also has the power to investigate and take action against companies thought to be operating anti-competitive practices in more than one European Union member country (see 7.3).

Marketing standards and codes of practice

Keen to assure consumers of their concern for product quality and ethical marketing, some industries have drawn up voluntary codes of practice which member firms are encouraged to follow. In many ways these are useful additions to the marketing strategies of firms.

▼ Trademarks which give the consumer quality assurance

- **British Standards Institution (BSI):** The BSI sets quality and safety standards for a wide range of products. Products meeting the BSI standards are awarded the **kitemark** to indicate that they have reached the necessary standards. Products awarded the kitemark will have a competitive advantage over rival products which fail to display the symbol to the consumer.
- **Professional and trade associations:** Members of trades often set up professional associations in order to protect their interests and improve their reputation with consumers. Examples include the Federation of Master Builders and Association of British Travel Agents (ABTA). These organizations usually specify a code of practice governing the behaviour of members, and consumers can appeal to the associations if they feel that a particular code of practice has been breached.
- **Independent Television Commission (ITC):** The ITC regulates advertisements appearing on television and has its own Code of Advertising Standards and Practice. Certain products and services, including cigarettes, spirits, private investigation agencies, and gambling, may not be advertised on TV. There are also strict rules about advertising aimed at children and about the use of child actors or models in adverts.
- **Advertising Standards Authority (ASA):** The ASA was set up in 1962 to monitor the standard of advertisements in the UK. It covers all advertisements in newspapers, magazines, posters, direct marketing, sales promotions, cinema, videos, and Teletext.

  The ASA safeguards the consumer by ensuring that the rules contained in the **British Code of Advertising Practice** are followed by any organization that prepares and publishes advertisements.

The essence of good advertising

The British Code of Advertising Practice states that all advertisements should be:

- Legal, decent, honest and truthful
- Prepared with a sense of responsibility to the consumer and to society
- In line with the principles of fair competition generally accepted in business

As well as receiving and investigating complaints from consumers, the ASA advises advertisers, agencies, and publishers how to avoid misleading advertising. If an advertisement is found to be misleading or offensive, the ASA will act to have it changed or withdrawn. Failure to comply with its rulings may lead to adverse publicity in the ASA's monthly report of judgements.

The work of the ASA is financed by a levy of 0.1% on UK advertising expenditures. One criticism, therefore, of the ASA is that it is funded by the very people it is attempting to police, namely the advertising industry.

Advertising on radio is regulated by the **Radio Authority**.

Portfolio Activity 12.5 

Coca-Cola raided by European Union officials

Officials from the European Commission have raided Coca-Cola offices in three countries in an attempt to establish whether the soft drinks group has violated competition rules, it emerged last night.

Commission officials seized internal company documents from Coca-Cola offices in Germany, Austria and Denmark on Tuesday in a series of dawn raids. Authorities also took records from three Coca-Cola bottlers, one of which is based in London.

A Coca-Cola spokesperson said "We can confirm that the European Commission made unannounced visits to several of our offices and the offices of some of our bottling partners. Their purpose was to review internal files relating to commercial practices with retailers and other customers".

The Commission is said to be concerned that Coke has been abusing its dominant position by offering retailers incentives to increase sales volumes, forcing them to stock the full range of Coca-Cola drinks and to stop selling competitors' products.

Officials launched the raids after a tip-off, although the Commission refused to confirm reports that Coca-Cola's rivals had launched formal complaints about the soft drinks group's commercial practices. Commission competition investigations are frequently triggered by complaints from rivals.

Coca-Cola was last night adamant that it had done nothing wrong. The company said "We believe we are within full compliance of all competition laws and regulations and we are co-operating fully with the authorities".

If the company is found to have abused its dominant position, it could be fined as much as 10 percent of its European turnover.

The Times, 10.7.1999

Volvo admits rigging prices

Volvo has admitted rigging the prices of cars in Britain by restricting the level of discounts offered to customers. An investigation by the Office of Fair Trading (OFT) found that dealers were threatened with loss of bonuses if they offered discounts beyond certain levels.

The secret price-fixing agreement between March 1995 and early 1996 was condemned as a "disgraceful case" by the Director General of the OFT. He said "This demonstrates a blatant disregard for UK law and an indifference to the exploitation of customers'.

The OFT has accepted an undertaking from Volvo Cars UK, now a subsidiary of Ford, that it will not support price-fixing cartels. Volvo said yesterday that the price-fixing was not a company policy but that a limited number of staff had acted against company policy by indicating support for dealer pricing agreements.

The Times, 27.7.1999

1. In both cases, describe why the two companies were acting against 'the public interest' and how they were being 'anti-competitive'.
2. What else could be done by governments, in addition to those actions reported in the articles, to control the anti-competitive behaviour of the two organizations?

Key words:

Stakeholders – people or organizations that have an interest in or are able to influence business decisions and actions

Pressure groups – groups of people or organizations who groups of people or organizations who seek to influence the actions and decisions of firms and governments

Competition policy – measures taken by government to control the behaviour of firms that are thought to be anti-competitive and acting against the public interest

Competition Commission – the UK competition authority. It has the task of implementing UK competition policy and has the power to ban behaviour which damages the interests of consumers or which abuses monopoly power

Monopoly – a producer with a commanding position over the market supply of a particular good or service. A pure monopoly will supply 100% of a particular market

Advertising Standards Authority – an independent body that monitors the standard of advertisements in the UK and attempts to enforce the British Code of Advertising Practice

Key Activity

1. **Produce a marketing strategy for a new or existing product**. Your strategy will need to include evidence and information about
   - how the strategy is based on the principles of marketing
   - how you have used sources of primary and secondary marketing information
   - how you have analysed the impact of the external environment on your marketing decisions
   - how you analysed the marketing context and decided on an appropriate strategy
   - how you developed a coherent mix of strategies (product, price, promotions, place, customer service) to meet consumer needs

2. **Write up your marketing strategy in a detailed report**. Use a word processor and graphics package to design and produce your report. Structure the chapters of your report as follows:

   The product: Technical and design information about your chosen product. This can be an existing good or service, or a new one you have designed yourself. Your chosen product can be something as simple as a new local car-cleaning or taxi service, or as sophisticated as a new computer game, a new European service introduced by a low-cost airline, or a new on-line retail service with international appeal.

   For existing products, or ones similar to your new product, try to find out who produces them, where they are produced, their production costs, how they are promoted, priced and distributed, and the service features the different producers offer their customers.

   Market research: This should contain researched information about the existing or likely market for your product, i.e. the existing or potential consumers of your product, the features and promotions they like and respond to, where they buy or would like to buy, the prices they want or expect to pay, the customer service features they require, who are your business rivals and how are they likely to react to your marketing strategy.

   Explain why you need market information and the sources you will use to obtain it. These should be primary and secondary sources. For example, you can design a questionnaire to interview existing or potential consumers of your chosen product. Data you collect can be presented in graphs. For example, you could use bar or pie charts to show the percentage of people interviewed who would be willing to pay different prices for your chosen product, or who liked or disliked proposed new design or promotional features.

   Analysing the market: What are your marketing aims? Present an analysis of the business environment that will affect the design and success of your marketing strategy. This should be based on information you have researched about the market for your product, including what consumers want, the marketing strategies and likely actions of business rivals, and external constraints such as industry codes of practice and consumer protection laws. Use PESTLE or SWOT models to present this information.

   Customer service: The customer service features required to make your marketing strategy effective and close sales.

   For each of the elements of your chosen marketing strategy (product features, price, advertising and promotions, distribution, customer service) you must explain in full the reasons for your choices based on your analysis of the market and external business environment.

3 Prepare and give a talk with slides to present your marketing strategy to your class group. Your presentation will need to show how your marketing strategy will work effectively.

Useful references

Advertising Standards Authority (*www.asa.org.uk*)
2 Torrington Place, London WC1E 7HW

British Standards Institution (*www.bsi-global.com*)
389 Chiswick High Road, London W4 4AL

Competition Commission (*www.Competition-Commission.org.uk*)
New Court, Carey Street, London WC2A 2JT

Office of Fair Trading (*www.oft.gov.uk*)
Fleetbank House, 2–6 Salisbury Square, London EC4V 8JX

Test your knowledge

1 Which of the following are **not** examples of external environmental influences on a business?

- **A** Government economic policy
- **B** Organization structure
- **C** New competition
- **D** Changes in employment law

Questions 2–4 share the following answer options:

- **A** Horizontal diversification
- **B** Conglomerate diversification
- **C** Vertical diversification
- **D** Divestment

Which of the above strategies do the following describe?

2 A coffee supplier opens a chain of coffee shops

3 A bank takes over ownership of a supermarket chain

4 A highly diversified manufacturer sells off its car parts business

Questions 5–7 share the following answer options:

- **A** Consolidation
- **B** Market development
- **C** Market penetration
- **D** Diversification

Which of the above marketing strategies suggested by the Ansoff matrix do the following describe?

5 A UK retail chain opens outlets overseas

6 A Japanese car manufacturer located in Europe seeks to maintain its share of the European car market

7 The Airbus Integrated Company of Europe plans to outsell the US aircraft manufacturer Boeing in the global market for passenger jets

Questions 8–10 share the following answer options:

- **A** Dogs
- **B** Stars
- **C** Cash cows
- **D** Question marks

Which of the following products or businesses are described by the Boston matrix titles above?

8 A product with a high market share but little further growth potential

9 A business which an organization should divest from

10 A product that is currently underperforming expectations but could, with some further development, grow market share significantly

Questions 11–13 share the following answer options:

- **A** Consumers Protection Act
- **B** Trade Descriptions Act
- **C** Sale of Goods and Services Act
- **D** Trademark Act

Which of the above laws do the following promotions break?

11 An advert which claims a new skin cream will make people look 10 years younger

12 A leaflet advertising a competition to win a car. The advert displays a Porsche but the prize is a Volvo.

13 A shop sign that reads '50% off all prices' but only applies to cash sales

14 **a** What is a marketing strategy?

b Describe and contrast PESTLE and SWOT analysis. How can they help a business to develop marketing strategies?

c Describe the work of the Advertising Standards Authority and how it may constrain the choice of marketing strategy by a business.

15 Explain, using diagrams, the Ansoff matrix and Boston matrix. Using examples, explain how these tools can be used to help a business develop and choose between different marketing strategies.

Human Resources

unit 4

About this unit

People with the skills and know-how that businesses need are called human resources. If businesses are to achieve their objectives, they must plan their human resources function so they have the right number of employees with the right kinds of qualifications and training to meet the needs of the business. A successful business is one that identifies the human resources it needs to be successful, and is then able to recruit, retain and manage these key resources.

You may have part-time working experience and will know first-hand how important it is for a business to keep employees motivated in work, to monitor their performance and to help them continually develop through additional training to meet the changing needs of the business in a competitive environment.

In this unit you will look at how businesses can plan and manage their human resources.

chapter 13 Human Resources Planning

This chapter looks at how businesses can plan for and manage their human resource requirement.

What you need to learn

Businesses have to plan carefully to ensure they have the right number of suitable employees for their needs. To do this they need a good understanding of the **labour market** in the areas where they operate. You need to be able to consider the effects of the following labour market factors for **human resources planning**:

- **availability of labour**
- **local employment trends**
- **local skills shortages**
- **competition for employees**

Human resources planning also involves looking at how labour is organized within the business. You need to understand why businesses must take account of factors when making decisions about their internal staffing. The factors include:

- **labour turnover**
- **sickness and accident rates**
- **age, skills and training**
- **succession**

You need to know how to use statistics to analyse these factors where appropriate.

In the event of a dispute between employers and employees, both parties may refer for assistance to the **Advisory, Conciliation and Arbitration Service (ACAS)**, to **Employment Tribunals**, the law courts or **European Court of Justice**, or to **Trade Unions** and **Employer's Associations.**

Section **13.1**

Managing human resources

What is human resourcing?

The most valuable resource in any business organization is its people, or **human resources**. There is a direct relationship between the quality of the workforce and business success.

The purpose of **Human Resource Management (HRM)** is to ensure that the employees of an organization are used and developed in such a way that the employer obtains the greatest possible benefit from their abilities. In order to do this, human resource managers must give careful thought to the needs of their employees and the financial and psychological rewards that they receive from their work. The human resource manager must, therefore, work closely with other managers in other departments, including production, marketing, sales, finance, etc.

Human resources are much more difficult to manage than natural or man-made resources, partly because conflicts can occur between the aims of the organization and those of their employees, and partly because there is increasingly a desire among employees to share in decision-making about their working environment.

The role and responsibilities of a Human Resources Department

Within a small business, responsibility for human resource management will rest with the owners. Most medium-to-large organizations, however, will have a whole specialist division of employees devoted to staff matters and welfare. It is the role of the **Human Resources Department** (or **Personnel** Department) to manage human resources within an organization (see 4.2).

The functions of a Human Resources Department are many, including:

- Forecasting future manpower and skill needs in the business
- Recruitment and selection of staff with the right skills and experience for the job
- Providing employment advice and information
- Notifying terms and conditions of employment to new employees
- Managing changes in the terms and conditions of existing workers, for example, due to the introduction of new technology, relocation, or internal reorganization
- Developing and promoting induction courses and training for employees
- Handling staff promotions and transfers
- Developing and administering staff appraisal procedures
- Developing and administering grievance procedures to handle employee complaints
- Handling employee discipline and dismissal
- Implementing non-discriminatory legislation
- Implementing health and safety procedures

▼ Recruitment

▼ Consultation

▼ Training

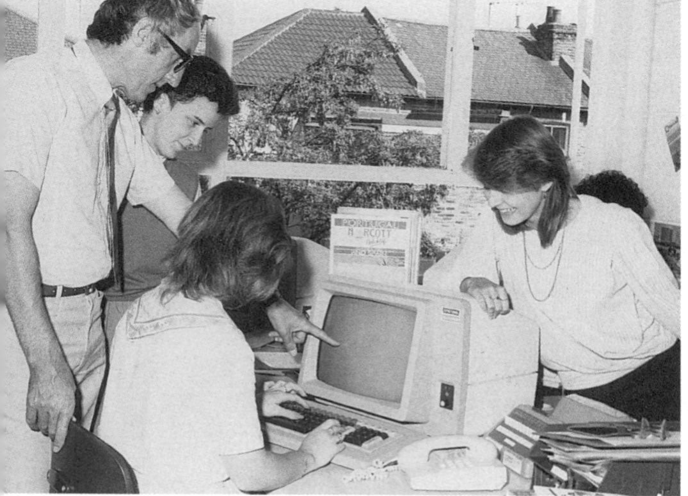

- Administering pay, non-financial rewards, and conditions of service, such as holiday entitlements and maternity pay
- Developing good industrial relations and employee consultation
- Taking part in negotiations with employees on pay and conditions and other aspects of their employment

In general, therefore, the human resources function in a business concerns:

- planning for and meeting the changing human resources requirement of the business so that it is able to achieve its objectives
- meeting legal rights and responsibilities the business has towards its employees and managing disputes when they occur
- motivating employees and managing their performance

All of these functions tend to be reinforcing: employees who lack motivation, are poorly trained or rarely consulted, and/or who perceive health risks due to poor environmental management at work, are unlikely to work as effectively as they could towards the achievement of organizational goals.

If employers are to get the best from their employees, they must consider their responsibilities to their staff. Some of these responsibilities are required legally, such as good health and safety procedures (see 15.2). Others are ethical and are part of being a good employer, such as giving employment advice and information, handling discipline and grievances in a fair and sympathetic manner, and consulting on a regular basis with employees or their representatives on matters of mutual concern.

The key function of human resource planning is examined in this chapter, while the next chapter looks at how businesses recruit and select employees to meet their resource requirements.

Chapter 15 considers how organizations can motivate, monitor, and manage the performance of their employees. The legal rights and responsibilities of employers appear in all three chapters in this unit because the way the human resource function is carried out in business is governed so much by them.

Key words:

Human Resource Management (HRM) - the use and development of employees in an organization in the most productive way in order to meet the goals of the organization

Section 13.2 Planning human resources

What is human resources planning?

Human resources planning involves:

- forecasting the type and number of employees an organization will require in the future to continue to meet business objectives or to meet new objectives
- identifying sources of labour with the right skills and qualifications the business needs
- planning the recruitment and selection of employees to meet the human resources requirement

Identifying and planning for future human resource requirements is extremely important in business. Imagine if the Police did not plan their resource requirements for the football season. Many matches would be under-policed. Or imagine a hospital that did not plan to hire more staff to work in a new hospital wing. There would not be enough doctors and nurses to care for the patients admitted to the new wing.

Similarly, suppose a firm installs new machinery to expand production but has no idea how many more workers it requires, or the skills they need to operate the new equipment. The machinery will remain idle until the firm can hire more employees. However, if it hires more employees than it actually needs wage costs will be higher than they need to be. Or it may hire too few employees and the workforce will be overstretched which may eventually cause ill-feeling, demotivate the employees and result in a costly dispute (see 13.3).

To create a plan for human resources an organization will need a great deal of data and other information on its existing workforce from internal sources and on the availability of skilled labour locally from external sources.

Statistical techniques can be used to help human resources planning but data collection and analysis can be very time consuming and expensive, and may still not yield robust results. Forecasting will be always be subject to uncertainty.

Internal sources of information

Over time an organization will collect a great deal of information on its employees. This will usually include:

- the total workforce differentiated by grade/position, job role, age, skills, qualifications, and time with the organization
- the number of employees known to be leaving, for example, due to resignation or retirement
- the number of new employees about to join the organization
- the average length of time employees stay with the organization, and the reasons why they leave
- the average time taken off by employees due to sickness, ill health, maternity, bereavement and other factors

Calculating labour turnover

This information can be used to calculate the rate of **labour turnover**. This is rate at which existing employees tend to leave the organization. If the rate of labour turnover increases over time it means employees are on average spending less time in employment with the organization before they leave.

For example, consider the staff profiles for three organizations in Figure 13.1.

▼ *Figure 13.1: Staff profiles for three organizations*

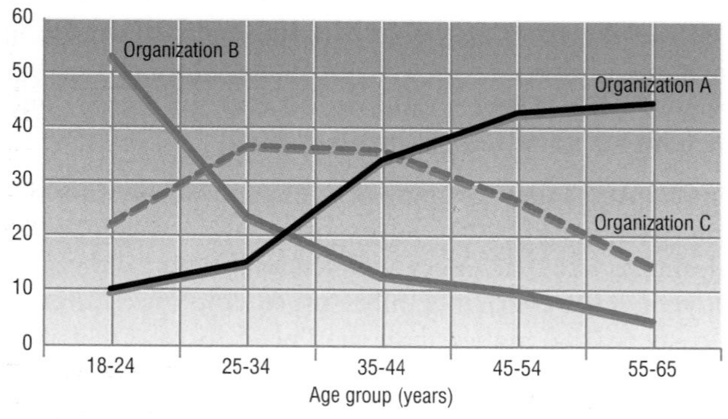

The profile for organization A suggests most employees have been with the organization for many years. Labour turnover is very low. This is not necessarily a good thing. Perhaps employees at organization A find the work too easy, or are paid too generously for what they do.

Some degree of labour turnover is desirable because it brings in people with new ideas and skills. Organization A has an ageing workforce. They may be set in their ways which means the organization may find the introduction of new working methods and equipment will meet with resistance. The organization will also face significant redundancy costs if it has to shed labour because so many of its employees have been with there for so long.

In contrast, labour turnover is relatively high at organization B. The 'average' employee has only been with the organization for 15 months. However, organization B does have a relatively youthful workforce, and is clearly able to attract new recruits. However, younger workers do tend to change job more frequently than older employees, and will not have the experience or commitment to the organization that older workers may have.

Organization B will have to consider why its employees tend to move on relatively quickly and take action, as appropriate, if something is at fault. For example, is motivation and staff morale low? Are pay levels and working conditions in rival organizations better? Are they recruiting the right employees in the first place? Improving pay and other working conditions relative to other firms can help attract new employees, motivate existing employees and lower turnover and absenteeism (see 15.2).

Calculating the rate of labour turnover

Imagine there are 200 employees in a business. Some are new employees that have only been with the business a few months, but most employees have been with the business for between 2 and 7 years. A few employees have been employed by the business for over 20 years. However, the average length of stay for any employee is 5 years. The rate of labour turnover is, therefore, 200/5 = 40. That is, on average 40 employees may need to be replaced each year to keep the workforce constant at 200 employees.

If labour turnover increased it would be reflected in a fall in the average length of stay by an employee in the business. For example, if the average length of stay fell to 4 years then the turnover rate would have risen to 200/4 = 50, an increase of 25%.

An organization can track changes in the rate of labour turnover over time by calculating a stability index. In the example above the index will rise from 100 to 125. Variations in labour turnover, especially when it is increasing, suggests instability and may reflect problems in the workplace; demotivated staff, poor recruitment, inadequate pay and benefit levels, low levels of training, lack of career opportunities, etc. An organization will need to investigate the causes and take actions to reduce turnover to an acceptable and stable level.

A high level of labour turnover could impose significant costs on organization B. These could include:

- significant costs devoted to increased recruitment and selection activity
- overtime payments to existing employees who work extra hours to cover vacant posts
- higher costs associated with potentially lower levels of output and poorer quality work from new inexperienced employees
- training and development costs for the new, inexperienced employees
- making incentive payments linked to length of stay to encourage employees to stay longer with the organization

However, it is possible that organization B may not be concerned with high labour turnover. The jobs may not require skilled workers or much training. Costs can be kept low because employees tend to leave or are sacked before they become entitled under law to redundancy pay, unfair dismissal protection, maternity or sick pay, and other employment benefits.

Organization C may have got it just about right. Labour turnover is neither too high nor too low. It retains a core of experienced existing workers who have been in active employment for some years, many with organization C for some time, and is able to recruit younger workers into junior and apprenticeship positions. Some may end up staying with the organization for a relatively long time so that the organization will not lose the investment it has made in their training and development.

Absenteeism

Workplace accidents and ill-health imposes significant costs on business in terms of lost output and revenues, sick pay and increased staff costs to provide cover for absent employees (see Portfolio Activity 1.5).

Worryingly, employee sickness and health problems may be a direct result of poor working conditions in the workplace, and injuries may be caused from inadequate training with potentially dangerous equipment and a lack of protective clothing. Constant pressure on employees to increase their performance can cause high levels of stress.

However, absenteeism among employees can be a symptom of factors other than illness or injury. Domestic problems and child care commitments may prevent employees from coming into work. Rail strikes can also cause absence if employees have no other means of getting to and from their place of work. But of more concern to an organization will be absenteeism due to low morale among demotivated staff.

Take up your sick bed and work

Absenteeism is costing the nation's businesses £10bn a year. As a result, some companies are taking a greater interest when their employees call in ill.

Unless you happen to work for a pharmacist, it's a safe bet that your boss will be delighted to see the end of the flu epidemic. After fielding countless sniffling phone calls from staff croaking that they really, honestly, can't make it in to the office, employers are looking forward to having a full complement of staff once again.

They shouldn't get excited too soon, however. Latest reports reveal that absenteeism is now one of the biggest problems facing the British workplace - whether or not we're at the height of the flu season. In a study by Gee Publishing, 40% of the 311 companies polled said that absence levels had risen during the previous three years, and one in five said absence was a major problem. In response, many companies are putting in place new and often controversial measures to persuade their employees to come to work.

It's not difficult to see why employers are concerned about staff taking sickies. The financial consequences are severe - absenteeism can cost a company 3% of its payroll, a national total of more than £10bn a year, according to the CBI. To persuade staff to make that little bit more effort to get into work, the Institute of Personnel and Development (IPD) has found that many employers are making sweeping changes in their procedure for employees calling in sick, as well as in the content of their return-to-work interviews. Some organizations are even providing a figure for the number of 'acceptable' days' absence, which raises the rather alarming prospect of workers having to drag themselves out of their wheelchairs once they have exceeded their monthly backache quota.

The Guardian, 2.8.2000

Rising levels of absenteeism over time need to be investigated. Temporary increases may occur for short periods of time due to flu and other contagious illnesses. However, a steady increase in absentee levels may reflect more serious staff problems that need to be put right.

A survey of employees in spring 1999 found that 5% of women and 3.8% of men had been absent from work for at least one day in the week preceding the survey. These findings have remained fairly steady over time. However, sickness absence rates do tend to follow a seasonal pattern, with rates being higher during winter months.

Investigating labour market conditions

Forecasting labour and skills requirements

The rate of labour turnover and levels of absenteeism, can be calculated for employees in different age groups in different grades, job roles, and with different skills.

A high level of turnover among younger, inexperienced employees and especially those in part-time or temporary jobs, may be expected and acceptable. However, an organization will be concerned if the turnover of its core employees - those with highly valued skills including senior managers - is high or rising.

In turn, an organization will use this information to project:

- the number of posts that are likely to become vacant over time, by grade/position, job role
- the types and levels of skills the organization will need to replace those of employees who will leave
- the additional number of employees that will be required simply to provide cover during periods of staff sickness and other absences

The human resources function will then need to investigate how it can best meet the labour and skill requirements it has identified, and consider what problems it may have in doing so. This requires an examination of employment trends and the availability of labour with the right skills from external information sources detailing national and local labour markets. For example, it may be able to identify that the skills it requires are in short supply compared with a high demand for them. It may, therefore, need to offer very generous pay and benefits packages to attract employees with these skills away from rival firms, and to their existing employees to stop them leaving.

What is the labour market?

The labour market consists of all those people willing and able to supply themselves for work and all those organizations willing and able to employ them. Demand and supply conditions in the labour market will determine the price of labour (i.e. wage and salary levels) and quantity of labour employed, just like demand and supply conditions in goods markets determine the price of those goods and the amount sold (see 5.3).

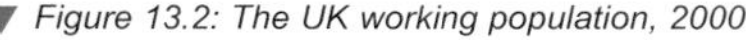
Figure 13.2: The UK working population, 2000

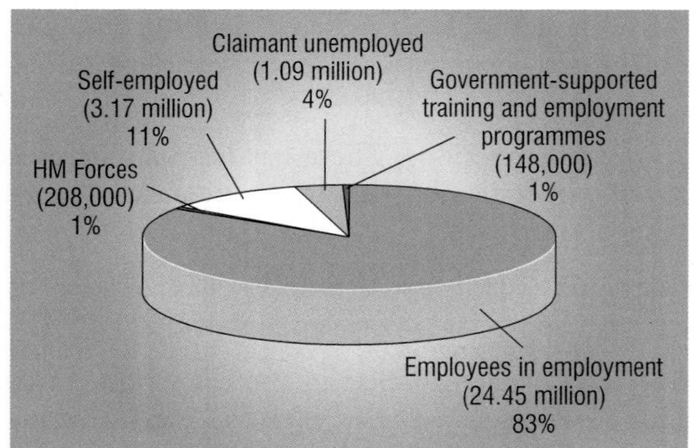

Labour Market Trends, September 2000

At a national level the total supply of labour will consist of the total labour force or **working population.** The working population in the UK includes:

- employees in employment
- the self-employed
- claimant unemployed
- HM forces
- people on government-supported training and employment programmes

In early 2000 the working population in the UK was just over 29 million, of whom 27.7 million were in employment - the highest level since records began in 1959. This compares with a working population of 26.6 million in 1979. This growth in the total labour supply in the UK is the result of an increase in the number of people over 16 years of age and a rise in economic activity among women.

The combined effect of low birth rates and low death rates in the UK has been to increase the proportion of over-16-year-olds in the total UK population (around 60 million people in 2000). The increase in the birth rate during the early 1960s fed through to the working population in the 1980s as many of those people joined the labour force for the first time after finishing school and college.

The working population has also increased in the UK because more females are economically active. This means they are in employment or actively seeking employment. The **economic activity rate**, also known as the **participation rate**, expresses the working population as a percentage of the total resident population of working age. In 1999, the participation rate in the UK was 63%. That is, 63 out of every 100 adults were participating in the total labour force.

▼ *Figure 13.3: Economic activity rates: by gender and age*

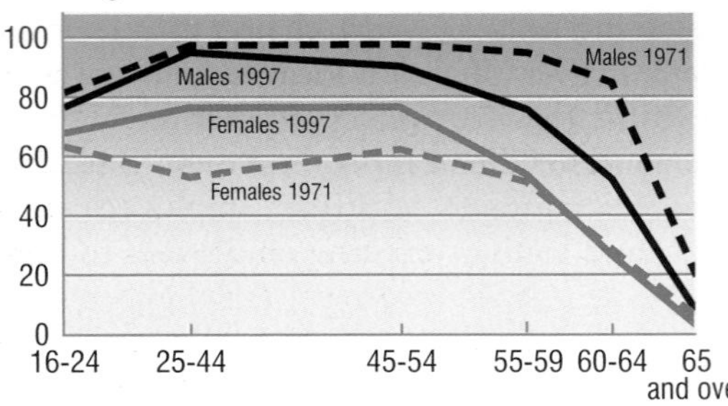

Social Trends, 1999

In 1971, just over half of women in the 25-to-44 age group were economically active. This increased to over 75% by 1997. At the same time, participation by males has been falling. In 1971, 98% of men aged 45 to 54 were economically active; by 1997 this had fallen to 91% (see Figure 13.3).

Overall, participation in the labour force by adult females has increased from 43% in 1971 to 55% in 2000 while economic activity among adult males has fallen from 79% to around 72%. Projections for the UK indicate a further narrowing of participation rates by gender. In 2011 it is estimated that 58% of all women will be economically active, compared with 70% of all men.

▼ *Attitudes towards women going to work have changed significantly.*

Why have female participation rates increased?

The reasons for the dramatic rise in participation rates among females are complex, but a number of key factors can be identified:

- **Changes in social attitudes** - for example, the trend towards later marriage, falling birth rates, and the increasing emancipation of women from a traditional domestic role. The aspirations of many households to increase their income and wealth have also, in part, been realized by wives going out to work.
- **Changes in the availability of jobs.** There has been an increase in the availability of part-time jobs, which has encouraged more women to join the labour force.
- **Legislation concerning equal opportunities** has helped to improve the pay and conditions of women at work (see 15.2).

The overall impact of rising female participation in the UK labour force and falling male participation rates on the sex distribution of the working population has been significant. In 1950, women made up less than a third of the working population. By 2000, they accounted for over 55% of the total labour supply.

According to official figures, occupations in which most women work are also those containing the most part-time workers: clerical and secretarial, childcare and catering, personal services, and sales. This would appear to support the view that women are attracted to occupations which can offer them flexibility to meet domestic commitments. There are also occupations in which more women work than men. These include health associate professionals (nurses, midwives, etc.) and teachers.

Unemployment

People who are unemployed are part of the available labour supply. The **claimant count** records the number of people claiming unemployment-related benefits each month. These are currently the Jobseeker's Allowance (JSA) and National Insurance Credits claimed at Employment Service local offices.

▼ *Figure 13.4: Claimant unemployment, UK 1970–2000*

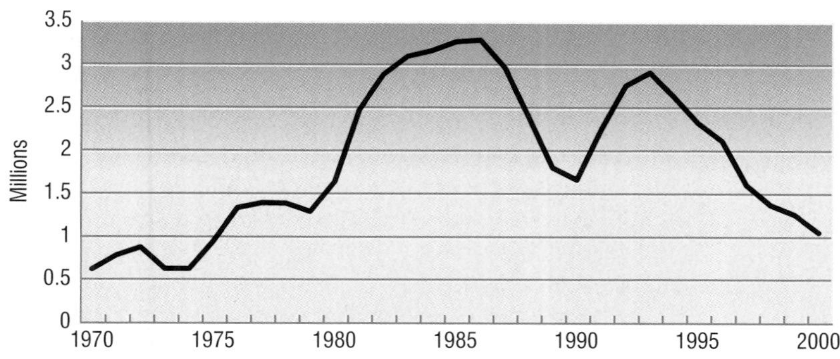

Economic Trends, Annual Supplement 2000

During the 1950s and 1960s, the level of unemployment in the UK was relatively low and stable, fluctuating between a low of 280,000 in 1951 and a peak of 612,000 employees in 1963. However, the level of unemployment increased steadily throughout the 1970s and 1980s and by 1986 had peaked at 3.3 million, or 11.1% of the total workforce (see Figure 13.4). The level of unemployment then fell back but increased again to almost 3 million people during the economic recession in 1993. Unemployment has fallen every year since and by the middle of 2000 was under 1.1 million, or just 3.7% of the working population.

There will always be some level of unemployment in the economy as people move between jobs, or become temporarily unemployed due to seasonal variations in labour demand, for example, in the tourist industry. However, the significant increase in the level and variation in unemployment between the early 1960s and 1990s is argued to be the result of two major factors: economic recession and industrial change.

▼ *Table 13.1: UK employees in employment: by sex and industry*

Employees in employment: by sex and industry
United Kingdom — **Thousands**

	1971	1981	1989	1993	1999
All industries	22,139	21,892	22,661	21,613	23,913
of which					
Males	13,726	13,487	11,992	10,992	12,199
Females	8,413	9,686	10,668	10,651	11,723
Manufacturing	8,065	7,253	5,187	3,913	3,984
Services	11,627	13,580	15,627	16,219	18,304
Other	2,447	2,340	1,847	1,481	1,625
Employees in employment					
Agriculture, forestry and fishing	450	363	330	326	317
Mining and quarrying; energy and water supply	2,080	1,649	1,176	593	287
Manufacturing of metal goods, equipment, vehicles, etc.	3,709	2,923	2,351	1,878	1,796
Other manufacturing	3,074	2,360	2,125	2,035	2,188
Construction	1,198	1,130	1,082	865	1,092
Wholesale and retail trade; catering and repairs	3,686	4,172	4,730	4,747	4,086
Transport and communication	1,556	1,425	1,362	1,317	1,462
Banking, finance, insurance, etc	1,336	1,739	2,627	975	1,036
Other services	5,049	6,197	6,908	8,998	11,720

Annual Abstract of Statistics, 1982, 1990, 1994, 2000

- **Economic recession:** During the early 1980s and early 1990s the UK economy suffered from a series of very severe and prolonged recessions. A recession is characterized by falling levels of demand for many goods and services, rising unemployment and falling national income. Falling consumer, business and/or government spending on goods and services at home or from overseas will reduce sales and firms will tend to cut back production. During a recession, therefore, unemployment tends to increase rapidly and remain high as firms cut their existing workforces and level of new recruitment.
- **Industrial change:** Employment in service industries has grown significantly while employment in manufacturing has declined (see 5.7). Between 1971 and 1999 almost 4 million jobs were lost from UK manufacturing industries. Just under half of these jobs were lost during the economic recession of the early 1980s. Over the same period the proportion of total value of UK output produced by manufacturing industries fell from 41% to around 20%. In 1999 just under 4 million people were employed in UK manufacturing, a figure which had remained fairly steady since 1995. In contrast, the service sector in the UK employed around 18 million people in 1999 (75% of all employees) and produced 70% of the value of UK total output.

Portfolio Activity 13.1 

Study the data on employees in employment in Table 13.1.

1. Describe the trends in (a) male and female employment, and (b) employment in the manufacturing and service sectors.
2. Draw line graphs, if possible using a computer spreadsheet, to illustrate the trends you have described in Question 1.
3. **(a)** Identify from the table an industry in each of the following industrial sectors (see also 5.7 for help).
   - The primary sector
   - The secondary sector
   - The tertiary sector

   (b) Calculate the change in the numbers employed in each industry between 1971 and 1999.

   (c) Investigate the reasons for the change in the numbers employed in each industry.

   (d) How is the distribution of employment between the three main industrial sectors likely to change in the future? Give reasons to support your forecast.
4. Identify an industry that is a major employer in your area. What changes have taken place in the numbers employed locally in this industry? How does this change compare with patterns of employment in the industry nationally?

▼ *Figure 13.5: Claimant count rate: by sub-region, March 2000*

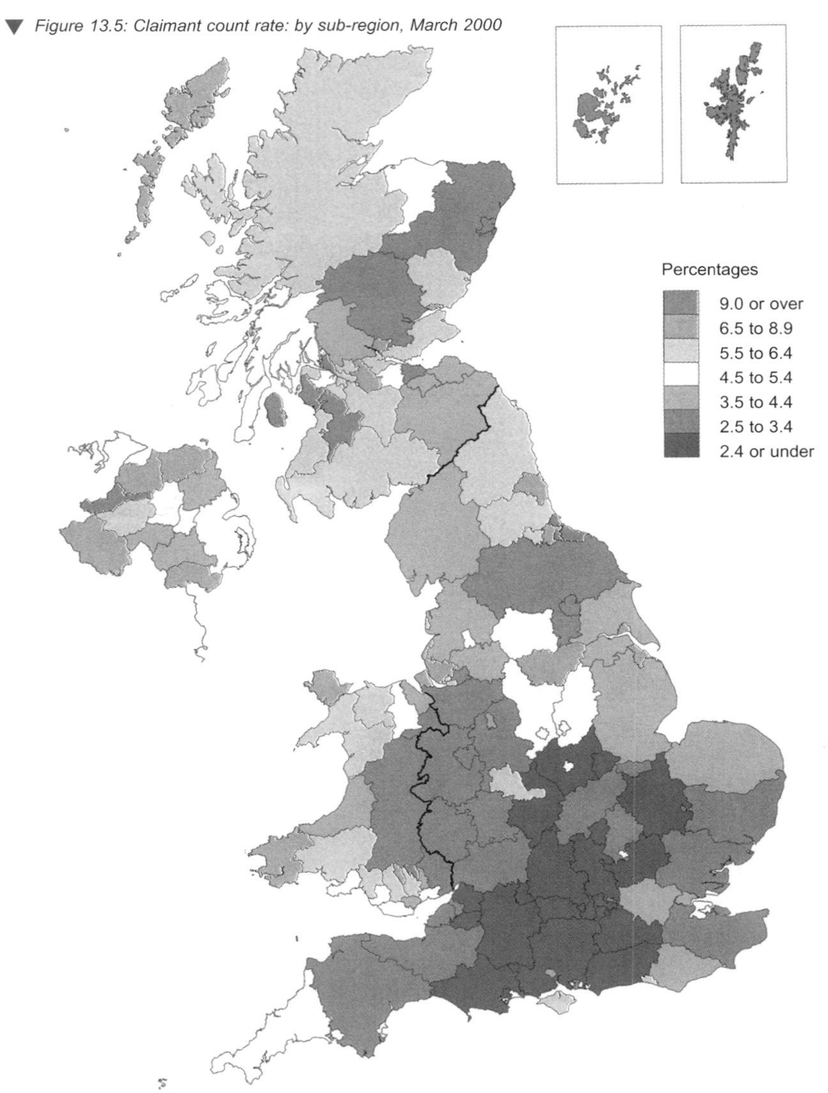

Source: Office for National Statistics
Regional Trends, 2000

Levels of employment differ markedly between different regions of the UK. This will reflect differences in the location of different industries and regional variations in consumer demand. As such regional unemployment rates will also vary because the products of industries in some areas have suffered falling demand while the markets for others have been expanding (see Figure 13.3).

Table 13.2 shows regional variations in employment in different industries. In general, it shows that employment in areas in the north of England, Scotland and Wales is concentrated more in manufacturing industries than in services. Conversely, services tend to employ a higher proportion of workers in the south of England than in most other areas, especially in banking and financial services and public administration. This reflects the concentration of government departments and international banking in London. The table also shows that female employment is concentrated in services.

▼ *Table 13.2 : Employees (%) in employment; by industry and gender, September 1998*

PERCENTAGES AND THOUSANDS

	Agriculture, hunting, forestry, & fishing	Mining quarrying. (inc oil & gas extraction)	Manu-facturing	Electricity gas, water	Con-struction	Distribution, hotels and catering, repairs	Transport storage & commun-ications	Financial & business services	Public Administra-tion and defence	Education social work & health services	Other	Whole economy (=100%) (thousands)
Males												
Great Britain	1.8	0.5	24.4	0.8	7.4	20.9	8.1	17.9	5.9	8.2	4.0	11,976
North East	1.1	0.6	30.9	1.1	9.9	17.0	6.9	11.3	7.1	10.0	4.0	458
North West	1.3	0.2	28.8	0.8	7.7	21.3	8.0	14.3	5.6	8.2	3.9	1,327
Yorkshire and the Humber	1.7	0.7	30.3	0.9	7.9	19.6	7.8	13.4	5.3	8.7	3.6	1,012
East Midlands	2.4	0.8	33.6	0.8	7.7	19.5	7.3	12.6	4.5	7.8	3.1	878
West Midlands	1.6	0.3	35.9	1.0	6.6	19.1	6.8	13.4	4.8	7.2	3.3	1,158
East	2.8	0.3	23.6	0.9	8.0	22.3	8.9	17.5	4.4	7.6	3.6	1,075
London	0.1	0.2	9.9	0.3	5.2	21.8	10.6	32.3	6.4	7.4	5.8	1,853
South East	1.9	0.2	19.5	0.8	7.0	23.2	8.0	21.6	5.7	8.1	3.9	1,703
South West	3.0	0.5	23.9	1.1	7.7	22.0	7.0	15.2	7.4	8.7	3.5	973
England	1.7	0.4	24.4	0.8	7.2	21.1	8.2	18.6	5.7	8.0	4.0	10,436
Wales	2.9	0.7	31.3	0.6	8.1	18.4	6.1	10.6	7.4	9.5	4.3	518
Scotland	3.1	2.2	21.5	1.2	9.9	19.6	7.6	14.1	7.1	9.4	4.2	1,022
Females												
Great Britain	0.8	0.1	10.2	0.3	1.6	24.9	3.4	19.4	5.9	28.4	5.0	11,358
North East	0.3	0.1	11.6	0.4	1.6	25.2	2.9	12.5	8.1	32.1	5.1	462
North West	0.5	—	11.3	0.3	1.5	26.4	3.4	16.3	6.3	29.4	4.4	1,294
Yorkshire and the Humber	0.7	0.1	11.9	0.3	1.9	25.2	3.0	15.7	6.4	30.1	4.7	945
East Midlands	1.2	0.1	16.6	0.3	1.7	24.2	3.0	14.8	5.0	28.8	4.4	790
West Midlands	0.8	0.1	14.3	0.4	1.4	24.3	2.9	17.0	5.1	29.1	4.6	1,022
East	1.6	0.1	9.9	0.4	1.8	26.0	4.0	19.3	4.5	27.7	4.8	1,005
London	0.1	0.1	5.7	0.1	1.1	23.1	4.6	31.7	5.7	21.3	6.5	1,760
South East	1.3	-	7.9	0.3	1.7	24.2	4.0	22.1	4.9	28.4	5.1	1,648
South West	1.1	0.1	9.1	0.4	1.6	26.6	2.8	16.6	6.5	30.8	4.6	938
England	0.8	0.1	10.2	0.3	1.6	24.9	3.6	20.1	5.7	27.9	5.0	9,861
Wales	0.8	0.1	11.7	0.2	1.9	24.6	2.1	12.3	7.3	33.9	5.0	489
Scotland	0.9	0.4	9.5	0.5	1.6	25.2	2.8	16.0	7.2	30.9	4.9	1,008

Regional Trends 2000

Table 13.3: UK Employees: by gender and occupation, 1991 and 1999

Employees[1]: by gender and occupation, 1991 and 1999

United Kingdom	Percentages			
	Males		Females	
	1991	1999	1991	1999
Managers and administrators	16	19	8	11
Professional	10	11	8	10
Associate professional and technical	8	9	10	11
Clerical and secretarial	8	8	29	26
Craft and related	21	17	4	2
Personal and protective services	7	8	14	17
Selling	6	6	12	12
Plant and machine operatives	15	15	5	4
Other occupations	8	8	10	8
All employees[2] (=100%)(millions)	11.8	12.4	10.1	10.8

1 At Spring each year. Males aged 16 to 64, females aged 16 to 59.
2 Includes a few people who did not state their occupation. Percentages are based on totals which exclude this group.
Source: Labour Force Survey, Office for National Statistics

Social Trends, 2000

▼ *Evidence of a tight labour market for lawyers*

Young City lawyers pay price for salary rise

Law firms in London are increasing the salaries of their first year associates by as much as 30%. Recruits to elite law firms can command salaries of £35,000 to £40,000.

The rises are a response both to US law firms and to staff joining dot.coms. According to the Law Gazette, the start was made by Gunderson Dettmer Stough Villeneuve Franklin and Hachi, a small law firm in California's silicon valley which raised first year associates' basic salaries to $125,000 (£83,000).

The rest of silicon valley followed suit, and in weeks the revolution had spread to New York; these firms also raised salaries in their London offices, initially paying a 'mid-Atlantic rate'.

A survey of 30 US law firms in the City found that newly qualified solicitors could earn up to £102,000 plus bonuses. In response English firms joined the bandwagon. Clifford Chance was the first, offering first year assistant solicitors an unprecedented £42,000 base salary plus bonuses.

The Guardian, 7.9.2000

Occupations and skills

There is not one labour market but many for different types of employment according to skills and qualifications. The **Standard Occupational Classification** (SOC) classifies some 374 occupation groups into nine major categories for the purpose of data collection and the examination of employment trends by government and business. The nine categories of occupation are displayed in Table 13.3.

Women employees outnumbered men in clerical and secretarial occupations by nearly three to one in Spring 1999, while there were nearly twice as many men as women managers and administrators. However, there has been some breakdown in traditional gender differences. For example, Table 13.3 shows the proportion of women who were managers and administrators increased from 8% in 1991 to 11% in 1999.

Changing occupational patterns are related to changes in consumer demands, industrial structure and technology. Rising demand for labour with particular skills can result in a tight labour market - the demand for workers outstrips the supply of workers with those skills. Competition for these workers will be fierce with rival organizations attempting to attract skilled employees through higher wages, more holidays and other working conditions. In contrast, falling demand for labour with old unwanted skills is likely to result in rising unemployment and wages falling behind other occupations.

Manual and non-manual labour

Within the SOC we can distinguish between manual and non-manual labour. We normally think of manual labour as undertaking physical work 'by hand', or with the aid of machinery, rather than work 'with the mind', but in fact this distinction is an imperfect one. A more appropriate division is between 'white-collar workers' who are largely office-based, and manual workers on the shop or factory floor, or out in the open on a building site or farm. However, most manual jobs will require the fulfilment of some administrative or 'white-collar' functions, for example, filling out delivery sheets, invoices, etc.

▼ Manual and non-manual occupations

Skilled, semi-skilled, or unskilled labour?

In the SOC, manual jobs are found in the following groups:

- Craft and related occupations
- Plant and machine operatives
- Other occupations, e.g. construction workers

Since the mid-1980s, there has been a marked increase in the number of non-manual employees in the UK. This is a reflection of the growth of the services, particularly in the financial and business services sector of the economy (see 5.7).

Skilled and unskilled labour

Manual work can require either **skilled, semi-skilled,** or **unskilled** labour, depending on the precise nature of the work. For example, we might consider an electronic engineer to be skilled, a bricklayer to be semi-skilled, and an agricultural labourer who undertakes a variety of tasks on a farm to be unskilled.

Similarly, non-manual work can be either skilled - for example, a computer programmer - or unskilled - for example, an office messenger. However, in many cases the distinction between what is skilled and unskilled is hard to draw. For example, a photocopy machine operative, who might be regarded as largely unskilled, will still require some skills in order to respond to people's requests, operate the machine effectively, and if necessary undertake some routine maintenance. Similarly, the agricultural labourer referred to above might need skills necessary to operate farm machinery and drive tractors.

In general, workers are considered skilled if they need to undergo intensive education and/or training in order to carry out their job.

Skill shortages

Skill shortages exist when there are not enough workers with the right skills to do the jobs that need doing. A shortage of appropriate skills can be a constraint on the growth of UK industry and its ability to compete with foreign rivals.

Employers' indications of recent or expected recruitment difficulties or hard-to-fill job vacancies are commonly used to measure skill shortages.

Skill Needs in Britain is an annual report by the Department for Education and Employment (DFEE), based on a survey of organizations employing 25 or more employees. The 1999 report suggested that recruitment problems among employers had increased, with 23% of employers surveyed experiencing recruitment problems, in 1998 compared with just 5% in 1992 (see Table 13.4). More detailed findings of the report were as follows:

- **Skill shortages in industries:** an analysis of hard-to-fill vacancies by industrial sector revealed the highest incidence in distribution and consumer services (25%) and in transport, public administration and other services (25%).

Portfolio Activity 13.2 

Consider the following occupations:

HGV driver
Computer programmer
Window cleaner
Marine biologist
Army cadet
Road sweeper
Stand-up comedian
Doctor
Hotel porter
Office cleaner
Secretary
Filing clerk
Holiday rep
Science teacher
Shop assistant
Book editor
Film cameraman
Interior designer
Bricklayer
Economist
Immigration officer
Hairdresser

Make a brief investigation of each occupation and try to decide:

- To which group in the Standard Occupational Classification each occupation belongs
- Whether the occupation is manual or non-manual
- Whether the occupation can be considered skilled, semi-skilled, or unskilled

Using this information, draw and complete a table like the one started below.

Occupation	SOC	Manual/Non-manual	Skilled/Un-skilled
Bus driver		manual	semi-skilled
Accountant			

▼ *Table 13.5: Skills which are lacking in existing employees*

	1997	Per cent 1998
Computer literacy or knowledge of information technology	55	56
Customer handling skills	54	53
General communication skills	52	55
Technical and practical skills[1]	51	64
Management skills	48	47
Literacy skills[2]	22	19
Numeracy skills[2]	–	18
Team-working skills	n/a	47
Problem-solving skills	n/a	39
Managing own development	n/a	37

Base: all employers who say a skill gap exists - 1990 (606)

1 In 1997 this was categorized solely as 'practical skills'

2 In 1997 there was a single category for 'literacy and numeracy skills'

Source: Skill Needs in Britain, 1999

▼ *Table 13.4: Establishments reporting current hard-to-fill vacancies by industry sector*

	1991	1992	1993	1994	1995	1996	1997	Per cent 1998
Manufacturing	6	5	7	11	18	17	15	19
Mining, utilities and construction	8	2	4	5	10	9	13	11
Distribution and consumer services	8	7	11	14	23	17	24	25
Finance and business services	7	3	5	8	17	15	21	23
Transport, public admin and other services	7	6	5	10	14	17	15	25
Total	7	5	6	11	16	17	18	23

Base: All employers

Source: Skill Needs in Britain, 1999

- **Skill shortages in occupations:** hard-to-fill vacancies were most often reported for personal and protective services, associate professional and technical, and clerical and secretarial occupations.
- **Rising skill needs:** over 60% of employers in the survey reported rising skill needs in each year since 1990. Skill needs have risen due to the introduction of new technology, a shift towards highly-skilled occupations, and new workplace practices. As production processes have become more automated and computerized, the role and skills required of workers have changed. Fewer workers are being asked to

specialize in one task. Instead, more workers are now needed to undertake a number of separate tasks within a firm. This is known as **multi-skilling.**

Job-related training can help to close a skills gap by teaching workers new skills or improving ones they already have.

Local Training and Enterprise Councils (TECs) and Chambers of Commerce also collect and publish information on skills needs and shortages in local businesses.

Survey on skills shortages

THE national co-ordination body of Britain's local training and enterprise councils (TECs), and TEC National Council, has published the latest results of its survey on skills, pointing to continued skills shortages, with demand growing especially in the managerial, engineering, technical and IT sectors. The growth in demand for these skills will be met only with difficulty from the existing labour market in the next year, the TEC National Council predicts.

In all, 67 of the 78 TECs and chambers of commerce, training and enterprise (CCTEs) in England and Wales responded to the latest round of the survey, accessing a collective sample of over 50,000 businesses and 112,000 individuals surveyed by the individual TECs and CCTEs. Over 80 per cent of these said that employers in their area were reporting 'some' or 'significant' recruitment difficulties, although many of the sectors affected were those with low levels of pay or unsociable hours. A total of 46 per cent of TECs and CCTEs reported some shortages of skills in their area, and another 33 per cent reported significant skills shortages. The area with the greatest report of shortages was among qualified engineers, technicians, mechanics and fitters: 27 per cent of respondents cited this as an area with shortages.

Labour Market Trends, July 1999

Wage differentials

The fact that some people work more hours than others does not necessarily explain why there are large differences in the earnings of people in different occupations (see Figure 13.6). **Wage differentials** (differences in the earnings of different people) can be explained by differences in the demand for and supply of labour. For example:

- Workers with skills which are in high demand by firms will tend to receive higher wages than those with old redundant skills, especially if the skilled workers are in short supply.
- Some jobs are dangerous or involve working unsociable hours. If individuals were not compensated, in the form of higher wages, for factors such as risk of injury or unsociable hours then the supply of labour to those occupations will be deficient and firms will find it difficult to recruit workers. For example, miners traditionally received much higher wages than workers in other manual occupations.
- Some jobs require long periods of education and training. This might discourage people from studying to become doctors, lawyers, or other professionals. Wages in these jobs therefore tend to be high because the supply of labour to these occupations is relatively low.

▼ *Table 13.6 : Average gross weekly earnings for full-time employees, July 1999*

Region	Manual (£)	Non-manual (£)
South East	329.2	469.7
East	325.9	439.0
South Western	300.2	407.4
West Midlands	311.8	423.3
East Midlands	311.0	404.5
Yorkshire & the Humber	328.3	400.5
North West	316.3	411.2
North East	307.9	384.4
England	319.3	455.2
Scotland	309.7	391.7
Wales	308.6	404.8
Great Britain	317.9	449.3

Labour Market Trends, December 1999

- If consumer demand for a particular good or service is high, firms making those products are likely to have a high demand for labour. This will tend to push up the wages of those workers in demand.
- In some areas of the UK an abundant supply of unemployed labour has tended to depress wage levels. This has resulted in **regional wage differentials** (see Table 13.6).
- Wage rates can also reflect regional differences in the cost of living. For example, many firms offer a 'London weighting allowance' to attract workers to jobs in London and the South East where living costs tend to be higher than elsewhere in the country.

However, some wage differentials can arise for reasons other than those connected with demand and supply conditions in labour markets. This is because:

- Workers often lack information about the availability of jobs and the wage rate they attract, and how these compare with other occupations. Finding out this information can be costly. Looking for a job involves much time and effort. As a result some workers work for less pay than they could simply because they are unaware of better paid vacancies elsewhere.

Portfolio Activity 13.3

Choose at least five different job adverts with different levels of pay from your local papers.

1. Using the information presented in each advertisement, write down the reasons why you think the wage rates may differ between each job.
2. What methods of payment and any other benefits are being offered in each case?
3. If employers are faced with a shortage or surplus of workers to fill the posts they advertise, how might the payments advertised in each case change?

▼ *Figure 13.6 : Average gross weekly earnings by main occupational group, April 1999*

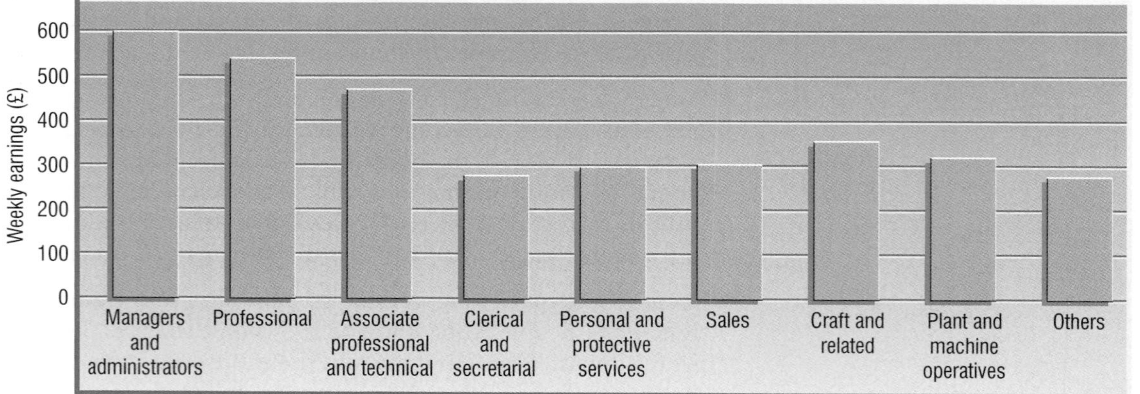

New Earnings Survey, 1999

▼ *Average gross weekly earnings, April 2000*

Non-manual workers £443

Manual workers £315

Male workers £442

Female workers £327

- Some employers may discriminate against groups of people. The most common forms of discrimination are refusing to employ women or ethnic minorities in jobs for which they are qualified, employing them only at lower wages, or insisting on higher qualifications than necessary where they are employed at the same wage rate as others.
- Some groups of workers may be powerful enough to force their employers to pay them high wages. Some employers also have immense power and may be able to force their workers to accept low wages. The government, for example, is the main employer in the UK of teachers, civil servants and nurses, and is therefore virtually the only source of demand for these type of workers.

Average earnings and hours of work

Table 13.7 shows that average gross weekly earnings (including overtime and any performance related pay – see 15.2) of all full-time employees on adult rates working a full week in April 2000 were £400. The gap between earnings in non-manual and manual occupations has widened over time, so that average manual earnings at £315 per week were around 75% of non-manual earnings of £443 per week.

The average working week of full-time employees was 40 hours, of which 2.1 hours were for paid overtime. The average working week for manual workers stretched to 43.9 hours, while non-manual employees worked just over 38 hours. Because of these differences in hours worked each week, the gap between average manual and non-manual weekly earnings does not appear as wide as the divergence between their average hourly earnings. Non-manual employees averaged £11.64 per hour in April 2000, manual workers £7.23.

Male and female wage differentials have been closing over time, in part due to legislation concerning equal pay opportunities (see 15.2).

The average gross weekly earnings of women in April 2000 were £327, representing 72% of average male earnings of £442 per week. This difference in pay is often used as an indication of sex discrimination in the UK labour market. However, the average earnings of women will be lower than those of men for many reasons not necessarily related to discrimination: women tend to work in traditionally lower-paid occupations and industries, and many work part-time. Women employees also worked on average around three hours less than men per week in April 2000.

Types of employment

Employees in employment

The nature of employment has changed over time. In 1999 some 80% of the total UK workforce were employed by someone else. Most are employed on a **full-time** basis but over time the proportion of workers employed on a part-time or temporary basis has increased.

Table 13.7: Levels of average pay and hours in April 2000

	Men			Women			Men and Women		
	Manual	Non-Manual	All	Manual	Non-Manual	All	Manual	Non-Manual	All
Average gross weekly earnings (£)	335	526	442	222	347	327	315	443	400
Average gross hourly earnings including overtime (£)	7.54	13.49	10.68	5.56	9.37	8.71	7.23	11.64	10.01
Average total weekly hours	4	39.0	41.4	39.9	37.0	37.5	43.6	38.1	40.0
Average weekly overtime hours	4.9	1.1	2.7	1.9	0.6	0.8	4.3	0.9	2.1

Labour Market Trends, December 1999

Figure 13.7: Full and part-time employment: by gender

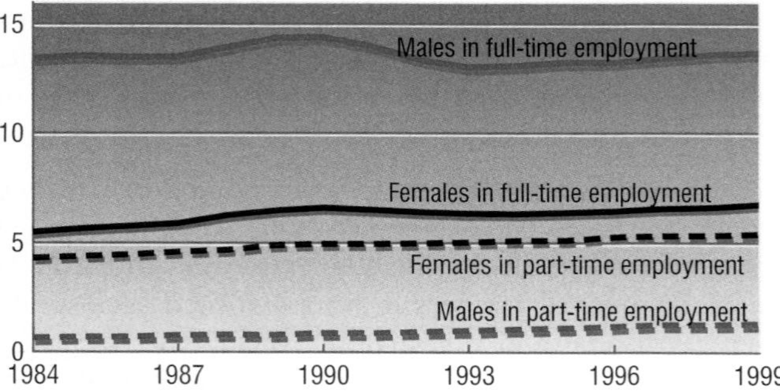

Social Trends, 2000

A **part-time employee** is officially defined as a person who normally works less than 30 hours a week excluding lunch breaks and overtime work. Some part-time employment may be the result of job sharing whereby two or more workers are employed to carry out one full-time job between them.

In 2000 around 6.9 million jobs in the UK were part-time compared with around 20.1 million full-time jobs. However, part-time employment has generally been on an upward trend since the early 1980, especially among women.

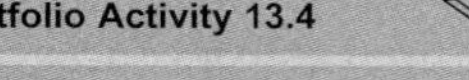

Portfolio Activity 13.4

1. How many part-time staff are employed in your school/college (a) in total, and (b) as a proportion of all employees? Interview the head of the school/college and ask him/her why part-time workers are employed, their occupations, and how levels of part-time employment have changed over the last 2–5 years.

2. Repeat Question 1 for another business organization - for example, a large retail outlet - and compare your findings with those from your school/college.

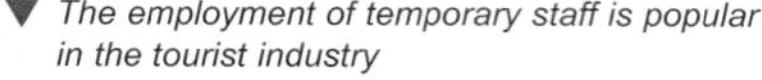

The employment of temporary staff is popular in the tourist industry

Temporary workers do not have permanent contracts of employment with their employers. Most are employed on contracts of between 6 and 12 months (see Figure 13.8). They are used by firms to provide extra help during busy periods or to cover for employees, who are absent through for example, illness, maternity leave, paternity leave, study leave, or secondment to other organizations. A temporary worker might also be employed to fill a job vacancy until the person selected for the job is able to take up the post. Industries which experience seasonal fluctuations in the demand for their products or services will often employ workers on a temporary basis when demand is high. This is especially the case in tourism and construction.

Why has part-time employment increased?

- **More jobs require only a limited labour input:** Many employers only require certain workers for a few hours each day or week because that is all it needs for them to complete their tasks. Classic examples are cleaners, typically employed for a few hours before or after normal working hours, and catering employees commonly working mid-morning to mid-afternoon.
- **More people want to work part-time:** Employment on a part-time basis allows a worker increased flexibility. This might be especially important to women with dependent children.
- **To retain valuable staff who can no longer work full time:** Employing a worker on a part-time basis means a firm can still make use of the worker's skills and use them to train a possible future replacement.
- **To match employment levels to peaks in product or service demand:** One industrial sector - distribution - dominates part-time work. This is partly a reflection of the increased flexibility in trading hours as a result of late night opening and Sunday trading. Supermarkets and department stores tend to employ part-timers to work lunchtimes and late nights, especially at weekends, to match predictable variations in customer demand. Part-timers are particularly attractive to employers in these situations because they rarely qualify for overtime rates of pay beyond the standard working day.
- **Staffing levels can be adjusted easily:** One advantage claimed for part-time employment is that higher levels of turnover among staff allows a firm to cut their workforces on a voluntary basis, without the need for redundancies, when the need arises.
- **To reduce labour costs:** Employers are only required to pay National Insurance Contributions (NICs) for an employee if he or she earns over a specified threshold each week. In 2001–02 the threshold was £87 per week. An employer will not have to pay NICs for part-time workers with earnings less than this each week.

Until 1994, part-time workers were also relatively cheaper to employ because they did not qualify for the same terms and conditions as full-time staff, namely sick pay, holidays, periods of notice and redundancy payments. Only those employees who worked 16 hours each week or more held the same legal rights as full-time workers. European regulations introduced to the UK in 1994 governing the employment rights of part-time workers made them eligible for the same holiday, redundancy pay and other entitlements as full-time workers, pro-rated to the number of hours they worked (see 15.2).

▼ *Figure 13.8: Duration of employment of temporary employees, UK Spring 1999*

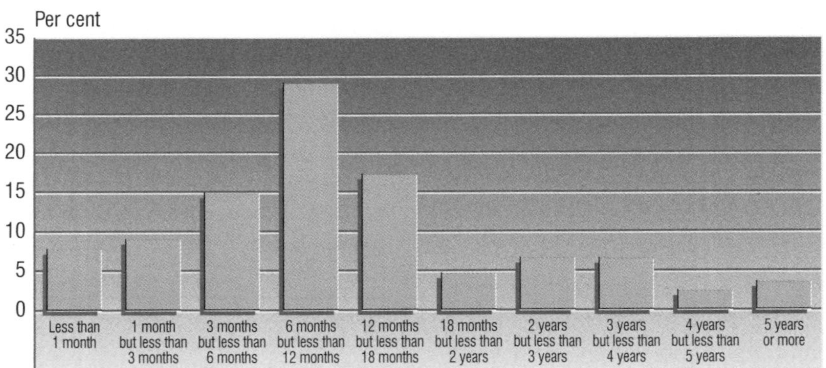

Labour Market Trends, November 1999

▼ *Figure 13.9: Temporary employees: by gender*

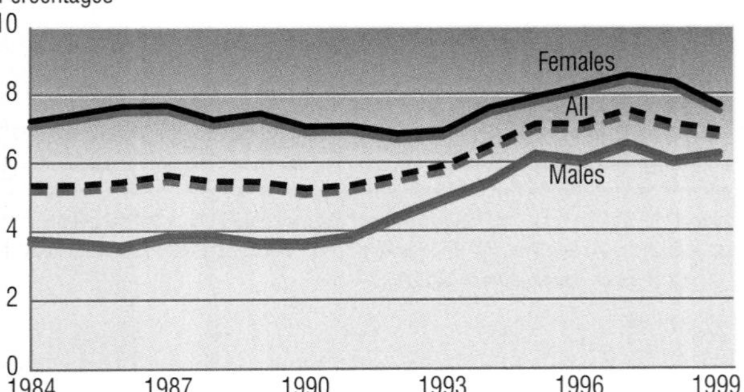

1 As a percentage of all employees. Temporary employees are those who assess themselves to have either a seasonal or casual job, a job done under contract or for a fixed period, or were temporary for some other reason, At spring each year.

Social Labour Force Survey, Office for National Statistics

Social Trends 2000

During the first half of the 1990s an increasing number of employers used temporary workers to help meet their changing requirements. The proportion of men working in temporary jobs increased rapidly between 1991 and 1995 from 3.9% to 6.3% (see Figure 13.9). Since then it has fluctuated and in 1999 6.3% of male employees were in temporary jobs. In contrast, women are more likely to work in temporary jobs. In 1992 6.8% of female employees were in temporary jobs. By 1998 this had risen to 8.7% but has since fallen back. In 2000 there were around 1.6 million temporary employees in the UK - around 7% of total employment.

Types of temporary worker

Examples of temporary workers include:

- Many temporary workers are employed as **seasonal workers**. Many jobs in the tourist and construction industries are seasonal jobs involving work only during the summer.
- Some temporary workers may be required to 'fill gaps' at short notice, for example, when a full-time employee has gone sick or is on leave. Temporary workers needed at short notice are often recruited from employment agencies and called **'temps'**.
- Some workers may be employed for one-off projects on short-term contracts because they have specialist skills required by a business. Workers may also be hired on short-term contracts to provide support services to an organization such as cleaning, equipment maintenance and catering.
- **Casual workers** may be employed on a day-to-day basis, usually with no formal contract of employment. They may be required to help out in a shop, office or on a building site for example, and will usually receive 'cash in hand' for their efforts. Because casual workers are paid in cash only when they are needed this type of work is often called 'unofficial employment'. As such, casual workers do not qualify for any of benefits that officially employed people do, such as holidays, sick pay, pensions or redundancy payments.

Self-employment

Self-employment refers to those people who start their own business organizations or who work on short-term contracts for other businesses. The growth in self-employment was one of the most significant changes to the labour market in the UK during the 1980s. In 1981 around 2.1 million people were registered as self-employed. This had grown to 3 million by 1988 and has remained fairly stable since. Around 16% of all male employees were self-employed in 1999 and 7% of female employees.

Around 75% of the self-employed were male in 1999, with around 27% employed in construction industries. In contrast, most self-employed females are employed in distribution, hotels and restaurants, public administration, education and health services (see Table 13.9).

▼ *Table 13.9: Self-employment: by gender and industry, Spring 1999*

United Kingdom	**Males**	**Females**	**Percentages All persons**
Construction	27	2	21
Distribution, hotels and restaurants	18	23	19
Banking, finance and insurance	19	18	19
Public administration, education and health	5	24	10
Manufacturing	7	7	7
Agriculture and fishing	7	4	6
Transport and communication	8	3	6
Other services	8	19	11
All industries[1] (=100%)(millions)	2.4	0.8	3.2

1 Includes those in energy and water supply industries for which figures are not shown separately because of the small sample sizes. Also includes those who did not state industry and those whose workplace was outside the United Kingdom, but percentages are based on totals which exclude these groups.

Labour Force Survey, Office for National Statistics

Social Trends, 2000

Why has the demand for self-employed labour increased?

- **The need for specialist skills**: Self-employed people with specialist skills can be employed by organizations who need those skills for a relatively short period of time - for example, to provide legal advice, instal a new computer network, or provide staff training. Many construction firms employ self-employed workers with specialized building skills, such as electricians, bricklayers, plasterers, interior decorators, etc.
- **To match skills and staffing levels to changes in demand:** Employing self-employed people for short periods can help an organization cope with peaks in demand for their goods or services.
- **More workers prefer to be self-employed:** As a result, self-employed workers may be more motivated - absenteeism may be lower and productivity higher.
- **To reduce costs:** An increasing number of larger organizations have downsized and sub-contracted non-core functions such as catering and cleaning to smaller external organizations. Larger firms can insist on quality at competitive rates from small organizations or individuals willing to undertake these functions. For example, many local and central government department functions were 'market tested' in the early 1990s as part of the UK Government's policy of privatization (see 6.5).

Why has the supply of self-employed labour increased?

- **Changes in the structure of consumer demand:** There has been an increase in consumer demand for more specialized and personalized products which can best be met by small firms and self-employed individuals.
- **Technological advance:** Technological change has brought sophisticated equipment such as computers and software within a price range that self-employed people can afford. Thus editors, designers and illustrators may produce work for publishers such as Oxford University Press using specialist equipment in their own homes.
- **Worker attitudes and demographic effects:** Increasing worker dissatisfaction with their employment, pay and promotion prospects may have grown. Self-employment allows a person to be their own boss, choose their own hours of work, and to specialize in those activities they either enjoy the most and/or are best able to do.
- **The business cycle:** The opportunities for individuals to become self-employed and be successful will tend to rise during economic booms when the demand for goods and services is buoyant. However, rising unemployment during economic recessions and a general lack of job vacancies may force individuals into self-employment. This was likely to be a significant explanatory factor underlying growth in the number self-employed during the early to mid-1980s.
- **Government policy:** The UK Government encourages people to become self-employed by providing free advice and financial help. The Government continues to pay the Jobseeker's Allowance to unemployed workers who become self-employed for the first six months of their self-employment.

Non-contract employment

This is unofficial employment. An employer is required by law to provide a contract of employment to any employee within two weeks of their appointment (see 14.5). However, by providing an employment contract an employee is entitled to certain rights, such as sick pay, holidays, etc. The employer may also be liable for additional National Insurance Contributions. Because of these additional costs of employment, some employers may employ workers on a casual basis without an employment contract and pay them cash 'in hand'. The employee may also benefit by not declaring this income for income tax purposes. 'Unofficial' employment and cash-in-hand payments are part of the so-called **black economy.**

Sources of information about labour markets and employment trends

A business can use market research to find out about local and national labour market conditions to inform its human resources planning. A business can collect its own information or it can draw on information collected and made available by other organizations. You can draw on the same useful references below to complete the Key Activity at the end of this unit.

- **Internal sources** of information on wage levels, employee numbers and skills, labour turnover and absenteeism should be readily available to a business from staff records.
- The **classified pages of local and national newspapers** can reveal the types of jobs being advertised by rival organizations, the skills they will

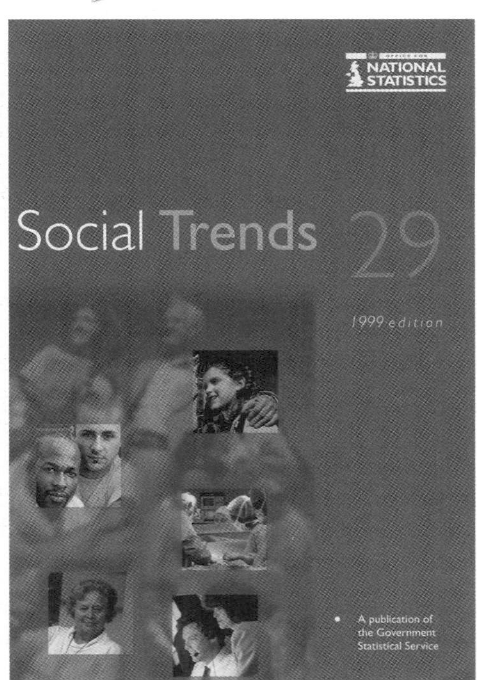

▲ *The publications, Labour Market Trends and Social Trends, contain a wealth of useful information for business on employment issues and labour market conditions*

require and the pay and other benefits they are offering prospective employees. If the business is to compete for similar labour, it will need to offer similar or better pay and benefits.

- Local **employment agencies** can also be helpful in providing details on local vacancies, pay levels and skills needs, the number and types of people looking for work.
- **Regional Development Agencies (RDAs), Chambers of Commerce, Training and Enterprise Councils (TECs)** and **Local Enterprise Councils (LECs)** are useful sources of local employment and business information (see 20.5).
- **Trade unions and employer associations** collect and make available information on employment, skills, wage costs and training in the occupations and industries they represent (see 13.3).
- The **Department for Education and Employment (DfEE)** publishes information on changing skills needs and training initiatives (see 15.2). Contact the DfEE on-line at ***www.dfee.gov.uk.***
- The Government's **Office for National Statistics** collects and publishes regional and national information on wages, employment and skills. By far the best source for information on all aspects of employment is their monthly publication *Labour Market Trends*. The magazine also contains a list of useful e-mail and telephone contact points in the ONS and other government departments to assist with published statistical information.

Other useful ONS publications include:

– *The New Earnings Survey*

– *The Monthly Digest of Statistics*

– *Social Trends*

– *Regional Trends*

– *Annual Abstract of Statistics*

College and larger public libraries are more likely to hold these publications as reference materials. Alternatively, these publications are available to buy from **The Stationery Office Ltd** (contact 0870 600 5222 for information on how to place an order or for a list of local Stationery Office bookshops).

You can contact the ONS on-line at ***www.ons.gov.uk.***

Key words:

Labour turnover - the rate at which employees leave an organization

Working population - the total supply of labour in an economy, consisting of all those willing and able to work

Economic activity rate - the working population expressed as a percentage of the total resident population of working age. People who are economically active are those willing and able to supply themselves for work

Claimant count - the official count of the number of people claiming unemployment-related benefits in the UK each month

Employees in employment - people employed by business organizations on a full or part-time, permanent or temporary basis

Black economy - unofficial trading activities undertaken to avoid taxes, other duties and business regulations

Wage differentials - differences in earnings between different people in different occupations, industries, and regions

Part-time employee - a person who normally works less than 30 hours a week excluding lunch breaks and overtime work

Short-term contract - an employment contract that is time limited, normally between 6 months and 2 years

Standard Occupational Classification (SOC) - a government classification of occupations into nine major categories for the purpose of data collection and the examination of employment trends

Manual labour - workers in occupations which involve a significant amount of physical effort

Non-manual labour - workers in occupations, often desk-based, which require more written skills and much less physical effort

Skilled labour - workers who have a trained ability and are considered expert in their particular occupation

Skill shortage - when the demand for labour with particular skills outstrips the supply of labour with those skills

Multi-skilling - training workers to carry out several tasks

Skills gap - the difference between the skills possessed by existing employees and the skills their employers would like them to have

Section 13.3 Managing employee relations

What happens when it all goes wrong?

Sometimes relations between an individual employee or a group of employees and their employer may sour and disputes can arise. The role of the Human Resources Department is to anticipate situations that might cause problems and take actions to prevent these from happening and damaging the business. However, it is not always possible to prevent disputes.

Grievance procedures

If an employee has a complaint, then their grievance should be discussed freely with senior managers and a compromise position reached. For example, an employee may simply be concerned about a lack of clean towels in the toilets or an absence of vegetarian meals in the canteen. These can be easily remedied. However, far more serious are complaints over possible breaches of the law. Where employment and other laws have been breached by an employer, the business may face legal action which can be very damaging in terms of bad public relations and if significant fines are imposed.

Employee grievances may arise due to:

- Incorrect calculation of pay
- Being overlooked for promotion

▼ Poor facilities?

▼ Harassment

- Unfair allocation of overtime
- Poor physical working conditions
- Not being allowed time off
- Sexual or racial harassment
- A line manager being rude or unreasonable

However, the most common grievance against employers is unfair dismissal (see 15.3).

Many organizations have a formal **grievance procedure** to deal with complaints from individual employees. A typical grievance procedure will allow both sides in a dispute to present their case to their department manager. The manager will examine the facts and then present his or her decision on what action should be taken, if any. If the employee is not satisfied with the decision they can take their case to more senior managers, or in some cases even a joint consultative committee of unions and management representatives. If the employee is still not satisfied with the outcome, they can apply to have the case examined by an employment tribunal.

Industrial disputes

Sometimes disagreements can arise between an organization and its entire workforce. Such large-scale disputes can occur for a number of reasons:

- **Pay**: Employees will often demand higher wages if the cost of living is rising or if other groups of workers are getting larger pay rises. Employees may also demand higher pay if their firm is making large profits, or if management are giving themselves large pay rises. A business may be reluctant to pay higher wages if output and sales have not increased, because it will reduce profits.
- **Changes in working practices**: Disputes may occur if employers attempt to change the way in which work is done without consulting employees, or if workers feel that the new arrangements are not as good as before. For example, an employer may introduce shiftwork in an attempt to reduce overtime working. Employees may try to resist these changes.
- **Changes in hours and conditions of work**: Employees will also tend to push for a shorter working week and longer holidays. This again will reduce output and raise costs for an employer, and may be resisted.
- **Redundancies**: Sometimes employers will cut the size of their workforce in an attempt to reduce their costs. New technology may be introduced which requires less labour input. Employees who risk being made redundant may fight to keep their jobs.

Resolving disputes

There are a number of ways employers and employees can attempt to settle their disagreements. These include:

- **Negotiation** between employers and trade unions
- Seeking the help of the **Advisory, Conciliation, and Arbitration Service (ACAS)**
- Taking the dispute to an **employment tribunal**
- Seeking **civil legal action**
- Appealing to the **European Court of Justice**

We will now consider these options in more detail.

Trade union negotiation

A **trade union** is an organization of workers whose main purpose is to represent the interests of its members (workers) in the workplace. Unions play a key role in resolving disputes between employers and individual employees and with their entire workforce.

Employees in many organizations, whether production operatives or managers, can belong to a trade union. Many trades unions for professional and managerial workers prefer to call themselves **staff associations.**

Several unions or staff associations can represent the interests of workers in the same workplace. For example, teachers and other staff in schools or colleges may belong to the National Union of Teachers (NUT), the Professional Association of Teachers (PAT), or the National Union of Public Employees (NUPE), among others.

Employees who belong to a trade union can seek the help and advice of union officials if they feel they have been unfairly treated or harassed by their employer or by another member of staff. The union official will be able to present the views and rights of the aggrieved employee to representatives of the employer.

Collective bargaining

The process of negotiating over pay and working conditions between trade union and employer representatives is called **collective bargaining.**

Collective bargaining may be organized so that a negotiated settlement determines pay and conditions for all firms in a particular industry, or in local agreements between particular companies and their own workers.

In addition to bargaining on wages and conditions, unions and employers will also negotiate about redundancies and the introduction of new technology.

What happens if negotiations fail?

If a union and an employer fail to reach agreement, they may enlist the help of the **Advisory, Conciliation and Arbitration Service (ACAS)** to resolve the dispute.

If these further negotiations with unions and ACAS fail, and if one side feels that the other has broken the law, the dispute may be taken to a court of law or to an informal type of court for settling employment disputes called an **employment tribunal.**

Finally, both parties can appeal to the highest court in Europe for a decision, the **European Court of Justice.**

▼ *Striking workers picketing their place of work*

Industrial action

When negotiations fail, trade unions may resort to the following types of industrial action to put pressure on their employers:

- **Overtime ban** - when workers refuse to work more than their normal hours. Many firms rely on overtime to meet production targets and deadlines.
- **Work-to-rule** - when workers comply with every rule and regulation at work in order to slow down production.
- **Go slow** - working deliberately slowly.
- **Sit-in** - when workers refuse to leave their place of work, often in an attempt to stop their firm from being closed down.
- **Strikes** - when negotiations between unions and employers fail, a trade union may recommend that their members withdraw their labour and refuse to work. A strike can be **official,** if it has been voted for by the majority of workers and has the backing of the union, or **unofficial** if it is called by workers without the support of their union. Under law, no strike action can be called until a full postal ballot of union members has been conducted and independently scrutinized. Unions are liable for any damages/losses suffered by business organizations as a result of strike or other actions.

Workers on strike may **picket** their firms by standing outside trying to persuade other people - fellow workers or members of other unions not involved in the dispute - not to enter the premises. However, going on strike will mean a loss of wages for workers, and can result in them losing their jobs if the firm is forced to reduce production as a result of lost customers and profits.

In extreme cases, an employer may retaliate by locking workers out of the firm with no pay.

Employee and employer associations

The aims of trade unions

The trade union movement started more than a hundred years ago. Workers, dissatisfied with poor pay and working conditions, organized themselves into groups to negotiate with 'one voice' against powerful employers. The main functions of trade unions are largely unchanged today being:

- to defend employee rights
- to secure improvements in working conditions, including health and safety
- to secure adequate pay for their members
- to secure improvements in sick pay, pensions and industrial injury benefits
- to provide education, training, and recreational and social amenities for members
- to encourage firms to increase worker participation in business decision making

Membership of trade unions in the UK has been declining. In the late 1970s over 50% of people in work belonged to a union. By 1998 this had fallen to just 31%, around 8 million workers. Union membership has declined as employment in manufacturing industries has fallen. Participation in unions is now highest in professional and lowest in sales occupations.

▼ *Trade unions in Great Britain, 1976-1997*

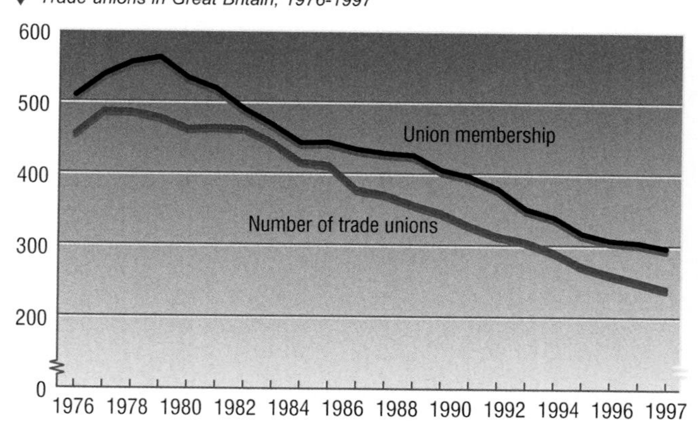

Labour Market Trends, July 1999

Types of Trade Union

There are a number of different types of trade union:

- General unions represent workers from many different occupations and industries. For example, the Transport and General Workers Union (TGWU) represents all sorts of clerical, manufacturing, transport and commercial workers.
- Industrial unions represent workers in the same industry, for example, the Communications Workers Union (CMU) and the Iron and Steel Trades Confederation (ISTC).
- Craft unions are often small and few in number today. They usually represent workers with the same skill across several industries, such as the Graphical, Paper and Media Union (GPMU) and the Amalgamated Engineers and Electrical Union (AEEU).
- Non-manual unions and staff associations represent workers in professional and commercial jobs. For example, the National Union of Teachers and Royal College of Nursing. UNISON is the largest union in the UK with 1.4 million members representing local government, health service, and other public sector workers.

Many large firms have a single union agreement with their employees. This means one union will represent all the workers in their place of work. Employers benefit by only having to negotiate on wages and working conditions with one single union rather than many.

The structure of a trade union

Every union in the UK is entirely independent and self-governing, but many are affiliated to the Trade Union Congress (TUC). The TUC represents the union movement in discussions with employer associations, the media and the UK and European Union Governments.

The TUC is headed by the general council, which is the TUC's executive decision-making body. It meets every year to discuss and establish policy. Each union can send delegates to the meeting, to debate and vote on policy.

The internal structure of trade unions varies widely, but there is a typical pattern extending from full-time union officials in the union headquarters to union members in factories, shops and offices.

Typical structure of a trade union

- **General Secretary** - Head of a union
- **National Executive** - Policy-making group. An important role of the executive is to negotiate pay and conditions with employers
- **Full-time Officials** - Union members at headquarters who assist local branches
- **Union Branches** - These co-ordinate the affairs of union members at a localized level
- **Shop Stewards** - Conduct day-to-day business of the union in their places of work as well as carrying out the job they were employed to do

What are employers associations?

These organizations exist to provide employers with help and advice, for example, on legal matters and calculating tax, and to represent their views in discussions with trade unions and Government. For example, the National Farmers Union (NFU) represents the views of farm owners and managers. Other examples include the Society of British Aerospace Companies and the Federation of Small Businesses.

Many employers associations belong to the Confederation of British Industry (CBI) along with many trade associations and over 250,000 different companies. The CBI is a very influential national organization representing the interests of many different employers in discussions with unions and Governments. It also collects and publishes up-to-date information on industrial trends. such as wage costs and sales, and on how well UK firms are performing.

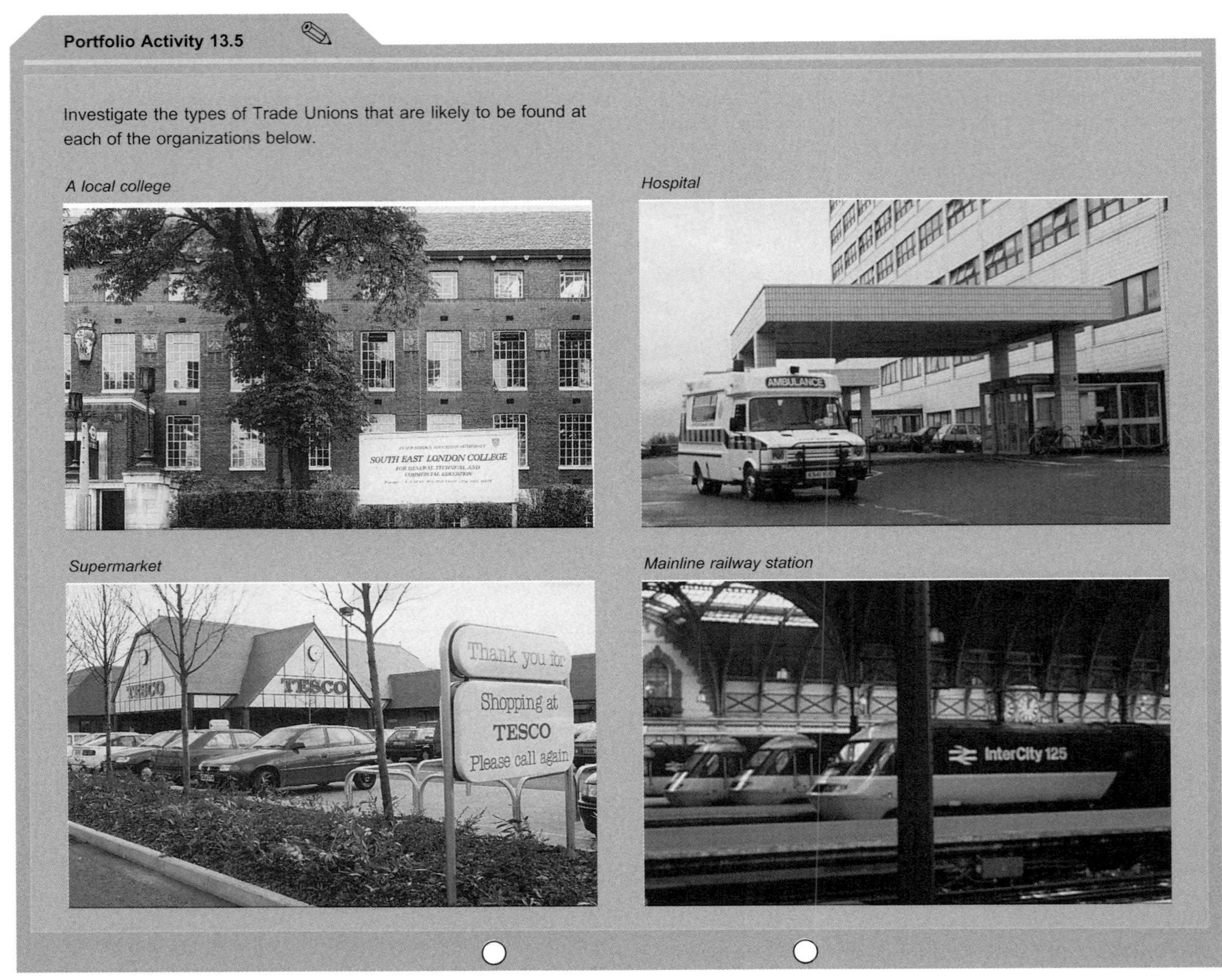

The Advisory, Conciliation and Arbitration Service (ACAS)

If negotiations between employer and employee representatives fail to reach a settlement that is acceptable to both sides, they may ask for the help of the **Advisory, Conciliation and Arbitration Service (ACAS).**

ACAS is an independent organization set up by the government in 1975 to help settle disputes between employers and employees. It publishes a code of good practice which employers may wish to follow when dealing with their employees.

The main aim of ACAS is to improve relations between employers and employees by bringing opposing parties together and attempting to find solutions to disputes.

When employers and employees are unable to agree, they may wish to talk with an independent organization like ACAS. In its conciliation role, ACAS will listen to both sides in a dispute and look for possible common ground. When asked to arbitrate, ACAS will listen to all the people involved in a dispute and make a decision for both sides on what to do. Sometimes both sides in a dispute may agree in advance to accept whatever ACAS decides.

ACAS in Northern Ireland is known as the **Labour Relations Agency**.

Employment tribunal

If an employee, or group of employees, feels that an employer has treated them unfairly and broken employment law, they can take their case to an **employment tribunal.**

An employment tribunal is rather like a court of law. It is less formal than the type of court you often see on television, but it has the authority to settle cases under a range of employment laws, such as wrongful or unfair dismissal or discrimination.

Each tribunal is made up of three people - a legally trained chairperson, plus one employer and one employee representative. They will listen to each side in the dispute and then make their recommendations. They can either reject the claim or make one of three decisions in favour of the employee, which the employer is legally bound to abide by. These are that:

- the employee is to be given back their old job
- the employee is to be given another job
- the employee is to be compensated

Figure 13.10: The employment tribunals process

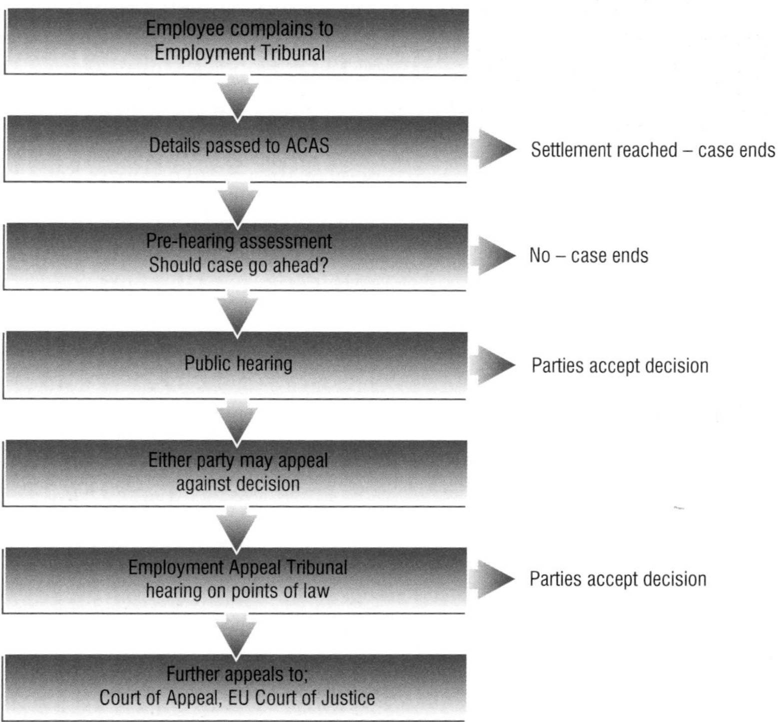
Employee complains to Employment Tribunal
Details passed to ACAS
Settlement reached – case ends
Pre-hearing assessment Should case go ahead?
No – case ends
Public hearing
Parties accept decision
Either party may appeal against decision
Employment Appeal Tribunal hearing on points of law
Parties accept decision
Further appeals to; Court of Appeal, EU Court of Justice

Both employer and employee have the right to appeal against a decision by the employment tribunal.

The Employment Rights Act 1996

This law simplifies the work of employment tribunals and allows them different ways to solve industrial and employment disputes. To speed up the process of settling disputes an employment tribunal can decide a case without a full hearing or in some situations, without a formal hearing at all.

In addition, the Employment Rights Act enables the Arbitration, Conciliation and Arbitration Service to provide an arbitration scheme to settle unfair dismissal disputes without using the law and without going to an employment tribunal. The Act also encourages employers and employees to use the internal appeals systems within their organizations to resolve unfair dismissal cases. It allows financial awards in settlement of cases of unfair dismissal to be reduced if the employee failed to use the procedures of the business, or raised if the employer failed to use them.

Civil legal action

Instead of going to an employment tribunal, an employee may decide to seek compensation for unfair dismissal by taking their employer to court. However, this can be expensive because it involves employing a solicitor, and sometimes a barrister as well. If the employer wins the case, then the employee may have to pay both sets of legal costs.

Because court cases can involve bad publicity, employers may sometimes wish to make an out-of-court settlement with a former employee, or suggest that both parties go to arbitration with an independent body deciding the outcome of the case.

The European Court of Justice

The **European Court of Justice** is run by judges from the member countries of the European Union (see 7.3). The role of the court is to settle cases where European Union laws or directives are concerned.

An employee, or employer, can appeal to the European Court if they believe that British courts have failed to apply European laws correctly.

The European Court is often used as a last resort to settle a disagreement between employees and firms if they have failed to reach a satisfactory settlement in a UK court.

EU directives

The European Union has passed a number of directives which aim to give workers in member countries the same basic employment rights. These include:

- A maximum working week of 48 hours
- Freedom to join unions and take strike action
- Equal treatment for part-time and full-time workers
- Access to appropriate training and re-training opportunities
- Equal treatment for men and women
- The right to be consulted on changes in organization, new working methods, mergers, and redundancies
- Protection of rights of pregnant women, with working hours and conditions to be adapted if the job endangers health
- Freedom to move between EU member states for work and to enjoy the same terms and conditions of employment, such as pay and holidays, as native workers, and have equal recognition of qualifications

Portfolio Activity 13.6 

1. You are an ACAS negotiator. Produce a short report setting out how you propose to bring together the two sides in the dispute. (*Hint*: what common ground can be established?)
2. Roleplay the dispute in groups of three. One member of the group should play the union leader, the other the employer's representative, and the third, the ACAS conciliator. Set a time limit of two periods of ten minutes for negotiations, separated by a five-minute break.
3. Present the results of your negotiations in the form of a newspaper report, using desktop publishing software. Each group member should write the article from the perspective of their particular role.

ITN staff support strike call

Last-ditch talks are to be held at ITN to avert strikes over changes to shifts which staff say will cause major disruption to their lives.

Journalists and technicians will stage a 24-hour walkout on January 27 and a four-hour stoppage on January 31 unless there is a breakthrough during talks at the conciliation service ACAS next week.

Members of the Broadcasting Entertainment Cinematograph and Theatre Union (Bectu) and National Union of Journalists (NUJ) voted by 80% majorities to back industrial action at a mass meeting yesterday.

Gerry Morrissey, Bectu's assistant general secretary, said: 'The changes put forward by ITN erode our members' family lives, which is totally unacceptable. The company can afford to introduce family-friendly working practices but refuses to do so.'

Managers want night working for all employees in plans to turn the station into a 24-hour news channel and to service its new contract to provide GMTV with news from next month.

ITN said it understood changes would alter the working lives of some individuals.

But its primary concern was job security and, to achieve that, it would have to be flexible enough to deliver services demanded by existing customers while branching out into new ones.

The Guardian, 15.1.2000

Key words:

Employment tribunal - a courtroom which is less formal than the law courts, where industrial disputes can be settled

ACAS - an independent organization providing unbiased advice, arbitration, or conciliation as required, in order to help settle industrial disputes

Civil action - the seeking of redress or settlement of disputes in the courts

European Court of Justice - legal body with the power to pass judgements on European laws, when these are in dispute

Trade Union - an organization representing the interests of its members, usually workers in a particular trade or industry

Trade Union Congress (TUC) - national coordinating and policy-making body for entire union movement in UK

Employers' association - an organization representing the views of companies within an industry

Industrial relations - the relationship between employers and their employees and/or employee representatives

Strikes - withdrawal of labour as a result of an industrial dispute

Collective bargaining - the process of negotiation between workers and employer representatives

Test your knowledge

1. Which of the following is not an objective of human resources planning in a business?
   - **A** Forecasting future skills needs
   - **B** Measuring labour turnover
   - **C** Purchasing protective clothing and uniforms for staff
   - **D** Planning the recruitment and selection of new employees

2. Which of the following is a possible advantage to a business of high labour turnover?
   - **A** Increased resources devoted to recruitment and selection
   - **B** Redundancy costs will be low or zero
   - **C** Increased training costs for new employees
   - **D** Increased overtime payments for existing workers

3. Which sector of the economy employs the largest number of workers in the UK?
   - **A** Manufacturing industries
   - **B** Extraction industries
   - **C** Service industries
   - **D** Craft industries

Question 4–6 relate to the answers given below:

Aspects of employment in the UK which have displayed significant growth since the early 1980s include:

- **A** Part-time employment
- **B** Temporary employment
- **C** Self-employment
- **D** Teleworking

Which of the above are likely to be associated with the following demand- and supply-side factors in labour markets?

4. Seasonal work

5. Increasing economic activity among women with dependent children

6. Improved communications technology

7. Which of the following are **not** included in the measure of the labour force or working population in the UK?
   - **A** Claimant unemployed
   - **B** Self-employed
   - **C** Students
   - **D** HM forces personnel

Questions 8–10 relate to the following identified employment trends:

- **A** An increase in the number of women at work
- **B** An increase in the number of people self-employed
- **C** An increase in the demand for skilled labour
- **D** A fall in the number employed in manual occupations

Which of the above trends could be explained by the following?

8. The introduction of robotic technology

9. Deindustrialization

10. Changes in social attitudes

11. The most likely outcome from a shortage of skilled labour in the UK is:
    - **A** More government re-training programmes
    - **B** Skilled workers demanding higher wages
    - **C** The increased use of labour with lower skills
    - **D** Falling production costs

12. The most up-to-date and in-depth statistics on employment in the UK are available in:
    - **A** Annual Abstract of Statistics
    - **B** Social Trends
    - **C** Labour Market Trends
    - **D** Monthly Digest of Statistics

13. Which of the following is unlikely to be a feature of a tight labour market?
    - **A** Rising wages
    - **B** Increased labour turnover
    - **C** Rising unemployment
    - **D** Increasing recruitment activity

14. In 2000, some 7 million workers in the UK were part-time employees.
    - **a** Explain two reasons for the growth in the number of part-time workers employed in UK firms over time.
    - **b** Give one example of:
      - i A skilled manual occupation
      - ii A non-manual occupation
    - **c** What has happened to the demand for skilled labour in the UK? What effect is this likely to have had on the wages of skilled workers?

chapter 14 Recruiting and Selecting Employees

This chapter identifies and evaluates recruitment and selection procedures used by business to fill job vacancies.

SO, WHAT MAKES YOU THINK YOU CAN DO THIS JOB THEN?

What you need to learn

Business need to recruit staff for a variety of reasons. You need to know why and how decisions to recruit staff are made. These include:

- **the growth of the business**
- **changing job roles within the business**
- **filling vacancies created by resignation, retirement and dismissal**
- **internal promotion**

You should understand that the **recruitment process** can be costly, in terms of resources devoted to the process and costs associated with recruiting poor performing staff. Therefore, it is important to accurately select people for interview. Businesses need to be very clear about the requirements of the job and about the kind of person they are looking for. You need to understand the ways in which they do this through:

- **preparing person specifications and job descriptions**
- **carefully planning how and when to advertise**
- **identifying the strengths and weaknesses of job applications, curriculum vitae and letters of application**
- **shortlisting candidates**

You need to understand how **recruitment interviews** are planned, carried out and evaluated.

You should be able to understand the legal and ethical responsibilities relating to equal opportunities, and know the key implications for recruitment of the following legislation:

- **Equal Pay Acts 1970/1983**
- **Sex Discrimination Acts 1975/1986**
- **Race Relations Act 1976**
- **Disability Discrimination Act 1995**

You will also need to identify:

- **the appropriate use of different methods of assessment such as psychometric and aptitude testing**
- **good interview techniques**
- **criteria for evaluating the recruitment process**

You need to understand the importance of recruiting and maintaining a **flexible workforce** if a business is to remain competitive. You need to know about the different bases for recruiting people for a flexible workforce, including:

- **different modes of employment**
- **different terms and conditions**
- **core employees**
- **part-time, temporary and contract labour**

You need to know how contracts of labour help a business to achieve a flexible workforce are put together. You should understand the key elements of legislation that seeks to protect the rights of employees in relation to **employment contracts**

Section **14.1**

Recruitment and selection

▼ *Recruitment*

The terms **recruitment** and **selection** are often confused. It is useful to make the following distinction:

- **Recruitment** is the first part of the process to fill a job vacancy. It refers to those activities that will generate a pool of suitable job applicants.
- **Selection** is the next stage, i.e. assessing job applicants by various methods, choosing between them, and making an offer of employment to the right candidate.

Since the 1980s, the UK labour market has undergone significant change. Unemployment has produced an over-supply of labour. The number of young people in the population is falling. Many more women are seeking employment. Employment laws have changed. Manufacturing industry has been in decline, to be replaced by high technology and service industries, such as retailing and finance. Competition has become global and fierce in many industries. Consequently, there is growing pressure to get selection right.

The activity of recruitment and selection has therefore had to adapt to overcome the following problems:

- Fewer jobs but larger numbers of applicants
- A need to comply with laws on sex and race discrimination
- Shortages of certain types of skilled labour

There is increasing competition among employers for young workers and those with valuable skills. Employers have also introduced more flexible working practices, such as multi-skilling and job sharing, and adapted their recruitment policies to tap alternative sources of labour - for example, older workers, women, and the disabled.

The need for effective recruitment and selection

An organization will seek to recruit new staff if it has identified vacancies in the business because

- it is expanding production, and needs more employees with the same skills as existing staff
- key staff have left for other jobs, retired or been dismissed, and need to be replaced
- some staff have been promoted to more senior positions within the organization, leaving their previous jobs vacant
- it has introduced new technology, so employees with skills in the use of the new equipment are required
- the organization has restructured and job roles have changed so new employees with different skills and aptitudes are required (see 2.4 and 2.5)

It is the role of the human resources manager to identify the need for these human resources, to attract the best candidates for new posts, and then to choose, or recruit, the most suitable candidate to fill the vacancy. If a candidate selected is unsuitable, or fails to be motivated by the work, then the business will fail to achieve the best from its human resources.

▼ *Figure 14.1: The recruitment and selection process*

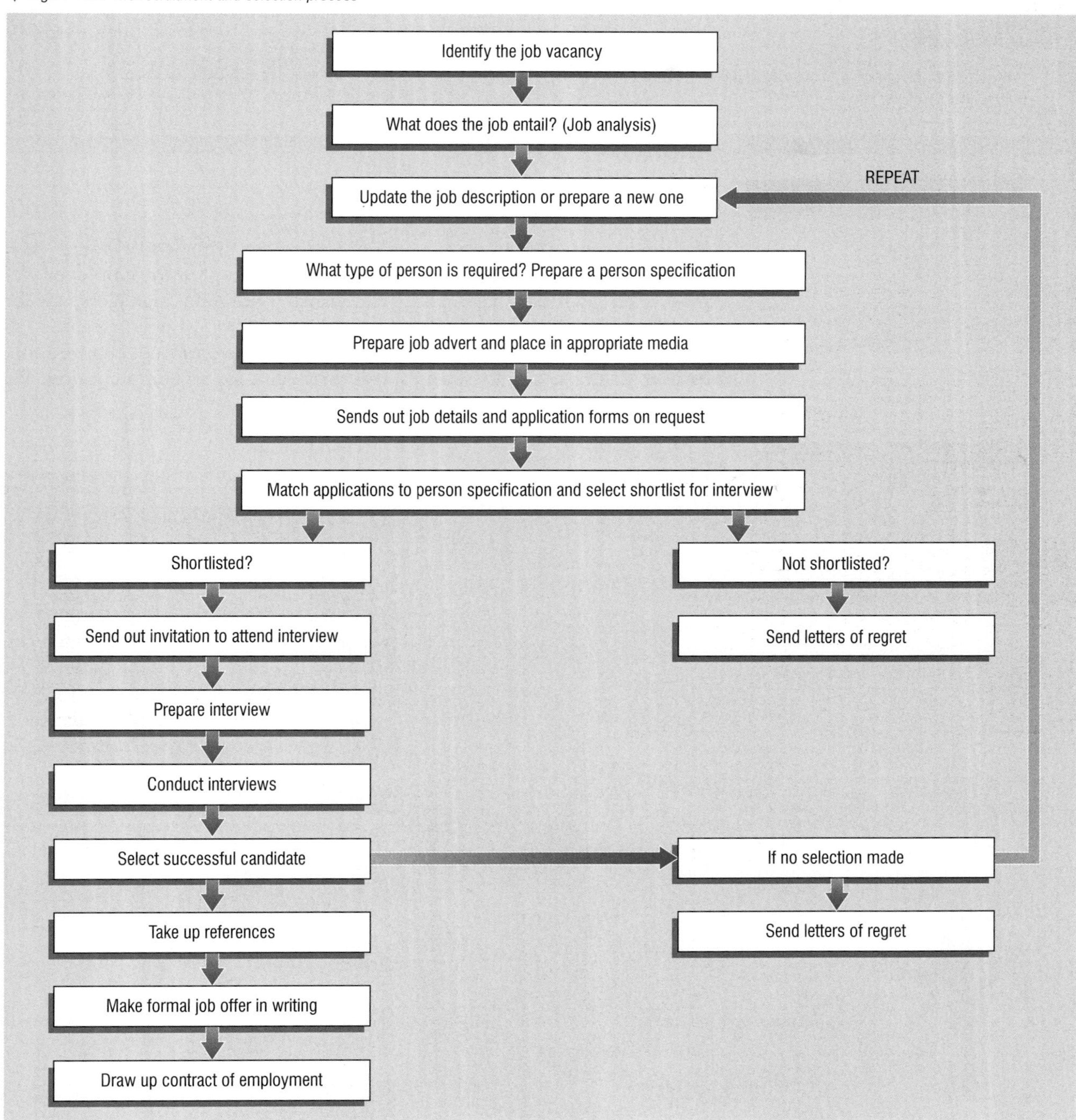

Selecting an unsuitable candidate to fill a job vacancy can also raise business costs. Output will be lower than it could otherwise be, and more training may be needed. The cost of employing an unsuitable air-traffic controller, for example, could be catastrophic. The process of recruitment and selection, therefore, needs careful planning and handling to minimize costs and minimize the risk of error.

Key words:

Recruitment - the process of generating job applicants, for example from a job advertisement

Selection - assessing the suitability of applicants for a job

Section 14.2 The recruitment process

If a job vacancy in a business is additional to the present workforce - say, because of a new or increased activity - then the need for the employee will most likely already have been established with line managers, senior managers, and personnel. However, the majority of job vacancies in business occur as replacements for people who have retired, changed job, or been dismissed. In these cases, it is important for a firm to consider the

Portfolio Activity 14.1 

Look at the jobs pictured. For each one, discuss and list:

1. The various tasks and activities involved
2. The skills the job holder must possess
3. Criteria that could be used to assess the appropriate rate of pay for the job and worker performance.

following questions:

- Is the post still needed?
- Should the tasks and responsibilities of the job be changed?

Questions like these will also arise when the organization is changing, perhaps because of the introduction of new technology. They may be answered by carrying out a **job analysis**. This is the study of what a job entails, namely, the tasks, skills, and training that are required to carry out the job effectively. Job analysis can also be used to decide on the appropriate wage rate for the job, and in staff appraisal and performance monitoring once the post has been filled.

The job description

Once a business has analysed what a job involves, the next step is to prepare a **job description**. This will contain many of the following elements:

The job description

General information

- Job title
- Position in the organizational structure, for example, director, manager, supervisor, etc.
- Department/division
- Name and location of employing firm
- Working conditions, salary details, and other benefits

Job content information

- Main tasks and responsibilities (can be in order of priority)
- General tasks, e.g. post holder should become familiar with administrative arrangements in the office
- Specific tasks, e.g. produce a report
- Purpose of tasks, e.g. to design a new sportswear range
- Methods involved, e.g. use of *EXCEL* computer spreadsheet, etc.
- Supervisory/management duties

Performance criteria

- For example, dates for the completion of certain tasks, quality standards, etc.

Special competencies

- Qualifications and skills considered vital to the post, for example, a degree in chemistry, a clean driving licence, fluency in a foreign language, etc.

Sample job descriptions

Job title: Business Assistant
Responsible to: Group Financial Director
A. Summary of main responsibilities and activities
Help to collate financial reporting information
Maintenance of financial information
Collection, collation, and distribution of marketing materials from and to regional offices
Maintenance of customer lists, customer profiles
Assist in development of marketing materials
Setting up and implementing administrative procedures relating to the above

B. Specific responsibilities

1. Staff
(No staff currently reporting to Business Assistant)

2. Planning
Plan and manage own time to achieve mutually agreed delivery schedules
Provide advice and input into product planning process

3. Confidential information
Privy to client data, reference groups, and customer information database
Privy to group financial information of a confidential nature

4. Contacts
Liaison with product managers
Liaison with personnel at regional offices
External marketing consultants and Public Relations organizations

C. Working conditions
Based at group head office in Warrington
Maybe occasional foreign travel
Salary approx. £30,000+ p.a.
37.5 hours per week (Flexible: core hours 10.00 - 16.00 Mon-Fri)
Additional benefits (subject to medical qualification)
- PPP Private Health Insurance
- Permanent Health Insurance to 75% of salary
- Life Insurance 4 times salary

Job title: Secretary
Reporting to: Financial Controller
Hours of work: 09.00 - 17.30 Mon - Fri
Significant working relationships:
All managers and secretaries
All Staff Divisions
Corporate Payroll

Overall purpose:
To provide an administrative and secretarial function to the Financial Controller and his department

Principal responsibilities:

1. Copy typing department correspondence and reports
2. Filing
3. Making meeting and buffet arrangements
4. Receiving visitors and providing hospitality required
5. Making travel arrangements as necessary
6. Send outgoing faxes
7. Mail distribution to department
8. Order and control stationery for department
9. Provide secretarial support for other staff when required
10. Maintain an internal document logging system for department
11. Any other tasks necessary to ensure the smooth running of the department and division

Training:
Wordprocessing package
Graphics package

Qualifications and personal skills:
Typing
Wordprocessing
Secretarial
Must be able to deal with people

Job title: Sales Assistant

Reports to: Store Manager

Overall purpose:
To carry out a range of duties specified by Store Manager

Specific duties:
Greeting and helping customers
Selling
Operating till
Stock taking
Stock retrieval
Shelf-filling

Every job within an organization will have a written job description, usually drawn up immediately prior to the appointment of an employee. Job descriptions can be modified over time to reflect changes in the organization, its business objectives, technology used, products, working conditions, etc. A job description allows a firm to tell applicants what is expected of them, and helps the personnel department to select suitable candidates. Once in post, the performance of the employee can be judged on how well they carry out the tasks identified in their job description.

▼ *The right person for the job?*

The person specification

A **person specification** describes in broad terms the skills, qualifications, abilities, and personal qualities needed to perform a particular job as described in a job description. The specification forms the basis for the selection of the most suitable job applicant.

A person specification is likely to include many of the following elements:

The person specification

Previous experience and qualifications

- Is experience required or will training be given?
- Evidence of previous experience and qualifications, if necessary, e.g. HGV licence, references from former employers
- Formal education and training qualifications required, e.g. GCSEs, A levels, NVQs, university degrees, postgraduate studies, etc.

Special aptitudes

- For example, is the person able to work under pressure? Flexible and adaptable? Good memory?
- Personal qualities and motivation
- For example, is the person willing to take on responsibility? Ambitious? Able to work independently? A 'self-starter'? Reliable and personable?

Special circumstances

- For example, will the person need to travel? Work unsociable hours?

(Note: For some jobs, physical attributes will also be specified for example, a minimum height requirement for people wishing to join the police.)

Sample person specifications

Job title: Business Assistant

A. Physical attributes

Minimum

Good health record. Few absences from work. Tidy appearance.

Desirable

Smart appearance, creates good impression on others

B. Mental attributes

Above average intelligence, good communication skills

C. Qualifications

Minimum

Higher education in a business discipline, e.g. business administration

Desirable

Further education in Public Relations and Marketing

D. Experience, training, and skill

Minimum

Experience of positions involving similar duties

Experience in using PCs as part of daily work, e.g. wordprocessing, spreadsheets, and presentations

Desirable

Conversational ability in German and French

Job title: Financial Accounts Clerk

Appearance: Needs to be well-groomed and smartly dressed - suits preferred

Desirable personal qualities:

- Self-starter
- Able to work independently
- Abundance of common sense
- Sense of humour
- Mature
- Outgoing and lucid communicator
- Open personality, willing to accept change/challenge
- Willing to accept responsibility

Qualifications and skills:

- Excellent writing skills
- Experience of business and marketing environment
- Numerate
- Not phased by technical activities
- GCSE pass in English and Maths required as minimum

Training:

- Bookkeeping skills

Job title: Sales Assistant

Qualities/Skills:

Neat and tidy appearance

Personable, able to get on with people

Reliable and trustworthy

Numerate

Physically fit

Aged 16 - 18 years

Training given:

Operation of till

Stock taking and ordering procedures

Portfolio Activity 14.2 

1. Select two employees in an organization you are familiar with. One should be of managerial grade, the other a shop-floor worker. From observations of both employees at work, and from interviews, make a list of the tasks they must perform and the skills and qualities they need.
2. From your observations, develop a job description and person specification for the jobs performed by your chosen employees.
3. If possible, discuss the accuracy of your job and person specifications with a personnel manager.

Attracting suitable job applicants

If vacancies exist, then it is up to the personnel department to find suitable staff to fill them. However, in the short term, if a firm is short of funds for additional workers, it may be possible to reorganize the workload so as to fill gaps created by vacant posts. Alternatively, existing workers may be offered overtime as an interim measure before new workers can be hired.

Vacancies will often be filled by **external recruitment**, through adverts placed in local or national newspapers, or Jobcentres. However, some vacancies may be filled by **internal recruitment**, usually by staff on promotion, although this is likely to create vacancies elsewhere in the organization.

Internal recruitment

The advantages of filling a vacancy from the existing workforce in a company rather than from outside are:

- Promotion opportunities can motivate existing workers
- It is more reliable, because existing workers and their abilities will be well-known to the company, while external candidates are not
- An existing worker may feel more committed to the company and the achievement of its goals
- Internal recruitment is relatively cheap and quick

However, there can also be disadvantages:

- Advertising a job internally limits the number of applicants
- External candidates may be more suitable
- It creates vacancies elsewhere in the organization
- External recruitment will still be necessary if no suitable internal candidate can be found

External recruitment

Many vacancies are filled from external sources. This can be time-consuming, expensive, and uncertain, but with careful planning it is possible to minimize these costs.

Choosing the most appropriate method of attracting external candidates will often depend on the type of job and type of employee a business wants. Even during a period of high unemployment, certain types of employee who possess scarce skills may be difficult to find, and employers may have to resort to specialized, and possibly expensive, means of recruitment.

- **Unsolicited applications.** A business will sometimes receive applications from candidates who either call personally looking for work, or write letters of enquiry. Their applications can be placed on file until a suitable vacancy arises.
- **Links with educational establishments.** Many employers maintain links with schools, colleges, and universities. For example, the 'milk round' involves companies visiting universities around the country each year, with the aim of generating interest in posts among final-year students.
- **Trade Unions.** Some employers recruit certain types of workers through appropriate Trade Unions, who are able to endorse candidates as having the necessary skills to undertake a job (see 13.3).
- **Professional associations:** A business can use these if they need to find employees with very specialized skills. For example, professional bodies, such as the Institute of Chartered Surveyors or British Medical Association, have an employment service for their members.
- **Government agencies:** It is in the interest of the UK Government to help people get jobs to keep unemployment low. The government, therefore, provides a number of free services to people looking for work, and to employers who want to fill vacancies. The **Careers Service** collects information about local job vacancies and distributes them to local schools/colleges and training establishments etc. **Jobcentres** will advertise posts on behalf of employers and select suitable candidates for interview. The service is free and most useful for advertising skilled, semi-skilled and unskilled manual and clerical jobs. Employers may also fill some vacancies with people from **government-supported training schemes.** The cost of employing a trainee can be paid for or heavily subsidized by the government.
- **Employment and recruitment agencies:** These business organizations specialize in recruiting and selecting suitable employees on behalf of other organizations. Businesses will often use their services to fill temporary vacancies. Some well-known agencies are Office Angels, Reed Employment, Brook Street and Kelly Services.

  An employer informs the agency of a vacancy, and the agency will then submit a suitable candidate from its register. When a candidate is appointed, the employer pays a fee to the agency. The main advantage of this is time and administration saved by the employer.

  Some agencies specialize in the recruitment and selection of managerial and professional staff, and will complete the entire recruitment process for an employer, including job analysis, job and person specification, sending out application forms, and interviewing suitable candidates. The employer is then presented with a shortlist of candidates for further interview.

  Very senior managers or executives are sometimes recruited through a process called **headhunting,** whereby suitable candidates with known specialisms are approached discreetly to discuss a possible appointment with another employer.

Portfolio Activity 14.3 

You are head of human resources at Flinchem Plc, a major UK manufacturer of kitchen appliances which are sold all over the world. You have asked a professional recruitment agency to help you find a new Finance Director for the company. The agency has produced two adverts for the job. One is a good advert, the other is not.

1. Use the good advert to produce a check list of all the things a job advert should contain.
2. Compare your list from task 1 with the poor advert. What is wrong with the advert? How could it be improved? Use a word processor program on a computer to redesign the advert.
3. Where would you advertise the job? Give reasons and try to find out how much it will cost.

Finance Director **£65,000**

Dynamic kitchen appliance maker seeks an experienced finance director. She will be a key member of the board and work closely with the Chief Executive.

To apply you must be a graduate and qualified accountant with a minimum of 2 years experience of finance and marketing, and the ability to work under stress. You will be required to manage the financial reporting process, establish internal controls and procedures, co-ordinate planning and company administration, and assess the potential for e-commerce.

If you are interested in this exciting opportunity contact

High Profile Search Associates on 01894 715354

London

Finance Director

c£65K+benefits

An outstanding opportunity for an entrepreneurial, commercially biased person to join a dynamic listed white goods company. The company, established 3 years ago, has an innovative new product due for market launch next year in the UK and thereafter across Europe, the United States and Asia. The successful candidate will be a key member of the Plc Board of directors and work closely with the Chief Executive to create a company that will generate growth over the next five years of trading.

The Role

- Manage monthly financial reporting against agreed budgets
- Establish internal controls and procedures
- Define the IT framework
- Co-ordinate planning against the agreed basis
- Monitor and summarise product variable costs
- Manage cash planning against agreed basis
- Establish company book-keeping procedures and ensure key issues such as banking, payment of payroll etc. have back-up processes
- Co-ordinate the activities of all company administration procedures to ensure a smooth flow of key business data
- Address the opportunity for electronic commerce

The Person

- A graduate, qualified accountant
- A minimum of 2 years experience as the Finance Director of a company with a turnover of at least £20M
- A background in consumer goods or where retail product marketing is strategically important
- Be fully conversant with UK statutory and tax legislation
- Demonstrate a proven ability to work under pressure, often with limited resources
- Possess an optimistic outlook and demonstrate a "can do" attitude
- Desire to be a proactive, key member of the executive team
- Have an ability to build strong relationships across all levels, both internally and externally
- Age 30 to mid 40's

Internet Recruiting Shows Rapid Growth

Finding well-qualified applicants quickly at the lowest possible cost has long been a primary goal for recruiters. To accomplish that aim, more companies are using online sources.

A survey of over 200 companies in the US showed two-thirds considered the Internet more cost-effective than most or all other available recruitment methods. Companies that had used the Internet longer or posted more jobs rated the Internet's cost-effectiveness higher than did other firms.

Internet users responding to another survey cited these advantages, among others: access to more people and a broader selection of applicants, the ability to target the type of people needed, access to people with a technical background who know computers, convenience and quicker response and turnaround, ease of use, and economy.

Adapted from HR Magazine on-line, April 2000

The main disadvantages of using an agency, apart from cost, is that the employer loses some control over the recruitment and selection process. Staff recruited through agencies also tend to stay in jobs only a short time.

- **Advertising.** The most popular method of recruitment is to advertise the vacancy and invite candidates to apply to the company.

  Job advertisements should aim to produce a small number of well-qualified candidates quickly and cheaply. It is important to make sure that the right advertisement is placed in the right media at the right time. For example, it would be inappropriate to advertise a post for specialist chemical engineers in a mass circulation newspaper like the *Sun,* or to broadcast the vacancy on Radio 1. Adverts for jobs, just like adverts for goods and services, should be aimed as closely as possible at their target audience (see 10.3).

Advertising to get the job done!

If advertising is be cost-effective and attract suitable candidates, the following principles need to be observed:

1. The adverts should contain enough clearly stated and relevant information for people to be able to tell what the job involves and whether they would be suitable candidates. The key elements should be:
   - A job title
   - Brief details of the job
   - Experience, skills, and qualifications required
   - Training given
   - Pay and working conditions
   - A brief description of the organization, including location, whether it has an equal opportunities policy, etc.
   - How to apply - for example, by phoning for further details and an application form, or submitting a letter of application and Curriculum Vitae (CV)

   In all cases, the information provided must be accurate and honest.
2. The medium chosen for the advertisement should be appropriate. This will depend on factors such as the type of job, the number of vacancies, and the budget available. Where a large number of vacancies exist, mass advertising in national newspapers or on TV may be appropriate, although expensive. For example, the police and armed services sometimes advertise for new recruits on TV.

   Some newspapers print specialized job supplements devoted to different types of job on particular days of the week. For example, *The Guardian* advertises jobs in computing every Thursday.
3. The response to the advert must be carefully analysed. For example:
   - How many candidates applied?
   - Were the applicants suitable for the job?
   - Did the advert reach its target audience?

   This will help a company to plan and design future job advertisements.

Key words:

Job analysis - a study of the tasks, skills, and training that are required to carry out a job

Job description - a summary of what a job entails

Person specification - a profile of the type of person required to do a job

Internal recruitment - filling a job vacancy in an organization from its existing workforce

External recruitment - generating job applicants from outside the organization, for example, by using private employment agencies or advertising in newspapers

Section 14.3 Applying for a job

There are a number of ways of inviting people to reply to a job advertisement. For example, they can be asked to:

- Apply for and complete an application form
- Prepare a Curriculum Vitae (CV)
- Write a letter of application

Information provided by job applicants should always be treated confidentially by the business organization receiving it.

The application form

This is sent to applicants on request, usually with further job details. Application forms are often used by business organizations to ensure that important details are not missed out, and that information about candidates is supplied in a logical and uniform manner. This enables information to be processed easily and conveniently, often within a computer database. Standardization also makes for easier comparison of candidates.

The layout and design of an application form will depend on the type of job and level of information required. However, in general, an application form will request the following details:

- **Personal details:** name, address (permanent and temporary if applicable), telephone number, date of birth, marital status
- The **name of the post** applied for
- **Education history:** schools, colleges, universities attended, with dates
- **Details of educational and professional qualifications:** exam grades, and dates taken. (*Note*: There are many different types of qualification. The form should allow for these. For example, students in Scotland are not able to list GCSEs and A levels among their educational attainments.)
- **Employment history/previous experience:** names and addresses of former employers, posts held, dates, reasons for leaving. (*Note*: The word **experience** can refer to both **work experience**, and the **skills** the applicant thinks s/he has. The application form should make it clear which meaning is intended.)
- **Medical history:** serious illnesses, disabilities. (These can only be requested if knowledge of them is vital to the execution of the job.)
- **Ethnic origin:** the Commission for Racial Equality code of practice recommends that employers include questions about applicants' ethnic origin on job application forms in order to allow monitoring.
- **Interests:** leisure- and work-related; positions of responsibility held at school - for example 'Prefect' - or in organizations related to applicants' leisure pursuits - for example, 'Treasurer of local Rambler's Association'
- **Other information:** for example, why is the applicant interested in the job? What qualities do they have that make them suited to the job?

Portfolio Activity 14.4 

1. Select 5-10 different job advertisements for posts at different levels within organizations in different industrial sectors. Check that each advertisement requests the applicant to apply for an application form.
2. Apply for the application forms by writing to the advertised addresses, or by telephoning.
3. Compare and contrast the application forms you receive. Make a list of the main features you think a good application should have. Which of the application forms do you think is (a) the most effective and (b) the least effective? Give reasons.

- **References:** usually, names and addresses of two referees who are able to confirm the applicant's character and suitability for the job.

Most application forms, especially those for higher-level jobs, will contain a mixture of **closed questions** (e.g. 'Please give details of your educational qualifications') and **open-ended questions** (e.g. 'Give reasons why you feel suited to this type of work'). It is important that questions are neither offensive nor illegal (for example, 'Have you got AIDS?' would not be allowed). It is also important for forms to provide enough space for applicants to write their answers.

An application form should make clear where and to whom the completed form should be sent, and the closing date for applications. The completed application provides the basis for selection and is a vital document in an employee's personnel record.

Tips on filling out application forms

1. Take a photocopy of the form and practise answering the questions in rough.
2. Read all the instructions carefully.
3. Always write clearly in black or blue ink (and use block capitals if asked to do so).
4. Answer questions in full. Do not leave any large gaps. If something does not apply to you, write N/A ('not applicable').
5. Remember to sign and date your completed form.
6. Take a photocopy of your completed form for future reference, should you be called for interview.
7. Ensure that the form is returned promptly to the employer.

▼ *Figure 14.2: Example of an application form*

JOB APPLICATION FORM

Please complete this side of the form in BLOCK CAPITALS

Surname (Mr/Mrs/Miss/Ms) | Forenames

Address (including postcode) | Previous name (if applicable)

Telephone number | Date of birth

Names and addresses of schools/colleges since age 11 | Dates attended

From ... to

From ... to

From ... to

Examinations taken or about to be taken

GCSE	Date	Grade	GNVQ	Date	Grade	A & A /S levels	Date	Grade

Please list any other courses and qualifications taken or about to be taken

Course/examination	Date	Grade

If you have shorthand/typing qualifications please indicate speeds

Shorthand ... wpm

Audio ... wpm

Typing ... wpm

Please give details of any work experience you have had, including Saturday and holiday jobs

Employer's name and address	Dates of employment	Duties

Please complete this side of the form in your own handwriting unless unable to do so because of physical disability

Indicate your interests and activities – include involvement in voluntary work, clubs and societies, hobbies and sport

Inside school | Duties

Outside school | Duties

Provide examples of where you have worked as part of a team. What was your role/contribution?

Please give details of special achievements and/or positions of responsibility (e.g. prefect, Duke of Edinburgh's Award)

Outline any activities you have planned and organized, and how you achieved your results

Please indicate why you are interested in this post, the reasons why you consider yourself suitable and how you see your future with this company

Signed | Date

The Curriculum Vitae (CV)

Much of the information an application form is designed to extract from a candidate can be provided from a **Curriculum Vitae** or **CV**. Although potentially less structured than an application form, a CV provides a broad summary of the applicant's life and education, and career achievements to date. A job applicant will frequently send a CV along with a letter of application, or application form.

A carefully prepared CV, preferably typed or wordprocessed, is the means by which an applicant will promote themselves to an employer. It is often the first contact between applicant and prospective employer. If it fails to make an impact, then any other efforts the applicant may make will be wasted.

A CV should be no longer than 3–4 sides of A4 paper, and in general should include the following headings:

- Personal details
- Educational history and qualifications
- Training and professional qualifications

Curriculum Vitae

Personal details

Name: Dawn MARTIN

Date of Birth: 6 September 1983

Address: 69 Westbank Road, Tolworth, Surrey KT5 9GR

Telephone: 020-83307-2345

Education history

1994 - 1999: Tolworth Girls School, Fullers Way North, Tolworth, Surrey
1999 - 2001: Kingston College of Further Education, Kingston-upon-Thames, Surrey

Qualifications

GCSE Subjects:
Art A
Biology C
English Language B
French A
History B
Mathematics C
Statistics C

Vocational A level Subjects:
Advanced Business Distinction
Advanced Art and Design Merit

Work experience

Vacation and temporary posts
June - Sept 1999: Sales Assistant, Bentalls Department Store, Kingston-upon-Thames
June - Sept 2000: Receptionist, Hotel Antoinette, Kingston-upon-Thames
November 2000: Work Placement at Nutmeg UK, assisting manager in design studio

Positions of responsibility

1996: Captain of hockey team
1999: Fifth form prefect
2000: Editor of student magazine

Interests
Watercolour painting, tennis, swimming, rock music, reading

Other information

Special skills
Typing (90 wpm) using Microsoft Word
User experience of Microsoft *Excel*
Full driving licence for 7 months
Good oral and written French

References
Academic: Mrs B Sure, Department of Art and Design, Kingston College of Further Education, Kingston-upon-Thames KT1 2AQ, Tel: 020-8546-4661
Work Experience: Mr D Jones, Nutmeg UK Ham Trading Estate, Richmond, Surrey, Tel: 020-8947-6666
Personal: Mrs G Peterson, 45 Park Avenue, Surbiton, Surrey KT6 7NT, Tel: 020-8303-0567

- Employment history and posts held/work experience
- Positions of responsibility held
- Interests
- Other information
- References

Tips on preparing a CV

1. Assemble all the facts about yourself.
2. Prepare a first draft. Use a wordprocessor if possible, as this will make it easier to correct and edit your CV to suit the requirements of different jobs.
3. Use plain white A4 paper and leave enough white space between your details to make presentation attractive and uncluttered.
4. Layout, for example, headings and sub-headings, font size and type, should be consistent.
5. Sentences should be short, to the point, and display a good grasp of English grammar and vocabulary. Try not to be either boring or too fancy.
6. Technical details should be presented in a way that can be understood by a non-specialist reader.
7. Edit and correct mistakes.
8. Print, read through, and redraft if necessary.

Portfolio Activity 14.5

1. Produce an up-to-date CV for yourself using a wordprocessor.
2. If possible, ask a human resources officer to evaluate your CV. Failing this, present your CV to a careers adviser in your school/college, or to a colleague, and ask them to evaluate your CV against the following checklist:
   - Is the content and coverage right?
   - Do major achievements stand out?
   - Is it concise and to the point?
   - Is spelling and grammar correct?
   - Is the layout pleasing?
   - Is it easily understood?
   - Does it create an overall good impression?

The letter of application

Sometimes job applicants may simply be invited to write a letter of application. However, more usually an applicant will use this as a covering letter for a completed application form or CV.

Many employers prefer letters of application to be handwritten. Good handwriting is a requirement in many jobs, particularly in clerical and administrative occupations, and firms may need to see evidence of an applicant's handwriting skills, rather than just a wordprocessed or typewritten application. Handwriting may also be analysed in some cases. The science of **graphology** - the assessment of a person's character from their handwriting - is popular in the USA and some European countries, and is now being used by a number of recruitment agencies in the UK.

Writing a letter of application probably requires more skill than simply filling in an application form or preparing a CV. A letter of application should have a clear structure and give the following information:

- The applicant's reasons for applying for the job
- Skills and knowledge the applicant has acquired that are particularly relevant to the job

- Details of relevant experience and qualifications (if not already provided in a supporting CV)

Tips on writing a letter of application

1. Prepare a first draft.
2. Use plain white A4 paper and try not to write more than one side.
3. Write your permanent address in the top right-hand corner.
4. Write the name and address of the person you are sending your letter to on the left-hand side immediately below your own address.
5. Date the letter below the application address.
6. Use the correct conventions for addressing letters. A letter beginning 'Dear Sir/Madam' should end 'Yours faithfully'. If 'Dear Mr X' is used, the letter should be signed 'Yours sincerely'.
7. Start your letter with a reference to the post you are applying for, and where and when it was advertised.
8. Use good English and try to keep your paragraphs short and to the point.
9. Do not repeat details that are contained in an accompanying CV, but make reference to your attached CV in your letter.
10. Redraft your letter until you are satisfied with it.

Portfolio Activity 14.6

This letter of application has been received in response to the advertisement for a data processing assistant. It has been rejected by the employer.

1. List what you think is wrong with the letter, and why.
2. How would you improve the letter? Prepare a new draft.

Data Processing Assistant

Circa £16,000 pa salary depending on experience

A small established busy firm seeks a full-time data processing assistant who will probably be aged 18–25. The main role would involve complex database selections being processed and output to numerous media in various formats. The ability to communicate with non-technically minded people is essential since client liaison would be required. Should the successful candidate show the right aptitude, training would be provided to progress into network management and programming. Education to A-level standard or equivalent with some computing experience necessary.

57 Letsby Avenue
Trumpington
Cambridge
CR2 1BZ

Ms M Lyes
Personnel Department

Dear Ms Lyes

I would like to apply for the job you advertised recently. I am very interested in computing and think it would be very interesting and rewarding job that I am well suited to carry out.

I am 18 years old and have been studying at college for the last two years. I have just competed courses in Business and Leisure and Tourism. At school I took exams in Maths, English, History, Art, and Computing. I have my own computer at home and am familiar with a number of wordprocesing and spreedsheet programs. Many of my assignments in the two GNVQ courses were completed using a computer. Computer studies was my best subject at school and I got a grade B in the GCSE. I have just enrolled at my college for part-time evening study in A level Computer studies.

I was a fifth form prefect at school and captain of the football team. I am curently working part-time at a local library. this allows me time to pursue my hobbies of photography and looking after my aquarium. At the library I have to check incoming and outgoing books, collect fines, order and shelve books and advise customers on library collections.

I am currently preparing my CV and will send this to you within the next few days. Should you require a reference you should contact;

Mr A Young
Head of Computer Studies
Milton High School
Cambridge

My thanks in advance of your consideration.

Yours faithfully

D J Moore

D J Moore (Mr)

References

A **reference** is a confidential statement about a person's character and abilities by a third party, known as a **referee.**

An employer will often request a job applicant to supply two or three referees. One will normally be a personal referee, such as a family friend; the other will be a former or present employer, or, if the applicant is still at school or college, a teacher or tutor. A clear, unbiased description of a candidate's abilities by a former employer can be extremely valuable in selection.

References are normally only taken up by an employer if a candidate is being seriously considered for appointment or has been **shortlisted** (see 14.4). A reference can take many forms:

- **Reference letter** - a formal and confidential written testimonial
- **Reference form** - a structured form of open and closed questions supplied by the prospective employer for the referee to complete
- **Telephone reference** - some organizations may phone referees. Answers to questions, and the tone of voice of the referee may reveal if they are being totally honest about the applicant.
- **Medical references** - these may be required if an employee wishes to join a company pension scheme, or if a job requires specific health standards.

Prospective employers need to treat references with caution. An applicant will naturally choose referees who they think will write complimentary things about them. An applicant who does *not* choose his or her present employer as a referee should therefore be viewed with some suspicion (although this may of course be because the applicant does not want them to know they are thinking of leaving). The present employer of an applicant may also be less than truthful on occasion. For example, they may provide a glowing reference because they secretly hope to get rid of an unsuitable employee.

For these reasons, employers do not usually take up references. Many will already be confident of their chosen candidate's character and abilities from their application and interviews.

Key words:

Application form - a standardized set of questions prepared by an organization for job applicants to complete

Curriculum Vitae (CV) - a written summary of a job applicant's life, education, and career achievements

Letter of application - a written letter by a job applicant summarizing information otherwise provided in a CV or an application form

References - a confidential statement about a person's character and abilities by a third party

Section 14.4 Selection

Once a firm has assembled a pool of applicants for a post, the process of selection can begin. However, the organization may be faced with the prospect of processing a large number of candidates. It is therefore often necessary to select a smaller group - or **shortlist** - of the most suitable

candidates for interview. This process is sometimes known as **pre-selection.** Although often rather crude, it is common practice when job advertisements generate a large response.

The process of pre-selecting begins with human resource managers comparing individual applications with the person specification. The aim at this stage is to identify attributes which show candidates to be suitable for the job, and also pinpoint any shortcomings, such as poor presentation, which will either rule them out, or necessitate special training if they are appointed. From this comparison, managers will decide who to invite for interview, and who will be rejected and sent a **letter of regret.** In all cases, selection should be objective and impartial. All applicants should be judged on their own merits - even those who may be internal candidates and known to the pre-selection panel.

Where there are many applicants, pre-selection can be very time-consuming. Carefully designed application forms can help by making comparison easier. Some pre-selection procedures will award points to applicants for information which matches the requirements in the person specification - for example, the number of exams passed at grade C and above, previous work experience, etc. Those with the most points will be shortlisted.

Testing

Pre-selection methods used by some organizations include the setting of **tests** for candidates to complete. For example:

- **Tests of numeracy and written communication.** The ability to write good, clear English is an important requirement in many clerical and administrative occupations. Similarly, shop assistants may be set simple arithmetic tests.
- **Practical tests.** These are designed to test whether the candidate can do what they claim to be able to do. For example, a secretary may be set a test to verify a claim to type 100 words per minute.
- **Intelligence tests.** These test applicants' powers of deduction, analysis, and reasoning. The Civil Service often uses these to test candidates for specialist posts. For example, a candidate may be asked to complete a number series, identify the pattern in a line of dominoes, sort jumbled sentences into their correct order, etc.
- **Psychometric and personality tests.** The current trend in job analysis is to concentrate on key behavioural requirements of a job, for example, stamina and mental agility, initiative, working with others, etc. These type of tests may reveal aspects of a candidate's behaviour and attitude to work, and different working practices.
- **Medical tests.** These are used to check specific health standards which are required for a job - for example, a train driver's hearing or colour vision. Medical tests can also be used to protect a firm against claims. For example, an employee may claim that their respiratory problems have been caused by the materials and chemicals they work with. Checking the results of a medical test taken prior to their appointment may reveal that the employee had always suffered from this problem.

Tests require careful design, and the process of compiling and validating tests can be a lengthy and expensive undertaking.

Final selection

The final stage of the selection process is usually the **interview** of shortlisted candidates. Interviews involve a face-to-face meeting between a candidate and his or her prospective employer. An interview is designed to include questions to test achievement and aptitude, and is at present the most commonly used method of personality assessment.

▼ *One-to-one interview*

▼ *Panel interview*

▼ *Bored interview!*

There are three main types of selection interview:

1. A **one-to-one interview** between interviewee (the candidate) and interviewer (a representative of the employer)
2. A **panel interview** involving several interviewers, for example, a senior manager, departmental manager, and personnel manager. Panel interviews have certain advantages:
   - Each interviewer can specialize in asking different questions.
   - All the interviewers can take part in a joint assessment of the candidate, reducing the risk of personal bias.

   However, there can also be disadvantages:
   - Questioning may be disorganized and repetitive unless questions are planned and agreed before an interview.
   - The candidate may feel less at ease.
3. A **board interview** with many more representatives of the employer. For example, boards of over 20 interviewers are not uncommon in the selection of senior civil servants. In addition to the advantages of panel interviews, the board interview is useful to reveal the behaviour of the candidate under stress. However, large numbers of interviewers can make the final assessment of the candidate very difficult.

   Sometimes sequential interviews are used in the pre-selection process. A further shortlist of candidates can be drawn up on the basis of their performance during a first interview. Successful candidates may then be invited back for a second interview before final selection is made. Sequential interviews are often used in the selection of senior managers.

Planning an interview

Poorly planned and structured interviews can give an organization a bad image and may result in the selection of an unsuitable candidate. It is therefore important for an employer to plan for an interview. The following steps can be followed:

1. Decide (a) is a test required? (b) is the interview to be one-to-one or panel?
2. If a panel interview, select and invite members.
3. Organize a room and facilities for the interview. Make sure the room is quiet and private. If necessary, check access arrangements for any disabled candidates.

4. Send clear instructions on time, date, and venue of interview to candidates and panel members. (Be sure to allow ample time for the interview to be conducted: 30–40 minutes is usual.)

5. Be familiar with the job description and person specification for the post. (Send copies to panel members.)

6. Compare the written application of each candidate with the job description, so that the interviewers can decide where clarification or further information is needed.

7. Make a note of questions to ask each candidate. Some 'control' questions should be common to all candidates in order to aid comparison between them. These might include problem-solving questions, or more open questions, such as 'What qualities do you think a good manager should have?', 'Why do you want to work here?', 'What were your favourite subjects at school?'

8. Agree list of questions between panel members.

Conducting the interview

A well-conducted selection interview should fulfil four main aims:

- To discover information about the candidate's motives and behaviour in order to assess personality
- To check factual information already supplied by the candidate
- To inform the candidate about the job applied for, and the company
- To be fair, so that each candidate feels they have an equal chance and leaves with a favourable impression of the organization

Whether or not an interview fulfils these aims will depend much on the skill and judgement of the interviewers and the questions they ask.

How to conduct an interview

1. Immediately prior to the start of interviews, check the arrangements and facilities are satisfactory. For example, check the seating plan, lighting, refreshments. If interviews are to be conducted across a desk, clear it of any unnecessary equipment. Make sure the room will not be disturbed.

2. Begin the interview with a few remarks and questions designed to welcome the candidate and put them at their ease. For example, 'Did you manage to find your way here OK?'

3. Explain the purpose of the interview to the candidate. For example, will selection be made for the job on the basis of this interview, or is it part of a sequence of interviews used in the process of pre-selection?

4. Ask probing questions. Do not accept candidates' replies to questions at face value. If a candidate says s/he was responsible for a particular activity, or has operated a piece of machinery before, further questions should be asked to find out whether this was in fact the case.

5. As a rule of thumb, in an interview lasting 30 minutes the candidate should be expected to talk for around 20. During this time, interviewers should look interested in what the candidate says, and if necessary make occasional comment to encourage him or her to say more.

6. Observe each candidate during interview. Body language can provide vital clues about the candidate's honesty, personality, and level of stress. For example, observe how they are they sitting, eye movements, and eye contact, arm and hand movements.

7. At the end of the interview, ask the candidate if they would like to ask any questions.

8. Find out whether, if offered the job, the candidate would still want it, and when they could start.

9. Finally, indicate when the interview is over, thank the candidate for attending, and tell them what the next step will be - for example, whether they will be contacted by letter or telephone, and how long they can expect to wait for a reply.

10. Write down any notes on the candidate for your future reference after the interview. Making notes during interview itself may unsettle the candidate.

After the interview

Once all the interviews have been conducted, the interviewer or panel must make their decision on which candidate to appoint. They will compare notes and make a thorough analysis of all the information they have collected on each candidate. Having made their choice, they will then:

- **Send a letter of confirmation.** The successful candidate should be informed promptly, usually by telephone and/or in writing. A letter should confirm essential details such as start date, wage rate/salary, hours of work, and holidays. Offers of employment may be made subject to satisfactory references, and may be conditional on passing a medical exam, university degree, etc.

- **Draw up the contract of employment.** Under the UK employment law, a new employee is entitled to a written statement of the main terms and conditions of their employment within 13 weeks of appointment (see 14.5).

- **Validate the selection process.** The selection decision can be validated by observing the successful candidate's progress and behaviour once s/he has been working in the job for some time.

What if no appointment is made?

If no suitable candidate can be found to match the organization's specifications, no appointment will be made, and the post will be re-advertised. Internal candidates who fail interviews should be given the chance to discuss their failure with managers at a follow-up meeting, otherwise their motivation can suffer.

What about the candidate?

So far we have focused on how a business organization can prepare and conduct an interview. However, most people reading this book are likely to be more concerned with what they can do as candidates to improve their chance of being successful in interview and getting an offer of a job. Here are some helpful hints.

Helpful hints for interviewees

- Acknowledge an invitation for interview promptly, preferably by letter.
- Make any necessary travel and overnight accommodation arrangements well before the interview.
- Find out about the organization, so that you can appear resourceful and knowledgeable during the interview.
- Prepare some questions to ask your interviewers about the job and the organization. For example, 'How has your company been affected by the single European market?', 'What training can I expect to be given?', 'What are the prospects for promotion?'. Questions about pay and holidays are not recommended. You can find out these details after the interview.
- Wear appropriate clothes. For most jobs, this will mean a suit for a man, and skirt and blouse for a woman.
- Hair should be neat and tidy. Jewellery and make-up should be kept to a minimum.
- Arrive no more than 10 minutes before your interview. Do not be late!
- Do not discuss your interview with other candidates who may be waiting. Only make polite conversation.
- Wait to be asked to sit down. Sit upright during interview and appear alert, but more importantly - relax!
- Do not be afraid to ask your interviewers to repeat or clarify questions.
- Take your time. Pause for thought before answering questions.
- Be positive. Speak clearly and with confidence, but always be polite.
- Be truthful. Probing questions will catch you out.
- Look at your interviewers when listening to their questions, and when speaking.
- Be aware of your body language. Do not slouch or keep looking away, and try not to be nervous or use exaggerated hand movements.
- Thank your interviewers and shake hands at the end of the interview.

▼ *DO!*

▼ *DON'T!*

Ethical and legal obligations

Matching the right candidate to the right job is essential if an organization is to accomplish set objectives. However, despite careful planning and conduct of the recruitment and selection process, the wrong person may still be chosen. This may be for a variety of reasons. For example, the most suitable candidate may have suffered from nerves during the interview, or may simply have had an off day. Studies have shown that most interviewers form their impression of the candidate within the first few minutes, and spend the rest of the time asking questions that simply reinforce their view. We are all influenced by subjective factors when judging people, for example, how they speak, their school and social background, physical attractiveness, etc. It is important for interviewers not to let these factors cloud their judgement.

The recruitment and selection process relies on both the job applicant and the employer being fair, honest, and truthful. A job advertisement must provide an accurate description of both the job and person required. For example, if the job involves weekend work, it must say so. Similarly, information supplied by a candidate on application forms, CVs, or during interview should be truthful. Failing to disclose information, or giving false information, will invalidate a contract of employment and could lead to dismissal if discovered.

Care must also be taken by an organization to ensure that recruitment and selection procedures do not infringe current employment legislation concerning discrimination. Equal opportunity laws make it an offence for recruiting firms to discriminate on grounds of sex, race, religion, disability, age, Trade Union membership, or against ex-offenders. Job advertisements, application forms, and interviews should be carefully worded to avoid potentially discriminatory statements or questions.

However, it *is* legal to advertise for a person of a particular sex or race if it is a genuine requirement of the job - for example, an attendant for male toilets will need to be male, and an Asian actor portraying an Asian character in a TV programme will need to be Asian.

Many large organizations have developed their own equal opportunities policies which include specific procedures to be followed when hiring employees.

Legal obligations are considered in more detail in Section 15.2.

Don't ask!

The following are examples of questions and statements that should be avoided. All are potentially discriminatory and offensive. They have little or no relevance to whether the candidate is capable of doing the job.

'Are you married, Mrs Smith?'

'Male technician required in small engineering company'

'How many children do you have?'

'Have you made arrangements for your children to be looked after during the school holidays?'

'Young girl required for secretarial duties'

'Do you think you are capable of doing this job, Miss Jones?'

'People over 50 need not apply'

'How would you react if a work colleague told a racist joke in your presence?'

'Disabled person needed for simple office duties'

Key words:

Shortlisting - selecting a handful of the most promising candidates for interview from the entire set of job applications

Interview - the most common method of personality assessment, involving a face-to-face meeting between a candidate and employers' representatives

Section 14.5 The contract of employment

When a person is offered a job, the offer will be subject to certain terms and conditions. These may be explained to that person at an interview and will usually be set out in a letter confirming appointment. Figure 14.3 shows an example of a letter confirming the appointment of a new employee.

Employers are required to provide both full-time and part-time workers with a written statement of their terms and conditions of employment within 13 weeks of their starting a job.

▼ *Figure 14.3: A letter confirming employment*

Leigh Limited
12-18 Green Street
Newtown
Newshire NX4 7YY

Ms K Jennings
34 Saunders Close
Newtown
Newshire NX7 8RG

14 May 200X

Dear Karen

Appointment as Receptionist

We are pleased to confirm your appointment for the above post. The terms and conditions of your appointment are given below.

1. The job will start on 1 June 200X.
2. You will be paid a salary of £15,000 per year, payable monthly in arrears into your bank account.
3. Your work performance against targets set by your manager will be reviewed every six months. Salary will also be reviewed at the same time.
4. Hours of work are from 8.15 am to 5.30 pm from Monday to Thursday and from 8.15 am to 4 pm on Friday. You will also be required to attend a special sales evening for our customers at the factory every two months. Hours will include attendance at this evening between 6 pm and 10 pm. The date of each sales evening will be given one month in advance and will be paid at a rate of £8 per hour as overtime. This sum may be reviewed at the six-monthly salary review.
5. The appointment is subject to two weeks' notice in writing.
6. Your line manager will be the head of administration.
7. This appointment is subject to a 1-month probationary period. If performance is satisfactory after this period, the probationary period will end. If performance is unsatisfactory, the probationary period may be extended or the employment may be terminated at the discretion of your line manager.
8. Sickness must be notified as early as possible, ideally at least one hour before start of work. Sickness of up to five working days requires a self-certification form. A longer period of sickness requires a doctor's certificate. Statutory Sick Pay (SSP) will be paid where appropriate for a period up to 20 weeks in a year. After that period, any entitlement to SSP will be paid by the Department of Social Security.
9. Holiday entitlement accrues at one day per month in the first year of employment and one and a half days per month thereafter. Holiday entitlement may be taken after three months' employment and notice of at least three weeks is required.
10. At all times, conduct befitting a representative of our firm when dealing with the public will be expected.

Any grievances relating to this employment should follow the company grievance procedure. Grievances in the first instance should be referred to your line manager, thereafter to the managing director in writing.

Please sign and return the enclosed copy indicating your acceptance of these terms and conditions.

Yours sincerely

Allan Salt

Allan Salt
Administration Manager

Terms and conditions

A contract of employment is drawn up by the employer and signed by the employee. It is a legally binding agreement and can be enforced in law. A contract can contain any details, but as a minimum it must contain the following:

* *Name of employer and employee*
* *Date on which employment started*
* *Date on which employment will end if the contract is for fixed term only*
* *Job title*
* *Rates of pay, payment intervals, and method of payment*
* *Normal hours of work and related conditions, such as meal breaks*
* *Holiday entitlement, holiday pay, and public holidays*
* *Conditions relating to sickness, injury, and maternity pay*
* *Pension arrangements*
* *Length of notice to quit to and from employee*
* *Disciplinary rules and procedures*
* *Arrangements for handling employee grievances*

Other conditions may cover topics such as trade union membership, dress codes, the need for confidentiality, work locations, etc.

All of the above are called the **expressed terms** - that is, terms which are openly agreed between employer and employee. Because the range of expressed terms can be enormous, some organizations will not provide full written details in a contract, but will instead direct employees to company handbooks, where the rules of the company and other matters are set out in more detail.

In addition, there will be unwritten **implied terms** which are assumed to be part of a contract. For example, employees will be expected to work towards the achievement of organizational goals, obey reasonable orders from their managers, wear suitable and acceptable clothing, and produce good quality work. Both employer and employee are expected to be trustworthy, act in good faith, and exercise due care to ensure health and safety in the workplace.

Types of employment contract

Employment contracts can differ in the terms and conditions they offer an employee. Increasingly employment contracts are being designed to give employers more flexibility in human resource planning and management.

Permanent full-time employment: Employees who work under contract for an unspecified period of time for 30 or more hours each week are full-time workers who have a permanent contract of employment. Their contract to work for an employer will only end when the employee leaves, retires, is sacked or made redundant.

In 1999 around 17 million workers in the UK had permanent full-time contracts.

Permanent part-time employment: A growing number of workers are employed to work fewer than 30 hours each week. These people are defined as part-time employees. Many have permanent contracts which specify a date to begin work in an organization but will give no date when employment might end. Some part-time contracts are for term time working only. These allow working parents to spend the school holidays at home looking after their children.

In 1999 there were 6.8 million part-time employees in the UK. Over 83% of these workers were female (see 13.2).

Fixed-term contract employment: Fixed-term contracts can involve full-time or part-time work but will only last for fixed period of time, typically up to 6 months to two years. Fixed-term contracts will specify a start date and an end date for the employment. For example, many jobs in the tourist industry are seasonal and so workers are hired on contracts for summer months only.

A growing number of workers are employed on fixed-term contracts in order to carry out a particular task for an employer. This gives employers the advantage that they can change the number of workers they employ to suit their needs by simply hiring more staff for short periods of time or by not renewing the contracts of existing staff when they expire. Workers on short fixed-term contracts are often called temporary.

Fixed-term contracts are increasingly being offered to what are being called 'external workers'. These are people who provide support services and advice to business organizations. They will include agency 'temps', the self-employed and workers sub-contracted from other firms (see 14.6).

Portfolio Activity 14.7 

1 Study the letter in Figure 14.3 on page 406.

  a What are the expressed terms in the offer of employment?

  b What implied terms do you think Karen will be expected to work to in her job?

2. In the first few months of her appointment Karen is asked to do the following:

- Wear more business-like clothes in reception instead of jeans and tee-shirts. Karen has agreed in order to pass her probationary period, but intends to wear what she likes once this period is over.
- Pop out to the local Chinese takeaway to get the managing director some lunch because he is too busy to do it himself. Karen refuses because she is meeting someone for lunch.
- Wash the senior sales manager's car during a quiet period when she has little to do. Karen refuses point blank.
- Attend a sales evening in four weeks' time. Karen has already booked to go to a concert that night and refuses to attend. The company has offered to reimburse her ticket if she is unable to sell it to someone else.
- Attend a three-day training course in customer care. Karen does not want to go because the training centre is 50 miles away and would involve a long train journey. Her employer will pay the cost of the travel.
- After two months' employment, Karen has asked to take two days' holiday in three weeks' time. It is a busy period for the firm and her request is refused. Karen feels this is an injustice and intends to discuss the matter with the senior human resources manager.

Discuss whether the organization was right to ask Karen to do these things, and if Karen was right to refuse or feel aggrieved.

Key words:

Employment contract - a written statement by an employer of the general and specific terms and conditions of a particular job role and position within their organization

Expressed terms - formal terms agreed between the employer and employee in the contract of employment

Implied terms - terms not written down in the employment contract but nevertheless expected to be conformed with by the employer and employee

Section 14.6 Change at work

Towards a flexible workforce

Since the early 1980s, the composition of the UK labour force has changed significantly. There has been a significant rise in the number of workers who are either self-employed, working part-time, or in temporary jobs, relative to the number of full-time workers (see 13.2). There has also been an increase in the number of workers engaged on short-term contracts.

These changes at work were prompted by the need to create workforces that are flexible to the changing needs of organizations and can be adapted more easily to new products and methods of working.

Many organizations have achieved flexibility by dividing their workforces into 'core', 'periphery', and 'external' groups.

- **Core workers.** These are full-time employees who are multi-skilled in performing varied and mainly key tasks. They will tend to be offered good pay and conditions, and a high degree of job security. This is achieved at the cost of employing 'peripheral' groups of workers, who can be hired and fired as necessary to match changes in consumer demand for a firm's products.

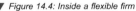

▼ *Figure 14.4: Inside a flexible firm*

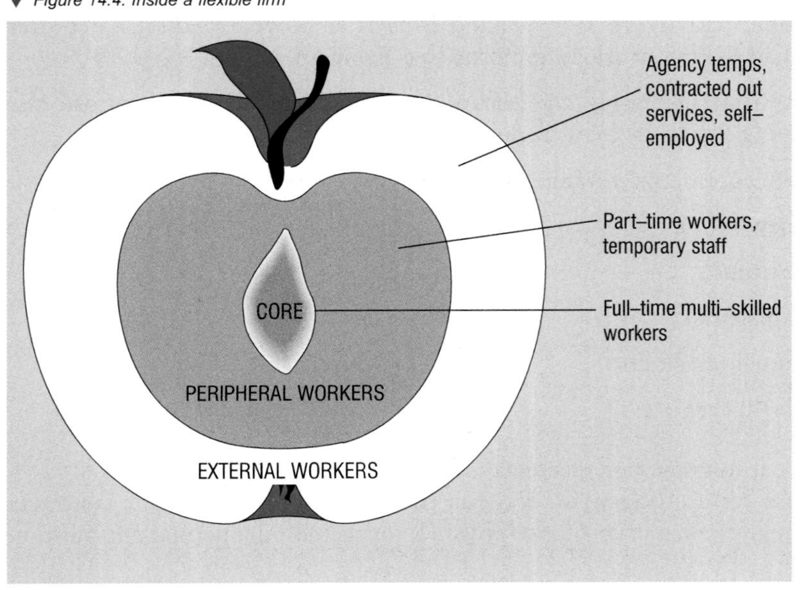

- **Peripheral workers.** These are temporary and part-time workers who may receive less favourable pay, conditions, and benefits.
- **External workers.** These are workers who are not directly employed by the firm, such as agency temps, self-employed workers, and sub-contracted workers from other firms. External workers will tend to carry out non-core functions, such as catering, cleaning, computer maintenance, Public Relations, etc. Consultants may also be employed for special one-off projects such as designing and installing new office equipment or advising on new factory locations.

Re-engineering

The term **re-engineering** refers to the way businesses overhaul themselves as part of a process of continuous change. Re-engineering is associated with reducing the size of the business organization, or **downsizing.** As the name suggests, this leads to fewer, but more highly skilled, workers in the 'core', doing more complex and varied work. Downsizing in UK organizations was especially apparent during the economic recession of the early 1980s and again at the beginning of the 1990s, when profits were squeezed by falling consumer demand and there was a need for businesses to trim costs. Increasing competition between firms globally has since increased cost pressures and the need for flexiblility in production to respond effectively to consumer expectations on price and quality product. (see 7.1).

Portfolio Activity 14.8 

1. Investigate whether it is possible to divide employees in your school/college into core and peripheral workers. Identify the occupations of core and peripheral workers. Are any tasks undertaken by external workers?
2. Contrast the information you have collected from your school/college with another organization with which you are familiar.
3. What do you think are the advantages to both organizations of structuring their workforce into core, periphery and external workers? If possible, try to confirm your views by interviewing head teachers and personnel managers in both organizations.

Other ways to achieve labour flexibility

Increasingly, business organizations are creating workforces that are flexible in terms of skills and the hours they work, so that staffing levels can be adjusted easily to match the fluctuations in consumer demand that occur each week, season, or with cyclical variations in the level of economic activity. In 1997 around 24% of employees in the UK reported they had flexible working patterns (see Table 14.2).

Apart from increasing the use of **non-standard labour**, firms are also achieving flexibility by introducing the following measures:

- New contractual arrangements
- Teleworking
- Flexitime
- Shift work
- Annualized hours
- Job sharing

New contractual arrangements

As jobs have changed, so too has the nature of employment contracts. Although the majority of jobs are still contracted on a permanent full-time basis, an increasing number of employees are being offered short-term contracts for fixed periods of time.

Until 1995 employees only acquired rights, such as protection against unfair dismissal and compensation for redundancy, if they had been in employment for two years or more. Changes in employment laws since have equalized the rights of full-time and part-time workers and those on short-term contracts. By offering contracts for periods of less than two years, firms could avoid the costs associated with these employment rights, and be more flexible in their ability to 'hire and fire' staff to match changing needs.

However, organizations can also negotiate changes to existing long-term employment contracts, for example by:

- Changing hours of work
- Reducing the wage rate
- Introducing performance-related pay
- Altering holiday entitlements
- Introducing new working practices, e.g. Sunday working or night-time shifts
- Re-location
- Introducing additional duties and responsibilities
- Introducing new technology

Of course, workers may resist these changes in negotiations with employees which, if appropiate, will be conducted by via Trade Union representatives (see 13.3).

Introducing changes to existing contracts without the agreement of staff can result in a breach of contract and worker dissatisfaction. This is liable to be reflected in lower productivity and work quality. However, workers may simply be given an ultimatum by their employer either to accept new contracts or face redundancy. To avoid this, many long-term contracts now contain clauses which specifically require the employee to accept change and adapt to the changing needs of the organization.

Teleworking

Home working is a growing feature of the UK labour market. It can be observed in most industries, with particular concentrations in the South East and in the financial and business services sector. So-called teleworking has become feasible because of technological advance. Home workers are now able to keep in touch with their main office via modem links on personal computers, by fax machines, and even with new videophones (see 3.2). However, the number of teleworkers in the UK is still relatively small - less than 3% of the employed workforce in 1997.

Annualized hours systems

Under this system, instead of working a specified number of hours each week, workers are contracted to work a given number of hours over

▼ *Table 14.1 Homeworking[1]: by gender and occupation, Spring 1997*

United Kingdom	Percentages		
	Males	Females	All persons
Professional	2.8	2.4	2.7
Managers and administrators	1.9	5.8	3.2
Associated professional and technical	4.6	4.8	4.7
Clerical and secretarial	1.3	4.8	3.9
Personal and protective services	–	5.2	3.7
Sales	1.3	0.8	1.0
Craft and related	0.5	10.5	1.3
Plant and machine operatives	–	3.0	0.7
All occupations[2]	1.4	4.0	2.6

1 Percentage of those in employment in each occupation who were homeworkers excluding those on government training and employment schemes. Homeworkers covers those who work mainly in their own home but excludes those who work in the same grounds or buildings as their home, those who work in different places using their home as a base and those who sometimes do work at home.

2 Includes those with other occupations and those who did not state their occupation.

Source: Labour Force Survey, Office for National Statistics
Social Trends 1999

▼ *A typical home office*

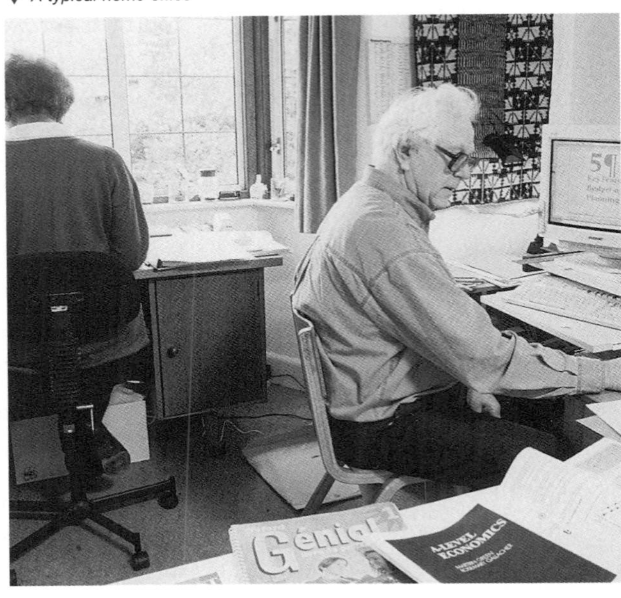

▼ *Advantages and disadvantages of teleworking*

Advantages to the firm	Disadvantages to the firm
• With more staff working at home, a firm will be able to reduce overall floorspace requirements and associated costs	• Possible loss of management control over home working staff
• Avoidance of commuting can be a significant incentive for employees, while employers may benefit from reduced wage claims to cover rising public transport fares, petrol prices, and parking charges	• Cost of equipment • Communication problems/unavailability of staff for meetings called at short notice
• Home working can motivate staff, reduce stress associated with travel and the office environment, and increase productivity	• Difficulty of on-job training

a 12-month period. This means a business can vary the number of hours from week to week or seasonally to meet its requirements - for example, to match fluctuations in consumer demand.

Flexitime

Unlike the annual hours system, **Flexitime** gives the employee the ability to choose, within limits, when to start work and when to finish during the working day, as long as a specified number of hours are completed each week. Work in excess of agreed hours can normally count towards extra leave. Because some people like to start early and others will want to start later each morning, a business organization will benefit from an extended period of staff cover in its offices. However, there may be some additional costs to a business. For example, firms will need to pay extra for lighting and heating because workers on Flexitime may be starting earlier and others leaving later at night.

▼ Table 14.2: Employees with flexible working patterns[1]: by gender, Spring 1997

United Kingdom	Percentages		
	Males	Females	All persons
Full-time employees			
Flexible working hours	8.9	14.7	11.0
Annualized working hours	4.2	4.3	4.2
Four and half day week	2.8	2.5	2.7
Term-time working	1.0	4.9	2.4
Nine day fortnight	0.5	0.2	0.4
Any flexible working pattern[2]	18.0	27.2	21.2
Part-time employees			
Flexible working hours	6.2	7.6	7.3
Annualized working hours	2.5	3.3	3.2
Term-time working	4.9	10.0	9.1
Job sharing	1.1	2.6	2.4
Any flexible working pattern[2]	18.0	24.9	23.8

1 Percentages are based on totals which exclude people who did not state whether or not they worked a flexible working arrangement.
2 Includes other categories of flexible working not separately identified.

Source: Labour Force Survey, Office for National Statistics Social Trends 1999

Flexitime tends to be a feature of office-based jobs: it is not very practical for retail outlets or manufacturing plants to allow workers to turn up for work when they want to.

Shift work

Firms that wish to remain operative for more than 8 or 9 hours each day will require their employees to work in **shifts.** Shift work involves using different groups of workers in rotation. For example, a manufacturer who wants to keep running 24 hours a day may employ workers on three shifts: 10pm – 6 am, 6am – 2pm, and 2 pm – 10 pm. Similarly, shops which open from 8am to 9pm may use two or three overlapping shifts, complemented by part-time workers. Workers on night shifts will often be paid an additional shift allowance.

Job sharing

As the name suggests, **job sharing** involves dividing up a full-time job between two or more part-time workers. The main problem is a possible lack of continuity in the job. Those sharing the job need to keep each other informed of the tasks undertaken and their decisions.

Reasons for change

There are a number of reasons why firms are introducing more flexible working practices and arrangements. These include:

- **Competitive market pressures.** Increasing competition for consumers has meant that firms must reduce their costs if they are to be in a position to cut prices. They also need to be able to react quickly to changes in consumer wants.

  By creating flexible workforces, organizations can match staffing levels more closely to peaks and troughs in consumer demand. If all employees were on long-term contracts for full-time employment, cutting labour requirements during periods of low or falling consumer demand would result in high redundancy payments.

- **To improve productivity**. If a firm is able to produce more output with the same, or fewer, resources, then productivity will increase, and the cost per unit of output produced will fall. If a firm is to be competitive, it must match the productivity gains of rival firms (see 1.1).

- **To reduce costs/improve quality.** An increasing number of larger organizations have downsized and sub-contracted non-core functions such as catering and cleaning to smaller external organizations. Larger firms can insist on quality at competitive rates from small organizations or individuals willing to undertake these functions. For example, many local and central government department functions were 'market tested' in the early 1990s as part of the government's policy of privatization (see 3.5).

- **Diversification.** Rather than producing just one product or service, most medium-to-large organizations produce many different ones, sold in different markets all over the world. Producing a range of products spreads the risk of falling demand or a hold-up in supplies for any one product. However, employees both at the managerial level and on the shop floor must have the necessary skills and be flexible enough to adapt them as required.
- **To motivate employees.** Core workers can be motivated by performance-related pay and job security (see 15.2). However, even peripheral workers may be motivated by the flexibility offered by part-time or temporary work.
- **To adapt to technological changes.** New technology requires new skills and methods of working. In many cases, new technology has also enabled firms to reduce the size of their workforces without reducing output.
- **The need for new skills.** Sometimes firms will not have all the skills they need within their existing workforce. Advancing technology and changing consumer demands create a need for new skills. These skills may be bought into a firm on a temporary basis - for example, a consultancy advising on the introduction of computerized production lines - or may be acquired on a semi-permanent basis, through the employment of self-employed people on renewable short-term contracts.

Implementing and monitoring change

There are three fundamental elements that will make changes to working methods and conditions successful in a business. These are:

- Planning
- Training
- Monitoring

Planning

Changes need to be planned carefully. A business will need a clear idea of how they will effect production, costs and revenues, and how manpower and equipment requirements might change. Explaining the need for change to employees and working out how best to minimize any negative impacts on them is important if workers are to accept changes and continue to work towards the goals of the organization.

Training

Where new production processes, technology and/or methods of working are introduced, training will be very important if employees are to be able to adopt these changes and use equipment effectively. Business managers will need to identify and meet the training needs of employees (see 15.2).

Monitoring

The success of measures designed to make working conditions and labour forces more flexible can be measured in the following ways:

- **Impact on productivity.** Output per employee should be higher than before. A firm will hope to produce more with less labour input.
- **Impact on efficiency.** Costs should be lower and profit margins higher.

- **Impact on quality.** Product quality and/or customer services should have improved, and waste reduced as a result.

However, the effects of increasing flexibility are not felt by firms alone. Individuals can also feel the impact of changes in working practices - both positive and negative:

- **Stress.** The separation of workforces into core, periphery, and external groups of workers will result in unemployment for those unfortunate enough not to be retained as 'core' workers. Full-time workers who lose their jobs may find that they have to take part-time or temporary jobs instead to earn a living. Short-term contracts and contracting out can also lead to increased job uncertainty.
- **Job satisfaction.** On the positive side, those lucky enough to retain their jobs may benefit from the increased flexibility that Flexitime and annualized hours systems give them. Teleworking also relieves people of the need to commute to and from work every day, while job sharing and part-time work may suit many people who have other commitments during the day, for example, meeting children from school, doing voluntary work, or running a small business as a sideline.

Key words:

Non-standard labour - Non-full-time workers who are employed either on fixed or short-term contracts or on a more permanent part-time basis

Flexible firm - a firm that divides its workforce into core, peripheral, and external groups

Core workers - full-time employees performing mainly key functions within an organization

Peripheral workers - temporary and part-time workers who tend to be employed to match fluctuations in demand

External workers - sub-contracted labour performing non-core activities such as catering

Downsizing - reducing the size of a business organization by focusing production and the workforce on core functions

Teleworking - employees working from home

Annualized hours - a system of contracting employees to work a specified number of hours each year, rather than a specified number of hours each week

Flexitime - a system which allows workers to choose the time they start and finish work each day within specified hours

Job sharing - when two or more part-time workers share the same full-time job

Re-engineering - looking at, and redesigning from first principles, the structure, job roles, and tasks within an organization

Useful references

Dale, M. '**Successful Recruitment and Selection**' (Kogan Page, 1995)

Roberts, G. '**Recruitment and Selection**' (Institute of Personnel and Development, 1997)

Flexibility on-line magazine at ***www.flexibility.co.uk***

HR Magazine on-line at ***www.shrm.org/docs/Hrmagazine.html***

People Management on-line magazine at ***www.peoplemanagement.co.uk***

Institute for Employment Studies (*www.employment-studies.co.uk*)
Mantell Building, Falmer, Brighton BN1 9RF

Institute of Personnel and Development (*www.ipd.co.uk*)
IPD House, Camp Road, London SW19 4UX

Internet key words search: **HRM, recruitment, recruitment agency**

Test your knowledge

1 Which of the following external sources of recruitment is a business seeking an experienced finance manager most likely to choose?

A Local Jobcentre

B University 'milk round'

C Professional recruitment agency

D Trade Union

2 Employers often like job applicants to submit a letter of application for an advertised job because:

A It reveals information not included in an application form

B It is more personal

C It makes shortlisting easier

D It reveals handwriting ability

3 A person specification is designed to:

A Analyse the authority and responsibility involved in a job

B Identify the qualities a worker needs to do a specific job

C Set performance criteria for a job

D Identify the various tasks involved in a job

4 A job selection interview should fulfil all of the following functions except:

A Inform candidates about the job and the organization

B Allow the assessment of the candidate's personality

C Check factual information provided by each candidate

D Agree terms and conditions of employment

5 A company has expanded into new premises and is seeking additional employees. Which of the following represents the usual order of recruitment and selection procedures?

A Advertise; applications; shortlist; interviews; appoint

B Advertise; shortlist; interviews; applications; appoint

C Applications; interviews; shortlist; advertise; appoint

D Advertise; applications; interviews; shortlist; appoint

6 A Curriculum Vitae (CV):

A Provides a summary of career details and ambitions

B Provides a summary of personal details and achievements

C Provides a summary of education and professional qualifications

D Provides a summary of personal details and career ambitions

7 A job description should include the following information except:

A Job title and position

B Job tasks and responsibilities

C Personal qualities and attributes

D Job performance criteria

Questions 8–10 share the answer options below:

A Keeping eye contact with your interviewers

B Asking questions about the organization

C Asking questions about training and promotion prospects

D Appearing relaxed and confident

If you were being interviewed for a job, which of the above would you use to demonstrate the following?

8 Showing that you are interested in developing your career

9 Showing long-term interest in the job and the company

10 Showing you are telling the truth and can be trusted

11 Shortlisting is:

A Drawing up a list of questions to ask during interview

B Making a list of questions to print on an application form

C Setting criteria by which to judge candidates

D Selecting candidates for interview from applications

Questions 12–14 share the answer options below:

A Apply by telephone

B Request and complete an application form

C Write a letter of application

D Provide a Curriculum Vitae and covering letter

Which of the above is likely to be the most appropriate method of applying for the following jobs?

12 A full-time job in a local newsagent's

13 A senior marketing manager in a large multinational

14 Part-time casual work delivering leaflets

Questions 15–17 share the following answer options:

Working practices are becoming more flexible due to:

A Flexitime

B Job sharing

C Teleworking

D Annualized hours

Which of the above practices do the following describe?

15 Working from home using ICT

16 Dividing a full-time job between two or more part-time employees

17 Agreeing to work a set number of hours each year

18 **a** What is the main purpose of recruitment and selection in a business organization?

b What is the difference between a job description and a person specification? Why are they required?

c List three items of information a job description and a person specification each will contain.

d Suggest two ways a person could apply to fill a job vacancy.

e List five items of information a job applicant should provide to a future potential employer.

19 **a** Suggest three ways in which a firm may recruit job applicants externally.

b List four headings you would expect to find in a CV.

c What is the purpose of shortlisting?

d Suggest at least three criteria on which job applicants might be judged for shortlisting.

e What is the difference between a panel interview and a board interview?

f How and why should a candidate prepare for a job interview?

g How and why should an interviewer prepare to interview job candidates?

20 **a** Many firms seeking to increase labour flexibility have divided work tasks into core, peripheral, and external activities, and are employing workers on different terms and conditions. Explain what these terms and conditions are in each case.

b Suggest and explain two other ways a firm might introduce labour force flexibility.

c Suggest and explain two reasons why firms are introducing more flexible staffing arrangements and working conditions.

d What impact could the changes in working conditions you have discussed have on employees? Explain your answer.

chapter 15 Managing Employee Performance

This chapter investigates how and why organizations motivate, manage and appraise the performance of their employees.

What you need to learn

A business needs to manage the performance of its employees effectively if it is to remain competitive. You should be aware of the importance of **employee motivation** and the significance of both **financial and non-financial incentives** in enhancing employee performance. You should be able to identify the influence of a number of **motivation theories** on the way in which businesses manage their employees:

- **Taylor's principles of scientific management**
- **Maslow's hierarchy of needs**
- **McGregor's Theory X and Y**
- **Herzberg's motivators and hygiene factors**

You need to develop an understanding of the working environment within which businesses attempt to manage the performance of their employees. In particular, you should know key aspects of legislation, such as the maximum number of hours employees can work in a week, regulations governing leave arrangements (including maternity and paternity) and minimum wage rates.

You should be aware of how **training and development** may motivate and enhance the performance of employees and the need for businesses to invest resources in training and development programmes.

You should also be aware of the need for competitive businesses to link performance reviews and evaluations to training and development.

You need to be able to explain and give examples of the following training methods and activities:

- **induction training**
- **mentoring**
- **coaching**
- **apprenticeships**
- **in-house training**
- **external training**

Training can be **on-the-job** or **off-the-job** to **develop skills** that are specific to the employing organization, or skills that may be in demand by many organizations. You should recognize how nationally recognized training structures, such as **Investors in People** and **Individual Learning Accounts**, and nationally recognized qualifications, including NVQs and GNVQs, can contribute to business training and development programmes.

You need to explain and give examples of the following methods that businesses use to manage the performance of their employees:

- **performance reviews and appraisals**
- **self-evaluation**
- **peer evaluation**
- **target setting for individuals and groups**
- **measuring individual and group output/production**

Section 15.1

Motivating employees

Why is employee performance important?

In a competitive business environment competing organizations will be under constant pressure to improve product quality and reduce prices in order to meet rising consumer expectations before and better than rival businesses do. Business organizations must do this by continually improving the productivity of its resources (see 1.1). This means increasing the output of a good or service from a given input of materials, capital goods and labour, and producing that output better, faster and cheaper than before.

At the heart of many productivity gains are employees. It is their skills and their level of motivation that will determine the level of productivity in a firm given a fixed input of materials and equipment. Even if a firm introduces new and more productive equipment and materials, it is employees that will need to purchase them, use them to produce goods and services, account for them, market them and sell them effectively. A key task of the Human Resources Department in an organization is to manage and improve the performance of all employees in the organization, that includes managers at all levels, operatives, office staff, sales teams and even staff within the Human Resources Department.

Why do people work?

If a business organization is to motivate workers to achieve higher levels of productivity and quality, it must first understand why people go to work. The obvious explanation is 'because they need the money'. However, money is not the only need that is satisfied by working. A combination of factors, financial and non-financial, give an employee **job satisfaction**, including:

I STILL SAY JIM'S NOT THE SAME SINCE HIS POOLS WIN

- Adequate wages and fringe benefits, e.g. pension, company car
- Holiday entitlement
- Pleasant working environment
- Challenging and interesting job tasks
- Variety in the working day
- Opportunities to learn and try new ideas
- Availability of training
- Working as part of a team
- Being consulted on management decisions
- Responsibility
- Regular feedback on performance
- Recognition for good work through pay bonuses or promotion
- Social relationships inside and outside of work with colleagues and managers

A satisfied worker is likely to be more productive, and more committed to the organization and the attainment of its business goals.

JOB SATISFACTION LEADS TO:-
• LOWER ABSENTEEISM
• HIGHER MORALE
• BETTER CO-OPERATION
• LOWER STAFF TURNOVER
• INCREASED MOTIVATION
• HIGHER PRODUCTIVITY
• MORE PROFIT
• GOOD CORPORATE IMAGE

Working conditions are the key to employee satisfaction

When people go to work they will expect to receive a number of benefits from their employers and to work in environments that are both pleasant and safe.

The main **working conditions** of any type of employment are:

- hours of work, including overtime
- levels and methods of payment, and other benefits
- holiday entitlements
- job security
- the physical environment of the workplace, which should be clean, safe and healthy to work in
- opportunities for career progression
- training and development opportunities

If employing organizations fail to meet or exceed the expectations of employees they are likely to become dissatisfied, reduce their work effort and eventually leave resulting in the costly recruitment and training of new employees. It is, therefore, the job of senior managers and the Human Resources Department in an organization to make sure working conditions for all staff are satisfactory and to meet or exceed the legal requirements governing working conditions. Laws governing pay, health and safety in the workplace and equal opportunities are especially important.

Working conditions and legal requirements, and how they can affect employee performance, are considered in detail in the next section.

Working methods and job design

As organizations have become more aware of the importance of motivation, many have introduced new methods of working to take account of the needs of their employees to enjoy their work, display their creativity and feel a sense of achievement and responsibility. It is argued that designing jobs with employees' needs in mind will increase quality, productivity and added value (see 1.1) and reduce production costs, absenteeism and staff turnover (see 13.1).

Various methods have been devised to incorporate workers needs into jobs. These include:

- **Job enlargement.** This attempts to make a job more varied by removing the boredom associated with repetitive operations. It involves 'enlarging' the scope of a job by adding similar tasks without increasing worker responsibility. For example, instead of an employee bolting the bumpers onto a new car s/he may also be allowed to fix doors and bonnets. Job enlargement is often criticized because it simply adds one dull task to another.

- **Job rotation.** Instead of enlarging jobs, workers can be organized into small groups and trained to carry out all the jobs in the group. Workers can then swap or rotate their jobs on a regular basis to provide variety.

Job rotation is often important in the training of work supervisors or managers. However, if each of the jobs performed is equally boring, motivation is hardly likely to improve as a result.

- **Job enrichment.** This attempts to increase the sense of challenge and achievement in a job. A job may be enriched by giving workers:

  - a greater variety of tasks
  - more freedom in deciding how to plan tasks, order materials, etc.
  - regular feedback on job performance
  - more involvement in analysing and changing physical aspects of their working environment, such as temperature control, office or plant layout, lighting, etc.

  However, some workers may resent an increase in their responsibility, while others may find it hard to cope with the added pressure. In other cases, technology may be a constraint. For example, jobs associated with the operation of specialized machinery and assembly-line techniques may never be particularly meaningful.

- **Teamworking.** This involves dividing the workforce into teams and giving them responsibility for areas such as the planning and execution of their work, quality control, and physical aspects of their environment such as the layout of equipment and furniture. Teamwork allows a greater range of skills and experience to be used in problem-solving and fosters cooperation, rather than competition, among team members.

Five steps to job satisfaction

1. A job should include all those tasks necessary to complete a finished product or process so that workers can feel a sense of achievement
2. Workers, or teams of workers, should take responsibility for the quality of the work and their output
3. Workers should be able to carry out a variety of tasks
4. Employees should be able to prioritize their work and regulate the speed at which they work
5. Employees should have the opportunity to work in groups and socialize with other workers

Advantages of teamworking	Disadvantages of teamworking
• Variety of skills leads to greater efficiency	• Decision-making can be slow, especially in large groups
• Problem-solving is easier - 'two heads are better than one'	• Some members may be inhibited by dominant personalities within the team and prevented from making what could have been good suggestions
• Individuals feel less inhibited about making suggestions and decisions with the backing of others - 'strength in numbers'	• Some teams may develop norms and attitudes at odds with the organization, for example, 'Don't work too hard - they won't thank you for it!'
• Groups may develop a team spirit	• Team discussions may involve 'too much talk and not enough action'
• Workers are motivated by team membership and committed to the achievement of group and organizational goals	

Redesigning jobs to give employees more control over their work, greater responsibility and challenge, and more involvement in business decision making has been labelled **empowerment**. However, some people suggest a number of employers may be abusing the idea that employees like to feel empowered by using it as an excuse to increase employee workload.

The importance of communication

Perhaps the most basic motivational requirement for senior managers is simply to communicate well with their employees. Communication can satisfy such basic human needs as recognition, security and a sense of belonging. Managers can praise staff for their efforts, ask their opinions on organizational issues, and involve them in decision-making. In this way managers can change the attitudes of workers so that they are more positive about their work and employers, and embrace the organizational culture (see 2.6).

If managers want to modify employee behaviour they must ensure that feedback is appropriate and consequences occur as a result of that behaviour. For example, if a new employee who arrives on time for work is praised and rewarded in some way, the probability of that employee arriving on time more often is increased. Conversely if an employee who is late is reprimanded or punished in some way, for example, by loss of earnings, they are less likely to arrive late again. An appropriately designed system of feedback and appraisal, underpinned by rewards and punishments, can reinforce good behaviour and help eliminate bad behaviour and poor performance.

Theories of employee motivation and behaviour

Underlying many of the initiatives and strategies used by employers to motivate their employees to greater performance and productivity are a number of behavioural theories developed from research findings. Here are a few notable examples, some dating back quite a long time:

Taylor's principles of scientific management

Frederick Taylor (1856–1915) was an American engineer who pioneered work studies and spent many years researching ways of increasing productivity in factories by making work tasks easier and quicker to perform. He initiated the time and motion study which broke down jobs into a series of small consecutive but repetitive tasks. The 'best' or 'correct' time for each task or 'motion' could be recorded and employees motivated to achieve it.

According to Taylor, labour productivity could be improved by different workers in a production sequence specialize in a particular task. That is, productivity would improve with repetition of each task and if employees were rewarded with higher wages and bonus payments for their increased output. Each task could be observed and the time taken to complete it noted.

The major problem for Taylor was devising a pay rewards scheme that was acceptable to both employees and their employers. He also overlooked how repetition of a task can de-motivate an employee through boredom.

Maslow's hierarchy of needs

In 1968, the American psychologist Abraham Maslow devised what he called a hierarchy of human needs. He claimed people initially worked in return for a wage that would provide enough income to satisfy their basic or 'physiological' needs for food, clothing and shelter. Once these were satisfied, individuals were motivated by higher needs, such as the need for job security and protection from danger in healthy, safe, orderly and pleasant working environment. A person then seeks acceptance by others, esteem and eventually the fulfillment of self-actualization needs to be creative and develop to his or her full potential. This hierarchy of needs can be visualized in the pyramid diagram below.

Many people have questioned the realism of such a structured approach to human needs and Maslow has also been criticized for producing a theory that primarily reflects the values of employees in professional and managerial occupations, i.e. 'one size does not fit all'.

▼ *Maslow's hierarchy of needs*

Theories of employee motivation and behaviour

McGregor's Theory X and Y

Douglas McGregor suggests in his book 'The Human Side of Enterprise' (1960) that employers will adopt one of two possible extreme views of their employees and what motivates them.

According to **Theory X** 'work-centred' employers assume their employees

- dislike work and responsibility, and will try to avoid both
- have little ambition and need constant direction at work
- do not like responsibility or change
- will have no commitment to the organization they work for or its objectives
- are motivated only by money and threat of pay or job loss

In contrast, 'people-centred' employers who subscribe to the alternative **Theory Y** assume their employees

- like working and seek responsibility
- do care about the objectives of their organization
- like to be fully employed and developed to their full potential
- like variety in work and are motivated by interesting tasks
- are not motivated simply by money or threats

These categories are too broad and too extreme to be entirely useful in human resource planning and management. The workforce in an organization may contain different employees who conform to both theories, or display muted elements of both. The same employees may also move between these categories over time as their working environment, expectations and attitudes change.

Herzberg's motivators and hygiene factors

Federick Herzberg developed his ideas in 1966. From his research he listed those factors which improve job satisfaction and those which, if improved or handled correctly, would reduce or at least prevent job dissatisfaction.

Motivators to improved job satisfaction include

- having a sense of achievement
- receiving recognition for good work and effort
- the nature of the work itself - whether it is challenging, interesting and rewarding
- being given and trusted with responsibility
- opportunities for promotion, pay and career advancement

Hygiene factors, or potential dissatisfiers at work, include

- rules and regulations
- wage and salary levels, and the availability of other 'fringe' benefits
- the working environment and provision of social facilities
- the style of supervision and management
- job status
- job security

Portfolio Activity 15.1

Which, if any, of the motivation theories considered above can you identify from the examples in the articles below?

When Quality is a Way of Life

India may not be the first place to conjure up images of industrial efficiency or total quality management. But that is now all changing and one company stands out as a benchmark for others to follow.

The truck and excavator company Telco (Tata Engineering and Locomotive Company) has developed a peculiarly Indian approach to quality and worker participation.

'Quality and productivity are essential in helping us to compete worldwide', says Sarosh Ghandy, resident director in Jamshedpur. 'We are investing in our "software": building on the skills, commitment and involvement of our workers'.

The company launched its own in-house 'human relations at work' (HRW) training programme in 1982. The focus is a three-day course, attended so far by 18,000 of Telco's 20,000 employees. The aim is to empower the workforce to take responsibility.

The visible manifestation has been the birth of shop-floor quality circles. Now nearly 1,300 voluntary groups of 10 to 12 people, involving the bulk of the workforce, meet for an hour each week to iron out problems - and discuss how to tackle alcoholism, family debt and communal tension in their townships.

One group bailed out a colleague who became heavily in debt after personal problems. Another group repaired a fault on a metal press which had baffled German engineers.

Each year, employees make 100,000 suggestions for improvements, saving Telco nearly £2m, says Ghandy. The company is now making 16,000 more trucks with 6,000 fewer workers and has enjoyed a strike-free industrial record over the last 21 years.

Financial Times, 25.9.1993

Nurses seek end to irregular shift patterns

The Royal College of Nursing has called on employers to end irregular shift patterns and to adopt flexible, family-friendly working hours. It called for the change after a Mori poll of more than 1,000 of its members revealed that nine out of 10 thought that staffing levels were 'critical' to improving care.

The survey also found that the requirement to work irregular shifts was deterring potential recruits. Respondents with family-care commitments said they found it particularly difficult to juggle these shifts.

Only a third of nurses participating in the poll said that pay was the most pressing issue.

Personnel Management on-line, 22.4.2000

Charities set to raise top scientists' salaries

The leading cancer and cardiac research charities are set to raise the salaries of their senior academics in an attempt to stop them from being poached by rich pharmaceutical companies, US "ivy league" universities, and rival biomedical research charities.

It could mean some science professors, who are pioneers in the war against cancer and heart disease, will be awarded pay packets worth about £100,000 per year - nearly three times the amount earned by some arts and humanities professors.

The pay rises are being considered by the Cancer Research Campaign, Imperial Cancer Research and the British Heart Foundation.

Financial Times, 21.6.1999

Engineers find nuts and bolts of trade come from innovation

In a factory in Yorkshire, engineers are hunched over computer screens, using design methods that helped develop the space shuttle to draw up industrial products made in millions and costing just 6p each.

Welcome to the world of nut-making, a business that has been around 500 years and is a crucial part of manufacturing industries from washing machines to cement plants.

Forty years ago Britain was virtually self-sufficient in nuts and had dozens of factories. Now most UK fastener plants concentrate on relatively expensive items such as special rivets for the aerospace industry.

One of the few remaining nut manufacturing businesses is Philidas, part of the Haden MacLellan engineering group.

It has retained a niche in this highly competitive business by adding design and manufacturing skills over the past 10 years to compensate for Britain's relatively high labour costs and the strength of the pound.

"We have to focus on quality and high technology products," says Bob Fisher, managing director of Philidas's main manufacturing unit in Pontefract. "Above all we have to be good at solving customers' problems."

Among Philidas's innovations is a design of nut that contains a tiny serrated edge in the thread. This ensures that when being fastened to a bolt during the assembly of a car component the nut removes any paint on the bolt, ensuring both parts screw together easily without the nut "sticking".

Philidas has also developed "team-based" manufacturing methods in which individual workers do a variety of machining and forging steps, and are each responsible for quality.

Such ideas - which encourage worker involvement and cut the number of defective parts - have played a crucial part in keeping up with competitors, Mr Fisher says.

Financial Times, May 2000

Key words:

Working conditions - the physical, financial and other elements which make working in particular organization and job attractive

Empowerment - giving employees more control over their work and more responsibility

Job enlargement - increasing the number of tasks within a job without increasing responsibility

Job rotation - allowing employees to swap their jobs

Job enrichment - making a job more interesting and challenging through greater task variety and responsibility

Teamworking - splitting employees into groups to complete tasks together

Motivation theories - different views of what motivates people in work which can assist the design of strategies to improve employee performance

Section 15.2 Working conditions and legal requirements

This section considers how employers can provide the right working conditions to satisfy a number of laws and regulations, and to motivate their employees to greater performance.

Portfolio Activity 15.2 

1. Consider the two employees in the pictures below. How do you think their working conditions might compare?

▼ *Full-time permanent construction site supervisor. Studied engineering at college for three years. Currently on day release to study management skills with a view to possible promotion to site manager. Starts work at 7.30 am every day, sometimes including Saturday and Sunday. Current salary around £2,300 per month including overtime. Five weeks holiday each year.*

▼ *Full-time administration assistant in a government department on short-term contract. Hoping to have contract extended or made permanent. Able to work flexitime as long he is in before 10 am and doesn't leave until after 4.30 pm. Any additional hours worked can be totalled and added to basic leave of 22 days per year. Salary currently £15,000 per year. Has received some computer training.*

2. Collect information on the jobs of two people you know. One should be a permanent full-time employee and the other either part-time, temporary, self-employed, or employed on a short-term contract. From interviews and your own observations and knowledge of the work they do, compare their working conditions and write up your findings in a short word-processed report.

Hours of work and holiday entitlement

All employees will have agreed hours they are expected to work each day, week, month or year, depending on the precise form of agreement. The basic working week in the UK is 37.5 to 40 hours each week for manual workers and 35–38 hours for non-manual workers. However, due to overtime, many workers work longer than the basic week, especially in manual occupations.

Actual hours and days worked will vary between jobs. Some employees - for example, staff in shops - may have to arrive and leave work at the same time every day to coincide with opening and closing times. Many shop workers are also obliged to work some Saturdays and Sundays in return for days off during the week. The Sunday Trading Act 1994 restricts most larger shops to six hours trading only on Sundays. Most office staff work what is considered the 'normal' working week from 9 am to 5.30 pm Monday to Friday each week. Shiftwork and flexitime also mean hours of work can vary widely between industries and occupations.

▼ *Table 15.1: Average weekly hours[1] worked by full-time employees: by industry and gender, Spring 1998*

United Kingdom — **Hours per week**

	Males	Females	All
Agriculture and fishing	49.1	43.9	48.2
Transport and communication	48.0	41.3	46.6
Energy and water supply	47.6	40.8	46.5
Construction	46.5	39.5	45.9
Distribution, hotels and restaurants	46.3	40.9	44.3
Manufacturing	45.3	40.7	44.2
Banking, finance and insurance	45.4	40.1	43.3
Public administration, education and health	44.4	40.9	42.4
Other services	45.3	41.0	43.5
All industries	45.8	40.7	44.0

[1] Total usual hours including paid and unpaid overtime and excluding meal breaks worked in main job only.
Source: Labour Forces Survey, Office for National Statistics

Social Trends, 1999

How the times are changing

In the past, employment contracts would often require workers to work a fixed number of hours, usually around 38 each week, between set times - for example, 9am to 5pm. However, a large number of employees are now working different patterns (see 14.6).

- **Shiftwork** involves working blocks of hours each day in order to keep a factory, shop or office running 24 hours each day. Each day is usually divided into 3 shifts of 8 hours each. Staff may be able to vary which shift they work each day.
- **Annualized hours systems** set the total number of hours an employee will work over each 12-month period. It is then up to the employer and employee to agree when, how long and how often to come to work.
- **Flexitime** enables an employee to choose what time to start and leave work each day around agreed core hours they must be at work, say between 10 am to 4 pm.

The European Working Time Directive

European and UK law introduced the following rights and protections for workers in October 1998:

- a limit of an average of 48 hours a week a worker can be required to work
- a limit of an average 8 hours work in 254 hours which nightworkers can be required to work
- a right for nightworkers to receive a free health assessment and free health insurance
- a right to a minimum 11 hours rest a day
- a right to uninterrupted rest of 24 hours once every 7 days (or 48 hours over 14 days)
- a right to take rest periods of at least 20 minutes if the working day is longer than six hours
- a minimum of 4 weeks annual paid leave

The **European Working Time Directive** was introduced to European Union members countries, including the UK, in 1998. It limits the number of hours an employee can be required to work each to an average of 48. However, workers can choose to work more than 48 hours each week if they wish, and some workers are exempt, e.g. doctors and army personnel.

The EU Working Time Directive also requires workers to receive a minimum of four weeks paid holiday each year. Many employers give their workers more holiday than this because they know the amount of annual leave their workers are entitled to is an important working condition for them. Good workers may leave a business if another firm offers them longer holidays.

Pay

Wages and salaries

Wages and salaries are payments made to workers.

- Workers who receive a **salary** normally receive the same amount of money each month, regardless of the number of hours they work each day, week, or month. Monthly payments will simply be calculated as 1/12th of an agreed annual salary. The amount received by a worker is only likely to change if they are promoted, demoted, or receive a pay rise. Workers in clerical, managerial, and professional occupations tend to be paid salaries.
- Workers who receive **wages** are normally paid by the hour at the end of each week or month. The more hours they work per day, week, or month, the more pay they will receive. Often, work outside of normal hours, for example, early in the morning, late in the evening, or at weekends, will be paid at overtime rates which may be 1.5 times or twice the normal hourly wage rate. Manual workers are usually paid an hourly wage rate and are required to 'clock on and off' as proof of the number of hours they have worked.

Gross and net earnings

The total earnings of an employee each week or month will consist of wages plus any overtime and other payments such as bonuses. It is usual for an employer to deduct income tax and national insurance contributions from the gross earnings of their employees before they are paid. Payments after these deductions have been made are known as **net earnings**. Self-employed workers are responsible for paying their own taxes direct to the government tax authority, the Inland Revenue.

Deductions from pay

By law, employers are only allowed to make the following deductions from an employee's wage or salary:

- Statutory deductions required by law, i.e. national insurance and income tax

- Voluntary contributions agreed in writing by an employee, e.g. trade union subscriptions, give-as-you-earn donations to charities, subscriptions to clubs and societies, additional pension contributions, etc.

Motivation and financial rewards

Time rates

Most employees receive wages or salaries based on the number of hours they work each week or year. Time rates are, therefore, used to reward workers for the amount of productive time they spend in work.

Performance Related Pay (PRP)

PRP is a term used to describe systems that link the pay of workers to some measure of individual, group or organizational effort. In recent years, PRP schemes have been extended from manual workers to non-manual/white collar occupations. These incentive payment schemes can take many forms:

- **individual payments by results** or piecework, where an individuals earnings are totally or partially based directly on individual performance, usually in terms of the quantity or value of output they produce.
- **group payment by results** where the output or sales related performance pay is divided between a group of workers according to some pre-determined formula.
- **plant or enterprise wide bonuses**, in which all employees receive a bonus, usually linked to profits
- **merit pay**, where the employee receives a level of bonus or basic pay linked to an assessment and appraisal of their performance by their superiors. This system is popular in white collar occupations.
- **financial participation**, for example, profit-sharing and share option schemes, whereby individual employees receive a reward in terms of cash or company shares, the size of which will normally depend on company profits over a given period. Government legislation has encouraged these schemes. Under the All Employee Share Ownership Plan (Aesop) workers could receive (in 2000/01) up to £6,000 of free shares a year from their employer free of tax and national insurance.
- **commission** will often be paid to workers involved in sales, such as insurance and double glazing salespeople, financial advisers and travel agents. In some cases, the wage payment to an employee will consist entirely of commission based on a percentage of the value of sales they achieve and can therefore be an incentive to effort. For other employees the commission may be paid in addition to a basic wage or salary.

Other payments

These can include generous travel and subsistence allowances to employees who are away on business, interest free loans for rail and bus travel tickets, moving expenses for new employees, and more generous payments to employees who are off work due to sickness or maternity than required by law.

Fringe benefits or non-monetary rewards

These are 'payments' to labour in a form other than money, for example, free medical insurance, occupational pension schemes, subsidized canteens and company cars. They can also include performance-related gifts such as 'free' holidays. The provision of 'fringe benefits' in addition to wages or salaries can make a job more attractive to a potential supply of labour. Some, like company cars, can give a job added status, despite the fact that taxes on company car perks have increased in recent years.

For the employer the provision of fringe benefits may work out cheaper than additional payments of wages or salaries. For example, a firm can take advantage of discounts for corporate membership of healthcare schemes or from the bulk purchase of company cars from a manufacturer.

▲ *Financial and other rewards are key motivators*

All employees, unless they are on very low wages, have to pay **National Insurance Contributions (NICs).** These allow them to claim government benefits such as:

- Jobseeker's allowance (unemployment benefit)
- Retirement pension
- Child benefit
- Statutory sick pay (SSP)

- Statutory maternity pay
- Widow's benefit
- Industrial disability benefit

To make sure people only claim what they are entitled to, everyone is issued with their own national insurance number by the Department of Social Security (DSS).

Unless a worker is self-employed, the employer will calculate and deduct NICs from the employee's weekly or monthly pay, details of which will be recorded on their pay slip.

Income tax is paid by both employed and self-employed people, the amount depending on how much they earn in a tax year (from 6 April one year to 5 April the next). Employers are responsible for calculating the amount of income tax each employee is liable for and then deducting this amount from their weekly or monthly pay. This is known as the **Pay-As-You-Earn (PAYE)** scheme.

Wage legislation

Wage protection for UK employees is provided by the **Wages Act** 1986. This sets out conditions for payments to workers, excluding redundancy payments, expenses or loans, and some other deductions.

Wage protection is also covered by the **Equal Pay Acts 1970/1983**. These state that an employee doing the same or broadly similar work to a member of the opposite sex within the same organization is entitled to the same rate of pay and conditions, for example, relating to duties, holidays, overtime, and hours.

National minimum wage legislation introduced in 1999 set the minimum wage for employees over 21 years of age at £3.60 per hour, and at £3 per hour for employees aged between 18 and 21 years. These rates are revised upwards from time to time. The main rate will be raised to £4.10 per hour from October 2001.

There are also regulations governing minimum payments for redundancy, and during sickness, maternity and holidays.

▼ *UK coal mines were once thought to offer their employees jobs for life. Few mines ara still working in the UK today*

Job security

Most employees today want to work in a secure job where they can plan ahead knowing they are unlikely to be made redundant. But in practice this is becoming increasingly rare.

Temporary employment, for example, in summer and holiday jobs, is perhaps the least secure form of employment. But even permanent jobs cannot be entirely safe in an ever-changing business environment. For example, many years ago, people living and working in coalmining towns and villages in the UK thought they had jobs for life. Fathers, sons, and even grandsons worked in the local pits. Today, few coal mines exist and most mining jobs have disappeared due to advances in mining technology, competition from cheaper coal imports from overseas, and a switch in household demand towards cleaner sources of fuel, namely electricity and gas.

Changes in technology, competition from rival firms at home and overseas, changes in consumer demand - can all lead to changes in numbers employed in different industries and occupations. However,

▼ *Secure jobs?*

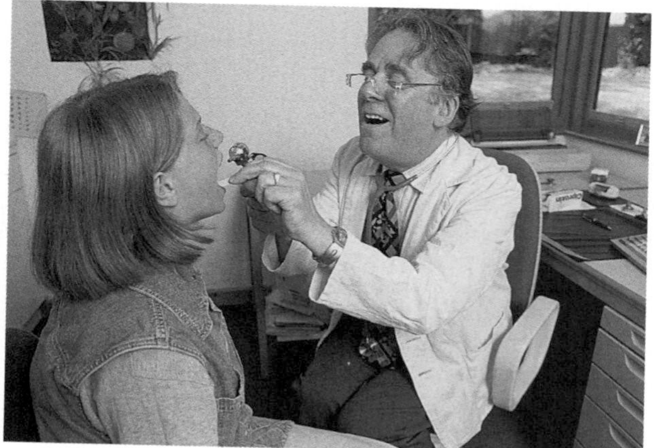

some jobs are less affected by these changes than others. For example, traditionally secure jobs include:

- **Teaching** - because there will always be school children and students who need to be taught
- **Doctors** - because people will always get ill
- **Emergency services** - such as the police and fire brigade

In the past, office jobs in the public sector were often considered to be among the most secure. Civil servants in government departments provide advice to whichever political party forms the UK government. They do not have to make a profit, nor are they affected by competition or consumer demand. However, more recently jobs in the civil service have become less secure as the UK government has cut staff numbers in a bid to reduce costs. Personal computers have also done away with a number of tasks which in the past were carried out by office workers.

The working environment

Working conditions vary greatly from industry to industry and from organization to organization. For example, consider the physical aspects of an office compared with a large iron and steel foundry. The office is probably air-conditioned, carpeted, attractively decorated, and quiet. The steel plant is likely to be hot, dirty, smelly, noisy, and potentially hazardous to workers' health.

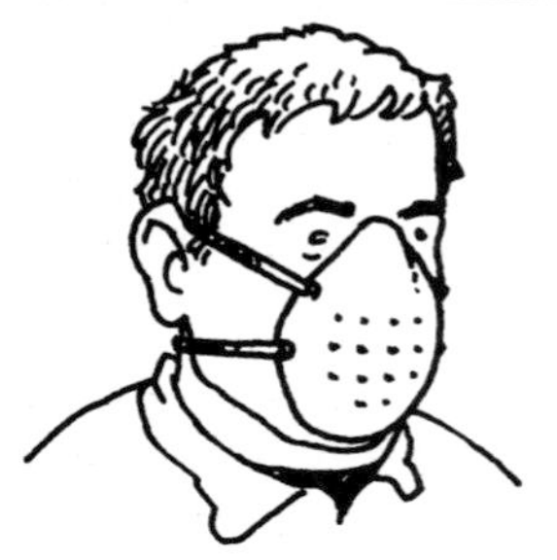

Even within the same industry working conditions can vary widely. For example, contrast the worker on an outside market stall with the assistant in a plush department store, or the policeman on the beat with an inspector in an office, or machine operators in a large modern computer-aided manufacturing plant with those in an old run-down factory.

In a typical week in the UK, around nine workers are killed as a result of accidents in the workplace. Many more receive injury or suffer health problems related to working, from stress to breathing disorders. It is not surprising that firms are required by law to provide, as far as possible, a healthy and safe environment for their workers and customers. A firm that fails to take into account the health and safety of its workers will not only find it difficult to recruit and retain its staff, but will fail to meet targets for output, sales, and profits (see also 1.4).

▼ *Pleasant working environment?*

▼ *Unpleasant working environment?*

▼ *Health and safety at work*

Measures that can make a workplace safer, healthier, and more pleasant to work in include:

- Providing protective clothing, goggles, breathing masks if appropriate
- Providing ear protectors against excessive noise
- Training staff in health and safety matters
- Maintaining safety equipment and clothing
- Allowing breaks for lunch and tea so that workers do not become tired
- Providing First Aid kits and medical officers
- Controlling workplace temperatures
- Installing filters to reduce air pollution
- Refurbishing offices and canteens

How necessary these measures are will depend on the materials and processes being used and the nature of the environment. For example, office workers will need to be aware of fire drills and precautions relating to the prolonged use of computer screens, the movement of office furniture, etc. In contrast, many manufacturing plants are by their very nature noisy, smelly and potentially hazardous places to work in, and stricter health and safety measures will be needed.

Health and safety policy

Every employer should produce a written statement of their policy on health and safety, including details of how the policy should be carried out. This will include details of safe working practices, how accidents should be reported, First Aid representatives, etc. All employees should be made familiar with these details and are expected to comply with them.

Large organizations can also set up safety committees to discuss health and safety issues and how improvements can be made. Senior and junior staff are usually represented on these committees, including any trade union safety representatives who are able to check on the day-to-day operation of the policy. This will include inspecting safety equipment and other possible hazards, investigating accidents and employee complaints, and talking with Health and Safety Executive inspectors.

Sick as a building

Blocked or stuffy nose, dry eyes, dry throat, headaches, and lethargy are some of symptoms of Sick Building Syndrome.

How to Deal with Sick Building Syndrome: Guidance for Employers, Building Owners and Building Managers is the first published HSE guidance on the subject.

Solutions can be simple and cheap and employers are advised to do the simplest things first. For example:

- look for the obvious such as a breakdown in the air-conditioning system;
- check the symptoms, to see how widespread they really are, or whether they are confined to a particular group or area;
- ask staff if they know of any problem or likely causes; and
- if this doesn't solve the problem, the building services and the maintenance and cleaning procedures should be checked.

Employment Gazette, April 1995

Health and safety law

The 1974 **Health and Safety at Work Act** requires employers to 'ensure as far as is reasonably practicable, the health, safety, and welfare at work of all staff.'

The Act requires:

- Firms to provide all necessary safety equipment and clothing free of charge
- Employers to provide a safe working environment
- Union-appointed representatives to have the right to inspect the workplace and investigate the causes of any accident

The Act also requires employees to take reasonable care to avoid injury to themselves or to others by their work activities, and to cooperate with employers and others in meeting statutory requirements. Employees must not interfere with or avoid anything provided to protect their health, safety, or welfare.

There are also a number of European Union regulations on health and safety at work. These cover the provision and use of work equipment, including the use of computer keyboards and screens, the provision and availability of protective clothing, manual handling operations, and workplace conditions.

Health and safety laws and regulations are enforced in the UK by the **Health and Safety Executive (HSE)**. The HSE is a government organization.

Career progression

It is the role of the Human Resources Department in a business to provide good workers with career opportunities and to develop them so that they can gain new skills and take on more responsibilities and challenges. Many workers will want to develop their careers by getting promotion to more senior jobs with more pay. A business that provides few opportunities for career development and promotion will frustrate their workers who are worthy of promotion. If workers are dissatisfied, their work may suffer and they may seek career opportunities with other firms. A business could lose its best workers and fail to recruit new ones, and will eventually be unable to meet its aims and objectives.

Defining what is meant by a 'career' is difficult. Simply working in the same job or a number of different jobs during your working life would not normally be thought of as a career, especially if those jobs involve mundane, repetitive work.

A career normally means working your way up an organization, gaining more experience, and taking on more responsibility in return for more pay. However, not everybody wants to progress in this way. Some people prefer to try out new things, and move from one department to another within the same organization - for example, from production to marketing to finance - broadening their experience as they go.

Portfolio Activity 15.3 

Investigate and report on career opportunities in a business sector of your choice, such as catering, construction, manufacturing, insurance, or retailing.

As a guide, here are some questions you might need to research if you choose health care provision as your business sector:

- What types of jobs are available?
- How can people apply to be a hospital porter or ambulance driver?
- How can people become nurses?
- What qualifications and experience will they need to be promoted to a sister or matron?
- What qualifications and training do people need to become doctors?
- What areas can doctors and nurses specialize in - for example, radiology, physiotherapy, maternity?
- How can doctors become consultants and surgeons?
- What are the main responsibilities of each job?

Opportunities for training

Training workers to improve their existing skills and learn new ones can be very important to a business. Training workers can improve the amount and quality of work they do.

Going back to school

When it comes to job loyalty, it might be a surprise to learn that money is not the number one issue. Instead recent surveys have shown that a happy working environment and good training are top of the list. Money only comes third.

One of the most effective ways of holding onto valued staff is not to give bigger and bigger bonuses but to train them. People want to be rewarded and developed, according to John Miskelly, managing director at JM Management Services.

While most new skills are learnt 'on the job', training reinforces what has been learnt and gives the individual concrete recognition of the skills he or she has gained.

Training increases the skills available within the company and can help it to achieve higher standards.

London Evening Standard, 11.1.1995

The need for training

Technological progress, changes in consumer wants, and competitive pressures in product markets mean that businesses must continually evaluate how they are organized and their needs for different skills. Training, therefore - whether for machine operatives, office or shop assistants, or managers - should be an ongoing process throughout an employee's career. It is the role of the human resources department to monitor the training needs of the organization and the individual employee, and to provide this training as and when required.

In general, the following training needs will arise within an organization over time:

- Organization of induction courses to introduce new employees to the goals and workings of the organization, and their particular jobs
- Improvement of the skills of existing workers to achieve higher levels of productivity and to reduce production costs
- Facilitation of the successful introduction of new equipment, products, and processes
- Reorganization of job roles and tasks within the organization
- Preparation of individual employees for promotion
- Raising employees' awareness of health and safety to reduce accidents
- Promotion of new skills among existing workers
- Creation of a flexible workforce with a wide variety of skills to adapt to change. This is known as **multi-skilling.**

For employees, training will lead to improved motivation simply because it allows staff to do their jobs better and because it raises confidence and improves promotion prospects.

From the employers' perspective, training may improve employee productivity and bring new ideas and working methods to a firm. Training can also improve health and safety procedures and so reduce accidents. It may also lead to a more positive attitude among workers and so reduce employee turnover (see also 13.1).

People as an asset

Increasingly, successful firms are recognizing that their staff are an asset to be invested in, rather than a cost to be minimized. Investment in this human capital through good induction, training, and career development are of as much benefit to particular businesses as they are to individual employees. This culture is best seen in the Investors In People Award, increasingly sought-after by firms as proof of their commitment to their staff.

Investors In People is a national standard designed to help British business get the most from employees. In order to gain this status a firm must:

- Make a public commitment from the top to develop all employees to achieve its business objectives
- Regularly review the training and development needs of all of its employees
- Take action to train and develop staff on recruitment and throughout their employment
- Regularly evaluate investment in training and development to assess achievement and improve future effectiveness

Investors In People is designed to be more than a training initiative: it aims to install permanent systems for continuous improvement and sustained quality within the human resources management of an organization, so as to provide the basis for future business success.

INVESTORS IN PEOPLE

However, training can be expensive. Firms will tend to restrict training to what is entirely necessary and will often only train employees who are likely to stay with the firm for a long time. Permanent full-time workers will, therefore, tend to receive more training than their temporary and part-time colleagues. Training for these workers will tend to be short lived and 'on the job'. It will also focus only on the skills they need to carry out their immediate tasks, such as operating an electronic cash register, and on essential health and safety matters.

Types of training

New employees are often introduced to their organization through a programme of **induction training.** This involves learning about the way the business works and what other staff do. For example, it may contain information about:

- The history and development of the business
- On-site facilities, such as canteens and toilets
- Rules and safety procedures
- Relationships between different jobs
- Employee benefits and services

Once in a job, an employee may receive training to develop their work skills. This can be **on-the-job** or **off-the-job** training.

When training is on-the-job, employees are trained while they are carrying out their normal duties at their place of work. This can take a number of forms:

- **Mentoring** - when a new worker is shown what to do by an experienced worker. It can vary from simply sitting next to a machine operator or attending meetings with another office employee.
- **Coaching** - in the same way as athletes are coached, a trainee employee can be coached by an experienced worker.
- **Job rotation** - involves an employee training to do different jobs over short periods of time, either to become multi-skilled or simply to gain knowledge of the way in which the whole company functions. This is often an important element in the training of management trainees.
- **Apprenticeships** - here, the training is normally sufficiently long and thorough to ensure that very little extra training will ever be necessary, apart from some occasional updating of worker skills and knowledge.

Off-the-job training will involve employees attending courses and training programmes away from their normal jobs:

- **In-house courses** are run by firms for their own employees. Some large organizations, like banks and building societies, even have their own residential training centres or colleges offering a variety of courses run by specialist training officers.

- **External courses** may be run by another employer or at a specialist training centre, or by a supplier of new equipment who is willing to train workers how to use it.
- **Vocational and professional courses** are provided by colleges, universities, and increasingly schools, as a means of supporting what is learnt in the workplace. Vocational courses, such as NVQs, provide training in competencies or job-related skills. Professional courses, for example, in accountancy, engineering, or law, are normally completed by university graduates entering these professions in order to develop their careers.

Government training and development initiatives

The UK government provides incentives and help for people entering work for the first time and for existing employees to train in new skills. It has also introduced legislation to give employees the right to take time off to complete studies. The Government believes skills development is vital to help improve the global competitiveness of UK industry and to generate wealth and jobs in the economy.

Individual Learning Account (ILA)

The ILA is a way of helping people in work pay for learning for their personal development. The ILA is:

- an 'account with government' enabling people to take up discounts for training courses, books and stationery
- a source of information about learning opportunities linked to other government initiatives
- a mechanism to make it easier for employers to support employees' individual development aspirations

Anyone aged 19 can open an account through a variety of ways including the Internet and telephone services. ILA customer service centres manage the administration of the scheme and form a key contact point for learning providers. The holder of an ILA will receive an annual statement of 'learning record' to summarize their learning and training. The statement can be used to demonstrate skill development to their employers or when applying for a new job.

National Traineeships

For school and college leavers aged 16 and upwards, National Traineeships provide an opportunity to get the qualifications and experience that young people will need for the jobs of the future. They offer structured programmes of training designed by employers to meet industry standards.

People who are accepted on to a National Traineeship receive a training agreement which sets out what is expected of them and their employer. The trainee will also have a plan setting out each stage of their training, and where they can expect the training to take place.

The aim is that the trainee will be employed, and will be paid wages. Where this is not the case the trainee will be linked to an employer, or group of employers, and paid an allowance by the Government.

Modern Apprenticeships

Most industries have an approved Modern Apprenticeship programme. These are available to mainly 16- and 17-year-old school and college leavers with the ability to gain high-level skills in their chosen careers and qualifications (to at least NVQ Level 3) which are recognized and wanted by employers. Most Modern Apprentices will be employed and paid wages. Where this is not possible they are linked to an employer, or group of employers, and paid an allowance.

At the end of June 1998 there were over 116,000 young people on Modern Apprenticeships in England and Wales.

▼ *People in training on Modern Apprenticeships: by sector and gender, 1998*

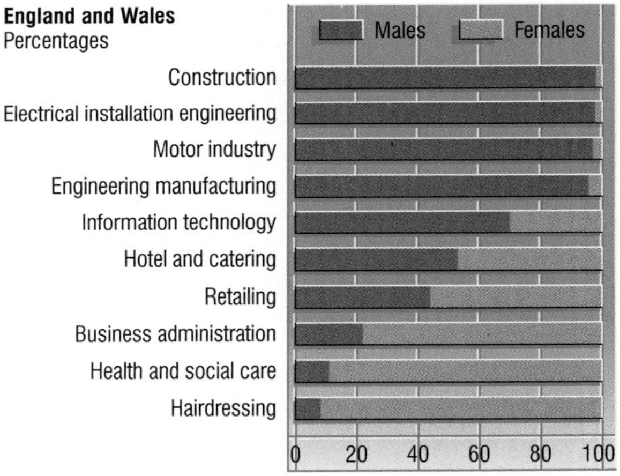

Source: Department for Education and Employment

Social Trends 1999

Right to Time Off for Study and Training

The Right to Time Off for Study or Training is part of the Teaching and Higher Education Act 1998. Employees aged 16 or 17, who are not in full-time secondary or further education and who have not achieved a certain standard in their education/training, are entitled to reasonable paid time off during normal working hours to study or train for a qualification which will help them towards achieving that standard, and improve their future employment prospects.

The 'standard of achievement', which determines both eligibility for the right and that which the young person should seek to attain, is Level 2 (i.e. 5 GCSEs at grades A–C, an NVQ level 2, an Intermediate GNVQ, or equivalents).

Was it worth it?

Training can be expensive. A good employer will evaluate the effectiveness of training courses for their workers to see if they have offered value for money. Key questions employers should ask are:

- What skills have workers acquired? For example, can they operate new machinery, implement health and safety procedures, build a brick wall?
- How has job performance or productivity improved?
- What do employees think about their training? Questionnaires at the end of courses can ask workers what they feel the training course has achieved, and how it could be improved.
- What are the benefits to the firm? Have business goals, such as increased profitability, improved customer relations, been achieved?

Evaluation is simple when the result of the training is clear - for example, if workers are now able to operate new machinery. But it is much more difficult when the benefits of training may only be revealed over a longer period of time, as in the case of improved management techniques or communication skills.

Portfolio Activity 15.4 

1. Investigate on-the-job and off-the-job training in an organization.
   - What skills/qualifications do the employees need in the organization?
   - What methods are used/courses available to train employees?
   - What use is the organization and its employees making of Government training initiatives?
   - What are the organization's immediate and potential future training needs?
   - How is the organization responding to these needs?
   - Does the organization keep a record of employee training and attendance on courses? What do these records show?
   - What further opportunities for training could the organization make use of?

   Draw up a short report on methods of training, benefits of training, and training needs in your chosen organization.
2. What other methods are used by the organization to motivate employees and gain their co-operation?

▼ *Equal opportunities at work*

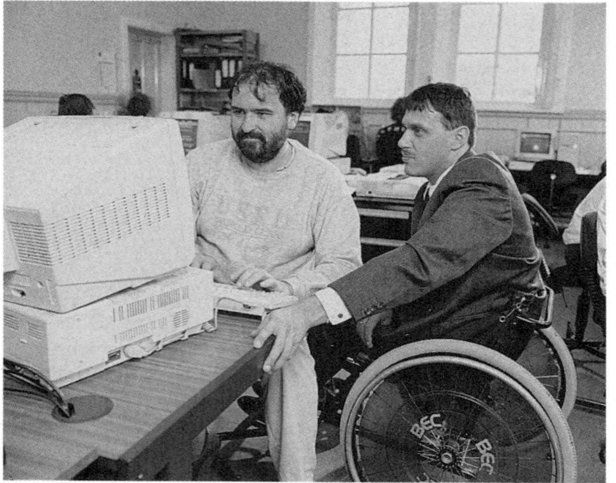

Equal opportunities at work

All employees have a right not to be discriminated against at their place of work. It is the responsibility of an employer to make sure that equal opportunities laws are observed in all aspects of their relationship with employees. This means that the wording of job adverts, the selection of new employees, wage and salary levels, attendance on training programmes, selection of employees for promotion or dismissal, must all be free from discrimination on grounds of sex, marital status, race, religion, or disability.

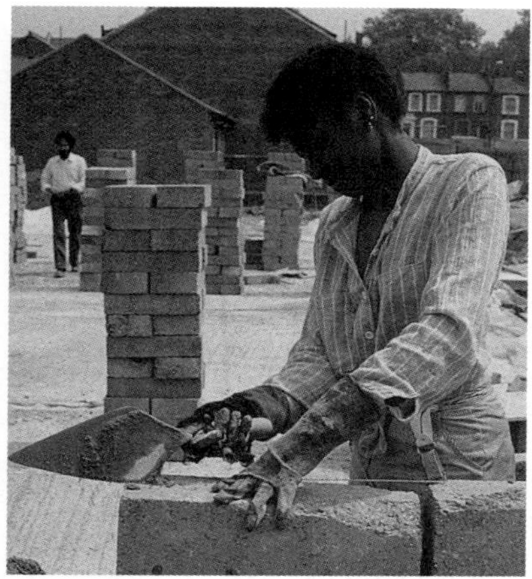

Types of unlawful discrimination

Discrimination at work can take a number of forms. Few are legal:

- **Direct discrimination** occurs when a person is treated less favourably than another because of their sex, race, religion, disability, etc. For example, this may occur when a pregnant woman is selected for redundancy, or a West Indian person is overlooked for promotion or paid less simply because of the colour of his or her skin.
- **Indirect discrimination** occurs when certain people would find it hard to meet a specific requirement. For example, advertising a job for people who are over six feet tall or who have red hair.
- **Victimization** occurs when a person is treated less favourably after claiming they have been discriminated against repeatedly. For example, a female worker could claim she has been victimized if she is made redundant or moved to a less well paid job because she had complained that her boss was sexually harassing her.

Legal discrimination

Discrimination is only legal where it involves a 'genuine occupational qualification'. This means it is possible to advertise, recruit, train, promote, and dismiss employees on grounds of their different skills, performance, and behaviour at work.

Discrimination on grounds of age is not illegal in the UK, although it is considered to be unfair by many people.

Job advertising

It is legal for an employer to express a preference for one type of a person over another in a job advert if there is a genuine occupational qualification for the job concerned. For example, advertising for the following is legal:

- For a coloured actor to appear in a TV programme
- For a female housemistress to work in a girls' boarding school
- For a male attendant for a male toilet
- For male applicants for jobs in countries overseas which may have laws or customs that prevent women doing some types of work
- For a West Indian person to communicate with and understand the needs of West Indian people in a community project

Equal opportunities at the BBC

'The BBC is committed to equal opportunities for all, irrespective of race, colour, creed, ethnic or national origins, gender, marital status, sexuality, disability, or age.

'We are committed to taking positive action to promote such equality of opportunity, and our recruitment, training, and promotion procedures are based on the requirements of the job.'

Equal opportunities policy

Although not required to do so by law, many firms have written their own equal opportunities policies which attempt to remove discrimination in the selection, payment, training, and promotion of their workers. Leading public and private sector organizations, such as Rank Xerox, Shell UK, British Airways, the BBC, and government departments have all adopted these type of policies.

Anti-discrimination legislation

A number of laws have been passed by the UK government to protect workers rights not to be discriminated against. The main laws are:

- **The Disability Discrimination Act 1995** makes it illegal for an employer to treat a disabled person less favourably than someone else because of their disability. It requires schools and colleges to provide information for disabled people. It also allows the Government to set minimum standards so that disabled people can use public transport more easily. The Act set up the National Disability Council to advise the Government on discrimination against disabled people.

  Under the Act, employers and people who provide goods and services to the public must take reasonable measures to make sure that they are not discriminating against disabled people. For example, this could mean removing physical obstructions by, say, widening doors or fitting ramps to enable disabled people to use their services. Firms providing services are not allowed to charge a disabled person more to meet the cost of making it easier for them to use their services. People who sell or let property for rent must ensure that they do not unreasonably discriminate against disabled people.

  If a disabled person feels that they have been unfairly treated in the provision of goods and services or selling of land, they can go to court to seek damages for any financial loss or injury to their feelings. There is no upper limit on the amount of damages that can be paid for injuries to feelings.
- **The Race Relations Act 1976** states that is illegal for an employer to discriminate on grounds of colour, race or ethnic origin in employment, education, training and the provision of housing and other services.
- **The Sex Discrimination Acts 1975/1986** makes it illegal to discriminate against a person on grounds of sex or marital status whether in job adverts, interviews, selection, training, promotion, dismissal and terms of employment. The 1986 act removed restrictions on the hours women could work each week.
- **The Fair Employment (NI) Act** In Northern Ireland contains much of the same legislation as the above laws.

If employees feel that they have been discriminated against they can take their case to an employment tribunal. They can also ask for the help of the Equal Opportunities Commission (EOC), a government body set up in 1975 to

- promote equal opportunities through codes of good practice
- investigate complaints of discrimination
- provide legal advice and financial help when a case goes to court or employment tribunal
- monitor the pay gap between men and women
- review the Equal Pay Act
- issue notices preventing an organization from discriminating

Key words:

EU Working Time Directive - Europe-wide legislation on minimum employee rights, covering the right to rest periods and holidays, and the maximum number of hours an employee can work per day/week

Wage rate - the rate of pay per hour or per period of time for a particular job

Salary - the yearly rate of pay for a particular job unrelated to hours worked

Net earnings - employee earnings after overtime and bonus payments have been added, and income tax and national insurance contributions deducted

Performance-related pay - systems which link pay and other financial rewards to individual, group or organizational performance

Fringe benefits - non-monetary employee rewards

PAYE - Pay As You Earn income tax system

Multi-skilling - training employees in a wide variety of skills to increase labour productivity

Induction training - training new employees to teach them how the business operates

On-the-job training - training employees while they are carrying out their normal duties. It can involve coaching by experienced staff and apprenticeships

Off-the-job training - training conducted away from the workplace through courses and internal or external training programmes. These can include vocational and professional training courses leading to recognized qualifications

Section **15.3**

Performance review and appraisal

Why appraise employee performance?

Regular and systematic monitoring and appraisal of the work performance of employees at all levels within an organization is now commonplace and of primary importance in business. **Performance appraisal** has a number of important benefits both for employers and for the employees undergoing appraisal:

- **It provides a check on the recruitment process:** Did the right employees get selected? An organization will have taken care to ensure that the successful candidates met with certain criteria in terms of skills and personal qualities. Some may have been tested formally. However, it is only when an individual is actually in work that the organization can monitor and assess their qualities and abilities, their attitude to working and if they 'fit' the organizational culture (see 2.6).
- **It can motivate employees:** Employees can be motivated to greater effort and quality in their work if they are given positive and constructive feedback on their performance from their colleagues and managers. In many cases, the performance appraisal will be used as the basis, either at individual or team level, to determine pay increases and bonus payments under performance related pay schemes (see 15.2). Performance appraisals can also be used to check on the effectiveness over time of motivational strategies introduced by the organization to increase work performance and productivity (see 15.1).
- **It can identify employee potential:** How well an employee performs in their current job can provide managers with an insight into how well they might perform in other or more senior positions. The appraisal process may show that an employee has skills or intellectual capabilities which he or she is not using fully. The employee may then be offered a new or redesigned job to motivate them and make better use of those abilities. A good performance appraisal result may increase the employees chances of promotion and this may help to motivate the employee in their current role.
- **It can help identify training and development needs:** If an employee displays a lack of competence in some areas of their work, for example, if they are finding it difficult to work with newly installed equipment, then appropriate training can be arranged. Similarly, employees identified as having the potential for promotion can be given the training they need now to prepare them for more senior positions.
- **It can provide documentation for disciplinary action:** An employee may need to be disciplined or even dismissed if their performance, and/or their attitude to work and colleagues, is significantly and consistently at fault. Appraisal records will provide documentary evidence of poor performance, the chances the employee was given to improve and any training offered should the employee challenge their employers action through his or her Trade Union or at an Employment Tribunal (see 13.3). The employer will need to demonstrate they have followed

necessary guidelines, gave ample warnings and acted fairly on all occasions.

- **It may reveal other problems:** Sometimes the performance of otherwise good employees can suffer because they have health or other personal problems at home, or are experiencing difficulties with other staff, for example, from racial or sexual harassment. A formal and well-handled appraisal may reveal these problems and appropriate help offered or action taken.

The performance appraisal, therefore, can be used to control employee behaviour, but more importantly to motivate and develop employees. A business that fails to appraise and reward employee performance effectively is unlikely to develop a workforce that will commit to the achievement of its objectives, work to increase productivity and strive to maintain the competitiveness of the business.

Performance appraisal methods

There are a number of different ways in which organizations appraise the performance of their employees. These include:

- performance reviews and evaluations
- self-evaluations
- peer evaluations
- achievement of individual or group targets
- measuring productivity

The precise method used will often depend on the type of work carried out by the employee. For example, peer evaluations by work colleagues will often be used in offices where the employee works as part of a team. Sales teams may be measured by the amount of revenue they generate, while manufacturing workers are more likely to be set output targets and assessed against them.

It is likely that a performance appraisal system within an organization will combine a number of different methods and will also consist of informal and formal elements.

Formal appraisal systems...

- involve formal appraisal interviews where views can be exchanged
- involve the completion of confidential appraisal reports which are then kept on file
- assess performance against an agreed set of criteria
- are completed usually every 12 months for all employees, to an agreed timetable
- will be completed by the immediate manager of the employee, and usually countersigned by a more senior manager

But...

- employees may get anxious about them and may mistrust them
- can be an administrative burden
- may come as a shock, especially if the assessment is critical, if the employee has not been given feedback throughout the appraisal period

Informal appraisal systems...

- rely on verbal feedback rather than formal written evaluations
- can identify areas of weakness in performance early on to give the employee a chance to improve in those areas or go on training courses
- provide a chance to give early warnings about poor performance

But...

- may be irregular an haphazard
- managers may avoid confrontation on difficult issues
- constructive criticisms may be misunderstood by the employee

▼ *Figure 15.1: An example of a formal appraisal report*

Performance and Development Assessment Record | Staff in Confidence

Section 1 : Job holder's details

Name: ______________________

Pay number: ______________________

Job title: ______________________

Date started present job: ______________

Job purpose and main responsibilities:

____

____

____

Section 2 : Achievement of objectives

Comment on how well overall the job holder met their objectives:

____

____

____

____

Section 3 : Competencies

Competence	*Rating*	*Comments*
Personal effectiveness	☐	
Appearance	☐	
Communication skills	☐	
Initiative	☐	
Technical expertise	☐	
Teamwork	☐	
Quality of work	☐	

Section 4 : Overall performance assessment

Give a rating for overall performance using the scale below (refer to guidance notes):

A	B	C	D	E	***(Tick appropriate box)***
Exceptional	Very good	Good	Reasonable	Unacceptable	

Comment on the overall performance of the job holder, noting any pressures or personal factors which may have affected performance, and on key development activities which have contributed towards objectives.

____

____

____

____

Signed (by manager) : ______________________ Date: ______________

Name (CAPITALS) : ______________________

Signed (by job holder) : ______________________ Date: ______________

Name (CAPITALS) : ______________________

Performance reviews and evaluations

The supervisor or manager of the employee will monitor and review their performance at work over time. A formal appraisal report is usually completed at the end of every 12-month period of review, but there may be short interim reports every three or six months (see Figure 15.1).

The appraisal report will provide written comments on the employee's achievements against targets and their performance under a number of headings, such as communication skills, use of IT, dealing with pressure or technical expertise. The appraiser may also give the employee a score under each heading as well as an overall marking for performance for the year.

The report will be discussed at a formal appraisal interview between the employee and the manager. At this meeting they will discuss the managers' reasons for comments made in the report and any scores given. The employee will usually have the chance to challenge these views and, if appropriate, agree revisions before the report is finalized. The interview will also agree objectives, targets and key tasks for the employee to complete over the next 12-month period and will identify any training needs, if appropriate.

Self-evaluations

The employee being appraised completes these. The employee will evaluate their own performance over time against an agreed list of criteria. They will also list their achievements and areas where they think they need to improve. The self-evaluation can be compared with the assessment completed by the manager to examine where their perceptions agree or disagree, and why.

Peer evaluations

These are performance reports completed by colleagues that the employee has worked with recently or continues to work with on regular basis. They can be employees who are in more senior or less senior positions than the employee being appraised, or at the same level within the organization hierarchy (see 2.4). For this reason, peer evaluations are often called **360 degree feedback exercises.**

Peer evaluations can be formal letters or reports, or informal verbal reports, directed to the employee being appraised and his or her appraiser. They will often be used to compile comments for the formal appraisal report.

Setting individual or group targets

Performance measurement can be a relatively simple task if the employee, or a group of employees in a team, is set targets at the beginning of each appraisal period to achieve by the end of that period. These may be:

- **quantitative targets**, for example, produce 1,000 units, increase sales revenues by 10% or reduce average costs by 5%
- **qualitative targets**, such as improve written skills or product quality
- **timescale targets**, for example, deliver a report on waste management by

July 2001, attend a management training course in April 2002, answer all customer enquiries within 10 working days of their receipt

Targets should be challenging but realistic. There is no point setting a target that is so difficult to meet there is little chance of anyone doing so. It is also important to understand why targets have not been met when appraising an employee or team. There may have been reasons beyond their control. The achievement of many qualitative targets can be especially difficult to judge unambiguously.

An example of the types of competencies an office assistant might be assessed against and how they can demonstrate their achievement

Competence	Activity
Communication skills	Speaks clearly Writes clear messages
Dealing with pressure	Thinks before acting Responds positively when placed under immediate work demands
Efficiency	Works quickly without making mistakes Knows rules and procedures Own work area is tidy and well ordered
Initiative	Works out how to deal with urgent items without being told
Flexibility	Deals effectively with unplanned and unexpected work
Team skills	Supports other team members effectively Shares information Contributes to team discussions
Analytical thinking	Does simple analysis Checks accuracy of data and information
Use of IT	Makes effective use of word processor and spreadsheet packages

...and some of the things a senior manager might be judged on

Competence	Activity
Communication skills	Explains complex issues simply Communicates a clear vision of what must be done and why
Credibility	Demonstrates a clear understanding of issues Shows concern to be taken seriously
Dealing with pressure	Deals effectively with heavy work loads over long periods
Efficiency	Looks for efficiency savings in whole processes Able to prioritize tasks and use of time
Improving results	Demonstrates drive and enthusiasm Sets long-term challenging goals for self and others
Influencing skills	Makes persuasive arguments and effective presentations Listens to others' views Works out effective influencing strategies
Initiative	Takes unprompted action to address deep, difficult problems or issues Thinks well ahead and identifies action plans

Appraisal techniques

An appraisal system may make use of a number of different techniques:

Competence rating: The competencies of the employee are graded on a scale which ranges from excellent to unacceptable. The competencies against which the employee is assessed will depend on the type of work undertaken.

Written commentary: The appraising manager will summarize and comment on features of the employee's abilities and achievements. In case the manager cannot remember all the notable achievements of the employee it is useful to combine this with peer and self-evaluation reports. This will also help to reduce any bias the manager has in favour or against the employee.

Achievement of objectives: Having set a series of objectives for the employee, the manager will then compare performance with these identified targets. Some objectives are fairly easy to measure, for example, completing a piece of work by a given date or reaching a sales target, but many are open to interpretation, such as, improving written skills.

Critical incident reporting: These are irregular reports by the appraising manager recording examples of particularly good or bad work.

Examples of rating scales used in appraisals

It is usual to compare the performance of the employee with others at the same grade in the organization or against what is generally expected of an employee at that level:

Employee performance... (tick box applicable)

- ☐ is significantly above requirements of the job
- ☐ is above the requirements of the job
- ☐ fully meets the requirements of the job
- ☐ is below the requirements of the job
- ☐ is unacceptable

Where comparisons are not made the abilities and competencies of the employee may be rated simply as very good to very poor:

Employee performance is (tick box applicable)

- ☐ Very good
- ☐ Good
- ☐ Fair
- ☐ Poor
- ☐ Very poor

Performance ratings may also be combined with a numerical scoring system:

Very good ⟵				⟶ Very poor
1	2	3	4	5

Measuring productivity

Production workers and managers are often set targets in terms of increasing output year on year. Sales teams and managers may be set targets in terms of increasing revenues. Their actual productivity over time can be measured against these productivity targets (see 1.1).

However, it is also possible to measure productivity gains in many service industries where there is no physical output or financial measures available. For example, teachers may be judged on improving the exam results of their students, doctors may be judged on the number of patients they see each day, postal workers may be judged against how quickly it takes them to complete their rounds, and the average time taken to process applications and arrange job interviews could be used as a measure of the productivity of a Human Resources Department.

Designing an appraisal system

If an performance appraisal system is to achieve its objectives, and not cause resentment among the employees being appraised and those undertaking the assessments, then it is vital that:

- management is fully committed to the appraisal system
- the system is easy to understand and to complete

- managers who appraise employees receive appropriate training for this role and are given clear guidelines to follow when completing reports
- enough time to complete the appraisal process is made available
- employees are fully informed about the process and the criteria against which they are to be appraised
- employees receive regular feedback on performance so that comments in a year end report should be a surprise
- it is a two-way process which allows employees to comment on their appraisals, agree changes with their appraisers if appropriate, or formally record their own remarks

▼ *Figure 15.2: A typical disciplinary and dismissal procedure*

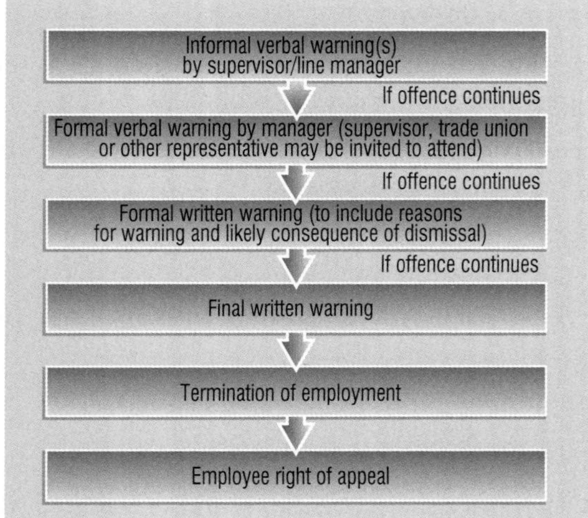

Disciplinary and dismissal procedures

If employee performance is continually poor and shows little sign of improving then it may be necessary to discipline the employee in some way, or even to dismiss the employee.

An important function of any Human Resource Department is to outline and operate the **disciplinary procedure.** This is the process whereby employees may be disciplined for failing to meet the terms of their contract.

A disciplinary procedure usually involves a series of steps: a verbal warning; a written warning, if the offence persists; a final written warning, and dismissal (if the final written warning is made within twelve months of the first). Alternatively, in the event of a serious breach of company rules (such as theft, or deliberate and dangerous contravention of health and safety rules), an employee may be suspended or dismissed immediately. The employee should be given the right to appeal and independent assessment at any stage in the disciplinary procedure.

Terminating employment

A contract of employment will end when an employee leaves for another job after an agreed period of notice has been given, or if s/he retires, dies, or is dismissed.

In law, there are five reasons for dismissal which are considered 'fair' and legal:

- **Redundancy** - when employees are surplus to requirements, possibly due to a decline in business, the introduction of new technology, or structural reorganization. Employees have the right to receive compensation for redundancy, based on their length of service and level of wages.
- **Gross misconduct** - i.e. theft, fraud, wilful disobedience, or negligence which involves a breach of contract.

- **Incompetence** - when the worker is clearly not able to do their job and has produced sub-standard work.
- **If continued employment contravenes laws** - for example, if a heavy goods vehicle driver has been banned for drink driving.
- **Substantive other reasons** - e.g. refusal to accept changes in working practices.

Some employees who have been disciplined or dismissed by an employer may feel aggrieved and wish to challenge the decision. They can do this by following the **grievance procedure** within their organization or by seeking outside help from a number of organizations such as **ACAS (the Advisory, Conciliation and Arbitration Service), an Employment Tribunal, the European Court of Justice**, or even by taking **civil legal action** against their employer.

Unfair dismissal is defined in law as follows:

- Where employers have failed to give the required period of notice as set out in the contract of employment in the case of redundancy
- Where employees have been dismissed for going on strike, while others who have done the same have not been dismissed
- Where employees have been dismissed for joining or refusing to leave a Trade Union
- Where employees have been dismissed on grounds of sex, race, or religion
- Where employees have been 'wrongfully' selected for redundancy
- Where employees have been dismissed due to illness or pregnancy

Grievance procedures and supporting organizations are considered in detail in Section 13.3.

Portfolio Activity 15.5 

In groups, suggest different competencies you think the following employees should demonstrate in their work, and the types of activities they do that could demonstrate level of achievement. After you have done this try to find out how their performance is judged in reality.

A newly trained nurse
A newly qualified school teacher
A bricklayer on a major construction site
A sales assistant in a department store
A finance office assistant in a major company

An experienced senior staff nurse
A school headmaster/mistress or principal
A construction site manager
The sales director at a department store
The finance director of a major company

Suggest some strategies you would use to motivate the above employees to improve their performance.

Key words:

Performance appraisal - an assessment of the work performance, competencies and attitudes of an employee

Appraisal system - the process, reporting methods and techniques used to monitor, review and appraise the performance of employees

360° feedback - reviews and evaluations of an employee's performance by work colleagues at different levels in their organization

Disciplinary procedure - a set of formal rules and processes governing the undertaking of disciplinary actions against employees who breach their contracts of employment

Key Activity

You are to produce a detailed analytical report on how one large organization manages its human resources. Your report must:

- accurately describe the responsibilities of the Human Resources Department in the organization
- explain why effective human resource management is vital to the business. In this section you should refer to and describe actual examples of how the business is using, or has used, its human resource function to improve competitiveness
- describe how human resource requirements are planned for by the business. Then create your own plan for human resources within the business from an analysis of relevant information on internal staffing (pay levels, turnover, absenteeism, skills, forecast vacancies, etc.) and local labour market conditions (employment trends, availability of skilled labour, level of competition for employees, etc.)
- describe how the business recruits and selects employees for vacant posts. This should also identify features of key recruitment documents, how they are used to identify and select candidates for interview, and how they are used in interview
- explain the purpose of performance management and describe how the business's approach may have been influenced by different motivation theories
- identify key aspects of the organization's training and development programme(s) and explain the importance of these programmes to the overall performance of the business. Analyse the relationship between training and development in the business, performance management and motivation theories. Suggest how and why training may conflict with cost and profit considerations, at least in the short run
- explore one of the above human resource functions in depth. Give examples of how the work is carried out and critically examine how well the function is carried out

First, produce an action plan to complete your report. This should include pre-arranged interviews with those members of the organization who carry out the human resources function, site visits, and target completion dates for the different sections of your report

Then develop your report on a computer using word processing software. Supporting statistical data should be presented in graphs and tables where appropriate.

Finally, produce a draft report to send to the Human Resources Department in the organization for their comment. Use their comments to finalize your report.

Useful references

See also Chapter 14

Equal Opportunities Commission (*www.eoc.org.uk*)
Customer Contact Point, Arndale House, Arndale Centre, Manchester M4 3EQ

Health and Safety Executive (*www.hse.gov.uk*)
Rose Court, 2 Southwark Bridge, London SE1 9HS

Internet key words search: **employee performance appraisal, employee motivation, training**

Test your knowledge

Questions 1–3 share the following answer options:

A Equal Pay Act

B Health and Safety at Work Act

C Race Relations Act

D Sex Discrimination Act

Which of the above laws would an organization be breaking if it:

1 failed to give workmen working with chemicals protective clothing?

2 sacked a woman because she was pregnant?

3 advertised a job for 'English male drivers only'?

4 Which of the following reasons for dismissing an employee would be unfair?

A For joining a trade union

B For redundancy due to a fall in sales of the product

C For very poor time keeping

D For sexual harassment

5 Which of the following is a legal responsibility of an employer?

A To ensure that health and safety standards at work are met

B To give staff regular training

C To provide a quiet place to rest during breaks

D To ensure that food can be bought on the premises for staff

6 Under health and safety legislation who has a legal responsibility to report any health and safety hazards?

A Both employers and employees

B Employees only

C Company owners

D Customers

7 A friend of yours claimed she has been unfairly dismissed by her employer because she is pregnant. What would you advise her to do?

A Take her case to the European Court of Justice

B Nothing

C Write to her employer demanding redundancy pay

D Take her case to an Employment Tribunal

Questions 8–10 share the following answer options:

A Job enlargement

B Job rotation

C Job enrichment

D Empowerment

Employers may motivate employees by redesigning their jobs. Which of the above describes:

8 Increasing the scope and variety of work tasks without increasing employee responsibility?

9 Organizing employees into groups and training them to carry out all the different jobs of that group?

10 Enhancing job variety and giving an employee more freedom to organize their work?

Questions 11–13 share the following answer options:

A A new employee learning about the business

B Off-the-job training

C On-the-job training

D Vocational training

Which of the above best describes:

11 Attending a college course on day release?

12 A new employee learning about the business?

13 A new employee being coached by an experienced worker?

14 **a** Contrast two theories of employee motivation

b Suggest how an employer might use them to design strategies to motivate their employees to greater performance

c What is the difference between on-the-job and off-the-job training?

d Explain why employee training and development is important in business.

15 **a** What is Performance Appraisal?

b Suggest ways you might judge the performance of (i) a senior marketing manager, and (ii) a skilled manufacturing worker.

c What is a peer review?

d Explain four reasons why performance appraisal is important in business.

Business Finance

About this unit

External confidence in the management of any large business is determined by its financial performance. You can look at the financial pages of any national newspaper to see how true this is. Shareholders in limited companies and other business stakeholders - major consumers, competitors, financial institutions, employees and even Government in some cases - will keenly await the latest information on the financial performance of business organizations.

Good financial management is vital to continued business success. That means that a business must record every financial transaction. Even the very smallest transaction will be audited so that the final accounts of a business accurately reflect the value of the business assets, its expenditures, sales and profits, at the end of each accounting period. Public confidence in a business and the confidence of its employees rely on good accounts. The tax authorities will also be concerned that final accounts are accurate so that a business pays the right amount of tax on its profits.

In this unit you will discover how businesses manage their finances and about key indicators of the financial health of a business. You will need to understand routine aspects of financial recording and management, and how financial performance is monitored and forecast. You will learn how to interpret financial information to make judgements about the effectiveness of a business, and find out how important financial management is for effective business planning.

chapter 16 Recording Financial Transactions

This chapter examines the various kinds of business documentation that are used to record financial transactions and provide the foundation for the creation of accounting records.

I'M FOLLOWING THE AUDIT TRAIL!

What you need to learn

Every business has to meet internal and external reporting requirements to monitor its financial performance and to meet legal and other requirements.

You need to know the range of documents used by businesses and how and why these are used to record **financial transactions**. You need to know how each contributes to the flow of financial information.

Purchase documents include **purchase orders** and **goods received notes**.

Sales documents include **invoices**, **delivery notes**, **credit and debit notes**, and **customer account statements**.

Payments can be **cash** or non-cash, such as **by cheque**, **automated methods**, **credit card** or **debit card**.

Receipts are proof of payment documents. They include **sales receipts**, **cheques**, **paying-in slips** and **bank account statements**.

Financial documents provide an **audit trail** - the means by which financial transactions can be traced and checked. You will need to understand the management of these documents and explain their use and importance.

Correct completion of documents is essential. Wrongly completed documents can result in inaccurate accounting methods and misleading information about financial performance.

Section **16.1**

What are financial transactions?

Types of financial transaction

Trade takes place when business organizations supply goods and services to consumers in return for money or other goods and services. A **financial transaction** takes place whenever a person or organization pays money to another person or organization for goods and services ordered or received.

Many millions of financial transactions take place each and every day all over the world. Whenever you buy an ice cream or can of drink in a sweet shop you are making a financial transaction. You pay money to the shopkeeper to receive the ice cream or drink. When you travel on a bus or train you will pay for a ticket which allows you to use the service.

Inward and outward transactions

Because most firms are not just producers but also consume goods and services they not only receive payments but also make payments to other people and organizations. That is, most firms will receive money and also pay money out. This means there are two types of financial transaction in business:

- **Inward transactions**
- **Outward transactions**

Inward and outward transactions

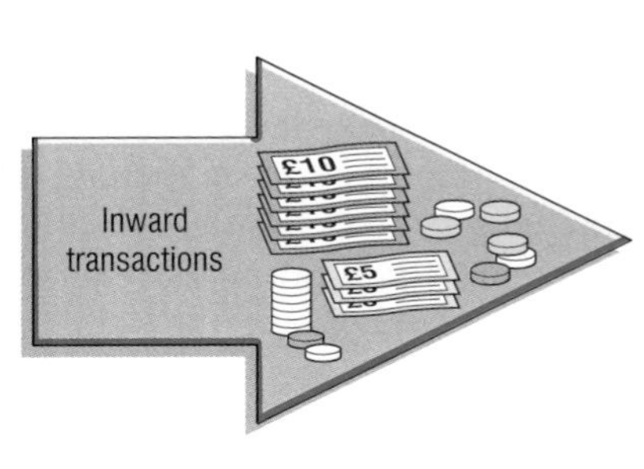

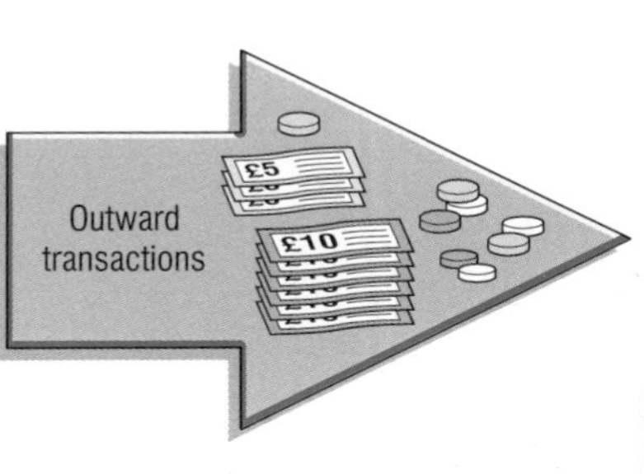

Inward transactions are payments of money received by a firm. For most business organizations inward transactions will include:

- Payments for goods and services sold to members of the public
- Payments for goods and services sold to other businesses
- Loans of money from banks and other lenders

Other organizations can receive inward transactions in other forms. For example, limited companies can receive money from the sale of shares, charities will receive donations and the government receives money in the form of taxes.

Outward transactions are payments made by a firm to other firms or people. A firm will usually make payments for:

- Wages for the hire of workers
- Raw materials and component parts from suppliers
- Services, such as cleaning, maintenance, insurance, and advertising
- Fixed assets such as premises, machinery, vehicles, and other equipment
- Overheads such as telephone charges, stamps, stationery, rent and rates
- Loan repayments and interest charges
- Any Value Added Tax (VAT) collected on goods and services sold will also have to be returned to the Government's Customs and Excise Department.

Whenever a business exchanges goods and services for money it is important that it keeps detailed and accurate records. Every purchase made by one firm or person is a sale to the firm that receives money in payment. An outward transaction is a payment for goods and services. An inward transaction is a sale.

Payment is made once an **invoice** is issued following an order for goods and services. An invoice will contain details of goods and services supplied, how much is owed by the customer and when payment is due (see 16.3).

Cash or credit?

In general, businesses sell their goods and services to individual and business customers in one of two main ways:

- **Cash sales** - which means that goods and services are paid for immediately they are received either by cash or by cheque. Most shops sell goods and services on this basis. When you buy a bar of chocolate or a CD you will normally pay for it there and then.
- **On credit** - which involves the customer 'buying now and paying later'. Sales on credit can take a number of forms.

  Trade credit is often given by suppliers to their main business customers. They are allowed up to 30, 60, or even 90 days to pay in full for the goods and services they have ordered and received.

  Credit sales are a popular method used by mail-order firms. The customer is allowed to spread payments for goods received over a number of weeks. Relatively low price items, such as a pair of jeans, can usually be paid for in regular weekly amounts over 12–24 weeks, while high price items, such as a widescreen TV, can be paid for over 52 weeks or sometimes even more. The customer owns the goods received after the first instalment has been paid for.

  Hire purchase (HP) also allows the customer to pay for the for goods or services they have received in regular (monthly) instalments, often including an interest charge, over anything from 6 months to a number of years. Unlike credit sales, a HP agreement will normally require the customer to pay a deposit of 10% or even 20% of the total price immediately the goods or services are ordered or received, and these do not become the property of the customer until the final payment has been made.

  HP is a popular method of payment used by smaller firms to buy the machinery and other equipment they need. Many suppliers are now offering interest-free HP in an attempt to encourage customers to buy their goods and services.

Debtors and creditors

People and organizations to whom goods or services have been sold on credit are known as **debtors**. The business organization that allows customers to pay on credit is, therefore, known as their **creditor** until those customers finally pay for the goods and services they have received.

Allowing customers to pay on credit can encourage sales because they are able to spread their payments. This will be an especially important advantage for individual and business customers who have limited incomes and/or savings. However, for the supplier there is always a risk that the customer may default - that is, not pay up. This will involve spending time and money chasing the debt in writing and even legal action through a court if they still fail to pay (see 17.3).

Why document financial transactions?

Financial information is essential to all organizations engaged in productive activities. It is important that all financial transactions are recorded, that records are kept up to date, and that information can be retrieved easily when required, for the following reasons:

- **To monitor business performance:** Business managers need financial records in order to measure how well their organization has performed (see 19.1). This will assist them in future business planning.
- **To record all purchases and sales:** A business will need to keep track of total purchases and sales so that the firm can know how much money they owe to suppliers and how much is owed to them by their debtors.
- **To produce final accounts:** Business owners and managers need to see financial accounts at the end of the financial year in order to judge the total worth of the business and how much profit or loss has been made. Limited companies are required by law to produce annual accounts (see 18.1).
- **To fulfil legal requirements:** Organizations are required by law to produce accounts so that the tax authorities can calculate how much corporation tax and VAT they are liable to pay.
- **To confirm mutual understanding between buyer and seller**. Any exchange of goods or services between organizations and individuals is a transaction. A transaction is a two-way process. It will involve one firm making a purchase and another making a sale. It is, therefore, important that both buyers and sellers can confirm arrangements for orders, delivery dates, prices and methods of payments. This can only be done by making sure each has a copy of relevant documents.

For all of these reasons, accurate financial records must be maintained. The recording of financial information is called **book-keeping**. These records are based upon the many thousands or millions of transactions made by firms each day. In the vast majority of firms, the daily and weekly transactions are far too many to be remembered, so every sale or purchase, or business expense, must be recorded for subsequent entry into the book-keeping system.

Using documents

Recording information about transactions often requires a lot of paperwork. To speed this process up, businesses have devised special documents to use. Invoices, order forms, purchase documents, bank paying-in slips, and sales invoices are just a few of the kinds of documents used to record transactions. Information from these documents is then transferred to the book-keeping system in order to record totals for sales, purchases, and other business expenses.

Financial documents are required not only to assist business managers in remembering transactions, but also to provide evidence that the transactions actually took place. For example, it might be tempting for some business managers to attempt to hide sales in order to avoid tax, but a quick check through the invoices raised by the firm by independent auditors (accountants) will usually reveal the true picture.

Portfolio Activity 16.1

Imagine that you are a sole trader running a small newsagent's shop. List the different kinds of financial transactions that you would regularly need to undertake; suggest how you would record them, and the types of documents you would need.

Undertake research into any small business that you know. Find out about the different kinds of documents that the business uses, and why it uses them. Compare these with your original list.

▼ *Figure 16.1: Documents involved in a typical business transaction*

Example: The household insurance department in a large insurance company head office purchases new office equipment from a stationery and office supplies company

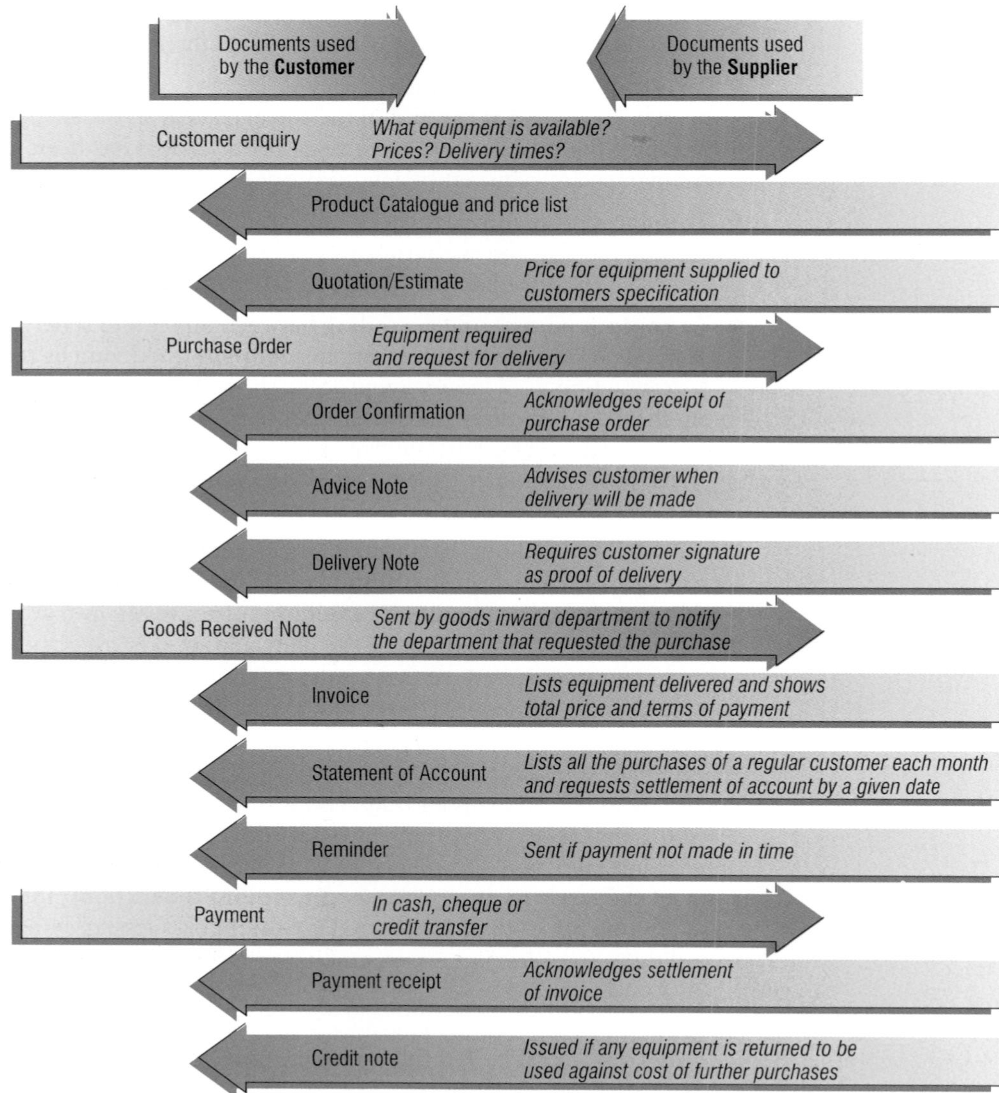

Section 16.2 Purchase documents

Making purchases

The function of the Purchasing Department in a business is to buy in materials of the right quality, in the right quantities, at the right time, and at the lowest cost (see 4.2). Every pound saved by purchasing is an extra pound made in profits, so it is essential that purchasing works efficiently. The different stages in the purchasing process require different kinds of documentation.

Before any documentation is drawn up, the Purchasing Department will make enquiries with different suppliers in order to get a range of **estimates** or **quotations** as to the best deal available. Once the best supplier is identified, a purchase order is drawn up. This is a legal offer to the supplier.

▼ *Figure 16.2: An example of a purchase order*

Iles Textiles Ltd
21 Bedford Way
London WC2
Tel: 020-7123-6789
Fax: 020-7123-6780
VAT Reg No. 4333 5432 18

Purchase Order No. 9285

To: Computer Supplies Ltd
1 Megadrive Way
Milton Keynes MK6

DATE	DESCRIPTION	QTY	CAT.No	PRICE	TOTAL
24.8.200X	PIII 700MHz 256 Mb RAM 21" Monitor Keyboard and mouse	1	928/C	£1,250	£1,250
Other charges				**Delivery**	£30
Deliver to above address				**Sub-total**	£1,280
				VAT @ 17.5%	£224
				Total	£1,504

Authorized by: J. Iles **for Iles Textiles Ltd.**

The purchase order

Figure 16.2 shows an order for computer equipment made by Iles Textiles Ltd.

An order for goods and/or services to be supplied should specify:

- The purchaser's name and address for delivery of goods and for receipt of payment documentation
- Precise details of the goods or services being purchased, including make, model number, unit price, VAT payable
- The total price
- The delivery date required. If delivery by a certain date is very important, this should be stated clearly on the order.
- The order should be signed by someone with sufficient authority to approve it.

A copy of the **purchase order** will also be forwarded by the Purchasing Department to the Accounts Department. When the supplier sends the request for payment, called an **invoice**, the Accounts Department can compare this bill with the original order to check that the goods in question were actually ordered by the firm and at the price stated on the invoice.

▼ *Figure 16.3: An example of an invoice*

INVOICE

Computer Supplies Ltd

1 Megadrive Way
Milton Keynes MK6
Tel: 01908-6566
Fax: 01908-6560
VAT Reg No. 234 8899 14

To: Iles Textiles Ltd
21 Bedford Way
London WC2

DATE	Order No	Account No.	Invoice No
8.9.200X	9285	702316	18967

QTY	Description	Cat No.	Unit Price	Total
1	PIII 700MHz 256 Mb RAM 21" Monitor Keyboard & mouse	928/C	£1250	£1250
1	Delivery		£30	£30
			Sub-total	£1280
			Cash discount	- £32
			Total (ex. VAT)	£1248
			VAT @ 17.5%	+ £218.40
			Total due	+ £1466.40

Terms:
Payment due 30 days from date of invoice.
Cash discount of 2.5% if payment received within 10 working days from date of invoice

E & OE

Purchase invoice

A supplier demands payment for goods delivered to a customer by sending an **invoice.** The invoice will detail the name and address of the supplier and customer. Sometimes the address for the invoice is different from the address for delivery of goods. For example, when delivering goods to a chain store, the goods will go to the main warehouse or to individual stores, but the invoice requesting payment will go to the Accounts Department at the company's head office.

An invoice will normally contain the following information:

- Customer's account number
- Invoice reference number
- A full description of the goods supplied and their reference numbers
- Unit price of the goods
- If the charge for delivery is included in the price, the invoice states 'carriage paid'
- Total price
- Deductions for any cash or trade discounts
- The total net price after including VAT and any deductions
- The date by which the invoice should be paid
- Some businesses may also include a **remittance advice note** with their invoices. This may take the form of a tear off slip summarizing the main points on an invoice. The buyer simply returns this with the payment so that it is easily matched to the correct transaction.

An invoice is a legal document. Firms must keep all their invoices in order to provide evidence of the amount they have spent on purchases, both for VAT inspectors and for the Inland Revenue. VAT-registered businesses can claim back VAT paid on purchases, and some may be tempted to claim they have purchased more than they really have. Similarly, a firm may be tempted to mislead the tax authorities by claiming more purchases were made than actually occurred in order to reduce the profit declared in the accounts and so reduce corporation tax liability. Both practices are illegal.

To the firm making a purchase, an invoice from a supplier is known as a **purchase invoice** because the payment made by the purchasing firm to settle it will be entered as a debit in their business accounts.

Figure 16.3 shows the invoice sent by Computer Supplies to Iles Textiles Ltd following delivery of the computer they ordered, using the purchase order in Figure 16.2.

Cash discounts

In order to speed up the payment of invoices, many suppliers offer a **cash discount**. This discount is a percentage of the goods total (usually around 2.5%) which the buyer can deduct if he or she pays immediately rather than waiting until the end of the period specified on the invoice.

Trade discounts

In addition to a discount for paying cash, some suppliers also give a discount to regular customers, called **a trade discount**. For example, most retailers will receive trade discount from their suppliers. The discount is deducted from the invoice total and will often vary with the quantity purchased. Bigger discounts tend to be given for bigger orders.

▼ *Figure 16.4: An example of a Goods Received Note*

Iles Textiles Ltd

GOODS RECEIVED NOTE

Supplier:
Computer Supplies Ltd
1 Megadrive Way
Milton Keynes MK6

GRN NO: 2546
Date: 6.9.200X
Re; Delivery Note: 10/6789

ORDER NO.	QTY	DESCRIPTION	REF NO:
9285	1 (2 boxes)	PIII 700MHZ 256 Mb RAM Keyboard + Mouse 21" monitor	928/C

Received by: A Bowme

for Iles Textiles Ltd.

Invoice errors and omissions

The abbreviation E & OE on an invoice stands for 'errors and omissions excepted', which means that if the supplier has made any mistakes or left anything off the invoice, the supplier has the right to correct the mistake later and demand full payment.

Goods received note (GRN)

Before paying for the goods, Iles Textiles Ltd Accounts Department will need signed proof that the goods have actually been received by their firm. This is usually in the form of a **goods received note** signed by a representative of the purchasing firm on delivery of the goods. Once the purchase order, purchase invoice, and goods received note are compared and found to agree, the invoice is paid.

Key words:

Purchase order - a request for the delivery of goods or services sent to a supplier

Invoice - a request for payment from a supplier

Goods received note - proof that goods have been delivered, completed by a representative of the firm that ordered them and then sent to the Accounts Department

Cash discount - a deduction from the total price on an invoice in return for immediate payment

Trade discount - a deduction made by a supplier to regular customers, often for making bulk purchases

Remittance advice note - form summarizing details on an invoice that is returned by the buyer with payment

Section **16.3**

Sales documents

Making a sale

The main objective of the Sales Department in an organization is to generate sales and to record revenues accurately, so that it can judge how well it is meeting its targets. In making sales, fulfilling customer orders, and obtaining payments, a Sales Department will issue a variety of documents.

Orders received

When a purchase order is received from a customer, the details are recorded by the Sales Department. The Sales Department then has to check that the firm can meet the order and supply the goods in the right quantity at the right price by the date requested in the order. The Sales Department may then send a **written acknowledgement** to the customer to confirm receipt of their order and giving precise details of the delivery date and time.

If goods are to be in transit for some time, the Sales Department may also send an **advice note** to tell the customer that the goods are on their way. This will give details of the date the goods were despatched, and how they have been sent - for example, by parcel post or courier.

▼ *Figure 16.5: An example of a delivery note*

Computer Supplies Ltd

1 Megadrive Way
Milton Keynes MK6
Tel: 01908-6566
Fax: 01908-6560
VAT Reg No. 234 8899 14

Ref No: 10/6789

Delivery address: Iles Textiles Ltd
21 Bedford Way
London WC2

Delivery date: 6.9.200X

DATE	Order No	Account No.	Invoice No
5.9.0X	9285	702316	18967

QTY	Catalogue No.	Description
1	928/C	PIII 700MHz 256 Mb RAM 21" Monitor Keyboard & mouse

Delivery by: Parcel Express
No. of items: 2 (CPU and Monitor separate)
Goods received by: ____________ **(signature)**
____________ **(please PRINT name)**

G Hubble

G Hubble
Sales Manager
Computer Supplies Ltd

Please retain this copy as proof of receipt

Delivery note

When goods are delivered by vehicle, either by the supplier or by an outside carrier, the driver is given a **delivery note** (see Figure 16.5). This gives a full description of the goods and states the number of packages. On receipt of the goods, the customer is able to check delivered items against the note in order to identify any errors or damage. The delivery note is usually carbonated with two copies. It is signed by the customer, and one copy is kept by the driver as proof that the goods were delivered as required.

Sales invoice

After delivering goods or services, a supplier will send an invoice to the customer. The invoice requests payment for the goods or services delivered and gives information on any discounts included in the final price and the date by which payment must be made (see 16.2). To the selling organization the invoice is a **sales invoice.** Sales on credit are entered as a credit in the accounts of the business.

▼ *Figure 16.6: An example of a credit note*

Computer Supplies Ltd
1 Megadrive Way
Milton Keynes MK6
Tel: 01908-6566
Fax: 01908-6560
VAT Reg No. 234 8899 14

To: Iles Textiles Ltd
21 Bedford Way
London WC2

CREDIT NOTE NO. CN3457

DATE	Reference Invoice No.	Customer Account No.
22.9.200X	18436	702316

QTY	Description	Cat No.	Unit Price	Total
4	CD-Recordable discs (box of 10)	344/D	£10	£40
			Sub-total	£40
			Cash discount	£0
			Total (ex. VAT)	£40
			VAT @ 17.5%	+£7
			Total credit	£47

Reason for credit:
Diskettes returned as faulty

Credit and debit notes

A **credit note**, often printed in red, is issued by the sales department to a customer if a deduction needs to be made from an invoice. This may be because:

- The supplier has made a mistake and overcharged
- Goods were not delivered because they were lost or stolen in transit
- The customer has returned unsatisfactory or faulty goods

Figure 16.6 shows a credit note issued by Computer Supplies Ltd to Iles Textiles Ltd after they had returned four boxes of CD-R discs which were found to be faulty from an earlier delivery.

A **debit note** will be sent to a customer if the amount on their invoice is insufficient - for example, if payment is late and is subject to a surcharge, or where boxes or crates used to deliver goods were on loan but have not been returned.

Statement of account

When a firm regularly uses the same supplier, it is likely to receive a number of invoices each month. In this case, rather than send out lots of individual invoices, it is more efficient for the supplier to send out a statement of account summarizing all the purchases made by that customer each month. It is also more convenient for a customer to make one payment each month than to have to make numerous payments to settle each separate invoice. The monthly statement shows the amount owed or balance outstanding at the beginning of the month, adding any invoices raised during the month, and deducting any payments received. The balance left at the end of the month is the amount owed. The monthly statement is, therefore, both a summary of transactions made during the month and a request for payment.

▼ *Figure 16.7: Example of a monthly statement of account*

Computer Supplies Ltd

1 Megadrive Way
Milton Keynes MK6
Tel: 01908-6566
Fax: 01908-6560
VAT Reg No. 234 8899 14

Account No: 702316

Iles Textiles Ltd
21 Bedford Way
London WC2

Statement date: 30.9.200X

Date	Details	Debit (Dr)	Credit (Cr)	Balance
1.9.0X	Balance brought forward	£700.60		£700.60 Dr
8.9.0X	Goods Invoice No. 18967	£1466.40		£2167.00 Dr
20.9.0X	Payment-thank you		£2500.00	£333.00 Dr
22.9.0X	Refund CN.3457		£47.00	£286.00 Cr
25.9.0X	Goods Invoice No. 19543	£560.00		£274.00 Dr
		Balance now due		£274.00 Dr

Terms: Payment by 14.10.200X required

Figure 16.7 shows the account of Iles Textiles Ltd with Computer Supplies Ltd for the month of September 200X. Included are references to the purchase order in Figure 16.2 and the credit note in Figure 16.6. A further order for supplies was made by Iles Textiles during the month. This was invoiced by Computer Supplies Ltd on the 25th September.

Portfolio Activity 16.2 

1. Based on the purchase order below from P Lewis Builders Merchants, design and complete a sales invoice from Johnson Office Supplies (preferably using a computer desktop publishing package). The invoice number is 9513. The VAT rate is 17.5%. Goods are subject to a 15% trade discount and a 5% cash discount if paid for within ten days of the invoice date.
2. Include the following information on your sales invoice and explain what is meant by each term:

   Product code or catalogue number, Unit price, Carriage paid, E & OE , Cash Discount 5 days , Deliver to ... , Sub-total, VAT
3. Prepare a flowchart to show each of the firms involved and the departments concerned in processing the documentation generated by the purchase order by P Lewis Builders Merchants.
4. Explain why the accounts department of P Lewis Builders Merchants will need to see a copy of a purchase order, purchase invoice, and goods received note for the same transaction before it pays for goods delivered.

P Lewis Builders Merchants

4 West Hill Way, Bromley BR4 05N

Tel: 020-8466-0001, Fax: 020-8466-0002

VAT Reg No. 2867 0823 9

Purchase Order No. 909867

To: Johnson Office Supplies

98 High Street, Coulsdon

DATE	DESCRIPTION	QTY	CAT.No	PRICE	TOTAL
7.6.200X	Photocopy paper	30	P567/2	£5 per ream	£150.00
	Tippex fluid	20	P345/7	£1.50	£50.00
	Staplers	2	P23/1	£4.25	£8.50
Other charges				Delivery	£2.00
Deliver to above address				Sub-total	£210.50
				VAT @ 17.5%	£36.84
				Total	£247.34

Authorised by: P Lewis

P Lewis

Key words:

Advice note - informs the customer that ordered goods have been despatched.

Delivery note - statement issued to the purchaser on taking delivery of goods, listing the items that have been despatched

Sales invoice - request sent out by a supplier for the payment of credit sales

Statement of account - a summary of all the purchases made by a regular customer in a month and the balance of money owed to the supplier

Credit note - notice of a reduction in the amount on an initial invoice, for example, if a customer has been overcharged, goods are lost in transit, or are returned as faulty

Debit note - notice of an increase in the amount owed on an initial invoice, for example, if a customer has been undercharged

Section **16.4**

Payment documents

Making payments

Most financial transactions are settled with cash payments. Cash is used primarily by individual customers making relatively small purchases 'over the counter'. However, for larger sums of money and for goods and services ordered over the telephone or Internet, non-cash payments will be used. Business organizations settling invoices will tend to use non-cash methods of payment. These are:

- **cheques**
- **automated methods (BACS and EDI)**
- **credit cards**
- **debit cards**

Once goods or services have been received by a purchasing firm and the Finance or Accounts Department has checked that the purchase order, goods received note and sales invoice all match, payment will be made. Each year around 3 billion cheques are used to make payments in the UK and around 3 billion payments are made by automated methods (see Figure 16.8).

▼ *Figure 16.8: Non-cash transactions, by method of payment*

United Kingdom
Billions

4
3
2
1
0
1985 1987 1989 1991 1993 1995 1997

Cheques
Automated payments[1]
Credit and charge cards[2]
Debit cards[3]

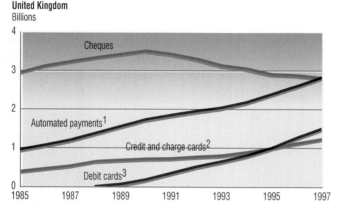

1 Includes direct debits, standing orders, direct credits, inter-branch automated items and CHAPS transactions.
2 Visa, Mastercards, travel/entertainment cards and store cards.
3 Visa Delta and Switch cards in all years; includes Electron cards from 1996 and Solo cards in 1997.

Source: Association for Payment Clearing Services

Social Trends 1999

Payment by cheque

Most business debts are settled by cheque. A cheque can be written for any amount. Unless it is made payable to 'cash', a cheque is simply a way of arranging a transfer of money between two bank or building society accounts. The person or firm who owns the account from which money will be debited is known as the **drawer**. The person or firm named on the cheque to receive payment is called the **payee**. Each cheque

▼ *Figure 16.9: An example of a cheque*

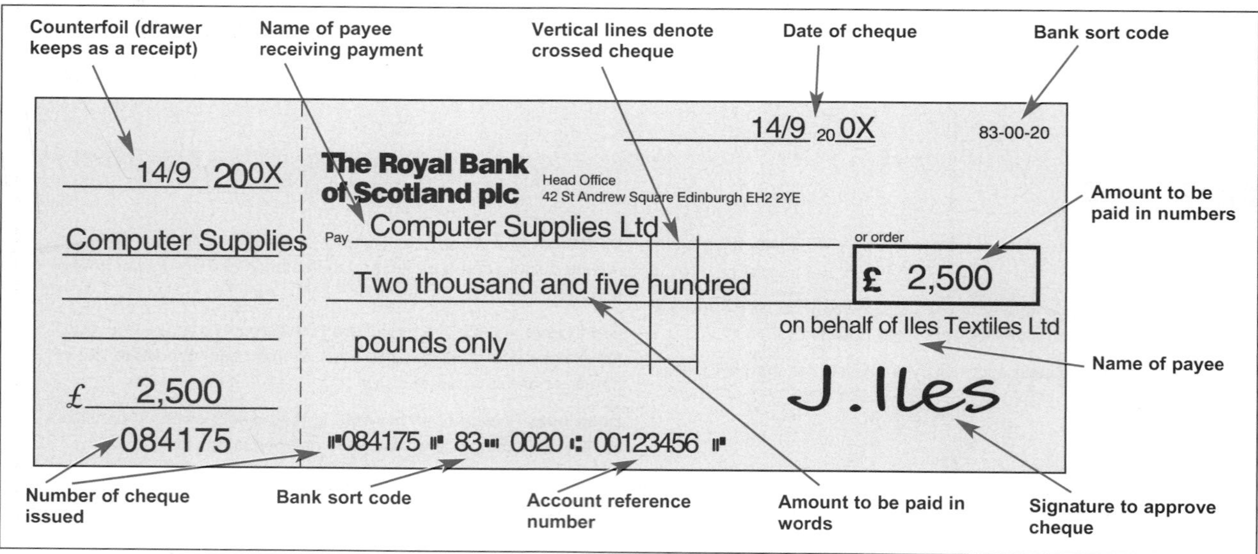

has a serial number, a sort code to identify the bank or building society, and the drawer's account number. It is usual to write out the sum to be paid in figures as well as in words on a cheque so that the precise amount cannot be mistaken. The drawer must also sign each cheque with his or her usual signature.

In all but the smallest firms, cheques can only be signed by authorized staff, usually in the Accounts Department. For larger sums, signatures of two staff are often required, one at a senior managerial level.

In most business organizations, employees who are in a position to order goods and services by raising purchase orders are not in a position to make payment for them as well by writing cheques. This provides an important safeguard against fraud. Clearing banks also keep specimen signatures of those staff authorized to sign cheques in order to provide further checks.

Cheque validation

A cheque is valid if:

- It is written in ink or printed
- It is signed by the drawer who is paying the money
- The amount in words is the same as the amount in numbers
- The cheque is made payable to someone or to the bearer (the person holding the cheque)
- The cheque is dated and is not more than six months old

Figure 16.10: Payment by cheque - an example

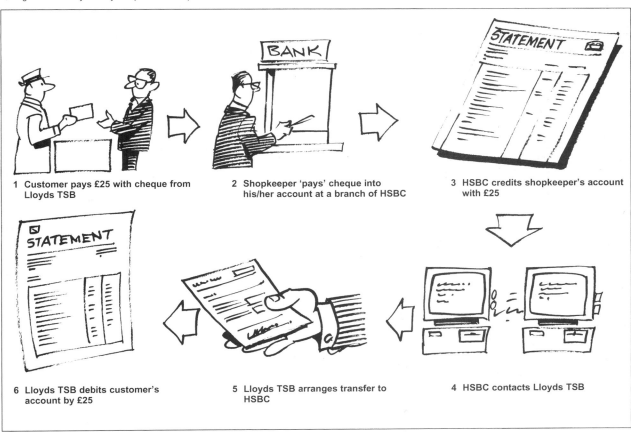

1 **Customer pays £25 with cheque from Lloyds TSB**

2 **Shopkeeper 'pays' cheque into his/her account at a branch of HSBC**

3 **HSBC credits shopkeeper's account with £25**

4 **HSBC contacts Lloyds TSB**

5 **Lloyds TSB arranges transfer to HSBC**

6 **Lloyds TSB debits customer's account by £25**

Cheques can be either **open** or **crossed.**

- A **crossed** cheque has two parallel lines across it. This signifies that it must be paid into the payee's account, regardless of who presents the cheque at a bank for payment. This safeguards the drawer and payee against theft. For additional security, the words 'A/C payee' are often written between the two lines to make sure that the cheque can only be paid into the payee's account.
- An **open** cheque, which does not have the two lines, can be cashed over a bank counter to whoever presents it.

▼ *Most businesses will not accept cheques as payment unless they are backed by a cheque card*

Cheque cards are issued by banks and building societies to their reliable account-holders. These are used to guarantee payment of the cheque even if the account upon which it is drawn does not contain enough money to cover it. However, certain conditions apply:

- The maximum sum guaranteed must be as stated on the cheque card (either £50 or £100)
- The cheque card number should be copied onto the back of the cheque
- The name and signature on the cheque should match those on the cheque card

Bankers' Automated Clearing Services (BACS)

Paying by cheque and taking cheques and other payments to and from banks can be time-consuming. In order to speed up payments to regular suppliers, many firms send the money from their bank account through the banking system to the bank account of the supplier, using computer links. These transfers of funds are made using a system known as **BACS** (Bankers' Automated Clearing Service).

A bank customer wishing to make regular payments completes a standing order form telling the bank who to pay, how much to pay them, and how often. The bank will then input these instructions to a computer and the payments will be made automatically.

Where the amounts paid regularly are likely to vary, the customer can change the amount using an 'autopay' version of the BACS system. This is usually achieved by giving the details on each series of payments to the bank on computer disk, or by sending the information via the telephone network using a modem (see 3.3). The banks provide the software programs which create the required format. Today, most workers, especially those in medium-to-large organizations, are paid their wages directly into their bank or building society accounts through BACS. Each worker will receive a monthly statement telling him or her how much money will be credited to their account after deductions for income tax, National Insurance contributions, and perhaps a company pension or season ticket loan repayments.

▼ *Figure 16.11: How the Bankers' Automated Clearing Service works*

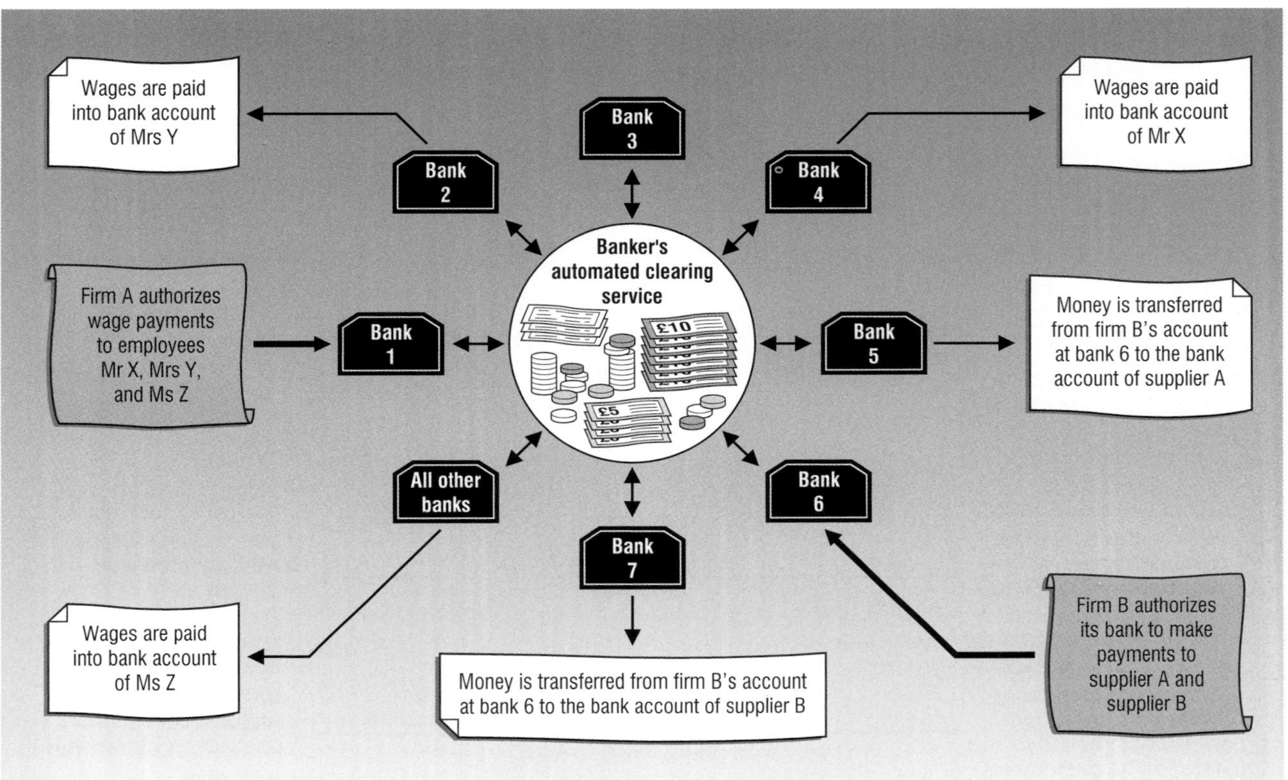

Electronic Data Interchange (EDI)

Just as it is possible for computer users to communicate with each other via the Internet, it is also possible for businesses to send purchase and sales information to each other using e-commerce (see 11.1). All of the documents considered in this chapter can be completed, stored and transmitted electronically using **EDI.**

EDI is used mainly by medium-to-large manufacturing and retailing organizations using Just-In-Time production and inventory controls where speed of delivery is an important concern (see 1.2). Bar-code readers can monitor the movement of goods in and out of the organization and maintain up-to-date records of stocks. When stock levels fall to a pre-set minimum, the central computer automatically sends an order for more stock electronically to the supplier. Payment can also be automated and made electronically via BACS. Using EDI, administration costs and staff can be reduced to a minimum.

▼ *Electronic Data Interchange reduces the need to record details of transactions by hand*

Bank

Customer

Supplier

Modem

Modem

Modem

Telephone network

Purchase order is completed on computer screen and sent via electronic mail to a supplier

Supplier receives electronic transmission of the order

Supplier completes invoice on computer screen and sends it via electronic mail to customer

Customer receives electronic invoice and authorizes bank via electronic mail to pay money into supplier's account

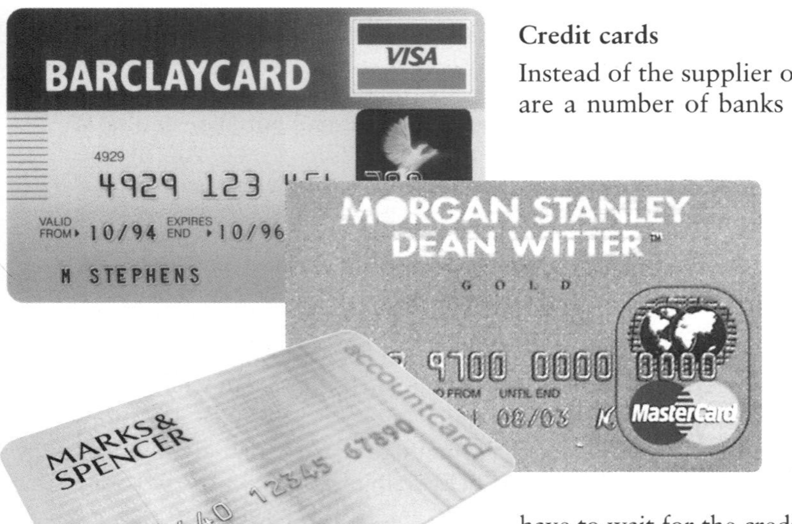

▲ *Credit and store card purchases totalled £80 billion in the UK in 1999*

Credit cards

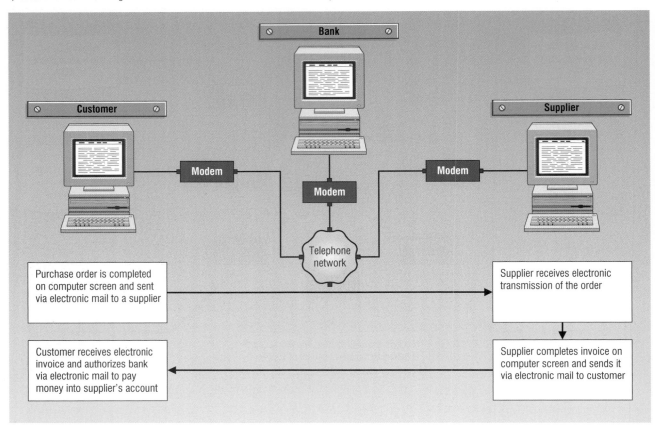

Instead of the supplier offering direct credit terms to their customers there are a number of banks and other financial organizations that issue cards that can be used to 'buy now and pay later'. Visa, Mastercard, American Express and Diners Club are all examples of credit card companies that provide credit cards. Many large retail organizations also offer their customers store credit cards which can be used only in their shops. For example, Marks and Spencer has its own credit card. In contrast, some companies like Tesco issue their customers with general-use Visa credit cards.

A business can supply goods and services to a customer using a credit card company but will then have to wait for the credit card to settle their bill. Suppliers will need to send proof of the sale to the credit card company before they will pay. The credit card company will then expect the cardholder to pay them by cheque or BACS, usually between 4 and 6 weeks after the sale was made (see Figure 16.12).

Each month the cardholder will receive a statement of their transactions using their credit card from the credit card company. The card user can then decide whether to pay the balance in full or in part. If payment is made in full no interest is charged. Interest is charged only on the outstanding balance and can be quite high.

▼ Figure 16.12: How a credit card can be used to make a purchase

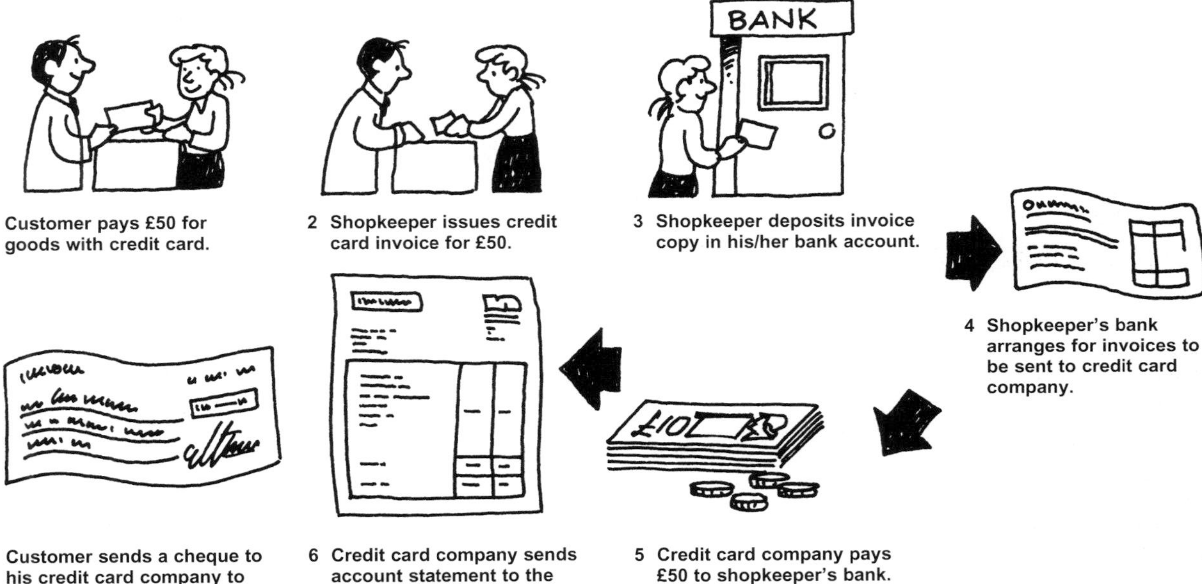

BANK
£10
1 Customer pays £50 for goods with credit card.
2 Shopkeeper issues credit card invoice for £50.
3 Shopkeeper deposits invoice copy in his/her bank account.
4 Shopkeeper's bank arranges for invoices to be sent to credit card company.
5 Credit card company pays £50 to shopkeeper's bank.
6 Credit card company sends account statement to the customer listing all his purchases with his credit card.
7 Customer sends a cheque to his credit card company to settle his account balance.

How credit card purchases are authorized

A business that is offered payment by credit card must check that the card is acceptable and gain necessary authorization. Most organizations can do this electronically today, but a number of smaller businesses may still rely on manual methods.

Electronic methods

New technology means that businesses can obtain authorization from credit card companies quickly and easily:

- A sales assistant will swipe the card through a special terminal which then transmits card details through to a central computer in the appropriate credit card company.
- The computer checks that the card is not listed as stolen and then checks that the card holder has not spent over the limit.
- A sales voucher with purchase and card details is then issued by the terminal. The card holder signs this and keeps the top copy as a proof of purchase.

▼ Printed electronically

12:27 13/08/0X
COMPLETED
B & Q PLC

NEW MALDEN
Till 8

02357423.6767 608658

VISA
No: 2033005731376667
Expiry date: 08/04

THANK YOU
£25.95 Sign below

Manual authorization

- First of all the business should check that the card is not a stolen one. This can be done by looking at up-to-date lists of stolen card numbers issued by the major credit card companies or by telephoning the appropriate credit card company. Using the telephone can be slow if the credit card company is busy.

- The telephone can be used to call the credit card company to check that the customer has enough money left to spend on their card to pay for the goods or services. If they have, the credit card company will issue an authorization code to write on the sales voucher. This code guarantees that the business will be paid by the credit card company.
- If the checks prove satisfactory the seller fills out a carbonated sales voucher. Card details are printed on to the voucher using a special imprinting device operated by hand. Purchase details are then written in before the customer signs it and receives the top copy as proof of purchase. The second copy is sent to the credit card company for payment while the third and fourth copies are kept by the supplier.

▼ *Completed by hand*

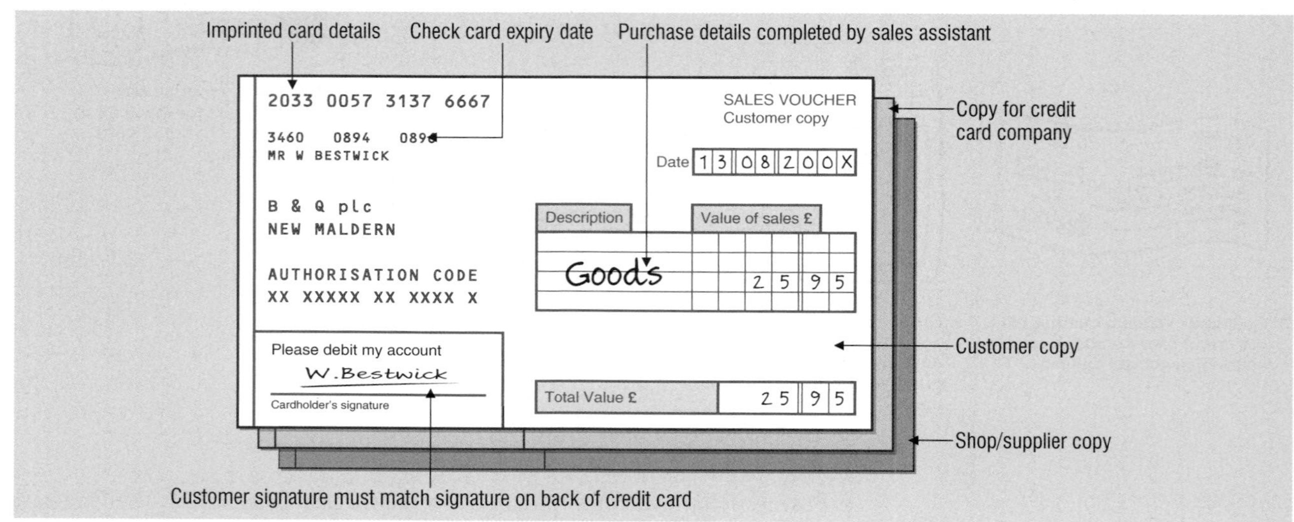

▲ *Switch and Connect debit cards are provided by the UK banking system*

Debit cards

Payment by debit card is immediate and does not give the holder credit. The person or business with a debit card must have a bank account. As soon as the debit card is used to make a purchase the amount is deducted from their account electronically and credited to the bank account of the business making the sale.

The advantage of debit card payment for the seller is that the payment is immediate. Cheques have to be taken to their bank and may take several days before they are 'cleared' for payment by the customers bank. Credit card payments can also take time to process and will involve charges levied by the credit card company.

To facilitate debit card purchases the seller must possess an electronic cash register linked to the EFTPOS system (Electronic Funds Transfer at Point Of Sale). When the card is swiped through the electronic register, details of the purchase are relayed to the card users bank and the amount to be paid is deducted automatically from their account and credited to the account of the business that has sold them the goods or services.

The register will issue a voucher as a record of the payment which must be authorized with the signature of the debit card user to show they have agreed to the transaction.

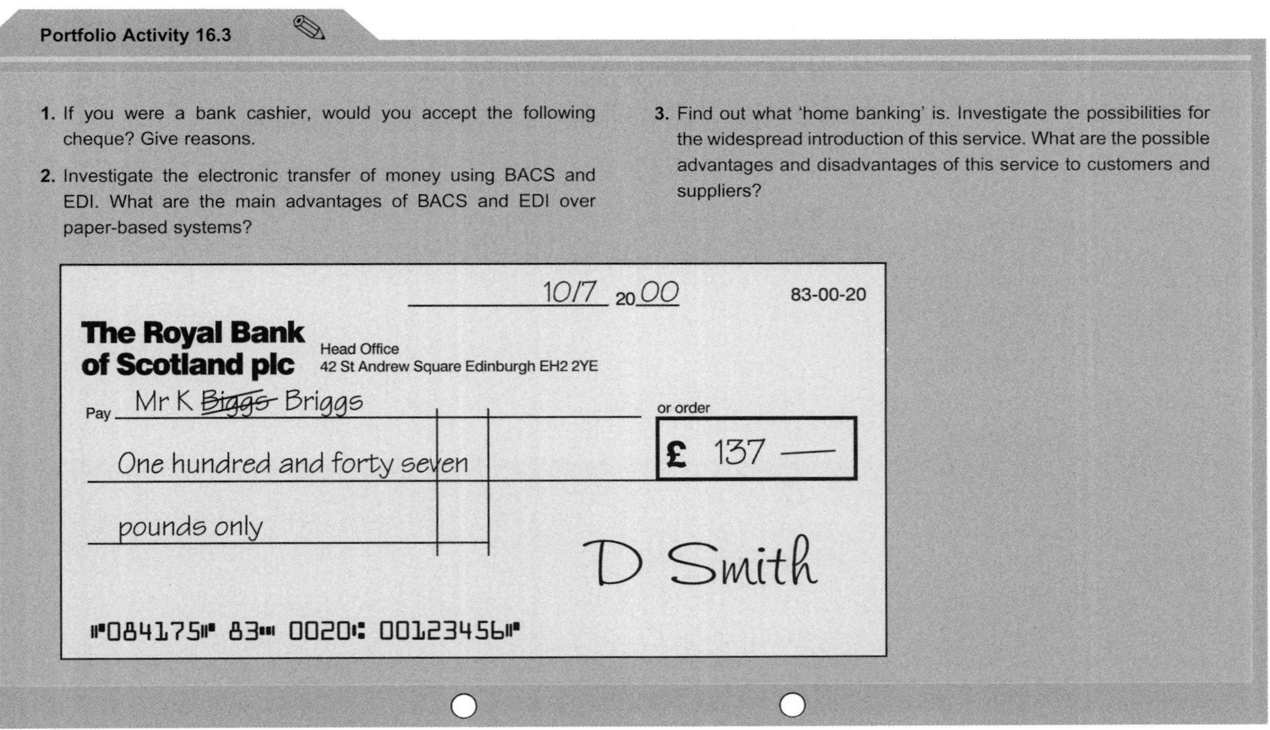

Portfolio Activity 16.3

1. If you were a bank cashier, would you accept the following cheque? Give reasons.
2. Investigate the electronic transfer of money using BACS and EDI. What are the main advantages of BACS and EDI over paper-based systems?
3. Find out what 'home banking' is. Investigate the possibilities for the widespread introduction of this service. What are the possible advantages and disadvantages of this service to customers and suppliers?

Key words:

Cheque - a written instruction to a bank or building society to transfer money from the account of the cheque drawer to a named payee

BACS (Bankers' Automated Clearing System) - a computerized system which transfers money between accounts without the need for cash or cheques

Cheque card - a guarantee that a cheque will be honoured up to a specified limit, usually £50 or £100

EDI (Electronic Data Interchange) - the interchange of financial documents and other information between organizations using computers linked by modems

Section **16.5**

Receipts documents

The proof of purchase

When you buy a good or service in a shop, you will receive a receipt as **proof of purchase.** Similarly, when an organization makes payment it will require proof that payment has been made for its own records and for the purpose of informing the tax authorities about its expenses.

A number of documents can provide proof that a transaction has taken place.

▼ *Figure 16.13: An example of a sales receipt*

WELCOME
TO
WH SMITH LTD

	£
Stationery	15.95
Newspaper	0.50
Book	22.50
Balance due	38.95
CASH	50.00
CHANGE	11.05

4280 07 5 1615 11:03:0X
21SEPT0X

THANK YOU FOR SHOPPING AT WH SMITH LTD
KINGSTON-UPON-THAMES

Sales receipts

A **sales receipt** is usually issued when payment for goods or services received is immediate. It can take many forms, but will include the following information:

- The name and address of the organization that has made the sale
- The date the transaction took place
- A description of the goods or services purchased
- The cost of each item
- The total cost of all items
- The method of payment

Portfolio Activity 16.4 

Assume that you work in the spare components section of Speed Ltd, a large garage. Usually the computer system prints out receipts for customers. However, today the system is not working and you must design your own receipt. N Mansell has just purchased a new set of tyres for £250 and paid in cash. Produce a handwritten receipt for the customer.

Paying-in slip

When a firm pays in cash and cheques to its bank, it will complete a **paying-in slip** or **bank giro credit** slip. The slip, along with cash and cheques, is handed to the cashier. The bank cashier will stamp and initial both the slip and the counterfoil. The counterfoil acts as the customer's receipt. The paying-in slip counterfoil allows the business to check that the subsequent entries on its bank statement are correct.

▼ *Figure 16.14: A bank giro credit slip*

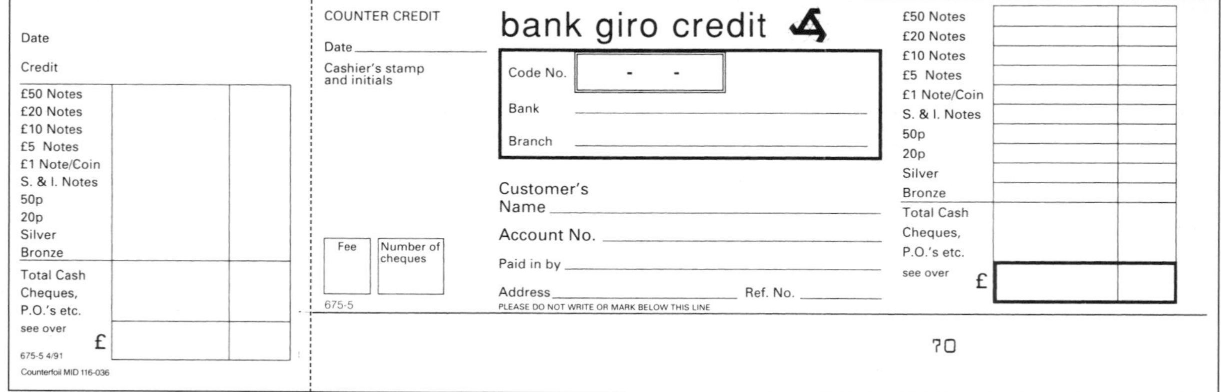

Date
Credit
£50 Notes
£20 Notes
£10 Notes
£5 Notes
£1 Note/Coin
S. & I. Notes
50p
20p
Silver
Bronze
Total Cash
Cheques, P.O.'s etc.
see over
£
675-5 4/91
Counterfoil MID 116-036

COUNTER CREDIT
Date
Cashier's stamp and initials
Fee
Number of cheques
675-5

bank giro credit

Code No. - -
Bank
Branch
Customer's Name
Account No.
Paid in by
Address
Ref. No.
PLEASE DO NOT WRITE OR MARK BELOW THIS LINE

£50 Notes
£20 Notes
£10 Notes
£5 Notes
£1 Note/Coin
S. & I. Notes
50p
20p
Silver
Bronze
Total Cash
Cheques, P.O.'s etc.
see over
£

70

Paying-in slips can be used to show the following information:

- The date money was paid into the account
- The bank (or building society) branch at which money was paid in
- The branch sort code
- The account-holder's name
- The number of the account to be credited
- The amount to be credited
- The name and signature of the person paying in the money

Portfolio Activity 16.5

1. Obtain a blank paying-in slip from a local bank.
2. Use the paying-in slip to pay the following amounts into your bank account (make up a number for the account).

Cheques	Notes	Coins
£420.00	12 x £50 = £600	143 x £1 = £143
£34.25	9 x £20 = £180	130 x 50p = £65
£500.00	30 x £10 = £300	60 x 20p = £12
£67.50	5 x £5 = £25	100 x 10p = £10
£121.47		500 x 5p = £25
£59.98		800 x 2p = £16
		200 x 1p = £2

Bank statement

A **bank statement** provides a summary of receipts and payments made to and from a bank account. Building societies also provide their account-holders with regular statements.

A bank statement can be checked for any mistakes against documentary proof that the transactions have been made, such as entries on cheque counterfoils, counterfoils issued when Switch or Connect debit cards are used, and paying-in counterfoils. This process is known as **bank reconciliation.** Differences between the bank statement and the firm's records may arise due to:

- Clerical errors causing figures to be wrongly entered or missed out
- Payments made into the bank which have not been entered in the firm's records
- Cheques presented to the bank which have not yet been cleared.
- Bank charges representing interest on loans or overdrafts and/or charges for other services (some current accounts also pay interest on credit balances)

Figure 16.15 shows the bank statement of account of Iles Textiles Ltd for September 200X. Note the drawing of the cheque for £2,500 by Computer Supplies Ltd on 20.9.200X as shown in the customer account statement in Figure 16.7.

▼ *Figure 16.15: Example of a bank statement*

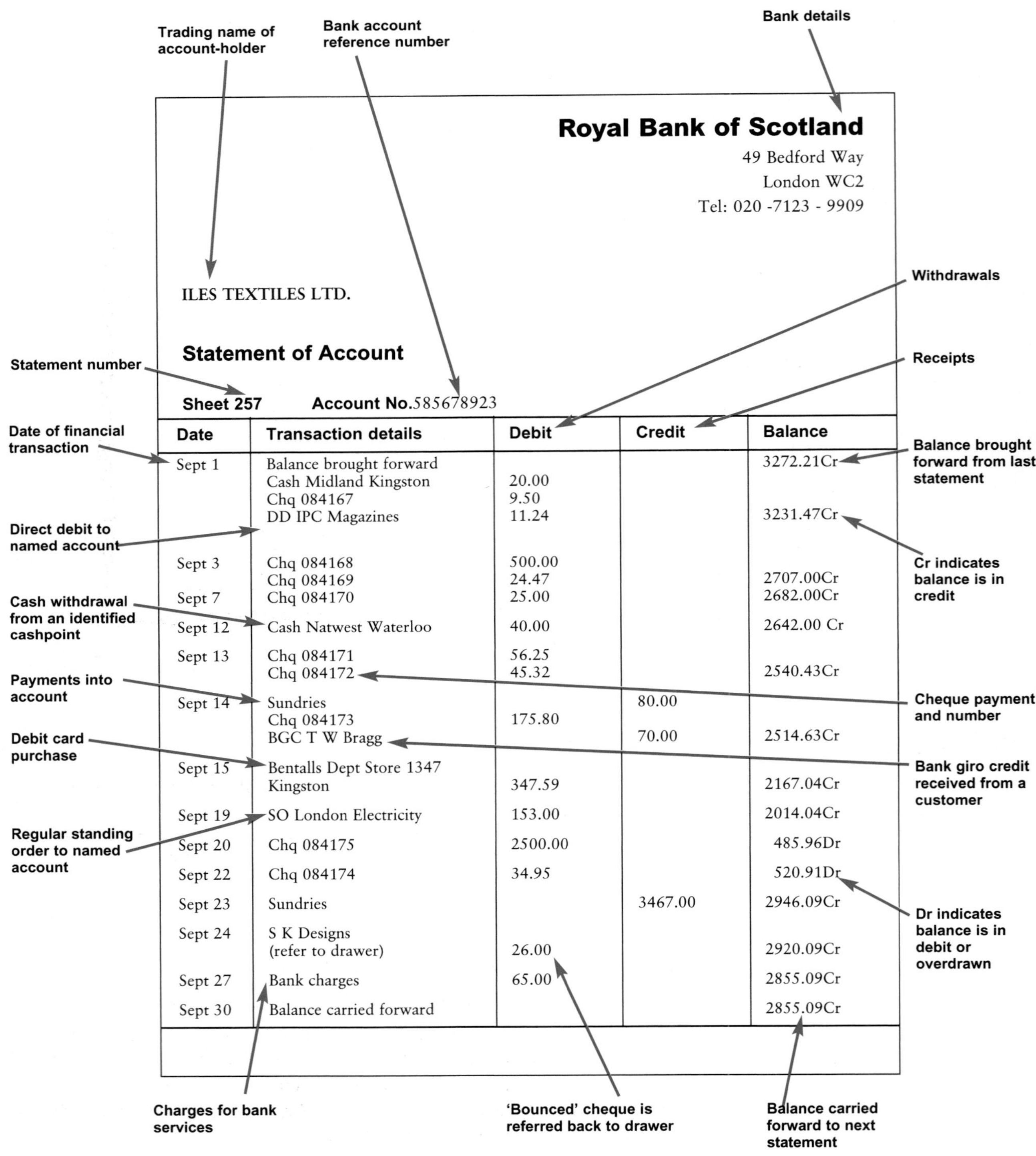

Royal Bank of Scotland
49 Bedford Way
London WC2
Tel: 020 -7123 - 9909

ILES TEXTILES LTD.

Statement of Account

Sheet 257 **Account No.**585678923

Date	Transaction details	Debit	Credit	Balance
Sept 1	Balance brought forward			3272.21Cr
	Cash Midland Kingston	20.00		
	Chq 084167	9.50		
	DD IPC Magazines	11.24		3231.47Cr
Sept 3	Chq 084168	500.00		
	Chq 084169	24.47		2707.00Cr
Sept 7	Chq 084170	25.00		2682.00Cr
Sept 12	Cash Natwest Waterloo	40.00		2642.00 Cr
Sept 13	Chq 084171	56.25		
	Chq 084172	45.32		2540.43Cr
Sept 14	Sundries		80.00	
	Chq 084173	175.80		
	BGC T W Bragg		70.00	2514.63Cr
Sept 15	Bentalls Dept Store 1347 Kingston	347.59		2167.04Cr
Sept 19	SO London Electricity	153.00		2014.04Cr
Sept 20	Chq 084175	2500.00		485.96Dr
Sept 22	Chq 084174	34.95		520.91Dr
Sept 23	Sundries		3467.00	2946.09Cr
Sept 24	S K Designs (refer to drawer)	26.00		2920.09Cr
Sept 27	Bank charges	65.00		2855.09Cr
Sept 30	Balance carried forward			2855.09Cr

Portfolio Activity 16.6 

1. Create a table in a computer word processing package in which to enter a bank statement.
2. Use the statement to record the following transactions made by a business account-holder during one month. Entries should appear in date order:
3. Remember to calculate and show the 'balance carried forward' to the next statement.

Date	Details	Amount
1	Balance brought forward	–£24
	Drawings:	
4	Cheque No. 15326	£35.25
7	Cheque No. 15327	£157.50
15	Cheque No. 15328	£12.99
12	Cheque No. 15329	£79
25	Cheque No. 15330	£230.70
9	Standing order to British Gas	£50
10	Cash dispenser	£60
18	Cash dispenser	£40
14	Standing order to N&P Building Society	£380
14	SWITCH Tesco Superstore	£49.45
28	SWITCH Houghtons Garage	£16.75
21	Bank Charges	£10.25
	Receipts:	
1	Credit transfer from XYZ Ltd	£1,425.50
8	Cheque No.26893 received	£56.90
18	Cheque No.99901 received	£10.25

Key words:

Sales receipt - a proof of purchase

Paying-in slip (or bank giro credit) - form used to identify the account into which accompanying cash or cheques must be paid

Bank statement - a summary of payments to and from a bank account

Bank reconciliation - the process of checking bank statement entries against actual payments and receipts documents

Section **16.6**

The accuracy and security of financial records

The consequences of incorrect completion of documents

A business uses its documentation on purchases, sales, payments, and receipts to complete its annual accounts (see 18.1). However, errors and omissions are inevitable - for example, recording the wrong price for an item, calculating VAT incorrectly, not adding up prices correctly, or mislaying an order or cheque payment.

Failing to complete documents accurately can cause problems for an organization:

- **Incorrect purchases:** If purchases are incorrect, this could lead to the wrong materials being bought in, which in turn could lead to expensive re-ordering, a slowdown in production and possible waste if the materials cannot be returned.
- **Incorrect sales:** If sales are incorrect, customers may be supplied with the wrong goods, leading to returns and a poor business image.
- **Incorrect payments and receipts:** If receipts and payments records are incorrect, this could lead to over- or undercharging of customers, late payment, disputes, and consequently dissatisfied customers and suppliers.
- **Incorrect accounts:** If there are errors in documentation relating to purchases, sales, or expenses, the final accounts will be incorrect and the business owners may get the wrong impression about the value of their firm and the profit it has made. The tax authorities also use the accounts to calculate the amount of tax a firm is liable to pay. If they discover any mistakes in the accounts, the firm could be fined heavily.
- **Misleading information on past business performance:** As decisions on how to manage the business are based on accounting records, the business could be badly managed as a consequence of incorrect or sloppy handling of basic financial documentation. This could lead to future financial difficulties.

The need for security

Whatever the methods used to purchase and pay for goods and services, a business must be aware of the risk of theft and fraud. For example, following the death of newspaper tycoon Robert Maxwell in 1991, it was discovered that he had illegally transferred over £400 million from his employees' pension fund to finance other business ventures. In order to minimize the risk of theft or fraud and to protect both the firm and the reputation of individual employees, it is necessary to have a series of checks and financial controls.

For example:

- **Use an audit trail.** The primary safeguard in maintaining financial records is to provide an audit trail. An **audit trail** is simply a means of checking the passage of a transaction through a business by checking through the records and documentation, from the generation of a purchase order or sale to the stage where the payment appears in the bank statement. If there is no audit trail - that is, if the transaction disappears somewhere in the firm and no further records can be found - the firm is open to fraud, because the transaction will be impossible to check.

By law, each year external independent auditors will sample some transactions in companies and follow the audit trail in the documentation through from beginning to end. Today, much of the audit trail is held on computer.

- **Use only authorized personnel to countersign orders and cheques.** Allowing just anybody to authorize payments opens a firm to risk of fraud because some employees may be tempted to issue payments to bogus companies operated by their friends or family. Ensuring that only staff with appropriate levels of seniority always sign purchase orders and cheques provides some control. For large transactions, often two signatures will be required. Clearing banks also maintain sample copies of authorized signatories in order that they can check the transactions of their customers.

When payment is made by cheque, it is also important to make sure it is crossed. Most cheque slips supplied by banks have two lines and the words 'A/C payee' already printed across them (see 16.4).

- **Always cross-check documents.** Checking of documents against external source documents such as invoices and goods received notes also provides a means of ensuring that the business only pays for what it has received.
- **Give responsibility for receiving goods and paying for goods to different people.** If the same person in an organization takes delivery of goods and makes payment for them they could defraud their employer or be tempted to steal. This is because they could lie about goods being delivered but still make payment. Or pay money to a bogus company operated by a friend or family member without having received any supplies.
- **Install security equipment.** This can include video cameras in delivery bays and at checkouts and the installation of safes in which to deposit money during the day to reduce the risk of theft.

Portfolio Activity 16.7 

Your school or college will have its own financial controls to assist with security. Arrange for one member of your group to contact the finance department of your school/college to set up a presentation on these procedures. Follow this up with questions and answers from your group.

Contact another organization if you can, and find out what kinds of controls they use. (Alternatively see if you can get a representative of a local accountancy firm to come in and give a presentation on the kinds of procedures which are typically used in firms - with some examples of bad, as well as good, practice.)

Prepare a short report comparing and contrasting the two presentations and suggest your own ideal system, giving reasons for your choice.

Key Activity

Tracey Lane has set up a new restaurant called 'Nibbles' on your local high street. Tracey has no experience of keeping financial records and is worried that she will either get into trouble with the tax authorities, or go out of business through lack of knowledge. Tracey has agreed to pay you to help her with recording financial transactions.

1. Produce a brief report for Tracey explaining:

   A Why she needs to keep accurate records of financial transactions

   B The main kinds of documents she should keep

2. Design, preferably using computer software, the main documents she will use on a regular basis. Include copies of these in your report.

3. Tracey has already been trading for a brief period and has made the transactions given below. She would like you to fill in the documents you have designed to show them.

   - A local business, Office Solutions, has an account with 'Nibbles'. Office Solutions regularly entertain clients at the restaurant and usually prefer to pay on receipt of a statement each month rather than on invoice. Transactions this month include:

Day 8	Meals	Invoice no. 765	£250
Day 11	Take away	Invoice no. 892	£50
Day 21	Meals	Invoice no. 969	£100
Day 25	Payment	Invoice no. 223	£50

   - B Kennington has also opened a business account and incurred a meals bill for £300, net of VAT, on day 25. Nibbles offers a 2% discount for payment within 5 days.
   - Office Solutions would like a receipt for a £150 payment they made on the 16th day of last month.
   - 'Nibbles' delivers food to parties and business functions and requires customers to sign on receipt of the order. Aldhouse Bricks Co. of Leigh in Kent have ordered a buffet for 50 people to be delivered in 10 sealed packs in two months time on the 18th day.

4. Tracey now needs to order more supplies as follows:

   10 chickens at £3 each

   50 lbs of potatoes @ 35 pence per pound

   20 lbs of salmon at £2 per lb

   20 lbs of steak at £4 per lb

   50 bottles of wine at £5 per bottle

   Supplies are bought from L Thomas of Whitehead Street, London E1.

   Draw up an appropriate purchase order for her, then complete a cheque for full payment to L Thomas.

5. Tracey usually pays her invoices using cheques. Explain in your report to her how, and why, she could make use of electronic banking methods instead.

6. Tracey hopes to be able to expand in future and so would like to take on other staff to assist her, especially with paperwork and administration. You have been asked to write a brief report explaining the kinds of steps she could take in order to reduce the risks of fraud or misunderstandings and so improve security.

Useful references

Moynihan, D. and Titley, B. '**Intermediate Business**' 2nd edn (Oxford, 2000) Chapter 9

Test your knowledge

1. The primary function of financial documentation in business is to:
   - **A** Provide information for lenders, for example, the bank
   - **B** Provide information for the government
   - **C** Provide information which will assist in monitoring and controlling the business
   - **D** Provide information for the registrar of companies

2. The person who signs a cheque to make payment is:
   - **A** The person who is paying the money
   - **B** The branch bank manager
   - **C** The person to whom the cheque is paid
   - **D** The person who pays the cheque in to the bank account

Questions 3–5 share the following answer options;

- **A** An audit trail
- **B** Checking invoices against purchase orders
- **C** Requiring two authorized personnel to sign orders
- **D** Checking invoices against goods received notes

Which of the above security measures could reduce the risk of the following situations occurring?

3. Paying invoices for goods not ordered.

4. Authorizing payment for goods not delivered.

5. Authorized personnel making fraudulent payments to their own bank account.

6. Which of the following would a firm send to a supplier requesting delivery of goods?
   - **A** Statement of account
   - **B** Purchase order
   - **C** Goods received note
   - **D** Invoice

Questions 7–9 share the following answer options:

- **A** A sales invoice
- **B** A delivery note
- **C** A statement of account
- **D** A sales receipt

Which of the above documents would be used to:

7. Provide proof that a purchase has been made?

8. Inform a customer of the value of goods supplied and terms of payment?

9. Request payment for goods delivered?

Questions 10–12 share the following answer options:

- **A** Delayed payments
- **B** Delivery of the wrong goods
- **C** Misleading the tax authorities
- **D** Unhappy customers cancelling further orders

Which of the above problems could be caused by the following sources of error?

10. Unclear instructions on a purchase order

11. Overcharging VAT on an invoice

12. Making an error in the final accounts

13. **a** What is a purchase order and what information should it contain?

    b What is the difference between a goods received note and a delivery note? Explain why they are needed.

    c What is the purpose of a sales invoice and what information should it contain?

    d Explain why it is important to check invoices against orders and goods received notes.

    e How is a cheque able to be both a method of payment and a receipt?

chapter 17 Cashflow Forecasting and Management

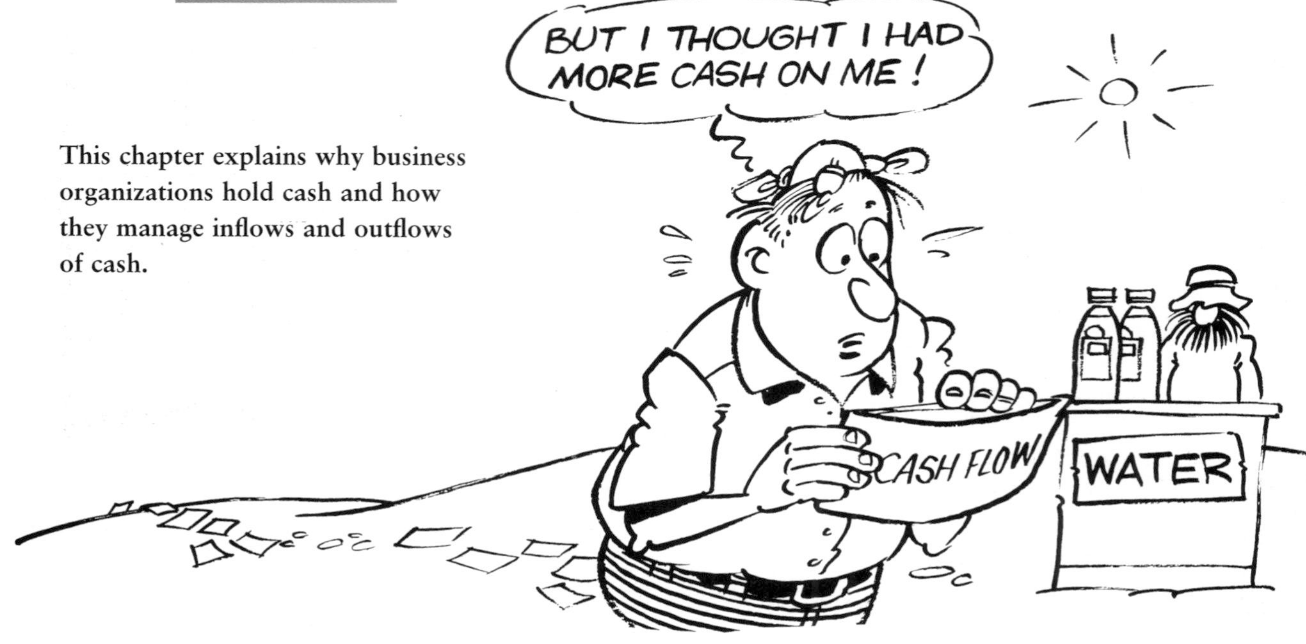

BUT I THOUGHT I HAD MORE CASH ON ME!
CASH FLOW
WATER

This chapter explains why business organizations hold cash and how they manage inflows and outflows of cash.

What you need to learn

All businesses need to manage their finances. A key element of this is **cashflow management**.

Businesses need to hold sufficient cash to meet day-to-day running expenses, debts and unexpected business costs. You will need to know what **working capital** is and how businesses manage their cash to meet their working capital requirements.

Liquid assets are those assets which can be quickly coverted into cash. Without enough liquidity, even a profitable firm can be forced to close down if it cannot meet working capital requirements.

A **cashflow forecast** provides a business with an estimate of future cash inflows and cash outflows. Forecasting cashflows helps managers to plan ahead to ensure their business has enough liquidity to pay off debts and expenses. The forecasts will also be used by people and organizations who lend money to the business to examine whether or not it will be able to make repayments.

Cashflow forecasts will be derived from spending plans in the **capital budget** and projections of running costs and revenues in the **trading forecast**. The capital budget will include the cost of purchasing or hiring premises, machinery and other fixed assets.

Cashflow difficulties in business can be caused by a variety of factors, including overtrading, the purchase of too many fixed assets, overstocking, poor credit control, and uncertainty and seasonal variations in sales.

You will need to know how **cashflow problems** can arise and why they need to be solved. This involves examining **credit control** and other methods that businesses use to maintain their cashflow, for example, by seeking additional finance, selling off stocks, delaying payments to creditors, and changing pricing policies.

Section 17.1 Why is cash important?

Portfolio Activity 17.1 

1. From the articles below, explain why holding cash is important in business.
2. Why do you think it is possible for 'companies that are profitable on paper' and those 'working at full capacity' to run out of cash?
3. Attempt to find out how much cash a business organization that you are familiar with will hold on an average day on the premises, and in bank and building society deposits. Establish the reasons why this amount of cash is held by the business.

Common obstacles for young companies

3. Forecast are rarely accurate
The future in business never unfolds to plan. There is likely to be a divergence from forecasts almost from the moment they are made. Common variations are that sales fall below budget, costs are higher and the pricing of the product or service is set too low.

As a result most new companies run into cashflow problems, requiring refinancing or worse. Companies that are profitable on paper frequently go bust because they run out of cash.

Atlantech was so obsessed by cash that for the first three years in business - by which time annual sales were heading for £5m - it ran its business mainly on a cash basis.

From the Financial Times, 25.4.1999

Cashflow holds back investment

Fresh clues about why companies have not been quicker to invest in the recent recovery - in spite of rapidly rising profits - emerged yesterday in a City research bulletin.

An analysis by Barclays de Zoete Wedd, the UK brokers, suggests that part of the problem may lie in the way cash is distributed across the corporate sector.

Although rising profitability left the sector as a whole sitting on a £13bn cash mountain last year - a 20-year high - it would appear that those sectors that need to invest are short of spare money, while cash-rich sectors are often facing considerably lower capacity pressures.

The research finds that retail and distribution companies enjoyed a cashflow surplus last year. However, most retailers are reporting relatively high levels of spare capacity, not least because consumer spending remains muted and retail capacity was sharply expanded in the late 1980s.

The manufacturing sector as a whole also reported a cash surplus. But the engineering, vehicles and textiles and clothing sectors had a cashflow deficit - even though a Confederation of British Industry survey this week suggested that more engineering groups were working at full capacity.

Mr Robert Barrie, economist at BZW, said: "Manufacturing companies have not been investing despite growing capacity pressures. The evidence is that this may be because their cashflow position is weaker than expected."

Financial Times, 28.4.1995

The importance of cash

All businesses need cash to pay for outward financial transactions (see 16.1).

Any business will need to pay its bills with cash either in the form of notes and coins held by the firm, or by converting a variety of assets which are of value into cash. Assets which can be turned into cash quickly are known as **liquid assets**. The term **liquidity** refers to the ability to exchange such assets for cash without a loss of value.

Cash is the most liquid asset a firm can hold. It refers to notes and coins held on business premises or in bank or building society current accounts which can be withdrawn at short notice, usually by using a cheque to make payment. Cash is part of, but not the same as, **working capital**, which is money used to meet the day-to-day running expenses of a business (see 23.1). Working capital includes other current assets, such as money owed by debtors, which will need to be paid before the cash is available to the business to pay bills.

If a firm runs short of cash, it may be able to exchange some of its assets for cash. However, some assets may be **illiquid**, i.e. difficult to convert into cash quickly. For example, it might be difficult to sell partly-finished products or raw materials very quickly in order to pay a bill. Even if these assets could be sold, there is no guarantee that they would be worth as much to others as they are to the firm selling them. For example, stocks of soft lead, enamel paint, and partly-finished toy soldiers will be of limited value to firms other than toy makers, and even then will only be of worth to those firms wishing to make lead toy soldiers.

Other assets might be easier to sell and have a more definite value, for example, a factory building, vehicles, and plant and machinery. But even the sale of these can take time, and if a firm has to sell these kinds of assets in order to meet a bill, it may then find it difficult to continue trading. Because of these problems, wise business managers always ensure that they hold sufficient cash as one of their assets to meet bills.

It is possible to imagine a whole 'spectrum of liquidity', that is, a range of assets that could be converted into cash by a business, given a long enough period of time (see Figure 17.1).

▼ *Figure 17.1: A simple liquidity spectrum*

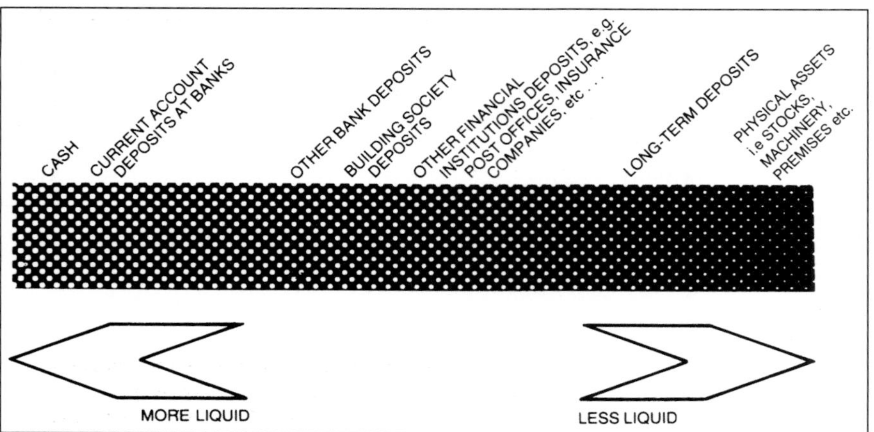

How much cash should a business hold?

Knowing exactly how much cash to hold, and being able to forecast future cash requirements, is one of the most important and difficult jobs facing business managers. A business can be very profitable 'on paper', but if it invests all of its cash into new machinery and plant, it may not have the funds available to meet day-to-day bills. When this happens, a firm is said to be **insolvent.**

If a firm is insolvent, it may be forced to borrow money from banks and other lenders at high rates of interest. If interest rates rise quickly, an otherwise profitable firm may find itself unable to meet its debts. At this point, creditors - the people or other firms to whom the firm owes money - may decide to demand repayment. The firm will then have to stop trading and shut down in order to be able to sell off key assets such as premises and machinery to meet bills. This is known as **liquidation.**

At first, it may seem odd that a profitable business could end up in this situation. However, cashflow problems may occur because of the time difference between receiving revenues from sales and making payments. For example, wages and salaries have to be paid out in cash each month, and raw materials must also be paid for, usually before the finished product can be sold to a customer. Thus, a firm incurs a number of cash costs before the good or service it produces is ready for sale. Even then, it may have to grant up to three months credit to customers, making a lengthy time-lag between paying out cash and receiving cash from sales. A business may, therefore, appear profitable 'on paper' - that is, revenue owed to the firm may be greater than its costs - but it can lack the liquidity needed to survive.

The continuous flows of cash into and out of a firm is often referred to as the **cashflow cycle** (see Figure 17.2).

▼ *Figure 17.2: The cashflow cycle*

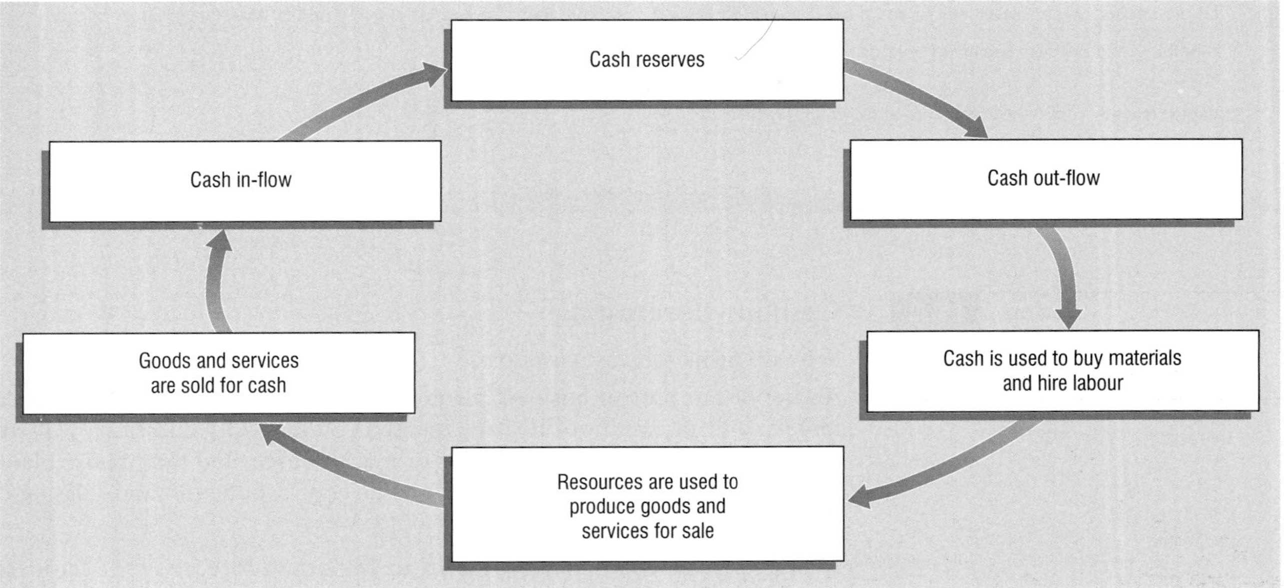

The difference between cash and profit - an example

Top Chocs has just started selling high-quality chocolates imported from Belgium. The sole trader firm sells an average of 500 boxes per month. Top Chocs sells the boxes for £10 each, making sales of £5,000 in the first month of trading.

The boxes of chocolates cost £5 each to buy, and the total wage bill for the firm is £1,500 per month. Rent costs are £500 per month, and insurance and energy costs add another £200 per month.

REVENUES	
500 boxes x £10	= £5,000
COSTS	
Chocolates (500 boxes)	= £2,500
Wages	= £1,500
Rent	= £ 500
Insurance and energy	= £200
	£4,700
PROFIT	
Revenues - Costs	= £300

Thus, after subtracting trading costs from sales revenues, Top Chocs has made a trading profit of £300 in its first month of operation. However, the owner, Ms Soft-Centre is worried, because even though she is making a profit on paper, her bank balance has fallen.

When the chocolates are imported, foreign suppliers will only despatch orders for 150 or more boxes to UK customers. Because Top Chocs sells four types of chocolate box, this means she has had to buy a total of 600 boxes at a total cost of £3,000 (600 x £5).

By the end of the first month, Ms Soft-Centre had spent the following cash sums:

Chocolate	£3,000
Rent	£ 500
Wages	£1,500
Insurance	£ 100
Energy	£100
	£ 5,200

In other words, the £300 profit was made on the quantity of chocolate boxes actually sold, but because so much stock had to be purchased initially, the firm is worse off in terms of cash holdings by a sum of £200, being the difference between sales revenue and total costs. The remaining extra stock will no doubt be profitably sold in the future, but in the meantime the Top Chocs' cash balance has been reduced by a profitable transaction.

Key words:

Cash - notes and coins and money held in bank or building society current accounts

Liquid assets - assets which can be converted into cash

Liquidity - the ability to exchange assets for cash without a loss of value

Illiquid assets - assets which cannot easily or quickly be converted into cash

Insolvency - when a firm does not have enough assets to pay its debts

Liquidation - selling off a firm's assets after the collapse of the business

Section **17.2**

Cashflow forecasting

Why do firms forecast cashflows?

An important part of business planning and management is the setting of targets, and preparation of plans to achieve them. Organizations will set objectives, such as increasing profits or market share, and then devise plans for the use of materials and labour, the level of production and sales, and the cash requirements to meet their objectives.

Making plans involves making forecasts. Important forecasts for a business are:

- **Capital budget** – this involves forecasting the timing and amount of necessary expenditures on premises, machinery, vehicles and other fixed assets (see 18.2 and 22.1). New fixed assets will be needed to replace old assets or to expand a new or existing business.
- **Trading forecast** – this involves forecasting spending on activities that enable the firm to produce and sell goods and services. These include forecasts of spending on raw materials, wages, telephones, power, rent and rates, and all other day-to-day running costs. Sales revenues resulting from trading activities will also be forecast.
- **The cashflow forecast** – this is a forecast of expected cash in-flows from sales and any other incomes, for example bank loans, and expected cash out-flows to pay for the bills forecast to arise in the capital budget and trading forecast.

We shall now consider the purposes and format of a cashflow forecast.

Cashflow smoothing

An important aspect of business success is to plan ahead and forecast inflows and outflows of cash, in order to be able to anticipate future difficulties and take appropriate action. If a forecast shows that the business is likely to run short of cash in a particular month, because cash outflows exceed cash inflows, managers can either decide to cut costs now, or attempt to raise revenues in future in order prevent the shortfall from happening. It is much better to be able to take time in deciding what should be cut, than to be forced into a rush decision.

A **cashflow forecast statement** is simply a budget for cash. It lists all expected monthly receipts and payments over a given period of time -

usually six or twelve months - so that the firm can identify when cash will be short or in surplus. Using this information, the firm can then arrange a loan to cover a cash shortfall or, if a cash surplus is likely to be earned at another time in the year, save it for use later in the year, when cash reserves are low.

Using cashflow forecasting to even-out cash surpluses and deficits into the future is sometimes known as **cashflow smoothing**. A firm will be able to test the impact on cashflow of different forecasts of spending on fixed assets and trading activities, and different assumptions about the future level of sales. In this way it will be able to have courses of action planned in case the firm runs short of cash.

Monitoring business performance

The cashflow forecast also provides a useful method by which business managers can monitor the performance of the firm. The forecast can be used to compare actual cashflow with plans on a regular basis, so as to help identify any differences which may require attention.

Raising capital

In addition, a cashflow forecast can be used to illustrate the future prospects for a business to a potential lender. For example, a bank manager will want to be assured that the firm will have sufficient cash each month to meet loan repayments. A healthy cashflow forecast can increase the confidence both of new and existing investors in the business.

The cashflow forecast statement

The precise format of a cashflow forecast statement will vary between firms. However, within any forecast there will be three main sections:

- **Receipts:** details of cash inflows from various sources, for example, revenues from cash sales, cash from debtors, and injections of new capital from loans or share sales. Interest payments on any surplus cash invested in a bank deposit account or other interest-bearing accounts can also produce cash for a business.
- **Payments:** details of cash outflows to pay for various items such as wages and salaries, purchases of raw materials and fixed assets, and overheads, such as telephone and electricity bills, office supplies, rent and rates, which tend not to vary with the level of output (see Chapter 22). Loan repayments, including any interest, will also be included within this section.
- **Summary balance**: this section at the bottom of the forecast statement sums total receipts and payments for each month. The net cashflow is then added to the cash balance available at the beginning of each month to give the closing balance of cash available at the end of each month.

Figure 17.3 shows an example of a cashflow forecast for a firm over a period of eight months. The **cash inflow** in each month represents expected monthly cash. The firm has also just received a bank loan of £2 million in January to replace some old equipment. Sales invoices outstanding since the previous December are also repaid in February, to add £800,000 to cash inflows.

▼ *Figure 17.3: Example of a cashflow forecast*

ALL FIGURES £000'S

Month	Jan	Feb	Mar	Apr	May	June	July	Aug
RECEIPTS: (cash inflows)								
Cash sales	3,000	2,500	1,900	1,800	1,800	1,500	1,200	1,000
Cash from debtors		800		500		500		300
Loan capital	2,000							
Interest payments						100		
Total receipts (A)	**5,000**	**3,300**	**1,900**	**2,300**	**1,800**	**2,100**	**1,200**	**1,300**
PAYMENTS: (cash outflows)								
Cash purchases (incl. VAT)	3,000	2,000	2,500	2,000	2,000	2,000	1,500	1,500
Credit purchases (incl. VAT)	500							
Wages/salaries	820	800	800	800	800	800	800	800
Overheads:								
Rent/rates	150	150	150	150	150	150	150	150
Transport	30	26	19	17	17	17	12	12
Hire Purchase	5	5	5	5	5	5	5	5
Leasing payments	25	25	25	25	25	25	25	25
Loan repayments		100	100	100	100	100	100	100
Electricity			60	60				
Gas			13	10				
Telephone			25	25				
Post	4	3	2	2	2	2	2	2
Insurance	6	6	6	6	6	6	6	6
VAT			-2,000			1,600		
Other expenses	30	25	25	25	25	25	20	20
Total payments (B)	**4,570**	**3,140**	**1,730**	**3,130**	**3,130**	**3,225**	**4,220**	**2,620**
Net Cashflow (A-B)	**430**	**160**	**170**	**-830**	**-1,330**	**-1,225**	**-3,020**	**-1,320**
+ Opening Bank Balance	**1,000**	**1430**	**1590**	**1760**	**930**	**-400**	**-1525**	**-4545**
= Closing Bank Balance	**1,430**	**1,590**	**1,760**	**930**	**-400**	**-1,525**	**-4,545**	**-5,865**

The forecast sales figures for each month could be based on previous experience or, in the case of a new business, on the average cash sales made by similar-sized competitors in the industry, or from market research into consumer demand for the firm's products. Financial advisers and accountants may also be able to help a new business forecast its cashflow. However, it is important to remember that a cashflow forecast only shows cash receipts, and that actual sales may be quite different to the cash figure if some sales are made on credit.

Cash outflows in the form of purchases, wages, and overheads are given each month. Again, these figures represent the expected cash payments made. Spending plans in the capital budget and trading forecast may differ from cash outflows - for example, if the firm is allowed credit by materials suppliers, or if assets are bought on hire purchase.

The **net cashflow** for each month is given as total receipts minus total payments. This information can be usefully plotted on a graph (see Figure 17.4).

▼ *Figure 17.4: A graphical representation of the cashflow forecast in Figure 17.3*

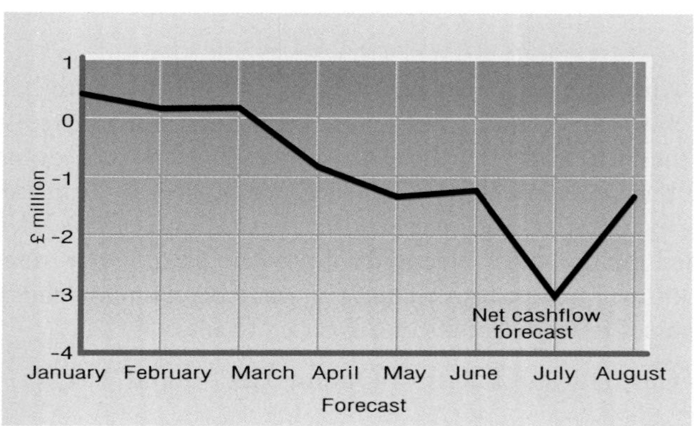

Inflows and outflows will affect the balance of cash held by the firm at the bank. In Figure 17.3, the business started with a bank balance of £1 million. The last rows of the cashflow forecast show the opening balance at the bank, and the impact on this balance of the net cashflow each month. Opening balance plus net cashflow gives the closing balance at the bank each month. The closing balance then becomes the opening bank balance in the next month.

The cashflow forecast in Figure 17.3 predicts a cash surplus in the first three months of the trading period, and then a deficit in each of the remaining five months, reflecting the seasonal nature of sales. However, due to the strong cashflow performance in the first few months, the forecast shows that the bank balance of the business is able to stay in credit for the first four months, before going into debit. The looming negative balance of nearly £6 million in August, not helped by a large VAT payment made to Customs and Excise in June at a time when sales were falling, will force the firm to plan ahead in an attempt to cover the expected cash deficit. Possible solutions to this cashflow problem are discussed in Section 17.3 below.

The timing of cash inflows and outflows

Credit periods

The example above illustrates the importance of correct timing when calculating cashflow figures. Purchases and sales are not necessarily entered into the cashflow when they happen, but are entered when a cash receipt or payment occurs. Given trade credit periods of up to three months, the time difference between entering transactions into the accounts and cashflow entries can be very significant (see 16.1). For example, a business may make sales on credit today of £10,000. A figure of £10,000 is entered into the accounts immediately, and is used in calculating the profit figure. However, the cashflow will only show the £10,000 cash received when it is paid to the firm in a few months' time.

Wages and salaries

It is usual to pay employees at the end of each month in arrears. This helps to delay cash outflows, often until cash receipts for each month are available to pay the wages bill.

Value Added Tax (VAT)

VAT is a percentage tax added to the price of many goods and services. Some goods, known as zero-rated, are exempt from VAT. Examples of zero-rated goods include children's clothes, books, food, and rail fares. Rates and wages and salaries are also exempt from VAT. The current rate of VAT is 17.5% in the UK, but this may be changed from time to time in the budget (see 6.2).

Traders are legally required (except if zero-rated) to collect VAT on their sales on behalf of the Customs and Excise Department. This is known as **output tax**.

In 2000/01, a firm with an anticipated turnover of £45,000 or more had to register for VAT with the Customs and Excise Department. If a business is VAT-registered, then the trader may reclaim any VAT it has paid on its own purchases as a business expense. VAT is likely to be paid by firms on purchases of stock, fixed assets, and overhead expenses. Since 1994 VAT has also been levied on gas and electricity bills but at a lower rate. Reclaimed VAT is known as **input tax**. This VAT may be claimed against the tax the trader passes on to Customs and Excise. That is:

VAT payable to Customs and Excise = Output Tax – Input Tax

For example, a firm makes sales of £571,428 in a given month, on which £100,000 will be owed to Customs and Excise in VAT (**output tax**). To produce the goods for these sales, the firm purchased £200,000 of stock, and of this sum, 17.5% or £35,000 was paid in VAT (**input tax**). The business can reclaim the input VAT it has paid and so only passes on the difference of £65,000 between output VAT and input VAT (i.e. £100,000 – £35,000) to Customs and Excise.

Since the output tax will nearly always be greater than the input tax, businesses will almost certainly end up paying some cash to the Customs and Excise Department for VAT. This is because output tax is based on selling prices, whereas input tax is based on cost prices of materials bought into the business before value is added (see 1.1).

Only zero-rated firms, for example, those in the food industry, are not required to charge VAT on their sales. However, they may have to pay out large sums in input VAT on purchases of raw materials and components. In this case, the Customs and Excise Department will owe the trader money. Zero-rated traders can reclaim this input tax every month, thereby boosting cashflow.

In the case of quickly-growing small firms, there is often a temptation to use VAT as a source of extra finance by delaying payment to Customs and Excise, so that total receipts including VAT can be used to boost net cashflow. However, fines for late payment of VAT are severe, and the costs of these fines would more than outweigh the benefits gained from using VAT money for a short period.

It is essential to make correct estimates as to the timing and size of VAT payments. At 17.5% of sales revenue, VAT can have a major impact on cash inflows and outflows.

Portfolio Activity 17.2 

Completing a cashflow forecast can be time-consuming. Incorrect entries may also be overlooked and carried forward from one month to the next. Because of this, many businesses prefer to set up a spreadsheet on a computer. In this way, cashflow and closing balances at the end of each month can be automatically recalculated each time a new figure is entered into an appropriate cell.

1. Load a spreadsheet package, for example EXCEL or LOTUS 123, on to your computer and set up the cashflow forecast statement from Figure 17.3.
   - Enter appropriate formulae to sum column totals for receipts and payments each month.
   - Also enter formulae to calculate net cashflow each month, by subtracting the cell containing total payments from the cell containing total receipts.
   - Enter formulae to calculate the opening balance and closing balance and to carry forward the closing balance each month.
   - Check that your spreadsheet works before proceeding.
2. Use your spreadsheet to adjust the cashflow forecast in Figure 17.3 to allow for the following additional flows:
   - A VAT bill for £600 is received in March but paid in April. The firm has paid £300 of VAT input tax which can be offset against this bill.
   - The firm delivered goods to a customer with an invoice for £400 in April. The sum was paid in June.
   - There was an unpaid energy bill for £200 outstanding in August.
   - Sales on credit worth £600 were made in February. Payment was received in May.
   - Sales on credit worth £400 were made in June. Payment was received in August.

Key words:

Capital budget - a plan for future purchases of fixed assets such as premises, machinery and other equipment

Trading forecast - a plan for production (raw material purchases, wage payments), overheads and sales in a business

Cashflow forecast statement - a prediction of all expected monthly business receipts and payments over a future time period, to show the forecast cash balance at the end of each month

Cashflow smoothing - using a cashflow forecast to plan the management of cash to smooth out surpluses and deficits and minimize the need to borrow capital externally

Net cashflow - total cash inflows less total cash outflows

Output tax - Value Added Tax (VAT) collected by business as a percentage of their sales of certain goods and services which must be paid to the Customs and Excise Department

Input tax - VAT on purchases made by a business which can be reclaimed as a business cost from the Customs and Excise Department

Section **17.3**

Cashflow problems

Causes of cashflow shortages

A business that fails to forecast cashflow accurately will fail to manage and control its working capital. The result can be a shortage of liquidity, which may force the business to sell important assets and therefore lead to a reduction in future profitability. Alternatively, the firm may have to borrow at high rates of interest, which will drain away profits. In the worst case, a lack of liquidity can lead to closure.

Cashflow difficulties may arise because of the following:

- **Overtrading.** A firm that attempts to increase the scale of production too quickly without regard to the impact of growth on cashflow, is said to be **overtrading.** Increased sales create the need for more cash to pay for extra raw materials and work in progress. Without having secured long-term funds in advance, the business is forced into delaying payment to creditors and attempting to obtain early payment from debtors. If a creditor insists on early payment, the firm may have to go into liquidation.
- **Too many fixed assets.** Spending too much money buying fixed assets, such as new plant and machinery, is a significant drain on business cash reserves. It may be better to lease fixed assets or purchase them on HP, rather than pay for them up-front in full.
- **Overstocking.** Another difficulty is caused when too much stock is purchased. The more specialized the stock is, the harder it will be to sell off quickly in a cashflow crisis in order to raise working capital. Large quantities of stock also tie up cash unnecessarily, which could be used to earn interest. Stocks may also become obsolete if fashions or technology change, or if there is a fall in demand for the product.
- **Too much credit.** A firm may raise its capital internally from its owners, or externally by borrowing (see 23.2). The larger the proportion of capital raised through borrowing, the larger will be the interest payments which the business has to make. If interest rates rise, the burden of interest payments faced by a heavily indebted firm will also increase. These payments are likely to be a severe drain on cashflow and profit.
- **Poor credit control.** Many small firms find themselves faced with cashflow difficulties either because sales are less than expected, or because credit customers take longer than expected to pay their debts. Often this is due to poor credit control, and the granting of credit to firms who are themselves experiencing cashflow difficulties.
- **Inflation.** Cashflow difficulties may arise because the general level of prices rises by more than was anticipated. If, for example, wages and raw materials costs rise suddenly and unexpectedly, then cash reserves may be used up, leaving too little cash for other eventualities. Firms often underestimate the impact of rising prices on their costs in their cashflow forecasts. Both capital budgets and trading forecasts should allow for an anticipated increase in prices over the forecast period.
- **Seasonal fluctuations.** Some businesses are seasonal, with cash inflows and outflows varying by time of year. For example, firework manufacturers may spend money throughout the year in producing fireworks, but find that their main source of cash inflow is in the weeks leading up to 5 November. While this may be anticipated, it takes very careful planning and discipline to ensure that the cash inflow is held over, to be spread across the full year.

Solving cashflow problems

The main ways of solving a cashflow crisis are either to foresee the problem and take preventative action (such as cutting cash outflows or raising inflows), or to find additional sources of finance to cover the deficit.

Specific cashflow remedies might include the following:

- **Negotiate short-term finance.** It may be possible to negotiate an overdraft with a bank in order to cover a potential cashflow difficulty. The disadvantage of this is that interest will have to be paid on the money borrowed, and if the firm is already in difficulty, it may be hard to find a lender to borrow from.
- **Convert current assets into cash.** A business may be able to sell some of its stock in order to raise cash. Debtors can also be chased for payment, or offered discounts to pay up more quickly.
- **Factoring:** late payment of invoices for goods delivered can cause considerable financial hardship for many firms. **Debt factoring** involves a specialist company, known as a **factor**, paying off the unpaid invoices of supplies in return for a fee.

  It is common for a factoring company to agree to pay 80% of the amount of the invoice on issue, paying the remaining 20% when the debtor settles the invoice with the factor. This provides the creditor with early payment of debts and leaves the chasing-up of payments to the factoring company.
- **Sell off fixed assets and lease back.** Fixed assets owned by a business, such as plant, vehicles, and machinery can be sold off to raise cash. The amount raised from the sale of fixed assets is known as their **net realizable value.** This may be less than their '**book value**' (i.e. cost price less an allowance for depreciation – see 18.2).

  However, fixed assets will be needed to produce goods and services for sale. By leasing these assets, a firm agrees to rent them for a fixed period from a leasing company, and is therefore able to carry on production (see 23.2). However, the regular monthly payments made to a leasing company will increase cash outflows over the period of asset hire.
- **Alter pricing policy.** Sometimes cutting product selling prices can result in increased cash sales if the quantity sold rises by a sufficiently large amount. If this happens, demand for the product is said to be **price- elastic** (see 5.6).
- **Tie cash outflows to sales.** This means that spending on items other than current wages and production supplies is postponed until after a target level of sales revenue has been reached. For example, a firm may delay replacing equipment and non-essential consumables until sales have picked up.
- **Improve credit control.** Most businesses need to employ some form of **credit control** system. Credit arrangements are clearly of benefit to the person or business that is buying goods and services, but they can cause problems for the suppliers.

Every business will need cash to make payments. It is, therefore, vital that a business is able to collect money owing to it quickly and with ease. If a firm adopts a 'tight credit' policy, it means it may limit the amount of credit it allows, reduce repayment periods, and give credit only to its most valued and reliable customers. This will reduce the risk of bad debts and improve cash-flow.

An 'easy credit' policy of allowing customers longer to pay and larger credit limits, may be used to encourage sales, particularly if the firm is entering a new market, or to clear old stocks of finished goods. It may also be designed to help out valued customers who may be experiencing financial difficulties of their own.

Avoiding cashflow problems

Businesses can adopt some practical strategies right from the start of trading, in order to minimize the risk of future cashflow crises. For example:

- Avoid reliance on a few big customers. If one closes down or switches supplier, it will hit cashflow very badly.
- Send out invoices as quickly as possible. If a contract involves a long period of work before a final invoice can be sent out, agree in advance to invoice at key points as the work progresses.
- Give debtors an incentive to pay up quickly by offering discounts for prompt payment. Be firm with late payers.
- Try to arrange to pay large bills in instalments.
- Once a good relationship has been built up with suppliers, try to re-negotiate credit and discounts with them in order to reduce costs.
- Avoid carrying too high a level of stock. Stock is important, but it represents business capital tied up, and can be costly if financed by a bank loan on which interest is paid.

Each system will differ but, in general, good credit control will involve the following:

- **Credit checks:** The bank at which a firm keeps its accounts will often be willing to enquire into the credit status of a potential customer by contacting their bank to see if there have been any problems.
- **Establishing a credit limit for each customer:** This will often be based on the bank's report on the customer's creditworthiness. If the value of orders exceeds this limit, the firm should investigate and, if necessary, either insist that outstanding invoices are paid first, or simply refuse the order.
- **Making sure outstanding invoices are 'aged':** By keeping an **aged debtors list** of customer names, including the date at which they received credit and the amount, a firm can easily identify customers as their debts fall due for payment at the end of an agreed credit period. Conversely, a firm can also keep an **aged creditors list** in which to record the names of their creditors, the amount of credit they were extended, and when payment falls due. This will help ensure they do not overlook paying their suppliers.
- **Sending out reminders:** Each debtor should be sent a copy of their invoice with 'reminder' stamped across it or written in a covering letter around 10 days before their payment falls due.
- **Chasing bad debts:** A **bad debt** is caused by a debtor failing to pay an outstanding invoice for goods or services delivered. Bad debts can cause cash-flow problems, especially in smaller firms who may be forced out of business if they lack the money to pay for resources to continue production. It is usual for a firm to chase up outstanding debts first with a payment reminder. If this does not work, the next step is a strongly worded letter or personal visit to the debtor. As a last resort the firm may threaten and eventually be forced to take legal action to recover monies owed to it.

Key words:

Overtrading - when a firm expands too quickly without obtaining the necessary long-term finance

Net realizable value - the value at which old fixed assets can be sold off

Book value - the cost price of replacing old fixed assets less an allowance for their depreciation

Debt factoring - short-term finance to cover unpaid invoices

Useful references

Hawkins, A. '**The Managing Cashflow Pocketbook**' (Management Pocketbooks paperback, 1996)

Learn how to create your own **cashflow forecasts** on-line with Biz/ed net at ***bized.ac.uk***

Key Activity

Hot Pizza Ltd is a small chain of two fast food outlets which started business on 1 January. Miss Katrina Sorrento is the principal shareholder in the company. Other shareholders in the company include her sister and brother. You are a friend of the family, and have been asked to provide business and financial advice.

1. Miss Sorrento has asked you to produce a cashflow forecast for the new company over the twelve-month period to next December. You decide to set up a spreadsheet model (like that in Figure 17.3) to calculate total expected receipts and payments each month, so that you can examine the effect on cashflow of a variety of assumptions. You base your forecast on the following information provided by Miss Sorrento:
   - The Sorrento sisters used £20,000 of their savings to start the business on 1 January.
   - Miss Sorrento arranges to have stock worth £5,000 delivered every quarter on the first day of the month, starting in January. This must be paid for in cash two months after delivery.
   - Her brother uses his savings to buy a van for £5,000 cash, and pays £3,000 cash for fixtures and fittings. He also decides to buy a personalized number plate for the van, registration P1ZA 1 for £1,000 cash.
   - Hot Pizza sales in January are expected to be low, at around £1,000 for the month, but thereafter steady sales of £3,000 per month are expected.
   - Miss Sorrento has taken on a contract to supply pizzas to the staff of the local hospital each weekday. This is on a credit basis, and is in addition to the £3,000 expected sales per month. The hospital contract is expected to earn £500 a month, with payment received one month in arrears. The first month of the contract will be in March.
   - Hot Pizza Ltd will employ three staff in the two outlets at a total wage cost of £1,500 per month.
   - Energy costs are expected to be £500 per quarter.
   - Insurance for public liability, employee liability, equipment, and vehicle insurance will come to £400 per month.
   - Advertising and other miscellaneous expenses will total £250 per month.

   - The Sorrento's hope to be able to draw out a total of £1200 a month to live on.

   Remember to check that your spreadsheet and the formulae you have input are working correctly, by manually calculating the Hot Pizza cashflow forecast. Rectify any faults.
2. Miss Sorrento is unhappy with the notion that transactions only affect the cashflow when money is received or paid, not when a transaction is made. She asks you to explain the importance of cashflow timings and how this works. Write a brief explanatory note to her, using examples taken from her own cashflow situation. Also explain the possible consequences on the pizza business of incorrect forecasting.
3. Is the business viable with the initial capital and forecast expenses that the Sorrento family is putting in? What advice would you give them?
4. From your spreadsheet, produce a graph of cashflow, showing the net cashflow surplus or deficit month by month. Include this in your report to Miss Sorrento.
5. Miss Sorrento has asked you to consider an optimistic scenario in which cash sales are £1,000 more each month than first expected as from April. If this is the case, she thinks additional expenses will be as follows:
   - Two part-time workers should be employed at a total cost of £380 per month
   - Additional stock each quarter of £1,000
   - Increased energy costs of £100 per quarter
   - A bank loan of £2,000 in August to purchase two more large ovens

   Recalculate the cashflow forecast using this information. Describe how it compares with the first forecast.

Test your knowledge

1 The purpose of a cashflow forecast is to:

A Show the amount of profit made

B Provide a tool for managing cashflow

C Show expenses actually incurred

D Provide information on sales actually made

Questions 2–4 relate to the simple cashflow forecast for a four-month period shown below:

Month	Jan	Feb	Mar	Apr
Receipts £				
Sales	**500**	**800**	**600**	**1,300**
Payments £				
Wages	600	600	600	600
Energy costs	100	100	100	100
Raw materials	100	200	300	300
Administration costs	50	50	40	20
Total payments	**850**	**950**	**1,040**	**1,020**

2 In which month does cash inflow exceed cash outflow for the first time?

A January

B February

C March

D April

3 All of the following are true statements about the forecast except:

A The firm will need an overdraft in April

B The amount of overdraft needed in January is £350

C Cashflow will be negative in March

D The closing balance at the end of February will have been decreased by £150

4 Assume now that the firm borrows £500 in February. If nothing else changes, net cashflow in April will be:

A + £500

B 0

C – £160

D + £360

5 In a trading forecast, cash outflows may include all of the following except:

A Wages

B Energy costs

C Long-term creditors

D Rent

Questions 6–9 share the following answer options:

A An unplanned cash surplus

B An unplanned bank overdraft

C An increase in money owed by the firm

D No impact on cashflow

Which of the above impacts on cashflow would result from:

6 Some debtors unexpectedly going bankrupt?

7 Payment by a customer of a previously written-off debt?

8 Purchases of machinery not accounted for in the capital budget?

9 The firm experiencing an increase in credit sales?

10 A business has produced a cashflow forecast which predicts a closing balance at the bank at the end of the year of £5,000. The following mistakes are then discovered:

- Sales for the year should be £7,000 higher
- An increase in wages in the trading forecast of £4,000 was ignored

What should the new forecast for the closing balance be, taking into account these changes?

A £8,000 surplus

B £16,000 surplus

C £6,000 deficit

D £2,000 surplus

11 A cashflow forecast will show:

A Profit or loss

B Depreciation of assets

C Cash receipts and payments

D Balances on customer accounts

12 When a business applies for a loan it is usual to produce a cashflow forecast. The main reason for this is:

A The cashflow forecast gives the lender unlimited liability

B It is a legal requirement

C It shows that borrowing requirements have been accurately estimated

D It shows that the business has a good accounting system

13 A firm registered for VAT makes payments to the Customs and Excise Department every three months. Its cashflow forecast for the next three months has left out VAT. The likely consequence of this is that the firm:

A Will be charged too much VAT by its suppliers

B Pays Customs and Excise too much money

C May not have sufficient funds to make the VAT payment

D Will be exempt from payment

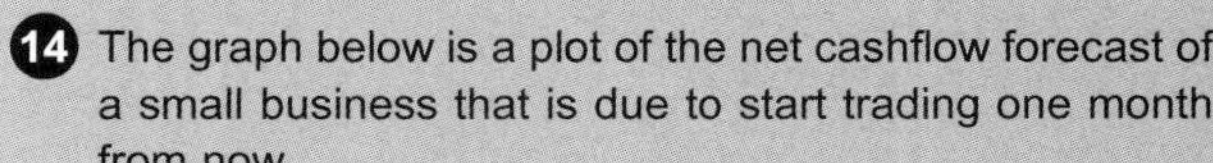

14 The graph below is a plot of the net cashflow forecast of a small business that is due to start trading one month from now.

What is the most likely explanation for the negative cashflow expected in the first four months of trading?

A Payment of VAT to Customs and Excise Department

B The receipt of a bank loan

C Sales on credit

D The purchase of fixed assets

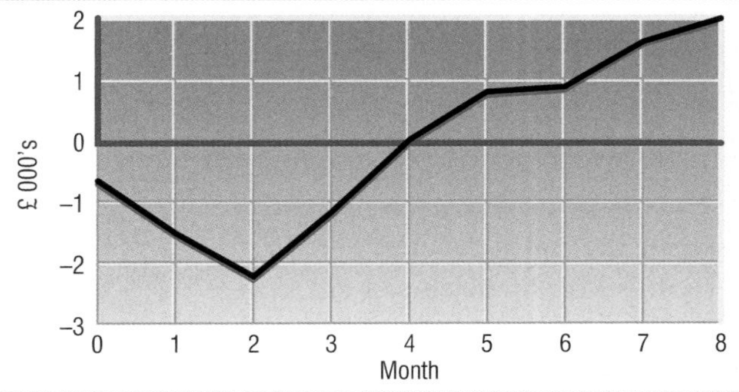

15 **a** What are the main purposes in business of producing forecasts of capital spending on fixed assets, sales and costs incurred in trading and cashflows? Explain your answer.

b Explain what might happen if a firm gets their forecasts wrong.

c Suggest and explain at least two reasons why a firm may make inaccurate forecasts of cashflow.

d Explain the difference between a cash inflow and cash outflow using examples of the various headings you would expect to find in a cashflow forecast.

chapter 18 Financial Accounts

WHAT WILL WE TELL THE SHAREHOLDERS?
PROFITS
£
MONTHS

This chapter investigates how to create the main accounting records kept by business - the profit and loss account and balance sheet.

What you need to learn

The **financial accounts** of a business will summarize records of financial transactions and performance over an **accounting period,** usually of 12 months' duration.

The **final accounts** of a business will be used by the tax authorities to assess its tax liability, by the business owners to monitor its performance, and to secure and maintain appropriate sources of finance.

A **balance sheet** is an account which records the assets and liabilities of a business. It is typically laid out in a vertical format which clearly shows the **working capital** in the business.

The accounting equation, **Assets = Liabilities + Capital**, underpins the construction of the balance sheet.

The **profit and loss statement** shows the profit or loss made by a business over an accounting period. It is made up of three parts: the **trading account** showing gross profit; the **profit and loss account** showing net profit after tax and interest; and the **appropriation account** showing how the final profit is distributed.

Completed financial documents, such as invoices and receipts, are used to keep up-to-date accounting records. Ledger accounts are summaries of the total amounts owed by and to the business. They are used to compile the final accounts at the end of each accounting period.

A **trial balance** will list all the balances on individual ledger accounts. Once the trail balance has been checked and sums to zero, the various entries can be transferred to the final balance sheet and profit and loss statement.

You need to understand how the information in financial documents is recorded and used to generate the final accounts of a business.

You should also be able to explain the concept of **depreciation** and how it can be calculated.

Section **18.1**

The purpose of accounts

Why do firms keep accounts?

All businesses need to keep financial records summarizing how well or how badly they are performing over time. These records will include financial data on costs, the value of assets, debts, sales, and profits. The final accounts of an organization summarize this financial information at the end of each trading period. The main financial summaries of a business are:

- The balance sheet
- The profit and loss statement

Accounting periods

It is normal to publish accounts on an annual 'financial year' basis, over the previous 12-month trading period, the start of which will normally have been determined by the date at which the business started to trade. For example, if a firm started trading on 1 July 2000, it may keep financial records over each 12-month period from 1 July each year to the following 31 June. It is not necessary to produce accounts running from 1 January to 31 December each year. Some large companies may even publish accounts more than once each year, for example, on a quarterly basis.

Business organizations produce accounts for a number of reasons:

- **To monitor business performance.** The final accounts provide a record of how well a business has performed over the last accounting period in terms of sales, cost control, and profits. These figures can be compared with those from earlier periods to see how business performance has improved (see 19.3). If business performance has worsened, managers can take action they think is appropriate to turn the fortunes of their organization around, for example, by cutting product prices, launching a new advertising campaign, streamlining the workforce, or employing new equipment.
- **To secure and maintain finance.** All businesses need capital to buy or hire assets such as premises, machinery, and land (see 22.1). Most business organizations raise capital from external sources such as banks and finance companies. These providers of finance will wish to use the accounts to judge whether or not the business will be in a position to repay loans. Similarly, before private investors are willing to buy shares in the ownership of a limited company, they will wish to know if the company is profitable and is able to pay its shareholders healthy dividends (see 19.4).
- **To meet legal requirements.** All firms must provide financial records to the Inland Revenue so that it can calculate corporation tax or income tax liabilities on their profits. The Customs and Excise Department will also need to check VAT liabilities. Limited companies are required by law to provide annual accounts to their shareholders and on request to the general public.

The role of accountants

It is the job of the accountant to keep financial records, and to turn these into a form that can be understood by business managers and other users of accounting information.

Businesses usually employ two kinds of accountant:

- **Financial accountants** are responsible for the production of final accounts in accordance with the various Companies Acts, in order to provide interested parties, such as the owners of the company, with an accurate picture of the firm's progress and financial position.
- **Management accountants** produce and use accounting information for internal management purposes. The management accountant may, for example, produce budgets and various forecasts in order to assist management in planning and controlling the business. Whereas the work of the financial accountant is made public in the annual report and accounts, the work of the management accountant is usually for confidential use only within a business.

By law, company accounts must be checked by independent accountants to ensure that they provide a 'true and fair view' of the position of the company. These independent accountants, called auditors, are hired to audit or check the company accounts before they are published. This is an important safeguard in helping to ensure that accurate information is presented to shareholders and other interested parties in the published accounts.

Financial statements

Limited companies are required by law to publish their accounts once a year, and to file these with the **Registrar of Companies** (see 2.2). These accounts are then made available to any member of the public who wishes to see them. The final accounts of a limited company will usually include the following sections:

Directors' report

This is a report written by the company directors in the annual accounts, which is required by the Companies Act 1985. The report usually:

- Reviews the development of the company during the year
- Informs shareholders of future developments
- Details the firm's health and safety policy
- Lists any political or charitable donations
- Lists directors' shareholdings and share options
- Details any changes in the membership of the board of directors
- States the amount of profit recommended to be paid as dividends to shareholders, and the amount to be retained for re-investment in the firm.

The chairman's statement

Large companies will often include a statement by the chairman in the accounts, although this is not required by law. The statement will normally include a review of the performance of different parts of the company and forecasts for the future.

Balance sheet

The balance sheet of a firm shows how the business has used its money, and where the money came from. The balance sheet contains two sections: the first lists the company assets (**capital**), the second summarizes what it owes (**liabilities**), on a particular date, for example, 31 December. The balance sheet is useful because it shows the value of the owners' investment in the firm at the given date. The balance sheet can also be used to calculate various statistical measures of the financial health and performance of the business (see 19.3).

The profit and loss account

The profit and loss account provides a picture of the firm's trading activities over the course of a trading period. It shows the sales revenues received, the direct and indirect trading costs incurred during the period, and the profit or loss made at the end of the period.

Cashflow statement

Large companies must also provide a cashflow statement which summarizes the sources and uses of cash over the accounting period.

Notes to the accounts

Notes to the accounts provide a detailed explanation of the accounts and how they have been constructed.

Auditor's report

The independent auditors are required by law to give an opinion on the accounts. They must state whether or not they feel that the accounts present a 'true and fair view' of the affairs of the company.

Portfolio Activity 18.1 

Public limited companies are required by law to provide copies of their annual accounts on request to any member of the public. Write to a selection of plcs that you are aware of in different business sectors, asking for copies of their latest published accounts.

On receipt, study the accounts. What information do they provide?

For what reasons have your chosen companies produced accounts? How does the performance of each company compare:

i Over time?

ii With the other companies in your selection?

What factors might explain any differences?

Key words:

Accounts - financial records showing the performance of a business over time, as used by owners, managers, the Inland Revenue, potential investors, and competitors

Financial accountant - a specialist employed by a company to produce financial accounts according to the requirements of the Companies Acts

Management accountant - a specialist employed by a company to produce financial information for internal purposes of planning and control of the business

Auditor - an independent accountant hired to check whether the company accounts provide a 'true and fair view' of the company performance

Section **18.2**

Creating a balance sheet

What is a balance sheet?

A **balance sheet** provides the following details about a business at a given point in time:

- **The value of fixed and current assets held**
- **Liabilities** - money owed by the business to external creditors
- **Capital** - money invested in the business by its owners

By presenting information on the value of fixed and current assets held by a business, a balance sheet will provide an indication of the total worth of that business. However, certain assets, such as customer loyalty to a branded product, or the good reputation of company among staff, suppliers and customers, which may have taken many years to develop, are difficult to value with any precision. These are often known as **intangible assets** because, although they are very important to the continued financial health of a business, they have no physical existence. Other intangible assets may include patents, copyrights, and trademarks.

Business assets

Firms will wish to hold some of their capital as cash in a bank account, to make any immediate or unforeseen payments. However, the purpose of raising finance is not usually to hold cash, but rather to buy the assets needed to operate as a business.

Businesses purchase two main kinds of tangible assets. These are:

- **Fixed assets**: for example, buildings, plant and machinery, and vehicles. These are physical assets which will in general last for a long period of time, usually defined as more than one year.

- **Current assets**: these are assets which are used up relatively quickly during trading. Current assets include:
  - Stocks of raw materials
  - Stocks of semi-finished goods (work in progress)
  - Stocks of finished goods
  - Money owed by debtors
  - Cash held in the business ('cash in hand')
  - Cash held in a bank account ('cash in tills')

Current assets are defined as those items which can be converted into cash within one year. Stocks can be sold to raise cash relatively quickly, and money owed by debtors can be called in for payment. Cash is needed by a business to fund day-to-day trading, for example, to pay wages or settle bills for electricity, gas, telephones, and other overheads. The amount of money available to a firm for this purpose is called **working capital** or **circulating capital.**

Working capital is equal to the value of current assets less any current liabilities, namely any outstanding bills yet to paid, and a bank overdraft (see 23.1).

Fixed and current assets are purchased with capital provided by the business owners, usually in the form of **share capital** (see 23.3), or from funds borrowed from external sources such as banks and trade creditors (see 23.2). All of the money used in a business to purchase assets is therefore owed to someone, either to the business owners or to other creditors. That is, all of the money invested in fixed and current assets by a business, is balanced pound for pound by its **liabilities.**

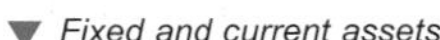
▼ *Fixed and current assets*

Liabilities

A liability refers to a sum of money owed. The liabilities of a business can be split into two kinds:

- **Liabilities to owners (shareholders' capital).** This represents the money invested by business owners in a firm, such as share capital, plus the accumulated profits made by the firm and not paid out to owners in previous years of trading. Accumulated profits retained by a business and not distributed to owners are known as **reserves**. Thus,

  Shareholders' Funds = Capital + Reserves

- **Liabilities to other creditors.** Businesses will often raise capital by borrowing money form external sources such as banks, or by withholding payment of invoices for goods delivered by a supplier for an agreed period of time.

  Current liabilities are those which normally have to be repaid within twelve months, for example:

  - Trade credits
  - Tax debts
  - Outstanding expenses (accruals)
  - Overdrafts

  Other liabilities may only need to repaid in full after a period of more than one year. These are known as **long-term liabilities**. For example:

  - Long-term loans
  - Loan stocks, i.e. debentures (see 23.3)

'A balance sheet must always balance'

The total value of all current and long-term liabilities of a business, including liabilities to its owners, is used to finance fixed and current assets. This relationship can therefore be represented in the following accounting equation:

Assets = Liabilities + Capital

Assets and liabilities in a balance sheet must always be equal, because the money needed to purchase business assets must have been financed from liabilities of one kind or another - hence the name 'balance sheet'.

An example of a balance sheet

Table 18.1 shows the types of asset and liability that might appear in the balance sheet of a limited company.

In Table 18.1 Leigh Ltd has liabilities totalling £160,000. Of this amount, £80,000 is money invested in the business by its shareholders. Profits retained by the business and not paid out in dividends to shareholders total £12,000. The firm has also obtained a bank loan of £20,000 and received goods and services on credit from trade suppliers worth £35,000. The firm also owes £13,000 to the Inland Revenue in corporation tax on last year's profits. Total money owed by the company is £160,000.

▼ *Table 18.1: Assets and liabilities in the balance sheet*

LEIGH Ltd
Balance Sheet as at 31.12.2000

Liabilities (Sources of capital)		**Assets (Uses of capital)**	
Capital and Reserves		**Fixed Assets**	
Shareholders' capital	£80,000	Premises	£90,000
Retained profit (Reserves)	£12,000	Computer equipment	£4,000
		Machinery	£30,000
Long-term Liabilities			
Bank loan	£20,000	**Current Assets**	
Current Liabilities		Stock	£10,000
		Debtors	£10,000
Trade creditors	£35,000	Cash at bank	£16,000
Taxation	£13,000		
Total Liabilities	£160,000	**Total Assets**	£160,000

On the other side of the equation, Leigh Ltd has used £160,000 to purchase various assets - premises valued at £90,000, computer equipment, and machinery costing £34,000, and current assets worth £36,000, which includes £16,000 held as cash to pay bills.

The balance sheet in Table 18.1 demonstrates that total assets must always equal total liabilities, because all of the capital a firm has must be owed to someone, either its owners, or people outside the business. Thus, whenever a transaction is made by the business, it will affect both assets and liabilities. For example, if Leigh Ltd decides to purchase more computer equipment costing £5,000 on credit, this will increase fixed assets by £5,000 and current liabilities **(trade creditors)** by £5,000. The balance sheet totals will also rise by £5,000. Similarly, when Leigh Ltd pays the £13,000 tax it owes to the Inland Revenue, this will reduce its cash holdings by £13,000, and the balance sheet totals will fall by £13,000.

Conventional balance sheet formats

Balance sheets are usually laid out in a vertical format. The advantage of this is that it clearly shows the **working capital** (current assets – current liabilities) of the firm: that is, the amount of money available to pay the day-to-day bills, which is a vital indicator of the financial health of a business.

An example of a vertical format balance sheet is given in Table 18.2.

Portfolio Activity 18.2

1. Input the balance sheet in Table 18.1 for Leigh Ltd into a suitable spreadsheet. Use sum commands to automatically calculate column totals for assets and liabilities, as individual number entries to the balance sheet are changed.
2. Check that your spreadsheet balance sheet always balances, after allowing for the following transactions taking place on 31.12.2000:

- Leigh Ltd decides to add to its vehicle fleet by purchasing a new van at a cost of £12,000 on Hire Purchase.
- The business decides to expand into new premises. It sells its existing premises and takes out a mortgage to pay for the additional cost of a £150,000 small factory and office unit.
- The Inland Revenue informs Leigh Ltd that it had overestimated its tax liability by £5,000.

The balance sheet and the law

The 1985 Companies Act requires that limited companies include the following information in their balance sheets or accompanying notes:

- Authorized capital - the amount of share capital the company is allowed to issue, as approved by the Registrar of Companies
- Called-up share capital - how much the company has actually raised from a share issue. Not all of the authorized capital may have been issued.
- The amount of share premium (over and above the face value of shares)
- Reserves (or retained profits)
- Details of fixed and current assets
- The method used to value fixed assets
- The total amount of depreciation in the value of fixed assets allowed for
- The value of any investments and shares held by the business in subsidiaries
- Any returns due from investments or shareholdings in subsidiaries
- Corresponding figures for the previous year for comparison

▼ *Table 18.2: An example balance sheet*

Notes		YEAR ENDING:	2000 £000	1999 £000
1		**Fixed Assets**		
		Intangible assets	5,256	
2		Tangible assets	49,999	47,094
		Investments	9,647	13,952
	(A)		**64,902**	**61,046**
3		**Current Assets**		
		Stocks	20,576	20,158
		Debtors and prepayments	28,845	44,881
		Cash at bank	9,200	37
	(B)		**58,621**	**65,076**
4	**(C)**	**Current Liabilities**		
		Amounts falling due within one year	26,770	35,774
5	**(D)**	**Net Current Assets**		
		[Working Capital) (B – C)	31,851	29,302
6	**(E)**	**Total assets less current liabilities**		
		[A+D)	96,753	90,348
7	**(F)**	**Long-term Liabilities**		
		Amount falling due in more than one year	(3,380)	(2,419)
8	**(G)**	**Provision for Liabilities and Charges**		
		Deferred taxation	(3,527)	(2,091)
9	**(H)**	**Net Assets**		
		(E – (F+G))	89,846	85,838
	(I)	**Capital and Reserves**		
10		Called-up share capital	9,363	9,361
11		Share premium account	33,530	33,502
12		Revaluations	-	-
13		Accumulated reserves	46,953	42,975
14		**Shareholders' funds (I = H)**	**89,846**	**85,838**

Company balance sheet terminology

1 **Fixed assets -** assets which will last for longer than one year, namely physical assets such as buildings, machinery, vehicles, etc. For the purpose of compiling a balance sheet, the estimated value of intangible assets such as customer loyalty, goodwill, patents, and trademarks, are also classed as fixed assets.

2 **Investments -** these are **financial assets**, usually shares held in other companies. If a company holds more than 50% of the shares of another company, that company is known as a **subsidiary**. If the holding is between 20% and 50%, the company is known as an **associated company**. Holdings of less than 20% are called **trade investments**. Investments may also include holdings of government bonds or deposits of foreign currency. Investments are included at cost in the balance sheet.

3 **Current assets** - assets which are generally used up in the business in less than one year, e.g. cash, stocks, debtors. Sometimes firms pay certain expenses in advance, for example, insurance premiums. Where these are paid in advance, for part of the next financial year they are **prepayments** and are counted as debtors.

4 **Current liabilities** - for example, creditors, overdrafts, accruals, or bills outstanding. Current liabilities include those debts which are likely to fall due within one year.

5 **Net current assets** - the difference between the value of current assets and current liabilities. This calculates the sum available to the business to pay for day-to-day running costs, otherwise known as working capital.

6 **Total assets less current liabilities** - fixed assets plus working capital.

7 **Long-term liabilities** - debts which do not need be settled within one year, e.g. bank loans, mortgages, debentures.

8 **Provisions for liabilities and charges** - money put aside to cover certain future liabilities, notably deferred taxation arising from timing differences between corporation tax liabilities on profits and claims for allowances against tax for capital expenditures and pension provisions, etc.

9 **Net assets** - the worth of the business to its owners, calculated by adding fixed assets to working capital and deducting long-term liabilities. The sum left represents the liability of the firm to its owners.

10 **Called-up share capital** - also known as **issued capital**. This is the amount of money received from selling shares valued at their face value. For example, selling 10,000 x £1.00 ordinary shares will give a company £10,000 of called-up share capital.

11 **Share premium** - because of a high level of demand for their shares, a company that issues shares may be able to charge more for them than their face value (see 19.4). For example, a firm may issue 10,000 ordinary shares with a nominal or face value of £1.00, but sell them for a market price of £1.50 each. In this case there is a premium of 50 pence per share over and above the face value. The share premium gives the business additional cash to use and is also a liability owed to the shareholders. Share premium is shown separately in the reserves section of the balance sheet.

12 **Revaluations** - because of inflation, the current value of some assets can be much higher than their original cost. Because of this, firms may wish to revalue their assets from time to time. Although not shown this balance sheet, this is common within the capital and reserves section of balance sheets. For example, if a firm revalues the property it owns, or if there is an appreciation in the value of its foreign currency holdings, then the value of fixed assets will increase, and liabilities in the form of reserves, shown by the revaluation account, will also rise.

13 **Reserves (or retained profits)** - some profits are retained each year in order to invest within the business. These retained profits are a liability of the firm to shareholders. Only a small part of the reserves will be held as cash; most of it will be re-invested in assets of different kinds.

14 **Shareholders' funds** - the total amount of money owed by the business to its owners. This should be exactly equal to net assets, because the total worth of the business belongs to its owner.

Portfolio Activity 18.3

You have been employed as an accountant to draw up a company balance sheet as at today's date, from the following information for XYZ Ltd. You may produce the balance sheet either manually or using a computer spreadsheet or accounting software.

Use the notes to Table 18.2 to help you.

At year end:	£000
Issued ordinary shares (400,000 × £2 each)	800
Retained profit	810
Trade creditors	700
Share premium account	270
Bank overdraft	310
Deferred taxation	120
Long-term loan	500
Debentures	360
Dividends payable	80
Buildings	1000
Machinery	1000
Vehicles	250
Cash at bank	750
Debtors	750
Prepayments	200

Depreciation

The **fixed assets** of a business, such as machinery and vehicles, are used over and over again in the production process. Each year, the value of fixed assets in the balance sheet will tend to fall due to wear and tear, or perhaps because changing technology makes some of them obsolete. A fall in the value of fixed assets is known as **depreciation** and represents a cost to business.

Each year a business must work out how much depreciation to allow for each fixed asset. That is, it must put aside a certain amount of money each year so that, when the asset wears out, it will have saved up enough to buy a replacement. The cost of depreciation appears as an expense in the profit and loss statement of a business (see 18.3).

▼ *Depreciation*

There are two main methods used by businesses to work out depreciation. These are:

- **The straight line method:** this divides the cost of the asset by the number of years it is expected to remain in service. For example, if a machine cost £1,000 and is expected to last 5 years, then the value of that machine will depreciate by £200 each year.
- **The reducing balance method:** this assumes that the depreciation charge in the earlier stages of the expected life of an asset will be greater than in later years. The value of the asset is therefore depreciated by a constant percentage each year. For example, if the value of the £1,000 machine is depreciated over 5 years at 25% each year then the depreciation charge in the first year will be £250, in the second year £187.50 (i.e. 25% of £750), in the third £140.63 - and so on, until all that remains after 5 years is the expected scrap value of the asset.

Key words:

Accounting equation - Assets = Liabilities + Capital

Balance sheet - a statement of a firm's assets and liabilities, the main purpose of which is to show the value of the business

Intangible assets - assets which have no physical existence, but which help to provide benefits for the firm, for example, suppliers' goodwill, customer loyalty to a branded product

Liabilities - money owed by the business to its owners or to external sources. These may either be current liabilities falling due within one year, or long-term liabilities which will need to be repaid some time after one year

Subsidiary - a company in which another company holds more than 50% of issued shares, i.e. has the controlling interest

Working capital - money available to a business to pay for its day-to-day running expenses

Called-up share capital - total funds raised through the issue of equities valued at their nominal or face value

Share premium - those funds raised from the sale of equities over and above their face value

Revaluation - a change in the book value of assets and liabilities due to a periodic revaluation of assets, for example, to allow for the effect of rising inflation on property values

Reserves - the total of retained profits held by a business over many years, shown as a liability to shareholders on a company balance sheet

Depreciation - an allowance made by a business for the fall in the value of its fixed assets over time

Section 18.3 The profit and loss statement

What is a profit and loss statement?

With the exception of charities, profit is the prime objective of most private-sector businesses and of organizations in the public sector (see 2.3). A profit is made when sales revenues, or turnover, exceed expenses. A loss, or **negative profit,** occurs when expenses exceed all revenues.

If a profit is made at the end of a trading period, some is likely to be paid out to the business owners, either in the form of drawings, or dividends on their shares. The remainder of the profit after tax will be retained in the business for future investment.

The profit and loss account shows how much profit or loss a firm has made during a trading period, usually over 12 months.

The calculation of profit and loss

The profit and loss statement of a business will be divided into three parts:

- The **trading** account
- The **profit and loss** account
- The **appropriation** account

An example is given in Table 18.3.

The trading account

The trading account shows sales revenues for the year, less the cost of these sales. The **cost of sales** refers to all costs of production associated with those goods and services actually sold.

▼ *Table 18.3: The profit and loss account of Mountain Bikes Retail Ltd*

MOUNTAIN BIKES RETAIL LTD

Profit and Loss Account for the year ended 31.12.2000

		£	
TRADING ACCOUNT	**Turnover**		**100,000**
	less cost of sales:		
	Opening stock (1.1.2000)	10,000	
	Add Purchases	60,000	
		70,000	
	less Closing stock (31.12.2000)	15,000	
			55,000
PROFIT AND LOSS ACCOUNT	**Gross profit**		**45,000**
	less expenses:		
	Heat and light	1,000	
	Printing and stationery	1,500	
	Advertising	750	
	Insurance	500	
	Wages & salaries (Admin only)	10,000	
	Business rates	1,500	
	Telephone	300	
	Provision for bad debts	1,300	
	Depreciation	2,000	
		18,850	
	Net profit		**26,150**
	add Non-operating income	1,250	
	less Interest payable	600	
APPROPRIATION ACCOUNT	**Profit before tax**		**27,400**
	less Corporation tax	6,825	
	Profit after tax		**20,575**
	less Proposed dividends	10,000	
	Retained profit for the year		10,575

It will often be necessary to adjust the cost of materials for changes in stocks over the trading period. The cost of sales for Mountain Bikes Retail Ltd in Table 18.3 is £55,000. This will consist mainly of the cost of purchasing bicycles for resale. However, it is likely that some of the bikes sold this trading period were purchased in the last period, while some of this period's stock may remain unsold until next year.

These adjustments can be made by adding purchases of stock made during the trading period to the opening stock (the value of stock held at the start of the year), and then deducting closing stock - that is, the value of stock left at the end of the trading period. This calculation gives the cost of stock actually sold during trading.

Cost of Sales = Opening Stock + Purchases – Closing Stock

The closing stock at the end of one period, therefore, is the opening stock in the next.

Thus:

Gross Profit = Sales Revenue – Cost of Sales

The difference between sales revenue and cost of sales is known as **gross profit.** In the example above, Mountain Bikes Retail Ltd made sales during the year of £100,000. It started the year with an opening stock of £10,000 and made purchases of £60,000, finishing the year with a closing stock of £15,000. Using the formula for cost of sales given above, this gives a cost of sales of £55,000 for the stocks of bikes, and a gross profit of £45,000.

The profit and loss account

The trading account gives the amount of profit made on trading activities - that is, on buying in stocks and then selling goods or services. However, gross profit is not the final profit available to the business managers to pay out to shareholders or to re-invest in their firm. Overheads and tax owed have to be deducted from profit first. In addition, firms may have extra income to add, known as **non-operating income**, which is not earned from trading, for example, interest on holdings of government bonds, and earnings from shares held in other companies.

The profit and loss account starts by deducting total operating expenses from gross profit. Expenses here are those **overheads** or indirect costs which are not incurred 'on the shop floor' as a result of the production of goods and services, for example, the wages of administrative staff, office supplies, business rates, etc. Thus,

Net (or Operating) Profit = Gross Profit – Expenses

Any expenses incurred but not yet paid must still be deducted from profit. For example, if a bill for water rates of £3,000 was received in December and not paid until the new financial year in January, the expense must still appear in the previous year's profit and loss account.

Many businesses will earn income from their own investments. This non-operating income must be added to net profit. In the example, Mountain Bikes Retail Ltd has a cash balance at the bank which earned £500 in interest in 2000, and the firm holds shares in a bicycle parts manufacturing company which have earned £750 in dividend payments, making a non-operating income of £1,250.

However, the firm took out a loan in the past and has paid £600 in interest during the year on this loan. This must be deducted from net profit before the tax liability can be calculated. Thus:

Profit before tax = Net profit + Non-operating Income – Interest Payable

▼ *Figure 18.1: Where do the profits go?*

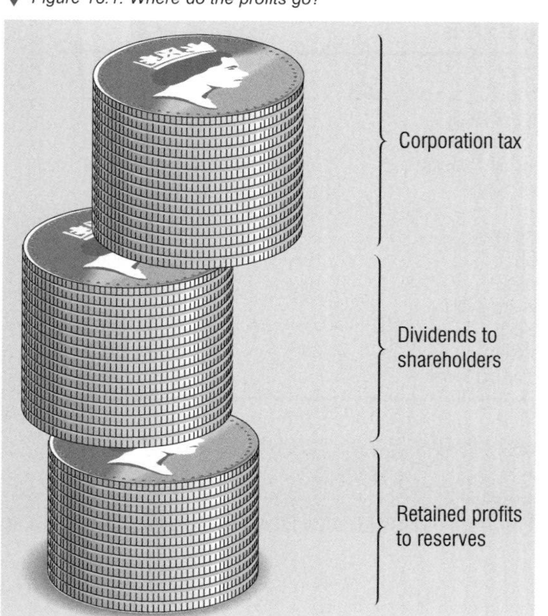

'Taxation' in company accounts refers only to corporation tax - that is, tax levied on company profits. Other taxes, including local business rates, are included as business expenses in the profit and loss account.

Appropriation account

The **appropriation account** shows what happens to the final profit - how much is distributed to shareholders as dividend payments, and how much is retained by the company to add to reserves.

Dividends are not an expense, because they do not affect the amount of profit made by a business. Rather, they are a way of using the profits which have been earned. In the case of Mountain Bike Retails Ltd, dividends of £10,000 have been paid out, leaving £10,575 as the profit retained by the business. This sum is allocated to accumulated reserves in the balance sheet and may, for example, be re-invested in new plant and machinery which increases the amount of fixed assets in the balance sheet.

Adjustments to the profit and loss accounts

Carriage inwards and outwards

This is a delivery cost. **Carriage inwards** is the cost of delivery paid by a firm's customers for goods received. It is therefore an additional source of revenue that should be added to turnover in the trading account.

On the other hand, when the firm takes delivery of materials or goods, it will have to pay for **carriage outwards**. This is an expense which will need to be deducted from gross profit in the profit and loss account.

Purchase returns

Money paid by the firm for any faulty goods or poor-quality materials subsequently returned to suppliers will have to be refunded. Unless refunds are subtracted from stock purchases in the trading account, gross profit will be understated.

Sales returns

Any finished goods returned by consumers in return for their money back will need to be subtracted from turnover in the trading account, otherwise gross profit will be overstated.

Discounts

Any discounts granted by the business in return for bulk purchases or prompt payment of outstanding sales invoices are counted as an expense, and deducted from gross profit in the profit and loss account.

Value Added Tax (VAT)

When companies charge VAT on goods or services, they are collecting the tax on behalf of the government and must pass this tax revenue on to the Customs and Excise department. It would, therefore, be wrong to include VAT at 17.5% in the value of sales turnover, because this would give the impression that profits were much higher. Thus, turnover excludes VAT in company accounts.

Bad debts

Sometimes customers may not pay for goods delivered or services received as agreed. These customers are known as **bad debtors**. When this happens, some adjustment will need to be made to the accounting figures to correct for bad or outstanding debts. Instead of reducing the sales figure, bad debts are considered to be an expense and are deducted from gross profit in the profit and loss account.

Portfolio Activity 18.4

Thomas Smith opened an art supplies shop ten years ago. Four years ago, he formed a limited company by selling shares in his business to two of his friends. With the money he raised, he opened a large art supplies discount warehouse.

Opposite is a summary of his transactions for a full 12-month accounting period. Produce a profit and loss statement for Thomas from these figures, and from the additional information provided below.

- At the start of the 12-month trading period, Thomas had no debtors or creditors, but did own £70,000 of stock left over from the previous period. Closing stock at the end of the trading period was valued at £55,000.
- Thomas owes his accountant £1,000 for work done during the year, and has promised his staff a Christmas bonus of £300 each, and £200 for the cleaner.
- Corporation tax is calculated as 20% of net profit. Dividends worth 40% of net profit after tax are paid to shareholders.

Year end totals	£
Cash sales	450,600
Cash received from credit sales	92,500
Purchase of stock	181,800
Wages (5 sales staff)	104,200
Drawings by Thomas	18,700
Cleaners' wages	10,000
Rent	26,000
Business rates	11,260
Electricity	4,500
Telephone	2,300
Postage and packing	1,170
Advertising	2,800
Depreciation	2,840
Interest on bank loan	300

How are the balance sheet and profit and loss statement related?

The balance sheet and profit and loss statement are linked in the following ways:

1. Profit belongs to the business owners, whether it is held in reserve by the business, or paid out to shareholders in dividends. Retained profit in a particular year increases the assets available to the business shown on the balance sheet, and at the same time increases the liabilities on the balance sheet owed by the firm to its owners. Accumulated reserves on the balance sheet represent the sum total of all of the retained profits held back during the life of the business.

   When a loss is made, this may be covered by drawing on reserves built up during previous years, as detailed in the balance sheet. If a business has no reserves, any loss would have to be paid for by borrowing money, or from a further sale of shares.
2. Allowances for depreciation reduce the value of fixed assets on the balance sheet, and are charged to gross profit as an expense.
3. Outstanding tax payments and dividends proposed but not yet paid to shareholders are shown as current liabilities on the balance sheet, and are also charged against profits as an expense.
4. Investments listed in the balance sheet as fixed assets may give rise to dividend or interest payments. This non-operating income is added to net profit in the profit and loss statement to obtain profit before tax.

Non-profit-making organizations

Private-sector organizations, such as charities or clubs and societies, which do not aim to make a profit from their activities are not required to produce a profit and loss account. Instead, they will normally draw up a **receipts and payments account** recording all monies received and paid out over a given period, along with an opening and closing cash and bank balance.

At the end of a trading period, these organizations may produce a more formalized **income and expenditure account**, following a very similar format to the profit and loss account. Local authorities must, by law, produce such an account at the end of each financial year.

Key words:

Profit and loss statement - an account showing the profit or loss made by a business over a period of time

Trading account - that part of the profit and loss statement which shows gross profit as being the difference between total sales and the cost of those sales

Cost of sales - the costs associated with the production of goods and services actually sold

Opening stock - the value of unsold stock held over from the previous trading period

Closing stock - the value of stock unsold at the end of the current trading period

Overheads - costs that are not linked directly to the production process, for example, rent, heating, and lighting

Non-operating income - income earned by a firm from investments and sources other than its own trading activities

Appropriation account - statement of how the profit after tax has been used by the company, either in payments to shareholders or in retained profits for re-investment

Net profit = gross profit less expenses

Section **18.4**

Trial balance and final accounts

In order to create the final accounts at the end of a trading period it is important that a business keeps accurate and up-to-date records of all business transactions throughout the period (see 16.1). The purpose of business documents for payments and receipts is to provide the information for these financial records.

Every business transaction has two elements. For example, if a firm buys stock for cash, its cash reserves will decrease, whilst its stock will increase. If instead the stock is bought on credit, the firm's liabilities to creditors will increase, and stock will increase. This twin effect is the basis for **double-entry book-keeping.**

Double-entry book-keeping is the system used by all firms where every transaction affects two different accounts. One account is said to be **credited** (added to) and the other is **debited** (taken from). This means that every transaction affecting a balance sheet or a profit and loss account will always have two effects. For example, if a company buys a new vehicle with cash, this will raise fixed assets and reduce the cash balance on the balance sheet.

Ledger accounts

The effects of business transactions are recorded in **ledger accounts.** Businesses will keep ledger accounts for:

- Sales (and money owed by debtors)
- Purchases (and money owed to creditors)
- Stationery expenses
- Rent and business rates
- Wages
- VAT
- Capital spending to buy fixed assets
- All other headings under which transactions are made

A **general ledger** will summarize all the details of incomes and expenditures entered into all the individual ledger accounts. Because entries in these accounts are often made on the left- or right-hand side of a 'T', they are also sometimes known as **'T' accounts.** Entries on the left are known as **debits**, whilst entries on the right are called **credits.** Most accounts will have entries on both sides (see Figure 18.2). At the end of a trading period, an accountant will want to use these accounts to produce the balance sheet and profit and loss statement.

Books of prime entry

Ledger accounts are summaries of the total amount owed by individual debtors and owed to individual creditors. However, on a day-to-day basis an organization will tend to record written details of invoices sent out and payments in so called **books of prime entry**. These include:

- **the sales daybook** – this records all the credit sales made by the organization from the invoices it has issued.
- **the purchase daybook** – this records all the credit purchases made by an organization and is prepared from invoices received from suppliers.
- **the returns books** – records credit notes issued or received from suppliers for returns. Goods returned by customers are known as **returns inwards** or sales returns. A **credit note** will be issued for each sale return (see 16.3). Issued credit notes will be entered into the **returns inward daybook**. On the other hand, goods that have been purchased by the organization but sent back to their supplier are known as **returns outwards** or purchases returns. Credit notes issued for these goods by their suppliers are entered into the **returns outward daybook.**
- **the cashbook** – records dates and details of payments and receipts. These can either be in the form of actual notes and coins paid out and received, or deposits and withdrawals to and from a bank or building society account.

At the end of each month entries into the daybooks for sales and purchases can be added up to provide totals to enter either as a credit or debit into the ledger accounts.

From trial balance to final accounts

Final accounts are produced by calculating the balance on each individual 'T' account at a particular date. For example, there is a balance of £425 on the sales account in Figure 18.2 at the end of May, and this is a credit balance. If May is the end of an accounting year, this is the sales figure that will be used in the trading account in the year-end profit and loss statement. In the same way, the balance on each 'T' account will provide a figure for either the balance sheet or profit and loss statement compiled at the end of an accounting period.

In practice, a business will have by the end of its financial year a wide range of accounts, listing many hundreds, thousands, or even millions of transactions, covering fixed assets, cash, debtors, creditors, expenses, accruals, prepayments, VAT, sales, bad debts, etc.

▼ *Figure 18.2: Examples of 'T' accounts*

Sales Account

Date	Debit	£	Date	Credit	£
			1 May	Balance b/d	200
2 May	Credit sales from Cam Ltd	100			
5 May	Returns from A Smith	75	10 May	Sales	250
			14 May	Cam Ltd	150
		425			
	Balance c/d	600	31 May		600
			31 May	Balance c/d	425

Purchases Account

Date	Debit	£	Date	Credit	£
			1 May	Returns	100
8 May	Paper	40			
15 May	Computer disks	50			
			18 May	Returns	50
29 May	Stock	500		Balance c/d	440
31 May		590			590
31 May	Balance c/d	440			

** c/d = carried down   b/d = brought down*

When is a transaction a debit or a credit?

A transaction will be a debit - i.e., recorded on the left of the 'T' account - if it is:

- An increase in assets, for example, the purchase of a car
- An expense to the firm, for example, wage payments
- A reduction in a liability, for example, a cash payment to a creditor

A transaction will be a credit - i.e. recorded on the right-hand side of the 'T' account - if it is:

- An increase in a liability, for example, an increase in creditors
- A reduction in the value of assets held, for example, the sale of a vehicle
- Income received, for example, sales revenue

The trial balance

Before using the figures in 'T' accounts to produce the final accounts, it is useful to check if the figures are correct. This check can be made by creating a **trial balance.**

A trial balance is simply a list of all the balances on the 'T' accounts, written as a simple column indicating whether each item is a debit or credit balance. Because each book-keeping transaction always has two matching effects, the sum of the debits should equal the sum of all the credits.

Thus, in the trial balance, the following equation should always hold:

Credits – Debits = 0

If this is not the case, then a mistake is likely to have been made somewhere in the accounts, and this will need to be corrected. It is much better to test the accounts using a trial balance than to go to the trouble of creating the balance sheet and profit and loss statement, only to find that the figures do not add up because of an error somewhere in the 'T' accounts.

▼ *Table 18.4: Example of a trial balance*

TRIAL BALANCE AS AT 31 DECEMBER 2000

'T' Accounts	Credit	Debit	Which final account?
	£	£	
Proprietor's capital	12,000		balance sheet
Plant and machinery		3,000	balance sheet
Depreciation		500	profit/loss
Freehold property		5,000	balance sheet
Opening stock		2,000	profit/loss
Purchases		1,000	profit/loss
Sales	10,650		profit/loss
Business rates		500	profit/loss
Wages		9,750	profit/loss
Sundry expenses		50	profit/loss
Cash account		750	balance sheet
Debtors		700	balance sheet
Creditors	600		balance sheet
Total Credits/Debits	**23,250**	**23,250**	

Once the trial balance sums to zero, the various 'T' account balances can be transferred to the balance sheet and profit and loss statement with more confidence that they are likely to be correct. Each trial balance item appears only once in the balance sheet or profit and loss statement. The value of closing stocks at the year end does not appear in the trial balance, but usually as a footnote underneath. Closing stock appears both in the balance sheet, as a current asset, and in the profit and loss account, as part of the cost of sales.

Key words:

Double-entry book-keeping - method of recording business transactions based on the idea that there are two aspects to all transactions, a source of funds and a use of funds

Ledger accounts - up to date records summarizing business transactions during a trading period. These are used to compile a trial balance

Books of prime entry - daily records of purchases, sales, returns and cashflows

'T' account - means of presenting individual transactions and a final balance in an account, using a simple 'T' layout

Trial balance - a list of credit and debit account balances in a business used to compile the final accounts. It is used as a means to establish whether all business transactions have been properly recorded

Key Activity

CRUMBZ!

You live in an area with a large number of office blocks. Although there are quite a few restaurants and eating places, you know that many office workers would rather have food delivered to their office than have to leave their place of work. You decide to set up a sandwich making and delivery service called 'Crumbz'.

1. Investigate and produce a financial plan detailing the types of assets (including fixed and working capital) you will need to purchase for your business, how much these are likely to cost, and the amount of finance you will need to raise to start up.
2. Write a short report explaining the basic accounting system you intend to use for your business, i.e. what financial documents, ledger accounts, trial balance and final accounts will you need to produce.
3. At the end of your second year of trading you have produced the trial balance below. You will now need to produce the year-end balance sheet and profit and loss statement from the trial balance. If possible, use a computer spreadsheet package with which you are familiar to input the information and to derive your final accounts. Remember to check for errors before printing out your final hard copies.

   (Alternatively, you may have access to business accounting software designed to help firms produce final accounts. What advantages does this business software offer your business over manual means of information-handling, or more conventional computer spreadsheets? If you do not have access to accounting software, you may wish to investigate the availability and facilities of such software designed for balance sheet applications. What advantages could this software offer your business and would they justify the cost of purchase?)

TRIAL BALANCE AS AT 31 DECEMBER

£

Capital introduced at 1 January	2,000
Cash	3,680
Cost of sales	10,300
Sales turnover	29,600
Drawings	12,000
Rent	2,800
Casual wages	3,800
Electricity	700
Office furniture and fittings	760
Debtors	4,300
Creditors	2,340
Other receipts	420
Telephone	320

Closing stock is £3910, opening stock was £6910

4. You have decided to employ a friend from school to run your office, answer the telephone, and take orders for food. You hope that your friend will eventually take over the book-keeping, and you decide to write him a brief report explaining why businesses need a trial balance, balance sheet, and profit and loss account, and how useful these are to business owners. Use examples taken from your own accounts produced under Task 2 above to illustrate points made in writing.

Useful references

Learn how to create your own **balance sheets** and **profit and loss statements** on-line with Biz/ed net at ***bized.ac.uk***

Look up company balance sheets and profit and loss statements from their **Annual Reports** on-line at

- ***www.reportgallery.com***
- ***www.carol.co.uk***
- ***www.news.ft.com***
- ***www.northcote.co.uk***

Access financial summaries on-line at

- ***www.hemscott.co.uk***
- ***www.hoovers.co.uk***

Test your knowledge

1 Which of the following is a current liability of a business?

A Buildings

B Stock

C Cash

D Overdraft

2 Which of the following is a long-term business liability?

A Vehicles

B An accrual for wages

C Creditors

D Debentures

Questions 3–5 share the following answer options:

A Business owners

B Employees

C Central government

D Suppliers

Which of the groups of people listed above will be interested in examining the final accounts of a limited company for the following purposes?

3 To negotiate pay and productivity agreements

4 To check business performance

5 To calculate liability for corporation tax

6 For a balance sheet to balance, only one of the following equations is correct and must hold. Which?

A Assets + Capital = Liabilities

B Fixed assets - Liabilities = Current Assets

C Gross Profit = Sales revenue – Cost of sales

D Assets = Liabilities + Capital

7 The main purpose of a balance sheet is to:

A Satisfy the Inland Revenue on tax liabilities

B Provide information for potential investors

C Show the value of the business

D Allow creditors to assess the firm's ability to repay debts

8 In which account would overhead expenses appear?

A Balance sheet

B Trading account

C Profit and loss account

D Appropriation account

9 The balance sheet will include information on:

A Sales

B Purchases

C Dividends paid

D Debtors

10 A link is provided between the balance sheet and profit and loss accounts through:

A Retained profit for a trading period

B Business expenses actually paid

C Fixed assets

D Sales

11 The purpose of a trial balance is to:

A Monitor business performance

B Calculate tax liabilities

C Check figures used to compile the final accounts

D Prepare a profit and loss statement

Questions 12 and 13 share the following answer options:

A £35,000

B £60,000

C £27,000

D £17,000

From the jumbled list of financial information for a small business given below, what is:

12 Net profit?

13 Profit after tax?

	£000
Corporation tax	8
Turnover	100
Non-operating income	5
Cost of sales	40
Expenses	30
Dividends payment proposed	10

14 a Why do firms keep financial accounts?

b What is the purpose of a trial balance in compiling final accounts?

c Explain the main differences between a balance sheet and a profit and loss statement.

chapter 19 Monitoring Financial Performance

PROFIT MARGINS ARE UP AND OVERHEADS ARE STABILIZING

This chapter explains how and why business organizations monitor the achievement of their financial targets and objectives.

What you need to learn

Another key element of sound financial management, in business, in addition to cashflow management, is **budgeting**.

Budgets help businesses to plan, set targets and control expenditures. **Variance analysis** involves investigating the reasons for differences between budget plans and actual results, as recorded in the business accounts.

To understand how budgets are used you need to know what they are, how they work and their particular purposes. You will need to be able to identify and interpret variance and explain the benefits of budgeting to businesses.

The information provided by final accounts can be interpreted in different ways. You need to understand how different stakeholders use **financial ratios** to assist them in interpreting accounts and in making judgements about the performance of a business.

You should be able to calculate and use:

- **liquidity (or solvency) ratios** - to measure the ability of a business to meet its debts
- **profitability ratios** - to measure how well a business is performing
- **activity (or performance) ratios** - to measure how efficiently a business is using its resources

You need to identify and compare financial ratios for different businesses, and how they have changed over time. You also need to understand the limitations of using financial ratios to make judgements about the effectiveness of businesses.

You also need to understand and explain how the following indicators can be used to show the performance of a public limited company:

- **movements in share prices**
- **dividends**
- **price earnings ratios**

Section 19.1 Accounting for business control

Setting business targets

Financial accounts, such as balance sheets and profit and loss statements, are used by business managers in order to plan and to control the activities of their organization.

The planning of business activities requires businesses to identify the long-term targets it wants to achieve in the future. These could be to:

- Maximize or increase profit
- Maximize or increase sales revenues
- Increase market share
- Expand into new or overseas markets
- Step up internal growth by increased investment in plant and equipment
- Promote external growth through the acquisition or takeover of other companies

Targets like these, which can be expressed in financial or money terms, are known as **quantitative targets.**

An organization may have other targets which are less easy to measure in money terms - for example, to improve the reputation of the business, or to increase loyalty among the workforce. Non-profit-making organizations, such as charities, may set targets such as increasing donations, saving more animals from exploitation, housing more homeless people, etc. Targets such as these are known as **qualitative**, or **non-financial targets.** How well an organization succeeds in meeting these targets is a matter of subjective judgement.

The objectives of The Body Shop

A qualitative target:

The Body Shop is against animal testing of cosmetic products and ingredients. We do not test our products or ingredients on animals. Nor do we commission others to do so. We never have and we never will.

We consider such tests to be morally and scientifically indefensible. We use our purchasing power to try to stop cosmetics ingredient suppliers animal testing. We also support and use alternative tests, inform the public and, most importantly, campaign to ban cosmetics tests on animals.

The Body Shop, Annual Report 1999

A quantitative target - Body Shop Group Turnover

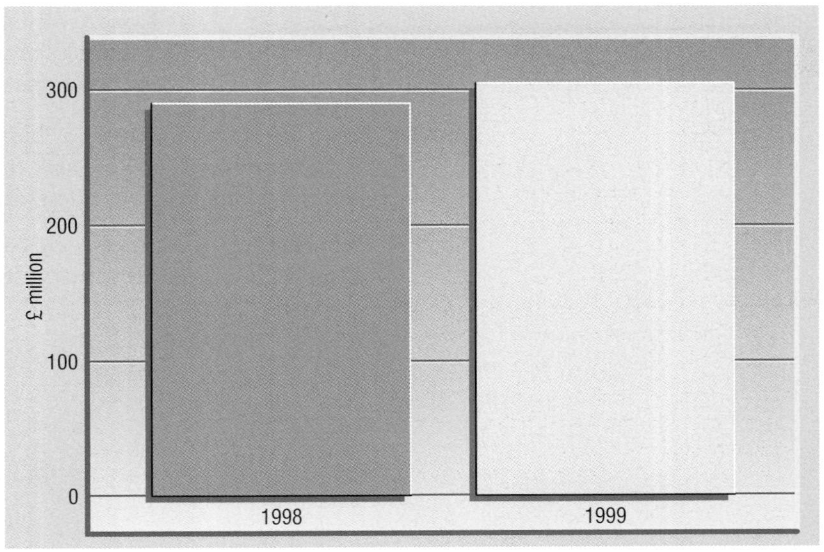

Business plans and targets can usually be found in the chairman's statement in the annual report and accounts of individual limited companies. The accounts themselves, including the profit and loss statement and balance sheet (see 18.1), represent an organization's progress to date in achieving its quantitative targets. The financial accounts of an organization can, therefore, be used to measure or monitor progress towards business objectives, as well as to set out targets for the future.

Reasons for monitoring business performance

In order to plan and control the running of a business, it is necessary to be able to identify the kinds of information that accounts can give, and how these can be interpreted to show how well a firm is doing.

Accounts can provide a way of monitoring:

- **Solvency:** whether or not a firm has enough assets (both fixed and current) to be able to trade into the future. For example, if a firm is short of cash, it may not be able to meet its debts and be forced to sell off fixed assets, such as machinery and vehicles. Cashflows can be monitored and forecast in order to make provision for periods when cash may be short (see 17.2).

▼ *Figure 19.1: Performance comparisons - over time, and with other firms*

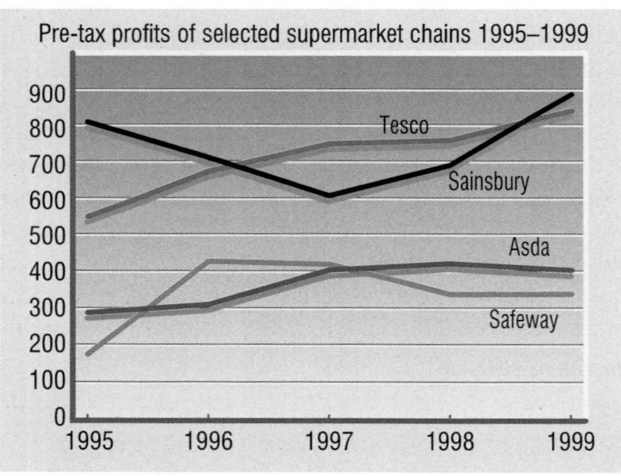

- **Profitability:** profit is one of the most significant measures of business performance. A firm will judge how well it has performed compared with past profit levels and with those of other firms in the industry.
- **Achievement of targets:** for example, has the firm achieved its target of a 10% increase in profits, a 5% growth in its market share, a 20% cut in operating costs, cut bad debts in half, etc.? Financial information can be used to identify areas where an organization can improve its performance. Actual results can be monitored and action taken if the firm appears to be off-target.
- **Tax:** a business can monitor and prepare for the amount of tax due to be paid to the Inland Revenue and Customs and Excise Department.
- **Financial requirements:** a business must monitor loan and credit repayments and make sure they do not fall behind, as this may jeopardize any future requests it makes for loans or credit.
- **Performance:** a business can compare its performance over time and with rival firms in the same industry and other industries.

Accounting information can also be used to:

- **Identify trends and forecast future performance:** in order to make an informed guess at the future performance of a business, it is useful to look at its past performance and see if there are any trends which might be expected to continue into the future. For example, if sales have on average risen by 10% each year, one might reasonably forecast sales to rise at this rate in the future. However, the past is not always the best guide to what might happen in the future. Market conditions are constantly changing. New suppliers entering the market, shortages of raw materials, changing consumer demand, new government policy - all these factors and more can affect the performance of a business. Judgement is, therefore, required.

▼ *Figure 19.2: Monthly sales of chocolate bars (£000) – an example*

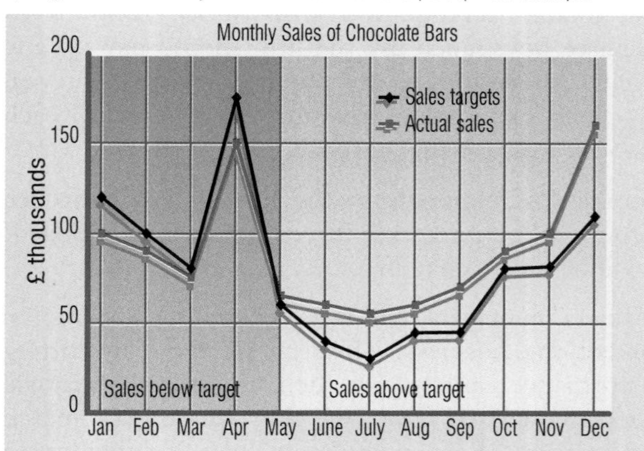

During the course of each trading period, a business will continually monitor whether or not it is 'on target' to achieve its objectives. If the firm is 'off target', or under-performing, managers can make changes to the operation of the business in order to move the firm back towards its goals. For example, a firm selling chocolate bars may aim to capture 25% of the market by the end of the year. To do this, it forecasts it must increase sales by 5% each month. If, midway through the year, sales of its chocolate bars are low and are being outstripped by sales of a competitor's product, the firm may plan a new advertising campaign to raise sales, or may even lower price to boost demand. Plotting actual sales against forecast sales on a graph is a useful way to monitor the achievement of this target (see Figure 19.2).

Similarly, a firm may set a target to increase annual profits by 10% over the previous year. If, at the end of the first quarter, profits are down, it can take action either to boost revenues or cut costs, for example, by buying materials from a cheaper source of supply.

Using accounting information to assist managers in planning, decision-making, and guiding a business is known as **management accounting.**

Who uses information on business performance?

A variety of people and organizations will wish to use data to monitor business performance:

- **Business owners** will want to see the accounts in order to know how well the firm is doing, how much profit is being made, and how much their investment in the firm is worth.
- **Employees** and **Trade Unions** may use published accounts to determine target pay settlements. If the accounts reveal that the company has gained a significant increase in profits, then employees may feel justified in asking for a large increase in their pay.

Key components of accounting information

In an efficient organization, monitoring is continual. To do this, financial information must be recorded accurately and be readily available, so that business managers can make decisions and take steps to ensure that their organization is working towards its targets. Such information will be available to business managers from the following sources:

- **Forecasts:** expectations of future costs, production levels, sales, stocks, input requirements, cash inflows and outflows, and profits.
- **Operating budgets:** used to plan the day-to-day use of resources in an organization. The operating budget will show expenditures and receipts agreed by business managers as required to meet set targets. Budgets will be prepared for all key areas of business activity: output, sales, inputs of labour and materials, overhead expenses, cash inflows and outflows (see 19.2).
- **The master budget:** a summary of total expenditure and expected receipts across the entire organization (see 19.2).
- **Aged creditors reports:** lists of suppliers to whom the organization owes money for goods and services delivered, with details of when each debt is due to be repaid.
- **Aged debtors reports**: lists of customers who owe the organization money, and how long each debt has been outstanding.
- **Balance sheet**: showing the assets and liabilities of a business at the end of each trading period (see 17.2).
- **Profit and loss statement:** a summary of all the financial transactions undertaken by a business within a trading period. It records total revenue and expenditure, and shows profit or loss (see 17.3).
- **Cashflow statement:** a summary of total cash inflows and outflows at the end of each trading period.
- Accounting information from the previous year's trading against which changes in performance can be judged.

- **Potential future investors,** including individuals and other organizations, will wish to see accounts in order to judge whether or not to invest in the company. Accounts allow investors to compare the performance of different companies over time.
- **Providers of finance,** such as banks and building societies, will wish to know the financial health of a business organization before lending it money, and to monitor its ability to repay.
- **Competing firms** will want to assess the financial strength and efficiency of a rival company by looking at its published accounts.
- The **Inland Revenue** will wish to see accounts to calculate how much tax the firm should pay on any profits. All businesses are required by law to reveal any profit or loss they have made at the end of each financial year for this purpose.
- **Suppliers of materials** to the firm will wish to see accounts before granting it credit, in order to judge if it will be able to pay invoices.
- **Business managers** will use accounting records to control the business. This can be done by setting performance targets and then monitoring financial performance to see if the outcomes match expectations. For example, managers might set a target for profit before tax to rise by 10% over a 12-month period. The actual percentage change in profit each week or month can then be compared with the 10% target. Accounts will provide a picture of the performance of a firm over time.

Business managers can make use of two important techniques to monitor the performance of their organization using financial information. These are:

- **Variance analysis**: this involves examining reasons for differences between business budget plans or forecasts and actual results.

- **Ratio analysis**: this involves comparing key financial figures from the final accounts.

These techniques are considered in detail in the following sections.

Key words:

Management accounting - using accounts to monitor the performance of a business and changing the way in which it is managed in order to improve performance

Quantitative targets - business targets which can be expressed in money terms

Qualitative targets - non-financial targets such as improving product quality

Solvency - the ability of a business to meet its debts

Section 19.2 Budgetary control

Preparing a budget

Budgeting allows business managers to improve their control over individual departments or divisions within their organization. **A budget** is a financial plan or statement which is agreed in advance. It is not a forecast, but a planned outcome which a firm hopes to achieve. It shows how much money is needed for spending, and how this expenditure might be financed. Most budgets will cover the next 12-month period, but some budget plans are drawn up for longer periods of time. For example, R&D may involve spending large amounts of money over many years.

The UK government also announces a budget each March for the economy as a whole (see 6.2). This is a statement of planned public expenditures and expected revenues in the coming financial year.

The preparation of budgets is an important aspect of business planning. Budgets will help an organization to:

- Appraise alternative courses of action - for example, identifying the costs and benefits of employing additional labour to raise output, or investing in new machinery instead
- Present information to potential lenders to raise finance
- Set business targets, as expressed by the amount and cost of resources shown in budget plans
- Monitor business performance by comparing plans with actual results

Drawing up a budget involves a number of steps, as illustrated in Figure 19.3.

▼ *Figure 19.3: Preparing a budget*

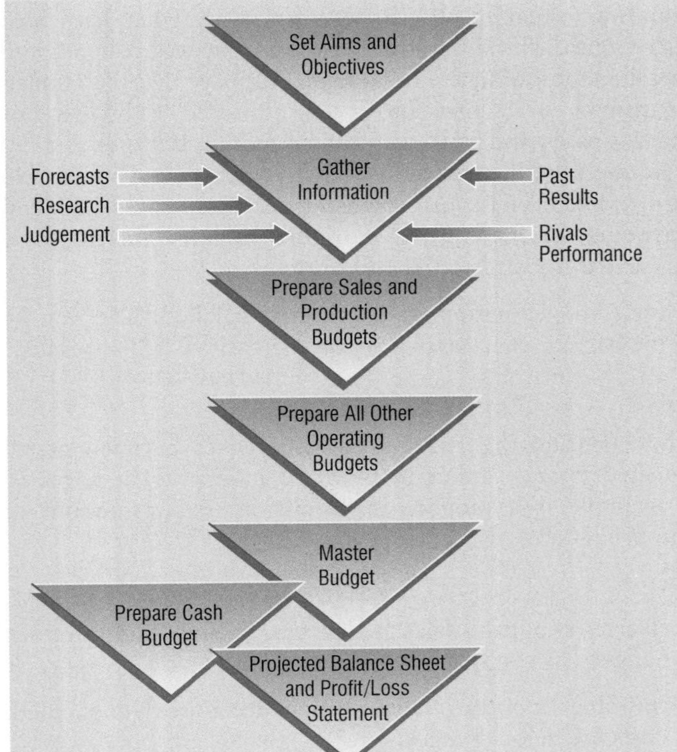

Stage 1: Decide upon a budget period. Most budgets are produced annually. It is usual for an annual budget to be broken down into quarterly or monthly budgets for easier control.

Stage 2: Agree business objectives and set targets. For example, to expand market share by 5%. In a large organization, individual targets will be agreed for each factory or office, or each department, area, or product to achieve. Targets should be challenging, but at the same time realistic.

Stage 3: Obtain information on which to base budgets. Most budgets are based on past spending levels, adjusted for the impact of price inflation on costs.

Stage 4: Prepare key operating budgets for sales, production, materials, labour, overheads, and cashflow, in line with agreed targets.

Stage 5: Draw up the master budget. This is a summary statement combining all individual budgets. It shows estimated revenues and planned expenditures and also, therefore, the expected profit.

Stage 6: Use the master budget and cash budget to prepare the projected balance sheet, to show the value of business assets and liabilities expected at the end of the budget period.

Types of budget

- **Zero-based budgets** are *not* based on past information. They ignore the past and make a fresh start. Each activity is evaluated against its relevance to the business, and whether or not the expenditure will yield benefits. For example, a firm that decides to install a computer network in its offices for the first time would have no past experience of computer costs. If it thinks computerization will increase output and efficiency by more than the cost of the equipment, then it will go ahead and prepare an IT budget based on cost estimates.
- **Flexible budgets** are adjusted over time in response to unforeseen changes in the level of activity in a firm. For example, the photocopying unit in a firm may need to buy a new machine to cope with an increased demand for photocopying minutes and reports, or an office may need to buy new computer equipment to replace a faulty machine.
- **Fixed budgets** remain the same, even if the level of activity in an organization differs from what has been predicted.

Monitoring budgets

If an organization is to be successful, it is important that it is always fully aware of its current financial situation. Business managers must therefore make sure that certain key areas of the organization are closely monitored:

- The **sales budget** shows planned revenues the firm hopes to achieve each month. This is calculated by multiplying predicted sales by the product prices the firm hopes to achieve.
- The **production budget** shows the amount of materials, labour hours, and machine hours needed to meet sales targets.

All other operating budgets for individual departments or activities will be based on the sales and production budgets. These will include budgets for labour and materials, overheads, and cashflow (see 17.2).

Summary budgets may also be drawn up separately for all capital and current expenditures. Current expenditures include wages, materials purchases, spending on power, and overhead expenses. Capital expenditures include spending on plant and machinery, vehicles, and other equipment that will remain productive for a long time. It will also include plans for loans to finance such expenditure.

It is possible to monitor business performance and the attainment of targets by comparing actual results, or outturn, with what had been planned for each month. The difference between what was planned and what is actual is called the **variance**. For example, suppose that the Human Resources Department in a firm has been allocated a budget for consumables, such as paper and pens, of £100 per month. If it spends £150 on these items in one month, then the variance is negative. That is, £50 more was spent than had been budgeted for. If the department is unable to cut back its spending on these items in future months, this negative variance will be carried forward to the end of the year.

At the end of each budget period, the projected balance sheet can be compared with the balance sheet drawn up on the basis of actual results.

Variance analysis

This involves investigating the reasons for differences between actual results and budgeted figures, either in terms of money or in terms of volumes - for example, the number of labour hours, or amount of materials used in production.

Variances can be:

- **Negative** or **adverse** - if outturn sales are less than planned, or if outturn costs exceed budget
- **Positive** or **favourable** - if outturn sales revenues are more than planned, or if outturn costs are below budget

Type of variance	Some reasons for variance
Sales variance	Unforeseen price changes Higher or lower sales volume than expected
Direct materials	Higher or lower prices than usual Increased wastage or inefficiency
Direct labour	Increased overtime working Negotiated pay settlement Cut in labour force Change in labour productivity
Overheads	Equipment breakdown Paper wastage Power cut Rise in price of materials

There are a number of important variances a firm will seek to monitor and analyse. The profit variance is usually the most important, showing the extent to which actual profit is greater or less than planned profit from the master budget.

Budgetary control, therefore, is the process of setting targets, preparing budget plans, monitoring those plans, and then analysing variances.

Figure 19.4: The process of budgetary control

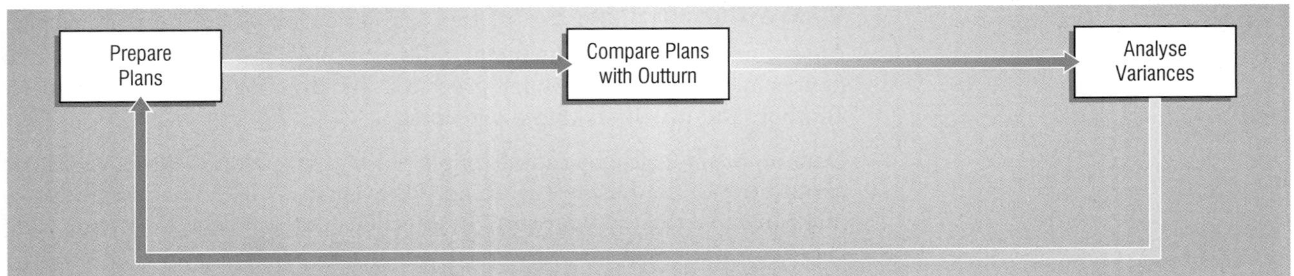

Portfolio Activity 19.1 

Examine the sales budget of the business organization below.

Month	Price	Sales targets (units)	Target revenues £	Actual revenues £	Variance +/-
January	£10	2000	20,000	21,000	
February	£10	1400	14,000	15,400	
March	£10	1200	12,000	12,500	
April	£10	1600	16,000	15,000	
May	£10	2200	22,000	18,200	
June	£12	2500	30,000	22,100	
July	£12	2700	31,400	29,500	

1. Suggest what information the sales budget may have been based on.
2. What is the danger of being too optimistic in the sales budget, and how might this impact on other operating budgets the business is likely to have drawn up?
3. Calculate the sales variances for each month.
4. What might have caused the large variances in sales?
5. How could management use this information?
6. Which variance(s) will the following factors affect? Are the factors adverse or favourable?
   - Discounts to customers who buy in bulk
   - Improved working conditions
   - Rise in staff absenteeism
   - Increasing competition from rival firms
   - Economic downturn
   - Favourable response to advertising campaign
   - Savings from contracting out office cleaning
   - Machine breakdown
   - Incorrect recording of hours worked
7. Investigate how budgets are prepared in a business organization with which you are familiar.

Key words:

Budget - a financial plan agreed in advance by managers

Sales budget - details of planned revenues

Production budget - details of factor inputs needed to achieve planned production targets

Current expenditure - spending on resources used up quickly, such as materials, labour, and power

Capital expenditure - spending on capital goods, such as plant and machinery

Master budget - a summary statement detailing the total budget for an organization, expected sales, and anticipated profits

Variance - the difference between an actual figure and a planned figure

Variance analysis - the investigation of reasons for variances

Section **19.3**

Ratio analysis

What is a financial ratio?

An accounting ratio or **financial ratio** is simply the comparison of two figures in company accounts produced by dividing one key figure by another, and usually taking a percentage.

Data on profit, sales, or capital employed in a firm alone tells us very little about how well a business is doing. **Ratio analysis** uses financial ratios to make meaningful comparisons of business performance over time and between different firms.

Even simple comparisons of financial data may reveal a great deal. For example, an investor has the choice of either placing money in a safe bank account and earning a guaranteed rate of interest, or risking money by buying shares which might provide a high rate of return - or none at all. Which is the best investment? A simple comparison of two figures could provide the answer. A bank account might pay 8% interest each year - that is, a return of 8 pence in every pound. If a firm received £100,000 in shareholders' funds and earned a profit of £5,000, this is only a return of 5%, which is significantly worse than the 8% which could be earned elsewhere. In this case, the investor would be better off placing savings in the bank. In making such a calculation, the investor is working out a financial ratio or comparing the return on savings with the return on an investment in shares.

The key accounting ratios used by business organizations are:

- **Liquidity ratios** - to measure the ability of a firm to meet its debts
- **Profitability ratios** - to measure how well an organization is doing
- **Activity ratios** - to measure how efficiently a firm is using its resources

Figure 19.5 presents the final accounts for Motorcade plc, a small car retail chain dealing in new and second-hand vehicles. Business managers at Motorcade are confident that performance has improved since 1999. We will use these accounts to show how financial ratios can be used to provide valuable information on business performance.

Liquidity ratios

The **liquidity** of a firm is measured by comparing those assets which can be turned into cash quickly, known as **current assets**, and those liabilities which have to be paid out in the short term, known as **current liabilities** (see 18.2).

▼ *Figure 19.5: Final acounts for Motorcade plc*

MOTORCADE PLC

Profit and Loss Statement for the year ended 31 December 2000

	2000 £000s	1999 £000s
Turnover	1,455	1,380
Less Cost of sales	935	905
Gross profit	520	475
Less overhead expenses	170	150
Net profit	350	325
Less Interest payable	47	39
Profit before tax	303	286
Less Taxation	76	71
Profit after tax	227	215
Less Dividends	180	170
Retained profits	47	45

MOTORCADE PLC

Balance Sheet as at 31 December 2000

	2000 £000s	1999 £000s
Fixed assets	778	743
Current assets		
Stock	218	201
Debtors	130	115
Cash at bank	23	33
	371	**349**
Creditors liabilities		
Creditors - amount falling due within one year	(185)	(180)
Net current assets	**186**	**169**
Total assets less current liabilities	**964**	**912**
Creditors - amount falling due after one year	(260)	(270)
Net assets	**704**	**642**
Capital and reserves		
Called-up share capital	307	257
Share premium account	350	340
Retained profits	47	45
Shareholders funds	**704**	**642**

If a firm has plenty of assets which can easily be converted to cash in order to meet liabilities which are due to be paid out soon, it is said to be **liquid.** If, however, it is **illiquid,** it may have to obtain an expensive bank loan or sell off important fixed assets, such as machinery, to raise cash in order to meet its business debts.

Liquidity ratios, also known as **solvency ratios**, are useful as they can give early warning of financial problems which might occur if there is a sudden demand for cash.

Current ratio

The ability of a firm to meet its short-term debts is measured by a liquidity ratio known as the current ratio, where:

$$\text{Current Ratio} = \frac{\textbf{Current Assets (£)}}{\textbf{Current Liabilities (£)}}$$

A generally accepted rule is that current assets should be about double current liabilities, to give a current ratio of 2:1. Any lower, and a firm could be in danger of running out of cash. A ratio any higher than 2:1 means that too much money is tied up in cash and not enough is being invested, either in interest-earning bank accounts or in capital equipment.

A ratio of less than 1:1 means that current liabilities exceed current assets, and the firm will not be able to pay its immediate debts and may have to sell some of its fixed assets.

Using the balance sheet for Motorcade plc in Figure 19.5, the current ratio may be calculated for 1999 and 2000 as follows:

Current ratios for Motorcade plc:

	1999	2000
Current assets (£000) : Current liabilities (£000) :	$\frac{349}{180} = 1.94{:}1$	$\frac{371}{185} = 2{:}1$

Motorcade PLC has therefore maintained a reasonable level of liquidity in both 1999 and 2000.

Acid test ratio

An alternative ratio for measuring liquidity is known as the **liquidity ratio** or **acid test ratio.**

$$\textbf{Acid Test Ratio} = \frac{\textbf{Current Assets (£) – Value of Stock (£)}}{\textbf{Current Liabilities (£)}}$$

The acid test ratio excludes stocks of finished products and materials from the calculation of current assets. That is, the ratio measures whether or not a business is able to meet its short-term debts without having to sell off stocks. This is because when a firm needs to raise cash quickly, it may be quite difficult to sell its stocks of finished goods.

As a general rule, an acid test ratio of 1:1, where current assets minus stocks equals current liabilities, is considered reasonably safe for a business, because it can meet all its short-term debts without having to sell off stocks. If the ratio falls below 1:1, then the firm could face problems if all its creditors demand to be paid in full at the same time. In this case, it would need to sell stocks to meet these debts and, should this not be possible, either borrow the money or sell fixed assets.

Acid test for Motorcade Ltd:

	1999	2000
Current assets less stock (£000): Current liabilities (£000) :	$\frac{349 - 201}{180} = 0.82$	$\frac{371 - 218}{185} = 0.83$

Using the acid test ratio, Motorcade displays a reasonable level of liquidity, although the business managers should be careful not to let this ratio fall any further below 1: 1 in future years by reducing their current liabilities.

Profitability ratios

There are a number of ratios which can be used to measure how well a business is doing. These are:

- Gross profit margin
- Net profit margin
- Return On Capital Employed (ROCE)

Gross profit margin

The gross profit margin is a measure of how much total profit is made as a percentage of sales. The ratio is a measure of trading efficiency. The higher the percentage, the better the business trading performance.

$$\textbf{Gross Profit Margin (\%)} = \frac{\textbf{Gross Profit (£)} \times \textbf{100}}{\textbf{Turnover (£)}}$$

Using the profit and loss statement in Figure 19.5 the gross profit margin for Motorcade PLC is calculated as follows:

	1999	2000
Gross Profit (£000) : Turnover (£000)	$\frac{475}{1,380} \times 100 = 34.4\%$	$\frac{520}{1,455} \times 100 = 35.7\%$

That is, in 2000 every £1 of sales at Motorcade generated just under 36 pence in profit - a very good result.

Net profit margin

Net profit is arrived at after overhead expenses, such as electricity, telephones, and gas, have been paid out from gross profit. The difference between gross and net profit therefore gives an indication of a firm's ability to control its costs. The higher the net profit margin, the smaller the difference between costs and revenues.

$$\textbf{Net Profit Margin (\%)} = \frac{\textbf{Net Profit (£)}}{\textbf{Turnover (£)}} \times \textbf{100}$$

The net and gross profit margins provide a useful means of judging business performance when comparing performance across two or more years. If gross margins stay constant but net margins decrease, this means that overheads must have increased during the year. With this information, management may wish to investigate cost control and budgeting for overhead costs.

For example, sales staff may spend increasing amounts on entertaining clients with expensive lunches in order to generate sales and earn more commission. Whilst gross profits will stay high due to extra sales, net profits may begin to fall, because of the increased expense involved in earning these extra sales. In this case, the self-interest of sales staff in earning high commission works against the good of the firm, because it leads to lower net profits. By monitoring changes in net profit margins over time, business managers can identify any potential future problems and take corrective action.

Motorcade plc net profit margins:

	1999	2000
Net Profit (£000) : Turnover (£000)	$\frac{325}{1,380} \times 100 = 23.5\%$	$\frac{350}{1,455} \times 100 = 24\%$

Return On Capital Employed (ROCE)

This ratio expresses the net profit of a business as a percentage of the total value of its capital invested in fixed and current assets.

$$\textbf{Return on Capital Employed (\%)} = \frac{\textbf{Net profit (£)}}{\textbf{Total Assets (£)}} \times \textbf{100}$$

The return on capital should ideally be higher than the rate of interest a business could earn by placing money in a bank or building society account. If not, then the business might just as well convert its assets to cash and put the money into an interest-earning account.

In limited companies, the business owners are its shareholders and they expect to be paid a dividend from company profits. They will clearly be interested in earning more from their money invested in shares than they would get from an interest-earning account, or from investing their money in another business venture. The ROCE ratio allows them to compare all these alternatives. In general, the more risky the business environment, the more the ROCE investors will expect to earn.

The higher the ROCE, the better for business owners. Profits are high, and therefore the dividends on their shares will be healthy. Judge for yourself if Motorcade plc is making a good return on capital employed, by comparing its rate of return with the rate that could currently be earned on savings accounts.

Return on capital employed in Motorcade plc:

	1999	2000
$\frac{\text{Net Profit (£000)}}{\text{Total Assets (£000)}}$	$\frac{325}{1{,}092} \times 100 = 29.7\%$	$\frac{350}{1{,}149} \times 100 = 30.5\%$

Return on net assets

This is very similar to ROCE, but measures the ratio on long-term capital only. Short-term sources of capital, such as creditors, are excluded. Deducting current liabilities from total assets in the balance sheet gives a figure for net capital employed or net assets.

$$\textbf{Return on Net Assets (\%)} = \frac{\textbf{Net Profit (£)}}{\textbf{Net Assets (£)}} \times 100$$

This ratio should be higher than ROCE, because net assets will be less than total capital employed.

Activity (or performance) ratios

There are a number of ratios which examine whether or not a business is using its resources efficiently. These include:

- Administration to sales
- Asset turnover
- Stock turnover
- Debt collection period

Administration expenses to sales

Another way in which a business can monitor how well it is controlling its costs is by calculating the ratio of administration or overhead expenses to sales revenue or turnover. The larger the percentage of sales revenues used to pay for administration expenses, the worse the cost control performance of the firm.

$$\textbf{Administration to Sales (\%)} = \frac{\textbf{Administration Expenses (£)}}{\textbf{Sales Revenue (£)}} \times 100$$

Administration expenses as a percentage of sales for Motorcade plc were as follows:

	1999	2000
$\frac{\text{Administration Expenses (£000)}}{\text{Turnover (£000)}}$	$\frac{150}{1{,}380} \times 100 = 10.9\%$	$\frac{170}{1{,}455} \times 100 = 11.7\%$

Motorcade plc has a good record of cost control. However, the slight rise in the proportion of total sales used to pay for overheads in 2000 may cause some concern for business managers, who may want to keep a tight control on these expenses in the following year.

Asset turnover

Since the net assets of a business represent the value of the capital invested in it, it is useful to see how many times a business can generate sales in a year equal to the value of its capital or net assets. **Asset turnover** is a measure of the number of times that net assets are 'turned over' in sales in a year. The more times this happens, the more productive the business is.

$$\textbf{Asset Turnover} = \frac{\textbf{Turnover (£)}}{\textbf{Value of Net Assets (£)}}$$

We can calculate the asset turnover ratio for Motorcade plc by taking sales revenues from the profit and loss statement and net assets from the balance sheet, as follows:

	1999	2000
Turnover (£000) : / Net Assets (£000) :	$\frac{1,380}{704} = 1.96$	$\frac{1,455}{642} = 2.26$

That is, in 2000 Motorcade generated sales of 2.26 times the value of its net assets.

Stock turnover

The **stock turnover ratio** measures the number of times in a year that a business sells the value of its stocks. It is a measure of business activity. The faster the rate of sales, the more times stocks will need to be replaced. If sales are poor, stocks will build up, indicated by a low and falling ratio, and production will have to be cut.

$$\textbf{Stock Turnover} = \frac{\textbf{Turnover (£)}}{\textbf{Value of Stocks (£)}}$$

The stock turnover ratio for Motorcade plc can be found by taking the sales figure from the profit and loss statement and the value of stocks figure from the balance sheet:

	1999	2000
Turnover (£000) : / Value of Stocks (£000) :	$\frac{1,380}{201} = 6.86$	$\frac{1,455}{218} = 6.67$

Therefore, Motorcade had to replace its stock of cars roughly 7 times in each year. Generally, the higher the rate of stock turnover, the better the sales performance of the firm. Ratios of around 6–7 are probably acceptable for a car dealer.

What is an acceptable level of stock turnover will vary with the type of business. For example, a high-quality jeweller may only replace his or her stock of expensive rings and necklaces once each year, whilst a bakery would expect to replace its stock of fresh bread every day, giving a ratio of 365.

Debt collection period

It is possible to measure how well a firm is controlling the giving of credit to its customers by calculating the average amount of time taken by debtors to pay their invoices.

Most firms give credit to their trade customers. The credit period will vary by the type of firm. Typically, firms will give trade customers up to 60 days to pay invoices for goods or services delivered. If debtors are taking longer than this to pay, it indicates that the firm may have given credit unwisely and could be left with bad debts. However, some large firms may give credit for 90 days, while some small firms may struggle if their debts are not repaid within 30 days.

Because it is assumed that debtors will pay their invoices in the near future, sales on credit are treated as a current asset in the balance sheet. However, the larger the proportion of sales accounted for by credit sales, the more serious the consequences for the business if some of the debtors fail to pay.

Businesses can calculate the average number of days it takes for debtors to settle their debts. To do this, it is first necessary to work out the figure for an average day's sales, by dividing total sales revenue by 365 days in a year. The next step is to calculate how many average days' sales is represented by the debtors figure:

$$\text{Debt Collection Period (Days)} = \frac{\text{Debtors (£)}}{\text{Average Daily Sales (£)}}$$

$$= \frac{\text{Debtors(£)}}{\text{Turnover (£)/365}}$$

For example, a firm may have average daily sales of £300 and total credit sales during a year of £6,000. This means that the debtors figure represents on average 20 days of sales revenues (i.e. £6,000/£300). That is, debtors take on average 20 days to settle invoices. Or, to look at it another way, it would take another 20 days of sales to cover the credit sales to debtors if they should all fail to pay up within an agreed period.

The average debt collection period in Motorcade plc can be found by taking sales in each year from the profit and loss statement in Figure 19.5 and dividing by 365, and then dividing this into the debtors figure found on the balance sheet:

	1999	2000
Debtors : / Turnover/365 :	$\frac{£115,000}{£3,780.80} = 30.4$ days	$\frac{£130,000}{£3,986.30} = 32.6$ days

In 1999, customers owing money to Motorcade paid up, on average, 30.4 days after receiving an invoice. In 2000, this had increased to an average of just under 33 days. As both figures are within the typical 60-day credit period, this does not indicate that the firm has a credit control problem. If the figure was greater than 60 days, this would indicate that some of the debtors had gone beyond the normal period of credit and so are unlikely to pay. In this case, the firm should review its policy on giving credit.

Long delays in receiving payments from debtors can create cashflow problems for a business. Businesses will, therefore, normally operate a system of credit control, using an aged debtors list (see 17.3). This lists the names and the 'ages' of the debts of all the firm's debtors. The business can then concentrate on collecting the oldest, or longest-outstanding, debts. Those debts that cannot be recovered after written warnings and even legal action are written off as bad debts.

Performance indicators

To complete the picture of past performance, there are a host of other indicators an organization might use. For example:

- Advertising costs per unit of sales
- Output per employee
- Average time taken to produce a unit of output
- Staff absenteeism
- Man days lost due to illness, machine breakdowns, disputes, etc.
- Number of faulty or sub-standard goods
- Number of customer complaints
- Average response time to customer orders

Portfolio Activity 19.2 

1. Write to a well-known public limited company of your choice, and ask them to send you a copy of their most recent annual report and accounts.
2. Study the profit and loss statement and balance sheet for your chosen company and calculate as many financial ratios as you can.
3. Comment briefly on the performance of your chosen company over the two-year period reported in the accounts.
4. What other information might be useful to examine the overall performance of the company?

The limitations of financial ratios

Although financial ratios are very helpful in analysing accounts, they have some important limitations.

- Accounting information alone cannot tell us everything about company performance. For example, accounts give no indication of changes in economic conditions, changes in the activities of a business - for example, the release of a new product - or about the quality of a firm's workforce, all of which can affect business performance.
- The balance sheet is simply a snapshot of performance at a particular moment. If the business is a seasonal one, like a seaside hotel, the balance sheet might look particularly healthy during the summer months, but this will not give a true picture of the overall performance of the business throughout the year.
- Different firms may compile their accounts in different ways - for example, in the way they value stocks, or account for the impact of price inflation on the value of assets such as land and buildings. This makes inter-firm comparisons difficult. Additionally, firms may have financial years which end on different dates, which also makes comparison difficult, especially where seasonal factors affect the business.

- Past performance may be a poor guide to future performance. Any analysis of past accounting information to inform future decision-making and business planning must be treated with caution.

Non-financial business objectives

Many firms have non-financial objectives which represent important targets that cannot be measured simply by looking at the financial performance of the company. Increasingly, firms are becoming aware of environmental issues and are setting targets relating to cleaning up their production processes, reducing waste, and repairing environmental damage caused by their past activities. Customer care is also important in an increasingly competitive business environment.

Objectives like these are usually outlined in the annual company report and accounts, together with a review of how well the company has progressed towards achieving them, for example, through buying wood from renewable sources and not from tropical rainforests, abolishing tests of cosmetics on animals, etc. With an increasing number of green consumers, firms are unlikely to be able to continue to make profits without taking an increasingly public environmental stance.

Portfolio Activity 19.3 

Here are a selection of accounting ratios for a firm, calculated over successive years. What do these ratios mean and what do they reveal about the performance of the business over time?

	1998	1999	2000
Gross profit as a percentage of sales	33%	35%	42%
Net profit as a percentage of sales	19%	21%	26%
Rate of return on capital employed	8%	9%	12%
Current ratio	1:1	1.4:1	2:1
Debt collection period	95 days	97 days	40 days
Stock turnover	5	5.2	6

Key words:

Ratio analysis - a way of interpreting accounting information by comparing two figures from company accounts, usually expressing one as a percentage of another, for example, profits as a percentage of turnover

Liquidity ratios - ratios measuring the extent to which assets, which can be quickly converted into cash, are available to a firm to meet its liabilities as they become due. These include the current ratio and acid test ratio

Profitability ratios - ratios that measure the profitability of a business

Net profit margin - measures a firm's ability to control overhead costs and expresses net profit as a percentage of turnover

Return On Capital Employed (ROCE) - a measure of the productivity of business capital, calculated by expressing the net profit of a business as a percentage of the value of its total assets

Activity ratios - ratios that examine how efficiently a firm is using its resources, including ratios for administration expenses to sales, stock and asset turnover

Asset turnover - the amount of times total sales generate the same value as the net assets of a business in a trading period

Stock turnover - the number of times in a year a firm has to replace its stock of finished or semi-finished goods

Debt collection period - the average number of days taken by debtors to pay their invoices

Aged debtors list - a list of debtors' names and the 'age' of their outstanding invoices

Section 19.4 Stock market performance

What is the stock market?

Issuing shares

Public limited companies are able to raise finance from the sale of new loans stocks and shares to people and other organizations on the stock market (see 2.2). The stock market consists of all those people and organizations that want to buy and sell stocks shares in public limited companies.

A **share** is simply part of a company offered for sale. The price printed on the front of a share certificate is its **face value**. That is, the price at which it is first offered for sale. The people and organizations that buy shares in a company become part owners of that company and are known as **shareholders.** Shares do not have to be repaid by the company that issued them. However, shareholders can sell their shares on to other people and firms. In contrast, loan stocks are repaid with a fixed rate of interest (see 23.3).

Public limited companies can issue different types of shares to raise finance. Ordinary shares are the most common. They are also known as equities. Equity holders have voting rights. That is, they can vote on who runs their company and the way it is run (see below).

The role of the Stock Exchange

Private limited companies can only sell shares to people connected with the business in some way, such as family, friends, workers, etc. (see 2.2). This limits their ability to raise finance through the issue of shares. However, a company that 'goes public', i.e. becomes a public limited company (plc), will obtain a listing on the Stock Exchange and be able to

Types of shares

Preference shares

These pay a **fixed dividend**. For example, a preference share worth 100 pence with a fixed return of 10% will pay a 10 pence dividend per year. However, if no profit is made, then no dividend is paid. If the shares are **cumulative preference shares**, profits not paid in one year will be paid in the next year in which profits are made.

Even if a company has a very profitable year, preference shareholders receive no more than the fixed rate of return, unless they hold **participating preference shares**. This type of share allows its holder to receive a sum out of profits in addition to their fixed dividend, after other shareholders have been paid their dividends.

Redeemable preference shares are issued for a specified period of time, after which they will be repaid by the company.

Preference shareholders are not usually allowed to vote for company directors at annual general meetings. Companies can raise capital by selling preference shares without the existing owners losing control.

Ordinary shares

These are the most commonly issued type of share. According to *ONS Financial Statistics*, UK companies raised around £12 billion from new issues in 1999, compared with just £137 million raised from the sale of new preference shares.

Ordinary shares (or **equities**) pay a dividend based on what is left from profits after interest on loans and dividends to preference shareholders have been paid, and after some profit has been retained for future investment.

Holding ordinary shares can be risky, because the price of the shares can go up and down, depending upon the performance of the company and the opinions of investors as to its future performance. In addition, the dividend payment may also fluctuate depending on the amount of profit made, and how much of this profit company directors decide to pay out to shareholders.

Owners of ordinary shares are allowed to vote. One vote per share is allowed, and voting takes place at the **annual general meeting (AGM)**. At the AGM, directors report on how the company has performed in the previous twelve months, and shareholders vote on whether or not they wish the present directors to continue in post.

advertise and sell a new issue of shares to members of the public from all over the world. The launch of a company's shares on the Stock Exchange is known as a **flotation.**

Before an organization can offer its shares for sale, the Council of the Stock Exchange will investigate it to ensure it is trustworthy and meets certain standards of practice and size. For example, a company must have authorized share capital of at least £50,000, of which it must sell at least a quarter. People will then buy shares in return for a share of any profits made, called a **dividend.** Once a share is sold, the company does not have to return the money to the shareholder. If shareholders want their money back, they can sell the shares to somebody else. If they are able to sell them for more than they paid, they will make a **capital gain.** The Stock Exchange provides a market for so-called 'second-hand securities' in plcs.

Stock Exchanges run markets for buying and selling new and second-hand loan stocks and shares, or **securities.** The main **Stock Exchange** in the United Kingdom is in London but it has offices in other parts of the country. It is part of the world stock market and has the following main functions:

- it determines the structure of the markets for different securities
- it makes rules and regulations for the way in which the markets work in order to protect the interest of people and firms who buy securities
- it supervises the conduct of the member firms buying and selling shares on the stock market
- it provides up-to-the-minute information on share prices and trading

Without the Stock Exchange it would be difficult for companies to raise capital. It would be difficult and possibly expensive for shareholders to search for other people and firms to sell their shares to. This would mean fewer shares are likely to be sold in the first place.

The are three main stock markets for shares in public limited companies. These are:

- **The UK equity market.** The Stock Exchange deals with the buying and selling of securities in thousands of large UK public limited company securities. A listed company is one that has been allowed by the council to sell its shares on the Stock Exchange. The total value of UK equities traded in 1999 was just over £1,400 billion.
- **The international equity market.** The London Stock Exchange has an international reputation for its strength in dealing in the shares of international companies. Two thirds of all share trading deals in London are in the shares of international companies. In 1998, international equity sales reached a high of £2,183 billion. On average each share deal was worth £386,000 compared with £64,000 for the average UK share transaction.
- **The Alternative Investment Market (AIM).** AIM is the London Stock Exchange's market for shares in small and growing companies. The requirements to join AIM are straightforward and there are few rules. There is no minimum size that a business has to be to join and no requirement to show a lengthy business history. The Alternative

Investment Market enables small firms to raise capital by having their shares traded widely. Firms wishing to join must employ an advisor from a list kept by the Stock Exchange. The role of the advisor is to ensure that the firm understands and complies with Stock Exchange rules.

▼ *Buying and selling shares is easy. Many market makers are now available on-line to buy and sell shares*

Buying and selling shares

The Stock Exchange is not open to the general public. This means that if a member of the public wishes to buy or sell some shares they must contact a share dealing firm (or **broker**) which is a member of the Stock Exchange.

The market in stocks and shares is worldwide and growing all the time. This means that share dealers must have very large sums of money in order to be able to buy and sell shares on the stock market. Because of the need for large sums of money, many professional share dealers on the Stock Exchange work for firms owned by banks and other large financial institutions.

A member of the public who wishes to buy or sell shares can either contact a broker for advice on stocks and shares or go to the nearest branch of their bank who will employ their own brokers. Even some Marks and Spencer stores and large supermarkets offer share-dealing services.

Brokers will buy and sell shares for the public for a fee known as **commission**. Suppose a customer wished to buy 1000 shares in Manchester United plc at no more than £10 a share. The broker and the customer agree a commission to be paid to the broker for undertaking the work. For example, this might be a charge of 1% of the total cost of the shares. The broker will now attempt to buy shares in Manchester United plc at the lowest possible price from other firms of brokers called **market makers**, usually by placing an order on the Stock Exchange computerized share-dealing system. Market makers are special brokers or dealers who create the market in shares. They do this by always being willing to buy and sell shares with other brokers or dealers. These market makers make their profit by selling shares they hold at a higher price than the price they paid for them.

Much of the share trading on the Stock Exchange is done using share information presented on computer screens around the world connected to the London Stock Exchange via the Internet. Market makers will display the prices at which they will buy and sell shares and the number of shares that they will trade. Market makers are in competition to offer the best prices and they make their profits by buying and selling shares at a profit.

Share prices are displayed on a continuously updated computer database called the **SEAQ (Stock Exchange Automated Quotation).** Up-to-the-minute share prices are available on information services around the world. The SEAQ screen shows a yellow strip which identifies the best bid and offer price for every SEAQ share, and it identifies up to four market making firms offering this price.

Share prices and company financial performance

Prices, profits and dividends

Movements in share prices can reveal much about how well companies are performing. Like the price of any other commodity, share prices reflect changes in market demand and supply conditions (see 5.1). The market price at which a 'second-hand' share is sold can be above or below its face value - the price it was first issued at.

Consider why people and other organizations buy shares in public limited companies. There are two main financial reasons:

1. because they want to make a **capital gain** from selling their shares at a higher price than they paid for them
2. because they want to receive **dividends**, or a share in the profits of the company

Thus, the people and firms who buy and sell shares will speculate on future share prices and dividends in the hope of making financial gains. Therefore, anything that could affect the eventual profits of a company will affect the prices of shares in that company and the likely dividend payouts shareholders can expect.

For example, if a company announces poor profits, shareholders may want to sell their shares in that company and buy shares in a more profitable one. The increase in supply of the company's shares on the stock market, coupled with falling demand for them, will cause the shares prices to fall.

In contrast, the demand for shares in a company and their market prices may rise significantly if shareholders think the company is about to merge with another large company. The formation of a larger, more powerful organization with potentially lower costs, a bigger market share and higher profits will mean that shareholders may receive larger dividend payouts on their shares. As the demand for the shares in the company rises relative to their supply, the prices at which the shares are traded will tend to rise. However, if the speculators are wrong and the merger does not go ahead, the demand for shares in the affected company, and their prices, may fall sharply again.

Bears, bulls and stags

The people and organizations who buy shares in the hope their price will rise so that they can sell them at a profit are called **bulls**. The stock market is called **bullish** if share prices are rising in general.

People and firms who sell shares in the hope their price will fall so that they can buy them back later at much lower prices are called **bears**. When share prices are falling the stock market is called **bearish**. 'Bears' buy the shares back despite their falling prices because they believe their prices will rise again in the long run and that dividend payments from company profits could be good.

People and firms who apply to buy up newly issued shares in the hope their price will rise quickly after dealing begins are called **stags**.

Shares can go up and down in price

The news article below illustrates just how risky it can be holding shares in companies. Some people have gained and lost fortunes overnight just because their shareholdings have unexpectedly jumped or fallen in value.

▼ *Financial Times Stockwatch*

Scotia disturbed by volatile market

Robert Dow, chief executive of Scotia, the biotechnology group, has warned that the recent share price volatility in the sector could prevent companies from raising money.

Over the past few weeks, biotech stocks in both the UK and US have risen sharply as many investors switched from internet and high-technology companies.

The rise was briefly halted last week, when a statement by the UK and US governments on gene research prompted selling.

It was "disturbing to be in a market so dominated by sentiment," said Dr Dow, adding that the price swings could hinder some companies' ability to raise funds.

Dr Dow said Scotia's shares - which closed down 6 per cent at 180p yesterday - had moved less than some of its rivals because the market was awaiting news of a partner for Foscan, its light-activated compound for the treatment of head and neck cancer.

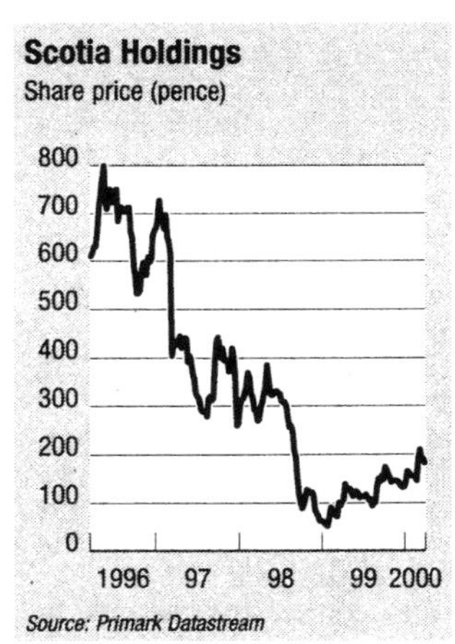

Financial Times, 24.3.2000

The prices at which shares in a company are traded on the stock market may fall because:

- the company is experiencing falling sales and market share
- there is increasing competition from other organizations
- the company is expected to announce low profits or has issued a poor profits warning
- actual profits are lower than expected
- dividend forecasts are lower than expected
- there is an unfavourable takeover bid by another company
- there are strikes and disruption by company workers
- a good senior manager announces s/he is leaving
- the company has lost a major business customer
- Government policies affect the company adversely, for example, increasing taxes on cigarettes will reduce the demand and potential for profit for cigarette producers
- the UK or world economy is moving into recession (this will tend to depress share prices generally)

In contrast, share prices in a company may rise if:

- company sales and market share are rising
- the company is expected to announce big gains in profits
- actual profits are higher than expected
- dividend forecasts are better than expected
- an favourable takeover bid is launched by another company
- there are improved productivity and lower costs
- a well-respected businessperson is elected to the board of directors
- the company has won significant new orders
- Government policies benefit the company - for example, reduced corporation taxes on profits
- the UK or world economy is booming (this will tend to boost share prices generally)

Shareholder ratios

If there are sufficient profits after tax, most companies will pay out a dividend twice a year, an **interim dividend** (for the first 6 months of their accounting or financial year) and a **final dividend** (at the end of the financial year). A dividend is declared as a percentage of the face value of a share, for example a 10% dividend would pay 5 pence on every £2 share in the company. A shareholder with 10,000 shares would, therefore, receive a total dividend of £500 (i.e. 10,000 × 5p). This doesn't sound a very good return on money invested in shares if £20,000 of shares in another company would earn more than £500 or earn more even if placed in a building society savings account.

However, because share prices can move up or down, it is more meaningful to use stock market prices rather than the face values of shares to calculate performance ratios such as the dividend yield and the price earnings ratio for shares.

Dividend yield

The dividend yield is the percentage return on the stock market price of a share. It is calculated as:

$$\textbf{Yield \%} = \frac{\textbf{Dividend paid}}{\textbf{Market price of share}} \times \textbf{100}$$

So if the dividend paid out is 10 pence a share and those shares are currently trading at £4 each, then the yield on them is just

$$\text{Yield \%} = \frac{10\text{ pence}}{400\text{ pence}} \times 100 = 2.5\%$$

This seems quite low. However, lower yields tend to reflect companies with growth potential. Companies that produce very high yields tend to be riskier investments. A fall in their profits could hit share prices and dividends significantly.

Earnings per share (EPS)

This shows the relationship between profits and the number of issued ordinary shares in a company. It is calculated as

$$\textbf{EPS} = \frac{\textbf{Net profit after tax}}{\textbf{Total number of ordinary shares issued}}$$

The earnings per share shows what ordinary shareholders could expect to be paid as a dividend. So, for example, if a company has made a net profit after tax of £150,000 and had issued 1.2 million ordinary shares then the EPS would be:

$$\text{EPS} = \frac{£150{,}000}{1{,}200{,}000} = 12.5\text{ pence}$$

Ordinary shareholders may not be paid a 12.5 pence dividend for each share they hold because some profit may be retained by the company to re-invest in new plant and machinery (see 18.3). However, retained profits are shareholders' funds and will eventually be returned to them, either as future dividends or capital gains on their shares, if they are used to boost profits further.

Share price indices

The **FTSE 100 Index** (often called the 'footsie') provides an up-to-date summary of the market prices of shares in the top 100 UK companies. It is recalculated every minute relative to a base value of 1,000 in 1984. At the close of trading on Monday 15 January 2001 the FTSE 100 index was 6170.3, which means the share prices of the top 100 companies had increased by an average of just under 617% since 1984.

Other share price indices are also available. For example, the Dow-Jones index tracks the prices of shares traded on the New York stock exchange in the USA and the Nikkei tracks the prices of shares traded on the Tokyo stock exchange in Japan.

▼ *FTSE 100 Index, 1.1.1996 – 15.1.2001*

Source: www.bloomberg.com

Price earnings ratio (P/E)

This is the market price of the share divided by the earnings per share.

$$\text{P/E ratio} = \frac{\textbf{Market price per share}}{\textbf{Earnings per share}}$$

Thus, a share with a market price of 400 pence and an EPS of 12.5 pence would have a P/E of:

$$\text{P/E ratio} = \frac{400 \text{ pence}}{12.5 \text{ pence}} = 32$$

The P/E ratio is one of the most widely used indicators of company performance. It calculates for a shareholder or would-be shareholder in a company, the true return on his or her investment in shares, even if not all company profits are returned as dividends.

Generally, companies with a good performance record and strong profits growth tend to have a high P/E ratio. In contrast, companies with a poor profits record will tend to have low P/E ratio. Investors in shares can, therefore, compare the P/E ratios of different companies to determine

Portfolio Activity 19.4

Play the Stock Market!

Imagine you have £10,000 to invest in the shares of different companies in different industrial sectors. Your holding of shares will be known as your **portfolio**. Choose your shares from those listed every day at the back of newspapers like the Financial Times and the Independent, or use information from on-line share dealing services like www.moneyworld.co.uk, or the guest prices pages at www.marketeye.co.uk.

Assume for the moment that you want to invest all your money in the shares of Rolls-Royce. The number of shares you can buy at a price of 200 pence per share would be 5,000. If the price of shares rose to 300 pence each the following week, your portfolio would be worth £15,000 (5,000 x 300 pence).

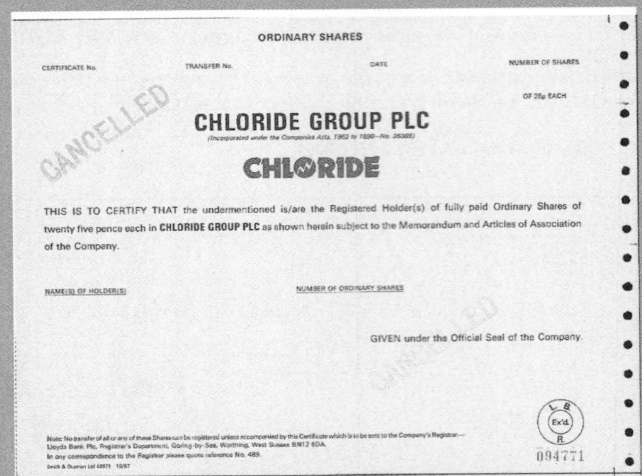

ORDINARY SHARES

CERTIFICATE No. TRANSFER No. DATE NUMBER OF SHARES

OF 25p EACH

CANCELLED

CHLORIDE GROUP PLC

(Incorporated under the Companies Acts, 1862 to 1890—No. 35365)

CHLORIDE

THIS IS TO CERTIFY THAT the undermentioned is/are the Registered Holder(s) of fully paid Ordinary Shares of twenty five pence each in **CHLORIDE GROUP PLC** as shown herein subject to the Memorandum and Articles of Association of the Company.

NAME(S) OF HOLDER(S) NUMBER OF ORDINARY SHARES

GIVEN under the Official Seal of the Company.

Note: No transfer of all or any of these Shares can be registered unless accompanied by this Certificate which is to be sent to the Company's Registrar— Lloyds Bank Plc, Registrar's Department, Goring-by-Sea, Worthing, West Sussex BN12 6DA.
In any correspondence to the Registrar please quote reference No. 489.

L B Ex'd. R

094771

The aim of this game is to double your money from capital gains. Compete against students in your class. The person with a portfolio worth nearest to £20,000 after six months wins.

To play you must follow these rules:

1. You are only allowed to hold shares in up to 10 different companies at any one time.
2. If you want to revise your portfolio, you may do so only on one day each week to be agreed by all the players in the game.
3. Every time you buy or sell shares, no matter what their value, you will have to pay a stockbroker £50 from your portfolio.

During the game:

- Obtain information on past company performance. Write to those companies you intend to buy shares in and ask for copies of their annual reports.
- Calculate an index number series of the average value of your shareholdings on the same day each week, using a computer spreadsheet. Compare the movement in the value of your share portfolio with changes in the FTSE 100. Is your portfolio performing better or worse than all other shares? If your portfolio is underperforming (i.e. the average value of your portfolio is falling or rising at a slower rate than the FT index) you may wish to reconsider your shareholdings and sell them in order to buy shares which are rising faster.
- Watch the market. Read the financial press, listen to the business news, get on-line company information, or use the on-line financial news at www.news.bbc.co.uk. What companies are about to announce profits? Are profit expectations high or low? How might changes in the UK and world economy affect your companies? How will these factors affect your decision to hold shares?
- Keep a detailed record of the shares you buy and sell on your computer spreadsheet, and justify your decisions in writing. You may discuss possible purchases with 'financial advisers' (e.g. your parents, guardians, or teachers).

▼ *How to read the Financial pages in newspapers (layout may differ)*

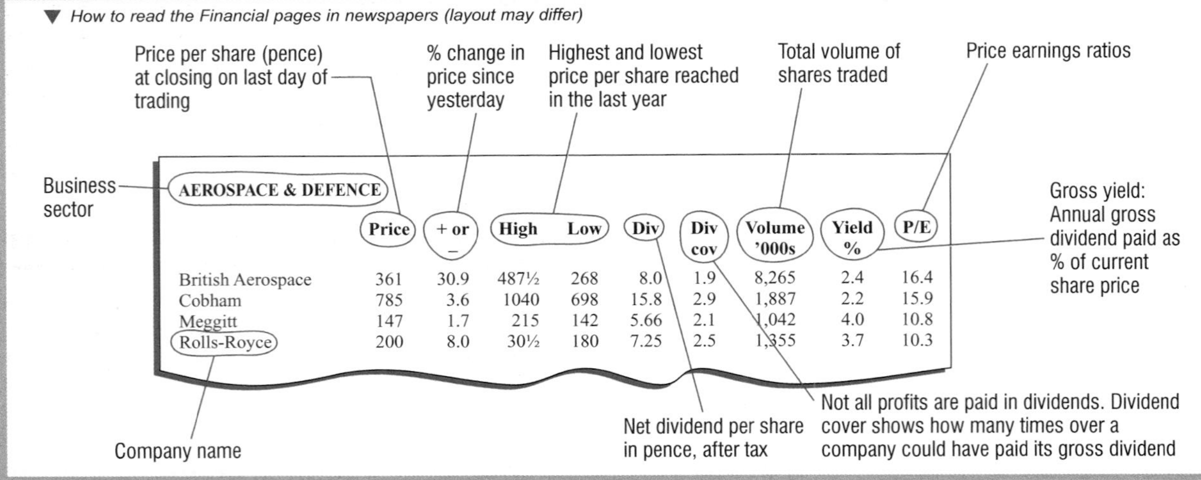

AEROSPACE & DEFENCE	Price	+ or –	High	Low	Div	Div cov	Volume '000s	Yield %	P/E
British Aerospace	361	30.9	487½	268	8.0	1.9	8,265	2.4	16.4
Cobham	785	3.6	1040	698	15.8	2.9	1,887	2.2	15.9
Meggitt	147	1.7	215	142	5.66	2.1	1,042	4.0	10.8
Rolls-Royce	200	8.0	30½	180	7.25	2.5	1,355	3.7	10.3

which shares are likely to be the better investment. However, P/E ratios, like share prices and the financial performance of companies that are used to calculate them, can change over time. So, it is also useful to look at how the P/E ratio of a company has changed over time. A rising P/E ratio is probably a good thing because it suggests improving company performance. A falling P/E ratio, unless a temporary event, could indicate fundamental company problems and a poor investment opportunity.

Key words:

Share - a certificate of part ownership in a limited company

Face value - the price at which shares are first issued

Listing - obtaining permission to sell shares through the Stock Exchange

Flotation - when shares are sold in a public limited company for the first time

Dividend - a proportion of company profits paid per share in that company

Capital gain - an increase in the market value of shares

Preference shares - shares which are entitled to a fixed dividend if sufficient profits are made

Ordinary shares - shares in the ownership of a limited company which allow their holders to vote at annual general meetings. Dividends are variable depending on profits.

Equities - ordinary shares

Price earnings ratio - the dividend paid out per share as a percentage of the closing price of that share on the stock market

Key Activity

1. Obtain the final accounts of two large public limited companies of your choice in the same industry.
2. You have been asked to advise a large bank that is keen to invest money in the shares of these companies. You are to produce a report containing the following information:
   - A brief history of each company
   - Objectives of each company
   - Why accounting information is used by business managers
   - Sources and key components of accounting information
   - How accounts can be used to examine financial performance
   - Evaluation of the financial performance of each company in terms of:
     - liquidity
     - sales
     - profits
     - costs
     - stock turnover
     - share prices
     - dividend payments
   - Whether each organization achieved its targets
   - Reasons for changes in the performance of each company over the two-year period contained in their accounts
   - An inter-firm performance comparison and an evaluation of any differences
   - Your recommendations to the bank - should they buy shares in one or both of these companies? Justify your choice.
3. Use ratio analysis to examine financial performance in your report. Make sure that any calculations are set out clearly and explained.

   To calculate financial ratios from information contained in company accounts, you may use a computer spreadsheet. You will first need to input information in an appropriate format from the profit and loss statement and balance sheets. You may then input formulae referring to the appropriate cells in each case to calculate the various ratios. Always check your calculations.
4. You should also consider any other means of measuring business performance, including performance in meeting non-financial objectives.
5. Also comment on how other factors, including the economic climate, government economic policy, and exchange rates may have affected performance.

Useful references

London Stock Exchange *(www.londonstockexchange.com)*
Information Department, London EC2N 1HP

Nasdaq Stock Market *(www.nasdaq.co.uk)*

Office for National Statistics *(www.ons.gov.uk)*
Public Enquiry Service, 1 Drummond Gate, London SW1V 2QQ

Use the following publications for share price information:

- Office of National Statistics, **'Financial Statistics'** published monthly by The Stationary Office
- **Financial Times** daily newspaper available at newsagents or on-line at *www.news.ft.com*

For the latest financial information on **company information and share prices**, visit:

- *www.fullcoverage.yahoo.com/Full_Coverage/Business/Stock_Markets*
- *www.news.ft-com*
- *www.ft-se.co.uk*

Internet key words search: **Annual Reports, Business, FTSE 100, Stock Market**

Test your knowledge

1 The acid test ratio is used to identify an organization's:

A Profitability
B Use of assets
C Ability to meet its debts
D Long-term liabilities

2 During a trading period, the rate of stock turnover is best described as:

A Total revenue from monthly sales of stocks
B The average level of stocks held per month
C The average cost per month of holding stocks
D The number of times that stocks levels are replaced

3 The ability of a firm to control credit can be measured by:

A Creditors divided by sales
B Debtors divided by daily sales
C Profits divided by debtors
D Debtors divided by creditors

4 Calculating the return on capital employed by a company provides information on:

A Profitability
B How efficiently assets are used
C Liquidity
D Capital structure

5 All of the following are financial performance ratios used by business organizations **except**:

A Return on net assets
B Asset turnover
C Stock turnover
D Acid test ratio

Questions 6–8 are based on the following jumbled financial information for an organization over a 12-month period.

	£000
Turnover	365
Fixed assets	400
Current assets	200
Current liabilities	50
Gross profit	90
Overheads	30
Debtors	60

6 The gross profit margin is:

A 45%
B 28.5%
C 15%
D 24.7%

7 The return on capital employed is:

A 15%
B 22.5%
C 10%
D 16.4%

8 The average debt collection period is:

A 60 days
B 6 days
C 10 days
D 75 days

9 The most likely reason for an adverse variance between the overheads budget and outturn is:

A A cut in the price of electricity
B A machine breakdown on the shop-floor
C An increase in the standing charge for telephone lines
D The purchase of a new, more efficient photocopier

10 If the budget for a particular business activity is zero-based, it means that:

A The business has planned not to spend any more money on it
B It is based on past information adjusted for inflation
C It is fixed until the end of the budget period
D It ignores past information in its preparation

11 A firm will wish to monitor its solvency because:

A It reveals how much profit it is making
B It reveals its ability to cover its debts
C It reveals its tax liabilities
D It reveals information on non-financial targets

12 Explain how and why business organizations monitor their performance using accounting and stockmarket information. Use examples to illustrate your answer.

Business Planning

About this unit

Central to the work of any business is its business plan. Without a well-researched and thought-through plan there is no way of judging whether or not the business is likely to succeed in meeting its objectives. Anyone who applies for start-up finance from a bank or other finance provider will need a clear plan. Providers of finance will then use the plan to judge the business idea and the ability of the owners to translate their objectives into actions.

Business planning is an entrepreneurial skill and can provide you with a firm basis for bringing your business idea to life. In this unit you will produce a plan for your new business venture. It will require you to use the knowledge and understanding you have developed in the other units of this book.

You will find out the market for your product and produce an effective marketing plan. This will involve forecasting potential demand for your product by understanding and analysing the demand and supply conditions of the market within which your business will operate.

You will consider the production of your product and the implications it has for the financial and marketing elements of your overall business plan. You will take account of the resources you will require to produce and market the product efficiently and effectively. You will also investigate financial aspects of your business and prepare a financial plan. This will help you to understand the importance of financial management in the effective planning of an organization.

unit 6

chapter 20 The Business Plan: Preparation and data collection

This chapter introduces the key issues to be considered when preparing the groundwork for a new business proposal in the form of a business plan.

What you need to learn

Businesses will have a range of financial **objectives** including, at the very least, to break even, or to maximize profits. Business managers need to plan in order to achieve objectives.

A standard format for outlining what an organization aims to achieve and how it aims to do this is known as a **business plan**.

Business plans are typically used by firms to present their ideas to potential lenders to raise finance, and as a tool for management to monitor progress towards business objectives.

A good business plan will show an appreciation of competing firms and products, the likely demand and repeat business for a product, and forecasts of sales volumes, values and profits.

Business activities usually have **legal and insurance implications**, and a good business plan will consider how these implications will be managed. The main areas of legislation a business will need to be aware of are employment, health and safety, environmental protection, and consumer protection. A business is required by law to have public, product, and employee liability insurance cover.

The key to good management is to organize the human, physical, and financial **resources** available, in order to achieve the targets or goals of the organization within a given time period. The business plan should detail the kinds of resources required to achieve business goals and how these will be managed.

A business must manage time effectively. Critical activities such as planning, marketing, production and selling should be identified and planned for accordingly.

A wide range of support and advice is available to **entrepreneurs** wishing to start up in business, including small-business advisers, local authority enterprise agencies, accountancy firms, Training and Enterprise Councils, local Chambers of Commerce, and many more. Much of this advice is provided free of charge, or at a low cost.

Section 20.1

So you want to be an entrepreneur?

Starting a new business

Business know-how, or the ability to organize and manage production, is known as **enterprise**. The people who have enterprise are known as **entrepreneurs**. They are the people who take the risks and decisions necessary to make a firm run successfully.

What do entrepreneurs do?

Innovate

Entrepreneurs have business ideas. Shami Ahmed started the 'Joe Bloggs' clothing company. Anita Roddick thought of The Body Shop.

Organize

Entrepreneurs hire resources and organize them to produce goods and services. They decide what to produce, where to locate business premises, methods of production, job specifications, how much labour and capital to employ, wage levels, and prices.

Take risks

Running a business is risky. An entrepreneur may borrow money, or use personal savings to invest in a business to pay for materials, premises, and labour. If the business fails, the entrepreneur will lose this money.

Useful skills in business

Personal skills

Working independently
Working with others
Evaluating your own strengths and weaknesses
Reliability under pressure
Judgement and foresight
Drive and determination

Organizational skills

Planning
Setting targets
Managing time and people
Monitoring and reviewing performance
Problem-solving
Information-seeking and handling

Communication skills

Oral and written skills
Negotiating
Presentation

Numerical skills

Gathering and handling data
Analysis
Mathematical/statistical
Graphical
Accounting and bookkeeping

Information technology

Hands-on experience of hardware and software

Starting a new business is not easy, because there are so many factors an entrepreneur cannot control, for example, legislation affecting the business, changes in taxes, economic conditions, consumer demand, and competition. About one in four businesses fail in their first few years.

Not everybody is suited to organizing and running a business. It means being able to manage yourself and others; to prioritize and organize your own time, and decide what to do, without anyone telling you. Some people enjoy managing themselves, while others prefer to work for someone else and have their work organized for them. Not everyone wants to be in a position of being entirely responsible for their own hours of work, their own earnings, and their own success or failure.

To be successful in business requires a variety of different skills. A small business may not be able to afford to buy in these skills from other people or organizations, and so many small business owners must be 'jacks of all trades'.

Small business owners and managers need to be able to communicate orally and in writing with a wide range of people, from customers and suppliers, to the Inland Revenue and Customs and Excise Department. As they often have to communicate figures to these organizations, skills in numeracy, such as accounting and book-keeping, are also valuable.

Running a business increasingly requires skills in information communication technology. Even the smallest businesses use computers to produce and store business letters and documents, for e-mail, for contacting customers and suppliers over the Internet. Many small businesses have also set up their own websites to advertise their products.

As well as these skills, it is necessary to be able to plan ahead, to manage others, to take decisions, and to solve problems. With an open mind, all of these skills can be learned.

▼ *Figure 20.1: A personal plan for self-employment*

	Achieved	To do	By when?	Support from?
The business Have you chosen a business idea that will suit your personal aptitudes and strengths? Have you identified and taken into account your strengths and weaknesses in relation to running the business on a day-to-day basis? Have you thought about contingency plans for running the business if you should become ill or have an accident? Have you considered your immediate, short-term (1-12 months) and long-term (1-5 years) objectives?				
Sales and marketing Have you identified your main selling points? Have you identified your target market segments and identified their characteristics, including their needs and purchasing behaviour? Have you estimated likely market share and growth of sales? Have you produced projected sales figures for your first year of trading? Have you analysed your strengths, weaknesses, market opportunities, and threats from competition? Have you decided how you will distribute your product? Have you a promotional strategy?				
Costs Have you estimated your costs? Do you know when you will have to pay the costs? Have you worked out break-even levels of output and price?				
Accounting and finance How much working capital will your business require? Have you created a cashflow forecast? Have you anticipated any cashflow problems and worked out a strategy to cope with them? Have you worked out how much you will need, and for what? Have you produced a business plan? Do you need an overdraft in the first year, and have you spoken to the bank about this? Have you identified grants and other sources of external finance which can be used?				
Fixed assets Do you know what fixed assets you will need? Have you worked out where to get them, and on what terms? Have you decided between leasing and buying?				
Location Have you identified a location for the business?				

The successful man is the one who finds out what is the matter with his business before his competitors do.

Roy L. Smith

The person who knows how will always have a job. The person who knows why will always be his boss.

Diane Ravitch

"You need:

- A burning wish to succeed
- A pride in being different
- A desire to be boss
- A realization that success is 90% hard work and tenacity, and only 10% talent!"

Dr Leah Hertz, authoress and businesswoman

In business, good organizational skills are absolutely essential because there is often no one else to tell you what to do and when to do it. Business owners and senior managers stand or fall on their own abilities.

Preparing a plan for business

In order to achieve success in business you need to plan in advance. This will help you to prioritize your objectives and avoid wasting time on unimportant issues.

When considering a business venture you need to investigate, consider and decide upon a wide variety of things. The best way to organize them is to create an **action plan**. The plan should list in order the key things that need to be done, and give timescales for completion, sources of information, advice, and support to be used along the way. An action plan can provide a very useful framework for actions to achieve your objectives.

An example of an action plan is given in Figure 20.1. Because each business is different, this plan will not be appropriate in every case, but it does list some of the important issues to be considered when setting up a new firm. Use this plan to help you devise and complete a personal plan for your business. In the 'Achieved' column, if your answer to a question is Yes, then you should say how; if your answer is No, give reasons.

Plans for your business idea should also consider the effect of statutory regulations. For example, a potential employee might wish to find out about law relating to equal opportunities, and how this might affect the interview process and employment in general. The action plan should also outline sources of useful advice and information.

Section 20.2 What is a business plan?

Portfolio Activity 20.1

1. What objectives do you think Helen Daniels had in starting her business, and how do you think her business objectives may have changed over time?
2. The article suggests Helen spent some time designing her product and planning her business before she got started. What sort of things do you think she would have tried to plan?
3. Imagine now that Helen had not spent time planning her business venture. How might this have hindered her success in business?

Helen Daniels Super duster

HELEN Daniels had become fed up of having to put a duster on the end of a ruler to clean behind her radiators.

"I've always been a one for finding the easiest and quickest way to do something," says the housewife from Haverhill, Suffolk.

"I was a painter and decorator for 16 years and always worked out the short cuts. like putting your brushes in cling-film long before everyone else started it."

Tired of dust flying around. Helen decided one day to take a strip of plastic about 28 inches long and attach two strips of interlining sewn together to make an inch-wide duster.

"It looked like a steam-rollered cricket bat," says Helen, 47.

"I showed to my brother who was in the house at the time, plumbing in my washing machine. He's always thought I was wired up the wrong way and he just laughed.

"He asked what it was called and I told him it was my Flatmate."

Eighteen months on, the Flatmate, which dusts and cleans behind tight spaces, is selling by the tens of thousands through the catalogues and shops of Lakeland.

The handy gizmo is soon to go on sale throughout Europe and Helen, who still packages all her Flatmates herself, has beeome a proficient businesswoman.

It was her son, Philip, 22, who initially convinced her that she had a good idea and that she should patent it.

Armed with advice and paperwork from the Patent Office, Helen did just that. She also hired a reputable patent agent and, with help and advice from the Government-sponsored Business Link, she produced a plan for her business and then set up her own firm.

"I then went about finding the right fabric to use. It was diffieult because the banks wouldn't help."

Eventually Helen found a fabric which soaked up liquids like a sponge.

With an industrial sewing machine found at a car boot sale, she made some prototypes and went off to sell her wares.

The rest, as they say, is history, with around 2,000 Flatmates being sold every week.

The Mirror, 10.4.1999

'Don't go into business to make money for money's sake. Choose something that fascinates you, like I did with the music industry. Since you're going to spend your life working on it, it is important you enjoy the work.

'Make sure there's an obvious need. If it's not being done well by somebody else, you can fill a gap in the market.'

▼ *Richard Branson, Virgin Group*

Starting a new business

If you think you have the right skills to set up and run a business, and to make it a success, then the first thing you need to do is to come up with a good business idea. So what is a 'good' business idea?

Evaluating a business idea

When evaluating your business idea, the key questions to ask are:

- Will you enjoy the work?
- Have you identified a gap in the market?
- Have you assessed the market potential?
- Who are your competitors?

Turning to the business itself, what is it that you want to produce? Is it a good or a service? Is the product something people will buy on a regular basis, such as food, or something that they are likely to want only every now and again, for example expensive jewellery or a carpet-cleaning service?

It is not always necessary to be innovative and make an entirely new product. You can provide a good or service that is already available - but do it better than the competition.

Many of the products we take for granted today started as the innovations of private individuals. For example, Percy Shaw became a multi-

▼ Product innovations

millionaire after inventing cats-eyes for roads as a result of seeing his car headlights reflected in some broken glass. Swedish brothers Gad and Hans Rausing made £5.2 billion from their invention, the Tetra Pak Carton.

A 'gap in the market'

Spotting a gap in the market means identifying a consumer want that is not being satisfied - either because a particular product is not available, or because existing products are unsatisfactory in some way. A business that is able to satisfy these consumer desires stands a good chance of succeeding.

For example, mobile phones have filled a gap in the market for improved communications. Microwave ovens filled a gap in the market for reduced cooking times, as the number of single working households increased and more women went out to work. Even if a good or service is generally available, a gap may still exist in the market at a local level. For example, a small village may not be served by a newsagent's shop or hairdressing salon.

The market for wine in the UK was expanding in the 1990s

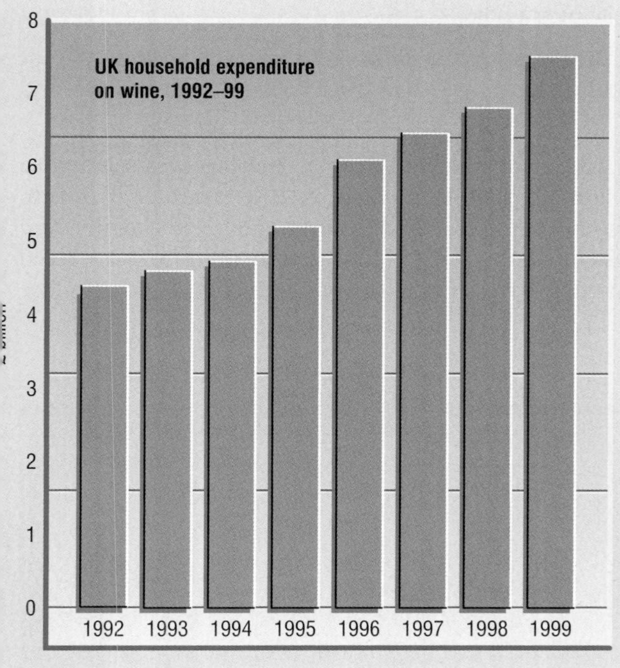

S Consumer Trends, 1999

Market potential

More opportunities for new business organizations exist in markets which are expanding. This means that sales of a particular good or service are rising. It is important for budding entrepreneurs to assess the future potential demand for their product ideas, by identifying trends in sales for similar products from published sources, such as the *Annual Abstract of Statistics*, or, in the case of entirely new products, by using primary market research to gauge consumer demand (see 9.3).

Market research can help to identify who is likely to buy your new products, and how much they are willing to pay. The target audience for your product and advertising can be identified by age, sex, income, lifestyle, and geographical location (see 9.4). Expanding markets in the 1990s and into the new millennium included mobile phones and other information communications equipment, DVD discs and players, air travel, organic foods, herbal drinks, Internet shopping, digital cameras, and widescreen televisions, to name a few.

Competition

Unless your good or service is unique, you can expect to encounter competition from rival business organizations. You can attempt to minimize competition by offering better quality and service, lower prices, faster delivery, better customer care and after-sales service, advertising, longer opening hours, and so on, and generally differentiating your product or service from that of your rivals.

It will be important to study the strengths and weaknesses of rival organizations in terms of price, promotion, quality, image, and customer care. Size and location will also be important. For example, it would be madness to think you could successfully compete against giant organizations such as Sony in the market for consumer electronics. Similarly, it would also be risky to open a hairdressing salon in an area already served by many competing salons.

Setting business objectives

One of the very first tasks for a budding entrepreneur is to identify business objectives for the short, medium, and long term. Once identified, these will provide the goals towards which the business works, and by which its success can be measured. Businesses may have many different objectives. However, all objectives will be reinforcing, and in financial terms, most will fall into one or other of the following categories:

- **To be subsidized:** some organizations may aim to operate at a loss in order to keep prices low, and will receive a subsidy from another source to break even. For example, central government continues to subsidize some loss-making passenger rail services in order to ensure that the public receives a reasonable and affordable level of service.
- **To break-even:** when a new business sets up, unless it has a very new and innovative product, it is unlikely that it will make a profit immediately. A more reasonable objective in the short term is simply to avoid making a loss, i.e. to break even. The break-even point is when total costs equal total revenues, and neither a profit nor a loss is made (see 21.2). The vast majority of entrepreneurs launching a new venture are quite pleased to be able to reach the target of breaking even by the end of their first year of trading.

  Non-profit-making organizations, such as charities, will always attempt to break even, spending no more than they receive in donations and other incomes.
- **To maximize sales and grow market share:** a new business seeking to establish itself may initially seek to increase sales as much as it can. In doing so, the new business can make sure employed labour and machinery is fully used. Many of the costs faced by a business are fixed no matter how many goods or services the business makes and sells (see

Portfolio Activity 20.2 

1. From your own knowledge and further research, identify markets that are currently expanding or contracting, and gather supporting information.
2. For the goods and services you have identified, list and explain possible reasons for their growth or decline in sales. Useful sources of data will include:

- *ONS Social Trends*
- *ONS Annual Abstract of Statistics*
- Newspapers and magazines
- Specialist marketing magazines
- Discussions with shop sales staff

22.2). For example, rent, business rates and insurance premiums are fixed. It makes sense to spread these costs over as much output as possible to achieve economies of scale (see 22.4). It is easier to increase sales when consumer demand for a product is growing. However, to increase sales faster than consumer demand is rising involves attracting sales away from rival producers. This means increasing market share at the expense of competing businesses (see 1.7). To do this, a new or established business will need to persuade consumers that its product is better than its rivals, through a combination of advertising and other promotions, improved quality, and lower prices. This will probably involve higher costs initially, but if the strategy is successful it can produce higher profits in the long run.

- **To maximize profits:** this is the ultimate goal of most private-sector business organizations. In order to make a profit, a firm must earn revenues in excess of total costs. To achieve this, it will need to meet a number of other shorter term (or tactical) objectives along the way, such as establishing a product and brand name, gaining market share and customer loyalty, etc. Similarly, large firms may subsidize new subsidiaries or products if they are aiming to enter a new market, in order to help them to get established.

The purposes of a business plan

Once an entrepreneur has a business idea and an agreed set of objectives, it is usual to set these out in a document known as a **business plan.** The plan will identify the objectives of the business, and detail how it intends to achieve them. It has been suggested that 'a business that fails to plan is one that plans to fail.' There is no set format for a business plan. The structure and content will vary widely from business to business, depending on its size, the nature of the product, and the expertise of the

Only the fittest survive

When the going gets tough, the main objective of any business is survival. About half a million new businesses start up every year in the UK. About one in four fail in their first few years of operation. Business survival is especially important in the early stages of trading, when consumers know little about the new company or their product, and when competition from existing firms in the market will be especially fierce. Survival is also important when there is a slump in consumer demand during an economic recession, or when a company is under threat of takeover by a rival firm.

Figure 20.2: Company insolvencies in England and Wales 1987–97

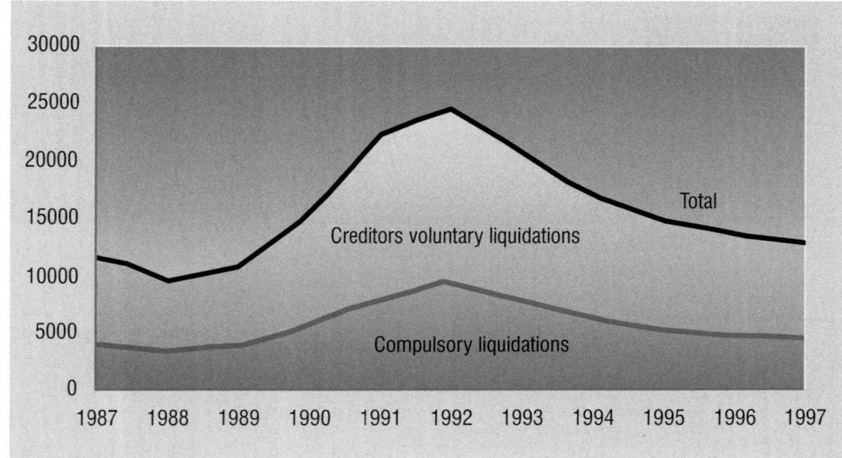

ONS Annual Abstract of Statistics 1999

writer. However, it is important for any business plan to consider the following five areas in some detail:

- Objectives
- How the business/product will be marketed
- How production will be organized, and the methods to be used
- Resource requirements (physical, human, and financial) and costs
- Sources of finance (see Chapter 23)

Producing a well-structured business plan is important for a number of reasons:

- **It is a valuable exercise for the owner(s).** It forces them to evaluate their business idea, market potential, and competition, assess their present financial situation, plan for the future, and set realistic output, sales, and profit targets.
- **To identify resource requirements.** For example, the plan will set out the business experience and skills of the owners, how many workers they will need, the skills they require, equipment and vehicle requirements, the size and location of suitable premises, and types and amounts of materials. Business start-up costs will also be identified, and the amount of external finance needed.
- **To support an application for finance.** A bank will insist on seeing a business plan before deciding to lend the owner(s) money. A plan will identify the key factors that will determine the success of the business, and how much of their own money the owners are willing to invest in the venture.
- **To monitor business performance.** The plan allows the business owner(s) to compare actual figures against projections. Forecasts of outputs, sales, cashflows, profit and loss statements, and balance sheets can be compared against outturn, usually every month or every three months.

Key words:

Entrepreneur - a person who starts up, owns, and runs a business

Business plan - a report detailing objectives, marketing strategy, production costings, and financial implications of a new business idea

Break-even - when revenues are equal to costs

Profit - an excess of revenues over costs

Section 20.3 Legal and insurance implications

Business law

An entrepreneur setting up a new business must have an understanding of the basics of business law. This is because being in business brings a wide variety of legal and other responsibilities which, if ignored, can be very costly and disruptive to the running of the organization. If a business does break the law, it is not an acceptable defence to plead ignorance. The major categories of law which affect businesses are as follows:

Employment law

The relationship between employers and their employees is regulated by a number of laws in the UK (see 15.2). The main ones are:

- Race Relations Act 1976
- Equal Pay Acts 1970, 1983
- Sex Discrimination Acts 1975, 1986
- Employment Rights Act 1978
- Wages Act 1986
- National Minimum Wage Act 1998
- European Working Time Directive 1998
- Employment Rights Act 1999

Together, these acts give employees legal rights including the rights to:

- A written statement of terms and conditions of employment
- Guaranteed payment of wages
- An itemized pay slip
- Statutory sick pay
- To return to the same job after illness
- Redundancy payments
- Maternity leave for female employees and the right to return to the same job afterwards
- Non-discrimination on grounds of sex, race, marital status, religion, and Trade Union membership
- Protection against unfair dismissal
- Notice of termination of employment
- Time off for public duties
- A limit on working time of an average of 48 hours a week
- Free health assessment and insurance for nightworkers
- Rest periods during the working day
- A minimum wage
- A minimum of 4 weeks annual paid leave

Health and safety

A number of laws have been in existence for many years to protect employees and members of the public from health and safety hazards at work (see 15.2). These include:

- The Factories Act 1961
- The Offices, Shops and Railway Premises Act 1963

- The Fire Precautions Act 1971
- The Health and Safety at Work Act 1974
- Control of Substances Hazardous to Health Regulations (COSHH) 1994
- Provision and Use of Work Equipment Regulations 1998

Health and safety legislation in the UK requires employers 'to ensure as far as is reasonably practicable, the health, safety and welfare at work of all staff'. Positive steps to prevent accidents and to promote health and safety must be taken by all organizations. Employers must:

- Develop and display a written policy on health and safety
- Maintain a safe working environment
- Provide safety equipment and, where appropriate, clothing free of charge
- Keep detailed records of accidents, and make regular assessments of health and safety risks in the workplace

All new businesses need to consider very carefully how they will ensure health and safety at work. The penalties for negligence on the part of employers can be very severe. New entrepreneurs should seek advice on health and safety before setting up in business.

Environmental protection

The Environmental Protection Act 1990 and a growing body of European legislation on the environment regulate the behaviour of firms in the UK, and these are enforced in the UK by the Environment Agency and the Scottish Environmental Protection Agency. Taken together, these laws control many thousands of different industrial processes, which might, if uncontrolled, cause noise or chemical pollution in the air, land, or water. Local authorities are also required by government to monitor some 30,000 industrial processes for unacceptable levels of pollution.

Firms breaking anti-pollution laws may be subject to heavy fines. Therefore, it is essential for new businesses starting out to establish whether or not any of their production processes are likely to contravene the law, and, if so, what it would cost to put this right. For example, does the business result in hazardous waste by-products? How can waste be kept to a minimum, and how can it be disposed of safely?

Portfolio Activity 20.3 

1. In groups, discuss the following questions arising from the articles:

   (a) In what ways can environmental and other kinds of legislation affect business costs?

   (b) If business costs in the UK rise, how and why might this affect international competitiveness?

   (c) What are the likely costs and benefits to producers, consumers, and citizens in the UK, of more legislation to protect the environment?

2. Survey any organization with which you are familiar in order to establish the kinds of costs which management feel are imposed by legislation of various kinds. Do they see the legislation as necessary? Would their views conflict with those of the general public? Report on your findings and prepare a short presentation to the rest of your group.

Energy levy plans fuel big consumers' anger

Plans to tax the energy used by businesses has unleashed a barrage of criticism against the government.

Critics argue that the levy, which ministers proposed in March, could damage the manufacturing industry, cost thousands of jobs and fail to help the environment.

But the government believes that the tax will bring clear environmental benefits. It would, it claims, help the country meet its short-term goals on stabilising greenhouse gas emissions and put it in a stronger position to meet the increasingly stringent targets needed to delay catastrophic climate change.

Big industrial energy users such as steel and chemicals companies have been leading the protests against the levy, arguing for discounts of up to 95 per cent. They have high energy costs, and argue that they are doing all they can to improve efficiency.

The levy, they claim, would merely make them uncompetitive against their overseas rivals and, according to research by Business Strategies, would cost 156,000 jobs over the next 10 years

Financial Times, 28.10.1999

CBI appeals for reinforcements on the green front

British businesses are starting to chafe under the weight of environmental regulation. They feel the government is creating laws without sufficiently balancing the costs and benefits. They also wish the government would make up its mind about environmental issues. These concerns reflected in a report published by the Confederation of British Industry (CBI). "At present too many businesses are falling foul of the pitfalls, rather than seizing the opportunities of environmental regulation," the CBI says.

A further problem is the effect of regulation on international competitiveness. A quarter of respondents to a CBI poll said they were experiencing difficulties gaining access to foreign markets, mainly because of eco-labelling schemes in other countries. According to the CBI, environmental regulators are not sufficiently sensitive to the costs that they impose.

Financial Times, 4.11.1994

Consumer protection law

A body of laws exist to protect consumers from misleading claims by producers and from the sale of goods of poor quality (see 12.5). These include:

- Food and Drugs Act 1955
- Weights and Measures Act 1963
- Trade Descriptions Act 1968
- Unsolicited Goods Act 1971
- Consumer Credit Act 1974
- Consumer Safety Act 1978
- The Sale of Goods Act 1979
- Foods Act 1984
- Consumer Protection Act 1987
- Food Safety Act 1990
- Trademark Act 1994
- Sale and Supply of Goods Act 1994

Together these acts make it illegal to:

- Prepare or sell food in unhygienic conditions
- Use false or misleading weighing equipment
- Give short measures
- Give false or misleading descriptions of goods and services
- Send goods to customers who have not ordered them and then demand payment
- Not provide consumers with copies of credit agreements
- Not provide correct and full details of credit arrangements
- Sell goods which might be harmful to consumers
- Sell goods that are not of merchantable quality
- Sell defective goods that may cause damage or harm to consumers or their property
- Copy the trademark, logo, or name of another business or product

In addition, legislation exists to control anti-competitive behaviour by firms, such as colluding to fix prices or predatory pricing to push new competitors out of a market (see 10.2). The Competition Commission in the UK is able to impose heavy fines on firms found guilty of restrictive practices (see 12.5).

Additional laws regulate opening times for shops and public houses, and forbid the sale of cigarettes, alcohol, and fireworks to children.

Other statutory requirements

Business start-up

Anybody who has been unemployed and is claiming the Jobseekers Allowance must notify their local Benefits Agency office if they find paid work or become self-employed. It is illegal to continue to claim benefits to cushion against the loss of income suffered while unemployed.

In some cases certain benefits may still be paid to people in work or starting their own business. For example, income support may be available

Portfolio Activity 20.4 

There are many other laws in the UK which can affect business, and which must be taken into consideration when starting up and running your business, and when planning business expansion. These include:

- Data Protection Act
- Insolvency Act
- Copyright Act
- Patents Act
- Business Names Act
- Partnership Act
- Companies Act
- Sunday Trading Act

Try to find out the various requirements of these laws. How might they affect a new or existing business?

to people on low wages and the Jobseekers Allowance may continue to be paid to unemployed people starting their own businesses during their first few months of trading.

Company registration

If the business a person starts up is a private limited company they will need to inform the governments Registrar of Companies based in Cardiff at Companies House (see 2.3).

The Registrar keeps details of all limited companies and requires them to send to Companies House a copy of their annual accounts each year (see 18.1). The company must also send in details each year of the company directors, their shareholdings, share capital issued and any company property that has been mortgaged.

Pension arrangements

A **pension** is a form of lifetime saving to provide an income for retirement from work. There are a number of different types of pension available to people in work.

- A **state pension** is payable on retirement to men over 65 years of age and women over 60 (the statutory retirement age for women is to be raised gradually to 65 years by the year 2010). The state pension is a relatively low flat rate decided each year by the government. In 2000–01 the state pension was £82 per week for a single person.
- If you want to have a bigger pension than the state pension when you retire, then it is likely you will need to pay regular amounts from your earnings into a **contributory pension** scheme. These savings build up over time with interest and pay out on retirement, usually in the form of a lump sum plus regular payments. The more you contribute, the more your pension is likely to be.

Some contributory pensions are also paid into by employers for their employees. Some may even operate their own company pension schemes run by the employer. Payments into the scheme by employees receive tax relief and are deducted from their wages.

Self-employed people must make their own arrangements for a pension with a bank or specialist pension fund provider. Payments can be offset against tax liabilities.

- In some cases workers may not have to pay into a pension scheme because their employer makes regular fixed contributions on their behalf, usually related to the amount they earn each month. These are called **non-contributory pensions**.

Taxation

Both employed and self-employed workers are required by law to pay income tax and National Insurance contributions (NICs). Self-employed people who employ staff of their own may also have to collect income tax and NICs on their behalf.

In addition, some self-employed workers must also register as eligible to pay Value Added Tax (VAT). When entering employment or self-employment, it is important to understand how these statutory requirements work.

Income tax

Self-employed and employed workers are taxed differently. An employee is taxed under the **Pay-As-You-Earn (PAYE)** system, whereby tax is deducted from their wage or salary 'at source' by their employer each week or month. Income tax is therefore automatic for employees, and all of the work in calculating the amount of tax due and when it should be paid is the responsibility of the employer. The employer must, therefore, organize the operation of the PAYE system for their employees.

A self-employed person must arrange to pay tax on their own earnings direct to the Inland Revenue. In order to do this, they must first tell their local tax office the date on which they propose to start being self-employed. Self-employed people normally pay tax in two instalments, in January and July of each year.

The general rule is that tax liability on self-employed earnings is based on profits made in the previous twelve months. This means that self-employed people pay tax one year in arrears. For example, a tax assessment for 2001–02 will be based upon earnings, net of expenses, in 2000–01. (A tax year runs from 6 April to 5 April the following year.) Because tax is paid in two lump sums, it is necessary to hold over enough earnings in order to meet the tax bill. This requires an element of self-discipline - another possible burden not placed on employees.

Allowable business expenses

As a self-employed person, you are able to deduct from your earnings any expenses which are wholly and exclusively incurred in carrying out your business. However, the tax authorities will require proof of the expenditure to be detailed in your business accounts.

Allowable business expenses can include:

- Cost of materials - for example, a self-employed decorator can deduct the cost of paints
- Goods bought for resale - for example, to sell in a shop
- VAT on purchases
- Wages and salaries of employees (including members of your family)
- Business travel
- Interest charges on loans and overdrafts
- Business insurance
- Professional fees - for example, payments to accountants, financial advisers, or solicitors
- Business gifts and entertaining staff and clients
- Subscriptions to professional and trade magazines
- Bad debts (i.e. non-payment of invoices by debtors)
- Running costs (overheads such as rent, rates, electricity and gas, telephone, cleaning, advertising, etc).

Corporation tax

Profits made by a business are liable for **corporation tax.** The tax is usually paid after the end of the company's trading year, and is based on a percentage of the company's profits.

In 2000–01, a company with more than £1.5m profit per year was taxed at a rate of 30%. Small companies with profits of between £50,000 and £300,000 paid 20%, and companies earning profits of less than £10,000 paid only 10%. In between these profit levels marginal tax rates applied.

National Insurance

Business owners who employ staff will need to deduct employees' **National Insurance Contributions (NICs)** from their wages and pay these to the Inland Revenue. In 2000–01 employee NICs were set at 10% of earnings between £76 and £535 per week. Earnings below £76 per week and additional earnings above £535 per week were zero-rated.

Employers also need to pay additional NICs from their own business funds for each person they employ earning over a specified threshold. In 2000–01 employers were required to pay the equivalent of 12.2% of the wage of any employee earning over £83 per week or £361 per month in Employers NICs.

Value Added Tax (VAT)

In the 2000–01 tax year, a business that expected sales to exceed £52,000 that year had to register for VAT with the Customs and Excise Department. VAT charged on goods or services sold to customers must be paid to the Customs and Excise Department every month or quarter, less any VAT paid on goods and services supplied to the business.

If an eligible business fails to register and subsequently claims not to have known about VAT, ignorance will not be accepted as a defence in law. Even if the business failed to charge VAT to its customers, Customs and Excise will still require that any VAT that should have been charged is passed on to them.

Business rates

Unless you run your small business from home, your business will have to pay a lump-sum tax to your local authority each year, based on the value of the business property.

Licences

Many kinds of business require licences in order to run. These include child-minding, money-lending, and gambling. In addition, taxis, food, and catering are covered by legislation governing business conduct.

When starting a new firm, it is sensible to consult with the local authority planning department, environmental health department, and trading standards office, in order to see how the business might be affected by existing regulations.

Insurance

Asset insurance

A large proportion of capital in a business will be invested in physical assets, such as buildings and machinery. **Asset insurance** aims to protect firms, through financial compensation, in the event of loss or damage to these assets. Because types of insurance and premiums vary, it is often worthwhile to seek the advice of a specialist **insurance broker**. Organizations will usually insure their assets against the following risks:

- **Fire:** damage to assets resulting from fire, flood, lightning, storms, riots, and vandalism.

- **Theft:** loss of assets through theft. Many businesses pay an extra insurance premium to cover assets both when they are on the firm's premises, and when they are authorized to be removed for use elsewhere (known as **all risks cover**). In such cases, it is essential to make sure that a sufficiently high insurance premium is paid to cover the full replacement value of the assets.
- **Disruption of trading:** this covers the firm against loss of earnings, usually as a result of claims under fire insurance cover. Fire and disruption of trading insurance, taken together, will pay for damage to assets, and compensate the firm for any loss of earnings due to damaged assets.

Firms are not required by law to take out asset insurance. However, it would be very foolish for a firm not to insure against this kind of loss or damage, given the high proportion of business capital that assets consume, and the difficulty of replacing them without financial compensation. Although premiums can be high, the consequences of a fire or theft on a business can be devastating.

Public, product, and employers' liability

Firms are, however, required by law to insure for public, product, and employers' liability. Again, the costs are justified, because a successful claim for damages by a member of the public or employee could bankrupt a firm.

Portfolio Activity 20.5 

1. From these articles, suggest why businesses need insurance.
2. Make a list of risks a business will need to insure against.
3. Try to confirm your list in Question 2 by talking to managers of an organization with which you are familiar, and/or by gathering information on cover provided by major insurance companies, such as the Prudential or Legal & General.

Hurricane Floyd hits Royal & Sun

EARTHQUAKES and Hurricane Floyd cost insurer Royal & Sun Alliance £42million in the last quarter, the group estimated yesterday. It said the three months to September 30 brought damage claims from the earthquakes in Turkey and Taiwan, Hurricane Floyd in the US and the Bahamas and Typhoon York in Hong Kong. The struggling British insurer is seen as vulnerable to a takeover.

Metro, 12.10.1999

QE2 passengers start moves to sue Cunard

A group of passengers who travelled on the Queen Elizabeth 2's ill-fated Christmas cruise from Southampton to the US have taken the first step in their intended legal action against Cunard, the ship's owner.

A claim letter has been sent to Cunard's offices in New York and Southampton by New York lawyers Kreindler & Kreindler ahead of the filing of a class action suit, probably this week.

"Each passenger has suffered damages of from $50,000 to $100,000," the letter states. Passengers are demanding a full fare refund plus damages for mental stress, physical injuries and impaired health.

The list of grievances includes:

- Exposure to asbestos dust and other noxious fumes.
- Fear from unsafe practices, including "blocked passageways to the deck areas in case of a need to evacuate the vessel, or to reach deck areas in an emergency".
- Lack of proper water, heat and air-conditioning as well as lack of agreed accommodation.

Financial Times, 30.1.1995

Other types of business insurance

- **Bad debts** - caused by customers not paying sales invoices
- **Fidelity guarantee** - to protect against theft and dishonesty by staff
- **Legal insurance** - to protect the organization from prosecutions for breaches of the law such as restrictive trading practices, river pollution, or unfair dismissal
- **Motor** - third-party insurance is a minimum legal requirement to protect passengers and pedestrians from injuries sustained through motor vehicle accidents

- **Public liability insurance:** firms must insure themselves against causing injury to a member of the public as a result of their business activities - for example, if a highly polished floor in a shop caused a customer to slip over and hurt themselves. Such insurance also covers loss or damage to customers' property. This is an important safeguard for the public and for firms, because without it, a claim from a member of the public for damages could easily bankrupt a business. The insurance is important for the public, because it guarantees them compensation if the firm is at fault.
- **Product liability insurance:** firms must also insure themselves against claims by members of the public for damages due to loss or injury caused by the use of their goods or services - for example, if an electrical product catches fire and causes damage, due to an internal fault. This insurance also covers a business for the legal costs which might be incurred in defending itself against claims made against it by a member of the public.
- **Employers' liability:** this provides protection against claims for compensation from employees involved in accidents at work.

Key words:

Employment law - legislation which defines the relationship between employers and their employees

Health and safety law - designed to protect workers and members of the public from hazards at work

Environmental protection laws - legislation to prevent harm or damage to the natural environment

Consumer protection law - designed to protect consumers from misleading claims and anti-competitive behaviour by business organizations

Asset insurance - insurance against damage to, or theft of, fixed assets such as machines and equipment, and disruption of trading

Pension - a saving scheme to provide income after retirement

Insurance broker - specialist adviser on insurance and insurance cover

Public liability insurance - compulsory insurance designed to protect members of the public and their property against loss or injury directly or indirectly caused by a business

Product liability insurance - compulsory insurance cover designed to protect consumers against loss or injury caused by the use of a firm's goods or services

Income tax - tax levied on personal income

National Insurance contributions - payments made by employees and employers to the government in the form of an insurance premium to help cover the cost of unemployment, sickness, bereavement, pensions, and other benefits

Corporation tax - tax levied on business profits

Value Added Tax - tax levied on the price of most goods and services

Section 20.4 Business resources

Planning, organizing and managing resources

In order to create a successful business, it is necessary to obtain and manage human, physical, and financial **resources** in order to achieve business goals within specific timescales. The hardest tasks in setting up a new business are to:

- Correctly identify the quantity and quality of resources required
- Obtain the resources needed at a reasonable cost

Portfolio Activity 20.6 

1. What kind of business costs are demonstrated in the article?
2. What has this entrepreneur done in order to minimize his costs?
3. Make a list of all other resources Charles Webb will require to run his business.

Charles Webb, proprietor of the Camden Bus estate agency in north London, is doing well selling flats to first-time buyers, Webb, 34, who set up the company seven years ago, was feeling flush and decided a company car was required. When your head office is a 1984 Route Traveller, what could be better for ferrying potential customers about than a black cab? The 'office' cost him £5,000 and his rent is £12,000 a year - about £15,000 less than conventional premises would cost in the same area. Rates too are less than half the going business rate for the area, at £1,500 a year - the initial calculation of £3,500 provoked complaints even from Webb's competitors in the area, demonstrating a rare streak of decency among estate agents. "We don't make heaps of money," admits Webb. "But we make a steady profit".

Daily Telegraph, 13.8.1994

- Manage the resources efficiently and effectively over a period of time, in order to achieve desired goals

This section considers some of the resource issues and questions which must be asked by entrepreneurs starting a new firm.

Human resources

Labour, or human resources, provides the physical and mental effort necessary to run a business. To be successful, a business needs the right management and workforce. The first step an entrepreneur should take when setting up a new business is to ask: 'Do I have the necessary experience and expertise to run this business? If not, how will I be able to run it and who else can help me?'

Sometimes the answer may prompt the entrepreneur to become an employee first in a similar kind of business, in order to 'learn the ropes'. It is clearly also very important to consider the kind of skills that would-be employees might need, and how staff with the right skills might be recruited. This might involve undertaking a survey of the employment market, in order to see what terms and conditions of employment staff are offered elsewhere (see 13.2).

Once the entrepreneur has identified whether or not the right management and staff can be found, it is necessary to look at the kinds of systems that will be needed to manage the human resources of the organization. As a business begins to grow and take on more staff, the owners will have to ensure that they can meet the requirements of employment legislation and can manage the deduction of income tax under the PAYE (pay-as-you-earn) system and the payment of National Insurance contributions. The costs of advertising, recruiting, and training staff must all be carefully estimated, because these will make up a significant proportion of the total costs of setting up a new business.

Physical resources

Physical resources include the premises that the business will operate from, the machinery and equipment it will use, and the stocks of materials and other consumables, such as paper, it will need to purchase. Choosing the right premises in the right location and at the right price is a key factor in the success of any new business, particularly a retail outlet.

Types of business premises can include:

- Shop
- Office
- Factory unit/Factory
- Farm
- Home

An increasing number of people are running small businesses from home, because it is often the cheapest and most convenient option. Many home businesses will either manufacture products that do not require a large amount of machinery and other equipment, such as stuffed toys or dried flower arrangements, or will provide services such as child-minding, cleaning, photography, or painting and decorating.

Because working from home changes the use of the property, it may be necessary to obtain planning permission from the local authority before the business can be established. Certain mortgages or leases also contain conditions which limit the use of the property.

Operating from home is not usually an option for people who start up new retail outlets or factories. A shop will need to be accessible by car and public transport, and near to other shops to pick up passing trade. A factory will need to house machinery and receive deliveries. The best location will, therefore, vary with the kind of business in question.

Choosing premises

When considering premises, traders should consider the following issues:

- Are there any plans which might change the character of the area in future, for example, new roads, office blocks, or changes to parking regulations?
- Are there any financial inducements to locate in the area? For example, is it a development area which qualifies for government financial assistance? (see 23.3)
- What local authority grants are available for new start-ups in the area?
- What is the availability of labour in the area?

Traders should also consider:

- The location of suppliers who will make regular deliveries to the business
- Ease of access, both for customers and for suppliers (e.g. locating in a restricted parking area may cause problems)
- Security of the premises, and how much it would cost to make them secure (wire grills, locks, alarms, etc.)
- Availability of facilities such as washbasins and toilets, and whether they meet health and safety requirements
- Storage facilities
- Floor area in relation to anticipated sales turnover and number of employees
- Fire exits, stairways, and lifts
- Space for expansion, car parking, etc.
- Costs of legal fees, rent, rates, refurbishment, and insurance
- Costs and other terms and conditions of the letting
- Local competition. For example, it would be unwise to set up yet another shoe shop in a small town already served by ten others

Once suitable premises have been found, it is necessary to consider carefully the basis on which the property will be occupied. If the land and and property are **freehold,** the owner can buy them outright and use them as they wish (subject to planning and local authority regulations). However, freehold ownership is not the norm for new businesses, because of the heavy financial commitment involved in taking out a commercial mortgage, and also because commercial properties tend to be available only on a **leasehold** basis.

Leasehold land or property is rented from its owner for a set number of years. This is the cheaper option, and the basis on which most firms operate.

If premises have been used for different purposes in the past, the entrepreneur will need to ask the local authority if formal planning permission is required for a 'change of use'. For example, a scheme to establish a wine bar in premises previously used as a furniture store will certainly need formal permission from the council. Obtaining planning permission will involve the local council investigating the views of other traders and local residents and considering any objections they may have. Some businesses may also require a special licence from the local authority to operate. For example, restaurants, bars, tobacconists, and nurseries all require a local authority licence. The licence may be removed at any time, if the local authority has evidence that the trader is not operating to the required standards.

Financial resources

When setting up a business, the owners need to consider:

- How much start-up capital they can raise from their own savings, or from family and friends
- The balance which needs to be raised from external sources

Calculating a realistic figure for the amount of external finance to be raised when starting a business is one of the most difficult tasks in business planning. Entrepreneurs are often unrealistic and underestimate the amount of money they will need. However, lenders, such as banks, are unlikely to be sympathetic if the business later starts to struggle because of a lack of finance.

Portfolio Activity 20.7 

1. Why do you think the bank manager asked Frank to prepare a business plan before considering his application for a loan?
2. Make a list of the type of questions the bank manager might have wanted the business plan to answer.
3. Make a list of the fixed assets, such as machinery, that Frank might have needed to start up and run his small bakery.
4. What 'hidden costs' was Frank unprepared for?
5. How does an overdraft differ from a loan? What do overdrafts tend to be used for in a business?
6. Why do you think the bank withdrew its support for Frank?
7. What 'cautionary tales' does the article tell about the pitfalls of starting a new business and arranging external finance? Make a list of useful tips for would-be entrepreneurs.

Crumbling fortune

When Frank Evans needed a loan to set up a business, Barclays Bank couldn't wait to lend him the cash.

The 53-year-old former truck driver had been made redundant and saw the bakers shop in Bacup, Lancashire, as an ideal little earner. His confidence was even boosted by the bank's own enthusiasm. But when the business hit a rocky patch, all that changed, and Frank is now in danger of losing his home.

The nightmare started in 1990. Frank visited his local Barclays Bank manager who asked him for a business plan. Frank saw an accountant, a business plan was prepared, and the bank manager visited the shop. He then suggested that Frank re-mortgage his house - on which he owed £6,500 - for £28,000. This would provide the £10,000 Frank would need to refurbish the bakery.

He also insisted Frank take out a mortgage care insurance. For £20.12 per month, the policy would provide £449 monthly income in case of sickness or accident.

Frank then set to work renovating the shop. Three months later Frank opened for business. He was soon earning £600 per week.

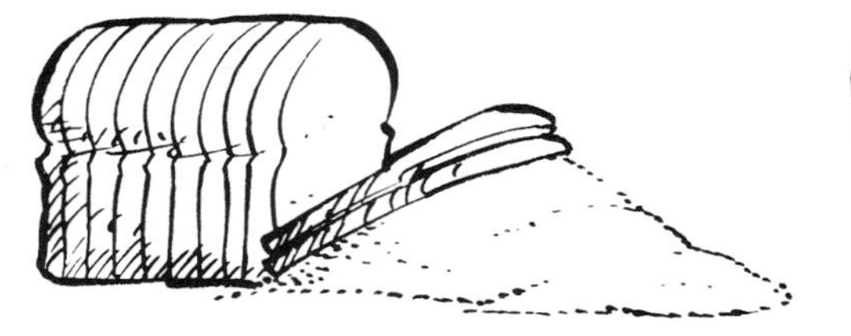

But refurbishing the run-down shop to Health and Safety standards cost more than he bargained for. He took out a loan for £5,000 and his overdraft went up to £6,000. As the expenditure was essential, he had no reason to doubt that Barclays would support him.

He was wrong. Seven months after opening, the bank manager told him there would be no more money. Frank managed to carry on for two more years until disaster struck and he had to go into hospital for three operations. The bakery was put up for sale and he was offered £20,000.

This amount fell far short of the £30,000 Frank had spent on improvements - and his years of hard work. The buyer, who also banked with Barclays, soon learned that Frank had financial problems. 'After that he kept knocking the price down,' says Frank. 'In the end I got only £7,000!'

Daily Mirror, 26.4.1994

A new business will require finance for:

- The purchase of fixed assets such as buildings, plant, and machinery
- Working capital, or the day-to-day financing requirements of the firm

In considering which sources of finance to use, business owners will need to carefully consider:

- The **total amount** of money required
- **How long** they need to borrow money for
- The **relative costs** of different sources of finance

A variety of external organizations will consider providing finance to businesses on different terms over different periods of time. These include banks, building societies, finance companies, and venture capitalists (see 23.2). Hire purchase and leasing should also be considered as methods of financing equipment.

Time management

Good management requires that resources are used to achieve particular goals within specified periods of time. For example, capital borrowed from a bank must be converted into goods and services for sale, and back into cash for repayment of the loan, within a period acceptable to the bank. One of the key issues in time management is the prioritizing of tasks, so that the most urgent ones are identified and carried out first. For example, when converting business premises, planning permission needs to be obtained *before* builders are contracted to make the alterations. Although this may seem obvious, when many hundreds of tasks need to be completed, the planning and organizing of tasks in this way is essential.

Businesses use two key techniques to help them plan and manage tasks:

- **Critical path analysis (CPA)** is a technique used to break down a project into its component activities, place them in the right sequence, and then decide when to carry them out. The aim is to identify the minimum amount of time required to complete the entire project.

  For example, in marketing there are a series of stages, including market research, research and development (R&D), test marketing, pricing, distribution, promotion, selling and after-sales service, which can be further broken down into key steps and prioritized (see Unit 3). Some of these activities are **critical,** such that if they are delayed, the whole project will take longer than expected. For example, the lead time between ordering and taking delivery of materials is critical in production.

  The objective of CPA is to schedule tasks in a way that minimizes time and costs. A series of lines, each one representing an activity, can be drawn in the form of a network diagram, or **PERT** chart **(Program Evaluation and Review Technique).** Adding the time each activity is expected to take allows a business to identify the **critical path** of the project – that is, the minimum time needed to complete it.

  Figure 20.2 shows a PERT chart for a project to install new computer equipment in an office. It shows that no activity in the network can be started until all preceding activities have been completed. To complete all the individual tasks would take 31 days. But because some tasks can be carried out at the same time, the whole project could be completed in 20 days. A delay in any one of the activities on the critical path will delay the whole project.

▼ *Figure 20.2: A PERT chart for installing new computer equipment*

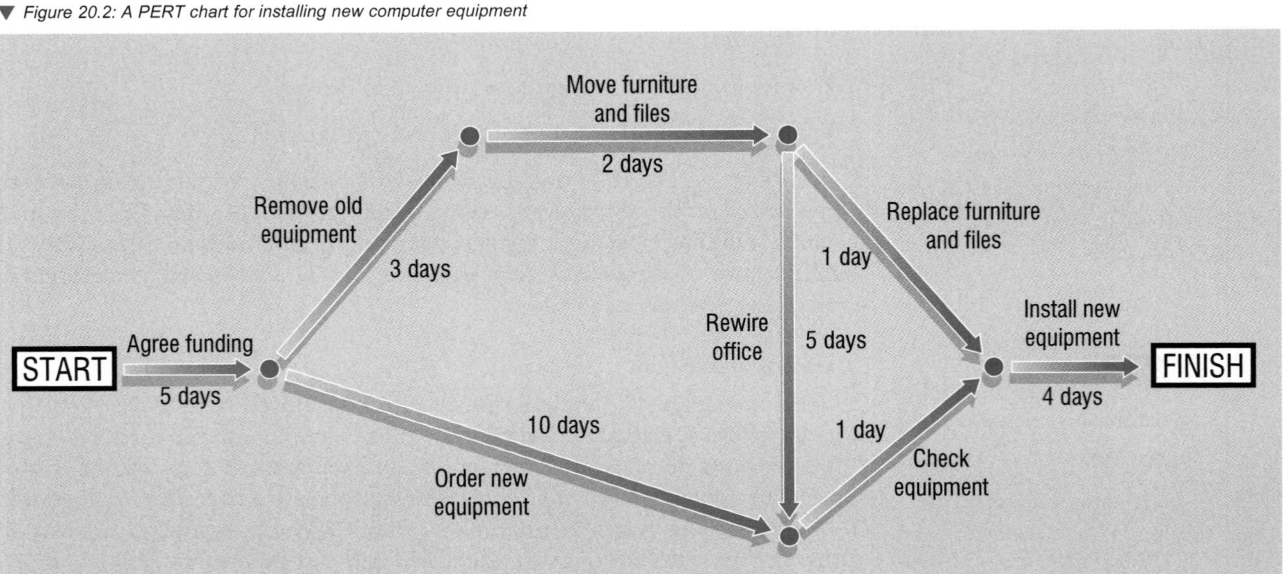

▼ *Figure 20.3: A GANNT chart for installing new computer equipment*

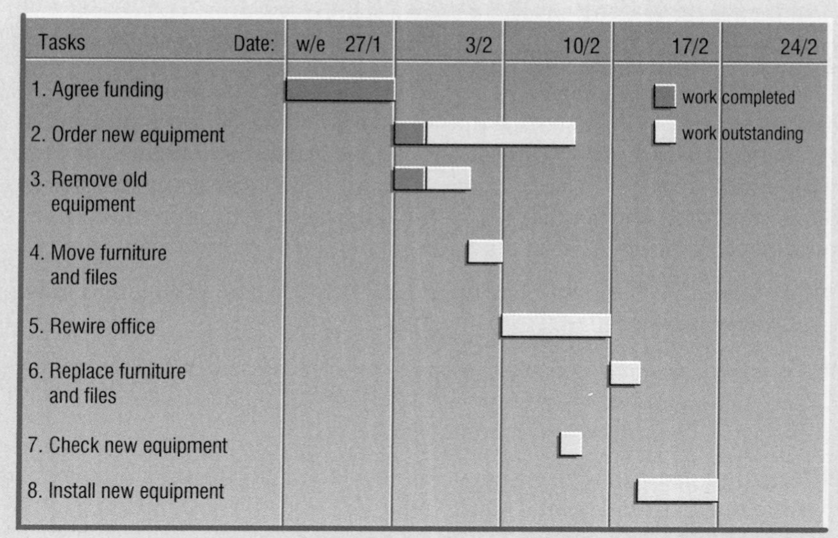

- A **GANNT chart** is simply a horizonal bar chart, each bar representing a different activity. The vertical axis records the different activities which need to be undertaken, and the horizontal axis records time. The length of each bar is determined by the amount of time needed to complete an activity. Bars can also be shaded to show how much work has been completed under each task (see Figure 20.3).

To prepare a GANNT chart, a manager will list all the activities necessary to complete a project, and then estimate the time required for each one. Progress is then checked against the chart. If the project is ahead of schedule, the manager may decide to move some employees to another project. If the project is behind schedule, extra labour may be required to finish it on time.

Portfolio Activity 20.8

A friend of yours knits jumpers with personalized designs. Business is good, but her knitting machine is slow and out of date. She has decided to replace it with new computerized equipment. At the same time, she wants to relocate her equipment and stores from her spare bedroom to a purpose-built extension at the back of her house. She has listed the following tasks she will need to complete, together with estimates of how long they will take to complete, as follows:

- Plan equipment needed (1 day)
- Place order for equipment (10 days to deliver)
- Remove old equipment (1 day)
- Remove furniture and storage cupboards from bedroom (1 day)
- Wire and fit new plug points in extension (3 days)
- Decorate extension (5 days)
- Order new stock of wools and cotton (1 day)
- Delivery of materials ordered (5 days)
- Install furniture and storage cupboards in extension (2 days)
- Set up new equipment in extension (1 day)

Your friend has asked you to:

1. Calculate the critical path for her project
2. Produce a PERT chart and a GANNT chart to illustrate the timing and sequencing of the tasks she needs to complete.

Key words:

Freehold property - property owned outright by the business

Leasehold property - property rented for a specified period from its owner

Critical Path Analysis (CPA) - diagrammatic technique used to plan and analyse the scheduling of activities in business projects

GANNT chart - type of bar chart used to assist in planning the timing and sequencing of activities in business projects

Section **20.5**

Potential support for a business plan

Why do businesses need support?

The main aims of a business plan are to raise finance from sources external to the business, such as banks, and to provide a means of monitoring and evaluating the progress of the business over time by comparing outturn with plans. Although a wide range of people may expect to see a business plan, would-be entrepreneurs are not expected to produce the business plan single-handed. A wide range of help and advice is available.

When writing a business plan for a new venture, the following kinds of expertise will be needed:

- **Financial:** to help construct a cashflow forecast, open a balance sheet and profit and loss statement (see 18.2–18.3), and advise on VAT, National Insurance, and income tax (see 20.3).
- **Legal:** to assist in registering a company and drawing up contracts with suppliers, customers, and staff.
- **Human resources:** to advise on employment law, advertising, recruitment, selection, and training (see Unit 4).
- **Production:** to help set up, run and manage production facilities, develop products, select suppliers, machinery, and premises, and negotiate contracts.
- **Sales and marketing:** to organize market research, create and implement a sales and marketing plan, determine product promotion, distribution and selling strategies, sales targets and after-sales service (see 8.1).
- **Management:** to assist in setting realistic and achievable deadlines and targets for parts of the business plan. This kind of experience is also needed in order to advise on establishing monitoring and review systems for the business.
- **ICT:** information communications technology has revolutionized the way businesses communicate with their employees, customers, suppliers and other organizations using electronic-mail and Internet websites (see 3.3). Computers are also used to producer and store business documents, create financial spreadsheets and information databases. However, keeping up with the latest developments in ICT, buying and installing equipment, and producing web-sites will require some technical knowledge.

For an existing business considering expansion into a new venture, advice on the above areas is likely to be available from staff already working in the accounts, administration, human resources, production, and sales and marketing departments. But for new businesses, advice and support from a variety of external sources will be required. Existing organizations can also take advantage of this support.

Barclays and Freeserve in web venture

Barclays yesterday moved to plug a gap in its internet strategy when it and Freeserve, the UK's largest internet service provider, each invested £10m to develop a web portal for small businesses.

The joint venture, as yet unnamed, will provide information and services such as payroll, tax, legal and employment advice for small businesses and sole traders.

Financial Times, 29.3.2000

▲ Business angels?

External sources of business support

A wide range of organizations and individuals can provide advice to business start-ups:

- **Accountants** will be able to assist with the creation of cashflow forecasts and initial accounts, as well as with setting up accounting systems in the new firm.
- **Banks** have special business start-up advisers at their local branches, who will offer help, particularly on finance, or suggest other sources of advice.
- **Independent financial advisers** can investigate and advise on the best sources of business finance and the costs involved, but will charge for this service.
- **Solicitors** can advise on all legal matters relating to the purchase of leases or freeholds, registration of companies or partnerships, and contracts.
- **'Business angels'** are individuals and organizations willing to invest money in small businesses in return for a share of the profits. ***(www.nationalbusangels.co.uk)***
- **Business Link** offers 'one-stop' shops, in many locations in England providing advice and counselling on all aspects of business start-up. Similar services are provided by the Business Shops network in Scotland, Business Connect offices in Wales, and EDnet - the Economic Development Network for Northern Ireland ***(www.businesslink.co.uk)***.
- **Training and Enterprise Councils (TECs)** and **Local Enterprise Companies (LECs)** can assist local business by providing information, advice, counselling and training services. Around 75 TECs operate in England and Wales, and 21 LECs in Scotland.
- **Local Enterprise Agencies (LEAs)** are companies limited by guarantee, typically set up as partnerships between the private sector and local

SMALL BUSINESS SUCCESS

BUSINESS LINK HELPS PR COMPANY SUSTAIN GROWTH

BUSINESS LINK

LONDON

For information on how Business Link can help your business call

07000 40 50 60

Meridian Public Relations enjoyed rapid expansion during its first four years in business, but last year this growth began to slow. Uncertain how best to remedy this, Managing Director Lisa Daitz realised she needed professional, independent advice. So she contacted Business Link.

Following a thorough review Business Adviser Judith Krichefski identified that Lisa's time needed to be managed more efficiently to allow her to focus on running the business rather than just running the office, and to delegate tasks to her managers. Lisa recalls, ***"Within no time at all Judith had a firm understanding of my business and the key issues facing me."***

Working closely with Lisa during the next few months, Judith:

- Developed a new business strategy, with agreed corporate objectives
- Implemented a new management structure, with defined responsibilities
- Conducted comprehensive research into target markets.

Today, the improved management structure gives Lisa the support she needs and the strategy provides direction for the business, enabling organic growth.

Lisa comments, ***"Working with Business Link has given us a new focus, which has helped us improve staff motivation, win major new contracts and most importantly, increase our profits."***

authorities, with support from central Government. They deliver business support services under contract to Training and Enterprise Councils (TECs), to Business Links and, increasingly, to overseas customers. The agencies' key purpose is to promote economic regeneration by helping small firms start-up. There are around 150 LEAs in England, the majority of which belong to the National Federation of Enterprise Agencies (***www.nfea.com***).

- Local **Chambers of Commerce** are run by local businesses to provide a network in which they can exchange ideas and experiences through meetings and workshops. Local Chambers can also assist with information on starting and running a business, training, organizing international trade missions, and completing export documentation. They represent business interests to local, national and international governments, through their membership of regional chambers (see for example, ***www.essexchambers.co.uk***, ***www.wwcc.co.uk***, ***www.oxlink.co.uk***) and the British Chamber of Commerce (***www.chamber.co.uk***).
- The **Confederation of British Industry (CBI)** can give support and advice to local businesses through a number of regional offices. The CBI is the UKs leading independent employers' organization representing the views of its membership of over 250,000 including many private sector enterprises, major public sector employers, some employer and trade associations, and Chambers of Commerce (***www.cbi.org.uk***).
- **Business in the Community (BITC)** works with some 650 of its member companies to help raise business awareness of community issues and encourage partnerships between the public, private and voluntary sectors. This includes sharing resources, including expertise and training, with small local businesses (***www.bitc.org.uk***).
- **The Advisory, Conciliation and Arbitration Service (ACAS)** offers free advice on employment issues (***www.acas.org.uk***) (see 13.3).
- The **Prince's Youth Trust** helps young people who are out of work or finding it hard to get started, by offering them low-cost loans up to £5,000 for business start-up, and grants for test marketing and towards community projects (***www.princes-trust.org.uk***).
- **UK Business Incubation (UKBI)** is an independent body which will work closely with other organizations, such as Business Links, TECs, UK Science Park Association, UK Business Innovation Centres, European Business Networks to promote the process of setting up new business 'incubation' projects in the UK. This will include: providing best practice information in terms of finance, management and marketing skills and technology transfer; encouraging partnerships in incubation, for example, by involving universities, business schools, venture capital companies and commercial companies in mentoring; exploring new business formats, such as networked companies, joint ventures and strategic alliances; and providing a central store of knowledge and advice to a wide range of private and public sector parties interested in business incubation (***www.ukbi.co.uk***).
- **The Department of Trade and Industry (DTI)** offers a wide range of business support (***www.dti.gov.uk***). This includes:

- free booklets for advice and guidance on starting a business, employing staff and raising finance
- help with regulations, innovation, environmental matters, and European matters, such as grants to help small and medium sized UK businesses adapt to the European single market (see 7.3)
- a range of services geared to helping businesses to export, including market research, sales leads and trade missions overseas
- the **Small Business Service** to provide free advice for small businesses
- the **Enterprise Zone** web-site offers on-line advice and links to other web-sites on all aspects of starting and running a business (***www.enterprisezone.org.uk***)
- the **Small Firms Loan Guarantee Scheme** guarantees repayments of loans from banks and other financial institutions to small businesses with viable business proposals (see 23.3)

- The **Department for the Environment, Transport and the Regions (DETR)** can provide advice on planning issues and reducing energy costs (***www.detr.gov.uk***).
- The **Department for Education and Employment (DfEE)** provides financial help and advice to the young, disabled and long-term unemployed to start-up their own businesses through the New Deal (***www.dfee.gov.uk*** and ***www.newdeal.gov.uk***).
- A host of specialist organizations and consultants exist to provide advice on every aspect of running a business from research and development to production and marketing, ICT systems and management structure. However, this advice may be expensive.

Useful references

Finch, B. '**30 Minutes to Write a Business Plan**' (Kogan Page, 1997)

Lane, M. '**The Effective Business Plan**' (Easyway Guides, 1998)

Langdon, K. '**The 101 Greatest Business Ideas of All Time**' (Capstone Publishing Ltd., 2000)

Larkin, G. A. '**12 Simple Steps to a Winning? Marketing Plan**' (Probus Publishing, 1992)

Stutely, R. '**The Definitive Business Plan**' (Financial Times Prentice Hall, 1999)

On-line help with business planning is available from

- the DTI web-site at ***www.dti.gov.uk***
- Ibis at ***www.ibisassoc.co.uk***
- The Biz/ed net at ***bized.ac.uk***

(where appropriate, use the site search functions on **business planning**)

Detailed information on **Acts of Parliament** can be found at the HMSO web-site at ***www.legislation.hmso.gov.uk/acts.htm***

Internet key words search: **Business ideas, Small businesses, Chambers of Commerce, Tecs, Lecs**

chapter 21

Marketing and Production Planning

This chapter examines how to prepare and complete a marketing and production plan for your chosen good or service.

What you need to learn

You will need to carefully identify and analyse the **market** for your chosen good or service to make informed judgements about likely sales levels. To do this you will need to understand:

- **the use of primary and secondary data in market research**
- **the factors affecting the demand for your product**
- **methods of identifying and analysing competition**

You must be able to identify your **target consumers** and demonstrate why they will be prepared to purchase your product. You should also be able to identify potential competitors and demonstrate why consumers may purchase your product rather than those marketed by competitors.

Based on your market analysis your **marketing plan** should describe and explain:

- **your choice or good or service and its distinctive features**
- **the price(s) of your products**
- **the methods you will use to promote your product**
- **how your product will be distributed to consumers**

You will also need to determine the **production process** for your good or service. This will involve you considering:

- **the quantity to be produced**
- **the plant, machinery and equipment you will need**
- **quality levels and means of assuring targeted quality**
- **the different stages of the production process**
- **the timing of production to meet customer requirements**

It will be important to relate your production decisions to aspects of your marketing plan.

You will need to judge your **resource requirements** for marketing and producing you product. These are:

- **natural resources**
- **artificial resources**
- **labour input and skill levels**
- **time**
- **financial**

You should also be aware of any legal, insurance, financial, environmental or technological constraints that you need to take into account when making your decisions.

Section **21.1**

Planning business objectives and timescales

The business plan

A new business that has considered in some detail its business idea and market potential, and has worked out plans that will help it achieve set objectives, will stand a better chance of survival than a business that has not. One in four new businesses fail in their first few years of operation. Drawing up a business plan can significantly improve the chances of survival.

In Chapter 20 we learned that the function of a business plan is to:

- Set business objectives and targets
- Identify resource requirements of the new business venture
- Support applications for finance
- Monitor business performance

The following table outlines the typical contents of a business plan, as suggested by a large firm of accountants.

Business plan checklist

Business	Description of the business
	Business objectives
	Ownership
	Key personnel
Management	Managers
	Missing skills, and how these will be provided
Products	Description of products
	Why products are better or different
Marketing	Major customers
	Size of market
	Predicted market share
	Major competitors
	Market strategy
	Pricing
	Methods of sale
	Average size of orders
	Advertising methods and costs
Production plan	Details of product design and development
	Raw materials needed and availability
	Suppliers
	Number of employees
	Skills required
	Training needed
	Premises location
	Equipment required and prices
	Lead times in delivery
Financial plan	Cashflow forecast
	Projected balance sheet
	Projected profit and loss statement
	Mechanisms for monitoring and review of accounting records

Ernst & Whinney: 'Starting Your Own Business'

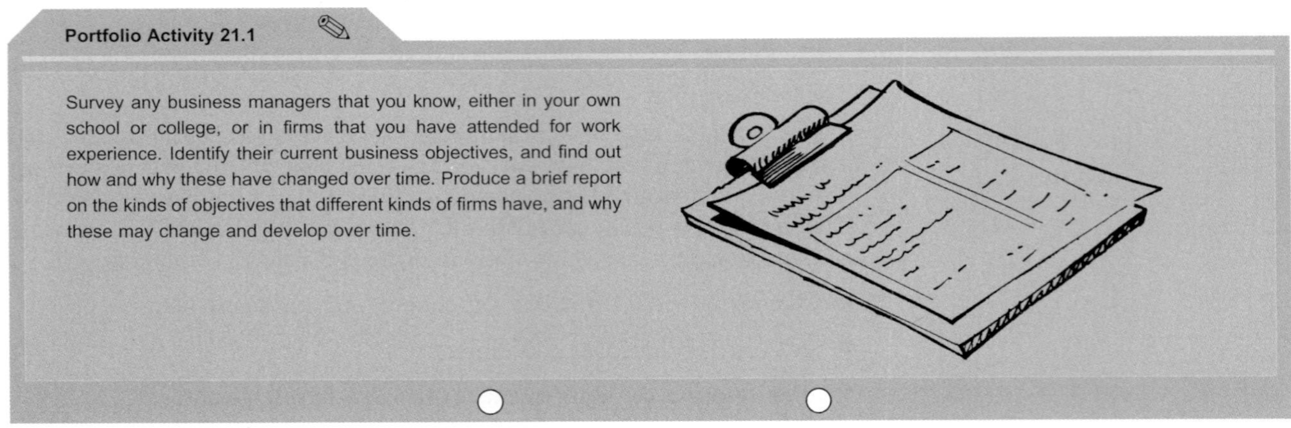

Portfolio Activity 21.1

Survey any business managers that you know, either in your own school or college, or in firms that you have attended for work experience. Identify their current business objectives, and find out how and why these have changed over time. Produce a brief report on the kinds of objectives that different kinds of firms have, and why these may change and develop over time.

Business objectives

Producing a business plan is an important means of clarifying business objectives. The plan should outline a range of objectives to be achieved over a period of time. A firm cannot hope to make a profit immediately, but is likely to set it as a long-term objective. In the short run, establishing the product and building sales are by far the most important objectives.

Objectives

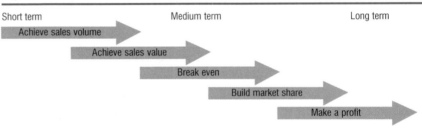

Short term — Medium term — Long term

Achieve sales volume

Achieve sales value

Break even

Build market share

Make a profit

- **To supply a good or service:** the first aim of any business that wants to be a success must be to produce a good or service that people either need or want. A business that aims to make a profit will stand no chance of doing so if people are not willing to buy their product.
- **To achieve sales volume:** if a business can supply the right product in the right place at the right time and at the right price, it has a good chance of making a sale. Setting price low initially and advertising will help to generate sales for a new product. However, selling at a low price at first is unlikely to make the business very profitable. When a business is new and output is low, the cost per unit of production is high, because fixed costs, such as rents, rates, and insurance, are spread over a small output (see 22.3). This usually leads to high prices in order to cover costs, and so makes the firm uncompetitive.

  A business may aim to achieve a higher level of output in order to expand production, and so achieve economies of scale (see 22.4). As output and sales rise, fixed costs are spread more evenly over a larger number of units, and so cost per unit falls. Therefore, a certain target sales volume may be a vital objective, enabling a firm to achieve a low enough level of costs to be competitive in the marketplace.

- **To achieve sales value:** some businesses may aim for high growth in the total cash value of their sales. This is likely to be true of firms which have spent a large amount on new capital equipment and have financed this with loans or other interest-bearing debt (see 23.2). In this situation, high sales value will be needed quickly in order to finance regular interest payments on the debt. A sales maximization objective may be reflected in the marketing strategy outlined by the firm in its business plan.
- **To break even:** covering business costs, or breaking even, is usually seen by entrepreneurs as an intermediate target to be reached along the way to profitability. A business that only manages to break even will not generate enough surplus capital for expansion or for unexpected costs. Break-even is therefore an acceptable short-term and – exceptionally – medium-term goal, but is not a sufficient target for a profit-seeking business in the long term. Non-profit-making organizations, such as charities, will always plan to break even and not to spend more than they generate in donations and other incomes.
- **To achieve market share:** once a product is established, a firm's medium-term objective may be to expand market share at the expense of rival organizations. In order to achieve a reasonable share of total sales in a market, a business must adopt a marketing mix geared for growth, including product, pricing, distribution, and promotion strategies (see 10.1). A business plan identifying this objective will need to indicate clearly how the firm would cope with competitors' responses.
- **Making a profit:** profit is the main motive for production in most private-sector firms (see 1.7). However, the importance of making a profit depends upon the stage an organization has reached in its development. Other objectives, including becoming established in the market, or removing competitors, may be more important in the short term. Profit is likely to be a long-term objective.

Portfolio Activity 21.2 

Using the article on the next page:

1. What motives do you think P&O had in importing cars from mainland Europe for re-sale in the UK?
2. What advantages might P&O have in the sales battle with the major car manufacturers and dealers, even though it is smaller and not in the car industry?
3. If existing car dealers had anticipated the P&O strategy, what plans could they have made to counteract P&O's actions?

P&O takes on the British car dealers

A FERRY company today launches the biggest challenge yet to high prices being charged to buy a car in Britain.

P&O Stena Line will import vehicles from the Continent, where they are generally cheaper, and re-sell them at up to 18 per cent less than the standard UK price.

The move is the first of its kind by a major British company and sends a clear signal to motor manufacturers the day after the Competition Commission delivered the long-awaited findings of its inquiry into British car prices.

Although several companies run schemes to help individuals make their own car purchases from Europe, P&O will offer a door-to-door service.

It has signed a deal with a vehicle importer to enable customers to order over the telephone. The cars will be delivered, with British registration and a year's road tax, to their homes.

P&O hopes to sell about 10,000 cars in its first year, a small fraction of the 2.2 million sold in Britain annually.

HOW THE PRICES COMPARE
Mercedes CL500
UK price: £83,045
P&O price: £63,900
Saving: £19,145
Range Rover 2.5D HSE
UK price: £48,705
P&O price: £41,310
Saving: £7,395
Jaguar XK8 Coupe
UK price: £50,955
P&O price: £44,480
Saving: £6,475
Toyota Land Cruiser 3.0TD VX Auto
UK price: £33,476
P&O price: £27,572
Saving: £5,854
BMW 528iSE
UK price: £31,095
P&O price: £27,225
Saving: £3,870
Renault Espace 2.2 RTX dt
UK price: £22,910
P&O price: £20,093
Saving: £2,817

Metro, 23.2.2000

Section 21.2 The marketing plan

Choosing the right mix

The marketing section of a business plan should aim to outline how the business intends to price, promote, distribute, and sell the product – the **marketing mix** (see 10.1).

Having a good product, with clever design, is not enough in itself to sell a product. In order to make sales, the product must be carefully targeted at those consumers who are likely to buy. This targeting requires that the product is designed to appeal, not just in its physical design, but also in its price, promotion, packaging, and distribution.

All aspects of a business are concerned with marketing, because everything a business does has some impact on sales, and ultimately profits. Marketing is a total approach to business which focuses on the needs of customers, from something as simple as the trading name of the business, the design of stationery, the helpfulness and knowledge of sales staff, to the price and quality of the product itself.

The marketing section of the business plan is very important, not just in encouraging business managers to organize their thoughts about how to achieve sales, but also in persuading potential lenders that the business will work. It should contain a realistic sales target (in terms of both volume and value) and details of how the marketing mix will be used to achieve it.

Your business market

This section provides an overview of some of the important marketing questions you will need to address in your business plan.

1. Is the market declining/static/increasing, and why?

____

____

____

2. Who are your major competitors?

____

____

____

3. What features of their products/services enable them to compete successfully with you?

____

____

____

4. What are your major strengths and those of your products/services that make you competitive in your business market?

____

____

____

5. What level of sales do you anticipate achieving?

   In the next 6 months £

   In the following 6 months £

6. What makes you certain of achieving these levels of sales?

____

____

____

7. What methods do you intend using to market and sell your products/services (e.g. advertising, direct mailing, trade fairs)?

	Cost (estimates)
____________	£ ________
____________	£ ________
____________	£ ________
____________	£ ________
____________	£ ________

Midland Bank, Credo - Planning The Business Plan

What's in a name?

You may choose to name your business after your own name. However, from a promotional point of view, it may be better to choose a trading name that reflects the product you are selling, or one that suggests a particular feature of the business, such as quality, speed of service, or value for money. For example, consider the following business names: General Motors; Richer Sounds; Prontaprint; Kwik Save. What do they tell you about these businesses?

Portfolio Activity 21.3

Survey the trading names of businesses in your local area, by visiting your town centre and/or looking in your local business phone directory.

Pick some business names, including those not well known to you. What do they tell you about the business, the product they sell, or the type of customer services they provide?

Now choose a business name for your own business idea. Conduct some market research to see if the name you have chosen is effective and will create the right image for your business.

▼ *Product features: consumers who buy watches are not just buying something from which to tell the time*

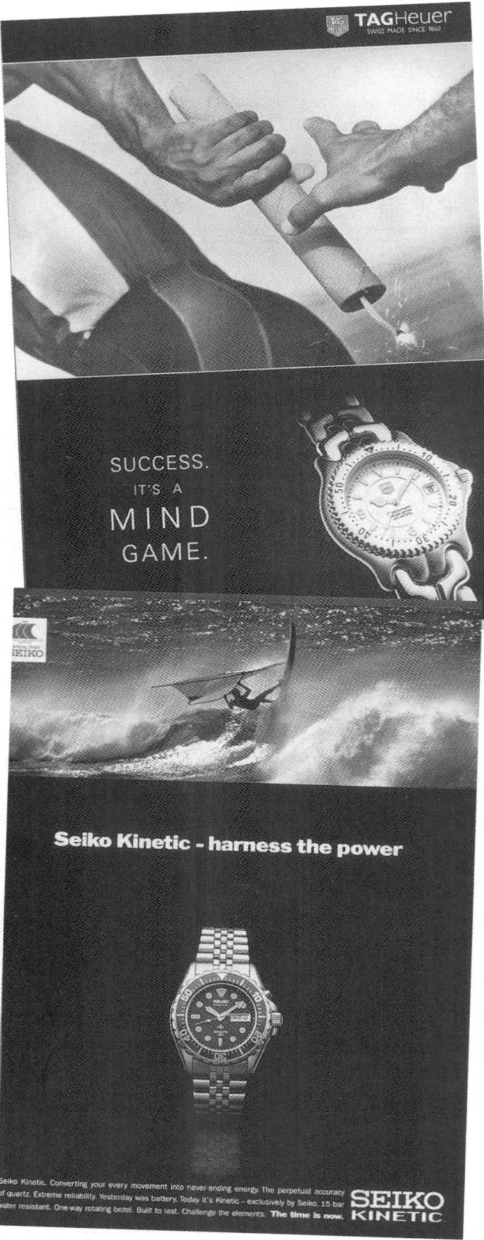

Product

Choosing the right product is vitally important. Unless your product is unique and you can create a want for it through advertising, it is important to produce a product for which the market is expanding. This will require research (see 9.1).

The appearance of a product, in terms of size, shape, colour, texture, taste, smell, labelling, brand image, and incorporated technology, will all influence the buying decision of the consumer.

Because consumers' desires are forever changing, it is important for a business to keep researching the market and adapting products accordingly. Product development - strategies, costs, and resources involved - is normally considered within a **production plan** (see 21.3).

Organizations will often use **best practice benchmarking** in product development. This involves observing the products and processes of rival companies, and then improving on them (see 1.2).

Methods of benchmarking can include taking apart rival products to see how they were made, analysing published data (for example, in company reports), or simply talking to suppliers, distributors, and customers.

Pricing

The price at which a product will sell will ultimately be determined by the forces of consumer demand and producer supply (see 5.5). If price is set too high, the product will not sell. If set too low, there will be an excess of demand which will force the firm to raise price, at least until they can expand output to meet the demand. How rival businesses will react to the price you choose is also very important.

Choosing the right price is, therefore, a key part of the marketing mix (see 10.1). But this does not mean that the good or service has to be cheap in order to attract customers. Consumers may be suspicious of a low price because it may suggest poor quality. Whatever price is charged should be consistent with all of the other marketing messages given by the marketing mix. For example, if the promotion, advertising, packaging, and retail outlets through which the product is distributed all suggest high quality, then the price should be correspondingly high.

Costs will also need to be taken into account in the pricing decision. If price fails to cover the cost of production, the firm will make a loss (see 5.5).

In the long term, the best price for a product is one that will maximize profits by creating the best combination of sales volume, price, and costs. However, in the short term, the goals for pricing

Value analysis

This is an attempt by business to ensure that the customer receives value for money from a good or service. All elements of the marketing mix are examined to eliminate unnecessary or wasteful effort, and expenditures checked in order to keep costs as low as possible without compromising product quality and reliability.

▼ Getting the price right is important

might be different. For example, price may be set low initially in order to build the business by gaining sales.

In practice, many small businesses take a lead from other businesses, by charging a similar price to that of their rivals.

Promotion

A good product will not sell, even if the price is right, if customers do not know it exists. Ensuring that the market knows about the firm's products is known as **product promotion** (see 10.3).

The key steps in efficient product promotion are as follows:

- Tell potential customers of the existence of the firm and/or its products
- Get customers to visit the firm and/or to see the products
- Encourage customers to buy
- Persuade customers to make a repeat purchase in future.

Effective promotion is about turning the target market into loyal and satisfied customers. A business outlining its promotional strategy for its business plan will therefore need to ask the following kinds of questions:

- **What is the promotion seeking to achieve?** The objectives of a promotion could be simply to ensure that customers know of the existence of a new business, or to persuade them to ask for further information, or to visit the business, or to place an order, and to continue to make repeat orders.
- **What kind of promotional message will achieve the objectives?** To create a persuasive message, a business needs to identify what is different or special about the product or business - that is, its **unique selling point**. If there is little about the product which is different, the owners need to ask what can be portrayed through advertising and promotions as being different - for example, quality, after-sales care, free gifts, helpful sales staff, etc. In this way, promotion creates a brand image in the mind of the consumer.

▼ Some promotional messages

Promotional media

- Television (including satellite and cable)
- National and local press
- Radio
- Cinema and video films
- Posters and leaflets
- Direct mailshots
- Exhibitions
- Websites (see 10.3)

- **What media will be used?** A wide variety of media can be used to communicate the firm's promotional message. These may vary from promotions on free carrier bags, to primetime television advertising. The choice of promotional medium is as important as the promotional message, because if the right message is sent out using the wrong media, the target market will not receive it, and the promotion will fail.

Clearly, the right media is not just the one which reaches the target market: the media also has to be affordable. Many small businesses use *Yellow Pages*, local newspaper advertising, specialist magazines and leaflets, as low-cost ways of reaching their target market.

A Meat-eoric Success:

Salami Man Sells An Extra 95 Tonnes

HE'S a walking, talking sausage who eats his own arms and has a wicked sense of humour - and he's proving that if you make the customers laugh, they are more likely to buy your product.

This unlikely character has increased sales of Pepperami, the savoury sausage snack, by 33% in six months, which converts into an extra 95 tonnes of Pepperami sold.

Daily Mirror, 26.10.1994

Distribution

Distribution is about where and how the product is sold (see 11.2).

In buying a product, consumers consider its place and method of sale along with the features of the product itself. For example, people buying bread and milk late on a Sunday evening or Bank holiday from a local 'corner shop' will often pay up to double the price they would pay at a supermarket on a weekday. This is simply because of the convenience of being able to shop late at night, when other stores are closed. In other words, the benefits of timing and ease of access to the local store are being sold along with the bread and milk.

A plan for distribution may be created by asking the following questions:

- **Who will buy the product or service?** The aim here is to identify a target market segment. This will help identify the kinds of outlet where the product should be distributed in order to reach the target market.
- **Why will customers buy?** The answer to this will reveal the package of features and benefits that customers will look for. If, for example, it includes 'good after-sales service', the product might need to be distributed through established department stores and high street shops. If not, then mail order or distribution through discount chains might be appropriate.

  Distribution will also involve a consideration of the cost, speed, and security of physically transporting products by road, rail, sea, or air.

Transport costs can often be a significant element in the total costs of a business.

Selling methods

The organization of sales and sales staff requires careful planning. Sales staff need to be carefully trained in order to acquaint them with the features of the product and how it can be favourably compared with competitors' products (see 11.3). The selling section of the marketing plan may aim to target particular types of customer, by choosing retail outlets in particular localities or by targeting 'direct' mailshots at certain customer groups. The sales section of the plan should make it clear how the business will:

- Influence customers' attitudes towards the product
- Make people desire the product
- Convince customers that buying the good is the right decision

Selling methods might include:

- Visiting customers
- 'Cold calling' by telephone or doorstep calls
- Direct mail and e-mailing to potential customers
- Telesales
- Trade magazines and trade fairs
- Contacting wholesalers
- Advertising in business directories and *Yellow Pages*
- Internet websites for e-commerce advertising and sales
- Posters and leaflet distribution
- Local and national radio advertising
- Free gifts and samples
- Cards in shop windows
- Catalogues and mail order
- Home demonstrations and sales parties in homes

Preparing a marketing budget

A good marketing plan will estimate the costs of the proposed marketing strategy, and express this in a **budget**.

A budget will enable the entrepreneur to evaluate whether or not the marketing plans are realistic. Once costed, the marketing plans could prove to be too expensive and so have to be scaled down; alternatively, the cost could be very modest and so allow some extra marketing effort. The budget will also provide a means by which the entrepreneur can monitor and control the operation of the marketing plan in practice, by carefully comparing actual marketing expenditure to planned expenditure.

The budget should estimate the amount likely to be spent on each aspect of the marketing plan. This will include market research, all types of advertising, promotions, distribution, and selling. The costs of many of these items can be estimated accurately. For example, press and leaflet advertising can be costed simply by contacting local newspapers and printers. Other items, such as the amount to be spent on selling expenses (e.g. expense accounts and training for sales staff), cannot be costed by contacting outside agencies, but will have to be estimated by business managers.

A number of different methods are used by firms in order to allocate funds to these kind of subjective budget headings. Methods can be based on:

- A fixed percentage of the next year's estimated sales value
- A fixed percentage of this year's sales value
- Estimates of what competitors spend
- Estimates of how much extra revenue an activity will generate

The marketing budget should also indicate how the planned expenditure will be phased across the year, usually using a monthly breakdown. The budget should be presented in a similar format to other kinds of operating budgets (see 19.2).

Timing and scheduling the marketing plan

In order to ensure that the marketing plan is successful, it is necessary to carefully work out priorities, and then schedule the timing of activities, so that the key marketing activities are carried out in the correct sequence. For example, the product must be designed, packaged, and priced *before* sales staff can be trained. Shop-counter promotions created to encourage consumers to sample the product can only take place once the product has been distributed - and so on.

Techniques such as the GANNT chart and Critical Path Analysis (CPA) can assist with the timing and scheduling of marketing activities (see 20.3).

Key words:

Marketing mix - the elements of a firm's marketing strategy designed to meet consumer wants and generate sales. The four main elements are: product, price, place, and promotion

Marketing plan - sets out how an organization will use the marketing mix to achieve its business objectives

Marketing budget - a forward plan of costed marketing activities

Unique selling points - features of a product or business that differentiate it from its rivals

Best practice benchmarking - observing the products and processes of rival companies in order to learn new and better ways of producing, marketing and selling

Section 21.3

The production plan

What is a production plan?

The aim of the production plan is to organize premises, machinery, labour, and raw materials efficiently, so that the firm can produce the goods required by customers in the right quantities and at the right time. The production plan will outline the action to be taken both immediately and in the medium-to-long term.

Portfolio Activity 21.4 

Using the article below:

1. What evidence is there to suggest that many British manufactured goods are poorly designed? Why is product quality important?
2. Why does the article suggest that planning for the introduction of new products is needed now, more than ever?
3. What kinds of strategies might be adopted by a new business in order to help get its product launch right?

Time for an Action Plan

The successful introduction of new products is one of the keys to profitable manufacturing, but, for many UK manufacturers, improving the process is still in its infancy.

This is one of the findings of an updated edition of *Manufacturing into the Late 1990s*, which has been prepared by the Department of Trade and Industry by Tony Roberts and Mark Smalley at PA Consulting group.

"Product design often takes years for many engineering-type products," he says. The complexity of new product introduction for many engineering products means it is less well understood than other industrial processes. It involves highly skilled people who are accustomed to working at their own pace.

The study gives advice to managers on how to improve their manufacturing responses to the challenges in the 1990s. It identifies four themes:

- Higher customer expectations. "Customer power continues to grow and to compete effectively you must satisfy existing and new customers profitably."
- Greater business complexity. Multi-technologies in the product and the manufacturing process, a wider product range, customization, and market niches.
- More uncertainty, stemming from a wider range of customers, shorter product lifecycles and more competition. This means greater uncertainty about the life of products and the investment decisions associated with them.
- Growing competitive and legislative pressure, such as that concerned with health and safety and product liability.

Because of these pressures successful new product introduction is seen as so important. The key ways to achieve this include getting designers close to customers, using multi-discipline teams with clear objectives about delivering their product on time, and having the design effort managed by a product director with clear authority to deliver.

Planning should also include the design of better factories, including flexible manufacturing processes with focused units which can handle variations in type of production for production runs of short lifecycle.

Roberts is encouraged by what has been happening in manufacturing. "There is a much greater awareness of the need for a strategy - something that makes sense of all of the elements of design and manufacture to produce a competitive and profitable business," he says.

A business may plan to vary the priorities for its product and production processes over time. The following table illustrates how this might be achieved.

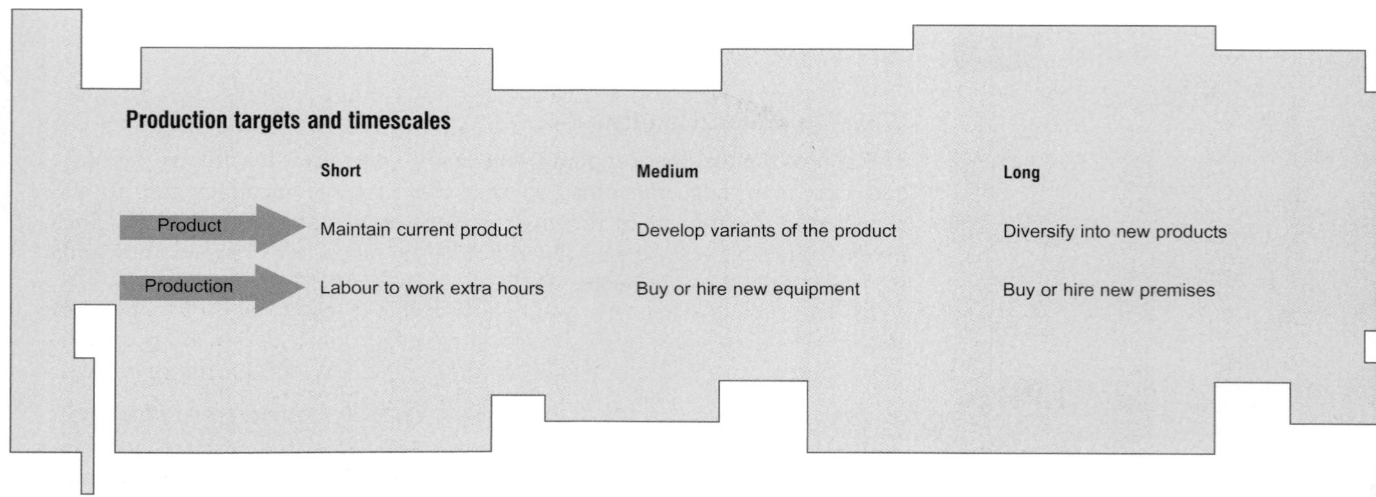

Production targets and timescales
Short
Medium
Long
Product
Maintain current product
Develop variants of the product
Diversify into new products
Production
Labour to work extra hours
Buy or hire new equipment
Buy or hire new premises

▼ *Job production*

▼ *Flow production*

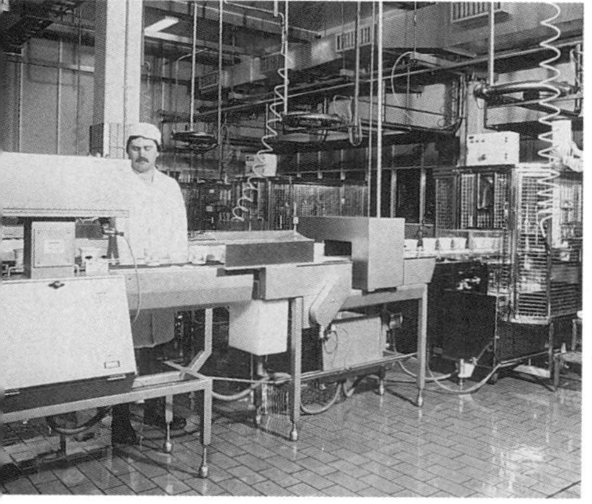

Types of production

The way in which production is organized will depend upon the method of production adopted by the business. Three possible methods are:

- **Job production:** this method is used for producing single or one-off orders, where each order is custom built. For example, personal services, such as hairdressing, painting and decorating, arranging flowers for weddings, are all examples of job production.
- **Flow production**: this method involves the manufacture of a product in a continuously moving process. Flow production is used to mass-produce identical products for huge national or international markets.
- **Batch production**: this method is used for producing a limited number of identical products to meet a specific order, for example, 1,000 calling cards, 50,000 pre-recorded video cassettes of a particular film, or runs of daily newspapers.

The precise method of production chosen will clearly depend on the answers to a number of questions:

- **What is the nature of the product?** For example, is it a personalized good or service? Do materials need careful handling?
- **What is the size of the market?** This will determine the volume of output required.
- **What is the nature of demand?** Will consumers purchase the product on a regular basis (e.g. washing powder), or infrequently (e.g. furniture and electrical goods)?
- **What is the capacity of the business?** If necessary, does the business have enough resources to produce on a large scale?

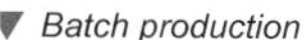 Batch production

Portfolio Activity 21.5 

Make a list of goods or services which have been produced using job production, flow production, and batch production, and suggest why these methods have been used in each case.

Resource requirements

Once the production method has been chosen and justified, it is possible to decide upon the kind of premises, equipment, raw materials, and labour that will be required to meet production targets.

Premises

Many individuals now run small businesses from home, for example, driving instructors, window-cleaners, and sandwich-makers. Operating from home can save money, but care needs to be taken to ensure that running a home business does not infringe local authority planning regulations or the conditions of the householder's mortgage. Most businesses are operated from **leased premises** (see 20.3).

It is useful in a production plan to draw a diagram of the premises and the layout of benches, counters, tables, machinery, and other equipment you intend to use.

Machinery

The production plan should identify the machinery and other equipment required, for example, tools and computers, and name some potential suppliers. This section should indicate whether or not the business intends to hire, lease, or buy equipment, and should also outline the estimated total cost of what it intends to do. The plan should detail the support available for servicing and maintaining the machinery, where this support will come from, and how much it will cost.

The impact of any plans to buy additional equipment in the future should also be outlined in the plan, as well as any staff training requirements to make full and effective use of new equipment.

Labour

Will production be labour-intensive or capital-intensive? The production plan should outline the firm's labour requirements - that is, numbers of employees, their skill levels, and previous experience required. The plan should indicate where these employees are to be found, how they will be recruited, methods of payment, and future training needs (see 15.2).

The cost of labour varies enormously across different regions in the UK. Labour costs in the South East are the highest in the country, while costs in parts of the North of England and Northern Ireland are among the lowest. The entrepreneur will need to consider the impact of the geographical location of the firm on its labour costs. A business requiring a large amount of unskilled labour might locate in a region with high unemployment and find that it can recruit cheaply. However, a business needing highly specialized labour, for example, those with computer system design skills, may need to locate near similar organizations, for example in 'Silicon Valley' in Cambridge, and may be forced to pay very high wages to attract staff from rival firms (see 13.2).

Materials and component parts

If the business needs materials and component parts, it is important that the entrepreneur identifies suppliers in advance who are able to supply them at the right quality in the right amounts at the right time, and who are prepared to trade on terms acceptable to the firm. Many suppliers will be cautious of giving credit to new and unknown businesses. Therefore, it is essential that the terms and conditions of supply are established before the business starts up.

This section should also outline the stock levels that the firm intends to carry.

Just In Time production (JIT)

Just In Time production is a system designed to reduce the costs of holding stocks of raw materials, work in progress, and finished goods, through careful scheduling of the production process. JIT is sometimes known as supply chain management, because it involves a great deal of work with suppliers to achieve high levels of quality and reliability in supplies.

JIT means that finished goods are produced to order and 'just in time' to be sold, thereby reducing storage times. Similarly, raw materials and components arrive at the factory 'just in time' to be used, thereby reducing storage costs (see 1.2).

Quality control objectives

Quality control aims to produce goods that:

- Satisfy consumer wants
- Work properly
- Can be repaired
- Conform to safety standards
- Are produced cost-effectively

A company that fails in quality control is unlikely to realize revenue, profit, or growth objectives.

Quality assurance

The production plan should also detail how product quality will be assured.

The production of poor-quality products, and the resulting search for weaknesses in production processes, use up valuable time and resources in a business. Errors are costly. Furthermore, should any poor-quality products reach consumers, company image and reputation can be damaged.

To prevent errors happening, organizations are increasingly turning to the techniques of **Total Quality Management (TQM).** This involves building-in quality checks at each and every stage in a production process, the aim being to identify problems and solve them *before,* rather than after, products have completed the production process (see 1.2).

Key words:

Production plan - this sets out details of design, product development, premises, machinery, materials to be used, and labour requirements.

Job production - completing one job before moving on to another

Flow production - continuous mass-production

Batch production - producing a limited number of identical products to meet a specific order. Work is completed for a whole batch before the next batch is begun

Just In Time production (JIT) - keeping stocks and work in progress to a minimum by ordering new supplies only when they are needed for production

Total Quality Management (TQM) - the continuous improvement of products and processes by focusing on quality at each stage of production

chapter 22 Financial Planning

This chapter sets out what is required in the financial plan for your business, and how to calculate your business costs.

What you need to learn

You will need to understand and use financial information to assess the viability of your business idea. To do this you will need to produce a **financial plan**. This will consist of:

- **budget plans**, including estimates of **start-up costs and working capital requirements**
- **break-even forecasts**
- **simple cashflow forecasts**
- **start-up and projected balance sheets**
- **projected profit and loss statements**
- **sources of finance**

You should demonstrate the viability of your business plan using your financial projections. You can do this by calculating your projected

- **return on capital employed**
- **profit margins**

You will also need to explain how you intend to evaluate the performance of your business over time by comparing your business outcomes against your forecasts of

- **costs and other budget plans**
- **sales and market share**
- **cashflows**
- **profits and profit margins**
- **returns on capital employed**

You will need to use a computer and software, such as a spreadsheet and graphics package, to develop and present your financial projections effectively.

Section 22.1 The financial plan

Making financial projections

Setting clear business objectives involves more than just producing words in a business plan. Business managers must translate their objectives into figures or targets expressed in money terms. **Financial plans** are needed to focus a firm on its targets and to help provide the entrepreneur with the answers to key questions once the business is trading. For example:

- What will be the costs of business start-up?
- What will be the fixed and variable costs of running the business?
- How much does the business need to produce and sell to cover the costs of the business and to make a profit?
- What will be the likely cash position of the business over time?
- How much profit is the business likely to make over time?
- How will the business costs be financed?

Figure 22.1 gives examples of the kind of questions an entrepreneur could be asked by a bank when starting up a new business venture.

The purpose of these questions is to establish how much money the firm will need to spend on its major cost items, including freehold or leasehold premises and rates, as well as plant, machinery, and equipment. Set against this are any assets which the entrepreneur can make available to a lender as security, and any capital to be provided by the entrepreneur.

In order to answer these questions you will need to forecast and analyse your **business costs**, and then produce projections of **cashflows**, **balance sheets** and **profit and loss statements**. You will then need to identify the possible sources of finance for your business venture (see Chapter 23).

Business costs

Sections 22.2–22.4 provide practical examples and guidance to help you forecast and analyse the likely costs of your business. These will include your business **start-up costs**, including the purchase of fixed assets such as premises, machinery and other equipment, and the costs of materials and labour which will vary according to how much of your good or service you intend to produce each week, month or year.

You will be able to use your business cost projections to carry out a **break-even analysis** (see 22.3). This means assessing how much you will need to produce and sell to cover the costs of running the business. Clearly, if this amount of output exceeds the level of demand you can expect from consumers for your product then you had better rethink your business strategy.

The cashflow forecast

Cashflow refers to the money which flows into and out of a business over a period of time, usually one year (see 17.2). A **cashflow forecast** should

▼ *Figure 22.1: A financial plan questionnaire*

Name of business ______ Type of business ______

Business address ______

Principal activities of business ______

Date business commenced ______

KEY PERSONNEL

Name	Position held	Salary

Please also attach details on separate sheet(s) of any additions to management team necessary for the growth of the business.

COST OF PREMISES

Freehold

Value (give basis and date) £ ______

Mortgate outstanding £ ______

Monthly repayment figure £ ______

Leasehold

Term of lease ______

Period outstanding ______

Option to renew YES/NO ______

Present rent per annum £ ______

Frequency of payment ______

Next rent review ______

Rates

Amount (half-yearly) £ ______

Date due (half-yearly) ______

Adapted from Banking Infomation Service Financial plan

PLANT AND MACHINERY, EQUIPMENT AND VEHICLES (EXISTING)

Description	Life expectancy	Value
		£

What capital expenditure do you anticipate during the next 12 months?

Please attach details on separate sheet.

PRODUCT OF SERVICE AND THE MARKET PLACE

Please give brief details of your product or service ______

Market size and potential (quote sources of information) ______

Major competitors and their existing market share ______

Has your product or service been market tested? ______

Please attach details on separate sheet together with firm orders, letters of intent, etc.

Marketing and sales methods including costs involved ______

ASSETS AVAILABLE AS SECURITY

Business (description)	Value (to include basis and date)
Personal (description)	Value (to include basis and date)

FINANCIAL REQUIREMENTS

Total cost of project £ ______

Own resources £ ______

Grants £ ______

Other sources (please specify) £ ______

£ ______

Bank requirements:

Overdraft (as per cashflow) £ ______

Loans and terms (years) £ ______

Other (please specify) £ ______

Total bank requirements £ ______

Total £

This Financial Plan to be used in conjunction with Cash flow Forecast in order to provide a comprehensive Business Plan.

▼ *Figure 22.2: A cashflow forecast proforma*

PERIOD (EG 4 WEEKS/MONTHS/QUARTERS)	Budget	Actual	Budget	Actual	Budget	Actual	Budget	Actual
Orders: Net of VAT								
Sales								
Receipts								
Cash Sales								
From Debtors								
Other Revenue Sources								
Total Receipts A								
Purchases								
Payments								
Cash Purchases								
To Creditors								
Wages/Salaries/PAYE								
RentlRates/lnsurance								
Light/Heat/Power								
Transport/Packing								
Repairs/Renewals								
VAT - Net								
HP Payments/Leasing Charges								
Bank/Finance charge/lnterest								
Sundry Expenses								
Tax								
Dividends								
Drawings/Fees								
Loan Repayments								
Capital Expenditure/lnflow								
Total Payments B								
A-B (net inflow) or C Cr								
B-A (net outflow) Dr								
Bank balance at end of D Cr								
previous period brought fwd ... Dr								
Bank balance at end of period Cr								
Carried fwd to aggregate (C&D) Dr								
Agreed overdraft facility								

Banking Information Service

be constructed for the first year of trading (some lenders ask to see forecasts for the first three years).

A cashflow forecast gives the estimated sum of cash inflows into a business, minus the sum of cash outflows. **Inflows** of cash can arise from cash sales, debtors paying cash, interest received, and sales of any assets. Cash **outflows** may be caused by cash purchases of stock, purchases of materials or of assets, or by settling debts owed to creditors. The cashflow forecast shows the net effect of cash inflows and outflows each month, and the impact of these on the firm's bank balance.

The advantage of cashflow forecasting is that it allows the business to spot in advance any shortfalls in cash during particular months, and to take appropriate action. If a deficit is anticipated, the firm can attempt either to reduce cash outflows in advance, or to raise cash inflows. Failing this, it can attempt to arrange an overdraft to cover the deficit. The cashflow forecast also allows the firm to identify where cash surpluses are likely to be made, and to plan to use these efficiently, for example, by investing the surplus or holding it over to meet a future deficit.

An example of a blank cashflow forecast statement is given in Figure 22.2. The forecast contains columns for both predicted and actual cashflow. By comparing the two, it is possible to identify differences or **variances** from the plan, and to investigate these as they happen (see 19.2).

A projected balance sheet

A potential lender will also require information about:

- The total capital (money) needed by a business
- What the business intends to do with its capital
- How much of the owner's money is being put into the firm
- Where the rest of the capital is to be raised from

This information is usually shown in the form of an **opening balance sheet.** A balance sheet is a statement of an organization's assets and liabilities at a particular point in time (see 18.2). Assets will include premises, machinery, and equipment owned by the firm, and holdings of cash, bank, or building society deposits, or sales on credit. **Liabilities** refer to money owed by the business to other people and organizations, for example, bank loans, hire purchase, leasing agreements, or purchases made on credit.

In the case of a new business, the balance sheet statement is likely to be drawn up for the first day of trading. It is common practice to include in a business plan both an opening balance sheet, and a projected balance sheet for the end of the first year of trading.

Figure 22.3 shows an opening balance sheet for a new business – Splash Decorating Services – and the balance sheet for the same business one year later.

The opening balance sheet shows the capital requirements of the firm, and what it intends to do with this capital in terms of distributing it between fixed and current assets (see 18.2). The balance sheet also shows, in the 'Financed by' section, how the business intends to raise its finance - in this case, by taking

▼ *Figure 22.3: Opening and projected balance sheet for Splash Decorating Services*

	OPENING BALANCE	PROJECTED BALANCE
	1.6.2001 £	31.5.2002 £
Fixed assets		
Machinery	2,000	1,600 (less 20% depreciation)
Vehicles	2,500	2,000 (less 20% depreciation)
(A)	4,500	3,600
Current assets		
Stocks	2,000	2,500
Debtors	–	500
Cash	1,500	2,000
(B)	3,500	5,000
Less Current liabilities (C)		
Trade creditors	2,500	1,850
(C)	2,500	1,850
Working capital (D=B–C)	1,000	3,150
Net assets (A+B)	**5,500**	**6,750**
Financed by		
Bank loan	4,500	4,500
Overdraft facility	–	1,000
Owners' savings	1,000	–
Net profit	–	**1,250**
	5,500	6,750

▼ *Figure 22.4: Projected profit and loss statement for Splash Decorating Services as at 31.5.2002*

	£	£
Turnover		45,000
Less Opening stock (1.6.2001)	4,500	
Add Purchases	12,000	
	16,500	
Less Closing stock (31.5.2002)	2,500	
		14,000
Gross profit		**31,000**
Less Rent	4,000	
Rates	500	
Light/heat	450	
Telephone/Post	150	
Insurance	250	
Hire Purchase	400	
Advertising	400	
Loan repayments	500	
Provisions for bad debts	300	
Depreciation	400	
Drawings	4,000	
Other expenses	750	
Total expenses	12,100	
Net profit		**18,900**

out a bank loan, and from the owners' savings. In this way, a start-up balance sheet can provide a great deal of useful information to a potential lender.

The projected balance sheet for the end of the first year shows the assets and liabilities the business expects to hold by 31 May 2002. By the end of the year, fixed assets such as machines and vehicles will have reduced in value because of depreciation (see 18.3). At the same time, the values for current assets and liabilities will change from their opening position, due to business trading.

In order to produce the end-of-year balance sheet forecast, the values of some of the balance sheet figures, such as stocks and cash, can be estimated from the cashflow forecast for the year. The firm will have some money owed from sales to debtors by the end of the year, and in this example, will have recorded its first profit, a predicted sum of £1,250.

The projected year-end balance sheet allows potential lenders to see the likely value of the business one year from starting trading, and so gives them an idea of the likelihood of the business being able to repay its loan.

The projected profit and loss statement

The profit and loss statement shows the profit made by a business during a particular trading period. It is calculated as total sales revenue minus total costs (see 18.3). Unlike a balance sheet, which gives a picture at a particular moment in time, the profit and loss statement shows profit made over a period of time.

Figure 22.4 provides an example of a projected profit and loss statement for Splash Decorating Services.

If a profit is projected after tax and other expenses, the business owners can then decide how much to retain in the business and how much to pay out to themselves. If a loss is projected, the owners can plan in advance how to raise the finance necessary to pay for the loss.

New firms are usually required to produce a projected profit and loss statement for their first year of trading in order to give potential lenders an estimate of how well the firm is likely to do. Once the business has started, managers are likely to produce a profit and loss statement every one to three months in order to monitor business performance (see Figure 22.5).

▼ *Figure 22.5: Proforma for monthly profit and loss statement forecast*

Month TOTAL £	**1**	**2**	**3**	**4**	**5**	**6**	**7**	**8**	**9**	**10**	**11**	**12**	
Sales Less opening stock Add purchases													
Gross profit (A)													
Expenses:													
Rent													
Rates													
Electricity													
Gas													
Advertising													
Insurance													
Stationery, postage													
Telephone													
Bank charges													
Loan repayments													
Hire Purchase													
Depreciation: equipment vehicles													
Provision for bad debts													
Owners' drawings													
Other expenses:													
______													
______													
______													
______													
Total expenses (B)													
Net profit/loss (A-B)													

Notes:

1 Opening stock should appear in Month 1 cost of sales. (Add purchases)

2 Allowance for depreciation of equipment and vehicles is usually entered in last month.

3 Drawings can be thought of as a monthly wage paid to the small business owner.

Monitoring and reviewing business performance

Once a new business is up and running, managers will want to monitor its financial performance very closely in order to be in a position to take immediate corrective action when required. Potential lenders will look for evidence that the business is going to be run according to principles of sound financial management, and will expect to see details of how this is going to happen in the business plan.

The main means of monitoring used by small firms are as follows:

1. Regular monitoring of cash inflows and outflows against the cashflow forecast.

2. Comparing actual sales and purchases against operating budget plans. A comparison of plans with outturn can be made using **variance analysis** (see 19.2). It is important for an organization to keep its costs as low as possible, and within budget.

3. Producing monthly or three-monthly profit and loss statements and balance sheets. These accounts can reveal a great deal about business performance. Financial performance can be monitored using **ratio analysis**, for example, measuring profit margins, return on capital employed, and liquidity ratios (see 19.3).

4. Monitoring **aged creditors lists** and **aged debtors lists** (see 19.3). This will tell a business how much is owed to suppliers and when payments have to be made, and how much is owed to the business for sales made on credit. Chasing up late payers may be required to keep cashflow projections on target and to provide funds, so that creditors can be paid on time.

5. Monitor achievements against other business objectives, such as growing market share or raising product awareness among consumers through a carefully planned promotional campaign (see 1.7). For example, the success or otherwise of the promotional campaign could be tested using market research (see 9.1).

Business planning

To be workable a business plan must be realistic; it must take account of the shortcomings of the firm and of the people involved. This will help to ensure that the plan is achievable within the resources available. For an average business, a three-year projection will be adequate, with the first year shown in detail, and the next two in outline. In quickly changing industries, such as computers or consumer electronics, the planning horizon may need to be shorter - perhaps 18 months to 2 years.

A business plan should not be seen as a rigid, inflexible answer to a firm's problems. Business conditions are continually changing, and a good business will adapt its plans to suit changes in the market or other circumstances. Business plans are only useful if they are realistic. A plan serves no purpose unless it can be delivered.

Research into small business growth and success both in the UK and USA suggests that there is a clear correlation between the amount of time invested in business planning and the ability of firms to sustain stable growth over time.

Section **22.2**

The costs of running a business

Identifying business costs

In most cases, running a business is all about making decisions on how best to use scarce resources in order to make a profit, where:

Profit = Sales Revenues – Costs

Every business decision, whether to launch a new product, change advertising methods, or to expand production, has cost implications. Because the primary purpose of most private-sector firms is to make a profit, it is essential that businesses are able to keep a tight control on their costs. Cost control is equally important to public-sector organizations and charities who do not seek to make a profit, but will nonetheless want to minimize the cost of their operations.

In order to control costs, it is first necessary to be able to identify business costs, calculate how much these costs are, and then to set targets for future cost levels.

Classifying costs

There are two main ways in which costs can be classified and calculated in order to assist managers in planning and controlling the operation of a business:

- **Direct and indirect costs** are definitions used for accounting purposes to calculate the level of profit before tax for a particular good or service.
- **Fixed and variable costs** are classified according to how they vary as the level of output of a good or service is varied.

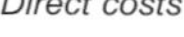

Direct costs

Direct costs

Costs which can be directly identified with a particular product or activity are known as **direct costs** or **prime costs**. These will include:

- **Direct materials:** the raw, or semi-finished materials and components used to make a product
- **Direct labour:** the wages of employees directly involved in making or assembling a product
- **Direct design costs:** costs incurred at the product planning stage
- **Other direct costs:** including the costs of power used in production, hire charges for machinery specifically employed in the production process, and the costs of any work subcontracted to other businesses
- **Depreciation:** an allowance made to cover a fall in the value of fixed assets, such as machinery, vehicles, computers, etc., due to wear and tear (see 18.2)

▼ *Indirect costs...*

Indirect costs

In most business organizations there will be costs which are not directly related to the production of a particular good or service, but which result from the operation of the entire organization. For example:

- Rent and business rates
- Lighting and heating
- Equipment maintenance
- Insurance
- Cleaning
- Sales and distribution costs, such as advertising and transport
- Bank charges on loans
- The wages and salaries of office staff, managers, accountants, etc.
- Depreciation of equipment used for administrative purposes

▼ *Indirect costs…*

These are all known as **indirect costs** or **overheads**.

The sum of direct and indirect costs gives the **total cost** of an organization's activities. It is important to know total cost in order to be able to work out **total profit**.

Fixed costs

Before a business can start production and make goods and services for sale it will need to pay for many costs. It will need to obtain premises, machinery and tools, office equipment, pay wages to office staff, and undertake market research. These are **start-up costs**. Starting up a business or developing a new product can be expensive and there will be no revenue to cover these start-up costs until the products are on sale and consumers are buying them.

Even when a business is up and running it will still need to pay many costs whether it is making and selling many or very few goods and services. **Fixed costs**, such as mortgage payments or rents on premises, interest charges on bank loans, lease charges for machinery, telephone bills and other overheads - that is, all indirect costs - tend not to vary with the amount of goods or services produced. For example, if it costs £5,000 each month to rent a factory in which to produce television sets this cost will be unchanged whether 1 or 1,000 television sets are produced. Clearly, it makes sense to try to spread these fixed costs over as much output as possible.

Variable costs

To expand production a firm is likely to need more materials or components, and more power to drive machinery, or to heat and light premises for longer periods. They may also need to take on more workers or employ existing workers on overtime to produce more.

Costs that vary with the level of output, such as materials, power, and the wages of production workers, are called **variable costs**. For example, if the variable cost of producing one television set is £100, then the cost of producing 1,000 television sets is likely to be £100,000, unless costs savings can be made from workers and machinery working much harder and improving their productivity (see 1.1).

Variable costs are, therefore, just the direct costs of productive activity.

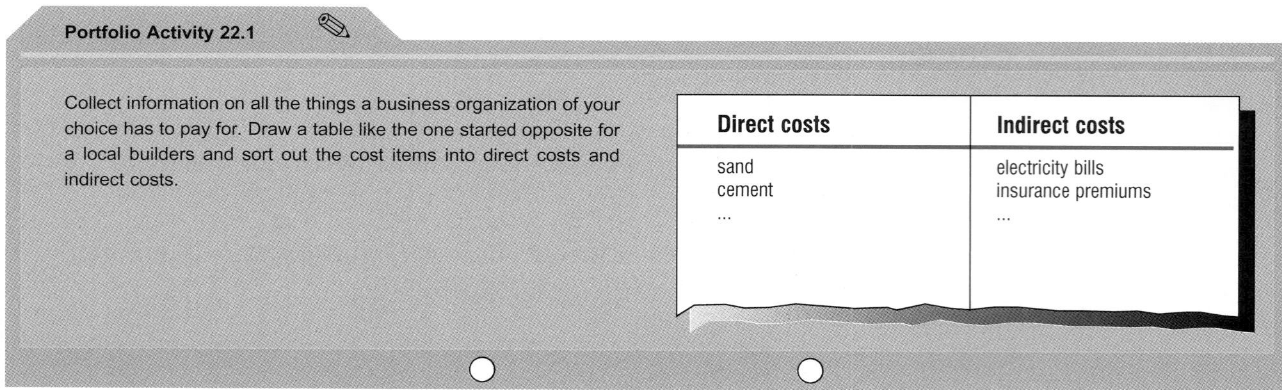

Portfolio Activity 22.1

Collect information on all the things a business organization of your choice has to pay for. Draw a table like the one started opposite for a local builders and sort out the cost items into direct costs and indirect costs.

Direct costs	Indirect costs
sand cement ...	electricity bills insurance premiums ...

MABEL'S MUGS (costs per month)

Direct costs		Indirect costs	
labour	£700	rent	£120
materials	£300	rates	£40
	£1,000	insurance	£35
		power	£30
		telephone	£25
		loan repayment	£35
		advertising	£15
			£300

Calculating the total cost of production

The **total cost** of producing a given level of output in an organization is the sum of its fixed and variable costs. Since the total costs of the same business is also the sum of its direct and indirect costs it follows that the total cost of producing a given level of output per period in any business is equal to:

Direct costs + Indirect costs = Fixed costs + Variable costs

Consider the following example. Mabel's Mugs is small pottery manufacturing business which makes large, hand-painted drinking mugs. Mabel, the owner of the business, has calculated that her direct costs are £1,000 each month, and her indirect costs are £300 each month. Total costs are, therefore, £1,300 per month.

These costs are based on Mabel's usual output of 500 mugs each month. That is, she allocates all her business costs to the production of her mugs. She would like to increase her output to 600 mugs each month. Her indirect costs are unlikely to increase simply because she has produced 100 more mugs. So, to find out how much extra 100 mugs would cost her she calculates that the variable cost of producing each mug in terms of labour and materials (her direct costs) is £2 (i.e. £1,000 / 500 mugs). Using this information Mabel calculates not only the total cost of producing 600 mugs each month but also other levels of output assuming her indirect costs remain fixed (see Table 22.1).

▼ *Table 22.1: How Mabel's Mugs costs vary with output*

Number of mugs per month	Fixed costs (£) per month	Total variable costs (£) for the level of output	Total cost (£) per month for the level of output
0	300	(£2 × 0) = 0	300
100	300	(£2 × 100) = 200	500
200	300	(£2 × 200) = 400	700
300	300	(£2 × 300) = 600	900
400	300	(£2 × 400) = 800	1100
500	300	(£2 × 500) = 1000	1300
600	300	(£2 × 600) = 1200	1500
700	300	(£2 × 700) = 1400	1700

So for example, Mabel calculates the total cost of producing 600 mugs is equal to £300 of fixed costs and £1,200 of variable costs – a total of £1,500 per month. If she increased production by 100 to 700 mugs per month her total variable costs will rise to £1,400 – an increase of £200. Fixed costs will be unchanged and so the total cost of making 700 mugs per month will be £1,700.

Will fixed costs always remain fixed?

As a firm expands output it may come to a point when its existing premises and amount of machinery are simply not enough to carry on producing more and more. That is, its productive capacity will be fully utilized - it has no spare capacity to produce any more output. If the firm is to expand production further it must take on larger premises and more machinery. The firm may also find it needs to take on more administrative staff to deal with orders, deliveries and payments. These fixed costs may not, therefore, always be fixed as firms expand production. For example, if Mabel's Mugs wanted to produce 1,000 mugs each month instead of 600 mugs it may need to buy a computer to help with office functions, a larger kiln in which to bake the clay mugs and a power-driven potter's wheel to replace one operated by foot. Fixed costs will rise.

Key words:

Direct costs - costs which can be directly related to the production of a particular good or service

Indirect costs - costs which cannot be directly related to the production of a particular good or service, for example, the costs of business administration

Overheads - indirect costs

Fixed costs - costs that do not vary with the level of output

Variable costs - costs that do vary with the level of output

Section 22.3

Calculating, analysing and presenting business costs

In the last section we learnt that **fixed costs**, such as rent, rates and other running expenses, do not vary with the level of output. Costs that do vary as a direct result of changes in the level of output, such as purchases of raw materials and wages, are called **variable costs**.

We will now consider how fixed and variable costs can be presented on graphs to help a business plan for future levels of production.

Figure 22.6: Fixed costs

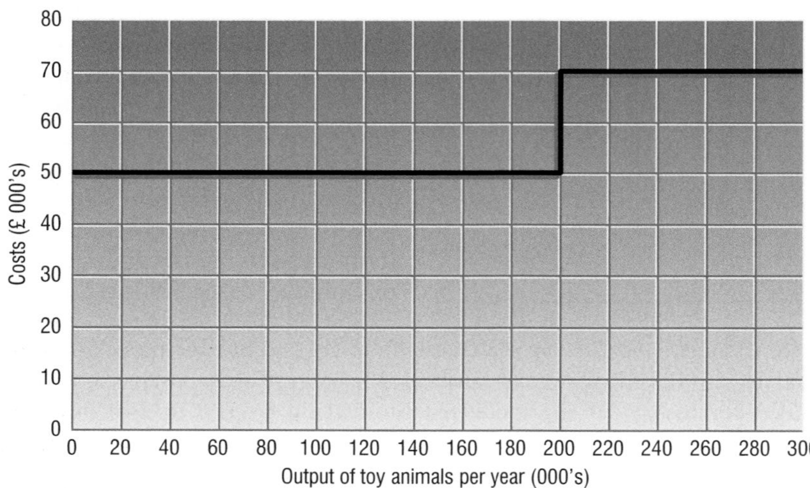

Fixed costs

Figure 22.6 depicts the relationship between fixed costs and output in a graph for a business making toy animals. It shows that fixed costs are £50,000 regardless of the amount produced, up to 199,999 units of product per year. If the firm wants to produce more than this, it will need to hire or buy larger premises and more machines. In the long run, therefore, fixed costs can be stepped up (or down), but will then remain fixed at their higher level of £70,000 at levels of output of 200,000 or more units per year.

Figure 22.7: Variable costs

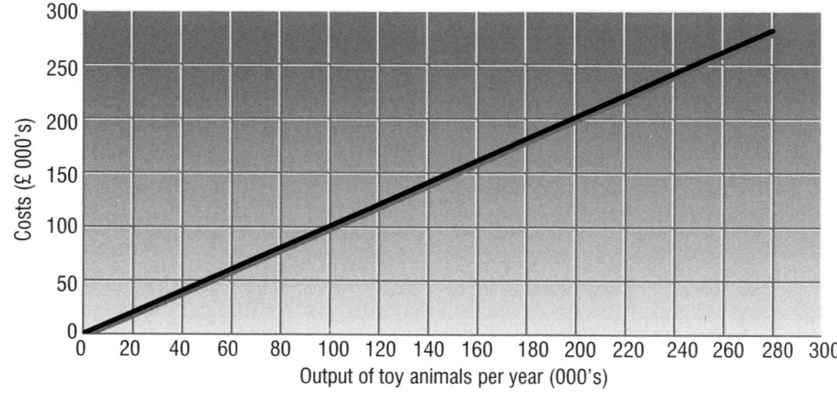

Variable costs

Figure 22.7 shows how variable costs vary with the amount of toy animals produced. The variable cost of each toy is £1. If the firm produces no toys, total variable costs will be zero. If the firm produces 200,000 toy animals, its total variable costs will be £200,000.

Output (Units of toy animals)	Fixed cost (FC)	Variable cost (VC)	Total cost (TC)
0	£50,000	0	£50,000
100,000	£50,000	£100,000	£150,000
200,000	£50,000	£200,000	£250,000

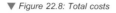

Semi-variable costs

Some costs do not fit neatly into the categories of 'fixed' and 'variable'. The cost of hiring labour is a good example. If a business employs ten people on a permanent basis, the total wage bill will be the same each week, regardless of the level of output. However, if the employees are asked to work overtime to produce more output, then the extra cost of their employment will be variable. Such labour costs are said to be **semi-variable**. Only if the employees' wages are linked directly to output, for example, through the payment of piece rates, will the whole wage bill be a variable cost to the business.

Other examples of costs which are often thought of as semi-variable are telephone and electricity charges. These consist of a fixed standing charge which is the same no matter how many calls are made or how much electricity is used, plus a variable charge dependent on the number of units used up.

Total costs

Adding fixed and variable costs together gives the total cost of production.

Total Cost (TC) = Fixed Cost (FC) + Variable Cost (VC)

The total cost of production is the cost of producing any given level of output. As output rises, total cost will increase because of variable costs. The relationship between total cost and output for the toy animal manufacturer is shown in Figure 22.8.

Figure 22.8: Total costs

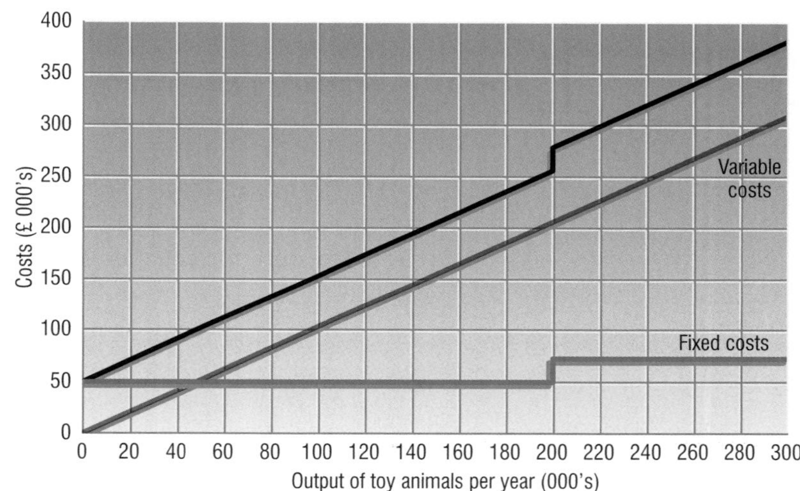

What is break-even analysis?

A business will often want to know how much they will have to produce and sell of a good or service at a chosen price before they make a profit. Classifying costs as fixed or variable allows managers to undertake this calculation, and to decide on appropriate selling prices for their products.

The **break-even level of output** is where total sales revenue is exactly equal to total costs. At this point, the firm makes neither a profit nor a loss. That is, the break-even point occurs where:

Total Revenue (£) = Fixed Costs + Variable Costs = Total Costs

Break-even analysis seeks to predict the level of sales a business will need to achieve in order to break even, and to determine how changes in output, costs, and/or price will affect the break-even point and their possible profits.

Calculating break-even point

A firm can calculate its break-even point if it knows its costs and the price it can charge for each unit of output. Consider the following example.

Geoff's Knitwear Ltd has fixed costs each year of £200,000, and variable costs of £5 per jumper produced. The jumpers are sold for £30 each. The break-even level of output for Geoff's Knitwear can be calculated as follows:

$$\text{Total Cost (TC)} = \text{Fixed Costs} + \text{Variable Costs}$$
$$\text{TC} = £200{,}000 + (£5 \times Q)$$

and:

$$\text{Total Revenue (TR)} = \text{Price} \times \text{Quantity Sold}$$
$$\text{TR} = £30 \times Q$$

(where Q is the quantity of jumpers produced and sold)

At break-even output, total cost equals total revenue. That is:

$$\text{TC} = \text{TR}$$
$$£200{,}000 + (£5 \times Q) = £30 \times Q$$

Thus, to solve the equation by finding Q:

$$£200{,}000 = £25 \times Q$$
$$\frac{£200{,}000}{£25} = Q$$
$$8{,}000 = Q$$

That is, Geoff's Knitwear must produce and sell 8,000 jumpers at a price of £30 each to break even. If more than 8,000 jumpers are sold, the firm makes a profit, while if less than 8,000 are made, the firm makes a loss.

We can check this calculation by returning to the formula TC = TR:

$$£200{,}000 + (£5 \times 8000 \text{ jumpers}) = £30 \times 8000 \text{ jumpers}$$
$$£200{,}000 + £40{,}000 = £240{,}000$$
$$£240{,}000 \text{ costs} = £240{,}000 \text{ revenue}$$

We can, therefore, be confident that 8,000 jumpers is the break-even level of output in Geoff's Knitwear Ltd.

▼ *Table 22.2: Schedule of outputs, costs and revenue for Geoff's Knitwear Ltd*

Jumpers per year (Q)	Total costs (£200,000 + (£5 x Q))	Total revenue (£30 x Q)
0	£200,000	0
2,000	£210,000	£60,000
4,000	£220,000	£120,000
6,000	£230,000	£180,000
8,000	£240,000	£240,000
10,000	£250,000	£300,000
12,000	£260,000	£360,000

Break-even charts

The break-even point can also be found by plotting total costs and total revenues on a **break-even chart.**

The first step is to calculate total costs and total revenue for a number of different levels of output. (As an absolute minimum, two levels of output should be chosen - zero and one other.) Table 22.2 is a schedule of outputs for Geoff's Knitwear Ltd, ranging from 0 to 12,000 jumpers per year, with corresponding costs and revenues. These figures can be used to plot the two line graphs in the break-even chart in Figure 22.9.

In a break-even chart, output or sales are measured on the horizontal (x) axis, while costs are measured on the vertical (y) axis. Break-even output is found at the point at which the total revenue line crosses the total cost line. The area between the two lines represents a loss when TC is greater than TR, and a profit when TC is less than TR.

▼ *Figure 22.9: Break-even chart for Geoff's Knitwear Ltd*

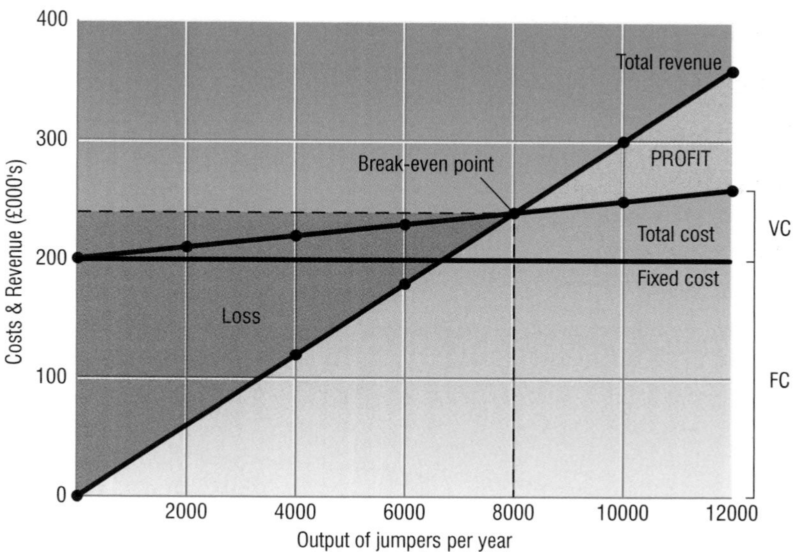

Portfolio Activity 22.2

Bear Necessities is a small toy firm producing hand-made teddy bears, owned by Bev Johnson. Bev rents a small factory unit on an industrial estate for £100 per week. She pays out £5 a week on heat and light (subsidized by the council), and £50 a week to repay a bank loan. She hires machinery at a cost of £45 per week, and employs her two brothers to help her make bears. At present, they pay themselves £1 for each bear they complete. Materials to make the bears cost £6, and foam costs £1. Bev initially charges £20.00 for each bear sold.

1. Calculate the total fixed costs of Bear Necessities and the variable cost per bear.
2. For the following levels of output of bears each week, calculate total costs, total revenue, and profit (or loss):

   (a) 5

   (b) 20

   (c) 40
3. What is the average cost per bear:

   (a) when 10 bears are produced each week?

   (b) if bear production is 40 per week?

   What do you conclude about the relationship between average cost and output? Why is this relationship unlikely to hold if bear production is expanded indefinitely?
4. Calculate how many bears Bev Johnson needs to produce and sell each week to break even.
5. What will happen to her break-even level of output if:

   (a) she finds a new supplier who offers her a bulk discount, such that material costs per bear fall to £4?

   (b) she has to reduce the price of each bear to £15 to encourage sales (costs are as calculated in Question 1)?
6. Suggest how break-even analysis can assist Bear Necessities in planning future production and prices.

'What if' analysis

Break-even charts are a useful business planning tool because they allow managers to project what might happen to the break-even output and profits if costs alter, or if the price of the product is changed. For example, if prices are cut, the break-even level of output will rise, since more units will need to be sold to cover production costs.

Figure 22.10: The impact of a price-rise on break-even

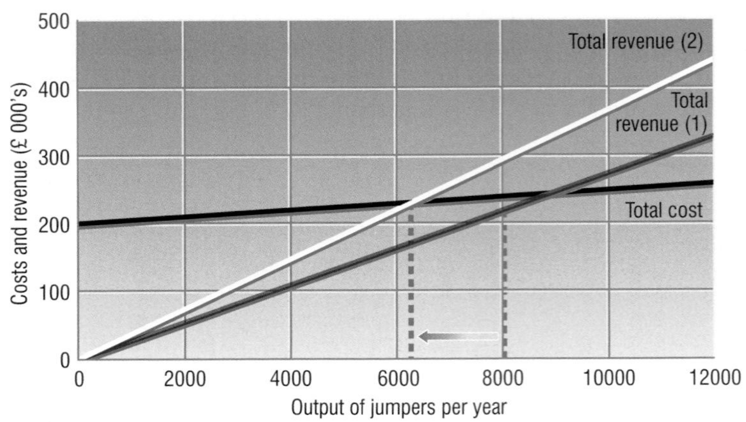

Figure 22.10 shows the effect of a price-rise to £37 per jumper on the break-even level of output for Geoff's Knitwear Ltd. Only 6,250 jumpers now have to be sold in order for the business to break even, rather than 8,000.

Figure 22.11: The impact of an increase in variable costs on break-even

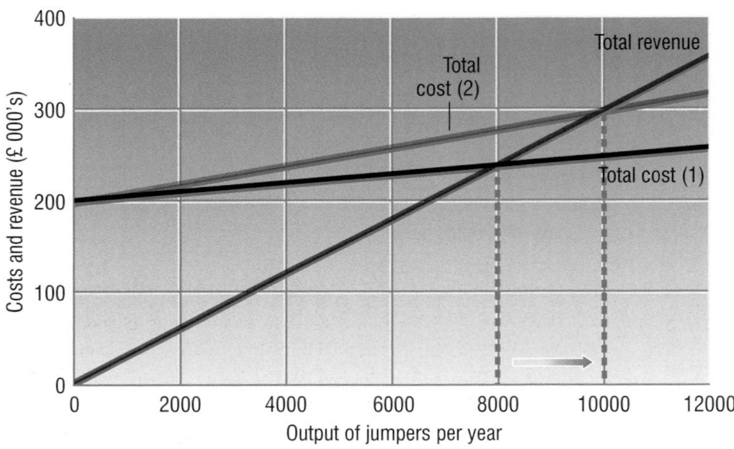

Figure 22.11 shows the impact of a rise in materials costs on the knitwear business. Variable costs per jumper are now £10. In order to break even, the company must now sell 10,000 jumpers per year. An increase in fixed costs would have a similar impact.

Figure 22.12: The margin of safety for Geoff's Knitwear Ltd

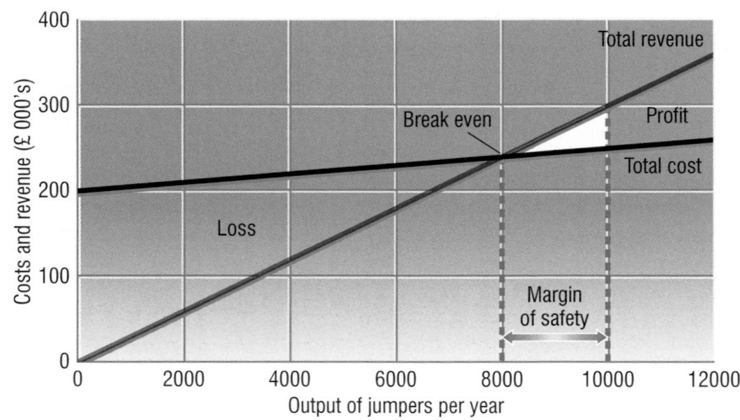

The margin of safety

Once a business has forecast the level of sales it must achieve at a given price in order to break even, it must then attempt to exceed this level in order to make a profit. In the example above, Geoff's Knitwear might plan to sell 10,000 jumpers next year - 2,000 more than required to break even. The firm would then be operating above break-even output and will therefore be in the area of profit. This difference between forecast sales and break-even output is known as the **margin of safety**. In other words, Geoff's Knitwear has incorporated a margin of safety of 2,000 units into its sales forecast. Sales of jumpers can therefore fall short of the forecast by up to 2,000 (or 20%) before the firm will start to make losses (see Figure 22.12).

Portfolio Activity 22.3

1. Input the following table into a computer spreadsheet:

FINANCIAL INFORMATION FOR SWIZZ MAGS LTD
Teen Dream Magazine (Retail Price £1.50)

Fixed costs per month £10,000
Variable cost per unit £0.25

Magazines per month	Total cost	Total revenue	Profit/Loss
0	?	?	?
4,000			
8,000			
2,000			
16,000			
20,000			
24,000			
28,000			

2. Input commands to automatically compute each cell in the columns for total cost, total revenue, and profit/loss for each level of output.
3. What is the break-even level of output?
4. Use the information to produce a break-even chart from your spreadsheet table. Make sure you use the following labels:
   - Area of profit/loss
   - Total cost and Total revenue
   - Costs and level of output
   - Break even point
   - Fixed costs and variable costs
5. For each of the following events in isolation, recalculate each column in your table, and then replot your break-even chart to show the effect of:

   (a) an increase in product price to £1.85

   (b) an increase in the variable cost per unit to 50 pence

   (c) an increase in fixed costs to £12,000 per month, due to an increase in insurance and business rates

Limitations of break-even analysis

Break-even analysis is a useful aid to business planning, but managers need to be aware of its limitations as a decision-making tool. For example:

- Break-even analysis assumes that the quantity of goods produced is actually sold, and that no stocks are held. In reality, however, firms will often need to build up stocks to cope with seasonal variations or unforeseen changes in demand. This means that they are sometimes likely to produce goods which are not sold.
- Break-even analysis also assumes that fixed costs are always fixed. However, when output expands, it may become necessary to install more plant and equipment, which can cause fixed costs to increase. Inflation will also affect costs.
- The conditions of demand and supply are constantly changing (see 5.1). That is, costs and the prices at which goods or services can be sold will not be static. As conditions change, it becomes harder to predict the break-even level of output.
- Break-even analysis relies on accurate cost and sales data. If data is inaccurate or forecasts poor, then break-even analysis will yield inaccurate advice. For example, if fixed costs have been underestimated, break-even analysis will suggest a lower level of sales will be needed to cover costs than will actually be the case and the firm will risk making a loss.

Key words:

Break-even - occurs where total revenue is equal to total cost, i.e. profit is zero

Break-even level of output - that level of output at which total sales revenue is equal to total cost

Break-even analysis - analysing price, output and cost information to determine the output a firm will need to produce and sell to break even

Margin of safety - a level of output over and above the break-even level to ensure that a firm can cover its costs and produce at a profit, even if costs were to rise or prices fall by some margin

Section 22.4

Calculating unit costs

Once the total cost of each product has been calculated, it is possible to calculate how much, on average it costs to produce each unit of output (or cost unit). This is particularly useful for a business to know.

A **cost unit** is simply a unit of product, the cost of which can be calculated and compared with revenues earned from its sale. A cost unit can be any good, for example, a car, a compact disc, a box of washing powder, a lawn mower, a chest of drawers and so on. Or the cost unit can be a service, such as one hour of labour from a car mechanic or hairdresser, one passenger mile on an aeroplane, train or bus, or one minute of time using a telephone.

Calculating average costs

The **average cost per unit** of output of a particular good or service produced can be calculated using the following formula:

$$\text{Average cost per unit} = \frac{\text{Total Cost of Output}}{\text{Total Output}}$$

Consider a manufacturer of toy dinosaurs. If the variable cost of producing each toy dinosaur is 50 pence and fixed costs are £150,000 per year, then the total cost of producing 200,000 toy dinosaurs each year will be £250,000, i.e.

Total variable costs = 200,000 × 50 pence =	£100,000
Total fixed costs per year =	£150,000
Total costs of 200,000 units per year =	£250,000

Thus, the average cost of each toy dinosaur is £1.25 (i.e. £250,000 / 200,000). If the business wanted to sell each toy for £2 it will make a profit of 75 pence per dinosaur, or a total profit of £150,000 if all 200,000 units are sold. That is, the price of £2 absorbs both direct and indirect production costs and leaves a surplus for profit.

In the same way we can calculate the average cost per unit of a service, for example one hour of labour from a car mechanic or one air passenger mile. All we would need to know is the total cost of both direct and indirect costs associated with these activities. So, for example, if a mechanic spends 7 hours working on a car at a total cost of £350 in labour, materials, power, administration and other overheads, then the average cost per labour hour is £50 (i.e. £350 / 7 hours).

Similarly, if it costs a total of £50,000 to fly 100 passengers 2000 miles - a total of 20,000 passenger miles - then the cost per passenger mile is £2.50 (i.e. £50,000 / 20,000 miles).

Calculating marginal cost

Sometimes it is useful for a business not just to know how much it costs on average to produce each unit of output but how much it would cost to produce just one more unit of output. If a firm wants to expand production it would like to know how much it will cost. It can then decide if this cost is worth paying. That is, will the sale of the extra output generate sufficient revenues to cover the cost of producing it?

Portfolio Activity 22.4 

Janine Nichols runs her own small craft business making soaps with natural herbal ingredients. She produces two soap products: 'Cool Blue' and 'Summer Meadow', which are sold to shops all over the UK.

Her costs of production each month are as follows:

Indirect costs		Direct costs	
Rent	£100	Cool Blue:	
Rates	£65	Labour	£120
Insurance	£35	Materials	£160
Power	£80		
Advertising	£25	Summer Meadow:	
Travel	£45	Labour	£150
Telephone	£25	Materials	£250
Loan repayment	£25		

Janine apportions her total indirect costs to the two products as follows;

Cool Blue 40%
Summer Meadow 60%

Output per month is currently 2,000 bars of Cool Blue soap and 4,000 bars of Summer Meadow soap.

Using this information;

1. Calculate the total cost of producing each level of output for each soap.
2. Calculate the average cost of producing one bar of Cool Blue soap and one bar of Summer Meadow.
3. Calculate the prices Janine should charge for each Cool Blue and Summer Meadow soap bar is she wants to earn of total profit of £560 and £960 on each brand respectively.
4. Summer Meadow is selling well and Janine would like to increase production by 1,000 bars per month. She has calculated that she will need to work longer and incur additional fixed costs (mainly power) of £50 per month. The variable cost of producing each bar of soap will remain the same.
   (a) Calculate the marginal cost of producing each extra bar of Summer Meadow soap.
   (b) Advise Janine whether you think it would be worth producing the additional 1,000 bars for sale at the same price you advised her to charge in task 3.

Consider the firm producing toy dinosaurs. It wants to expand production by 50,000 units. However, this will mean hiring extra machinery and moving to larger premises. The extra annual cost of machine hire, rent and rates is estimated to be £100,000. If the variable cost of producing each toy dinosaur is 50 pence then to produce an extra 50,000 toys each year will cost:

$$\begin{aligned}\text{Additional total variable costs} = 50{,}000 \times 0.50 \text{ pence} &= \pounds 25{,}000\\ \text{Additional fixed costs} &= \underline{\pounds 100{,}000}\\ \text{Total additional costs} &= \pounds 125{,}000\end{aligned}$$

This means that it would cost £2.50 to produce each one of the additional 50,000 dinosaurs (i.e. £125,000 / 50,000). Because the firm has chosen to price each dinosaur at £2 each it will not make a profit from the additional output unless it raises their price. However, this may price the toys beyond what consumers are willing to pay for them.

The additional cost of raising output is called the **marginal cost** of production. The marginal cost per unit of extra output is, therefore, calculated as follows:

$$\text{Marginal cost of an extra unit of output} = \frac{\text{Change in Total Cost}}{\text{Change in Total Output}}$$

Economies of scale

Economies of scale refer to the reductions in average cost per unit of output brought about by an increase in the scale or size of a firm. In general, as output is increased, the average cost per unit will tend to fall, as fixed costs are spread over more and more units of output.

For example, consider a power station generating electricity. Fixed costs of production are £10,000 per week regardless of how much electricity is produced. If 10,000 watts of electricity are produced each week, the average fixed cost per watt will be £1. Doubling output to 20,000 watts per week will reduce average fixed costs per watt to 50 pence. The variable cost per unit of output may also fall as output is increased. For example, the power station may be able to buy more gas and obtain a discount from suppliers.

Falling average costs are an important benefit to firms. If, however, average cost rises as output is increased, then a firm will experience **diseconomies of scale**, because it will be producing beyond its optimum level of output.

We can plot the relationship between average cost and output in a typical firm on a graph, as follows:

▼ *Figure 22.13: An average cost curve*

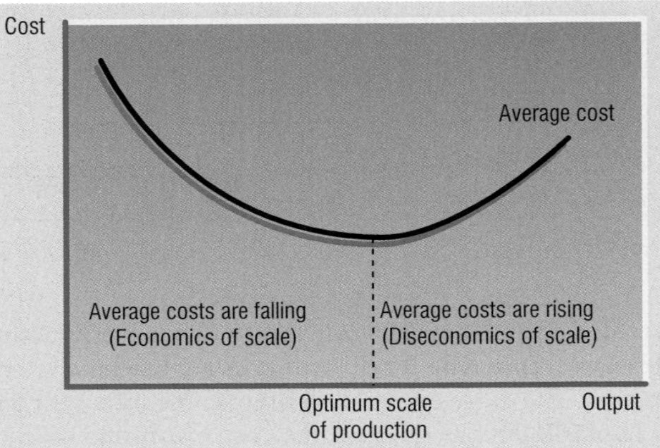

In general, the average cost curve for a given firm is U-shaped. At first, as the scale of production expands, there are cost savings resulting from increases in the scale of output. However, after a certain point, if the firm expands too much, production will become less efficient, and average costs will begin to rise. The firm will then experience diseconomies of scale. The optimum scale of production, or most efficient size of a firm, is therefore where the average cost of producing each car, toy, pair of shoes, therm of gas, microchip, etc., is at the lowest level possible. At this point, it will be possible to combine and organize resources in the most efficient or cost-effective way. Lowering average production costs will either increase the profit margin on that product, or allow the firm to lower price to attract more sales.

Economies of scale - the advantages of large-scale production

When a firm expands the scale of production, it has a chance to become more efficient and reduce average costs. This is because expansion can give business managers and owners a chance to reorganize the way in which their firm is run and financed. The advantages which result from this are known collectively as **internal economies of scale**, and include the following:

- **Financial economies.** A large firm may be able to obtain finance from a greater variety of financial institutions, for example, by selling shares on the Stock Market (see 23.2).
- **Marketing economies.** Large firms, with the necessary finance and storage space, can often take advantage of discounts for bulk purchases offered by suppliers. They may employ specialist sales teams to market their products, and will also have the financial resources to advertise widely through a variety of media to reach and expand their market.
- **Technical economies.** The research and development of new, faster, and more efficient processes and products is often very expensive. A large firm will be able to spread this cost across a large output, and can therefore afford to use a wider range of production methods. It will also be able to benefit from bulk carriers such as juggernauts, or in the case of oil companies, pipelines, and supertankers, to meet its vast distribution requirements.
- **Risk-bearing economies.** A large firm can attempt to minimize or spread risk in a number of ways not open to a smaller enterprise. It can buy materials in bulk from a number of suppliers to minimize the risk of a hold-up in supplies from one outlet. It may also diversify production lines - i.e. produce a range of different products for sale in case the demand for one falls.

Diseconomies of scale - the disadvantages of large-scale production

However, if a firm becomes too large, production may become inefficient. Average costs will rise. This is caused by diseconomies of scale, for example:

- **Management diseconomies.** Large firms can often suffer from too many layers of management, leading to communication problems.
- **Supply problems.** It may become difficult to secure the amount of materials or components required, at the right price and of the right quality, for large-scale production.
- **Labour diseconomies.** Large firms will use specialized mass-production techniques in an attempt to reduce average production costs. However, as production of the final product is divided up into many specialized tasks, workers may become bored with their repetitive and often monotonous jobs, and productivity and product quality may suffer.

Key words:

Cost unit - a unit of a good or service to which costs can be charged and compared with revenues

Marginal cost - the cost of producing an additional unit of output

Economies of scale - cost savings resulting from expanding the scale of production in a firm

Average cost - total cost divided by total output to give the cost per unit of output

Test your knowledge

1 All of the following business costs will usually be classified as direct costs **except**:

A Business rates

B Raw materials

C Production workers wages

D Depreciation

2 Depreciation as a business cost is:

A A fall in the value of foreign currency holdings

B A fall in the value of current assets

C A fall in the value of stocks held

D A fall in the value of fixed assets

3 Which of the following is **not** an indirect cost to business?

A The purchase of photocopying paper

B Allowances for the depreciation of machinery

C Office heating bills

D After sales care

Questions 4–6 share the following answer options:

A Passenger mile

B Call unit

C Labour hour

D Barrel

Which of the above cost units will be used by the producers of the following goods and services to compare unit costs and revenues?

4 Crude oil

5 Piano lessons

6 Coach travel

7 Which of the following costs is likely to vary with the level of output in a firm?

A Rent

B Overheads

C Component parts

D Insurance

8 Which of the following cost items are unlikely to vary with the level of output on a farm?

A Seeds

B Petrol for a tractor

C Business rates

D Fertilizer

9 A firm wants to expand production by 10,000 units over current levels of output. To do this it will need to hire additional machinery at a cost of £5,000 per year. If the cost of labour and materials to produce each unit of production is £3, what is the marginal cost of each additional unit?

A 70 pence

B £3.50

C £7

D £3

Questions 10–12 are based on the following information:

ABC Ltd has calculated that its fixed costs are £10,000 per month. Variable costs are £2 per unit produced.

10 What is the total cost of producing 5,000 units each month?

A £12,000

B £200,000

C £10,000

D £20,000

11 What is the average cost of producing each unit of the total output of 5,000 units per month?

A £4

B £2

C £40

D £20

12 If ABC Ltd wanted to earn a profit of £10,000 on the production and sale of 5,000 units per month, what price per unit should they charge?

A 60 pence

B £60

C £2

D £6

chapter 23

Sources of Finance for Your Business Plan

This chapter identifies the need for, and possible sources of, finance for your new business.

CON, BADGER STING & SONS
I HATE TO HURRY YOU ALONG MR SMYTHE BUT THE FIRST PAYMENT IS ALMOST DUE

What you need to learn

Your business will need **capital** for a wide variety of reasons including business start-up, expansion, introducing new technology, and R&D.

Capital is used to provide **long-term assets**, such as land, buildings, machinery, and equipment. **Working capital** is for the purchase of items to be consumed over a short period of time, such as materials, financing for work in progress and stocks of finished goods, and for paying off loans.

Most business organizations rely on bank **overdrafts** and **trade credit** to fund their working capital requirements.

Some capital may be raised internally within an organization from **owners' savings, retained profits, asset management**, and by improving the management of working capital.

Capital to finance business assets can also be raised externally from the **sale of shares** to investors, or via **loan capital** in the form of **loan stocks, bank loans, hire purchase, leasing, mortgages,** and **venture capital**.

All limited companies may issue **ordinary and preferences shares**, but only **public limited companies (plcs)** may trade their shares through the Stock Exchange.

A wide variety of institutions may assist in the raising of finance for business, including individual and institutional investors, banks, building societies, leasing and factoring companies, government agencies, and venture capital firms.

When choosing the best method of finance, you should consider the amount to be raised, the purpose for which the finance is required, the cost of finance, your status as a borrower, the general economic environment, and your level of **gearing** (ratio of debt finance to total finance).

Section **23.1**

Why do businesses need capital?

What is capital?

Your new business venture will need money to pay for the start-up and running costs you identified from Chapter 22. It is unlikely that you will have enough money to pay for everything from your personal savings, or that your business will generate enough revenue, at least initially, to cover many of your business costs. However, in time you will hope that your business will be a success and be able to fund continued production and even expansion from the revenues it generates. These objectives will be set out in your financial plans and projections.

Capital refers to money introduced into a firm by its owners to purchase **assets**, such as land, buildings, machinery, vehicles, and office equipment. Businesses need capital to finance business start-ups, to expand, to pay for research and product development, and to finance the introduction of new technology. This chapter considers the ways in which firms can 'raise capital'. You will need to investigate and select those ways which are most appropriate for your business venture.

Capital can be described in a number of ways, depending on how it is used by an organization:

- **Venture capital** is often used to describe money used to finance new business start-ups, mainly of private limited companies
- **Investment capital** is money used to buy new **fixed assets**, such as premises, machinery and other equipment that have relatively long productive lives
- **Working capital** is money used to pay the day-to-day running expenses of a business, such as materials, electricity, telephone bills, insurance, loan repayments, etc.

Working capital can be held in the form of the following **current assets**, which are used up by a business over a relatively short period of time:

- Cash 'in hand' and in bank or building society accounts
- Liquid assets, such as stocks and work in progress which can be sold quickly to raise cash
- Debtors – people and firms who owe money to the business. This money can be recalled to raise cash

Portfolio Activity 23.1 

You are a sole trader preparing to set up a newsagent's store. Before you can begin to trade, the shop you intend to buy will need re-fitting with shelves, a counter, a store room, lighting and heating, and a new shopfront.

1. Make a detailed list of all the things that you will need to spend money on. (Pay a visit to a local newsagent to help you.) Divide your list into fixed assets and current assets.
2. Make estimates of how much each list will cost you and justify these estimates.
3. Consider how you might raise the money to finance this expenditure.
4. If you intend to borrow money, consider how you might convince people and other organizations to finance your business.
5. Some sources of finance might be better for financing assets, and others for providing working capital. Investigate and explain.
6. How do you think your answers to Questions 1–5 would differ for a large chain of newsagency and stationery stores owned by a public limited company, for example, WH Smith?

Working capital is equal to the value of current assets less any current liabilities, namely any outstanding bills yet to be paid or bank overdrafts which will reduce the amount of cash available to your business.

Internal sources of finance

A business organization may already have some capital of its own to contribute to asset and working capital finance. The main sources of **internal finance** are:

- **Personal savings:** the use of personal savings remains an important, and often principal, source of finance for many small firms, especially sole traders and partnerships (see 2.2).
- **Retained profits:** ploughed-back or retained profits amount to around 50% of the total finance used by companies. These are a cheap source of finance because the funds are not borrowed and no interest need be paid for their use.

  In small businesses, including sole traders and partnerships, it is unlikely that there will be enough retained profit to use as a source of finance. Limited companies are more likely to make sufficient profits to provide reserves for the future. However, because all profits after tax belong to the business owners, any profits retained by managers must be justified to them.
- **Asset management:** a firm may raise funds by selling off some of its existing assets such as machinery or fixtures and fittings. Because asset sales tend to reduce the ability of a firm to trade, this is a fairly drastic means of raising finance.
- **Management of working capital:** by careful planning, it is possible to manage the flow of cash into and out of a firm so as to avoid the need for short-term finance (see 17.2). A surplus of cash one month can be saved to cover a deficit later on, when outflows of cash exceed inflows - for example, when a large bill for electricity or deliveries of materials has to be paid.

External sources of finance

Most firms will be unable to finance all their asset and working capital requirements from internal sources. They will therefore raise the money they need from external sources, such as banks and other financial institutions. Charities will rely on gifts, donations and membership fees.

In order to raise **external finance**, it is necessary for a business to produce a plan detailing how exactly it intends to use the finance raised.

It is good financial practice to match the source of finance with the kind of asset required. For example, it would not be a good idea to purchase a large piece of capital equipment which will pay for itself over ten years, with an overdraft requiring repayment in six months!

Because fixed assets, such as buildings and machinery, remain productive for a long time, a company will often be willing to pay for them over many years, and will seek sources of **long-term finance**. In contrast, **short-term finance** is available from a variety of sources to fund working capital requirements and enable firms to meet day-to-day bills and debts. As a rule of thumb, short-term finance is normally repaid within three years while medium- to long-term finance is repaid over many more.

Long- or short-term external finance?

Short-term finance	Long-term finance
To cover short-term losses and net outflows of cash	To purchase long-term or fixed assets including equipment
To meet working capital requirements	To finance expansion
To finance exports	To cover costs of long-term projects, for example, building a new office or factory
To puchase low-cost fixed assets, e.g. a new computer	

Figure 23.1 summarizes the various sources of external short- and long-term finance available to a business organization.

Figure 23.1: Sources of business finance

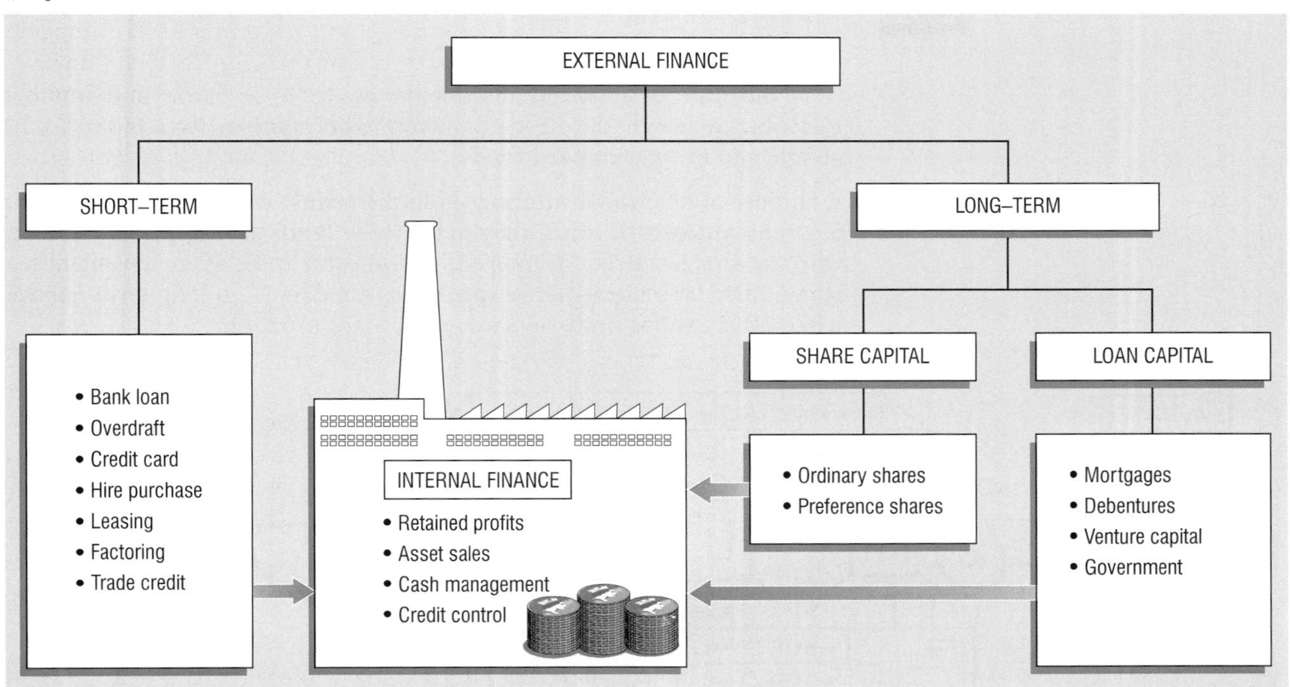

There are two main sources of long-term external finance. These are:

- **Loan capital:** this is any money borrowed over a period of time which has be repaid by an agreed date, usually with interest, either as a lump sum or in regular instalments (see 23.2).
- **Share capital:** limited companies are able to sell shares to raise finance (see 2.2). The sale of shares can raise very large amounts of money. Unlike a loan, share capital is **permanent** capital because it is not normally redeemed, i.e. a firm never has to repay shareholders' money. To get their money back, a shareholder must sell their shares to someone else.

Key words:

Capital - finance or money used in a business to purchase assets

Assets - resources owned by a business and used up in production

Fixed assets - business assets, such as plant and machinery, used over a long period of time

Venture capital - money used to finance a new business start-up

Investment capital - money used to buy plant and equipment

Current assets - assets used up over a short period of time, such as stocks of finished products and raw materials

Working capital - funds available for use in the day-to-day operation of the business

Internal finance - capital raised from sources inside a business from retained profits, the sale of assets, or by cash management

External finance - capital raised from sources outside a business

Loan capital - money borrowed by a business for a long period of time

Share capital - money raised by the sale of shares in a business

Permanent capital - money that never has to be repaid

Section 23.2

Raising loan capital

Financial intermediation

It is the task of **financial intermediaries**, such as banks and building societies, to match the needs of savers who want to lend money, with people and firms who need funds.

A number of financial institutions hold the savings of people and firms, and pay them interest. In turn, they make these funds available to borrowers, who are charged a rate of interest, and in some cases an arrangement fee. Some financial intermediaries specialize in medium- to long-term finance, while others concentrate on short-term loans of money.

▼ *Figure 23.2: Financial intermediation*

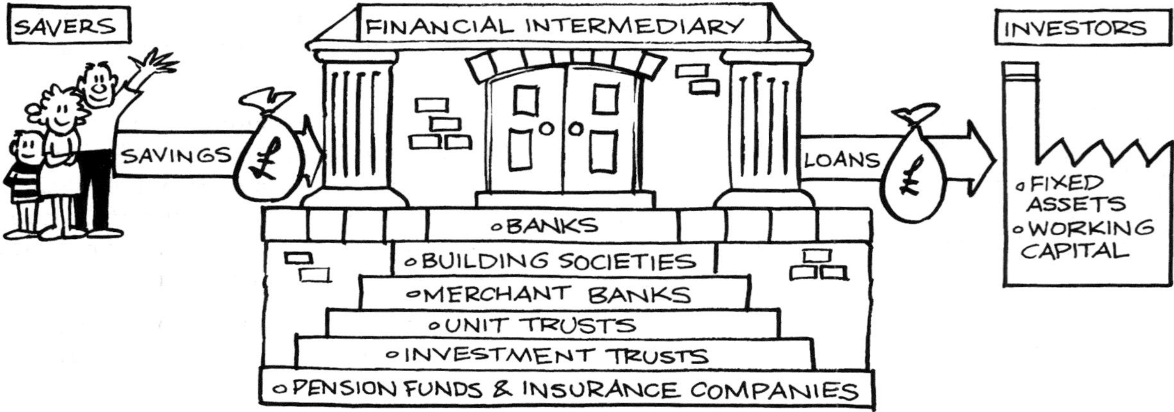

Securing finance

Many small businesses find it difficult to borrow money because they lack security. Your business is unlikely to be an exception. Loans may be **secured** or **unsecured**. Some financial institutions may insist on **security** or **collateral** against a loan, especially when the amount of money involved is large. This refers to an asset, or assets, of value equal to the amount borrowed, which is tied to the loan. In the event of non-payment or default, the lender is legally entitled to take possession of the secured assets, and to sell them to obtain their money.

▼ Credit cards provice a useful method of short-term finance

Assets most likely to be accepted as security for a loan include:

- Property
- Money saved in endowment and life insurance policies
- Shareholdings

Assets which lose their value quickly or are difficult to sell - for example, specialized machinery - are unlikely to be accepted by banks and other lenders as suitable forms of security.

The money market

Short-term finance is available on the **money market**. This is made up of people and firms who want to borrow money for relatively short periods of time, and those people and organizations willing and able to provide it.

The supply of short-term finance is dominated by the major commercial banks, also known as **clearing banks**, such as Lloyds TSB, Barclays, HSBC, and NatWest. These lend money to firms in the same way as they lend money to private individuals. Short-term finance is available in the form of a bank loan or overdraft. The major banks can also arrange, often through specialized companies which they own, other methods of finance, such as leasing and factoring services, and commercial mortgages.

Methods of short-term finance

- **Overdraft:** overdrafts are frequently used to ease cashflow problems associated with working capital requirements in many business organizations. Under an overdraft agreement, a bank allows a business to make payments or withdrawals in excess of the amount held in its account, up to a specified limit. Banks normally insist that overdrafts are paid off relatively quickly. Interest is charged on the amount of the overdraft on a daily basis, and is normally slightly lower than the rate charged on loans.

- **Bank loan:** banks can advance loans to businesses, to be repaid in regular fixed monthly instalments over an agreed period of time. Loan terms can be anything from six months to ten years, but most tend to be relatively short. Interest is charged on the total amount of the loan, and is normally fixed from the outset. A borrower is locked into that rate, even if interest rates fall during the period of the loan.

  Loans and overdrafts can be an expensive way of borrowing, but they are one of the most popular forms of short-term finance available to sole traders and partnerships (see 2.2).

- **Credit cards:** Visa, Access, American Express, and Diners Club are examples of credit card companies. Depending on the credit card, users can pay bills and make purchases, and defer payment until up to eight weeks later. Each month, users receive a statement of their transactions. They can then decide whether to pay the balance in full or in part. If payment is made in full, no interest is charged. Interest is charged only on the outstanding balance, but can be quite high.

- **Hire purchase:** this is a popular method of finance, often used by smaller firms to buy plant and machinery. A hire purchase agreement will normally require a firm to pay a deposit on equipment purchased, and then to pay off the balance, with interest, in regular instalments over a few months or several years.

  Hire purchase can be arranged through a bank or, more often, through a finance house. Because finance houses tend to be less selective in granting loans, their rates of interest tend to be higher. The finance house will buy the equipment for the buyer, and will be the legal owner of it until the last payment has been made. If the buyer is unable to pay the agreed instalments, the finance house can legally repossess the equipment.

- **Leasing:** Leasing is a way of paying rent for the loan of equipment for a fixed period. At the end of the period, the equipment is returned to its owner. The advantage is that businesses can get expensive equipment such as computer systems without making a large capital outlay. During the period of the lease, maintenance and servicing of equipment are the responsibility of the owner of the equipment rather than the lessee. Once the period of the lease is over, the firm can return the old computer system and lease a more up-to-date version.

  A number of specialist leasing companies will buy plant and machinery to order from a company wanting to rent the equipment. Over a long

Leasing

New lease on life

When Ian Dyson wanted to start a Sheffield bus company in 1990, he was faced with a problem. He and his three partners, all former senior depot managers for the nationalized bus company, had little money and less collateral. To achieve critical mass they needed at least 15 double-decker buses.

The solution was to buy 12-year-old vehicles – but who would finance such aged assets? After exploring a number of cul-de-sacs, including bank loans, Dyson found Close Asset Finance, a specialist leasing company.

Whereas banks were not interested in his collateral, Close Asset Finance took a view on the residual value of the assets in the event of default, entered a hire-purchase arrangement and Sheffield Omnibus was born. Four years later, the company has 85 buses, employs 220 people full-time and is still using leasing for its asset financing.

▼ *Figure 23.3: How leasing works*

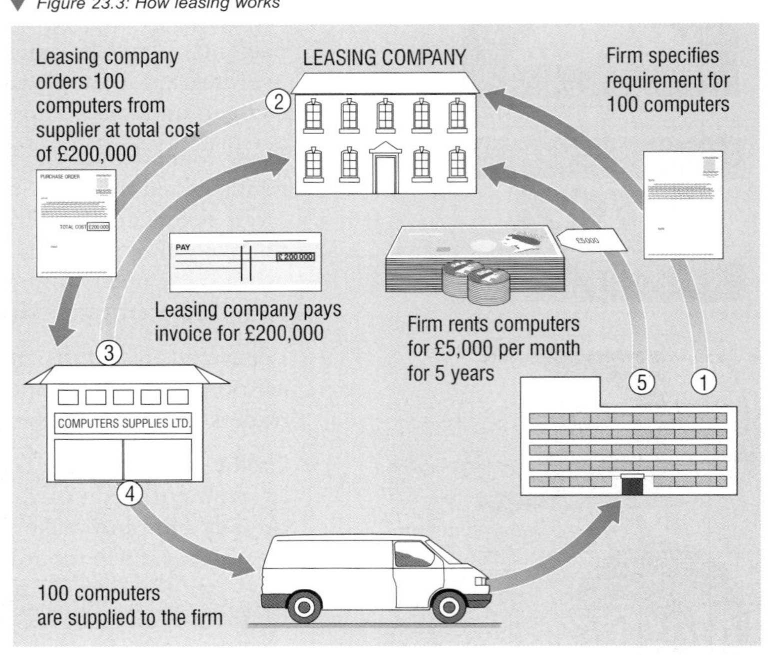
LEASING COMPANY
① Firm specifies requirement for 100 computers
② Leasing company orders 100 computers from supplier at total cost of £200,000
PURCHASE ORDER
TOTAL COST £200,000
PAY
£200,000
③ Leasing company pays invoice for £200,000
COMPUTERS SUPPLIES LTD
④ 100 computers are supplied to the firm
⑤ Firm rents computers for £5,000 per month for 5 years
£5000

period of time, leasing can be more expensive than buying equipment outright. Leasing is, however, an increasingly popular means of obtaining equipment.

- **Trade credit:** many businesses rely on their creditors as a form of short-term finance. Because most suppliers allow their customers to take somewhere between one and three months to pay for goods supplied, the debtor company can use what is effectively an interest-free loan of up to 90 days to pay other bills. Creditors will often give incentives in the form of cash discounts if payment is made earlier, but by delaying payment, the debtor can use money owed to finance other current assets.

  - **Factoring:** late payment of invoices for goods delivered can cause considerable financial hardship for creditors. **Debt factoring** involves a specialist company, known as a **factor**, paying off the unpaid invoices of supplies in return for an agreed fee.

  It is common for a factoring company to agree to pay 80% of the amount of the invoice on issue, paying the remaining 20% when the debtor settles the invoice with the factor. This provides the creditor with early payment of debts and leaves the chasing-up of payments to the factoring company.

What is the capital market?

The **capital market** brings together people and firms who want to borrow a lot of money for long periods of time with those who are willing and able to supply funds on this basis. Borrowers tend to be limited companies seeking to fund large-scale replacement of fixed assets or expansion.

Methods of long-term finance

- **Mortgages:** a commercial mortgage is a long-term loan, typically over 25 years, of up to approximately 80% of the purchase price of a business property. Business owners may also remortgage their existing premises in order to raise finance for use elsewhere in the business. The business premises provide security for the loan, and, in the event of a failure to repay regular instalments, the lender can take possession of the property.

  Mortgages are available from building societies and banks.

- **Venture capital:** start-up funds for new limited companies are available from specialist venture capital companies. These are commercial organizations specializing in loans to new and risky businesses who might otherwise find it difficult to raise finance. Investors in Industry (3i) plc, Pi Capital, Paribus, and the clearing banks are some of the biggest and best-known venture capital firms. These firms usually lend in return for shares in the ownership of the company (or **equity stakes**), hoping for an eventual capital gain on the value of their shares, rather than for interest or dividends.

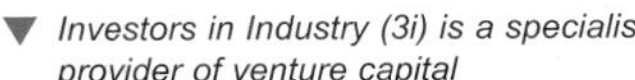

Investors in Industry (3i) is a specialist provider of venture capital

£9 million funding fuels growth at Steill

An innovative deal to invest £9 million in the Lanarkshire based Steill Group will propel the business into the UK premier division of facilities management. Growth of more than 50% is anticipated over the next 12 months and annual sales are targeted to hit £200 million by 2005, a five-fold increase on last year's figures.

In return for a 30% equity stake, Europe's leading venture capital company, 3i are investing £9 million to help fund Steill's ambitious plans to expand across the UK through organic growth and strategic acquisitions of other companies.

Taken from a 3i press release, 3.4.2000 ***(www.3i.com)***

Key facts about venture capital in the UK

- The UK industry is the largest and most developed in Europe accounting for nearly 50% of total annual European venture capital investment, and is second to the USA in world importance
- The UK venture capital industry has invested over £28 billion (nearly £23 billion in the UK) in up to 18,000 companies between 1983 and 1999
- A record £4.9 billion was invested in 1998, in over 1,300 companies, 26 times the number in 1984
- Most - 50% of venture capital financings are for expansion - specifically to help existing businesses expand and compete

Taken from the British Venture Capital Association (BVCA) 'Report on Investment Activity' ***(www.bvca.co.uk)***

Merchant banks also provide venture capital. These are financial institutions specializing in advice and financial assistance to limited companies, for example, to fund business expansion, takeovers of other companies, or management buyouts.

The venture capital industry in the UK has grown very quickly, providing a valuable source of finance to small firms and high-risk enterprises. Venture capital investments in the UK rose from £1.4 billion in 1989 to over £5 billion in 1999.

- **Loan stocks:** these are certificates issued for sale by limited companies, which acknowledge that the bearer has lent a company money and is to be repaid at a specified future date, known as **maturity**. Government is also able to borrow money by issuing loan stocks for sale to the general public.

Loan stocks are sold to raise finance - around £44 billion in 1999. They offer holders a fixed or floating rate of interest each year until the loan is repaid by the issuing company. If, during the period of the loan, the holder wishes to get their money back, the loan stock can be sold to another person or company. Loan stocks can be in the form of:

- **Debentures** issued by public limited companies (see 2.2)
- **Local government bonds** issued by local authorities
- **Gilt-edged securities** issued by central government, normally with maturities of between 10 and 20 years

A **debenture** may be secured or unsecured on specific property owned by the company. When debentures are issued, the company agrees to repay the loan with interest on maturity.

The Stock Exchange

The capital market is dominated by the **Stock Exchange** in London. The main function of the Stock Exchange is to provide a market where the owners of loan stocks and shares can sell them to other people and firms who want to buy them (see 19.4). The total market value of all stocks and shares traded on the Stock Exchange is called the **market capitalization.** At the end of March 2000, this value stood at £5,521 billion (see Figure 23.4).

The people and organizations that provide companies with capital by buying shares in them are called **investors**. Most shares traded in the UK are bought by investment trusts, unit trusts, pension funds, and insurance companies. These companies accept people's savings and use the money to invest in shares and government stocks. Dividends, interest on stocks, and capital gains in the value of shares are passed on, in part, to savers.

▼ *Figure 23.4: Total market value of securities quoted on the London Stock Exchange*

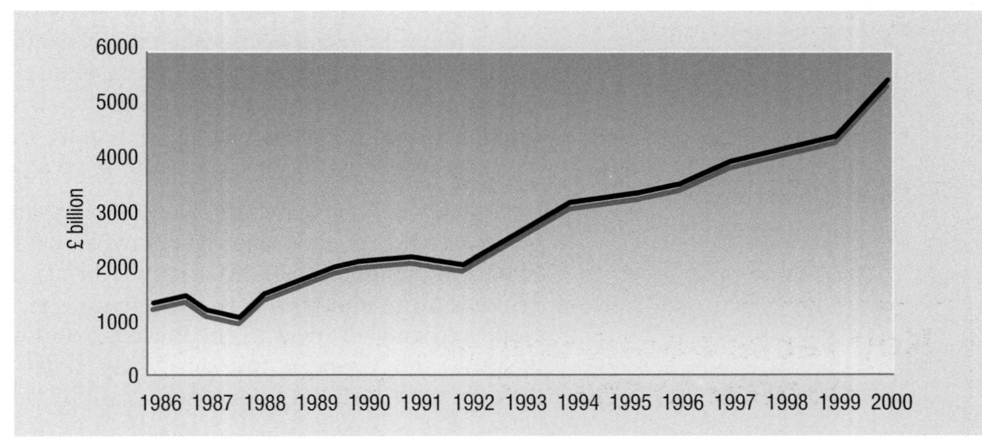

Selling shares

Shares can be sold to raise money for a business venture. This requires the formation of a **limited company** (see 2.2). If you wanted to own all the shares in your company, you would need to form a single-member company. However, to raise extra money to invest in your business you will need to sell shares in your new company to members of your family, friends or business associates. In doing so you will share ownership and any profits with your new shareholders.

To form a limited company you will need to draw up some legal documents with the help of a solicitor, and send copies of these to the government's Registrar of Companies. The **Articles of Association** define the internal rules of the company and give details such as the number of directors, voting rights of shareholders, and how profits are to be shared out. The **Memorandum of Association** gives details of company name, objective and capital (see 2.2).

The 'ready-made' limited company

A number of specialist organizations can help you form a new limited company quickly and easily, or can sell you one 'off the shelf' for as little as £100 or even less in some cases. These 'off-the-shelf' companies already have paperwork completed and their names registered. All they need is details of their new owners and directors and to start trading. By typing **limited company formations** into an Internet search engine you will be directed to the web sites of many of these organizations. Here are just two examples:

- Midlands Company Services Ltd ***(www.company-services.co.uk)***
- UK Business Formations Ltd ***(www.uk-business-formations.co.uk)***

To raise more money for your new business you may be tempted to 'float' your company on the stock market (see 19.4). This means forming a public limited company and issuing shares for sale to the general public. However, unless you keep over 50% of the value of shares issued you may lose control of your business.

There are far more small and medium-sized public limited companies (plc's) than there are giants like BP Amoco plc, Rolls-Royce plc, HSBC plc and BAA plc (to name but a few). However, floating a new company on the main stock market can be expensive. You will need to publish a detailed prospectus containing full details about your company, its history, future plans, financial results and an application form for shares. You may need to print many thousands of these to distribute to would-be investors, and you will also need to advertise the share sale in newspapers. The London Stock Exchange will also require you to submit very detailed business and financial information to it on a continuing basis.

In contrast, selling shares in your company on the **Alternative Investment Market (AIM)** is easier and less expensive (see 19.4). The London Stock Exchange designed the AIM with the needs of small companies in mind. There is no minimum size requirement (in terms of the amount of capital employed and turnover of the business) and no need to submit a detailed business and financial history. Many small companies, especially new 'hi-tech' start-ups, have floated successfully on the AIM.

Key words:

Financial intermediary - an institution, such as a bank or building society, which accepts deposits and uses this money to make loans

Collateral - an asset which provides security for a loan

Money market - the market for short-term finance, consisting of borrowers and lenders

Commercial banks - high street banks that accept deposits from, and make loans to, the general public and business organizations

Bank loan - money borrowed for a specified period from a bank that has to be repaid with interest, usually in equal monthly instalments

Overdraft - short-term finance provided by overdrawing from a bank account

Credit cards - issued by companies providing short-term credit for payments made with them. If full payment is made to the credit card company within a specified period, usually 6–8 weeks, no interest is charged

Hire purchase - taking delivery of goods after paying a deposit, and then paying the balance with interest in equal monthly instalments over an agreed period

Finance house - specialist providers of finance for hire purchase

Leasing - renting equipment for an agreed period, after which it can be bought at a discount or returned to the owner

Trade credit - when a supplier gives a customer time to pay for goods or services delivered

Creditor - a supplier who has granted trade credit

Factoring - borrowing money to cover unpaid invoices

Capital market - the market for long-term finance made up of borrowers and lenders

Commercial mortgage - a loan secured on the value of property

Venture capital - funds lent to high-risk (usually new) companies

Merchant banks - specialist banks for limited companies

Loan stocks - tradeable certificates sold by companies to raise long-term finance. At maturity, they entitle their holder to the face value at which they were sold, plus interest

Debentures - loan stocks issued by companies

Gilt-edged securities - loan stocks issued by government, often for up to 20 years

Stock Exchange - the UK market for the sale of loan stocks and shares issued by public limited companies and the government

Market capitalization - the value of shares quoted on the Stock Exchange

Investors - people and organizations who provide share capital

AIM - Alternative Investment Market for trading shares in new and small companies

Section 23.2 Financial help from government

The UK government offers a considerable amount of free advice and financial help to new and existing businesses to promote employment, new technologies, and economic growth. Financial assistance is available in the form of grants, income support, subsidies, tax allowances, and repayable loans. However, the amount and type of financial help made available can vary from industry to industry, by area and by size of business. For example, financial help for small farms is very different from that made available to large UK aerospace and defence equipment manufacturers.

Financial help for small businesses

The UK government can offer direct financial help to new and established small businesses in a number ways.

Small Firms Loan Guarantee Scheme

This scheme encourages banks and other financial institutions to lend money for periods of between two and ten years to small businesses and business projects which they would normally consider too risky to lend to. The Department of Trade and Industry (DTI) guarantees to repay up to 85% of a loan up to £250,000 (in 2000/01) if the small business borrower runs into trouble and is unable to repay.

The Smart Scheme

This provides grants to individuals and small/medium sized businesses to review, research, or develop technologies leading to commercial products. The following help was available in England in 2000/01:

- **Technology Reviews**: Grants of up to £2,500 for individuals and small and medium-sized firms towards the costs of expert reviews against best practice.
- **Technology Studies:** Grants of up to £5,000 for individuals and small and medium-sized firms to help identify technological opportunities leading to innovative products and processes.
- **Micro Projects:** Grants of up to £10,000 are available to help individuals and micro-firms with the development of low-cost prototypes of products and processes involving technical advances and/or novelty.
- **Feasibility Studies:** Grants of up to £45,000, awarded through competitions, for individuals and small firms undertaking feasibility studies into innovative technologies.
- **Development Projects:** Grants of up to 200,000 euro, awarded through competitions, for small and medium-sized firms undertaking development projects.
- **Exceptional Development Projects:** Also for small and medium-sized firms, a small number of *exceptional* high cost development projects may attract grants of up to 600,000 euro.

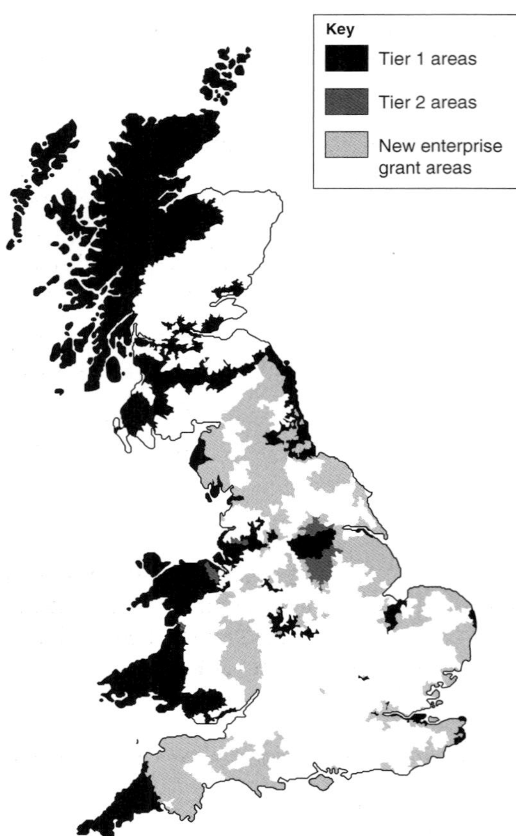

▼ *Figure 23.5: Assisted Areas 1999*

Regional Policy

Both the UK and European Union Governments operate a **regional policy** to encourage firms to locate and expand in areas which suffer from high unemployment and industrial decline. These areas are called **Assisted Areas** and firms in, or thinking of moving to, these areas, can apply for financial help called **Regional Selective Assistance (RSA).** This is a discretionary grant awarded to firms who can demonstrate their projects will safeguard or create jobs, particularly skilled jobs, and increase prosperity.

Assisted areas are reviewed from time to time by the UK Government because of changes in regional employment, investment, population, migration, and income patterns. In 1999 assisted areas were redrawn into three different groups as Figure 23.5 shows.

Tier 1 areas include Cornwall, Merseyside, South Yorkshire and West Wales and the Valleys. Northern Ireland is included as an area of exceptional concern. Firms in Tier 1 regions can apply for grants of up to 40 per cent towards new investment projects that safeguard or generate jobs.

Tier 2 areas include the Highlands and Islands area of Scotland, and parts of the East and West Midlands, the North East and West, Yorkshire and the Humber, North East Anglia, and some inner city areas in London. Firms in these areas can apply for grants of up to 20 per cent of the cost of new investment projects.

A third tier of **Enterprise Grant Areas** was introduced to provide assistance to small and medium enterprises employing less than 250 people. These areas include local authority districts with high unemployment, old coalfield areas, and rural development areas.

Regional Selective Assistance is provided through the Scottish Executive, the National Assembly for Wales, the Northern Ireland Office, and eight **Regional Development Agencies (RDAs)** in England.

In 1999–2000 RDAs had a total budget of over £1 billion to spend in their regions on:

- encouraging economic regeneration
- promoting business efficiency, investment and competitiveness
- promoting employment
- developing and improving workforce skills
- improving the environment

Other UK Government regional assistance

The assisted areas policy complements other programmes which aim to help business start-up and generate employment in different areas of the UK. In 2000 these included:

- The **Single Regeneration Budget**, which provides money to help 'regenerate' communities suffering from multiple problems including low levels of employment and skills, a lack of infrastructure, poor health and housing, and high levels of crime and drug misuse. SRB schemes range from grants for business start-up schemes, employment and training programmes, to community safety and drug abuse projects.
- **Employment Zones**, which target help at improving the employability of the long-term unemployed, including helping business start-up.
- **The Coalfields Enterprise Fund**, which targets financial help at small firms with high growth potential in areas blighted by the closer of coal mines in the 1980s and 1990s.

European Structural Fund Areas

Many of the assisted areas in the UK also qualify for additional help from the European Union, especially Tier 1 areas in which the average incomes of people are below many other areas. These are called 'objective one' areas under the terms of the **European Structural Fund.**

EU Objective	Types of area
1	Helping areas suffering general decline, deprivation and poor infrastructure (transport, schools, hospitals, etc.)
2	Assisting areas of industrial decline
3	Combating long-term unemployment
4	Helping workers adapt to industrial change
5a	Helping agriculture adjust to new conditions
5b	Rural development

Other objective one areas in Europe include eastern Germany, all of Greece, north-west Ireland, central and southern Spain, southern Italy and parts of Austria. Financial help is available in these areas to create jobs, invest in new skills and technologies, build new roads and schools, and improve the environment

Key words:

Assisted Areas - depressed areas, suffering from high unemployment and a lack of business opportunities, designated by Government as in need of financial assistance

Section 23.4 Choosing a method of finance

When selecting methods of finance to start your business you should use the following criteria:

- **Amount:** the larger the amount of capital you require, the less likely it is to be raised from internal sources. If large amounts of capital are required for long periods, then it may be worth the expense of raising finance through a share issue by forming a private limited company.
- **Cost:** you will want to raise capital in the cheapest way possible, both in terms of administration costs and interest charges. Selling shares can be expensive in terms of administration, advertising, etc., whereas borrowing for a short period of time on credit cards or by trade credit can be interest-free. However, share sales can raise large amounts of permanent capital for your firm.

  In general, the longer the period of a loan, and the more risk that you could fail to repay, the higher the rate of interest you will be charged.
- **Purpose:** many firms will tend to seek long-term sources of finance in order to spread the cost of fixed asset purchases, such as premises and new machinery, over a number of years. For example, mortgages can spread the cost of buying or building a new factory over 25 years. In contrast, you should consider funding the working capital requirements of your business from short-term sources, such as trade credit and overdrafts.
- **Status and size of the borrower:** small sole traders tend to be limited in their choices of finance, and will often lack assets to offer as security against a large long-term loan (see 23.2). The high failure rate of small businesses also tends to scare off potential lenders, who will only be willing to lend in return for a high rate of interest. You may therefore find it difficult to raise capital from a bank loan. In contrast, banks and other lenders regard lending to large, profitable companies such as Unilever and ICI, as being as safe as lending to the government. This means that these firms can raise finance more easily and at lower cost.
- **The economic environment:** economic factors can influence a firm's choice of finance. For example, in times of rising inflation, firms may find it of benefit to borrow at fixed rates of interest. If the general level of prices rises, then the real value of the sum paid back is reduced.

  During a recession, when sales and profits are likely to be falling, it would be unwise for a firm to take on hefty loan repayments, unless it can be sure of a future economic recovery So study current economic conditions carefully before choosing a method of finance.
- **Gearing:** the proportion of total finance raised in a firm from borrowing is called the **gearing ratio**, and has an important impact on how a company can raise further finance. It is not wise to make your business too highly-geared.

A high gearing ratio means that a firm has, in the past, raised a large proportion of its total capital through borrowing, and so has a large amount of fixed interest payments to make from future profits. This interest must still be paid on debt, even when profits are low or non-existent. This tends to make further borrowing a riskier form of raising finance than selling shares. With equities, no set amount must be paid to shareholders out of profits.

Portfolio Activity 23.2 

1. In each of the following cases, investigate and select the type of borrowing you think would best suit the circumstances. Justify your choices (more than one answer may be correct). In each case, what will be the approximate duration and cost of repayment? Will security be needed? What security could be offered?
   - A large multinational company wishes to borrow £20 million to finance the construction of a new factory.
   - A corner shop would like £5,000 to improve the decoration of the premises.
   - A furniture company is seeking finance to build up its stock of wood.
   - A private hospital would like to raise £50,000 for a new brain-scanning machine
   - A large British plc is considering the location of a new factory in the North East of England. The area has very heavy unemployment and the firm wishes to raise £1.5 million.
2. Identify, with examples, those sources of finance which would be most useful to a business for:
   (a) Long-term borrowing (over 5 years)
   (b) Medium-term borrowing (3–5 years)
   (c) Short-term borrowing (less than 3 years)

Key words:

Gearing ratio - the proportion of total finance raised by a company from borrowing

▼ *Some helpful advice*

Borrow your way to a big success

THE most popular way to finance a start-up or growing business is an overdraft.

Small businesses borrow £36 billion a year from the banks with around half of this in the form of overdrafts. Loans are increasing in popularity.

If the amount small firms owe seems frighteningly high, the amounts they paid into banks reached record levels of £31.7 billion last year, making the deficit only just over £4 billion.

Overdrafts are generally used to finance fluctuations in cash flow and it is a good idea not to owe more on your overdraft than you are owed by your customers.

Loans, on the other hand, are better bets for buying your business assets, your company vehicle, computers and office furniture.

The rate of interest you pay will be linked to the Bank of England base rate although fixed-rate lending is increasing in popularity as it gives small firms certainty about what they will actually have to pay each month. Generally the riskier your business venture, the higher rate of interest you are charged. In addition be prepared for your bank to demand security, usually the family home, against any loans.

Another option is to take out a personal loan instead of a business one. Once again shop around as rates vary. Marks & Spencer have a reasonable rate charging as little as 11.9 per cent APR on personal loans. Lombard Direct offer cheap rates starting at 9.9 per cent.

Although credit cards are not a way to finance a business start-up, they are a good way to help with cash flow. Pick a card with a good rate. Capital One charges 11.9 per cent.

As your business grows an invoice discounting or factoring service can help solve cash flow problems. This service run by companies like Lombard NatWest advances you a large proportion of your sales invoices upfront so you do not have to wait for customers to settle bills.

There are several schemes to help small firms to raise finance. Ring Business Link national signpost line on 0345 567 765 for details of your local Business Link.

Sunday Mirror, 25.10.1999

Key Activity

A. Preparing your Business plan

1. Think up a business idea (and possible alternatives). You can produce a good or service. Develop ideas for your product (or shop) design, including features, if appropriate, such as size, shape, colours, quality, incorporated technology, taste, smell, packaging, labelling, logos, level of service, and business trading name.
2. Evaluate your business idea(s) in terms of:
   - Market potential for the good or service
   - Level and strength of demand for the product
   - Number of potential customers
   - Likelihood of repeat trade
   - Competition

   The following sources of information may be useful:
   - Face-to-face interviews with consumers, using questionnaires
   - Government statistical publications
   - Newspapers and magazines
   - Surveys of local businesses
3. Investigate the materials you will need to make your product, and possible methods of production. For example, what ingredients would you need to produce chocolate cakes? Should you produce them individually or in large batches? Materials will also be important for many services, but methods of production will tend to be 'customized'.
4. Identify potential sources of support for your business idea.
5. Gather information on:
   - Your resource requirements, including availability of suitable premises, suppliers of materials, suitable labour
   - Legal and insurance requirements
   - Start-up costs
   - Realistic timescales in which to acquire resources and start your business idea
   - Potential sources of external finance

   Useful additional information sources to those you identified in Task 3 will include commercial property agencies, other business organizations, and Jobcentres.
6. Investigate suitable methods and costs of promoting your new business and product to customers, including advertising and publicity.
7. Draw up an action plan identifying the actions you need to take in order to finalize your business plan, with an appropriate timescale.

B. Producing your Business Plan

1. Prepare a business plan in five parts for a good or service of your choice. The purpose of the plan is to secure finance from a lender, and the plan should be produced with this in mind.

   The plan should contain a section on each of the following:
   - Your business objectives for the short, medium, and long term
   - An outline marketing plan covering your product idea, its market potential, pricing and promotion strategies, distribution, methods of selling, and a marketing budget. The marketing plan should suggest a schedule of timings for each of these items.
   - An outline production plan, covering product design, development, and production methods
   - The resource requirements of the business, covering human, physical, financial, and time resources
   - Financial data and forecasts, including a cashflow forecast, opening and projected balance sheet and profit and loss statement, and an outline of your proposed means of monitoring and reviewing business performance and your financial systems

     In each section, you must justify the choices you have made - for example, your choice of product, size and location of premises, production method.

     Where appropriate, graphs and tables should be included in the text of your plan. Useful illustrations will include:
   - A table of your business start-up costs
   - A bar chart of your expected monthly sales revenues
   - A line chart of your projected net cashflow
   - A break-even graph to show expected revenues and costs at different levels of output
   - GANNT and PERT charts of your planned marketing and production activities

   You should look closely at the Application of Number and Information Technology core skills when preparing your plan, in order to ensure that you produce the required evidence towards them.
2. Prepare and make a short presentation of the main points of your plan to your lender. Use a range of visual aids, including charts and graphs, and prepare a brief summary of the plan to hand out to the lender.

Using pre-prepared plans and proforma

Most high street banks can supply business plan forms on request from their small business services. Cashflow forecast and monthly profit and loss statement proforma are also available from them. The Banking Information Service is also able to supply these documents for you to complete.

Alternatively, use the proformas in Figures 22.2 and 22.5. However, in all cases it is suggested that you use printed plans and proforma only as a guide. Ideally, you should adapt them to meet your own requirements, using a wordprocessing and/or spreadsheet package.

Useful references

Financial advice for small businesses is available from:

- **The Department of Trade and Industry** ***(www.dti.gov.uk)***
  Enquiry Unit, 1 Victoria Street, London SW1H 0ET
- **Barclays Bank plc** ***(www.business.barclays.co.uk, www.smallbusiness.barclays.co.uk)***
  54 Lombard Street, London EC3P 3AH
- **HSBC Holdings plc** ***(www.banking.hsbc.com.uk)***
  10 Lower Thames Street, London EC3R 6AU
- **Lloyds TSB Group plc** ***(www.lloydstsbbusiness.com)***
  71 Lombard Street, London EC3P 3BS
- **National Westminster Bank plc** ***(www.natwest.co.uk)***
  41 Lothbury, London EC2P 2BP

On-line advice on **business taxation** is available from the **Inland Revenue** at ***www.inlandrevenue.gov.uk***

Index

Where more than one page reference is shown for a particular subject, pages containing main text and definitions are in bold if appropriate.